W9-AZH-021

This power source
belongs to:

given by:

I also pray that you understand
the incredible greatness of God's power
for us who believe him.

Ephesians 1:19

Dedicated to Katie, my beautiful daughter.

ACKNOWLEDGMENTS

With a project like this, where do you start? Simple, you start with your wife! Thank you, Michelle, for your patience, encouragement, and keen eye throughout the many late nights and early mornings, and for your deep reservoir of love that keeps me going. Thank you to the Scottish Bible Society (Doug, Colin, and Sharon) for your integrity, passion, and commitment to get the Word of God into the world of sport — in Scotland and around the world. Thank you to all those experts who helped shape and encourage the project, including Mary MacLeod, Barry Nicholson, Emma Cromwell, Alan Gray and the KICK TEAM, Dr Peter Walters, Christians in Sport, Gordon Thiessen, and Doug Reese — tothenextlevel.org.

A massive thanks to Graeme Hewitson, our graphic designer: for all your hard work, most excellent design, indefatigable coolness, and continuous friendship — your creative heart is a reflection of your Creator.

Visit Tyndale's exciting Web site at www.tyndale.com.

Holy Bible, New Living Translation, copyright © 1996, 2004 by Tyndale Charitable Trust. All rights reserved.

Notes copyright © 2004 by Steve Conner

The text of the *Holy Bible*, New Living Translation, may be quoted in any form (written, visual, electronic, or audio) up to and inclusive of five hundred (500) verses without express written permission of the publisher, provided that the verses quoted do not account for more than 25 percent of the work in which they are quoted, and provided that a complete book of the Bible is not quoted.

When the *Holy Bible*, New Living Translation, is quoted, one of the following credit lines must appear on the copyright page or title page of the work:

Scripture quotations marked NLT are taken from the *Holy Bible*, New Living Translation, copyright © 1996, 2004. Used by permission of Tyndale House Publishers, Inc., Wheaton, Illinois 60189. All rights reserved.

Scripture quotations are taken from the *Holy Bible*, New Living Translation, copyright © 1996, 2004. Used by permission of Tyndale House Publishers, Inc., Wheaton, Illinois 60189. All rights reserved.

Unless otherwise indicated, all Scripture quotations are taken from the *Holy Bible*, New Living Translation, copyright © 1996, 2004. Used by permission of Tyndale House Publishers, Inc., Wheaton, Illinois 60189. All rights reserved.

When quotations from the NLT text are used in nonsalable media, such as church bulletins, orders of service, newsletters, transparencies, or similar media, a complete copyright notice is not required, but the initials NLT must appear at the end of each quotation.

Quotations in excess of five hundred (500) verses or 25 percent of the work, or other permission requests, must be approved in writing by Tyndale House Publishers, Inc. Send requests by e-mail to: permission@tyndale.com or call 630-668-8300, ext. 8817.

Publication of any commentary or other Bible reference work produced for commercial sale that uses the New Living Translation requires written permission for use of the NLT text.

New Living Translation, NLT, and the New Living Translation logo are registered trademarks of Tyndale House Publishers, Inc.
ISBN 1-4143-0351-3
Printed in the United States of America.

Tyndale House Publishers and Wycliffe Bible Translators share the vision for an understandable, accurate translation of the Bible for every person in the world. Each sale of the *Holy Bible*, New Living Translation, benefits Wycliffe Bible Translators. Wycliffe is working with partners around the world to accomplish Vision 2025 — an initiative to start a Bible translation program in every language group that needs it by the year 2025.

Graphic Design by Graeme Hewitson of Viewfield Design, Glasgow, Scotland.

A NOTE FROM THE EDITOR

Aren't you glad God gave us a book? In your hand is the New Testament — God's Word, beginning with Jesus' arrival two thousand years ago to signal in a new era. Through God's Spirit the writers were influenced to write about Jesus, the key to our salvation; the influence he had; and the spread of Christianity. But this book is special! It is not just a mere history book, it is an invaluable source of power. Ask God to speak to you through these Scriptures, and he will. The Bible is food for your very inner reality — your soul. Reading the Bible is taking in valuable and delicious nutrition. This is the New Testament, but we hope that when you get fired-up about Scripture you will only thirst for more and start to read the Old Testament as well. Power up!

Of course, the writers of the Bible did not use 21st century English; the books of the Bible were originally written in Hebrew (Old Testament), Greek, and Aramaic. This edition of the Bible, the *New Living Translation,* has been meticulously translated — by loads of scholars — into our modern language. It has been seriously scrutinized, and the result is the Word of God in a modern, accurate, understandable version.

Read this!

The Colored Sidebars (Count On It, What Does It Mean?, Stats, Tips, Bible Hits, etc.) are interspersed throughout the Scripture to add insight into your sport and your faith in Christ. Many of the sidebars have a Bible verse in the box along with brief commentary to encourage you to live out your faith and understand the Scriptures better — but they are not the Scriptures! I hope the sidebars give you insight and bring clarity to the Word of God, but make sure they do not distract you. Put simply, the most powerful part of your book will be in black letters on the white pages!

All God's Best!

Steve

Steve Connor is International Director of Sports Outreach Association. The past eighteen years he has been helping develop sports ministry in the USA, England, and Scotland. Steve became a Christian when he was invited to a sports camp by his high school football coach. He was an NAIA two-time All-American at Azusa Pacific University and had a short and unillustrious career in the NFL. He has been chaplain to the NFL Europe's Scottish Claymores; he is also a speaker and has written six books. Steve is married to Michelle and has three children: Katie, Hayleigh, and Harry.

If you aim at **nothing,** you'll hit it every time

A **goal** not written down is merely a **wish**

a good coach will help the player do what they **do not want** to do (like train hard) so they will do what **they want** to do (achieve their potential)

who am I?
where am I going?
how am I going to get there? ▶

MONTHLY ACTION PLAN

PLANNING GUIDE

Developing a healthy game plan for life:

It is good to develop healthy habits that will help you to achieve your priorities and goals throughout your entire life. The Monthly Action Plan helps you map out a strategy for achieving your priorities and goals in a balanced healthy exercise.

1) Ask God to help you with this planning exercise.

2) Look at the pages in the back of your Bible (Spiritual Disciplines, Prayer List, Personal Goals, and Sport Goals) and fill them in where appropriate.
*If you need help, it is good to get a parent, coach, friend, or minister to help you plan your Monthly Action Plan.

3) As a monthly exercise, fill in the four boxes at the bottom of your Monthly Action Plan from the lists at the back of your Bible.

4) If you know you have competitions, church events, or other events already fixed in your year, mark them into your calendar above the boxes.

5) Review your Monthly Action Plan (Spiritual Disciplines, Prayer List, Personal Goals, and Sport Goals) daily, then honestly mark the boxes that you have worked on or prayed through during that day.

EXAMPLES:

Spiritual Disciplines

Prayer
I will aim to pray every morning

Faith Community I am going to not only attend my church weekly, I want to contribute 2 hours a week to the Sunday school.

Bible Reading I will aim at reading the Gospel of John this month, every morning before training and work hard at living out what I learn from it.

Prayer List

Friends I am going to pray for three friends from my list in the back of my Bible every day. (see back pages for bigger lists)

World I am going to pray for my political leaders and a section of the world every day for this month. (see back pages for bigger lists)

Personal I am going to pray (from my back list) that 'Thy will not my will' be done in certain areas of my life every day. (see back pages for bigger lists)

Personal Goals

Family This month I am going to work hard on encouraging my sister.

Work/School/Social This month I am going to focus on getting to work on time.

Challenge This month I am going to work hard on memorizing John 14:6

Sport Goals

Training This month I am going to focus on my ball handling skills.

Performance This month I am going to work on staying focused throughout the competition.

Competition Results This month I am going to do my best to keep the team unified throughout the competition.

TABLE OF CONTENTS

Introduction pages:

Acknowledgments

A Note from the Editor

Monthly Action Plan: Planning Guide

Matthew 1

Mark 37

Luke 59

John 93

Acts 121

Romans 155

1 Corinthians 175

2 Corinthians 195

Galatians 207

Ephesians 215

Philippians 225

Colossians 231

1 Thessalonians 237

2 Thessalonians 243

1 Timothy 247

2 Timothy 253

Titus 257

Philemon 261

Hebrews 263

James 279

1 Peter 285

2 Peter 291

1 John 295

2 John 302

3 John 303

Jude 305

Revelation 307

Final Section:

Notes

Monthly Action Plan: Goals Lists

Matthew

The first four books of the New Testament are called *Gospels* or *Good News*. Through the writers of the Gospels God gives us a clear, meticulous, and attractive view of Jesus Christ's amazing life.

All the biblical chronicles of Jesus' lineage, birth, life, teachings, miracles, crucifixion, and resurrection have their own flavor and style; but Matthew is one of three parallel accounts (along with Mark and Luke) called synoptic, which literally means "run along side each other." The synoptic Gospels are accounts of Jesus' life that have the same structure and similar pattern and record many of the same historical events in Jesus' life. Each book is inspired by God and has selected events in Jesus' life that address a particular concern or speak to a distinct audience.

Matthew gives a jam-packed and meticulous account of Christ's life. Matthew (Levi), formerly a despised tax collector working for an often corrupt government, was recruited by Jesus, and his response to follow Jesus changed his life forever. It is helpful to keep in mind that Matthew's target audience is Jewish – he writes to his own people to clearly explain that Jesus is the achievement of the Old Testament prophecies. Over and over he reveals to his readers how Jesus has fulfilled the prophecies of the Old Testament and that he is truly our King.

JANUARY M.A.P.

1

S.D.	P.L.	P.G.	S.G.
P. ☐	F. ☐	F. ☐	T. ☐
F. ☐	W. ☐	W. ☐	P. ☐
B. ☐	P. ☐	C. ☐	C. ☐

2

S.D.	P.L.	P.G.	S.G.
P. ☐	F. ☐	F. ☐	T. ☐
F. ☐	W. ☐	W. ☐	P. ☐
B. ☐	P. ☐	C. ☐	C. ☐

3

S.D.	P.L.	P.G.	S.G.
P. ☐	F. ☐	F. ☐	T. ☐
F. ☐	W. ☐	W. ☐	P. ☐
B. ☐	P. ☐	C. ☐	C. ☐

4

S.D.	P.L.	P.G.	S.G.
P. ☐	F. ☐	F. ☐	T. ☐
F. ☐	W. ☐	W. ☐	P. ☐
B. ☐	P. ☐	C. ☐	C. ☐

9

S.D.	P.L.	P.G.	S.G.
P. ☐	F. ☐	F. ☐	T. ☐
F. ☐	W. ☐	W. ☐	P. ☐
B. ☐	P. ☐	C. ☐	C. ☐

10

S.D.	P.L.	P.G.	S.G.
P. ☐	F. ☐	F. ☐	T. ☐
F. ☐	W. ☐	W. ☐	P. ☐
B. ☐	P. ☐	C. ☐	C. ☐

11

S.D.	P.L.	P.G.	S.G.
P. ☐	F. ☐	F. ☐	T. ☐
F. ☐	W. ☐	W. ☐	P. ☐
B. ☐	P. ☐	C. ☐	C. ☐

12

S.D.	P.L.	P.G.	S.G.
P. ☐	F. ☐	F. ☐	T. ☐
F. ☐	W. ☐	W. ☐	P. ☐
B. ☐	P. ☐	C. ☐	C. ☐

17

S.D.	P.L.	P.G.	S.G.
P. ☐	F. ☐	F. ☐	T. ☐
F. ☐	W. ☐	W. ☐	P. ☐
B. ☐	P. ☐	C. ☐	C. ☐

18

S.D.	P.L.	P.G.	S.G.
P. ☐	F. ☐	F. ☐	T. ☐
F. ☐	W. ☐	W. ☐	P. ☐
B. ☐	P. ☐	C. ☐	C. ☐

19

S.D.	P.L.	P.G.	S.G.
P. ☐	F. ☐	F. ☐	T. ☐
F. ☐	W. ☐	W. ☐	P. ☐
B. ☐	P. ☐	C. ☐	C. ☐

20

S.D.	P.L.	P.G.	S.G.
P. ☐	F. ☐	F. ☐	T. ☐
F. ☐	W. ☐	W. ☐	P. ☐
B. ☐	P. ☐	C. ☐	C. ☐

25

S.D.	P.L.	P.G.	S.G.
P. ☐	F. ☐	F. ☐	T. ☐
F. ☐	W. ☐	W. ☐	P. ☐
B. ☐	P. ☐	C. ☐	C. ☐

26

S.D.	P.L.	P.G.	S.G.
P. ☐	F. ☐	F. ☐	T. ☐
F. ☐	W. ☐	W. ☐	P. ☐
B. ☐	P. ☐	C. ☐	C. ☐

27

S.D.	P.L.	P.G.	S.G.
P. ☐	F. ☐	F. ☐	T. ☐
F. ☐	W. ☐	W. ☐	P. ☐
B. ☐	P. ☐	C. ☐	C. ☐

28

S.D.	P.L.	P.G.	S.G.
P. ☐	F. ☐	F. ☐	T. ☐
F. ☐	W. ☐	W. ☐	P. ☐
B. ☐	P. ☐	C. ☐	C. ☐

Spiritual Disciplines

Prayer

Faith Community

Bible Reading

Prayer List

Friends

World

Personal

(For designing your M.A.P. – Monthly Action Plan – see introduction pages)

Who am I....
Where am I going....
How am I going to get there?

nt:sport
MONTHLY ACTION PLAN

5

S.D.	P.L.	P.G.	S.G.
P. ☐	F. ☐	F. ☐	T. ☐
F. ☐	W. ☐	W. ☐	P. ☐
B. ☐	P. ☐	C. ☐	C. ☐

6

S.D.	P.L.	P.G.	S.G.
P. ☐	F. ☐	F. ☐	T. ☐
F. ☐	W. ☐	W. ☐	P. ☐
B. ☐	P. ☐	C. ☐	C. ☐

7

S.D.	P.L.	P.G.	S.G.
P. ☐	F. ☐	F. ☐	T. ☐
F. ☐	W. ☐	W. ☐	P. ☐
B. ☐	P. ☐	C. ☐	C. ☐

8

S.D.	P.L.	P.G.	S.G.
P. ☐	F. ☐	F. ☐	T. ☐
F. ☐	W. ☐	W. ☐	P. ☐
B. ☐	P. ☐	C. ☐	C. ☐

13

S.D.	P.L.	P.G.	S.G.
P. ☐	F. ☐	F. ☐	T. ☐
F. ☐	W. ☐	W. ☐	P. ☐
B. ☐	P. ☐	C. ☐	C. ☐

14

S.D.	P.L.	P.G.	S.G.
P. ☐	F. ☐	F. ☐	T. ☐
F. ☐	W. ☐	W. ☐	P. ☐
B. ☐	P. ☐	C. ☐	C. ☐

15

S.D.	P.L.	P.G.	S.G.
P. ☐	F. ☐	F. ☐	T. ☐
F. ☐	W. ☐	W. ☐	P. ☐
B. ☐	P. ☐	C. ☐	C. ☐

16

S.D.	P.L.	P.G.	S.G.
P. ☐	F. ☐	F. ☐	T. ☐
F. ☐	W. ☐	W. ☐	P. ☐
B. ☐	P. ☐	C. ☐	C. ☐

21

S.D.	P.L.	P.G.	S.G.
P. ☐	F. ☐	F. ☐	T. ☐
F. ☐	W. ☐	W. ☐	P. ☐
B. ☐	P. ☐	C. ☐	C. ☐

22

S.D.	P.L.	P.G.	S.G.
P. ☐	F. ☐	F. ☐	T. ☐
F. ☐	W. ☐	W. ☐	P. ☐
B. ☐	P. ☐	C. ☐	C. ☐

23

S.D.	P.L.	P.G.	S.G.
P. ☐	F. ☐	F. ☐	T. ☐
F. ☐	W. ☐	W. ☐	P. ☐
B. ☐	P. ☐	C. ☐	C. ☐

24

S.D.	P.L.	P.G.	S.G.
P. ☐	F. ☐	F. ☐	T. ☐
F. ☐	W. ☐	W. ☐	P. ☐
B. ☐	P. ☐	C. ☐	C. ☐

29

S.D.	P.L.	P.G.	S.G.
P. ☐	F. ☐	F. ☐	T. ☐
F. ☐	W. ☐	W. ☐	P. ☐
B. ☐	P. ☐	C. ☐	C. ☐

30

S.D.	P.L.	P.G.	S.G.
P. ☐	F. ☐	F. ☐	T. ☐
F. ☐	W. ☐	W. ☐	P. ☐
B. ☐	P. ☐	C. ☐	C. ☐

31

S.D.	P.L.	P.G.	S.G.
P. ☐	F. ☐	F. ☐	T. ☐
F. ☐	W. ☐	W. ☐	P. ☐
B. ☐	P. ☐	C. ☐	C. ☐

Psalm 25:5

Lead me by your truth and teach me, for you are the God who saves me. All day long I put my hope in you.

Personal Goals

Family

Work/School/Social

Challenge

Sport Goals

Training

Performance

Competition Results

Direction
FOLLOW it

Trust in the LORD with all your heart; do not depend on your own understanding. Seek his will in all you do, and he will show you which path to take.

PROVERBS 3:5-6

MATTHEW

The Ancestors of Jesus the Messiah

1

This is a record of the ancestors of Jesus the Messiah, a descendant of David and of Abraham:

[2]Abraham was the father of Isaac.

Isaac was the father of Jacob.

Jacob was the father of Judah and his brothers.

[3]Judah was the father of Perez and Zerah (whose mother was Tamar).

Perez was the father of Hezron.

Hezron was the father of Ram.

[4]Ram was the father of Amminadab.

Amminadab was the father of Nahshon.

Nahshon was the father of Salmon.

[5]Salmon was the father of Boaz (whose mother was Rahab).

Boaz was the father of Obed (whose mother was Ruth).

Obed was the father of Jesse.

[6]Jesse was the father of King David.

David was the father of Solomon (whose mother was Bathsheba, the widow of Uriah).

[7]Solomon was the father of Rehoboam.

Rehoboam was the father of Abijah.

Abijah was the father of Asa.

[8]Asa was the father of Jehoshaphat.

Jehoshaphat was the father of Jehoram.

Jehoram was the father of Uzziah.

[9]Uzziah was the father of Jotham.

Jotham was the father of Ahaz.

Ahaz was the father of Hezekiah.

[10]Hezekiah was the father of Manasseh.

Manasseh was the father of Amon.

Amon was the father of Josiah.

[11]Josiah was the father of Jehoiachin and his brothers (born at the time of the exile to Babylon).

[12]After the Babylonian exile:

Jehoiachin was the father of Shealtiel.

Shealtiel was the father of Zerubbabel.

[13]Zerubbabel was the father of Abiud.

Abiud was the father of Eliakim.

Eliakim was the father of Azor.

[14]Azor was the father of Zadok.

Zadok was the father of Akim.

Akim was the father of Eliud.

[15]Eliud was the father of Eleazar.

Eleazar was the father of Matthan.

Matthan was the father of Jacob.

[16]Jacob was the father of Joseph, the husband of Mary. Mary gave birth to Jesus, who is called the Messiah.

[17]All those listed above include fourteen generations from Abraham to David, fourteen from David to the Babylonian exile, and fourteen from the Babylonian exile to the Messiah.

John Wycliffe translated the first English Bible in 1382.

The Birth of Jesus the Messiah

[18]This is how Jesus the Messiah was born. His mother, Mary, was engaged to be married to Joseph. But before the marriage took place, while she was still a virgin, she became pregnant through the power of the Holy Spirit. [19]Joseph, her fiance, was a good man and did not want to disgrace her publicly, so he decided to break the engagement quietly.

[20]As he considered this, an angel of the Lord appeared to him in a dream. "Joseph, son of David," the angel said, "do not be afraid to take Mary as your wife. For the child within her was conceived by the Holy Spirit. [21]And she will have a son, and you are to name him Jesus, for he will save his people from their sins."

[22]All of this occurred to fulfill the Lord's message through his prophet:

[23]"Look! The virgin will conceive a child!

She will give birth to a son,

and they will call him Immanuel,

which means 'God is with us.'"

[24]When Joseph woke up, he did as the angel of the Lord commanded and took Mary as his wife. [25]But he did not have sexual relations with her until her son was born. And Joseph named him Jesus.

Visitors from the East

2

Jesus was born in Bethlehem in Judea, during the reign of King Herod. About that time some wise men from eastern lands arrived in Jerusalem, asking, [2]"Where is the newborn king of the Jews? We saw his star as it rose, and we have come to worship him."

[3]King Herod was deeply disturbed when he heard this, as

God helps your habits: Good habits come with understanding what God wants of you. Ask for God's help and have a determination to follow his plan for your life. Fill your life with good habits.

"You yourself must be an example to them by doing good works of every kind. Let everything you do reflect the integrity and seriousness of your teaching."

Titus 2:7

was everyone in Jerusalem. [4]He called a meeting of the leading priests and teachers of religious law and asked, "Where is the Messiah supposed to be born?"

[5]"In Bethlehem in Judea," they said, "for this is what the prophet wrote:

[6]'And you, O Bethlehem in the land of Judah,

are not least among the ruling cities of Judah,

for a ruler will come from you

who will be the shepherd for my people Israel.'"

[7]Then Herod called for a private meeting with the wise men, and he learned from them the time when the star first appeared. [8]Then he told them, "Go to Bethlehem and search carefully for the child. And when you find him, come back and tell me so that I can go and worship him, too!"

[9]After this interview the wise men went their way. And the star they had seen in the east guided them to Bethlehem. It went ahead of them and stopped over the place where the child was. [10]When they saw the star, they were filled with joy! [11]They entered the house and saw the child with his

profiles

Adam & Eve: They had it all!

God ended his creation with a spectacular finish — he created men and women in his own image. First he made Adam, who was in charge of caring for and nurturing God's creation. Next he made Eve, knowing it was not good for man to be alone. They had all the privileges of the Garden of Eden (Paradise), and they enjoyed perfect companionship with God. He gave them full reign over all Creation with one clear directive: *"You may freely eat the fruit of every tree in the garden — except the tree of the knowledge of good and evil. If you eat its fruit, you are sure to die" (Genesis 2:16-17).*
One day Satan, in the form of a serpent, shifted Eve's focus and desire from all the wonderful privileges she possessed to the one thing she was not allowed — the very thing that would hurt her. Eve willingly broke God's rules and listened to the serpent instead of God. Sadly, Adam also accepted the forbidden fruit and not only broke his relationship with God but caused all his descendants to inherit the same devastating fate: separation from God and death.

But God already had a plan for restoring his people; as the Gospel writer Luke emphasized, there would be a new Adam – sinless – who would take away the sin of the world. God's plan is Jesus.

mother, Mary, and they bowed down and worshiped him. Then they opened their treasure chests and gave him gifts of gold, frankincense, and myrrh. [12]When it was time to leave, they returned to their own country by another route, for God had warned them in a dream not to return to Herod.

The Escape to Egypt

[13]After the wise men were gone, an angel of the Lord appeared to Joseph in a dream. "Get up! Flee to Egypt with the child and his mother," the angel said. "Stay there until I tell you to return, because Herod is going to search for the child to kill him."
[14]That night Joseph left for Egypt with the child and Mary, his mother, [15]and they stayed there until Herod's death. This fulfilled what the Lord had spoken through the prophet: "I called my Son out of Egypt."
[16]Herod was furious when he realized that the wise men had outwitted him. He sent soldiers to kill all the boys in and around Bethlehem who were two years old and under, based on the wise men's report of the star's first appearance. [17]Herod's brutal action fulfilled what God had spoken through the prophet Jeremiah:
[18]"A cry was heard in Ramah—
weeping and great mourning.
Rachel weeps for her children,
refusing to be comforted,
for they are dead."

The Return to Nazareth

[19]When Herod died, an angel of the Lord appeared in a dream to Joseph in Egypt. [20]"Get up!" the angel said. "Take the child and his mother back to the land of Israel, because those who were trying to kill the child are dead."
[21]So Joseph got up and returned to the land of Israel with Jesus and his mother. [22]But when he learned that the new ruler of Judea was Herod's son Archelaus, he was afraid to go there. Then, after being warned in a dream, he left for the region of Galilee. [23]So the family went and lived in a town called Nazareth. This fulfilled what the prophets had said: "He will be called a Nazarene."

John the Baptist Prepares the Way

3

In those days John the Baptist came to the Judean wilderness and began preaching. His message was, [2]"Repent of your sins and turn to God, for the Kingdom

of Heaven is near." [3]The prophet Isaiah was speaking about John when he said,
"He is a voice shouting in the wilderness,
'Prepare the way for the LORD's coming!
Clear the road for him!'"
[4]John's clothes were woven from coarse camel hair, and he wore a leather belt around his waist. For food he ate locusts and wild honey. [5]People from Jerusalem and from all of Judea and all over the Jordan Valley went out to see and hear John. [6]And when they confessed their sins, he baptized them in the Jordan River.
[7]But when he saw many Pharisees and Sadducees coming to watch him baptize, he denounced them. "You brood of snakes!" he exclaimed. "Who warned you to flee God's coming wrath? [8]Prove by the way you live that you have repented of your sins and turned to God. [9]Don't just say to each other, 'We're safe, for we are descendants of Abraham.' That means nothing, for I tell you, God can create children of Abraham from these very stones. [10]Even now the ax of God's judgment is poised, ready to sever the roots of the trees. Yes, every tree that does not produce good fruit will be chopped down and thrown into the fire.
[11]"I baptize with water those who repent of their sins and turn to God. But someone is coming soon who is greater than I am—so much greater that I'm not worthy even to be his slave and carry his sandals. He will baptize you with the Holy Spirit and with fire. [12]He is ready to separate the chaff from the wheat with his winnowing fork. Then he will clean up the threshing area, gathering the wheat into his barn but burning the chaff with never-ending fire."

The Baptism of Jesus

[13]Then Jesus went from Galilee to the Jordan River to be baptized by John. [14]But John tried to talk him out of it. "I am the one who needs to be baptized by you," he said, "so why are you coming to me?"
[15]But Jesus said, "It should be done, for we must carry out all that God requires." So John agreed to baptize him.
[16]After his baptism, as Jesus came up out of the water, the heavens were opened and he saw the Spirit of God descending like a dove and settling on him. [17]And a voice from heaven said, "This is my dearly loved Son, who brings me great joy."

The Temptation of Jesus

4

Then Jesus was led by the Spirit into the wilderness to be tempted there by the devil. [2]For forty days and

Temptation (MATTHEW 4)

The temptation of Jesus was a preface to his formal ministry and followed forty days and nights fasting and praying in the desert of Judea. This was a tough test with Satan trying to sever Jesus' relationship with his Father. It was a brutal challenge, but it represented a victorious result for Christ and a shining example for us. Note how Jesus relied on his Father and the Holy Spirit for strength. It is also important to understand how Satan falsely used Scripture to tempt Jesus but failed as Jesus refuted him with Scripture in right context.

forty nights he fasted and became very hungry. ³During that time the devil came and said to him, "If you are the Son of God, tell these stones to become loaves of bread."

⁴But Jesus told him, "No! The Scriptures say,

'People do not live by bread alone,
but by every word that comes from the mouth of God.'"

⁵Then the devil took him to the holy city, Jerusalem, to the highest point of the Temple, ⁶and said, "If you are the Son of God, jump off! For the Scriptures say,

'He will order his angels to protect you.
And they will hold you up with their hands
so you won't even hurt your foot on a stone.'"

⁷Jesus responded, "The Scriptures also say, 'You must not test the LORD your God.'"

⁸Next the devil took him to the peak of a very high mountain and showed him the kingdoms of the world and all their glory. ⁹"I will give it all to you," he said, "if you will kneel down and worship me."

¹⁰"Get out of here, Satan," Jesus told him. "For the Scriptures say,

'You must worship the LORD your God
and serve only him.'"

¹¹Then the devil went away, and angels came and took care of Jesus.

The Ministry of Jesus Begins

¹²When Jesus heard that John had been arrested, he left Judea and returned to Galilee. ¹³He went first to Nazareth, then left there and moved to Capernaum, beside the Sea of Galilee, in the region of Zebulun and Naphtali. ¹⁴This fulfilled what God said through the prophet Isaiah:

¹⁵"In the land of Zebulun and of Naphtali,
beside the sea, beyond the Jordan River,
in Galilee where so many Gentiles live,
¹⁶the people who sat in darkness
have seen a great light.
And for those who lived in the land where death casts its shadow,
a light has shined."

¹⁷From then on Jesus began to preach, "Repent of your sins and turn to God, for the Kingdom of Heaven is near."

The First Disciples

¹⁸One day as Jesus was walking along the shore of the Sea of Galilee, he saw two brothers—Simon, also called Peter, and Andrew—throwing a net into the water, for they fished for a living. ¹⁹Jesus called out to them, "Come, follow me, and I will show you how to fish for people!" ²⁰And they left their nets at once and followed him.

²¹A little farther up the shore he saw two other brothers, James and John, sitting in a boat with their father, Zebedee, repairing their nets. And he called them to come, too. ²²They immediately followed him, leaving the boat and their father behind.

Crowds Follow Jesus

²³Jesus traveled throughout the region of Galilee, teaching in the synagogues and announcing the Good News about the Kingdom. And he healed every kind of disease and illness. ²⁴News about him spread as far as Syria, and people soon began bringing to him all who were sick. And whatever their sickness or disease, or if they were demon-possessed or epileptic or paralyzed—he healed them all. ²⁵Large crowds followed him wherever he went—people from Galilee, the Ten Towns, Jerusalem, from all over Judea, and from east of the Jordan River.

The Sermon on the Mount

5

One day as he saw the crowds gathering, Jesus went up on the mountainside and sat down. His disciples gathered around him, ²and he began to teach them.

The Beatitudes

³"God blesses those who are poor and realize their need for him,
for the Kingdom of Heaven is theirs.
⁴God blesses those who mourn,
for they will be comforted.
⁵God blesses those who are humble,
for they will inherit the whole earth.
⁶God blesses those who hunger and thirst for justice,
for they will be satisfied.
⁷God blesses those who are merciful,
for they will be shown mercy.
⁸God blesses those whose hearts are pure,
for they will see God.
⁹God blesses those who work for peace,
for they will be called the children of God.
¹⁰God blesses those who are persecuted for doing right,
for the Kingdom of Heaven is theirs.
¹¹"God blesses you when people mock you and persecute you and lie about you and say all sorts of evil things against

My closest friend is really messed up, but who am I to tell them to straighten out their life?

First, it is not your job to straighten out anybody's life. It's God's job, and he has been doing it for a long time. You do have a responsibility to pray for your friends and teammates and to have Jesus' life reflected in your life. Guide your friends to God when the opportunity arises, tell them you are praying for them, and when it is appropriate, tell them that some of their actions are breaking God's heart. Read the parable of the lost son (Luke 15:11-32). Remember prayer changes things.

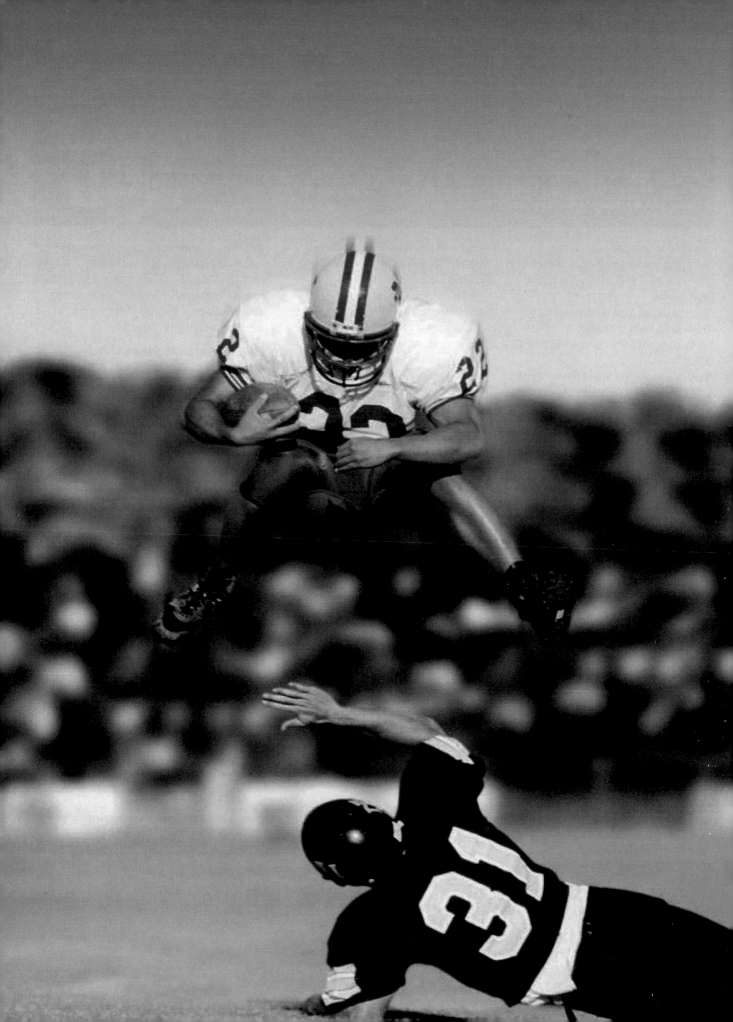

you because you are my followers. [12]Be happy about it! Be very glad! For a great reward awaits you in heaven. And remember, the ancient prophets were persecuted in the same way.

5:1-12 WHAT'S IT SAYING?

WHAT AM I GOING TO DO ABOUT IT?

Teaching about Salt and Light

[13]"You are the salt of the earth. But what good is salt if it has lost its flavor? Can you make it salty again? It will be thrown out and trampled underfoot as worthless.

[14]"You are the light of the world—like a city on a hilltop that cannot be hidden. [15]No one lights a lamp and then puts it under a basket. Instead, a lamp is placed on a stand, where it gives light to everyone in the house. [16]In the same way, let your good deeds shine out for all to see, so that everyone will praise your heavenly Father.

Teaching about the Law

[17]"Don't misunderstand why I have come. I did not come to abolish the law of Moses or the writings of the prophets. No, I came to accomplish their purpose. [18]I tell you the truth, until heaven and earth disappear, not even the smallest detail of God's law will disappear until its purpose is achieved. [19]So if you ignore the

least commandment and teach others to do the same, you will be called the least in the Kingdom of Heaven. But anyone who obeys God's laws and teaches them will be called great in the Kingdom of Heaven. [20]"But I warn you—unless your righteousness is better than the righteousness of the teachers of religious law and the Pharisees, you will never enter the Kingdom of Heaven!

Teaching about Anger

[21]"You have heard that our ancestors were told, 'You must not murder. If you commit murder, you are subject to judgment.' [22]But I say, if you are even angry with someone, you are subject to judgment! If you call someone an idiot, you are in danger of being brought before the court. And if you curse someone, you are in danger of the fires of hell.

[23]"So if you are presenting a sacrifice at the altar in the Temple and you suddenly remember that someone has something against you, [24]leave your sacrifice there at the altar. Go and be reconciled to that person. Then

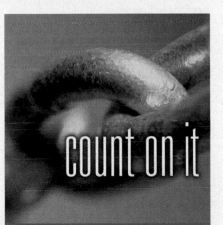

Get some rest!

There are times when you will feel stressed by your performance on and off the field. Sometimes you will be so exhausted that you feel you can't recharge mentally, physically, spiritually, and socially. What does God say? "Come to me, all of you who are weary and carry heavy burdens, and I will give you rest." (Matthew 11:28)
Count on it!

come and offer your sacrifice to God.

[25]"When you are on the way to court with your adversary, settle your differences quickly. Otherwise, your accuser may hand you over to the judge, who will hand you over to an officer, and you will be thrown into prison. [26]And if that happens, you surely won't be free again until you have paid the last penny.

Teaching about Adultery

[27]"You have heard the commandment that says, 'You must not commit adultery.' [28]But I say, anyone who even looks at a woman with lust has already committed adultery with her in his heart. [29]So if your eye—even your good eye—causes you to lust, gouge it out and throw it away. It is better for you to lose one part of your body than for your whole body to be thrown into hell. [30]And if your hand—even your stronger hand—causes you to sin, cut it off and throw it away. It is better for you to lose one part of your body than for your whole body to be thrown into hell.

Teaching about Divorce

[31]"You have heard the law that says, 'A man can divorce his wife by merely giving her a written notice of divorce.' [32]But I say that a man who divorces his wife, unless she has been unfaithful, causes her to commit adultery. And anyone who marries a divorced woman also commits adultery.

Teaching about Vows

[33]"You have also heard that our ancestors were told, 'You must not break your vows; you must carry out the vows you make to the LORD.' [34]But I say, do not make any vows! Do not say, 'By heaven!' because heaven is God's throne. [35]And do not say, 'By the earth!' because the earth is his footstool. And do not say, 'By Jerusalem!' for Jerusalem is the city of the great King. [36]Do not even say, 'By my head!' for you can't turn one hair white or black. [37]Just say a simple, 'Yes, I will,' or 'No, I won't.' Anything beyond this is from the evil one.

Teaching about Revenge

[38]"You have heard the law that says the punishment must match the injury: 'An eye for an eye, and a tooth for a tooth.' [39]But I say, do not resist an evil person! If someone slaps you on the right cheek, offer the other cheek also. [40]If you are sued in court and your shirt is taken from you, give your coat, too. [41]If a soldier demands that you carry his gear for a mile, carry it two miles. [42]Give to those who ask, and don't turn away from those who want to borrow.

Teaching about Love for Enemies

[43]"You have heard the law that says, 'Love your neighbor' and hate your enemy. [44]But I say, love your enemies!* Pray for those who persecute you! [45]In that way, you will be acting

5:44 Some manuscripts add *Bless those who curse you. Do good to those who hate you.* Compare Luke 6:27-28.

What are the five most significant things you could do with your life?

1.
2.
3.
4.
5.

action

WHAT AM I GOING TO DO ABOUT IT?

as true children of your Father in heaven. For he gives his sunlight to both the evil and the good, and he sends rain on the just and the unjust alike. 46If you love only those who love you, what reward is there for that? Even corrupt tax collectors do that much. 47If you are kind only to your friends, how are you different from anyone else? Even pagans do that. 48But you are to be perfect, even as your Father in heaven is perfect.

Teaching about Giving to the Needy

6

"Watch out! Don't do your good deeds publicly, to be admired by others, for you will lose the reward from your Father in heaven. 2When you give to someone in need, don't do as the hypocrites do—blowing trumpets in the synagogues and streets to call attention to their acts of charity! I tell you the truth, they have received all the reward they will ever get. 3But when you give to someone in need, don't let your left hand know what your right hand is doing. 4Give your gifts in private, and your Father, who sees everything, will reward you.

Teaching about Prayer and Fasting

5"When you pray, don't be like the hypocrites who love to pray publicly on street corners and in the synagogues where everyone can see them. I tell you the truth, that is all the reward they will ever get. 6But when you pray, go away by yourself, shut the door behind you, and pray to your Father in private. Then your Father, who sees everything, will reward you.

7"When you pray, don't babble on and on as people of other religions do. They think their prayers are answered merely by repeating their words again and again. 8Don't be like them, for your Father knows exactly what you need even before you ask him! 9Pray like this:
Our Father in heaven,
may your name be kept holy.
10May your Kingdom come soon.
May your will be done on earth,
as it is in heaven.
11Give us today the food we need,
12and forgive us our sins,
as we have forgiven those who sin against us.
13And don't let us yield to temptation,
but rescue us from the evil one.

14"If you forgive those who sin against you, your heavenly Father will forgive you. 15But if you refuse to forgive others, your Father will not forgive your sins.

16"And when you fast, don't make it obvious, as the hypocrites do, for they try to look miserable and disheveled so people will admire them for their fasting. I tell you the truth, that is the only reward they will ever get. 17But when you fast, comb your hair and wash your face. 18Then no one will notice that you

are fasting, except your Father, who knows what you do in private. And your Father, who sees everything, will reward you.

Teaching about Money and Possessions

19"Don't store up treasures here on earth, where moths eat them and rust destroys them, and where thieves break in and steal. 20Store your treasures in heaven, where moths and rust cannot destroy, and thieves do not break in and steal. 21Wherever your treasure is, there the desires of your heart will also be. 22Your eye is a lamp that provides light for your body. When your eye is good, your whole body is filled with light. 23But when your eye is bad, your whole body is filled with darkness. And if the light you think you have is actually darkness, how deep that darkness is! 24No one can serve two masters. For you will hate one and love the other; you will be devoted to one and despise the other. You cannot serve both God and money.

25"That is why I tell you not to worry about everyday life—whether you have enough food and drink, or enough clothes to wear. Isn't life more than food, and your body more than clothing? 26Look at the birds. They don't plant or harvest or store food in barns, for

6:13 Or *from evil.* Some manuscripts add *For yours is the kingdom and the power and the glory forever. Amen.*

TIPS

Progress:

By using balanced training principles, eating a nutrient-rich diet, and getting proper amounts of rest, almost every person can make incredible changes in his or her performance.

your heavenly Father feeds them. And aren't you far more valuable to him than they are? ²⁷Can all your worries add a single moment to your life?

²⁸"And why worry about your clothing? Look at the lilies of the field and how they grow. They don't work or make their clothing, ²⁹yet Solomon in all his glory was not dressed as beautifully as they are. ³⁰And if God cares so wonderfully for wildflowers that are here today and thrown into the fire tomorrow, he will certainly care for you. Why do you have so little faith? ³¹"So don't worry about these things, saying, 'What will we eat? What will we drink? What will we wear?' ³²These things dominate the thoughts of unbelievers, but your heavenly Father already knows all your needs. ³³Seek the Kingdom of God above all else, and live righteously, and he will give you everything you need. ³⁴"So don't worry about tomorrow, for tomorrow will bring its own worries. Today's trouble is enough for today.

Do Not Judge Others

7

"Do not judge others, and you will not be judged. ²For you will be treated as you treat others. The standard you use in judging is the standard by which you will be judged.

³"And why worry about a speck in your friend's eye when you have a log in your own? ⁴How can you think of saying to your friend, 'Let me help you get rid of that speck in your eye,' when you can't see past the log in your own eye? ⁵Hypocrite! First get rid of the log in your own eye; then you will see well enough to deal with the speck in your friend's eye.

⁶"Don't waste what is holy on people who are unholy. Don't throw your pearls to pigs! They will trample the pearls, then turn and attack you.

Effective Prayer

⁷"Keep on asking, and you will receive what you ask for. Keep on seeking, and you will find. Keep on knocking, and the door will be opened to you. ⁸For everyone who asks, receives. Everyone who seeks, finds. And to everyone who knocks, the door will be opened.

⁹"You parents—if your children ask for a loaf of bread, do you give them a stone instead? ¹⁰Or if they ask for a fish, do you give them a snake? Of course not! ¹¹So if you sinful people know how to give good gifts to your children, how much more will your heavenly Father give good gifts to those who ask him.

The Golden Rule

¹²"Do to others whatever you would like them to do to you. This is the essence of all that is taught in the law and the prophets.

The Narrow Gate

¹³"You can enter God's Kingdom only through the narrow gate. The highway to hell is broad, and its gate is wide for the many who choose that way. ¹⁴But the gateway to life is very narrow and the road is difficult, and only a few ever find it.

The Tree and Its Fruit

¹⁵"Beware of false prophets who come disguised as harmless sheep but are really vicious wolves. ¹⁶You can identify them by their fruit, that is, by the way they act. Can you pick grapes from thornbushes, or

action

7:7-12 WHAT'S IT SAYING?

WHAT AM I GOING TO DO ABOUT IT?

figs from thistles? ¹⁷A good tree produces good fruit, and a bad tree produces bad fruit. ¹⁸A good tree can't produce bad fruit, and a bad tree can't produce good fruit. ¹⁹So every tree that does not produce good fruit is chopped down and thrown into the fire. ²⁰Yes, just as you can identify a tree by its fruit, so you can identify people by their actions.

True Disciples

²¹"Not everyone who calls out to me, 'Lord! Lord!' will enter the Kingdom of Heaven. Only those who actually do the will of my Father in heaven will enter. ²²On judgment day many will say to me, 'Lord! Lord! We prophesied in your name and cast out demons in your name and performed many miracles in your name.' ²³But I will reply, 'I never knew you. Get away from me, you who break God's laws.'

STATS

At the first modern Olympic Games there were 241 male but no female competitors. Women were allowed to take part in the next Olympics in Paris. In the 1996 Games there were 3512 female competitors.

Lord of the Harvest (MATTHEW 9:35–10:42)
Jesus so far in his ministry had recruited disciples, taught, and performed miracles. At the end of chapter 9 we see Jesus very upset as he observed his people who were helpless and without someone to lead them safely. A weak analogy could be a gifted athlete who has no encouragement, guidance, or coaching and is spoiling their health by stupid and poor training. Jesus is concerned about his people and urges prayer to his Father, the Lord of the harvest, to send out workers. It is no coincidence that in the next passage we see Jesus training and mobilizing his top guys to do ministry.

BIBLE HIT

Building on a Solid Foundation

24"Anyone who listens to my teaching and follows it is wise, like a person who builds a house on solid rock. 25Though the rain comes in torrents and the floodwaters rise and the winds beat against that house, it won't collapse because it is built on bedrock. 26But anyone who hears my teaching and ignores it is foolish, like a person who builds a house on sand. 27When the rains and floods come and the winds beat against that house, it will collapse with a mighty crash."

28When Jesus had finished saying these things, the crowds were amazed at his teaching, 29for he taught with real authority—quite unlike their teachers of religious law.

Jesus Heals a Man with Leprosy

8

Large crowds followed Jesus as he came down the mountainside. 2Suddenly, a man with leprosy approached him and knelt before him. "Lord," the man said, "if you are willing, you can heal me and make me clean."

3Jesus reached out and touched him. "I am willing," he said. "Be healed!" And instantly the leprosy disappeared. 4Then Jesus said to him, "Don't tell anyone about this. Instead, go to the priest and let him examine you. Take along the offering required in the law of Moses for those who have been healed of leprosy. This will be a public testimony that you have been cleansed."

The Faith of a Roman Officer

5When Jesus returned to Capernaum, a Roman officer came and pleaded with him, 6"Lord, my young servant lies in bed, paralyzed and in terrible pain."

7Jesus said, "I will come and heal him."

8But the officer said, "Lord, I am not worthy to have you come into my home. Just say the word from where you are, and my servant will be healed. 9I know this because I am under the authority of my superior officers, and I have authority over my soldiers. I only need to say, 'Go,' and they go, or 'Come,' and they come. And if I say to my slaves, 'Do this,' they do it."

10When Jesus heard this, he was amazed. Turning to those who were following him, he said, "I tell you the truth, I haven't seen faith like this in all Israel! 11And I tell you this, that many Gentiles will come from all over the world—from east and west—and sit down with Abraham, Isaac, and Jacob at the feast in the Kingdom of Heaven. 12But many Israelites—those for whom the Kingdom was prepared—will be thrown into outer darkness, where there will be weeping and gnashing of teeth."

13Then Jesus said to the Roman officer, "Go back home. Because you believed, it has happened." And the young servant was healed that same hour.

Jesus Heals Many People

14When Jesus arrived at Peter's house, Peter's mother-in-law was sick in bed with a high fever. 15But when Jesus touched her hand, the fever left her. Then she got up and prepared a meal for him.

16That evening many demon-possessed people were brought to Jesus. He cast out the evil spirits with a simple command, and he healed all the sick. 17This fulfilled the word of the Lord through the prophet Isaiah, who said,

"He took our sicknesses
and removed our diseases."

The Cost of Following Jesus

18When Jesus saw the crowd around him, he instructed his disciples to cross to the other side of the lake.

19Then one of the teachers of religious law said to him, "Teacher, I will follow you wherever you go."

20But Jesus replied, "Foxes have dens to live in, and birds have nests, but the Son of Man has no place even to lay his head."

21Another of his disciples said, "Lord, first let me return home and bury my father."

22But Jesus told him, "Follow me now. Let the spiritually dead bury their own dead."

Jesus Calms the Storm

23Then Jesus got into the boat and started across the lake with his disciples. 24Suddenly, a fierce storm struck the lake, with waves breaking into the boat. But Jesus was sleeping. 25The disciples went and woke him up, shouting, "Lord, save us! We're going to drown!"

26Jesus responded, "Why are you afraid? You have so little faith!" Then he got up and rebuked the wind and waves, and suddenly all was calm.

27The disciples were amazed. "Who is this man?" they asked. "Even the winds and waves obey him!"

Jesus Heals Two Demon-Possessed Men

28When Jesus arrived on the other side of the lake, in the region of the Gadarenes, two men who were possessed by demons met him. They lived in a cemetery and were so violent that no one could go through that area.

29They began screaming at him, "Why are you interfering with us, Son of God? Have you come here to torture us before God's appointed time?"

30There happened to be a large herd of pigs feeding in the distance. 31So the demons begged, "If you cast us out, send us into that herd of pigs."

32"All right, go!" Jesus commanded them. So the demons came out of the men and entered the pigs, and the whole herd plunged down the steep hillside into the lake and drowned in the water.

33The herdsmen fled to the nearby town, telling everyone what happened to the demon-possessed men. 34Then the entire town came out to meet Jesus, but they begged him to go away and leave them alone.

Jesus Heals a Paralyzed Man

9

Jesus climbed into a boat and went back across the lake to his own town. 2Some people brought to him a paralyzed man on a mat. Seeing their faith, Jesus said to the paralyzed man, "Be encouraged, my child! Your sins are forgiven."

3But some of the teachers of religious law said to themselves, "That's blasphemy! Does he think he's God?"

4Jesus knew what they were thinking, so he asked

them, "Why do you have such evil thoughts in your hearts? ⁵Is it easier to say 'Your sins are forgiven,' or 'Stand up and walk'? ⁶So I will prove to you that the Son of Man has the authority on earth to forgive sins." Then Jesus turned to the paralyzed man and said, "Stand up, pick up your mat, and go home!"

⁷And the man jumped up and went home! ⁸Fear swept through the crowd as they saw this happen. And they praised God for sending a man with such great authority.

Jesus Calls Matthew

⁹As Jesus was walking along, he saw a man named Matthew sitting at his tax collector's booth. "Follow me and be my disciple," Jesus said to him. So Matthew got up and followed him.

¹⁰Later, Matthew invited Jesus and his disciples to his home as dinner guests, along with many tax collectors and other disreputable sinners. ¹¹But when the Pharisees saw this, they asked his disciples, "Why does your teacher eat with such scum?"

¹²When Jesus heard this, he said, "Healthy people don't need a doctor—sick people do." ¹³Then he added, "Now go and learn the meaning of this Scripture: 'I want you to show mercy, not offer sacrifices.' For I have come to call not those who think they are righteous, but those who know they are sinners."

A Discussion about Fasting

¹⁴One day the disciples of John the Baptist came to Jesus and asked him, "Why don't your disciples fast like we do and the Pharisees do?"

¹⁵Jesus replied, "Do wedding guests mourn while celebrating with the groom? Of course not. But someday the groom will be taken away from them, and then they will fast.

¹⁶"Besides, who would patch old clothing with new cloth? For the new patch would shrink and rip away from the old cloth, leaving an even bigger tear than before.

¹⁷"And no one puts new wine into old wineskins. For the old skins would burst from the pressure, spilling the wine and ruining the skins. New wine is stored in new wineskins so that both are preserved."

Jesus Heals in Response to Faith

¹⁸As Jesus was saying this, the leader of a synagogue came and knelt before him. "My daughter has just died," he said, "but you can bring her back to life again if you just come and lay your hand on her."

¹⁹So Jesus and his disciples got up and went with him. ²⁰Just then a woman who had suffered for twelve years with constant bleeding came up behind him. She touched the fringe of his robe, ²¹for she thought, "If I can just touch his robe, I will be healed."

²²Jesus turned around, and when he saw her he said, "Daughter, be encouraged! Your faith has made you well." And the woman was healed at that moment.

²³When Jesus arrived at the official's home, he saw the noisy crowd and heard the funeral music. ²⁴"Get out!" he told them. "The girl isn't dead; she's only asleep." But the crowd laughed at him. ²⁵After the crowd was put outside, however, Jesus went in and took the girl by the hand, and she stood up! ²⁶The report of this miracle swept through the entire countryside.

Jesus Heals the Blind

²⁷After Jesus left the girl's home, two blind men followed along behind him, shouting, "Son of David, have mercy on us!"

²⁸They went right into the house where he was staying, and Jesus asked them, "Do you believe I can make you see?"

"Yes, Lord," they told him, "we do."

²⁹Then he touched their eyes and said, "Because of your faith, it will happen." ³⁰Then their eyes were opened, and they could see! Jesus sternly warned them, "Don't tell anyone about this." ³¹But instead, they went out and spread his fame all over the region.

³²When they left, a demon-possessed man who couldn't speak was brought to Jesus. ³³So Jesus cast out the demon, and

I know I am supposed to have peace but I just keep feeling anxious.
You are definitely not alone on this one! Anxiety is a bell to remind us to pray. Ask God for help and keep asking him. Sometimes it is good to make a list of everything that is making you anxious and pray about each item on the list. Know that God wants what is best for you.

STAND POINT

When your performance is poor

10:31

So don't be afraid; you are more valuable to God than a whole flock of sparrows.

then the man began to speak. The crowds were amazed. "Nothing like this has ever happened in Israel!" they exclaimed. [34]But the Pharisees said, "He can cast out demons because he is empowered by the prince of demons."

The Need for Workers

[35]Jesus traveled through all the towns and villages of that area, teaching in the synagogues and announcing the Good News about the Kingdom. And he healed every kind of disease and illness. [36]When he saw the crowds, he had compassion on them because they were confused and helpless, like sheep without a shepherd. [37]He said to his disciples, "The harvest is great, but the workers are few. [38]So pray to the Lord who is in charge of the harvest; ask him to send more workers into his fields."

Jesus Sends Out the Twelve Apostles

10

Jesus called his twelve disciples together and gave them authority to cast out evil spirits and to heal every kind

of disease and illness. [2]Here are the names of the twelve apostles: first, Simon (also called Peter), then Andrew (Peter's brother), James (son of Zebedee), John (James's brother), [3]Philip, Bartholomew, Thomas, Matthew (the tax collector), James (son of Alphaeus), Thaddaeus, [4]Simon (the zealot), Judas Iscariot (who later betrayed him).

[5]Jesus sent out the twelve apostles with these instructions: "Don't go to the Gentiles or the Samaritans, [6]but only to the people of Israel—God's lost sheep. [7]Go and announce to them that the Kingdom of Heaven is near. [8]Heal the sick, raise the dead, cure those with leprosy, and cast out demons. Give as freely as you have received!

[9]"Don't take any money in your money belts—no gold, silver, or even copper coins. [10]Don't carry a traveler's bag with a change of clothes and sandals or even a walking stick. Don't hesitate to accept hospitality, because those who work deserve to be fed. [11]"Whenever you enter a city or village, search for a worthy person and stay in his home until you leave town. [12]When you enter the home, give it your blessing. [13]If it turns out to be a worthy home, let your blessing stand; if it is not, take back the blessing. [14]If any household or town refuses to welcome you or listen to your message, shake its dust from your feet as you leave. [15]I tell you the truth, the wicked cities of Sodom and Gomorrah will be better off than such a town on the judgment day.

[16]"Look, I am sending you out as sheep among wolves. So be as shrewd as snakes and harmless as doves. [17]But beware! For you will be handed over to the courts and will be flogged with whips in the synagogues. [18]You will stand trial before governors and kings because you are my followers. But this will be your opportunity to tell the rulers and other unbelievers about me. [19]When you are arrested, don't worry about

how to respond or what to say. God will give you the right words at the right time. [20]For it is not you who will be speaking—it will be the Spirit of your Father speaking through you.

[21]"A brother will betray his brother to death, a father will betray his own child, and children will rebel against their parents and cause them to be killed. [22]And all nations will hate you because you are my followers. But everyone who endures to the end will be saved. [23]When you are persecuted in one town, flee to the next. I tell you the truth, the Son of Man will return before you have reached all the towns of Israel.

[24]"Students are not greater than their teacher, and slaves are not greater than their master. [25]Students are to be like their teacher, and slaves are to be like their master. And since I, the master of the household, have been called the prince of demons, the members of my household will be called by even worse names! [26]"But don't be afraid of those who threaten you. For the time is coming when everything that is covered will be revealed, and all that is secret will be made known to all. [27]What I tell you now in the darkness, shout abroad when daybreak comes. What I whisper in your ear, shout from the housetops for all to hear! [28]"Don't be afraid of those who want to kill your body; they cannot touch your soul. Fear only God, who can destroy both soul and body in hell. [29]What is the price of two sparrows—one copper coin? But not a single sparrow can fall to the ground without your Father knowing it. [30]And the very hairs on your head are all numbered. [31]So don't be afraid; you are more valuable to God than a whole flock of sparrows.

[32]"Everyone who acknowledges me publicly here on earth, I will also acknowledge before my Father in heaven. [33]But everyone who denies me here on earth, I will also deny before my Father in heaven.

Winners walk the talk!

Why is it that we can painstakingly live out our faith in every aspect of our life, then completely ignore Christ in our sport? If we do not practice what we preach — the character and qualities of Christ working in us — then we slash the throat of our gospel message. We must live it on the field, in the locker room, and on the road. The best way to teach a concept is to model it. Make sport your mission! "In the same way, encourage the young men to live wisely. And you yourself must be an example to them by doing good works of every kind." Titus 2:6-7

Winners – live it!

34"Don't imagine that I came to bring peace to the earth! I came not to bring peace, but a sword.
35'I have come to set a man against his father,
a daughter against her mother,
and a daughter-in-law against her mother-in-law.
36Your enemies will be right in your own household!'
37"If you love your father or mother more than you love me, you are not worthy of being mine; or if you love your son or daughter more than me, you are not worthy of being mine. 38If you refuse to take up your cross and follow me, you are not worthy of being mine. 39If you cling to your life, you will lose it; but if you give up your life for me, you will find it.
40"Anyone who receives you receives me, and anyone who receives me receives the Father who sent me. 41If you receive a prophet as one who speaks for God, you will be given the same reward as a prophet. And if you receive righteous people because of their righteousness, you will be given a reward like theirs. 42And if you give even a cup of cold water to one of the least of my followers, you will surely be rewarded."

10:40-42 WHAT'S IT SAYING?

WHAT AM I GOING TO DO ABOUT IT?

WHAT DOES IT MEAN?

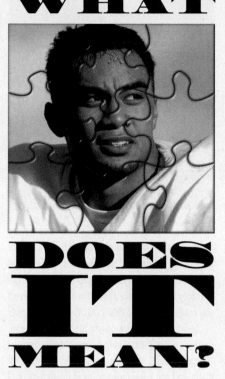

unpardonable sin

Jesus assures us that all our sins can be forgiven, even blasphemy (to speak irreverently and disrespectfully about or to God), except the deliberate refusal to acknowledge God's power – the Holy Spirit – in Christ. Many people worry that they have accidentally committed the *unpardonable sin*. The very fact they are concerned about committing the unpardonable sin, the blaspheming of the Holy Spirit, would suggest they haven't. To blaspheme is to willfully know God's truth and to speak or attribute the action of the Holy Spirit to Satan, not to speak out of ignorance or unbelief.

Jesus and John the Baptist

11

When Jesus had finished giving these instructions to his twelve disciples, he went out to teach and preach in towns throughout the region.

2John the Baptist, who was in prison, heard about all the things the Messiah was doing. So he sent his disciples to ask Jesus, 3"Are you the Messiah we've been expecting, or should we keep looking for someone else?"
4Jesus told them, "Go back to John and tell him what you have heard and seen—5the blind see, the lame walk, the lepers are cured, the deaf hear, the dead are raised to life, and the Good News is being preached to the poor. 6And tell him, 'God blesses those who do not turn away because of me.'"
7As John's disciples were leaving, Jesus began talking about him to the crowds. "What kind of man did you go into the wilderness to see? Was he a weak reed, swayed by every breath of wind? 8Or were you expecting to see a man dressed in expensive clothes? No, people with expensive clothes live in palaces. 9Were you looking for a prophet? Yes, and he is more than a prophet. 10John is the man to whom the Scriptures refer when they say,
'Look, I am sending my messenger ahead of you,
and he will prepare your way before you.'
11"I tell you the truth, of all who have ever lived, none is greater than John the Baptist. Yet even the least person in the Kingdom of Heaven is greater than he is! 12And from the time John the Baptist began preaching until now, the Kingdom of Heaven has been forcefully advancing, and violent people are attacking it. 13For before John came, all the prophets and the law of Moses looked forward to this present time. 14And if you are willing to accept what I say, he is Elijah, the one the prophets said would come. 15Anyone with ears to hear should listen and understand!
16"To what can I compare this generation? It is like children playing a game in the public square. They complain to their friends,
17'We played wedding songs, and you didn't dance, so we played funeral songs, and you didn't mourn.'
18For John didn't spend his time eating and drinking, and you say, 'He's possessed by a demon.' 19The Son of Man, on the other hand, feasts and drinks, and you say, 'He's a glutton and a drunkard, and a friend of tax collectors and other sinners!' But wisdom is shown to be right by its results."

Judgment for the Unbelievers

20Then Jesus began to denounce the towns where he had done so many of his miracles, because they hadn't repented of their sins and turned to God. 21"What sorrow awaits you, Korazin and Bethsaida! For if the miracles I did in you had been done in wicked Tyre and Sidon, their people would have repented of their sins long ago, clothing themselves in burlap and throwing ashes on their heads to show their remorse. 22I tell you, Tyre and Sidon will be better off on judgment day than you.
23"And you people of Capernaum, will you be honored in

heaven? No, you will go down to the place of the dead. For if the miracles I did for you had been done in wicked Sodom, it would still be here today. ²⁴I tell you, even Sodom will be better off on judgment day than you."

Jesus' Prayer of Thanksgiving

²⁵At that time Jesus prayed this prayer: "O Father, Lord of heaven and earth, thank you for hiding these things from those who think themselves wise and clever, and for revealing them to the childlike. ²⁶Yes, Father, it pleased you to do it this way!

²⁷"My Father has entrusted everything to me. No one truly knows the Son except the Father, and no one truly knows the Father except the Son and those to whom the Son chooses to reveal him."

²⁸Then Jesus said, "Come to me, all of you who are weary and carry heavy burdens, and I will give you rest. ²⁹Take my yoke upon you. Let me teach you, because I am humble and gentle at heart, and you will find rest for your souls. ³⁰For my yoke is easy to bear, and the burden I give you is light."

A Discussion about the Sabbath

12

At about that time Jesus was walking through some grainfields on the Sabbath. His disciples were hungry, so they began breaking off some heads of grain and eating them. ²But some Pharisees saw them do it and protested, "Look, your disciples are breaking the law by harvesting grain on the Sabbath."

STAND POINT

When you need to keep your cool

12:28-30

But if I am casting out demons by the Spirit of God, then the Kingdom of God has arrived among you. For who is powerful enough to enter the house of a strong man like Satan and plunder his goods? . . . someone who could tie him up and then plunder his house. Anyone who isn't with me opposes me, and anyone who isn't working with me is actually working against me.

³Jesus said to them, "Haven't you read in the Scriptures what David did when he and his companions were hungry? ⁴He went into the house of God, and they broke the law by eating the sacred loaves of bread that only the priests are allowed to eat. ⁵And haven't you read in the law of Moses that the priests on duty in the Temple may work on the Sabbath? ⁶I tell you, there is one here who is even greater than the Temple! ⁷But you would not have condemned my innocent disciples if you knew the meaning of this Scripture: 'I want you to show mercy, not offer sacrifices.' ⁸For the Son of Man is Lord, even over the Sabbath!"

Jesus Heals on the Sabbath

⁹Then Jesus went over to their synagogue, ¹⁰where he noticed a man with a deformed hand. The Pharisees asked Jesus, "Does the law permit a person to work by healing on the Sabbath?" (They were hoping he would say yes, so they could bring charges against him.)

¹¹And he answered, "If you had a sheep that fell into a well on the Sabbath, wouldn't you work to pull it out? Of course you would. ¹²And how much more valuable is a person than a sheep! Yes, the law permits a person to do good on the Sabbath."

¹³Then he said to the man, "Hold out your hand." So the man held out his hand, and it was restored, just like the other one! ¹⁴Then the Pharisees called a meeting to plot how to kill Jesus.

Jesus, God's Chosen Servant

¹⁵But Jesus knew what they were planning. So he left that area, and many people followed him. He healed all the sick among them, ¹⁶but he warned them not to reveal who he was. ¹⁷This fulfilled the prophecy of Isaiah concerning him:

¹⁸"Look at my Servant, whom I have chosen.
He is my Beloved, who pleases me.

I will put my Spirit upon him,
and he will proclaim justice to the nations.
¹⁹He will not fight or shout
or raise his voice in public.
²⁰He will not crush the weakest reed
or put out a flickering candle.
Finally he will cause justice to be victorious.
²¹And his name will be the hope
of all the world."

Jesus and the Prince of Demons

²²Then a demon-possessed man, who was blind and couldn't speak, was brought to Jesus. He healed the man so that he could both speak and see. ²³The crowd was amazed and asked, "Could it be that Jesus is the Son of David, the Messiah?"

²⁴But when the Pharisees heard about the miracle, they said, "No wonder he can cast out demons. He gets his power from Satan, the prince of demons."

²⁵Jesus knew their thoughts and replied, "Any kingdom divided by civil war is doomed. A town or family splintered by feuding will fall apart. ²⁶And if Satan is casting out Satan, he is divided and fighting against himself. His own kingdom will not survive. ²⁷And if I am empowered by Satan, what about your own exorcists? They cast out demons, too, so they will condemn you for what you have said. ²⁸But if I am casting out demons by the Spirit of God, then the Kingdom of God has arrived among you. ²⁹For who is powerful enough to enter the house of a strong man like Satan and plunder his goods? Only someone even stronger—someone who could tie him up and then plunder his house.

³⁰"Anyone who isn't with me opposes me, and anyone who isn't working with me is actually working against me.

³¹"Every sin and blasphemy can be forgiven—except blasphemy against the Holy Spirit, which will never be forgiven. ³²Anyone who speaks against the Son of Man can be forgiven, but anyone who speaks against the Holy Spirit will never be forgiven, either in this world or in the world to come.

³³"A tree is identified by its fruit. If a tree is good, its fruit will be good. If a tree is bad, its fruit will be bad. ³⁴You brood of snakes! How could evil men like you speak what is good and right? For whatever is in your heart determines what you say. ³⁵A good person produces good things from the treasury of a good heart, and an evil person produces evil things from the treasury of an evil heart. ³⁶And I tell you this, you must give an account on judgment day for every idle

word you speak. [37]The words you say will either acquit you or condemn you."

The Sign of Jonah

[38]One day some teachers of religious law and Pharisees came to Jesus and said, "Teacher, we want you to show us a miraculous sign to prove your authority."

[39]But Jesus replied, "Only an evil, adulterous generation would demand a miraculous sign; but the only sign I will give them is the sign of the prophet Jonah. [40]For as Jonah was in the belly of the great fish for three days and three nights, so will the Son of Man be in the heart of the earth for three days and three nights.

[41]"The people of Nineveh will stand up against this generation on judgment day and condemn it, for they repented of their sins at the preaching of Jonah. Now someone greater than Jonah is here—but you refuse to repent. [42]The queen of Sheba will also stand up against this generation on judgment day and condemn it, for she came from a distant land to hear the wisdom of Solomon. Now someone greater than Solomon is here—but you refuse to listen.

[43]"When an evil spirit leaves a person, it goes into the desert, seeking rest but finding none. [44]Then it says, 'I will return to the person I came from.' So it returns and finds its former home empty, swept, and in order. [45]Then the spirit finds seven other spirits more evil than itself, and they all enter the person and live there. And so that person is worse off than before. That will be the experience of this evil generation."

The True Family of Jesus

[46]As Jesus was speaking to the crowd, his mother and brothers stood outside, asking to speak to him. [47]Someone told Jesus, "Your mother and your brothers are outside, and they want to speak to you."

[48]Jesus asked, "Who is my mother? Who are my brothers?" [49]Then he pointed to his disciples and said, "Look, these are my mother and brothers. [50]Anyone who does the will of my Father in heaven is my brother and sister and mother!"

Parable of the Farmer Scattering Seed

13

Later that same day Jesus left the house and sat beside the lake. [2]A large crowd soon gathered around him, so he got into a boat. Then he sat there and taught as the people stood on the shore. [3]He told many stories in the form of parables, such as this one:

"Listen! A farmer went out to plant some seeds. [4]As he scattered them across his field, some seeds fell on a footpath, and the birds came and ate them. [5]Other seeds fell on shallow soil with underlying rock. The seeds sprouted quickly because

the soil was shallow. [6]But the plants soon wilted under the hot sun, and since they didn't have deep roots, they died. [7]Other seeds fell among thorns that grew up and choked out the tender plants. [8]Still other seeds fell on fertile soil, and they produced a crop that was thirty, sixty, and even a hundred times as much as had been planted! [9]Anyone with ears to hear should listen and understand."

[10]His disciples came and asked him, "Why do you use parables when you talk to the people?"

[11]He replied, "You are permitted to understand the secrets of the Kingdom of Heaven, but others are not. [12]To those who listen to my teaching, more understanding will be given, and they will have an abundance of knowledge. But for those who are not listening, even what little understanding they have will be taken away from them. [13]That is why I use these parables,

For they look, but they don't really see.
They hear, but they don't really listen or understand.

[14]This fulfills the prophecy of Isaiah that says,
'When you hear what I say,
you will not understand.
When you see what I do,
you will not comprehend.
[15]For the hearts of these people are hardened,
and their ears cannot hear,
and they have closed their eyes—
so their eyes cannot see,
and their ears cannot hear,
and their hearts cannot understand,
and they cannot turn to me
and let me heal them.'

Basketball was invented in 1891 by James Naismith. He set out to invent a game to occupy his college students and help them grow closer to God. He once said, "It is not what the boy does with the ball that is important, but what the ball does for the boy."

[16]"But blessed are your eyes, because they see; and your ears, because they hear. [17]I tell you the truth, many prophets and righteous people longed to see what you see, but they didn't see it. And they longed to hear what you hear, but they didn't hear it.

[18]"Now listen to the explanation of the parable about the farmer planting seeds: [19]The seed that fell on the footpath represents those who hear the message about the Kingdom and don't understand it. Then the evil one comes and snatches away the seed that was planted in their hearts. [20]The seed on the rocky soil represents those who hear the message and immediately receive it with joy. [21]But since they don't have deep roots, they don't last long. They fall away as soon as they have problems or are persecuted for believing God's word. [22]The seed that fell among the thorns represents those who hear God's word, but all too quickly the message is crowded out by the worries of this life and the lure of wealth, so no fruit is produced. [23]The seed that fell on good soil represents those who truly hear and understand God's word and produce a harvest of thirty, sixty, or even a hundred times as much as had been planted!"

Parable of the Wheat and Weeds

[24]Here is another story Jesus told: "The Kingdom of Heaven is like a farmer who planted good seed in his field. [25]But that night as the workers slept, his enemy came and planted weeds among the wheat, then slipped away. [26]When the crop began to grow and produce grain, the weeds also grew.

[27]"The farmer's workers went to him and said, 'Sir, the field where you planted that good seed is full of weeds! Where did they come from?'

[28]"An enemy has done this!' the farmer exclaimed.
"'Should we pull out the weeds?' they asked.

[29]"'No,' he replied, 'you'll uproot the wheat if you do. [30]Let both grow together until the harvest. Then I will tell the harvesters to sort out the weeds, tie them into bundles, and burn them, and to put the wheat in the barn.'"

Parable of the Mustard Seed

[31]Here is another illustration Jesus used: "The Kingdom of Heaven is like a mustard seed planted in a field. [32]It is the smallest of all seeds, but it becomes the largest of garden plants; it grows into a tree, and birds come and make nests in its branches."

Parable of the Yeast

[33]Jesus also used this illustration: "The Kingdom of Heaven is like the yeast a woman used in making

Keep your focus positive! Think about people or things that are truthful and good and try to do things the right way. When in doubt, think about the life of Jesus. "Fix your thoughts on what is true, and honorable, and right, and pure, and lovely, and admirable. Think about things that are excellent and worthy of praise."
Philippians 4:8

bread. Even though she put only a little yeast in three measures of flour, it permeated every part of the dough."

34Jesus always used stories and illustrations like these when speaking to the crowds. In fact, he never spoke to them without using such parables. 35This fulfilled what God had spoken through the prophet:

"I will speak to you in parables.
I will explain things hidden since the creation of the world."

Parable of the Wheat and Weeds Explained

36Then, leaving the crowds outside, Jesus went into the house. His disciples said, "Please explain to us the story of the weeds in the field."

37Jesus replied, "The Son of Man is the farmer who plants the good seed. 38The field is the world, and the good seed represents the people of the Kingdom. The weeds are the people who belong to the evil one. 39The enemy who planted the weeds among the wheat is the devil. The harvest is the end of the world, and the harvesters are the angels.

40"Just as the weeds are sorted out and burned in the fire, so it will be at the end of the world. 41The Son of Man will send his angels, and they will remove from his Kingdom everything that causes sin and all who do evil. 42And the angels will throw them into the fiery furnace, where there will be weeping and gnashing of teeth. 43Then the righteous will shine like the sun in their Father's Kingdom. Anyone with ears to hear should listen and understand!

Parables of the Hidden Treasure and the Pearl

44"The Kingdom of Heaven is like a treasure that a man discovered hidden in a field. In his excitement, he hid it again and sold everything he owned to get enough money to buy the field.

45"Again, the Kingdom of Heaven is like a merchant on the lookout for choice pearls. 46When he discovered a pearl of great value, he sold everything he owned and bought it!

13:44-45 WHAT'S IT SAYING?

WHAT AM I GOING TO DO ABOUT IT?

Parable of the Fishing Net

47"Again, the Kingdom of Heaven is like a fishing net that was thrown into the water and caught fish of every kind. 48When the net was full, they dragged it up onto the shore, sat down, and sorted the good fish into crates, but threw the bad ones away. 49That is the way it will be at the end of the world. The angels will come and separate the wicked people from the righteous, 50throwing the wicked into the fiery furnace, where there will be weeping and gnashing of teeth. 51Do you understand all these things?"

"Yes," they said, "we do."

52Then he added, "Every teacher of religious law who becomes a disciple in the Kingdom of Heaven is like a homeowner who brings from his storeroom new gems of truth as well as old."

Jesus Rejected at Nazareth

53When Jesus had finished telling these stories and illustrations, he left that part of the country. 54He returned to Nazareth, his hometown. When he taught there in the synagogue, everyone was amazed and said, "Where does he get this wisdom and the power to do miracles?" 55Then they scoffed, "He's just the carpenter's son, and we know Mary, his mother, and his brothers—James, Joseph, Simon, and Judas. 56All his sisters live right here among us. Where did he learn all these things?" 57And they were deeply offended and refused to believe in him.

Then Jesus told them, "A prophet is honored everywhere except in his own hometown and among his own family." 58And so he did only a few miracles there because of their unbelief.

The Death of John the Baptist

14

When Herod Antipas, the ruler of Galilee, heard about Jesus, 2he said to his advisers, "This must be John the Baptist raised from the dead! That is why he can do such miracles."

3For Herod had arrested and imprisoned John as a favor to his wife Herodias (the former wife of Herod's brother Philip). 4John had been telling Herod, "It is against God's law for you to marry her." 5Herod wanted to kill John, but he was afraid of a riot, because all the people believed John was a prophet.

6But at a birthday party for Herod, Herodias's daughter performed a dance that greatly pleased him, 7so he promised with a vow to give her anything she wanted. 8At her mother's urging, the girl said, "I want the head of John the Baptist on a tray!" 9Then the king regretted what he had said; but because of the vow he had made in front of his guests, he issued the necessary orders. 10So John was beheaded in the prison, 11and his head was brought on a tray and given to the girl, who took it to her mother. 12Later, John's disciples came for his body and buried it. Then they went and told Jesus what had happened.

Jesus Feeds Five Thousand

[13]As soon as Jesus heard the news, he left in a boat to a remote area to be alone. But the crowds heard where he was headed and followed on foot from many towns. [14]Jesus saw the huge crowd as he stepped from the boat, and he had compassion on them and healed their sick.

[15]That evening the disciples came to him and said, "This is a remote place, and it's already getting late. Send the crowds away so they can go to the villages and buy food for themselves."

[16]But Jesus said, "That isn't necessary—you feed them."

[17]"But we have only five loaves of bread and two fish!" they answered.

[18]"Bring them here," he said. [19]Then he told the people to sit down on the grass. Jesus took the five loaves and two fish, looked up toward heaven, and blessed them. Then, breaking the loaves into pieces, he gave the bread to the disciples, who distributed it to the people. [20]They all ate as much as they wanted, and afterward, the disciples picked up twelve baskets of leftovers. [21]About 5,000 men were fed that day, in addition to all the women and children!

Jesus Walks on Water

[22]Immediately after this, Jesus insisted that his disciples get back into the boat and cross to the other side of the lake, while he sent the people home. [23]After sending them home, he went up into the hills by himself to pray. Night fell while he was there alone.

[24]Meanwhile, the disciples were in trouble far away from land, for a strong wind had risen, and they were fighting heavy waves. [25]About three o'clock in the morning Jesus came toward them, walking on the water. [26]When the disciples saw him walking on the water, they were terrified. In their fear, they cried out, "It's a ghost!"

[27]But Jesus spoke to them at once. "Don't be afraid," he said. "Take courage. I am here!"

[28]Then Peter called to him, "Lord, if it's really you, tell me to come to you, walking on the water."

[29]"Yes, come," Jesus said.

So Peter went over the side of the boat and walked on the water toward Jesus. [30]But when he saw the strong wind and the waves, he was terrified and began to sink. "Save me, Lord!" he shouted.

[31]Jesus immediately reached out and grabbed him. "You have so little faith," Jesus said. "Why did you doubt me?"

[32]When they climbed back into the boat, the wind stopped. [33]Then the disciples worshiped him. "You really are the Son of God!" they exclaimed.

[34]After they had crossed the lake, they landed at Gennesaret. [35]When the people recognized Jesus, the news of his arrival spread quickly throughout the whole area, and soon people were bringing all their sick to be healed. [36]They begged him

WHAT DOES IT MEAN?

salt and light?

Jesus is giving us a very positive, action-oriented challenge in the word picture of salt and light. These are two things we may take for granted, but in Jesus' day they were really valuable and hard to come by. Salt was used to keep food from rotting and bring out its flavor. And light obviously helps us see and keeps us safely on the right path. Much the same, we Christians are to have a positive influence in the world around us and take a stand against the evil that rots God's creation. Also, we are to be proactive in shedding light on God's plan, which illuminates the path that God has desired the world to travel.

to let the sick touch at least the fringe of his robe, and all who touched him were healed.

Jesus Teaches about Inner Purity

15

Some Pharisees and teachers of religious law now arrived from Jerusalem to see Jesus. [2]"Why do your disciples disobey our age-old tradition?" they demanded. "They ignore our tradition of ceremonial hand washing before they eat."

[3]Jesus replied, "And why do you, by your traditions, violate the direct commandments of God? [4]For instance, God says, 'Honor your father and mother,' and 'Anyone who speaks disrespectfully of father or mother must be put to death.' [5]But you say it is all right for people to say to their parents, 'Sorry, I can't help you. For I have vowed to give to God what I would have given to you.' [6]In this way, you say they don't need to honor their parents. And so you cancel the word of God for the sake of your own tradition. [7]You hypocrites! Isaiah was right when he prophesied about you, for he wrote,

[8]'These people honor me with their lips,
but their hearts are far from me.
[9]Their worship is a farce,
for they teach man-made ideas as commands from God.'"

[10]Then Jesus called to the crowd to come and hear. "Listen," he said, "and try to understand. [11]It's not what goes into your mouth that defiles you; you are defiled by the words that come out of your mouth."

[12]Then the disciples came to him and asked, "Do you realize you offended the Pharisees by what you just said?"

[13]Jesus replied, "Every plant not planted by my heavenly Father will be uprooted, [14]so ignore them. They are blind guides leading the blind, and if one blind person guides another, they will both fall into a ditch."

[15]Then Peter said to Jesus, "Explain to us the parable that says people aren't defiled by what they eat."

[16]"Don't you understand yet?" Jesus asked. [17]"Anything you eat passes through the stomach and then goes into the sewer. [18]But the words you speak come from the heart—that's what defiles you. [19]For from the heart come evil thoughts, murder, adultery, all sexual immorality, theft, lying, and slander. [20]These are what defile you. Eating with unwashed hands will never defile you."

Bible FACTS

There are 30,442 verses — about 845,000 words — in the English Bible.

action

15:1-20 WHAT'S IT SAYING?

WHAT AM I GOING TO DO ABOUT IT?

The Faith of a Gentile Woman

²¹Then Jesus left Galilee and went north to the region of Tyre and Sidon. ²²A Gentile woman who lived there came to him, pleading, "Have mercy on me, O Lord, Son of David! For my daughter is possessed by a demon that torments her severely."

²³But Jesus gave her no reply, not even a word. Then his disciples urged him to send her away. "Tell her to go away," they said. "She is bothering us with all her begging."

²⁴Then Jesus said to the woman, "I was sent only to help God's lost sheep—the people of Israel."

²⁵But she came and worshiped him, pleading again, "Lord, help me!"

²⁶Jesus responded, "It isn't right to take food from

the children and throw it to the dogs."

²⁷She replied, "That's true, Lord, but even dogs are allowed to eat the scraps that fall beneath their master's table."

²⁸"Dear woman," Jesus said to her, "your faith is great. Your request is granted." And her daughter was instantly healed.

Jesus Heals Many People

²⁹Jesus returned to the Sea of Galilee and climbed a hill and sat down. ³⁰A vast crowd brought to him people who were lame, blind, crippled, those who couldn't speak, and many others. They laid them before Jesus, and he healed them all. ³¹The crowd was amazed! Those who hadn't been able to speak were talking, the crippled were made well, the lame were walking, and the blind could see again! And they praised the God of Israel.

Jesus Feeds Four Thousand

³²Then Jesus called his disciples and told them, "I feel sorry for these people. They have been here with me for three days, and they have nothing left to eat. I don't want to send them away hungry, or they will faint along the way."

³³The disciples replied, "Where would we get enough food here in the wilderness for such a huge crowd?"

³⁴Jesus asked, "How much bread do you have?"

They replied, "Seven loaves, and a few small fish."

³⁵So Jesus told all the people to sit down on the ground. ³⁶Then he took the seven loaves and the fish, thanked God for them, and broke them into pieces. He gave them to the disciples, who distributed the food to the crowd.

³⁷They all ate as much as they wanted. Afterward, the disciples picked up seven large baskets of leftover food. ³⁸There were 4,000 men who were fed that day, in addition to all the women and children. ³⁹Then Jesus sent the people home, and he got into a boat and crossed over to the region of Magadan.

Leaders Demand a Miraculous Sign

16

One day the Pharisees and Sadducees came to test Jesus, demanding that he show them a miraculous sign from heaven to prove his authority.

²He replied, "You know the saying, 'Red sky at night means fair weather tomorrow; ³red sky in the morning means foul weather all day.' You know how to interpret the weather signs in the sky, but you don't know how

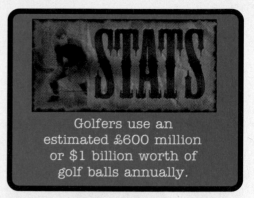

STATS

Golfers use an estimated £600 million or $1 billion worth of golf balls annually.

to interpret the signs of the times! ⁴Only an evil, adulterous generation would demand a miraculous sign, but the only sign I will give them is the sign of the prophet Jonah." Then Jesus left them and went away.

Yeast of the Pharisees and Sadducees

⁵Later, after they crossed to the other side of the lake, the disciples discovered they had forgotten to bring any bread. ⁶"Watch out!" Jesus warned them. "Beware of the yeast of the Pharisees and Sadducees."

⁷At this they began to argue with each other because they hadn't brought any bread. ⁸Jesus knew what they were saying, so he said, "You have so little faith! Why are you arguing with each other about having no bread? ⁹Don't you understand even yet? Don't you remember the 5,000 I fed with five loaves, and the baskets of leftovers you picked up? ¹⁰Or the 4,000 I fed with seven loaves, and the large baskets of leftovers you picked up? ¹¹Why can't you understand that I'm not talking about bread? So again I say, 'Beware of the yeast of the Pharisees and Sadducees.'"

¹²Then at last they understood that he wasn't speaking about the yeast in bread, but about the deceptive teaching of the Pharisees and Sadducees.

Peter's Declaration about Jesus

¹³When Jesus came to the region of Caesarea Philippi, he asked his disciples, "Who do people say that the Son of Man is?"

¹⁴"Well," they replied, "some say John the Baptist, some say Elijah, and others say Jeremiah or one of the other prophets."

¹⁵Then he asked them, "But who do you say I am?"

¹⁶Simon Peter answered, "You are the Messiah, the Son of the living God."

¹⁷Jesus replied, "You are blessed, Simon son of John, because my Father in heaven has revealed this to you. You did not learn this from any human being. ¹⁸Now I say to you that you are Peter (which means 'rock'), and upon this rock I will build my church, and all the powers of hell will not

conquer it. [19]And I will give you the keys of the Kingdom of Heaven. Whatever you forbid on earth will be forbidden in heaven, and whatever you permit on earth will be permitted in heaven."

[20]Then he sternly warned the disciples not to tell anyone that he was the Messiah.

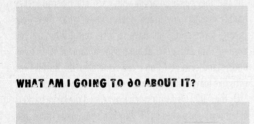

16:24-28 WHAT'S IT SAYING?

WHAT AM I GOING TO DO ABOUT IT?

Jesus Predicts His Death

[21]From then on Jesus began to tell his disciples plainly that it was necessary for him to go to Jerusalem, and that he would suffer many terrible things at the hands of the elders, the leading priests, and the teachers of religious law. He would be killed, but on the third day he would be raised from the dead.

[22]But Peter took him aside and began to reprimand him for saying such things. "Heaven forbid, Lord," he said. "This will never happen to you!"

[23]Jesus turned to Peter and said, "Get away from me, Satan! You are a dangerous trap to me. You are seeing things merely from a human point of view, not from God's."

[24]Then Jesus said to his disciples, "If any of you wants to be my follower, you must turn from your selfish ways, take up your cross, and follow me. [25]If you try to hang on to your life, you will lose it. But if you give up your life for my sake, you will save it. [26]And what do you benefit if you gain the whole world but lose your own soul? Is anything worth more than your soul? [27]For the Son of Man will come with his angels in the glory of his Father and will judge all people according to their deeds. [28]And I tell you the truth, some standing here right now will not die before they see the Son of Man coming in his Kingdom."

The Transfiguration

17

Six days later Jesus took Peter and the two brothers, James and John, and led them up a high mountain to be alone. [2]As the men watched, Jesus' appearance was transformed so that his face shone like the sun, and his clothes became as white as light. [3]Suddenly, Moses and Elijah appeared and began talking with Jesus. [4]Peter blurted out, "Lord, it's wonderful for us to be here! If you want, I'll make three shelters as memorials—one for you, one for Moses, and one for Elijah."

[5]But even as he spoke, a bright cloud came over them, and a voice from the cloud said, "This is my dearly loved Son, who brings me great joy. Listen to him." [6]The disciples were terrified and fell face down on the ground.

[7]Then Jesus came over and touched them. "Get up," he said. "Don't be afraid." [8]And when they looked, they saw only Jesus.

[9]As they went back down the mountain, Jesus commanded them, "Don't tell anyone what you have seen until the Son of Man has been raised from the dead." [10]Then his disciples asked him, "Why do the teachers of religious law insist that Elijah must return before the Messiah comes?"

[11]Jesus replied, "Elijah is indeed coming first to get everything ready for the Messiah. [12]But I tell you, Elijah has already come, but he wasn't recognized, and they chose to abuse him. And in the same way they will also make the Son of Man suffer." [13]Then the disciples realized he was talking about John the Baptist.

Jesus Heals a Demon-Possessed Boy

[14]At the foot of the mountain, a large crowd was waiting for them. A man came and knelt before Jesus and said, [15]"Lord, have mercy on my son. He has seizures and suffers terribly. He often falls into the fire or into the water. [16]So I brought him to your disciples, but they couldn't heal him."

[17]Jesus replied, "You faithless and corrupt people! How long must I be with you? How long must I put up with you? Bring the boy to me." [18]Then Jesus rebuked the demon in the boy, and it left him. From that moment the boy was well.

[19]Afterward the disciples asked Jesus privately, "Why couldn't we cast out that demon?"

[20]"You don't have enough faith," Jesus told them. "I tell you the truth, if you had faith even as small as a mustard seed, you could say to this mountain, 'Move from here to there,' and it would move. Nothing would be impossible.'"

Jesus Again Predicts His Death

[22]After they gathered again in Galilee, Jesus told them, "The Son of Man is going to be betrayed into the hands of his enemies. [23]He will be killed, but on the third day he will be raised from the dead." And the disciples were filled with grief.

Payment of the Temple Tax

[24]On their arrival in Capernaum, the collectors of the Temple tax came to Peter and asked him, "Doesn't your teacher pay the Temple tax?"

[25]"Yes, he does," Peter replied. Then he went into the house.

But before he had a chance to speak, Jesus asked him, "What do you think, Peter? Do kings tax their own people or the people they have conquered?"

[26]"They tax the people they have conquered," Peter replied.

"Well, then," Jesus said, "the citizens are free! [27]However, we don't want to offend them, so go down to the lake and throw in a line. Open the mouth of the first fish you catch, and you will find a large silver coin. Take it and pay the tax for both of us."

The Greatest in the Kingdom

18

About that time the disciples came to Jesus and asked, "Who is greatest in the Kingdom of Heaven?"

[2]Jesus called a little child to him and put the child among them. [3]Then he said, "I tell you the truth, unless you turn from your sins and become like little children, you will never get into the Kingdom of Heaven. [4]So anyone who becomes as humble as this little child is the greatest in the Kingdom of Heaven.

17:20 Some manuscripts add verse 21, *But this kind of demon won't leave except by prayer and fasting.* Compare Mark 9:29.

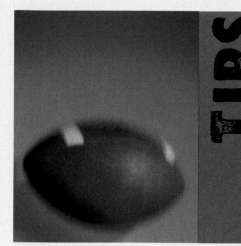

Overtraining:

"The more you work out, the stronger and more in shape you will get." No! No! No! This is one of the most damaging myths that ever reared its ugly head. Most professionals will admit that at some time they made this mistake. When you train, your body needs rest to allow it to regenerate. In order to maximize a training week, a lot of athletes will plan their training program so that they focus on different muscle groups on alternate days (e.g. Monday – focus on lower body, Tuesday – focus on upper body). It is important to note that while this allows an athlete to train every day, one complete day should be given for relaxation to allow the body to recover.

⁵"And anyone who welcomes a little child like this on my behalf is welcoming me. ⁶But if you cause one of these little ones who trusts in me to fall into sin, it would be better for you to have a large millstone tied around your neck and be drowned in the depths of the sea.

⁷"What sorrow awaits the world, because it tempts people to sin. Temptations are inevitable, but what sorrow awaits the person who does the tempting. ⁸So if your hand or foot causes you to sin, cut it off and throw it away. It's better to enter eternal life with only one hand or one foot than to be thrown into eternal fire with both of your hands and feet. ⁹And if your eye causes you to sin, gouge it out and throw it away. It's better to enter eternal life with only one eye than to have two eyes and be thrown into the fire of hell.

¹⁰"Beware that you don't look down on any of these little ones. For I tell you that in heaven their angels are always in the presence of my heavenly Father.

Parable of the Lost Sheep

¹²"If a man has a hundred sheep and one of them wanders away, what will he do? Won't he leave the ninety-nine others on the hills and go out to search for the one that is lost? ¹³And if he finds it, I tell you the truth, he will rejoice over it more than over the ninety-nine that didn't wander away! ¹⁴In the same way, it is not my heavenly Father's will that even one of these little ones should perish.

Correcting Another Believer

¹⁵"If another believer sins against you, go privately and point out the offense. If the other person listens and confesses it, you have won that person back. ¹⁶But if you are unsuccessful, take one or two others with you and go back again, so that everything you say may be confirmed by two or three witnesses. ¹⁷If the

person still refuses to listen, take your case to the church. Then if he or she won't accept the church's decision, treat that person as a pagan or a corrupt tax collector.

¹⁸"I tell you the truth, whatever you forbid on earth will be forbidden in heaven, and whatever you permit on earth will be permitted in heaven.

¹⁹"I also tell you this: If two of you agree here on earth concerning anything you ask, my Father in heaven will do it for you. ²⁰For where two or three gather together as my followers, I am there among them."

18:1-6 WHAT'S IT SAYING?

WHAT AM I GOING TO DO ABOUT IT?

Parable of the Unforgiving Debtor

²¹Then Peter came to him and asked, "Lord, how often should I forgive someone who sins against me? Seven times?"

²²"No, not seven times," Jesus replied, "but seventy times seven!

²³"Therefore, the Kingdom of Heaven can be compared to a king who decided to bring his accounts up to date with servants who had borrowed money from him. ²⁴In the process, one of his debtors was brought in who owed him millions of dollars. ²⁵He couldn't pay, so his master ordered that he be sold—along with his wife, his children, and everything he owned—to pay the debt.

²⁶"But the man fell down before his master and begged him, 'Please, be patient with me, and I will pay it all.' ²⁷Then his master was filled with pity for him, and he released him and forgave his debt.

²⁸"But when the man left the king, he went to a fellow servant who owed him a few thousand dollars. He grabbed him by the throat and demanded instant payment.

²⁹"His fellow servant fell down before him and begged for a little more time. 'Be patient with me, and I will pay it,' he pleaded. ³⁰But his creditor wouldn't wait. He had the man arrested and put in prison until the debt could be paid in full.

³¹"When some of the other servants saw this, they were very upset. They went to the king and told him everything that had happened. ³²Then the king called in the man he had forgiven and said, 'You evil servant! I forgave you that tremendous debt because you pleaded with me. ³³Shouldn't you have mercy on your fellow servant, just as I had mercy on you?' ³⁴Then the angry king sent the man to prison to be tortured until he had paid his entire debt.

18:10 Some manuscripts add verse 11, *And the Son of Man came to save those who are lost.* Compare Luke 19:10.

35"That's what my heavenly Father will do to you if you refuse to forgive your brothers and sisters from your heart."

Discussion about Divorce and Marriage

19

When Jesus had finished saying these things, he left Galilee and went down to the region of Judea east of the Jordan River. 2Large crowds followed him there, and he healed their sick.

3Some Pharisees came and tried to trap him with this question: "Should a man be allowed to divorce his wife for just any reason?"

4"Haven't you read the Scriptures?" Jesus replied. "They record that from the beginning 'God made them male and female.' 5And he said, 'This explains why a man leaves his father and mother and is joined to his wife, and the two are united into one.' 6Since they are no longer two but one, let no one split apart what God has joined together."

7"Then why did Moses say in the law that a man could give his wife a written notice of divorce and send her away?" they asked.

8Jesus replied, "Moses permitted divorce only as a concession to your hard hearts, but it was not what God had originally intended. 9And I tell you this, whoever divorces his wife and marries someone else commits adultery—unless his wife has been unfaithful.*"

10Jesus' disciples then said to him, "If this is the case, it is better not to marry!"

11"Not everyone can accept this statement," Jesus said. "Only those whom God helps. 12Some are born as eunuchs, some have been made eunuchs by others, and some choose not to marry for the sake of the Kingdom of Heaven. Let anyone accept this who can."

Jesus Blesses the Children

13One day some parents brought their children to Jesus so he could lay his hands on them and pray for them. But the disciples scolded the parents for bothering him.

14But Jesus said, "Let the children come to me. Don't stop them! For the Kingdom of Heaven belongs to those who are like these children." 15And he placed his hands on their heads and blessed them before he left.

action

19:27-30 WHAT'S IT SAYING?

WHAT AM I GOING TO DO ABOUT IT?

The Rich Man

16Someone came to Jesus with this question: "Teacher, what good deed must I do to have eternal life?"

17"Why ask me about what is good?" Jesus replied. "There is only One who is good. But to answer your question—if you want to receive eternal life, keep the commandments."

18"Which ones?" the man asked.

And Jesus replied: "'You must not murder. You must not commit adultery. You must not steal. You must not testify falsely. 19Honor your father and mother. Love your neighbor as yourself.'"

20"I've obeyed all these commandments," the young man replied. "What else must I do?"

21Jesus told him, "If you want to be perfect, go and sell all your possessions and give the money to the poor, and you will have treasure in heaven. Then come, follow me."

22But when the young man heard this, he went away very sad, for he had many possessions.

23Then Jesus said to his disciples, "I tell you the truth, it is very hard for a rich person to enter the Kingdom of Heaven. 24I'll say it again—it is easier for a camel to go through the eye of a needle than for a rich person to enter the Kingdom of God!"

25The disciples were astounded. "Then who in the world can be saved?" they asked.

26Jesus looked at them intently and said, "Humanly speaking, it is impossible. But with God everything is possible."

27Then Peter said to him, "We've given up everything to follow you. What will we get?"

28"Yes," Jesus replied, "and I assure you that when the world is made new and the Son of Man sits upon his glorious throne, you who have been my followers will also sit on twelve thrones, judging the twelve tribes of Israel. 29And everyone who has given up houses or brothers or sisters or father or mother or children or property, for my sake, will receive a hundred times as much in return and will inherit eternal life. 30But many who are the greatest now will be least important then, and those who seem least important now will be the greatest then.

Parable of the Vineyard Workers

20

"For the Kingdom of Heaven is like the landowner who went out early one morning to hire workers for his

The Rich Young Man (MATTHEW 19:16-30)

Along came what would seem to many a top recruit for Jesus' movement. He had morality, he had authority, he had bravado, and he had cash. Seem like all the ingredients to be headhunted for a top spot on God's team? Wrong! The man was trying to justify himself to God by his own good works. In God's economy the rich young man's good works were pretty weak. He was probably a good guy in many ways, but Jesus looked deep into his heart and saw him for who he was — a sinner who loved his possessions more than obedience to God. Jesus does not ask everyone to give up all their possessions, but if he gave you a direct command, would you obey? The disciples were pretty shocked at Jesus' response to the rich guy and asked "Who in the world can be saved?" Of course Jesus' reply is clear: "Humanly speaking, it is impossible. But with God everything is possible."

BIBLE HIT

19:9 Some manuscripts add *And anyone who marries a divorced woman commits adultery.* Compare Matt 5:32.

24

vineyard. ²He agreed to pay the normal daily wage and sent them out to work.

³"At nine o'clock in the morning he was passing through the marketplace and saw some people standing around doing nothing. ⁴So he hired them, telling them he would pay them whatever was right at the end of the day. ⁵So they went to work in the vineyard. At noon and again at three o'clock he did the same thing.

⁶"At five o'clock that afternoon he was in town again and saw some more people standing around. He asked them, 'Why haven't you been working today?'

⁷"They replied, 'Because no one hired us.'

"The landowner told them, 'Then go out and join the others in my vineyard.'

⁸"That evening he told the foreman to call the workers in and pay them, beginning with the last workers first. ⁹When those hired at five o'clock were paid, each received a full day's wage. ¹⁰When those hired first came to get their pay, they assumed they would receive more. But they, too, were paid a day's wage. ¹¹When they received their pay, they protested to the owner, ¹²'Those people worked only one hour, and yet you've paid them just as much as you paid us who worked all day in the scorching heat.'

¹³"He answered one of them, 'Friend, I haven't been unfair! Didn't you agree to work all day for the usual wage? ¹⁴Take your money and go. I wanted to pay this last worker the same as you. ¹⁵Is it against the law for me to do what I want with my money? Should you be jealous because I am kind to others?'

¹⁶"So those who are last now will be first then, and those who are first will be last."

Jesus Again Predicts His Death

¹⁷As Jesus was going up to Jerusalem, he took the twelve disciples aside privately and told them what was going to happen to him. ¹⁸"Listen," he said, "we're going up to Jerusalem, where the Son of Man will be betrayed to the leading priests and the teachers of religious law. They will sentence him to die. ¹⁹Then they will hand him over to the Romans to be mocked, flogged with a whip, and crucified. But on the third day he will be raised from the dead."

Jesus Teaches about Serving Others

²⁰Then the mother of James and John, the sons of Zebedee, came to Jesus with her sons. She knelt respectfully to ask a favor. ²¹"What is your request?" he asked.

She replied, "In your Kingdom, please let my two sons

sit in places of honor next to you, one on your right and the other on your left."

²²But Jesus answered by saying to them, "You don't know what you are asking! Are you able to drink from the bitter cup of suffering I am about to drink?"

"Oh yes," they replied, "we are able!"

²³Jesus told them, "You will indeed drink from my bitter cup. But I have no right to say who will sit on my right or my left. My Father has prepared those places for the ones he has chosen."

²⁴When the ten other disciples heard what James and John had asked, they were indignant. ²⁵But Jesus called them together and said, "You know that the rulers in this world lord it over their people, and officials flaunt their authority over those under them. ²⁶But among you it will be different. Whoever wants to be a leader among you must be your servant, ²⁷and whoever wants to be first among you must become your slave. ²⁸For even the Son of Man came not to be served but to serve others and to give his life as a ransom for many."

Jesus Heals Two Blind Men

²⁹As Jesus and the disciples left the town of Jericho, a large crowd followed behind. ³⁰Two blind men were

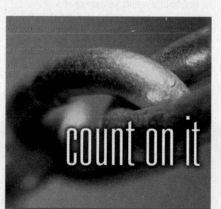

count on it

It's not easy!
It never says in the Scriptures you are going to have an easy life. Families break up, friends blow it, teams lose, and stuff happens. What God does promise is that he will comfort you in the tough times when you are hurting if you come to him. "God blesses those who mourn, for they will be comforted." (Matthew 5:4)
Count on it!

sitting beside the road. When they heard that Jesus was coming that way, they began shouting, "Lord, Son of David, have mercy on us!"

³¹"Be quiet!" the crowd yelled at them.

But they only shouted louder, "Lord, Son of David, have mercy on us!"

³²When Jesus heard them, he stopped and called, "What do you want me to do for you?"

³³"Lord," they said, "we want to see!" ³⁴Jesus felt sorry for them and touched their eyes. Instantly they could see! Then they followed him.

Jesus' Triumphant Entry

21

As Jesus and the disciples approached Jerusalem, they came to the town of Bethphage on the Mount of Olives. Jesus sent two of them on ahead. ²"Go into the village over there," he said. "As soon as you enter it, you will see a donkey tied there, with its colt beside it. Untie them and bring them to me. ³If anyone asks what you are doing, just say, 'The Lord needs them,' and he will immediately let you take them."

⁴This took place to fulfill the prophecy that said,

⁵"Tell the people of Israel,
'Look, your King is coming to you.
He is humble, riding on a donkey—
riding on a donkey's colt.'"

⁶The two disciples did as Jesus commanded. ⁷They brought the donkey and the colt to him and threw their garments over the colt, and he sat on it.

⁸Most of the crowd spread their garments on the road ahead of him, and others cut branches from the trees and spread them on the road. ⁹Jesus was in the center of the procession, and the people all around him were shouting,

"Praise God for the Son of David!
Blessings on the one who comes in the name of the LORD!
Praise God in highest heaven!"

¹⁰The entire city of Jerusalem was in an uproar as he entered. "Who is this?" they asked.

¹¹And the crowds replied, "It's Jesus, the prophet from Nazareth in Galilee."

Jesus Clears the Temple

¹²Jesus entered the Temple and began to drive out all the people buying and selling animals for sacrifice. He knocked over the tables of the money changers and the chairs of those selling doves. ¹³He said to them, "The Scriptures declare, 'My Temple will be called a house of prayer,' but you have turned it into a den of thieves!"

¹⁴The blind and the lame came to him in the Temple, and he healed them. ¹⁵The leading priests and the teachers of religious law saw these wonderful miracles and heard even

the children in the Temple shouting, "Praise God for the Son of David."

But the leaders were indignant. [16]They asked Jesus, "Do you hear what these children are saying?"

"Yes," Jesus replied. "Haven't you ever read the Scriptures? For they say, 'You have taught children and infants to give you praise.'" [17]Then he returned to Bethany, where he stayed overnight.

Jesus Curses the Fig Tree

[18]In the morning, as Jesus was returning to Jerusalem, he was hungry, [19]and he noticed a fig tree beside the road. He went over to see if there were any figs, but there were only leaves. Then he said to it, "May you never bear fruit again!" And immediately the fig tree withered up.

[20]The disciples were amazed when they saw this and asked, "How did the fig tree wither so quickly?"

[21]Then Jesus told them, "I tell you the truth, if you have faith and don't doubt, you can do things like this and much more. You can even say to this mountain, 'May you be lifted up and thrown into the sea,' and it will happen. [22]You can pray for anything, and if you have faith, you will receive it."

The Authority of Jesus Challenged

[23]When Jesus returned to the Temple and began teaching, the leading priests and elders came up to him. They demanded, "By what authority are you doing all these things? Who gave you the right?"

[24]"I'll tell you by what authority I do these things if you answer one question," Jesus replied. [25]"Did John's authority to baptize come from heaven, or was it merely human?"

They talked it over among themselves. "If we say it was from

told the older boy, 'Son, go out and work in the vineyard today.' [29]The son answered, 'No, I won't go,' but later he changed his mind and went anyway. [30]Then the father told the other son, 'You go,' and he said, 'Yes, sir, I will.' But he didn't go.

[31]"Which of the two obeyed his father?"

They replied, "The first."

Then Jesus explained his meaning: "I tell you the truth, corrupt tax collectors and prostitutes will get into the Kingdom of God before you do. [32]For John the Baptist came and showed you the right way to live, but you didn't believe him, while tax collectors and prostitutes did. And even when you saw this happening, you refused to believe him and repent of your sins.

Parable of the Evil Farmers

[33]"Now listen to another story. A certain landowner planted a vineyard, built a wall around it, dug a pit for pressing out the grape juice, and built a lookout tower. Then he leased the vineyard to tenant farmers and moved to another country. [34]At the time of the grape harvest, he sent his servants to collect his share of the crop. [35]But the farmers grabbed his servants, beat one, killed one, and stoned another. [36]So the landowner sent a larger group of his servants to collect for him, but the results were the same.

[37]"Finally, the owner sent his son, thinking, 'Surely they will respect my son.'

[38]"But when the tenant farmers saw his son coming, they said to one another, 'Here comes the heir to this estate. Come on, let's kill him and get the estate for ourselves!' [39]So they grabbed him, dragged him out

in the Scriptures?

'The stone that the builders rejected
has now become the cornerstone.
This is the Lord's doing,
and it is wonderful to see.'

[43]I tell you, the Kingdom of God will be taken away from you and given to a nation that will produce the proper fruit. [44]Anyone who stumbles over that stone will be broken to pieces, and it will crush anyone it falls on."

[45]When the leading priests and Pharisees heard this parable, they realized he was telling the story against them—they were the wicked farmers. [46]They wanted to arrest him, but they were afraid of the crowds, who considered Jesus to be a prophet.

Parable of the Great Feast

22

Jesus also told them other parables. He said, [2]"The Kingdom of Heaven can be illustrated by the story of a king who prepared a great wedding feast for his son. [3]When the banquet was ready, he sent his servants to notify those who were invited. But they all refused to come!

[4]"So he sent other servants to tell them, 'The feast has been prepared. The bulls and fattened cattle have been killed, and everything is ready. Come to the banquet!' [5]But the guests he had invited ignored them and went their own way, one to his farm, another to his business. [6]Others seized his messengers and

Basic lifts are best:

Using simple free weights (barbells and dumbbells) on basic multi-joint exercises, like the squat, bench press, shoulder press, and dead lift, is still the most effective means of resistance exercise ever invented. Scientific research has shown that many exercise machines lack the proper eccentric component of exercise that's necessary to stimulate and develop muscle strength and growth.

heaven, he will ask us why we didn't believe John. [26]But if we say it was merely human, we'll be mobbed because the people believe John was a prophet." [27]So they finally replied, "We don't know."

And Jesus responded, "Then I won't tell you by what authority I do these things.

Parable of the Two Sons

[28]"But what do you think about this? A man with two sons

of the vineyard, and murdered him.

[40]"When the owner of the vineyard returns," Jesus asked, "what do you think he will do to those farmers?"

[41]The religious leaders replied, "He will put the wicked men to a horrible death and lease the vineyard to others who will give him his share of the crop after each harvest."

[42]Then Jesus asked them, "Didn't you ever read this

insulted them and killed them.

[7]"The king was furious, and he sent out his army to destroy the murderers and burn their town. [8]And he said to his servants, 'The wedding feast is ready, and the guests I invited aren't worthy of the honor. [9]Now go out to the street corners and invite everyone you see.' [10]So the servants brought in everyone they could find, good and bad alike, and the banquet hall was filled with guests.

¹¹"But when the king came in to meet the guests, he noticed a man who wasn't wearing the proper clothes for a wedding. ¹²'Friend,' he asked, 'how is it that you are here without wedding clothes?' But the man had no reply. ¹³Then the king said to his aides, 'Bind his hands and feet and throw him into the outer darkness, where there will be weeping and gnashing of teeth.'

¹⁴"For many are called, but few are chosen."

Taxes for Caesar

¹⁵Then the Pharisees met together to plot how to trap Jesus into saying something for which he could be arrested. ¹⁶They sent some of their disciples, along with the supporters of Herod, to meet with him. "Teacher," they said, "we know how honest you are. You teach the way of God truthfully. You are impartial and don't play favorites. ¹⁷Now tell us what you think about this: Is it right to pay taxes to Caesar or not?"

¹⁸But Jesus knew their evil motives. "You hypocrites!" he said. "Why are you trying to trap me? ¹⁹Here, show me the coin used for the tax." When they handed him a Roman coin, ²⁰he asked, "Whose picture and title are stamped on it?"

²¹"Caesar's," they replied.

"Well, then," he said, "give to Caesar what belongs to Caesar, and give to God what belongs to God."

²²His reply amazed them, and they went away.

Discussion about Resurrection

²³That same day Jesus was approached by some Sadducees—religious leaders who say there is no resurrection from the dead. They posed this question: ²⁴"Teacher, Moses said, 'If a man dies without children, his brother should marry the widow and have a child who will carry on the brother's name.' ²⁵Well, suppose there were seven brothers. The oldest one married and then died without children, so his brother married the widow. ²⁶But the second brother also died, and the third brother married her. This continued with all seven of them. ²⁷Last of all, the woman also died. ²⁸So tell us, whose wife will she be in the resurrection? For all seven were married to her."

²⁹Jesus replied, "Your mistake is that you don't know the Scriptures, and you don't know the power of God. ³⁰For when the dead rise, they will neither marry nor be given in marriage. In this respect they will be like the angels in heaven.

³¹"But now, as to whether there will be a resurrection of the dead—haven't you ever read about this in the Scriptures? Long after Abraham, Isaac, and Jacob had died, God said, ³²'I am the God of Abraham, the God of Isaac, and the God of Jacob.' So he is the God of the living, not the dead."

³³When the crowds heard him, they were astounded at his teaching.

The Most Important Commandment

³⁴But when the Pharisees heard that he had silenced the Sadducees with his reply, they met together to question him again. ³⁵One of them, an expert in religious law, tried to trap him with this question: ³⁶"Teacher, which is the most important commandment in the law of Moses?"

³⁷Jesus replied, "'You must love the LORD your God with all your heart, all your soul, and all your mind.' ³⁸This is the first and greatest commandment. ³⁹A second is equally important: 'Love your neighbor as yourself.' ⁴⁰The entire law and all the demands of the prophets are based on these two commandments."

Whose Son Is the Messiah?

⁴¹Then, surrounded by the Pharisees, Jesus asked them a question: ⁴²"What do you think about the Messiah? Whose son is he?"

They replied, "He is the son of David."

⁴³Jesus responded, "Then why does David, speaking under the inspiration of the Spirit, call the Messiah 'my Lord'? For David said,

⁴⁴'The LORD said to my Lord,
Sit in the place of honor at my right hand
until I humble your enemies beneath your feet.'

⁴⁵Since David called the Messiah 'my Lord,' how can the Messiah be his son?"

⁴⁶No one could answer him. And after that, no one dared to ask him any more questions.

Jesus Criticizes the Religious Leaders

23

Then Jesus said to the crowds and to his disciples, ²"The teachers of religious law and the Pharisees are the official interpreters of the law of Moses. ³So practice and obey whatever they tell you, but don't follow their example. For they don't practice what they teach. ⁴They crush people with impossible religious demands and never lift a finger to ease the burden.

⁵"Everything they do is for show. On their arms they wear extra wide prayer boxes with Scripture verses inside, and they wear robes with extra long tassels. ⁶And they love to sit at the head table at banquets and in the seats of honor in the synagogues. ⁷They love to receive respectful greetings as they walk in the marketplaces, and to be called 'Rabbi.'

⁸"Don't let anyone call you 'Rabbi,' for you have only one teacher, and all of you are equal as brothers and sisters. ⁹And don't address anyone here on earth as 'Father,' for only God in heaven is your spiritual Father. ¹⁰And don't let anyone call you 'Teacher,' for you have only one teacher, the Messiah. ¹¹The greatest among you must be a servant. ¹²But those who exalt themselves will be humbled, and those who humble themselves will be exalted.

¹³"What sorrow awaits you teachers of religious law and you Pharisees. Hypocrites! For you shut the door of the Kingdom of Heaven in people's faces. You won't go in yourselves, and you don't let others enter either.*

¹⁵"What sorrow awaits you teachers of religious law and you Pharisees. Hypocrites! For you cross land and sea to make one convert, and then you turn that person into twice the child of hell you yourselves are!

¹⁶"Blind guides! What sorrow awaits you! For you say that it means nothing to swear 'by God's Temple,' but that it is binding to swear 'by the gold in the Temple.' ¹⁷Blind fools! Which is more important—the gold or the Temple that makes the gold sacred? ¹⁸And you say that to swear 'by the altar' is not binding, but to swear 'by the gifts on the altar' is binding. ¹⁹How blind! For which is more important—the gift on the altar or the altar that makes the gift sacred? ²⁰When you swear 'by the altar,' you are swearing by it and by everything on it. ²¹And when you swear 'by the Temple,' you are swearing by it and by God, who lives in it. ²²And when you swear 'by heaven,' you are swearing by the throne of God and by God, who sits on the throne.

²³"What sorrow awaits you teachers of religious law and you Pharisees. Hypocrites! For you are careful to tithe even the tiniest income from your herb gardens, but you ignore the more important aspects of the law—justice, mercy, and faith. You should tithe, yes, but do not neglect the more important things. ²⁴Blind guides! You strain your water so you won't accidentally swallow a gnat, but you swallow a camel!

²⁵"What sorrow awaits you teachers of religious law and you Pharisees. Hypocrites! For you are so careful to clean the outside of the cup and the dish, but inside you are filthy—full of greed and self-indulgence! ²⁶You blind Pharisee! First wash the inside of the cup and the dish, and then the outside will become clean, too.

²⁷"What sorrow awaits you teachers of religious law and you Pharisees. Hypocrites! For you are like whitewashed tombs—beautiful on the outside but filled on the inside with dead people's bones and all sorts of impurity. ²⁸Outwardly you look like righteous people, but inwardly

---

23:13 Some manuscripts add verse 14, *What sorrow awaits you teachers of religious law and you Pharisees. Hypocrites! You shamelessly cheat widows out of their property and then pretend to be pious by making long prayers in public. Because of this, you will be severely punished. Compare Mark 12:40 and Luke 20:47.*

FEBRUARY M.A.P.

1
S.D.	P.L.	P.G.	S.G.
P. ☐	F. ☐	F. ☐	T. ☐
F. ☐	W. ☐	W. ☐	P. ☐
B. ☐	P. ☐	C. ☐	C. ☐

2
S.D.	P.L.	P.G.	S.G.
P. ☐	F. ☐	F. ☐	T. ☐
F. ☐	W. ☐	W. ☐	P. ☐
B. ☐	P. ☐	C. ☐	C. ☐

3
S.D.	P.L.	P.G.	S.G.
P. ☐	F. ☐	F. ☐	T. ☐
F. ☐	W. ☐	W. ☐	P. ☐
B. ☐	P. ☐	C. ☐	C. ☐

4
S.D.	P.L.	P.G.	S.G.
P. ☐	F. ☐	F. ☐	T. ☐
F. ☐	W. ☐	W. ☐	P. ☐
B. ☐	P. ☐	C. ☐	C. ☐

9
S.D.	P.L.	P.G.	S.G.
P. ☐	F. ☐	F. ☐	T. ☐
F. ☐	W. ☐	W. ☐	P. ☐
B. ☐	P. ☐	C. ☐	C. ☐

10
S.D.	P.L.	P.G.	S.G.
P. ☐	F. ☐	F. ☐	T. ☐
F. ☐	W. ☐	W. ☐	P. ☐
B. ☐	P. ☐	C. ☐	C. ☐

11
S.D.	P.L.	P.G.	S.G.
P. ☐	F. ☐	F. ☐	T. ☐
F. ☐	W. ☐	W. ☐	P. ☐
B. ☐	P. ☐	C. ☐	C. ☐

12
S.D.	P.L.	P.G.	S.G.
P. ☐	F. ☐	F. ☐	T. ☐
F. ☐	W. ☐	W. ☐	P. ☐
B. ☐	P. ☐	C. ☐	C. ☐

17
S.D.	P.L.	P.G.	S.G.
P. ☐	F. ☐	F. ☐	T. ☐
F. ☐	W. ☐	W. ☐	P. ☐
B. ☐	P. ☐	C. ☐	C. ☐

18
S.D.	P.L.	P.G.	S.G.
P. ☐	F. ☐	F. ☐	T. ☐
F. ☐	W. ☐	W. ☐	P. ☐
B. ☐	P. ☐	C. ☐	C. ☐

19
S.D.	P.L.	P.G.	S.G.
P. ☐	F. ☐	F. ☐	T. ☐
F. ☐	W. ☐	W. ☐	P. ☐
B. ☐	P. ☐	C. ☐	C. ☐

20
S.D.	P.L.	P.G.	S.G.
P. ☐	F. ☐	F. ☐	T. ☐
F. ☐	W. ☐	W. ☐	P. ☐
B. ☐	P. ☐	C. ☐	C. ☐

25
S.D.	P.L.	P.G.	S.G.
P. ☐	F. ☐	F. ☐	T. ☐
F. ☐	W. ☐	W. ☐	P. ☐
B. ☐	P. ☐	C. ☐	C. ☐

26
S.D.	P.L.	P.G.	S.G.
P. ☐	F. ☐	F. ☐	T. ☐
F. ☐	W. ☐	W. ☐	P. ☐
B. ☐	P. ☐	C. ☐	C. ☐

27
S.D.	P.L.	P.G.	S.G.
P. ☐	F. ☐	F. ☐	T. ☐
F. ☐	W. ☐	W. ☐	P. ☐
B. ☐	P. ☐	C. ☐	C. ☐

28
S.D.	P.L.	P.G.	S.G.
P. ☐	F. ☐	F. ☐	T. ☐
F. ☐	W. ☐	W. ☐	P. ☐
B. ☐	P. ☐	C. ☐	C. ☐

Spiritual Disciplines

Prayer

Faith Community

Bible Reading

Prayer List

Friends

World

Personal

Who am I....
Where am I going....
How am I going to get there?

nt:sport

MONTHLY ACTION PLAN

5
S.D.	P.L.	P.G.	S.G.
P. ☐	F. ☐	F. ☐	T. ☐
F. ☐	W. ☐	W. ☐	P. ☐
B. ☐	P. ☐	C. ☐	C. ☐

6
S.D.	P.L.	P.G.	S.G.
P. ☐	F. ☐	F. ☐	T. ☐
F. ☐	W. ☐	W. ☐	P. ☐
B. ☐	P. ☐	C. ☐	C. ☐

7
S.D.	P.L.	P.G.	S.G.
P. ☐	F. ☐	F. ☐	T. ☐
F. ☐	W. ☐	W. ☐	P. ☐
B. ☐	P. ☐	C. ☐	C. ☐

8
S.D.	P.L.	P.G.	S.G.
P. ☐	F. ☐	F. ☐	T. ☐
F. ☐	W. ☐	W. ☐	P. ☐
B. ☐	P. ☐	C. ☐	C. ☐

13
S.D.	P.L.	P.G.	S.G.
P. ☐	F. ☐	F. ☐	T. ☐
F. ☐	W. ☐	W. ☐	P. ☐
B. ☐	P. ☐	C. ☐	C. ☐

14
S.D.	P.L.	P.G.	S.G.
P. ☐	F. ☐	F. ☐	T. ☐
F. ☐	W. ☐	W. ☐	P. ☐
B. ☐	P. ☐	C. ☐	C. ☐

15
S.D.	P.L.	P.G.	S.G.
P. ☐	F. ☐	F. ☐	T. ☐
F. ☐	W. ☐	W. ☐	P. ☐
B. ☐	P. ☐	C. ☐	C. ☐

16
S.D.	P.L.	P.G.	S.G.
P. ☐	F. ☐	F. ☐	T. ☐
F. ☐	W. ☐	W. ☐	P. ☐
B. ☐	P. ☐	C. ☐	C. ☐

21
S.D.	P.L.	P.G.	S.G.
P. ☐	F. ☐	F. ☐	T. ☐
F. ☐	W. ☐	W. ☐	P. ☐
B. ☐	P. ☐	C. ☐	C. ☐

22
S.D.	P.L.	P.G.	S.G.
P. ☐	F. ☐	F. ☐	T. ☐
F. ☐	W. ☐	W. ☐	P. ☐
B. ☐	P. ☐	C. ☐	C. ☐

23
S.D.	P.L.	P.G.	S.G.
P. ☐	F. ☐	F. ☐	T. ☐
F. ☐	W. ☐	W. ☐	P. ☐
B. ☐	P. ☐	C. ☐	C. ☐

24
S.D.	P.L.	P.G.	S.G.
P. ☐	F. ☐	F. ☐	T. ☐
F. ☐	W. ☐	W. ☐	P. ☐
B. ☐	P. ☐	C. ☐	C. ☐

29
S.D.	P.L.	P.G.	S.G.
P. ☐	F. ☐	F. ☐	T. ☐
F. ☐	W. ☐	W. ☐	P. ☐
B. ☐	P. ☐	C. ☐	C. ☐

Psalm 43:3

Send out your light and your truth; let them guide me. Let them lead me to your holy mountain, to the place where you live.

Personal Goals

Family

Work/School/Social

Challenge

Sport Goals

Training

Performance

Competition Results

(For designing your M.A.P. – Monthly Action Plan – see introduction pages)

your hearts are filled with hypocrisy and lawlessness. [29]"What sorrow awaits you teachers of religious law and you Pharisees. Hypocrites! For you build tombs for the prophets your ancestors killed, and you decorate the monuments of the godly people your ancestors destroyed. [30]Then you say, 'If we had lived in the days of our ancestors, we would never have joined them in killing the prophets.' [31]"But in saying that, you testify against yourselves that you are indeed the descendants of those who murdered the prophets. [32]Go ahead and finish what your ancestors started. [33]Snakes! Sons of vipers! How will you escape the judgment of hell?

[34]"Therefore, I am sending you prophets and wise men and teachers of religious law. But you will kill some by crucifixion, and you will flog others with whips in your synagogues, chasing them from city to city. [35]As a result, you will be held responsible for the murder of all godly people of all time—from the murder of righteous Abel to the murder of Zechariah son of Barachiah, whom you killed in the Temple between the sanctuary and the altar. [36]I tell you the truth, this judgment will fall on this very generation.

Jesus Grieves over Jerusalem

[37]"O Jerusalem, Jerusalem, the city that kills the prophets and stones God's messengers! How often I have wanted to gather your children together as a hen protects her chicks beneath her wings, but you wouldn't let me. [38]And now, look, your house is abandoned and desolate. [39]For I tell you this, you will never see me again until you say, 'Blessings on the one who comes in the name of the LORD!'"

Jesus Foretells the Future

24

As Jesus was leaving the Temple grounds, his disciples pointed out to him the various Temple buildings. [2]But he responded, "Do you see all these buildings? I tell you the truth, they will be completely demolished. Not one stone will be left on top of another!"

[3]Later, Jesus sat on the Mount of Olives. His disciples came to him privately and said, "Tell us, when will all this happen? What sign will signal your return and the end of the world?"

[4]Jesus told them, "Don't let anyone mislead you, [5]for many will come in my name, claiming, 'I am the Messiah.' They will deceive many. [6]And you will hear of wars and threats of wars, but don't panic. Yes, these things must take place, but the end won't follow immediately. [7]Nation will go to war against nation, and kingdom against kingdom. There will be famines and earthquakes in many parts of the world. [8]But all this is only the first of the birth pains, with more to come.

[9]"Then you will be arrested, persecuted, and killed. You will be hated all over the world because you are my followers. [10]And many will turn away from me and betray and hate each other. [11]And many false prophets will appear and will deceive many people. [12]Sin will be rampant everywhere, and the love of many will grow cold. [13]But the one who endures to the end will be saved. [14]And the Good News about the Kingdom will be preached throughout the whole world, so that all nations will hear it; and then the end will come.

[15]"The day is coming when you will see what Daniel the prophet spoke about—the sacrilegious object that causes desecration standing in the Holy Place." (Reader, pay attention!) [16]"Then those in Judea must flee to the hills. [17]A person out on the deck of a roof must not go down into the house to pack. [18]A person out in the field must not return even to get a coat. [19]How terrible it will be for pregnant women and for nursing mothers in those days. [20]And pray that your flight will not be in winter or on the Sabbath. [21]For there will be greater anguish than at any time since the world began. And it will never be so great again. [22]In fact, unless that time of calamity is shortened, not a single person will survive. But it will be shortened for the sake of God's chosen ones.

[23]"Then if anyone tells you, 'Look, here is the Messiah,' or 'There he is,' don't believe it. [24]For false messiahs and false prophets will rise up and perform great signs and wonders so as to deceive, if possible, even God's chosen ones. [25]See, I have warned you about this ahead of time.

[26]"So if someone tells you, 'Look, the Messiah is out in the desert,' don't bother to go and look. Or, 'Look, he is hiding here,' don't believe it! [27]For as the lightning flashes in the east and shines to the west, so it will be when the Son of Man comes. [28]Just as the gathering of vultures shows there is a carcass nearby, so these signs indicate that the end is near.

[29]"Immediately after the anguish of those days,

the sun will be darkened,
the moon will give no light,
the stars will fall from the sky,
and the powers in the heavens will be shaken.

[30]And then at last, the sign that the Son of Man is coming will appear in the heavens, and there will be deep mourning among all the peoples of the earth. And they will see the Son of Man coming on the clouds of heaven with power and great glory. [31]And he will send out his angels with the mighty blast of a trumpet, and they will gather his chosen ones from all over the world—from the farthest ends of the earth and heaven.

[32]"Now learn a lesson from the fig tree. When its branches bud and its leaves begin to sprout, you know that summer is near. [33]In the same way, when you see all these things, you can know his return is very near, right at the door. [34]I tell you the truth, this generation will not pass from the scene until all these things take place. [35]Heaven and earth will disappear, but my words will never disappear.

[36]"However, no one knows the day or hour when these things will happen, not even the angels in heaven or the Son himself. Only the Father knows.

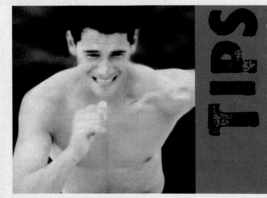

Lean gut myth:

Even though you see it on television, there is no such thing as spot-reduction. (We are not talking about getting rid of pimples by weight lifting - we're talking about making one specific part of your body lean!) Doing thousands and thousands of sit-ups will give you tight abdominal muscles, but they will do nothing to rid your midsection of fat. Nothing will rid the body of fat, unless it is a carefully orchestrated reduction in your daily energy intake; in other words, if you burn more calories than you actually take in.

³⁷"When the Son of Man returns, it will be like it was in Noah's day. ³⁸In those days before the flood, the people were enjoying banquets and parties and weddings right up to the time Noah entered his boat. ³⁹People didn't realize what was going to happen until the flood came and swept them all away. That is the way it will be when the Son of Man comes.

⁴⁰"Two men will be working together in the field; one will be taken, the other left. ⁴¹Two women will be grinding flour at the mill; one will be taken, the other left.

⁴²"So you, too, must keep watch! For you don't know what day your Lord is coming. ⁴³Understand this: If a homeowner knew exactly when a burglar was coming, he would keep watch and not permit his house to be broken into. ⁴⁴You also must be ready all the time, for the Son of Man will come when least expected.

⁴⁵"A faithful, sensible servant is one to whom the master can give the responsibility of managing his other household servants and feeding them. ⁴⁶If the master returns and finds that the servant has done a good job, there will be a reward. ⁴⁷I tell you the truth, the master will put that servant in charge of all he owns. ⁴⁸But what if the servant is evil and thinks, 'My master won't be back for a while,' ⁴⁹and he begins beating the other servants, partying, and getting drunk? ⁵⁰The master will return unannounced and unexpected, ⁵¹and he will cut the servant to pieces and assign him a place with the hypocrites. In that place there will be weeping and gnashing of teeth.

Parable of the Ten Bridesmaids

25

"The Kingdom of Heaven can be illustrated by the story of ten bridesmaids who took their lamps and went to meet the bridegroom. ²Five of them were foolish, and five were wise. ³The five who were foolish didn't take enough olive oil for their lamps, ⁴but the other five were wise enough to take along extra oil. ⁵When the bridegroom was delayed, they all became drowsy and fell asleep.

⁶"At midnight they were roused by the shout, 'Look, the bridegroom is coming! Come out and meet him!'

⁷"All the bridesmaids got up and prepared their lamps. ⁸Then the five foolish ones asked the others, 'Please give us some of your oil because our lamps are going out.'

⁹"But the others replied, 'We don't have enough for all of us. Go to a shop and buy some for yourselves.'

¹⁰"But while they were gone to buy oil, the bridegroom came. Then those who were ready went in with him to the marriage feast, and the door was locked. ¹¹Later, when the other five bridesmaids returned, they stood outside, calling, 'Lord! Lord! Open the door for us!'

¹²"But he called back, 'Believe me, I don't know you!'

¹³"So you, too, must keep watch! For you do not know the day or hour of my return.

25:14-30 WHAT'S IT SAYING?

WHAT AM I GOING TO DO ABOUT IT?

Parable of the Three Servants

¹⁴"Again, the Kingdom of Heaven can be illustrated by the story of a man going on a long trip. He called together his servants and entrusted his money to them while he was gone. ¹⁵He gave five bags of silver to one, two bags of silver to another, and one bag of silver to the last—dividing it in proportion to their abilities. He then left on his trip.

¹⁶"The servant who received the five bags of silver began to invest the money and earned five more. ¹⁷The servant with two bags of silver also went to work and earned two more. ¹⁸But the servant who received the one bag of silver dug a hole in the ground and hid the master's money.

¹⁹"After a long time their master returned from his trip and called them to give an account of how they had used his money. ²⁰The servant to whom he had entrusted the five bags of silver came forward with five more and said, 'Master, you gave me five bags of silver to invest, and I have earned five more.'

²¹"The master was full of praise. 'Well done, my good and faithful servant. You have been faithful in handling this small amount, so now I will give you many more responsibilities. Let's celebrate together!'

²²"The servant who had received the two bags of silver came forward and said, 'Master, you gave me two bags of silver to invest, and I have earned two more.'

²³"The master said, 'Well done, my good and faithful servant. You have been faithful in handling this small amount, so now I will give you many more responsibilities. Let's celebrate together!'

²⁴"Then the servant with the one bag of silver came and said, 'Master, I knew you were a harsh man, harvesting crops you didn't plant and gathering crops you didn't cultivate. ²⁵I was afraid I would lose your money, so I hid it in the earth. Look, here is your money back.'

²⁶"But the master replied, 'You wicked and lazy servant! If you knew I harvested crops I didn't plant and gathered crops I didn't cultivate, ²⁷why didn't you deposit my money in the bank? At least I could have gotten some interest on it.'

²⁸"Then he ordered, 'Take the money from this servant, and give it to the one with the ten bags of silver. ²⁹To those who use well what they are given, even more will be given, and they will have an abundance. But from those who do nothing, even what little they have will be taken away. ³⁰Now throw this useless servant into outer darkness, where there will be weeping and gnashing of teeth.'

The Final Judgment

³¹"But when the Son of Man comes in his glory, and all the angels with him, then he will sit upon his glorious throne. ³²All the nations will be gathered in his presence, and he will separate the people as a shepherd separates the sheep from the goats. ³³He will place the sheep at his right hand

STAND POINT

When you are dating

26:41

Keep watch and pray, so that you will not give in to temptation. For the spirit is willing, but the body is weak!

count on it

Get cleaned up!

Have you ever done something so bad you hope nobody will ever find out about it? Have you ever done something so bad you feel you can never be forgiven? God is in the business of forgiveness. Also, when you ask, he will make you totally clean. "If we confess our sins to him, he is faithful and just to forgive us our sins and to cleanse us from all wickedness." (1 John 1:9) **Count on it!**

and the goats at his left.

³⁴"Then the King will say to those on his right, 'Come, you who are blessed by my Father, inherit the Kingdom prepared for you from the creation of the world. ³⁵For I was hungry, and you fed me. I was thirsty, and you gave me a drink. I was a stranger, and you invited me into your home. ³⁶I was naked, and you gave me clothing. I was sick, and you cared for me. I was in prison, and you visited me.'

³⁷"Then these righteous ones will reply, 'Lord, when did we ever see you hungry and feed you? Or thirsty and give you something to drink? ³⁸Or a stranger and show you hospitality? Or naked and give you clothing? ³⁹When did we ever see you sick or in prison and visit you?'

⁴⁰"And the King will say, 'I tell you the truth, when you did it to one of the least of these my brothers and sisters, you were doing it to me!'

⁴¹"Then the King will turn to those on the left and say, 'Away with you, you cursed ones, into the eternal fire prepared for the devil and his demons. ⁴²For I was hungry, and you didn't feed me. I was thirsty, and you didn't give me a drink. ⁴³I was a stranger, and you didn't invite me into your home. I was naked, and you didn't give me clothing. I was sick and in prison, and you didn't visit me.'

⁴⁴"Then they will reply, 'Lord, when did we ever see you hungry or thirsty or a stranger or naked or sick or in prison, and not help you?'

⁴⁵"And he will answer, 'I tell you the truth, when you refused to help the least of these my brothers and sisters, you were refusing to help me.'

⁴⁶"And they will go away into eternal punishment, but the righteous will go into eternal life."

The Plot to Kill Jesus

26

When Jesus had finished saying all these things, he said to his disciples, ²"As you know, Passover begins in two days, and the Son of Man will be handed over to be crucified."

³At that same time the leading priests and elders were meeting at the residence of Caiaphas, the high priest, ⁴plotting how to capture Jesus secretly and kill him. ⁵"But not during the Passover celebration," they agreed, "or the people may riot."

Jesus Anointed at Bethany

⁶Meanwhile, Jesus was in Bethany at the home of Simon, a man who had previously had leprosy. ⁷While he was eating, a woman came in with a beautiful alabaster jar of expensive perfume and poured it over his head.

⁸The disciples were indignant when they saw this. "What a waste of money," they said. ⁹"It could have been sold for a high price and the money given to the poor."

¹⁰But Jesus, aware of this, replied, "Why criticize this woman for doing such a good thing to me? ¹¹You will always have the poor among you, but you will not always have me. ¹²She has poured this perfume on me to prepare my body for burial. ¹³I tell you the truth, wherever the Good News is preached throughout the world, this woman's deed will be remembered and discussed."

Judas Agrees to Betray Jesus

¹⁴Then Judas Iscariot, one of the twelve disciples, went to the leading priests ¹⁵and asked, "How much will you pay me to betray Jesus to you?" And they gave him thirty pieces of silver. ¹⁶From that time on, Judas began looking for an opportunity to betray Jesus.

action

26:26-30 WHAT'S IT SAYING?

WHAT AM I GOING TO DO ABOUT IT?

The Last Supper

¹⁷On the first day of the Festival of Unleavened Bread, the disciples came to Jesus and asked, "Where do you want us to prepare the Passover meal for you?"

¹⁸"As you go into the city," he told them, "you will see a certain man. Tell him, 'The Teacher says: My time has come, and I will eat the Passover meal with my disciples at your house.'" ¹⁹So the disciples did as Jesus told them and prepared the Passover meal there.

²⁰When it was evening, Jesus sat down at the table with the twelve disciples. ²¹While they were eating, he said, "I tell you the truth, one of you will betray me."

²²Greatly distressed, each one asked in turn, "Am I the one, Lord?"

²³He replied, "One of you who has just eaten from this bowl with me will betray me. ²⁴For the Son of Man must die, as the Scriptures declared long ago. But how terrible it will be for the one who betrays him. It would be far better for that man if he had never been born!"

²⁵Judas, the one who would betray him, also asked, "Rabbi, am I the one?"

And Jesus told him, "You have said it."

²⁶As they were eating, Jesus took some bread and

blessed it. Then he broke it in pieces and gave it to the disciples, saying, "Take this and eat it, for this is my body."

[27]And he took a cup of wine and gave thanks to God for it. He gave it to them and said, "Each of you drink from it, [28]for this is my blood, which confirms the covenant between God and his people. It is poured out as a sacrifice to forgive the sins of many. [29]Mark my words—I will not drink wine again until the day I drink it new with you in my Father's Kingdom."

[30]Then they sang a hymn and went out to the Mount of Olives.

Jesus Predicts Peter's Denial

[31]On the way, Jesus told them, "Tonight all of you will desert me. For the Scriptures say,

'God will strike the Shepherd,
and the sheep of the flock will be scattered.'

[32]But after I have been raised from the dead, I will go ahead of you to Galilee and meet you there."

[33]Peter declared, "Even if everyone else deserts you, I will never desert you."

[34]Jesus replied, "I tell you the truth, Peter—this very night, before the rooster crows, you will deny three times that you even know me."

[35]"No!" Peter insisted. "Even if I have to die with you, I will never deny you!" And all the other disciples vowed the same.

Jesus Prays in Gethsemane

[36]Then Jesus went with them to the olive grove called Gethsemane, and he said, "Sit here while I go over there to pray." [37]He took Peter and Zebedee's two sons, James and John, and he became anguished and distressed. [38]He told them, "My soul is crushed with grief to the point of death. Stay here and keep watch with me."

[39]He went on a little farther and bowed with his face to the ground, praying, "My Father! If it is possible, let this cup of suffering be taken away from me. Yet I want your will to be done, not mine."

[40]Then he returned to the disciples and found them asleep. He said to Peter, "Couldn't you watch with me even one hour? [41]Keep watch and pray, so that you will not give in to temptation. For the spirit is willing, but the body is weak!"

[42]Then Jesus left them a second time and prayed, "My Father! If this cup cannot be taken away unless I drink it, your will be done." [43]When he returned to them again, he found them sleeping, for they couldn't keep their eyes open.

[44]So he went to pray a third time, saying the same

things again. [45]Then he came to the disciples and said, "Go ahead and sleep. Have your rest. But look—the time has come. The Son of Man is betrayed into the hands of sinners. [46]Up, let's be going. Look, my betrayer is here!"

Jesus Is Betrayed and Arrested

[47]And even as Jesus said this, Judas, one of the twelve disciples, arrived with a crowd of men armed with swords and clubs. They had been sent by the leading priests and elders of the people. [48]The traitor, Judas, had given them a prearranged signal: "You will know which one to arrest when I greet him with a kiss."

[49]So Judas came straight to Jesus. "Greetings, Rabbi!" he exclaimed and gave him the kiss.

[50]Jesus said, "My friend, go ahead and do what you have come for."

Then the others grabbed Jesus and arrested him. [51]But one of the men with Jesus pulled out his sword and struck the high priest's slave, slashing off his ear.

[52]"Put away your sword," Jesus told him. "Those who use the sword will die by the sword. [53]Don't you realize that I could ask my Father for thousands of angels to protect us, and he would send them instantly? [54]But if I did, how would the Scriptures be fulfilled that describe what must happen now?"

[55]Then Jesus said to the crowd, "Am I some dangerous revolutionary, that you come with swords and clubs to arrest me? Why didn't you arrest me in the Temple? I was there teaching every day. [56]But this is all happening to fulfill the words of the prophets as recorded in the Scriptures." At that point, all the disciples deserted him and fled.

Jesus before the Council

[57]Then the people who had arrested Jesus led him to the home of Caiaphas, the high priest, where the teachers of religious law and the elders had gathered. [58]Meanwhile, Peter followed him at a distance and came to the high priest's courtyard. He went in and sat with the guards and waited to see how it would all end.

[59]Inside, the leading priests and the entire high council were trying to find witnesses who would lie about Jesus, so they could put him to death. [60]But even though they found many who agreed to give false witness, they could not use anyone's testimony. Finally, two men came forward [61]who declared, "This man said, 'I am able to destroy the Temple of God and rebuild it in three days.'"

[62]Then the high priest stood up and said to Jesus,

"Well, aren't you going to answer these charges? What do you have to say for yourself?" [63]But Jesus remained silent. Then the high priest said to him, "I demand in the name of the living God—tell us if you are the Messiah, the Son of God."

[64]Jesus replied, "You have said it. And in the future you will see the Son of Man seated in the place of power at God's right hand and coming on the clouds of heaven."

[65]Then the high priest tore his clothing to show his horror and said, "Blasphemy! Why do we need other witnesses? You have all heard his blasphemy. [66]What is your verdict?"

"Guilty!" they shouted. "He deserves to die!"

[67]Then they began to spit in Jesus' face and beat him with their fists. And some slapped him, [68]jeering, "Prophesy to us, you Messiah! Who hit you that time?"

Peter Denies Jesus

[69]Meanwhile, Peter was sitting outside in the courtyard. A servant girl came over and said to him, "You were one of those with Jesus the Galilean."

[70]But Peter denied it in front of everyone. "I don't know what you're talking about," he said.

[71]Later, out by the gate, another servant girl noticed him and said to those standing around, "This man was with Jesus of Nazareth."

[72]Again Peter denied it, this time with an oath. "I don't even know the man," he said.

[73]A little later some of the other bystanders came over to Peter and said, "You must be one of them; we can tell by your Galilean accent."

[74]Peter swore, "A curse on me if I'm lying—I don't know the man!" And immediately the rooster crowed.

[75]Suddenly, Jesus' words flashed through Peter's mind: "Before the rooster crows, you will deny three times that you even know me." And he went away, weeping bitterly.

Judas Hangs Himself

27

Very early in the morning the leading priests and the elders met again to lay plans for putting Jesus to death. [2]Then they bound him, led him away, and took him to Pilate, the Roman governor.

[3]When Judas, who had betrayed him, realized that Jesus had been condemned to die, he was filled with remorse. So he took the thirty pieces of silver back to the leading priests and the elders. [4]"I have sinned," he declared, "for I have betrayed an innocent man."

"What do we care?" they retorted. "That's your problem."

[5]Then Judas threw the silver coins down in the Temple and went out and hanged himself.

[6]The leading priests picked up the coins. "It wouldn't be right to put this money in the Temple treasury," they said, "since it was payment for murder." [7]After some discussion they finally decided to buy the potter's field, and they made it into a cemetery for foreigners. [8]That is why the field is still called the Field of Blood. [9]This fulfilled the prophecy of Jeremiah that says,

"They took the thirty pieces of silver—

the price at which he was valued by the people of Israel,

[10]and purchased the potter's field,

as the LORD directed."

Jesus' Trial before Pilate

[11]Now Jesus was standing before Pilate, the Roman governor. "Are you the king of the Jews?" the governor asked him. Jesus replied, "You have said it."

[12]But when the leading priests and the elders made their accusations against him, Jesus remained silent. [13]"Don't you hear all these charges they are bringing against you?" Pilate demanded. [14]But Jesus made no response to any of the charges, much to the governor's surprise.

[15]Now it was the governor's custom each year during the Passover celebration to release one prisoner to the crowd—anyone they wanted. [16]This year there was a notorious prisoner, a man named Barabbas. [17]As the crowds gathered before Pilate's house that morning, he asked them, "Which one do you want me to release to you—Barabbas, or Jesus who is called the Messiah?" [18](He knew very well that the religious leaders had arrested Jesus out of envy.)

[19]Just then, as Pilate was sitting on the judgment seat, his wife sent him this message: "Leave that innocent man alone. I suffered through a terrible nightmare about him last night."

[20]Meanwhile, the leading priests and the elders persuaded the crowd to ask for Barabbas to be released and for Jesus to be put to death. [21]So the governor asked again, "Which of these two do you want me to release to you?"

The crowd shouted back, "Barabbas!"

[22]Pilate responded, "Then what should I do with Jesus who is called the Messiah?"

They shouted back, "Crucify him!"

[23]"Why?" Pilate demanded. "What crime has he committed?"

But the mob roared even louder, "Crucify him!"

[24]Pilate saw that he wasn't getting anywhere and that a riot was developing. So he sent for a bowl of water and washed his hands before the crowd, saying, "I am innocent of this man's blood. The responsibility is yours!"

[25]And all the people yelled back, "We will take responsibility for his death—we and our children!" [26]So Pilate released Barabbas to them. He ordered Jesus flogged with a lead-tipped whip, then turned him over to the Roman soldiers to be crucified.

The Soldiers Mock Jesus

[27]Some of the governor's soldiers took Jesus into their headquarters and called out the entire regiment.

Not Just on Sundays!

God does not want us to be part-time Christians. It is not starting the race that counts, but how we finish. He wants us to persevere to the end. He also wants every area of our lives to be under his care and control. God knows that we cannot change on our own — we need help from others to encourage us and, more importantly, we need power from God. But he promises he will stay close. "And be sure of this: I am with you always, even to the end of the age." (Matthew 28:20)

Is my faith affecting every area of my life?

```
        Not at all——a little——things are happening——God is in control
          1———2———3———4———5———6———7———8———9———10


Mental:   1———2———3———4———5———6———7———8———9———10

Physical: 1———2———3———4———5———6———7———8———9———10

Social:   1———2———3———4———5———6———7———8———9———10

Spiritual: 1———2———3———4———5———6———7———8———9———10
```

[28] They stripped him and put a scarlet robe on him. [29] They wove thorn branches into a crown and put it on his head, and they placed a reed stick in his right hand as a scepter. Then they knelt before him in mockery and taunted, "Hail! King of the Jews!" [30] And they spit on him and grabbed the stick and struck him on the head with it. [31] When they were finally tired of mocking him, they took off the robe and put his own clothes on him again. Then they led him away to be crucified.

The Crucifixion

[32] Along the way, they came across a man named Simon, who was from Cyrene, and the soldiers forced him to carry Jesus' cross. [33] And they went out to a place called Golgotha (which means "Place of the Skull"). [34] The soldiers gave him wine mixed with bitter gall, but when he had tasted it, he refused to drink it. [35] After they had nailed him to the cross, the soldiers gambled for his clothes by throwing dice.* [36] Then they sat around and kept guard as he hung there. [37] A sign was fastened to the cross above Jesus' head, announcing the charge against him. It read: "This is Jesus, the King of the Jews." [38] Two revolutionaries were crucified with him, one on his right and one on his left.

[39] The people passing by shouted abuse, shaking their heads in mockery. [40] "Look at you now!" they yelled at him. "You said you were going to destroy the Temple and rebuild it in three days. Well then, if you are the Son of God, save yourself and come down from the cross!"

[41] The leading priests, the teachers of religious law, and the elders also mocked Jesus. [42] "He saved others," they scoffed, "but he can't save himself! So he is the King of Israel, is he? Let him come down from the cross right now, and we will believe in him! [43] He trusted God, so let God rescue him now if he wants him! For he said, 'I am the Son of God.'" [44] Even the revolutionaries who were crucified with him ridiculed him in the same way.

The Death of Jesus

[45] At noon, darkness fell across the whole land until three o'clock. [46] At about three o'clock, Jesus called out with a loud voice, "Eli, Eli, lema sabachthani?" which means "My God, my God, why have you abandoned me?"

[47] Some of the bystanders misunderstood and thought he was calling for the prophet Elijah. [48] One of them ran and filled a sponge with sour wine, holding it up to him on a reed stick so he could drink. [49] But the rest said, "Wait! Let's see whether Elijah comes to save him."*

[50] Then Jesus shouted out again, and he released his spirit. [51] At that moment the curtain in the sanctuary of the Temple was torn in two, from top to bottom. The earth shook, rocks split apart, [52] and tombs opened. The bodies of many godly men and women who had died were raised from the dead. [53] They left the cemetery after Jesus' resurrection, went into the holy city of Jerusalem, and appeared to many people. [54] The Roman officer and the other soldiers at the crucifixion were terrified by the earthquake and all that had happened. They said, "This man truly was the Son of God!"

[55] And many women who had come from Galilee with Jesus to care for him were watching from a distance. [56] Among them were Mary Magdalene, Mary (the mother of James and Joseph), and the mother of James and John, the sons of Zebedee.

The Burial of Jesus

[57] As evening approached, Joseph, a rich man from Arimathea who had become a follower of Jesus, [58] went to Pilate and asked for Jesus' body. And Pilate issued an order to release it to him. [59] Joseph took the body and wrapped it in a long sheet of clean linen cloth. [60] He placed it in his own new tomb, which had been carved out of the rock. Then he rolled a great stone across the entrance and left. [61] Both Mary Magdalene and the other Mary were sitting across from the tomb and watching.

The Guard at the Tomb

[62] The next day, on the Sabbath, the leading priests and Pharisees went to see Pilate. [63] They told him, "Sir, we remember what that deceiver once said while he was still alive: 'After three days I will rise from the dead.' [64] So we request that you seal the tomb until the third day. This will prevent his disciples from coming and stealing his body and then telling everyone he was raised from the dead! If that happens, we'll be worse off than we were at first."

[65] Pilate replied, "Take guards and secure it the best

you can." [66] So they sealed the tomb and posted guards to protect it.

The Resurrection

28

Early on Sunday morning, as the new day was dawning, Mary Magdalene and the other Mary went out to visit the tomb. [2] Suddenly there was a great earthquake! For an angel of the Lord came down from heaven, rolled aside the stone, and sat on it. [3] His face shone like lightning, and his clothing was as white as snow. [4] The guards shook with fear when they saw him, and they fell into a dead faint.

[5] Then the angel spoke to the women. "Don't be afraid!" he said. "I know you are looking for Jesus, who was crucified. [6] He isn't here! He is risen from the dead, just as he said would happen. Come, see where his body was lying. [7] And now, go quickly and tell his disciples that he has risen from the dead, and he is going ahead of you to Galilee. You will see him there. Remember what I have told you."

[8] The women ran quickly from the tomb. They were very frightened but also filled with great joy, and they rushed to give the disciples the angel's message. [9] And as they went, Jesus met them and greeted them. And they ran to him, grasped his feet, and worshiped him. [10] Then Jesus said to them, "Don't be afraid! Go tell my brothers to leave for Galilee, and they will see me there."

The Report of the Guard

[11] As the women were on their way, some of the guards went into the city and told the leading priests what had happened. [12] A meeting with the elders was called, and they decided to give the soldiers a large bribe. [13] They told the soldiers, "You must say, 'Jesus' disciples came during the night while we were sleeping, and they stole his body.' [14] If the governor hears about it, we'll stand up for you so you won't get in trouble." [15] So the guards accepted the bribe and said what they were told to say. Their story spread widely among the Jews, and they still tell it today.

The Great Commission

[16] Then the eleven disciples left for Galilee, going to the mountain where Jesus had told them to go. [17] When they saw him, they worshiped him—but some of them doubted! [18] Jesus came and told his disciples, "I have been given all authority in heaven and on earth. [19] Therefore, go and make disciples of all the nations, baptizing them in the name of the Father and the Son and the Holy Spirit. [20] Teach these new disciples to obey all the commands I have given you. And be sure of this: I am with you always, even to the end of the age."

27:35 Greek *by casting lots*. A few late manuscripts add *This fulfilled the word of the prophet: "They divided my garments among themselves and cast lots for my robe."* See Ps 22:18.
27:49 Some manuscripts add *And another took a spear and pierced his side, and out flowed water and blood.* Compare John 19:34.

Change your Form

"Pray for us, too, that God will give us many opportunities to speak about his mysterious plan concerning Christ. That is why I am here in chains. [4]Pray that I will proclaim this message as clearly as I should." Colossians 4:3-4

Good coaches can sustain the big picture while being flexible enough to adapt the team's strategy. Can we help the church do the same?

One summer morning I found myself in the vestry (back room) of an ancient Scottish church waiting to preach at a "special evangelistic service." Sitting next to me was the old "Beadle" (church caretaker) preparing himself to lead the procession (me) to the sanctuary! I was already a bit disheartened after peeking at the congregation - it was a sea of grey hair, not a young person in sight! I thought "My father-in-law would love this place because it would make him feel young."

I asked the Beadle, "How long have you served this church?" He paused, pondered, protruded his lower lip, squinted his eyes, shook his head, and said, "Eh, just over thirty years." I replied, "Wow! Over thirty years you must have seen a lot of changes here!" The old man again paused, pondered, protruded his lower lip, squinted his eyes, shook his head, and replied matter-of-factly, "No!" After the service, I thought to myself that if that old Beadle had served that church for two hundred years he would not have seen any change!

DEVOTIONAL

Two components of Christianity get confused: message and method. The gospel is the Good News to those who put their faith and trust in the resurrected Son of God, Jesus Christ. This message must be biblically based and convey spiritual truth: The message must never, ever change or be watered down. To dilute the gospel is to dilute its power.

However, the method can be different and open to change. There is no biblical mandate for how to share our faith. You may proclaim Christ formally and informally in a variety of ways. You can proclaim the gospel through speech, word, picture, song, and drama ... as long as biblical reliability and compassion are upheld. There is nothing sacred about the method. When one style of transmitting the message becomes more important than the message, your traditions are more important than the people outside the church.

If a coach or businessperson had the same results as many of our churches, they would have a team of athletes who had not changed their style in generations. Imagine golfing with wooden shaft clubs, high jumping into a sandpit, sprinting on cinders, or pole-vaulting with a wooden pole. If that does not hit home, how about living without penicillin or smallpox vaccinations?

Reflection
Do we value sitting in comfortable pews more than making disciples? Hold tight to the message not the method.

Prayer
Father, help me to understand the difference between truth and style.

"Disregard the immaterial."
Blake's dictum

Nicked with permission from: A Sporting Guide to Eternity, Steve Connor, Christian Focus Publications - ISBN 1-85792-746-X

Mark

Mark is the second of the four Gospels of Christ. Having four Gospels gives us a distinct view of Christ's life from different angles; yet, at the same time, all the books are consistent and harmonious. Remarkably, these books are written by very different men, yet all the Gospels have a complementary power, inspired by God, that reveals Jesus' life, character, mission, power, and purpose. Each account shows a special aspect of Jesus' history and lineage. Each writer starts Jesus' history from a different branch of his family tree to emphasize particular aspects of his life and authority.

John takes us back right to the beginning of time and the foundation of the world to reveal that Jesus was with his Father as the Creator and Sustainer of all things. Jesus is God.

Luke traces his account of Jesus back to Adam to explain that Jesus is the new Adam. Jesus is our Savior.

Matthew starts Jesus' life with King David to reveal that Jesus is the fulfillment of the Old Testament prophecies — a savior and new king will come from the line of King David. Jesus is our King.

Mark cuts to the chase and starts recording Christ's life as an adult: the Messiah-deliverer. This is a fast-paced, action-packed look at Jesus' life and ministry. Jesus calmed the sea, healed the sick, drove out demons, fed the 4,000, debated with religious leaders, and recruited, trained, and mobilized his followers. This is the shortest Gospel – most Bible scholars think that Matthew and Luke both used Mark as the model for their own book. Mark's target audience is the Gentiles (non-Jews), which arguably would have been mainly Roman. Mark, inspired by the Holy Spirit, deliberately selected and omitted sections of Jesus' ministry that we find in the other Gospels, which would have had little meaning to his unique audience. Mark keeps a very intense pace, emphasizing Jesus' action in the face of spiritual adversity. This Gospel emphasizes Jesus' servant-hood and sacrifice throughout, and we are challenged to do the same in complete surrender and commitment to Christ.

Improvement
LIVE it

MARK

John the Baptist Prepares the Way

1

This is the Good News about Jesus the Messiah, the Son of God. It began ²just as the prophet Isaiah had written:
"Look, I am sending my messenger ahead of you, and he will prepare your way.
³He is a voice shouting in the wilderness, 'Prepare the way for the LORD's coming! Clear the road for him!'"
⁴This messenger was John the Baptist. He was in the wilderness and preached that people should be baptized to show that they had turned to God to receive forgiveness for their sins. ⁵All of Judea, including all the people of Jerusalem, went out to see and hear John. And when they confessed their sins, he baptized them in the Jordan River. ⁶His clothes were woven from coarse camel hair, and he wore a leather belt around his waist. For food he ate locusts and wild honey.
⁷John announced: "Someone is coming soon who is greater than I am—so much greater that I'm not even worthy to stoop down like a slave and untie the straps of his sandals. ⁸I baptize you with water, but he will baptize you with the Holy Spirit!"

The Baptism and Temptation of Jesus

⁹One day Jesus came from Nazareth in Galilee, and John baptized him in the Jordan River. ¹⁰As Jesus came up out of the water, he saw the heavens splitting apart and the Holy Spirit descending on him like a dove. ¹¹And a voice from heaven said, "You are my dearly loved Son, and you bring me great joy."
¹²The Spirit then compelled Jesus to go into the wilderness, ¹³where he was tempted by Satan for forty days. He was out among the wild animals, and angels took care of him.
¹⁴Later on, after John was arrested, Jesus went into Galilee, where he preached God's Good News. ¹⁵"The time promised by God has come at last!" he announced. "The Kingdom of God is near! Repent of your sins and believe the Good News!"

The First Disciples

¹⁶One day as Jesus was walking along the shore of the Sea of Galilee, he saw Simon and his brother Andrew

The first international soccer game played between non-British sides took place in 1902 in Vienna when Austria beat Hungary 5–0.

throwing a net into the water, for they fished for a living. ¹⁷Jesus called out to them, "Come, follow me, and I will show you how to fish for people!" ¹⁸And they left their nets at once and followed him.
¹⁹A little farther up the shore Jesus saw Zebedee's sons, James and John, in a boat repairing their nets. ²⁰He called them at once, and they also followed him, leaving their father, Zebedee, in the boat with the hired men.

Jesus Casts Out an Evil Spirit

²¹Jesus and his companions went to the town of Capernaum. When the Sabbath day came, he went into the synagogue and began to teach. ²²The people were amazed at his teaching, for he taught with real authority—quite unlike the teachers of religious law. ²³Suddenly, a man in the synagogue who was possessed by an evil spirit began shouting, ²⁴"Why are you interfering with us, Jesus of Nazareth? Have you come to destroy us? I know who you are—the Holy One sent from God!"
²⁵Jesus cut him short. "Be quiet! Come out of the man,"

he ordered. ²⁶At that, the evil spirit screamed, threw the man into a convulsion, and then came out of him.
²⁷Amazement gripped the audience, and they began to discuss what had happened. "What sort of new teaching is this?" they asked excitedly. "It has such authority! Even evil spirits obey his orders!" ²⁸The news about Jesus spread quickly throughout the entire region of Galilee.

Jesus Heals Many People

²⁹After Jesus left the synagogue with James and John, they went to Simon and Andrew's home. ³⁰Now Simon's mother-in-law was sick in bed with a high fever. They told Jesus about her right away. ³¹So he went to her bedside, took her by the hand, and helped her sit up. Then the fever left her, and she prepared a meal for them.
³²That evening after sunset, many sick and demon-possessed people were brought to Jesus. ³³The whole town gathered at the door to watch. ³⁴So Jesus healed many people who were sick with various diseases, and he cast out many demons. But because the demons knew who he was, he did not allow them to speak.

Jesus Preaches in Galilee

³⁵Before daybreak the next morning, Jesus got up and went out to an isolated place to pray. ³⁶Later Simon and the others went out to find him. ³⁷When they found him, they said, "Everyone is looking for you."
³⁸But Jesus replied, "We must go on to other towns as well, and I will preach to them, too. That is why I came." ³⁹So he traveled throughout the region of Galilee, preaching in the synagogues and casting out demons.

Jesus Heals a Man with Leprosy

⁴⁰A man with leprosy came and knelt in front of Jesus, begging to be healed. "If you are willing, you can heal me and make me clean," he said.
⁴¹Moved with compassion, Jesus reached out and touched

Make time for God: Excuses are like elbows – we all have two of them! If you can make time for sports, friends, and entertainment, you can make time for God. It will be the best thing you do all day. "Before daybreak the next morning, Jesus got up and went out to an isolated place to pray."

(Mark 1:35)

him. "I am willing," he said. "Be healed!" [42]Instantly the leprosy disappeared, and the man was healed. [43]Then Jesus sent him on his way with a stern warning: [44]"Don't tell anyone about this. Instead, go to the priest and let him examine you. Take along the offering required in the law of Moses for those who have been healed of leprosy. This will be a public testimony that you have been cleansed."

[45]But the man went and spread the word, proclaiming to everyone what had happened. As a result, large crowds soon surrounded Jesus, and he couldn't publicly enter a town anywhere. He had to stay out in the secluded places, but people from everywhere kept coming to him.

2:1-5 WHAT'S IT SAYING?

WHAT AM I GOING TO DO ABOUT IT?

Jesus Heals a Paralyzed Man

2

When Jesus returned to Capernaum several days later, the news spread quickly that he was back home. [2]Soon the house where he was staying was so packed with visitors that there was no more room, even outside the door. While he was preaching God's word to them, [3]four men arrived carrying a paralyzed man on a mat. [4]They couldn't bring him to Jesus because of the crowd, so they dug a hole through the roof above his head. Then they lowered the man on his mat, right

down in front of Jesus. [5]Seeing their faith, Jesus said to the paralyzed man, "My child, your sins are forgiven."

[6]But some of the teachers of religious law who were sitting there thought to themselves, [7]"What is he saying? This is blasphemy! Only God can forgive sins!" [8]Jesus knew immediately what they were thinking, so he asked them, "Why do you question this in your hearts? [9]Is it easier to say to the paralyzed man 'Your sins are forgiven,' or 'Stand up, pick up your mat, and walk'? [10]So I will prove to you that the Son of Man has the authority on earth to forgive sins." Then Jesus turned to the paralyzed man and said, [11]"Stand up, pick up your mat, and go home!"

[12]And the man jumped up, grabbed his mat, and walked out through the stunned onlookers. They were all amazed and praised God, exclaiming, "We've never seen anything like this before!"

Jesus Calls Levi (Matthew)

[13]Then Jesus went out to the lakeshore again and taught the crowds that were coming to him. [14]As he walked along, he saw Levi son of Alphaeus sitting at his tax collector's booth. "Follow me and be my disciple," Jesus said to him. So Levi got up and followed him.

[15]Later, Levi invited Jesus and his disciples to his home as dinner guests, along with many tax collectors and other disreputable sinners. (There were many people of this kind among Jesus' followers.) [16]But when the teachers of religious law who were Pharisees saw him eating with tax collectors and other sinners, they asked his disciples, "Why does he eat with such scum?" [17]When Jesus heard this, he told them, "Healthy people don't need a doctor—sick people do. I have come to call not those who think they are righteous, but those who know they are sinners."

A Discussion about Fasting

[18]Once when John's disciples and the Pharisees were fasting, some people came to Jesus and asked, "Why don't your disciples fast like John's disciples and the Pharisees do?"

[19]Jesus replied, "Do wedding guests fast while celebrating with the groom? Of course not. They can't fast while the groom is with them. [20]But someday the groom will be taken away from them, and then they will fast.

[21]"Besides, who would patch old clothing with new cloth? For the new patch would shrink and rip away from the old cloth, leaving an even bigger tear than before.

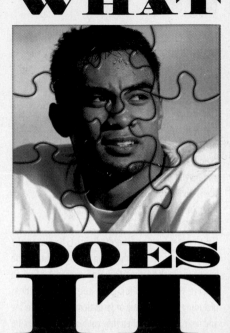

WHAT DOES IT MEAN?

Sea of Galilee

The Sea of Galilee is a lake 12.5 miles long and over 7 miles wide. It's about 60 miles northeast of Jerusalem with access to all surrounding nations and countries. It attracted the Lord Jesus and induced him to make this spot the center of his public ministry, his "own town" (Matthew 9:1).

The Sea of Galilee was famous for its fishing and attracted a large cross section of people. Capernaum was a coastal city where Jesus chose fishermen (Peter and his brother, Andrew, and James and John) to be disciples, and mobilized them to fish for people (Matt. 4:18, 22; Mark 1:16-20; Luke 5:1-11). It was here that Jesus showed his power by calming a horrific storm, and here that he showed himself to his disciples after his resurrection (John 21). It is also called the Lake of Gennesaret and the Sea of Tiberias.

22"And no one puts new wine into old wineskins. For the wine would burst the wineskins, and the wine and the skins would both be lost. New wine calls for new wineskins."

A Discussion about the Sabbath

23One Sabbath day as Jesus was walking through some grainfields, his disciples began breaking off heads of grain to eat. 24But the Pharisees said to Jesus, "Look, why are they breaking the law by harvesting grain on the Sabbath?"

25Jesus said to them, "Haven't you ever read in the Scriptures what David did when he and his companions were hungry? 26He went into the house of God (during the days when Abiathar was high priest) and broke the law by eating the sacred loaves of bread that only the priests are allowed to eat. He also gave some to his companions."

27Then Jesus said to them, "The Sabbath was made to meet the needs of people, and not people to meet the requirements of the Sabbath. 28So the Son of Man is Lord, even over the Sabbath!"

Jesus Heals on the Sabbath

3

Jesus went into the synagogue again and noticed a man with a deformed hand. 2Since it was the Sabbath, Jesus' enemies watched him closely. If he healed the man's hand, they planned to accuse him of working on the Sabbath.

3Jesus said to the man, "Come and stand in front of everyone." 4Then he turned to his critics and asked, "Does the law permit good deeds on the Sabbath, or is it a day for doing evil? Is this a day to save life or to destroy it?" But they wouldn't answer him.

There are 66 books in the Bible, 39 in the Old Testament and 27 in the New Testament.

5He looked around at them angrily and was deeply saddened by their hard hearts. Then he said to the man, "Hold out your hand." So the man held out his hand, and it was restored! 6At once the Pharisees went away and met with the supporters of Herod to plot how to kill Jesus.

Crowds Follow Jesus

7Jesus went out to the lake with his disciples, and a large crowd followed him. They came from all over Galilee, Judea, 8Jerusalem, Idumea, from east of the Jordan River, and even from as far north as Tyre and Sidon. The news about his miracles had spread far and wide, and vast numbers of people came to see him.

9Jesus instructed his disciples to have a boat ready so the crowd would not crush him. 10He had healed many people that day, so all the sick people eagerly pushed forward to touch him. 11And whenever those possessed by evil spirits caught sight of him, the spirits would throw them to the ground in front of him shrieking, "You are the Son of God!" 12But Jesus sternly commanded the spirits not to reveal who he was.

Jesus Chooses the Twelve Apostles

13Afterward Jesus went up on a mountain and called

out the ones he wanted to go with him. And they came to him. 14Then he appointed twelve of them and called them his apostles. They were to accompany him, and he would send them out to preach, 15giving them authority to cast out demons. 16Here are their names:

Simon (whom he named Peter),

17James and John (the sons of Zebedee, but Jesus nicknamed them "Sons of Thunder"),

18Andrew,

Philip,

Bartholomew,

Matthew,

Thomas,

James (son of Alphaeus),

Thaddaeus,

Simon (the zealot),

19Judas Iscariot (who later betrayed him).

Jesus and the Prince of Demons

20One time Jesus entered a house, and the crowds began to gather again. Soon he and his disciples couldn't even find time to eat. 21When his family heard what was happening, they tried to take him away. "He's out of his mind," they said.

22But the teachers of religious law who had arrived from Jerusalem said, "He's possessed by Satan, the prince of demons. That's where he gets the power to cast out demons."

23Jesus called them over and responded with an illustration. "How can Satan cast out Satan?" he asked. 24"A kingdom divided by civil war will collapse. 25Similarly, a family splintered by feuding will fall apart. 26And if Satan is divided and fights against himself, how can he stand? He would never survive. 27Let me illustrate this further. Who is powerful enough to enter the house of a strong man like Satan and plunder his goods? Only someone even stronger—someone who could tie him up and then plunder his house.

28"I tell you the truth, all sin and blasphemy can be forgiven,

---

Choose Your Side! (MARK 3:23-29)

The Christian life is a competition, a fight, a war in which we are the soldiers. As athletes we prepare mentally and physically, often at great sacrifice of time and effort, in order to win games. How much more, having identified our opponent, should we be prepared for a lifetime in the service of Christ? In a powerful illustration Jesus talked about a strong man (the devil) defending his possessions until an even stronger man (Jesus) comes along, overpowering and disarming him. We were all playing on the devil's team, but Christ has transferred us onto his team. The transfer fee is his precious blood. Come the final whistle, Satan's defeat is certain. CHOOSE YOUR SIDE – "Anyone who isn't helping me opposes me, and anyone who isn't working with me is actually working against me" (Matthew 12:30). Imagine being on a soccer field, and just as the ball comes to you, you think, *I don't know which goal I'm shooting for!* In the middle of the game there is no room for neutrality. Jesus says there is no room for neutrality in the spiritual battle. If you are not with him gathering into heaven, you are with the enemy scattering into hell.

BIBLE HIT

STAND POINT

When you have doubts

4:41

The disciples were absolutely terrified. "Who is this man?" they asked each other. "Even the wind and waves obey him!"

²⁹but anyone who blasphemes the Holy Spirit will never be forgiven. This is a sin with eternal consequences." ³⁰He told them this because they were saying, "He's possessed by an evil spirit."

The True Family of Jesus

³¹Then Jesus' mother and brothers came to see him. They stood outside and sent word for him to come out and talk with them. ³²There was a crowd sitting around Jesus, and someone said, "Your mother and your brothers are outside asking for you."

³³Jesus replied, "Who is my mother? Who are my brothers?" ³⁴Then he looked at those around him and said, "Look, these are my mother and brothers. ³⁵Anyone who does God's will is my brother and sister and mother."

Parable of the Farmer Scattering Seed

4

Once again Jesus began teaching by the lakeshore. A very large crowd soon gathered around him, so he got into a boat. Then he sat in the boat while all the people remained on the shore. ²He taught them by telling many stories in the form of parables, such as this one:

³"Listen! A farmer went out to plant some seed. ⁴As he scattered it across his field, some of the seed fell on a footpath, and the birds came and ate it. ⁵Other seed fell on shallow soil with underlying rock. The seed sprouted quickly because the soil was shallow. ⁶But the plant soon wilted under the hot sun, and since it didn't have deep roots, it died. ⁷Other seed fell among thorns that grew up and choked out the tender plants so they produced no grain. ⁸Still other seeds fell on fertile soil, and they sprouted, grew, and produced a crop that was thirty, sixty, and even a hundred times as much as had been planted!" ⁹Then he said, "Anyone with ears to hear should listen and understand."

¹⁰Later, when Jesus was alone with the twelve disciples and with the others who were gathered around, they asked him what the parables meant.

¹¹He replied, "You are permitted to understand the secret of the Kingdom of God. But I use parables for everything I say to outsiders, ¹²so that the Scriptures might be fulfilled:

'When they see what I do,
they will learn nothing.
When they hear what I say,
they will not understand.
Otherwise, they will turn to me
and be forgiven.'"

¹³Then Jesus said to them, "If you can't understand the meaning of this parable, how will you understand all the other parables? ¹⁴The farmer plants seed by taking God's word to others. ¹⁵The seed that fell on the footpath represents those who hear the message, only to have Satan come at once and take it away. ¹⁶The seed on the rocky soil represents those who hear the message and immediately receive it with joy. ¹⁷But since they don't have deep roots, they don't last long. They fall away as soon as they have problems or are persecuted for believing God's word. ¹⁸The seed that fell among the thorns represents others who hear God's word, ¹⁹but all too quickly the message is crowded out by the worries of this life, the lure of wealth, and the desire for other things, so no fruit is produced. ²⁰And the seed that fell on good soil represents those who hear and accept God's word and produce a harvest of thirty, sixty, or even a hundred times as much as had been planted!"

Parable of the Lamp

²¹Then Jesus asked them, "Would anyone light a lamp and then put it under a basket or under a bed? Of course not! A lamp is placed on a stand, where its light will shine. ²²For everything that is hidden will eventually be brought into the open, and every secret will be brought to light. ²³Anyone with ears to hear should listen and understand."

The Greek word for *Christian* appears only three times in the Bible: Acts 11:26; 26:28; and 1 Peter 4:16.

²⁴Then he added, "Pay close attention to what you hear. The closer you listen, the more understanding you will be given—and you will receive even more. ²⁵To those who listen to my teaching, more understanding will be given. But for those who are not listening, even what little understanding they have will be taken away from them."

4:21-25 WHAT'S IT SAYING?

WHAT AM I GOING TO DO ABOUT IT?

Parable of the Growing Seed

²⁶Jesus also said, "The Kingdom of God is like a farmer who scatters seed on the ground. ²⁷Night and day, while he's asleep or awake, the seed sprouts and grows, but he does not understand how it happens. ²⁸The earth produces the crops on its own. First a leaf blade pushes through, then the heads of wheat are formed, and finally the grain ripens. ²⁹And as soon as the grain is ready, the farmer comes and harvests it with a sickle, for the harvest time has come."

Parable of the Mustard Seed

³⁰Jesus said, "How can I describe the Kingdom of God? What story should I use to illustrate it? ³¹It is like a mustard seed planted in the ground. It is the smallest of all seeds, ³²but it becomes the largest of all garden plants; it grows long branches, and birds can make nests in its shade."

³³Jesus used many similar stories and illustrations to

TIPS

The stretch is not enough:

Stretching is often incorrectly considered a complete warm-up because it is commonly done during the first stage of training. In addition to the stretch, a walk to run that gradually increases heart rate will help the body get ready for action by raising the body temperature and increasing blood flow.

teach the people as much as they could understand. [34]In fact, in his public ministry he never taught without using parables; but afterward, when he was alone with his disciples, he explained everything to them.

Jesus Calms the Storm

[35]As evening came, Jesus said to his disciples, "Let's cross to the other side of the lake." [36]So they took Jesus in the boat and started out, leaving the crowds behind (although other boats followed). [37]But soon a fierce storm came up. High waves were breaking into the boat, and it began to fill with water.

[38]Jesus was sleeping at the back of the boat with his head on a cushion. The disciples woke him up, shouting, "Teacher, don't you care that we're going to drown?"

[39]When Jesus woke up, he rebuked the wind and said to the water, "Silence! Be still!" Suddenly the wind stopped, and there was a great calm. [40]Then he asked them, "Why are you afraid? Do you still have no faith?"

[41]The disciples were absolutely terrified. "Who is this man?" they asked each other. "Even the wind and waves obey him!"

Jesus Heals a Demon-Possessed Man

5

So they arrived at the other side of the lake, in the region of the Gerasenes. [2]When Jesus climbed out of the boat, a man possessed by an evil spirit came out

from a cemetery to meet him. [3]This man lived among the burial caves and could no longer be restrained, even with a chain. [4]Whenever he was put into chains and shackles—as he often was—he snapped the chains from his wrists and smashed the shackles. No one was strong enough to subdue him. [5]Day and night he wandered among the burial caves and in the hills, howling and cutting himself with sharp stones.

[6]When Jesus was still some distance away, the man saw him, ran to meet him, and bowed low before him. [7]With a shriek, he screamed, "Why are you interfering with me, Jesus, Son of the Most High God? In the name of God, I beg you, don't torture me!" [8]For Jesus had already said to the spirit, "Come out of the man, you evil spirit."

[9]Then Jesus demanded, "What is your name?" And he replied, "My name is Legion, because there are many of us inside this man." [10]Then the evil spirits begged him again and again not to send them to some distant place.

[11]There happened to be a large herd of pigs feeding on the hillside nearby. [12]"Send us into those pigs," the spirits begged. "Let us enter them."

[13]So Jesus gave them permission. The evil spirits came out of the man and entered the pigs, and the entire

herd of 2,000 pigs plunged down the steep hillside into the lake and drowned in the water.

[14]The herdsmen fled to the nearby town and the surrounding countryside, spreading the news as they ran. People rushed out to see what had happened. [15]A crowd soon gathered around Jesus, and they saw the man who had been possessed by the legion of demons. He was sitting there fully clothed and perfectly sane, and they were all afraid. [16]Then those who had seen what happened told the others about the demon-possessed man and the pigs. [17]And the crowd began pleading with Jesus to go away and leave them alone.

[18]As Jesus was getting into the boat, the man who had been demon possessed begged to go with him. [19]But Jesus said, "No, go home to your family, and tell them everything the Lord has done for you and how merciful he has been." [20]So the man started off to visit the Ten Towns of that region and began to proclaim the great things Jesus had done for him; and everyone was amazed at what he told them.

Jesus Heals in Response to Faith

[21]Jesus got into the boat again and went back to the other side of the lake, where a large crowd gathered around him on the shore. [22]Then a leader of the local synagogue, whose name was Jairus, arrived. When he saw Jesus, he fell at his feet, [23]pleading fervently with him. "My little daughter is dying," he said. "Please come and lay your hands on her; heal her so she can live."

[24]Jesus went with him, and all the people followed, crowding around him. [25]A woman in the crowd had suffered for twelve years with constant bleeding. [26]She had suffered a great deal from many doctors, and over the years she had spent everything she had to pay them, but she had gotten no better.

Proactive Player and Proactive Prayer (Mark 6:46)

Again we see Jesus in action. Jesus knows that one of the most important parts of his life is to stay in complete harmony with his Father. Prayer is action! Prayer gets God's purpose done. Before every big event and many small events, we see Jesus get away and pray. One great thing about athletes is that you are proactive. You don't just sit around and talk about life, you live it! God wants you not only to be a proactive player, but a proactive prayer. How are your goals being achieved in your training schedule?

BIBLE HIT

In fact, she had gotten worse. ²⁷She had heard about Jesus, so she came up behind him through the crowd and touched his robe. ²⁸For she thought to herself, "If I can just touch his robe, I will be healed." ²⁹Immediately the bleeding stopped, and she could feel in her body that she had been healed of her terrible condition.

³⁰Jesus realized at once that healing power had gone out from him, so he turned around in the crowd and asked, "Who touched my robe?"

³¹His disciples said to him, "Look at this crowd pressing around you. How can you ask, 'Who touched me?'"

³²But he kept on looking around to see who had done it. ³³Then the frightened woman, trembling at the realization of what had happened to her, came and fell at his feet and told him what she had done. ³⁴And he said to her, "Daughter, your faith has made you well. Go in peace. Your suffering is over."

³⁵While he was still speaking to her, messengers arrived from the home of Jairus, the leader of the synagogue. They told him, "Your daughter is dead. There's no use troubling the Teacher now."

³⁶But Jesus overheard them and said to Jairus, "Don't be afraid. Just have faith."

³⁷Then Jesus stopped the crowd and wouldn't let anyone go with him except Peter, James, and John (the brother of James). ³⁸When they came to the home of the synagogue leader, Jesus saw much commotion and weeping and wailing. ³⁹He went inside and asked, "Why all this commotion and weeping? The child isn't dead; she's only asleep."

⁴⁰The crowd laughed at him. But he made them all leave, and he took the girl's father and mother and his three disciples into the room where the girl was lying. ⁴¹Holding her hand, he said to her, "Talitha koum," which means "Little girl, get up!" ⁴²And the girl, who was twelve years old,

immediately stood up and walked around! They were overwhelmed and totally amazed. ⁴³Jesus gave them strict orders not to tell anyone what had happened, and then he told them to give her something to eat.

count on it

God will keep his promises

Friends, teams, coaches, and you yourself will eventually let you down. But Jesus Christ will never, never, never let you down. He is flawless! "For all of God's promises have been fulfilled in Christ with a resounding 'Yes' And through Christ, our 'Amen' (which means 'Yes') ascends to God for his glory." (2 Corinthians 1:20) **Count on it!**

Jesus Rejected at Nazareth

6

Jesus left that part of the country and returned with his disciples to Nazareth, his hometown. ²The next Sabbath he began teaching in the synagogue, and many who heard him were amazed. They asked, "Where did he get all this wisdom and the power to perform such miracles?" ³Then they scoffed, "He's just a carpenter, the son of Mary and the brother of James, Joseph, Judas, and Simon. And his sisters live right here among us." They were deeply offended and refused to believe in him.

⁴Then Jesus told them, "A prophet is honored everywhere except in his own hometown and among his relatives and his own family." ⁵And because of their unbelief, he couldn't do any mighty miracles among them except to place his hands on a few sick people and heal them. ⁶And he was amazed at their unbelief.

Jesus Sends Out the Twelve Disciples

Then Jesus went from village to village, teaching the people. ⁷And he called his twelve disciples together and began sending them out two by two, giving them authority to cast out evil spirits. ⁸He told them to take nothing for their journey except a walking stick—no food, no traveler's bag, no money. ⁹He allowed them to wear sandals but not to take a change of clothes. ¹⁰"Wherever you go," he said, "stay in the same house until you leave town. ¹¹But if any place refuses to welcome you or listen to you, shake its dust from your feet as you leave to show that you have abandoned those people to their fate."

¹²So the disciples went out, telling everyone they met to repent of their sins and turn to God. ¹³And they cast out many demons and healed many sick people, anointing them with olive oil.

The Death of John the Baptist

¹⁴Herod Antipas, the king, soon heard about Jesus, because everyone was talking about him. Some were saying, "This must be John the Baptist raised from the dead. That is why he can do such miracles." ¹⁵Others said, "He's the prophet Elijah." Still others said, "He's a prophet like the other great prophets of the past."

¹⁶When Herod heard about Jesus, he said, "John, the man I beheaded, has come back from the dead."

¹⁷For Herod had sent soldiers to arrest and imprison John as a favor to Herodias. She had been his brother Philip's wife, but Herod had married her. ¹⁸John had

Who are the top five people from history you admire?

1
2
3
4
5

BIG FIVE

been telling Herod, "It is against God's law for you to marry your brother's wife." [19]So Herodias bore a grudge against John and wanted to kill him. But without Herod's approval she was powerless, [20]for Herod respected John; and knowing that he was a good and holy man, he protected him. Herod was greatly disturbed whenever he talked with John, but even so, he liked to listen to him.

[21]Herodias's chance finally came on Herod's birthday. He gave a party for his high government officials, army officers, and the leading citizens of Galilee. [22]Then his daughter, also named Herodias, came in and performed a dance that greatly pleased Herod and his guests. "Ask me for anything you like," the king said to the girl, "and I will give it to you." [23]He even vowed, "I will give you whatever you ask, up to half my kingdom!"

[24]She went out and asked her mother, "What should I ask for?"

Her mother told her, "Ask for the head of John the Baptist!"

[25]So the girl hurried back to the king and told him, "I want the head of John the Baptist, right now, on a tray!"

[26]Then the king deeply regretted what he had said; but because of the vows he had made in front of his guests, he couldn't refuse her. [27]So he immediately sent an executioner to the prison to cut off John's head and bring it to him. The soldier beheaded John in the prison, [28]brought his head on a tray, and gave it to the girl, who took it to her mother. [29]When John's disciples heard what had happened, they came to get his body and buried it in a tomb.

Jesus Feeds Five Thousand

[30]The apostles returned to Jesus from their ministry tour and told him all they had done and taught. [31]Then Jesus said, "Let's go off by ourselves to a quiet place and rest awhile." He said this because there were so many people coming and going that Jesus and his apostles didn't even have time to eat.

[32]So they left by boat for a quiet place, where they could be alone. [33]But many people recognized them and saw them leaving, and people from many towns ran ahead along the shore and got there ahead of them. [34]Jesus saw the huge crowd as he stepped from the boat, and he had compassion on them because they were like sheep without a shepherd. So he began teaching them many things.

[35]Late in the afternoon his disciples came to him and said, "This is a remote place, and it's already getting late. [36]Send the crowds away so they can go to the nearby farms and villages and buy something to eat."

[37]But Jesus said, "You feed them."

"With what?" they asked. "We'd have to work for months to earn enough money to buy food for all these people!"

[38]"How much bread do you have?" he asked. "Go and find out."

They came back and reported, "We have five loaves of bread and two fish."

[39]Then Jesus told the disciples to have the people sit down in groups on the green grass. [40]So they sat down in groups of fifty or a hundred.

[41]Jesus took the five loaves and two fish, looked up toward heaven, and blessed them. Then, breaking the loaves into pieces, he kept giving the bread to the disciples so they could distribute it to the people. He also divided the fish for everyone to share. [42]They all ate as much as they wanted, [43]and afterward, the disciples picked up twelve baskets of leftover bread and fish. [44]A total of 5,000 men and their families were fed from those loaves!

Jesus Walks on Water

[45]Immediately after this, Jesus insisted that his disciples get back into the boat and head across the lake to Bethsaida, while he sent the people home. [46]After telling everyone good-bye, he went up into the hills by himself to pray.

[47]Late that night, the disciples were in their boat in the middle of the lake, and Jesus was alone on land. [48]He saw that they were in serious trouble, rowing hard and struggling against the wind and waves. About three o'clock in the morning Jesus came toward them, walking on the water. He intended to go past them, [49]but when they saw him walking on the water, they cried out in terror, thinking he was a ghost. [50]They were all terrified when they saw him.

But Jesus spoke to them at once. "Don't be afraid,"

There are no exact dimensions for the oval-shaped field (or pitch) used in Australian rules football. The suggested limits are 150 to 200 yards by 120 to 170 yards.

he said. "Take courage! I am here!" [51]Then he climbed into the boat, and the wind stopped. They were totally amazed, [52]for they still didn't understand the significance of the miracle of the loaves. Their hearts were too hard to take it in.

[53]After they had crossed the lake, they landed at Gennesaret. They brought the boat to shore [54]and climbed out. The people recognized Jesus at once, [55]and they ran throughout the whole area, carrying sick people on mats to wherever they heard he was. [56]Wherever he went—in villages, cities, or the countryside—they brought the sick out to the marketplaces. They begged him to let the sick touch at least the fringe of his robe, and all who touched him were healed.

Jesus Teaches about Inner Purity

7

One day some Pharisees and teachers of religious law arrived from Jerusalem to see Jesus. [2]They noticed that some of his disciples failed to follow the Jewish ritual of hand washing before eating. [3](The Jews, especially the Pharisees, do not eat until they have poured water over their cupped hands, as required by their ancient traditions. [4]Similarly, they don't eat anything from the market until they immerse their hands in water. This is but one of many traditions they have clung to—such as their ceremonial washing of cups, pitchers, and kettles.)

[5]So the Pharisees and teachers of religious law asked him, "Why don't your disciples follow our age-old tradition? They eat without first performing the hand-washing ceremony."

[6]Jesus replied, "You hypocrites! Isaiah was right when he prophesied about you, for he wrote,

[7]'These people honor me with their lips,
but their hearts are far from me.
Their worship is a farce,
for they teach man-made ideas as commands from God.'

[8]For you ignore God's law and substitute your own tradition." [9]Then he said, "You skillfully sidestep God's law in order to hold on to your own tradition. [10]For instance, Moses gave you this law from God: 'Honor your father and mother,' and 'Anyone who speaks disrespectfully of father or mother must be put to death.' [11]But you say it is all right for people to say to their parents, 'Sorry, I can't help you. For I have vowed to give to God what I would have given to you.' [12]In this way, you let them disregard their needy parents. [13]And so you cancel the word of God in order to hand down your own tradition. And this is only one example among many others."

[14]Then Jesus called to the crowd to come and hear. "All of you listen," he said, "and try to understand. [15]It's not what goes into your body that defiles you; you are defiled by what comes from your heart.*"

[17]Then Jesus went into a house to get away from the crowd, and his disciples asked him what he meant by the parable

7:15 Some manuscripts add verse 16, *Anyone with ears to hear should listen and understand.* Compare 4:9, 23.

MARK

Prophecies Fulfilled (MARK 8:22)

In the Old Testament a prophet named Isaiah made several predictions about Christ – 700 years before he was born. Here is one of them: Isaiah 35:4-5 says: "Be strong, and do not fear, for your God is coming to destroy your enemies. He is coming to save you. And when he comes, he will open the eyes of the blind and unplug the ears of the deaf." Jesus fulfilled all of Isaiah's predictions, including helping the blind and deaf – both the physically blind and deaf and the spiritually blind and deaf.

he had just used. [18]"Don't you understand either?" he asked. "Can't you see that the food you put into your body cannot defile you? [19]Food doesn't go into your heart, but only passes through the stomach and then goes into the sewer." (By saying this, he declared that every kind of food is acceptable in God's eyes.)

[20]And then he added, "It is what comes from inside that defiles you. [21]For from within, out of a person's heart, come evil thoughts, sexual immorality, theft, murder, [22]adultery, greed, wickedness, deceit, lustful desires, envy, slander, pride, and foolishness. [23]All these vile things come from within; they are what defile you."

7:7-23 WHAT'S IT SAYING?

WHAT AM I GOING TO DO ABOUT IT?

The Faith of a Gentile Woman

[24]Then Jesus left Galilee and went north to the region of Tyre. He didn't want anyone to know which house he was staying in, but he couldn't keep it a secret. [25]Right away a woman who had heard about him came and fell at his feet. Her little girl was possessed by an evil spirit, [26]and she begged him to cast out the demon from her daughter.

Since she was a Gentile, born in Syrian Phoenicia, [27]Jesus told her, "First I should feed the children— my own family, the Jews. It isn't right to take food from the children and throw it to the dogs."

[28]She replied, "That's true, Lord, but even the dogs under the table are allowed to eat the scraps from the children's plates."

[29]"Good answer!" he said. "Now go home, for the demon has left your daughter." [30]And when she arrived home, she found her little girl lying quietly in bed, and the demon was gone.

Jesus Heals a Deaf Man

[31]Jesus left Tyre and went up to Sidon before going back to the Sea of Galilee and the region of the Ten Towns. [32]A deaf man with a speech impediment was brought to him, and the people begged Jesus to lay his hands on the man to heal him.

[33]Jesus led him away from the crowd so they could be alone. He put his fingers into the man's ears. Then, spitting on his own fingers, he touched the man's tongue. [34]Looking up to heaven, he sighed and said, *"Ephphatha,"* which means, "Be opened!" [35]Instantly the man could hear perfectly, and his tongue was freed so he could speak plainly!

[36]Jesus told the crowd not to tell anyone, but the more he told them not to, the more they spread the news. [37]They were completely amazed and said again and again, "Everything he does is wonderful. He even makes the deaf to hear and gives speech to those who cannot speak."

Jesus Feeds Four Thousand

8

About this time another large crowd had gathered, and the people ran out of food again. Jesus called his disciples and told them, [2]"I feel sorry for these people. They have been here with me for three days, and they have nothing left to eat. [3]If I send them home hungry, they will faint along the way. For some of them have come a long distance."

[4]His disciples replied, "How are we supposed to find enough food to feed them out here in the wilderness?"

[5]Jesus asked, "How much bread do you have?"

"Seven loaves," they replied.

[6]So Jesus told all the people to sit down on the ground. Then he took the seven loaves, thanked God for them, and broke them into pieces. He gave them to his disciples, who distributed the bread to the crowd. [7]A few small fish were found, too, so Jesus also blessed these and told the disciples to distribute them.

[8]They ate as much as they wanted. Afterward, the disciples picked up seven large baskets of leftover food. [9]There were about 4,000 people in the crowd that day, and Jesus sent them home after they had eaten. [10]Immediately after this, he got into a boat with his disciples and crossed over to the region of Dalmanutha.

Pharisees Demand a Miraculous Sign

[11]When the Pharisees heard that Jesus had arrived, they came and started to argue with him. Testing him, they demanded that he show them a miraculous sign from heaven to prove his authority.

[12]When he heard this, he sighed deeply in his spirit and said, "Why do these people keep demanding a miraculous sign? I tell you the truth, I will not give this generation any such sign." [13]So he got back into the boat and left them, and he crossed to the other side of the lake.

Yeast of the Pharisees and Herod

[14]But the disciples had forgotten to bring any food. They had only one loaf of bread with them in the boat. [15]As they were crossing the lake, Jesus warned them, "Watch out! Beware of the yeast of the Pharisees and of Herod."

[16]At this they began to argue with each other because they hadn't brought any bread. [17]Jesus knew what they

were saying, so he said, "Why are you arguing about having no bread? Don't you know or understand even yet? Are your hearts too hard to take it in? [18]'You have eyes—can't you see? You have ears—can't you hear?' Don't you remember anything at all? [19]When I fed the 5,000 with five loaves of bread, how many baskets of leftovers did you pick up afterward?" "Twelve," they said.

[20]"And when I fed the 4,000 with seven loaves, how many large baskets of leftovers did you pick up?" "Seven," they said.

[21]"Don't you understand yet?" he asked them.

Jesus Heals a Blind Man

[22]When they arrived at Bethsaida, some people brought a blind man to Jesus, and they begged him to touch the man and heal him. [23]Jesus took the blind man by the hand and led him out of the village. Then, spitting on the man's eyes, he laid his hands on him and asked, "Can you see anything now?"

[24]The man looked around. "Yes," he said, "I see people, but I can't see them very clearly. They look like trees walking around."

[25]Then Jesus placed his hands on the man's eyes again, and his eyes were opened. His sight was completely restored, and he could see everything clearly. [26]Jesus sent him away, saying, "Don't go back into the village on your way home."

Peter's Declaration about Jesus

[27]Jesus and his disciples left Galilee and went up to the villages near Caesarea Philippi. As they were walking along, he asked them, "Who do people say I am?"

[28]"Well," they replied, "some say John the Baptist, some say Elijah, and others say you are one of the other prophets."

[29]Then he asked them, "But who do you say I am?" Peter replied, "You are the Messiah."

[30]But Jesus warned them not to tell anyone about him.

Jesus Predicts His Death

[31]Then Jesus began to tell them that the Son of Man must suffer many terrible things and be rejected by the elders, the leading priests, and the teachers of religious law. He would be killed, but three days later he would rise from the dead. [32]As he talked about this openly with his disciples, Peter took him aside and began to reprimand him for saying such things.

[33]Jesus turned around and looked at his disciples, then reprimanded Peter. "Get away from me, Satan!" he said. "You are seeing things merely from a human

count on it

Keep your focus

If you feel like you are floundering and need to make sense out of your life, remember you have a purpose: to worship God. In all you do you are to worship God. In worship, you will find focus and happiness! "The devil took [Jesus] to the peak of a very high mountain and showed him the kingdoms of the world and all their glory. 'I will give it all to you,' he said, 'if you will kneel down and worship me.' 'Get out of here, Satan,' Jesus told him. 'For the Scriptures say, "You must worship the LORD your God and serve only him.""'

(Matthew 4:8-10)

Count on it!

point of view, not from God's."

[34]Then, calling the crowd to join his disciples, he said, "If any of you wants to be my follower, you must turn from your selfish ways, take up your cross, and follow me. [35]If you try to hang on to your life, you will lose it. But if you give up your life for my sake and for the sake of the Good News, you will save it. [36]And what do you benefit if you gain the whole world but lose your own soul? [37]Is anything worth more than your soul? [38]If anyone is ashamed of me and my message in these adulterous and sinful days, the Son of Man will be ashamed of that person when he returns in the glory of his Father with the holy angels."

9

Jesus went on to say, "I tell you the truth, some standing here right now will not die before they see the Kingdom of God arrive in great power!"

The Transfiguration

[2]Six days later Jesus took Peter, James, and John, and led them up a high mountain to be alone. As the men watched, Jesus' appearance was transformed, [3]and his clothes became dazzling white, far whiter than any earthly bleach could ever make them. [4]Then Elijah and Moses appeared and began talking with Jesus.

[5]Peter exclaimed, "Rabbi, it's wonderful for us to be here! Let's make three shelters as memorials—one for you, one for Moses, and one for Elijah." [6]He said this because he didn't really know what else to say, for they were all terrified.

[7]Then a cloud overshadowed them, and a voice from the cloud said, "This is my dearly loved Son. Listen to him." [8]Suddenly, when they looked around, Moses and Elijah were gone, and only Jesus was with them.

[9]As they went back down the mountain, he told them not to tell anyone what they had seen until the Son of Man had risen from the dead. [10]So they kept it to themselves, but they often asked each other what he meant by "rising from the dead."

[11]Then they asked him, "Why do the teachers of religious law insist that Elijah must return before the Messiah comes?" [12]Jesus responded, "Elijah is indeed coming first to get everything ready for the Messiah. Yet why do the Scriptures say that the Son of Man must suffer greatly and be treated with utter contempt? [13]But I tell you, Elijah has already come, and they chose to abuse him, just as the Scriptures predicted."

Jesus Heals a Demon-Possessed Boy

[14]When they returned to the other disciples, they saw a large crowd surrounding them, and some teachers of religious law

STAND POINT

When you feel like quitting

9:23-24

"What do you mean, 'If I can'?" Jesus asked. "Anything is possible if a person believes." The father instantly cried out, "I do believe, but help me overcome my unbelief!"

were arguing with them. ¹⁵When the crowd saw Jesus, they were overwhelmed with awe, and they ran to greet him. ¹⁶"What is all this arguing about?" Jesus asked.

¹⁷One of the men in the crowd spoke up and said, "Teacher, I brought my son so you could heal him. He is possessed by an evil spirit that won't let him talk. ¹⁸And whenever this spirit seizes him, it throws him violently to the ground. Then he foams at the mouth and grinds his teeth and becomes rigid. So I asked your disciples to cast out the evil spirit, but they couldn't do it."

¹⁹Jesus said to them, "You faithless people! How long must I be with you? How long must I put up with you? Bring the boy to me."

²⁰So they brought the boy. But when the evil spirit saw Jesus, it threw the child into a violent convulsion, and he fell to the ground, writhing and foaming at the mouth.

²¹"How long has this been happening?" Jesus asked the boy's father.

He replied, "Since he was a little boy. ²²The spirit often throws him into the fire or into water, trying to kill him. Have mercy on us and help us, if you can."

²³"What do you mean, 'If I can'?" Jesus asked. "Anything is possible if a person believes."

²⁴The father instantly cried out, "I do believe, but help me overcome my unbelief!"

²⁵When Jesus saw that the crowd of onlookers was growing, he rebuked the evil spirit. "Listen, you spirit that makes this boy unable to hear and speak," he said. "I command you to come out of this child and never enter him again!"

²⁶Then the spirit screamed and threw the boy into another violent convulsion and left him. The boy appeared to be dead. A murmur ran through the crowd as people said, "He's dead." ²⁷But Jesus took him by the hand and helped him to his feet, and he stood up.

²⁸Afterward, when Jesus was alone in the house with his disciples, they asked him, "Why couldn't we cast out that evil spirit?"

²⁹Jesus replied, "This kind can be cast out only by prayer."

Jesus Again Predicts His Death

³⁰Leaving that region, they traveled through Galilee. Jesus didn't want anyone to know he was there, ³¹for he wanted to spend more time with his disciples and teach them. He said to them, "The Son of Man is going to be betrayed into the hands of his enemies. He will be killed, but three days later he will rise from the dead." ³²They didn't understand what he was saying, however, and they were afraid to ask him what he meant.

The Greatest in the Kingdom

³³After they arrived at Capernaum and settled in a house, Jesus asked his disciples, "What were you discussing out on the road?" ³⁴But they didn't answer, because they had been arguing about which of them was the greatest. ³⁵He sat down, called the twelve disciples over to him, and said, "Whoever wants to be first must take last place and be the servant of everyone else."

³⁶Then he put a little child among them. Taking the child in his arms, he said to them, ³⁷"Anyone who welcomes a little child like this on my behalf welcomes me, and anyone who welcomes me welcomes not only me but also my Father who sent me."

9:33-37 WHAT'S IT SAYING?

WHAT AM I GOING TO DO ABOUT IT?

Using the Name of Jesus

³⁸John said to Jesus, "Teacher, we saw someone using your name to cast out demons, but we told him to stop because he wasn't in our group."

³⁹"Don't stop him!" Jesus said. "No one who performs a miracle in my name will soon be able to speak evil of me. ⁴⁰Anyone who is not against us is for us. ⁴¹If anyone gives you even a cup of water because you belong to the Messiah, I tell you the truth, that person will surely be rewarded.

⁴²"But if you cause one of these little ones who trusts in me to fall into sin, it would be better for you to be thrown into the sea with a large millstone hung around your neck. ⁴³If your hand causes you to sin, cut it off. It's better to enter eternal life with only one hand than to go into the unquenchable fires of hell with

two hands.* ⁴⁵If your foot causes you to sin, cut it off. It's better to enter eternal life with only one foot than to be thrown into hell with two feet.* ⁴⁷And if your eye causes you to sin, gouge it out. It's better to enter the Kingdom of God with only one eye than to have two eyes and be thrown into hell, ⁴⁸where the maggots never die and the fire never goes out.'

⁴⁹"For everyone will be tested with fire. ⁵⁰Salt is good for seasoning. But if it loses its flavor, how do you make it salty again? You must have the qualities of salt among yourselves and live in peace with each other."

Discussion about Divorce and Marriage

10

Then Jesus left Capernaum and went down to the region of Judea and into the area east of the Jordan River. Once again crowds gathered around him, and as usual he was teaching them.

²Some Pharisees came and tried to trap him with this question: "Should a man be allowed to divorce his wife?"

³Jesus answered them with a question: "What did Moses say in the law about divorce?"

⁴"Well, he permitted it," they replied. "He said a man can give his wife a written notice of divorce and send her away."

⁵But Jesus responded, "He wrote this commandment only as a concession to your hard hearts. ⁶But 'God made them male and female' from the beginning of creation. ⁷This explains why a man leaves his father and mother and is joined to his wife, ⁸and the two are united into one.' Since they are no longer two but one, ⁹let no one split apart what God has joined together."

¹⁰Later, when he was alone with his disciples in the house, they brought up the subject again. ¹¹He told them, "Whoever divorces his wife and marries someone else commits adultery against her. ¹²And if a woman divorces her husband and marries someone else, she commits adultery."

Jesus Blesses the Children

¹³One day some parents brought their children to Jesus so he could touch and bless them. But the disciples scolded the parents for bothering him.

¹⁴When Jesus saw what was happening, he was angry with his disciples. He said to them, "Let the children come to me. Don't stop them! For the Kingdom of God belongs to those who are like these children. ¹⁵I tell

9:43 Some manuscripts add verse 44, 'where the maggots never die and the fire never goes out.' See 9:48.
9:45 Some manuscripts add verse 46, 'where the maggots never die and the fire never goes out.' See 9:48.

you the truth, anyone who doesn't receive the Kingdom of God like a child will never enter it." [16]Then he took the children in his arms and placed his hands on their heads and blessed them.

The Rich Man

[17]As Jesus was starting out on his way to Jerusalem, a man came running up to him, knelt down, and asked, "Good Teacher, what must I do to inherit eternal life?" [18]"Why do you call me good?" Jesus asked. "Only God is truly good. [19]But to answer your question, you know the commandments: 'You must not murder. You must not commit adultery. You must not steal. You must not testify falsely. You must not cheat anyone. Honor your father and mother.'"

[20]"Teacher," the man replied, "I've obeyed all these commandments since I was young."

[21]Looking at the man, Jesus felt genuine love for him. "There is still one thing you haven't done," he told him. "Go and sell all your possessions and give the money to the poor, and you will have treasure in heaven. Then come, follow me."

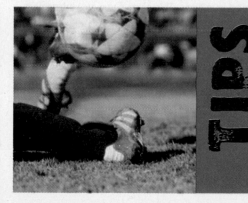

TIPS

If you don't use it, you lose it:

Improving and retaining flexibility depends on numerous variables, including genetic factors, age, and the state of training. Thus, your muscles' response to regular stretching is a function of these factors and is dependent on which muscle group you stretch. Generally, for healthy individuals, the longer, more frequently, and more intensely you stretch, the faster and more significant your improvement in flexibility will be. Likewise, once you stop your stretching discipline, the flexibility gains will be lost over time.

²²At this the man's face fell, and he went away very sad, for he had many possessions.

²³Jesus looked around and said to his disciples, "How hard it is for the rich to enter the Kingdom of God!" ²⁴This amazed them. But Jesus said again, "Dear children, it is very hard to enter the Kingdom of God. ²⁵In fact, it is easier for a camel to go through the eye of a needle than for a rich person to enter the Kingdom of God!"

²⁶The disciples were astounded. "Then who in the world can be saved?" they asked.

²⁷Jesus looked at them intently and said, "Humanly speaking, it is impossible. But not with God. Everything is possible with God."

²⁸Then Peter began to speak up. "We've given up everything to follow you," he said.

²⁹"Yes," Jesus replied, "and I assure you that everyone who has given up house or brothers or sisters or mother or father or children or property, for my sake and for the Good News, ³⁰will receive now in return a hundred times as many houses, brothers, sisters, mothers, children, and property—along with persecution. And in the world to come that person will have eternal life. ³¹But many who are the greatest now will be least important then, and those who seem least important now will be the greatest then."

Jesus Again Predicts His Death

³²They were now on the way up to Jerusalem, and Jesus was walking ahead of them. The disciples were filled with awe, and the people following behind were overwhelmed with fear. Taking the twelve disciples aside, Jesus once more began to describe everything that was about to happen to him. ³³"Listen," he said, "we're going up to Jerusalem, where the Son of Man will be betrayed to the leading priests and the teachers of religious law. They will sentence him to die and hand him over to the Romans. ³⁴They will mock him, spit on him, flog him with a whip, and kill him, but after three days he will rise again."

Jesus Teaches about Serving Others

³⁵Then James and John, the sons of Zebedee, came over and spoke to him. "Teacher," they said, "we want you to do us a favor."

³⁶"What is your request?" he asked.

³⁷They replied, "When you sit on your glorious throne, we want to sit in places of honor next to you, one on your right and the other on your left."

³⁸But Jesus said to them, "You don't know what you are asking! Are you able to drink from the bitter cup of suffering I am about to drink? Are you able to be baptized with the baptism of suffering I must be baptized with?"

³⁹"Oh yes," they replied, "we are able!"

Then Jesus told them, "You will indeed drink from my bitter cup and be baptized with my baptism of suffering. ⁴⁰But I have no right to say who will sit on my right or my left. God has prepared those places for the ones he has chosen."

⁴¹When the ten other disciples heard what James and John had asked, they were indignant. ⁴²So Jesus called them together and said, "You know that the rulers in this world lord it over their people, and officials flaunt their authority over those under them. ⁴³But among you it will be different. Whoever wants to be a leader among you must be your servant, ⁴⁴and whoever wants to be first among you must be the slave of everyone else. ⁴⁵For even the Son of Man came not to be served but to serve others and to give his life as a ransom for many."

Jesus Heals Blind Bartimaeus

⁴⁶Then they reached Jericho, and as Jesus and his disciples left town, a large crowd followed him. A blind beggar named Bartimaeus (son of Timaeus) was sitting beside the road. ⁴⁷When Bartimaeus heard that Jesus of Nazareth was nearby, he began to shout, "Jesus, Son of David, have mercy on me!"

⁴⁸"Be quiet!" many of the people yelled at him. But he only shouted louder, "Son of David, have mercy on me!"

⁴⁹When Jesus heard him, he stopped and said, "Tell him to come here."

So they called the blind man. "Cheer up," they said. "Come on, he's calling you!" ⁵⁰Bartimaeus threw aside his coat, jumped up, and came to Jesus.

⁵¹"What do you want me to do for you?" Jesus asked. "My rabbi," the blind man said, "I want to see!"

⁵²And Jesus said to him, "Go, for your faith has healed you." Instantly the man could see, and he followed Jesus down the road.

Jesus' Triumphant Entry

11

As Jesus and his disciples approached Jerusalem, they came to the towns of Bethphage and Bethany on the Mount of Olives. Jesus sent two of them on ahead. ²"Go into that village over there," he told them. "As soon as you enter it, you will see a young donkey tied there that no one has ever ridden. Untie it and bring it here. ³If anyone asks, 'What are you doing?' just say, 'The Lord needs it and will return it soon.'"

⁴The two disciples left and found the colt standing in the street, tied outside the front door. ⁵As they were untying it, some bystanders demanded, "What are you doing, untying that colt?" ⁶They said what Jesus had told them to say, and they were permitted to take it. ⁷Then they brought the colt to Jesus and threw their garments over it, and he sat on it.

⁸Many in the crowd spread their garments on the road ahead of him, and others spread leafy branches they had cut in the fields. ⁹Jesus was in the center of the procession, and the people all around him were shouting,

I really want to share my faith, but don't know how to start.

Great question! Follow Jesus' example and ask a pointed question. This shows you are interested in that person, and you are willing to listen to them. You cannot give good directions until you know where they are coming from. A good starting point is: "Do you know for sure that if you died tonight, you would go to heaven?"

I hate feeling like a hypocrite. I have a church life and a life with my friends. Any suggestions?

Facing the fact that trying to live two different lives will make you miserable is a good start. Jesus had strong words for those pretending to be genuine Christians. Find a friend to encourage you and hold you accountable. Be honest with your unchurched friends, and be a genuine Christian 24-7. If they do not like you for your faith, they are not true friends.

Winners live it out!

It is powerful to watch an athlete stay in control, especially when they are under pressure. It is often shocking that some of the most mature Christians, many of whom are leaders in their own churches, think that they can indulge themselves in improper behavior in competition. People who would never dream of being rude, cheating, fighting, or having a temper tantrum in their neighborhood, place of work, school, or church, act like idiots in sports. Why is it that we often feel we have license to exhibit poor sportsmanship? Don't compete like a fool; hold it together.

"Fools vent their anger, but the wise quietly hold it back." (Proverbs 29:11)

Winners – live it!

"Praise God!
Blessings on the one who comes in the name of the LORD!
[10]Blessings on the coming Kingdom of our ancestor David!
Praise God in highest heaven!"
[11]So Jesus came to Jerusalem and went into the Temple. After looking around carefully at everything, he left because it was late in the afternoon. Then he returned to Bethany with the twelve disciples.

Jesus Curses the Fig Tree

[12]The next morning as they were leaving Bethany, Jesus was hungry. [13]He noticed a fig tree in full leaf a little way off, so he went over to see if he could find any figs. But there were only leaves because it was too early in the season for fruit. [14]Then Jesus said to the tree, "May no one ever eat your fruit again!" And the disciples heard him say it.

Jesus Clears the Temple

[15]When they arrived back in Jerusalem, Jesus entered the Temple and began to drive out the people buying and selling animals for sacrifices. He knocked over the tables of the money changers and the chairs of those selling doves, [16]and he stopped everyone from using the Temple as a marketplace. [17]He said to them, "The Scriptures declare, 'My Temple will be called a house of prayer for all nations,' but you have turned it into a den of thieves."
[18]When the leading priests and teachers of religious law heard what Jesus had done, they began planning how to kill him. But they were afraid of him because the people were so amazed at his teaching.
[19]That evening Jesus and the disciples left the city.
[20]The next morning as they passed by the fig tree he

had cursed, the disciples noticed it had withered from the roots up. [21]Peter remembered what Jesus had said to the tree on the previous day and exclaimed, "Look, Rabbi! The fig tree you cursed has withered and died!"
[22]Then Jesus said to the disciples, "Have faith in God. [23]I tell you the truth, you can say to this mountain, 'May you be lifted up and thrown into the sea,' and it will happen. But you must really believe it will happen and have no doubt in your heart. [24]I tell you, you can pray for anything, and if you believe that you've received it, it will be yours. [25]But when you are praying, first forgive anyone you are holding a grudge against, so that your Father in heaven will forgive your sins, too.*"

The Authority of Jesus Challenged

[27]Again they entered Jerusalem. As Jesus was walking through the Temple area, the leading priests, the teachers of religious law, and the elders came up to him. [28]They demanded, "By what authority are you doing all these things? Who gave you the right to do them?"
[29]"I'll tell you by what authority I do these things if you answer one question," Jesus replied. [30]"Did John's authority to baptize come from heaven, or was it merely human? Answer me!"
[31]They talked it over among themselves. "If we say it was from heaven, he will ask why we didn't believe John. [32]But do we dare say it was merely human?" For they were afraid of what the people would do, because everyone believed that John was a prophet. [33]So they finally replied, "We don't know."
And Jesus responded, "Then I won't tell you by what authority I do these things."

Parable of the Evil Farmers

12

Then Jesus began teaching them with stories: "A man planted a vineyard. He built a wall around it, dug a pit for pressing out the grape juice, and built a lookout tower. Then he leased the vineyard to tenant farmers and moved to another country. [2]At the time of the grape harvest, he sent one of his servants to collect his share of the crop. [3]But the farmers grabbed the servant, beat him up, and sent him back empty-handed. [4]The owner then sent another servant, but they insulted him and beat him over the head. [5]The next servant he sent was killed. Others he sent were either beaten or killed, [6]until there was only one left—his son whom he loved dearly. The owner finally sent him, thinking, 'Surely they will respect my son.' [7]"But the tenant farmers said to one another, 'Here comes the heir to this estate. Let's kill him and get the estate for ourselves!' [8]So they grabbed him and murdered him and threw his body out of the vineyard.
[9]"What do you suppose the owner of the vineyard will do?" Jesus asked. "I'll tell you—he will come and kill those

STAND POINT

When you need an example of strength
14:36

"Abba, Father," he cried out, "everything is possible for you. Please take this cup of suffering away from me. Yet I want your will to be done, not mine."

11:25 Some manuscripts add verse 26, *But if you refuse to forgive, your Father in heaven will not forgive your sins.* Compare Matt 6:15.

MARK

farmers and lease the vineyard to others. [10]Didn't you ever read this in the Scriptures?

'The stone that the builders rejected
has now become the cornerstone.
[11]This is the LORD's doing,
and it is wonderful to see.'"

[12]The religious leaders wanted to arrest Jesus because they realized he was telling the story against them—they were the wicked farmers. But they were afraid of the crowd, so they left him and went away.

Taxes for Caesar

[13]Later the leaders sent some Pharisees and supporters of Herod to trap Jesus into saying something for which he could be arrested. [14]"Teacher," they said, "we know how honest you are. You are impartial and don't play favorites. You teach the way of God truthfully. Now tell us—is it right to pay taxes to Caesar or not? [15]Should we pay them, or shouldn't we?"

Jesus saw through their hypocrisy and said, "Why are you trying to trap me? Show me a Roman coin, and I'll tell you." [16]When they handed it to him, he asked, "Whose picture and title are stamped on it?"

"Caesar's," they replied.

[17]"Well, then," Jesus said, "give to Caesar what belongs to Caesar, and give to God what belongs to God."

His reply completely amazed them.

Discussion about Resurrection

[18]Then Jesus was approached by some Sadducees—religious leaders who say there is no resurrection from the dead. They posed this question: [19]"Teacher, Moses gave us a law that if a man dies, leaving a wife without children, his brother should marry the widow and have a child who will carry on the brother's name. [20]Well, suppose there were seven brothers. The oldest one married and then died without children. [21]So the second brother married the widow, but he also died without children. Then the third brother married her. [22]This continued with all seven of them, and still there were no children. Last of all, the woman also died. [23]So tell us, whose wife will she be in the resurrection? For all seven were married to her."

[24]Jesus replied, "Your mistake is that you don't know the Scriptures, and you don't know the power of God. [25]For when the dead rise, they will neither marry nor be given in marriage. In this respect they will be like the angels in heaven. [26]"But now, as to whether the dead will be raised—haven't you ever read about this in the writings of Moses, in the story of the burning bush? Long after Abraham, Isaac, and Jacob had died, God said to Moses, 'I am the God of Abraham, the God of Isaac, and the God of Jacob.' [27]So he is the God of the living, not the dead. You have made a serious error."

The Most Important Commandment

[28]One of the teachers of religious law was standing there listening to the debate. He realized that Jesus had answered well, so he asked, "Of all the commandments, which is the most important?"

[29]Jesus replied, "The most important commandment is this: 'Listen, O Israel! The LORD our God is the one and only LORD. [30]And you must love the LORD your God with all your heart, all your soul, all your mind, and all your strength.' [31]The second is equally important: 'Love your neighbor as yourself.' No other commandment is greater than these."

[32]The teacher of religious law replied, "Well said, Teacher. You have spoken the truth by saying that there is only one God and no other. [33]And I know it is important to love him with all my heart and all my understanding and all my strength, and to love my neighbor as myself. This is more important than to offer all of the burnt offerings and sacrifices required in the law."

[34]Realizing how much the man understood, Jesus said to him, "You are not far from the Kingdom of God." And after that, no one dared to ask him any more questions.

Whose Son Is the Messiah?

[35]Later, as Jesus was teaching the people in the Temple, he asked, "Why do the teachers of religious law claim that the Messiah is the son of David? [36]For David himself, speaking under the inspiration of the Holy Spirit, said,

'The LORD said to my Lord,
Sit in the place of honor at my right hand
until I humble your enemies beneath your feet.'

[37]Since David himself called the Messiah 'my Lord,' how can the Messiah be his son?" The large crowd listened to him with great delight.

Today's Olympic gold medals actually are sterling silver covered with a thin coating of gold.

[38]Jesus also taught: "Beware of these teachers of religious law! For they like to parade around in flowing robes and receive respectful greetings as they walk in the marketplaces. [39]And how they love the seats of honor in the synagogues and the head table at banquets. [40]Yet they shamelessly cheat widows out of their property and then pretend to be pious by making long prayers in public. Because of this, they will be more severely punished."

The Widow's Offering

[41]Jesus sat down near the collection box in the Temple and watched as the crowds dropped in their money. Many rich people put in large amounts. [42]Then a poor widow came and dropped in two small coins.

[43]Jesus called his disciples to him and said, "I tell you the truth, this poor widow has given more than all the others who are making contributions. [44]For they gave a tiny part of their surplus, but she, poor as she is, has given everything she had to live on."

action

12:28-31 WHAT'S IT SAYING?

WHAT AM I GOING TO DO ABOUT IT?

Jesus Foretells the Future

13

As Jesus was leaving the Temple that day, one of his disciples said, "Teacher, look at these magnificent buildings! Look at the impressive stones in the walls." ²Jesus replied, "Yes, look at these great buildings. But they will be completely demolished. Not one stone will be left on top of another!"

³Later, Jesus sat on the Mount of Olives across the valley from the Temple. Peter, James, John, and Andrew came to him privately and asked him, ⁴"Tell us, when will all this happen? What sign will show us that these things are about to be fulfilled?"

⁵Jesus replied, "Don't let anyone mislead you, ⁶for many will come in my name, claiming, 'I am the Messiah.' They will deceive many. ⁷And you will hear of wars and threats of wars, but don't panic. Yes, these things must take place, but the end won't follow immediately. ⁸Nation will go to war against nation, and kingdom against kingdom. There will be earthquakes in many parts of the world, as well as famines. But this is only the first of the birth pains, with more to come.

to get a coat. ¹⁷How terrible it will be for pregnant women and for nursing mothers in those days. ¹⁸And pray that your flight will not be in winter. ¹⁹For there will be greater anguish in those days than at any time since God created the world. And it will never be so great again. ²⁰In fact, unless the Lord shortens that time of calamity, not a single person will survive. But for the sake of his chosen ones he has shortened those days.

²¹"Then if anyone tells you, 'Look, here is the Messiah,' or 'There he is,' don't believe it. ²²For false messiahs and false prophets will rise up and perform signs and wonders so as to deceive, if possible, even God's chosen ones. ²³Watch out! I have warned you about this ahead of time!

²⁴"At that time, after the anguish of those days,
the sun will be darkened,
the moon will give no light,
²⁵the stars will fall from the sky,

home, he gave each of his slaves instructions about the work they were to do, and he told the gatekeeper to watch for his return. ³⁵You, too, must keep watch! For you don't know when the master of the household will return—in the evening, at midnight, before dawn, or at daybreak. ³⁶Don't let him find you sleeping when he arrives without warning. ³⁷I say to you what I say to everyone: Watch for him!"

Jesus Anointed at Bethany

14

It was now two days before Passover and the Festival of Unleavened Bread. The leading priests and the teachers of religious law were still looking for an opportunity to capture Jesus secretly and kill him. ²"But not during the Passover celebration," they agreed, "or the people may riot."

³Meanwhile, Jesus was in Bethany at the home of Simon, a man who had previously had leprosy. While he was eating, a woman came in with a beautiful alabaster jar of expensive

TIPS

Your pace is great:

Athletes all have a different capacity to learn skill and strategy. Work hard on staying focused, and feel free to ask the coach at an appropriate time for extra help.

⁹"When these things begin to happen, watch out! You will be handed over to the local councils and beaten in the synagogues. You will stand trial before governors and kings because you are my followers. But this will be your opportunity to tell them about me. ¹⁰For the Good News must first be preached to all nations. ¹¹But when you are arrested and stand trial, don't worry in advance about what to say. Just say what God tells you at that time, for it is not you who will be speaking, but the Holy Spirit.

¹²"A brother will betray his brother to death, a father will betray his own child, and children will rebel against their parents and cause them to be killed. ¹³And everyone will hate you because you are my followers. But the one who endures to the end will be saved.

¹⁴"The day is coming when you will see the sacrilegious object that causes desecration standing where he should not be." (Reader, pay attention!) "Then those in Judea must flee to the hills. ¹⁵A person out on the deck of a roof must not go down into the house to pack. ¹⁶A person out in the field must not return even

and the powers in the heavens will be shaken.

²⁶Then everyone will see the Son of Man coming on the clouds with great power and glory. ²⁷And he will send out his angels to gather his chosen ones from all over the world—from the farthest ends of the earth and heaven.

²⁸"Now learn a lesson from the fig tree. When its branches bud and its leaves begin to sprout, you know that summer is near. ²⁹In the same way, when you see all these things taking place, you can know that his return is very near, right at the door. ³⁰I tell you the truth, this generation will not pass from the scene before all these things take place. ³¹Heaven and earth will disappear, but my words will never disappear.

³²"However, no one knows the day or hour when these things will happen, not even the angels in heaven or the Son himself. Only the Father knows. ³³And since you don't know when that time will come, be on guard! Stay alert!

³⁴"The coming of the Son of Man can be illustrated by the story of a man going on a long trip. When he left

perfume made from essence of nard. She broke open the jar and poured the perfume over his head.

⁴Some of those at the table were indignant. "Why waste such expensive perfume?" they asked. ⁵"It could have been sold for a year's wages and the money given to the poor!" So they scolded her harshly.

⁶But Jesus replied, "Leave her alone. Why criticize her for doing such a good thing to me? ⁷You will always have the poor among you, and you can help them whenever you want to. But you will not always have me. ⁸She has done what she could and has anointed my body for burial ahead of time. ⁹I tell you the truth, wherever the Good News is preached throughout the world, this woman's deed will be remembered and discussed."

Judas Agrees to Betray Jesus

¹⁰Then Judas Iscariot, one of the twelve disciples, went to the leading priests to arrange to betray Jesus to them. ¹¹They were delighted when they heard why he had come, and they promised to give him money. So he began looking for an opportunity to betray Jesus.

MARCH M.A.P.

1

S.D.	P.L.	P.G.	S.G.
P. ☐	F. ☐	F. ☐	T. ☐
F. ☐	W. ☐	W. ☐	P. ☐
B. ☐	P. ☐	C. ☐	C. ☐

2

S.D.	P.L.	P.G.	S.G.
P. ☐	F. ☐	F. ☐	T. ☐
F. ☐	W. ☐	W. ☐	P. ☐
B. ☐	P. ☐	C. ☐	C. ☐

3

S.D.	P.L.	P.G.	S.G.
P. ☐	F. ☐	F. ☐	T. ☐
F. ☐	W. ☐	W. ☐	P. ☐
B. ☐	P. ☐	C. ☐	C. ☐

4

S.D.	P.L.	P.G.	S.G.
P. ☐	F. ☐	F. ☐	T. ☐
F. ☐	W. ☐	W. ☐	P. ☐
B. ☐	P. ☐	C. ☐	C. ☐

9

S.D.	P.L.	P.G.	S.G.
P. ☐	F. ☐	F. ☐	T. ☐
F. ☐	W. ☐	W. ☐	P. ☐
B. ☐	P. ☐	C. ☐	C. ☐

10

S.D.	P.L.	P.G.	S.G.
P. ☐	F. ☐	F. ☐	T. ☐
F. ☐	W. ☐	W. ☐	P. ☐
B. ☐	P. ☐	C. ☐	C. ☐

11

S.D.	P.L.	P.G.	S.G.
P. ☐	F. ☐	F. ☐	T. ☐
F. ☐	W. ☐	W. ☐	P. ☐
B. ☐	P. ☐	C. ☐	C. ☐

12

S.D.	P.L.	P.G.	S.G.
P. ☐	F. ☐	F. ☐	T. ☐
F. ☐	W. ☐	W. ☐	P. ☐
B. ☐	P. ☐	C. ☐	C. ☐

17

S.D.	P.L.	P.G.	S.G.
P. ☐	F. ☐	F. ☐	T. ☐
F. ☐	W. ☐	W. ☐	P. ☐
B. ☐	P. ☐	C. ☐	C. ☐

18

S.D.	P.L.	P.G.	S.G.
P. ☐	F. ☐	F. ☐	T. ☐
F. ☐	W. ☐	W. ☐	P. ☐
B. ☐	P. ☐	C. ☐	C. ☐

19

S.D.	P.L.	P.G.	S.G.
P. ☐	F. ☐	F. ☐	T. ☐
F. ☐	W. ☐	W. ☐	P. ☐
B. ☐	P. ☐	C. ☐	C. ☐

20

S.D.	P.L.	P.G.	S.G.
P. ☐	F. ☐	F. ☐	T. ☐
F. ☐	W. ☐	W. ☐	P. ☐
B. ☐	P. ☐	C. ☐	C. ☐

25

S.D.	P.L.	P.G.	S.G.
P. ☐	F. ☐	F. ☐	T. ☐
F. ☐	W. ☐	W. ☐	P. ☐
B. ☐	P. ☐	C. ☐	C. ☐

26

S.D.	P.L.	P.G.	S.G.
P. ☐	F. ☐	F. ☐	T. ☐
F. ☐	W. ☐	W. ☐	P. ☐
B. ☐	P. ☐	C. ☐	C. ☐

27

S.D.	P.L.	P.G.	S.G.
P. ☐	F. ☐	F. ☐	T. ☐
F. ☐	W. ☐	W. ☐	P. ☐
B. ☐	P. ☐	C. ☐	C. ☐

28

S.D.	P.L.	P.G.	S.G.
P. ☐	F. ☐	F. ☐	T. ☐
F. ☐	W. ☐	W. ☐	P. ☐
B. ☐	P. ☐	C. ☐	C. ☐

Spiritual Disciplines

Prayer

Faith Community

Bible Reading

Prayer List

Friends

World

Personal

(For designing your M.A.P. – Monthly Action Plan – see introduction pages)

Who am I....
Where am I going....
How am I going to get there?

nt:sport
MONTHLY ACTION PLAN

5

S.D.	P.L.	P.G.	S.G.
P. ☐	F. ☐	F. ☐	T. ☐
F. ☐	W. ☐	W. ☐	P. ☐
B. ☐	P. ☐	C. ☐	C. ☐

6

S.D.	P.L.	P.G.	S.G.
P. ☐	F. ☐	F. ☐	T. ☐
F. ☐	W. ☐	W. ☐	P. ☐
B. ☐	P. ☐	C. ☐	C. ☐

7

S.D.	P.L.	P.G.	S.G.
P. ☐	F. ☐	F. ☐	T. ☐
F. ☐	W. ☐	W. ☐	P. ☐
B. ☐	P. ☐	C. ☐	C. ☐

8

S.D.	P.L.	P.G.	S.G.
P. ☐	F. ☐	F. ☐	T. ☐
F. ☐	W. ☐	W. ☐	P. ☐
B. ☐	P. ☐	C. ☐	C. ☐

13

S.D.	P.L.	P.G.	S.G.
P. ☐	F. ☐	F. ☐	T. ☐
F. ☐	W. ☐	W. ☐	P. ☐
B. ☐	P. ☐	C. ☐	C. ☐

14

S.D.	P.L.	P.G.	S.G.
P. ☐	F. ☐	F. ☐	T. ☐
F. ☐	W. ☐	W. ☐	P. ☐
B. ☐	P. ☐	C. ☐	C. ☐

15

S.D.	P.L.	P.G.	S.G.
P. ☐	F. ☐	F. ☐	T. ☐
F. ☐	W. ☐	W. ☐	P. ☐
B. ☐	P. ☐	C. ☐	C. ☐

16

S.D.	P.L.	P.G.	S.G.
P. ☐	F. ☐	F. ☐	T. ☐
F. ☐	W. ☐	W. ☐	P. ☐
B. ☐	P. ☐	C. ☐	C. ☐

21

S.D.	P.L.	P.G.	S.G.
P. ☐	F. ☐	F. ☐	T. ☐
F. ☐	W. ☐	W. ☐	P. ☐
B. ☐	P. ☐	C. ☐	C. ☐

22

S.D.	P.L.	P.G.	S.G.
P. ☐	F. ☐	F. ☐	T. ☐
F. ☐	W. ☐	W. ☐	P. ☐
B. ☐	P. ☐	C. ☐	C. ☐

23

S.D.	P.L.	P.G.	S.G.
P. ☐	F. ☐	F. ☐	T. ☐
F. ☐	W. ☐	W. ☐	P. ☐
B. ☐	P. ☐	C. ☐	C. ☐

24

S.D.	P.L.	P.G.	S.G.
P. ☐	F. ☐	F. ☐	T. ☐
F. ☐	W. ☐	W. ☐	P. ☐
B. ☐	P. ☐	C. ☐	C. ☐

29

S.D.	P.L.	P.G.	S.G.
P. ☐	F. ☐	F. ☐	T. ☐
F. ☐	W. ☐	W. ☐	P. ☐
B. ☐	P. ☐	C. ☐	C. ☐

30

S.D.	P.L.	P.G.	S.G.
P. ☐	F. ☐	F. ☐	T. ☐
F. ☐	W. ☐	W. ☐	P. ☐
B. ☐	P. ☐	C. ☐	C. ☐

31

S.D.	P.L.	P.G.	S.G.
P. ☐	F. ☐	F. ☐	T. ☐
F. ☐	W. ☐	W. ☐	P. ☐
B. ☐	P. ☐	C. ☐	C. ☐

Psalm 48:14

That is what God is like. He is our God forever and ever, and he will guide us until we die.

Personal Goals

Family

Work/School/Social

Challenge

Sport Goals

Training

Performance

Competition Results

The Last Supper

[12]On the first day of the Festival of Unleavened Bread, when the Passover lamb is sacrificed, Jesus' disciples asked him, "Where do you want us to go to prepare the Passover meal for you?"

[13]So Jesus sent two of them into Jerusalem with these instructions: "As you go into the city, a man carrying a pitcher of water will meet you. Follow him. [14]At the house he enters, say to the owner, 'The Teacher asks: Where is the guest room where I can eat the Passover meal with my disciples?' [15]He will take you upstairs to a large room that is already set up. That is where you should prepare our meal." [16]So the two disciples went into the city and found everything just as Jesus had said, and they prepared the Passover meal there.

[17]In the evening Jesus arrived with the twelve disciples. [18]As they were at the table eating, Jesus said, "I tell you the truth, one of you eating with me here will betray me."

[19]Greatly distressed, each one asked in turn, "Am I the one?"

[20]He replied, "It is one of you twelve who is eating from this bowl with me. [21]For the Son of Man must die, as the Scriptures declared long ago. But how terrible it will be for the one who betrays him. It would be far better for that man if he had never been born!"

[22]As they were eating, Jesus took some bread and blessed it. Then he broke it in pieces and gave it to the disciples, saying, "Take it, for this is my body."

[23]And he took a cup of wine and gave thanks to God for it. He gave it to them, and they all drank from it. [24]And he said to them, "This is my blood, which confirms the covenant between God and his people. It is poured out as a sacrifice for many. [25]I tell you the truth, I will not drink wine again until the day I drink it new in the Kingdom of God."

[26]Then they sang a hymn and went out to the Mount of Olives.

Jesus Predicts Peter's Denial

[27]On the way, Jesus told them, "All of you will desert me. For the Scriptures say,

'God will strike the Shepherd,
and the sheep will be scattered.'

[28]But after I am raised from the dead, I will go ahead of you to Galilee and meet you there."

[29]Peter said to him, "Even if everyone else deserts you, I never will."

[30]Jesus replied, "I tell you the truth, Peter—this very night, before the rooster crows twice, you will deny three times that you even know me."

[31]"No!" Peter declared emphatically. "Even if I have to die with you, I will never deny you!" And all the others vowed the same.

Jesus Prays in Gethsemane

[32]They went to the olive grove called Gethsemane, and Jesus said, "Sit here while I go and pray." [33]He took Peter, James, and John with him, and he became deeply troubled and distressed. [34]He told them, "My soul is crushed with grief to the point of death. Stay here and keep watch with me."

[35]He went on a little farther and fell to the ground. He prayed that, if it were possible, the awful hour awaiting him might pass him by. [36]"Abba, Father," he cried out, "everything is possible for you. Please take this cup of suffering away from me. Yet I want your will to be done, not mine."

[37]Then he returned and found the disciples asleep. He said to Peter, "Simon, are you asleep? Couldn't you watch with me even one hour? [38]Keep watch and pray, so that you will not give in to temptation. For the spirit is willing, but the body is weak."

[39]Then Jesus left them again and prayed the same prayer as before. [40]When he returned to them again, he found them sleeping, for they couldn't keep their eyes open. And they didn't know what to say.

[41]When he returned to them the third time, he said, "Go ahead and sleep. Have your rest. But no—the time has come. The Son of Man is betrayed into the hands of sinners. [42]Up, let's be going. Look, my betrayer is here!"

Jesus Is Betrayed and Arrested

[43]And immediately, even as Jesus said this, Judas, one of the twelve disciples, arrived with a crowd of men armed with swords and clubs. They had been sent by the leading priests, the teachers of religious law, and the elders. [44]The traitor, Judas, had given them a prearranged signal: "You will know which one to arrest when I greet him with a kiss. Then you can take him away under guard." [45]As soon as they arrived, Judas walked up to Jesus. "Rabbi!" he exclaimed, and gave him the kiss.

[46]Then the others grabbed Jesus and arrested him.

action

14:35-42 WHAT'S IT SAYING?

WHAT AM I GOING TO DO ABOUT IT?

count on it

Little things matter!

Put in that extra effort to obey the Holy Spirit – that small voice from God. Work hard at keeping your motives pure. You may be tempted to cheat or cut corners. Don't! It will catch up with you. God is interested in the little things – they become big things! "Don't be misled – you cannot mock the justice of God. You will always harvest what you plant. Those who live only to satisfy their own sinful nature will harvest decay and death from that sinful nature. But those who live to please the Spirit will harvest everlasting life from the Spirit." (Galatians 6:7-8) **Count on it!**

[47] But one of the men with Jesus pulled out his sword and struck the high priest's slave, slashing off his ear. [48] Jesus asked them, "Am I some dangerous revolutionary, that you come with swords and clubs to arrest me? [49] Why didn't you arrest me in the Temple? I was there among you teaching every day. But these things are happening to fulfill what the Scriptures say about me." [50] Then all his disciples deserted him and ran away. [51] One young man following behind was clothed only in a long linen shirt. When the mob tried to grab him, [52] he slipped out of his shirt and ran away naked.

Jesus before the Council

[53] They took Jesus to the high priest's home where the leading priests, the elders, and the teachers of religious law had gathered. [54] Meanwhile, Peter followed him at a distance and went right into the high priest's courtyard. There he sat with the guards, warming himself by the fire.

[55] Inside, the leading priests and the entire high council were trying to find evidence against Jesus, so they could put him to death. But they couldn't find any. [56] Many false witnesses spoke against him, but they contradicted each other. [57] Finally, some men stood up and gave this false testimony: [58] "We heard him say, 'I will destroy this Temple made with human hands, and in three days I will build another, made without human hands.'" [59] But even then they didn't get their stories straight!

[60] Then the high priest stood up before the others and asked Jesus, "Well, aren't you going to answer these charges? What do you have to say for yourself?" [61] But Jesus was silent and made no reply. Then the high priest asked him, "Are you the Messiah, the Son of the Blessed One?"

[62] Jesus said, "I AM. And you will see the Son of Man seated in the place of power at God's right hand and coming on the clouds of heaven."

[63] Then the high priest tore his clothing to show his horror and said, "Why do we need other witnesses? [64] You have all heard his blasphemy. What is your verdict?"

"Guilty!" they all cried. "He deserves to die!"

[65] Then some of them began to spit at him, and they blindfolded him and beat him with their fists. "Prophesy to us," they jeered. And the guards slapped him as they took him away.

Peter Denies Jesus

[66] Meanwhile, Peter was in the courtyard below. One of the servant girls who worked for the high priest came by [67] and noticed Peter warming himself at the fire. She looked at him closely and said, "You were one of those with Jesus of Nazareth."

[68] But Peter denied it. "I don't know what you're talking about," he said, and he went out into the entryway. Just then, a rooster crowed.

[69] When the servant girl saw him standing there, she began telling the others, "This man is definitely one of them!" [70] But Peter denied it again.

A little later some of the other bystanders confronted Peter and said, "You must be one of them, because you are a Galilean."

[71] Peter swore, "A curse on me if I'm lying—I don't know this man you're talking about!" [72] And immediately the rooster crowed the second time.

Suddenly, Jesus' words flashed through Peter's mind: "Before the rooster crows twice, you will deny three times that you even know me." And he broke down and wept.

Jesus' Trial before Pilate

15

Very early in the morning the leading priests, the elders, and the teachers of religious law—the entire high council—met to discuss their next step. They bound Jesus, led him away, and took him to Pilate, the Roman governor.

[2] Pilate asked Jesus, "Are you the king of the Jews?"

Jesus replied, "You have said it."

[3] Then the leading priests kept accusing him of many crimes, [4] and Pilate asked him, "Aren't you going to answer them? What about all these charges they are bringing against you?" [5] But Jesus said nothing, much to Pilate's surprise.

[6] Now it was the governor's custom each year during the Passover celebration to release one prisoner—anyone the people requested. [7] One of the prisoners at that time was Barabbas, a revolutionary who had committed murder in an uprising. [8] The crowd went to Pilate and asked him to release a prisoner as usual.

[9] "Would you like me to release this 'King of the Jews'?" Pilate asked. [10] (For he realized by now that the leading priests had arrested Jesus out of envy.) [11] But at this point the leading priests stirred up the crowd to demand the release of Barabbas instead of Jesus.

[12] Pilate asked them, "Then what should I do with this man you call the king of the Jews?"

[13] They shouted back, "Crucify him!"

[14] "Why?" Pilate demanded. "What crime has he committed?"

But the mob roared even louder, "Crucify him!"

[15] So to pacify the crowd, Pilate released Barabbas to them. He ordered Jesus flogged with a lead-tipped whip, then turned him over to the Roman soldiers to be crucified.

The Soldiers Mock Jesus

[16] The soldiers took Jesus into the courtyard of the governor's headquarters (called the Praetorium) and called out the entire regiment. [17] They dressed him in a purple robe, and they wove thorn branches into a crown and put it on his head. [18] Then they saluted him and taunted, "Hail! King of the Jews!" [19] And they struck him on the head with a reed stick, spit on him, and dropped to their knees in mock worship. [20] When they were finally tired of mocking him, they took off the purple robe and put his own clothes on him again. Then they led him away to be crucified.

The Crucifixion

[21] A passerby named Simon, who was from Cyrene, was coming in from the countryside just then, and the soldiers forced him to carry Jesus' cross. (Simon was the father of Alexander and Rufus.) [22] And they brought Jesus to a place called Golgotha (which means "Place of the Skull"). [23] They offered him wine drugged with myrrh, but he refused it.

[24] Then the soldiers nailed him to the cross. They divided his clothes and threw dice to decide who would get each piece. [25] It was nine o'clock in the morning when they crucified him. [26] A sign was fastened to the cross, announcing the charge against him. It read, "The King of the Jews." [27] Two revolutionaries were crucified with him, one on his right and one on his left.*

[29] The people passing by shouted abuse, shaking their heads in mockery. "Ha! Look at you now!" they yelled at him. "You said you were going to destroy the Temple and rebuild it in three days. [30] Well then, save yourself and come down from the cross!"

[31] The leading priests and teachers of religious law also mocked Jesus. "He saved others," they scoffed, "but he can't save himself! [32] Let this Messiah, this King of Israel, come down from the cross so we can see it and believe him!" Even the men who were crucified with Jesus ridiculed him.

The Death of Jesus

[33] At noon, darkness fell across the whole land until three o'clock. [34] Then at three o'clock Jesus called out with a loud voice, *"Eloi, Eloi, lema sabachthani?"* which means "My God, my God, why have you abandoned me?"

[35] Some of the bystanders misunderstood and thought he was calling for the prophet Elijah. [36] One of them ran and filled a sponge with sour wine, holding it up to him on a reed stick so he could drink. "Wait!" he said. "Let's see whether Elijah comes to take him down!"

[37] Then Jesus uttered another loud cry and breathed his last. [38] And the curtain in the sanctuary of the Temple was torn in two, from top to bottom.

15:27 Some manuscripts add verse 28, *And the Scripture was fulfilled that said, "He was counted among those who were rebels."* See Isa 53:12; also compare Luke 22:37.

profiles

John the Baptist:

"He [Jesus] must become greater and greater, and I must become less and less" (John 3:30). John the Baptist (not to be confused with John the apostle) was related to Jesus and commissioned by God to usher in a new era – the era of Jesus, the Savior of the world. He was given a unique task: to be the voice in the wilderness, to prepare the way of the Lord – a prophesy proclaimed by Isaiah hundreds of years earlier (Isaiah 40:3). Through the Gospels and other historical evidence, we find John fulfilling his task flawlessly. The Baptist was a rugged individual who stayed focused on his task, attracted quite a crowd, and baptized hundreds of followers. He was asked often, "Are you the Messiah?" John constantly played down his role. He announced: "Someone is coming soon who is greater than I am — so much greater that I'm not even worthy to be his slave" (Luke 3:16). John's mission was to announce the coming of God's Kingdom through Jesus and the need for us to turn from our sin, which is symbolized in baptism. He was bold and did not apologize for his message. His boldness cost him his life, and his cousin Jesus mourned his death. John understood Jesus' ministry and his role in God's purpose. You also have a purpose: Jesus wants to live in you. Can you say in your life, "He must become greater and greater and I must become less and less"?

39When the Roman officer who stood facing him saw how he had died, he exclaimed, "This man truly was the Son of God!"
40Some women were there, watching from a distance, including Mary Magdalene, Mary (the mother of James the younger and of Joseph), and Salome. 41They had been followers of Jesus and had cared for him while he was in Galilee. Many other women who had come with him to Jerusalem were also there.

The Burial of Jesus

42This all happened on Friday, the day of preparation, the day before the Sabbath. As evening approached, 43Joseph of Arimathea took a risk and went to Pilate and asked for Jesus' body. (Joseph was an honored member of the high council, and he was waiting for the Kingdom of God to come.) 44Pilate couldn't believe that Jesus was already dead, so he called for the Roman officer and asked if he had died yet. 45The officer confirmed that Jesus was dead, so Pilate told Joseph he could have the body. 46Joseph bought a long sheet of linen cloth. Then he took Jesus' body down from the cross, wrapped it in the cloth, and laid it in a tomb that had been carved out of the rock. Then he rolled a stone in front of the entrance. 47Mary Magdalene and Mary the mother of Joseph saw where Jesus' body was laid.

The Resurrection

16

Saturday evening, when the Sabbath ended, Mary Magdalene and Salome and Mary the mother of James went out and purchased burial spices so they could anoint Jesus' body. 2Very early on Sunday morning, just at sunrise, they went to the tomb. 3On the way they were asking each other, "Who will roll away the stone for us from the entrance to the tomb?" 4But as they arrived, they looked up and saw that the stone, which was very large, had already been rolled aside. 5When they entered the tomb, they saw a young man clothed in a white robe sitting on the right side. The women were shocked, 6but the angel said, "Don't be alarmed. You are looking for Jesus of Nazareth, who was crucified. He isn't here! He is risen from the dead! Look, this is where they laid his body. 7Now go and tell his disciples, including Peter, that Jesus is going ahead of you to Galilee. You will see him there, just as he told you before he died."
8The women fled from the tomb, trembling and bewildered, and they said nothing to anyone because they were too frightened.

[Shorter Ending of Mark]

Then they briefly reported all this to Peter and his companions. Afterward Jesus himself sent them out from east to west with the sacred and unfailing message of salvation that gives eternal life. Amen.

[Longer Ending of Mark]

9After Jesus rose from the dead early on Sunday morning, the first person who saw him was Mary Magdalene, the woman from whom he had cast out seven demons. 10She went to the disciples, who were grieving and weeping, and told them what had happened. 11But when she told them that Jesus was alive and she had seen him, they didn't believe her.
12Afterward he appeared in a different form to two of his followers who were walking from Jerusalem into the country. 13They rushed back to tell the others, but no one believed them.
14Still later he appeared to the eleven disciples as they were eating together. He rebuked them for their stubborn unbelief because they refused to believe those who had seen him after he had been raised from the dead.*
15And then he told them, "Go into all the world and preach the Good News to everyone. 16Anyone who believes and is baptized will be saved. But anyone who refuses to believe will be condemned. 17These miraculous signs will accompany those who believe: They will cast out demons in my name, and they will speak in new languages. 18They will be able to handle snakes with safety, and if they drink anything poisonous, it won't hurt them. They will be able to place their hands on the sick, and they will be healed."
19When the Lord Jesus had finished talking with them, he was taken up into heaven and sat down in the place of honor at God's right hand. 20And the disciples went everywhere and preached, and the Lord worked through them, confirming what they said by many miraculous signs.

16:14 Some early manuscripts add: And they excused themselves, saying, "This age of lawlessness and unbelief is under Satan, who does not permit God's truth and power to conquer the evil [unclean] spirits. Therefore, reveal your justice now." This is what they said to Christ. And Christ replied to them, "The period of years of Satan's power has been fulfilled, but other dreadful things will happen soon. And I was handed over to death for those who have sinned, so that they may return to the truth and sin no more, and so they may inherit the spiritual, incorruptible, and righteous glory in heaven."

Luke was interested in the BIG PICTURE! He is credited not only with writing the Gospel we see before us but also the book of Acts, which is a what-happened-next sequel to Luke. This Gospel tells the story of Jesus' life and has special emphasis on the power of prayer and the power of the Holy Spirit. Luke reveals the special attention Jesus paid the poor and his "Power Habit" of praying before every tough decision or challenge he faced. As a historian, he placed special emphasis on the Old Testament prophecies that Jesus fulfills. We also get a great insight to Jesus' childhood, some of which is not recorded in the other Gospels.

Luke was commissioned to seek out and interview intimate friends of Jesus as well as people who had been directly impacted by his ministry and write a special account of Jesus' life. The list could have included Mary, the mother of Jesus; James, Jesus' brother; disciples of John the Baptist; and Jesus' very own top guys, including John and Peter. Luke became a close friend of the apostle Paul, who calls Luke, "the beloved doctor" (Colossians 4:14). This would make sense, because his writing style is clearly that of an educated man, and there are small hints that he wrote from a physician's point of view. The beloved doctor Luke's attention to detail and accuracy are present along with a structure that corresponds with the Gospels of Matthew and Mark.

Luke

Word of God
COUNT ON IT

LUKE

Introduction

1

Many people have set out to write accounts about the events that have been fulfilled among us. [2]They used the eyewitness reports circulating among us from the early disciples. [3]Having carefully investigated everything from the beginning, I also have decided to write a careful account for you, most honorable Theophilus, [4]so you can be certain of the truth of everything you were taught.

The Birth of John the Baptist Foretold

[5]When Herod was king of Judea, there was a Jewish priest named Zechariah. He was a member of the priestly order of Abijah, and his wife, Elizabeth, was also from the priestly line of Aaron. [6]Zechariah and Elizabeth were righteous in God's eyes, careful to obey all of the Lord's commandments and regulations. [7]They had no children because Elizabeth was unable to conceive, and they were both very old.

[8]One day Zechariah was serving God in the Temple, for his order was on duty that week. [9]As was the custom of the priests, he was chosen by lot to enter the sanctuary of the Lord and burn incense. [10]While the incense was being burned, a great crowd stood outside, praying.

[11]While Zechariah was in the sanctuary, an angel of the Lord appeared to him, standing to the right of the incense altar. [12]Zechariah was shaken and overwhelmed with fear when he saw him. [13]But the angel said, "Don't be afraid, Zechariah! God has heard your prayer. Your wife, Elizabeth, will give you a son, and you are to name him John. [14]You will have great joy and gladness, and many will rejoice at his birth, [15]for he will be great in the eyes of the Lord. He must never touch wine or other alcoholic drinks. He will be filled with the Holy Spirit, even before his birth. [16]And

The longest chapter in the Bible is Psalm 119, a celebration of God's Word.

he will turn many Israelites to the Lord their God. [17]He will be a man with the spirit and power of Elijah. He will prepare the people for the coming of the Lord. He will turn the hearts of the fathers to their children, and he will cause those who are rebellious to accept the wisdom of the godly."

[18]Zechariah said to the angel, "How can I be sure this will happen? I'm an old man now, and my wife is also well along in years."

[19]Then the angel said, "I am Gabriel! I stand in the very presence of God. It was he who sent me to bring you this good news! [20]But now, since you didn't believe what I said, you will be silent and unable to speak until the child is born. For my words will certainly be fulfilled at the proper time."

[21]Meanwhile, the people were waiting for Zechariah to come out of the sanctuary, wondering why he was taking so long. [22]When he finally did come out, he couldn't speak to them. Then they realized from his gestures and his silence that he must have seen a vision in the sanctuary.

[23]When Zechariah's week of service in the Temple was over, he returned home. [24]Soon afterward his wife, Elizabeth, became pregnant and went into seclusion for five months. [25]"How kind the Lord is!" she exclaimed. "He has taken away my disgrace of having no children."

The Birth of Jesus Foretold

[26]In the sixth month of Elizabeth's pregnancy, God sent the angel Gabriel to Nazareth, a village in Galilee, [27]to a virgin named Mary. She was engaged to be married to a man named Joseph, a descendant of King David. [28]Gabriel appeared to her and said, "Greetings, favored woman! The Lord is with you!*"

[29]Confused and disturbed, Mary tried to think what the angel could mean. [30]"Don't be afraid, Mary," the angel told her, "for you have found favor with God! [31]You will conceive and give birth to a son, and you will name him Jesus. [32]He will be very great and will be called the Son of the Most High. The Lord God will give him the throne of his ancestor David. [33]And he will reign over Israel forever; his Kingdom will never end!"

[34]Mary asked the angel, "But how can this happen? I am a virgin."

[35]The angel replied, "The Holy Spirit will come upon you, and the power of the Most High will overshadow you. So the baby to be born will be holy, and he will be called the Son of God. [36]What's more, your relative Elizabeth has become pregnant in her old age! People used to say she was barren, but she's now in her sixth

month. [37]For nothing is impossible with God."

[38]Mary responded, "I am the Lord's servant. May everything you have said about me come true." And then the angel left her.

Mary Visits Elizabeth

[39]A few days later Mary hurried to the hill country of Judea, to the town [40]where Zechariah lived. She entered the house and greeted Elizabeth. [41]At the sound of Mary's greeting, Elizabeth's child leaped within her, and Elizabeth was filled with the Holy Spirit.

[42]Elizabeth gave a glad cry and exclaimed to Mary, "God has blessed you above all women, and your child is blessed. [43]Why am I so honored, that the mother of my Lord should visit me? [44]When I heard your greeting, the baby in my womb jumped for joy. [45]You are blessed because you believed that the Lord would do what he said."

The Magnificat: Mary's Song of Praise

[46]Mary responded,

"Oh, how my soul praises the Lord.
[47]How my spirit rejoices in God my Savior!
[48]For he took notice of his lowly servant girl,
and from now on all generations will call me blessed.
[49]For the Mighty One is holy,
and he has done great things for me.
[50]He shows mercy from generation to generation
to all who fear him.
[51]His mighty arm has done tremendous things!
He has scattered the proud and haughty ones.
[52]He has brought down princes from their thrones
and exalted the humble.
[53]He has filled the hungry with good things
and sent the rich away with empty hands.
[54]He has helped his servant Israel
and remembered to be merciful.
[55]For he made this promise to our ancestors,
to Abraham and his children forever."

[56]Mary stayed with Elizabeth about three months and then went back to her own home.

The Birth of John the Baptist

[57]When it was time for Elizabeth's baby to be born, she gave birth to a son. [58]And when her neighbors and relatives heard that the Lord had been very merciful to her, everyone rejoiced with her.

[59]When the baby was eight days old, they all came for the circumcision ceremony. They wanted to name him Zechariah, after his father. [60]But Elizabeth said, "No! His name is John!"

[61]"What?" they exclaimed. "There is no one in all your family by that name." [62]So they used gestures to ask the baby's father what he wanted to name him. [63]He motioned for a

1:28 Some manuscripts add *Blessed are you among women.*

profiles

Peter:

Jesus asked Peter, "Do you love me more than these?" (John 21:15) It was a painful time in Peter's amazing relationship with his master. Christ's original commission for Peter was, "Come follow me, and I will show you how to fish for people" (Mark 1:17). Now Jesus had been crucified, resurrected, and had revealed himself to Peter on many occasions. It seemed that Peter was to return to his old life of fishing. His three-year dream of following this King seemed to be over. When Jesus appears to Peter (Jesus had named him Peter, which means "rock"), we see this impetuous man who had bragged that he would follow Jesus to death deny him three times. Now Jesus asks him again do you love me more than these? What was around Peter at this scene? His friends, fish and boats. Jesus slowly draws out the poison and grief Peter held inside him, asking him three more times, "Do you love me?" Jesus met Peter where he was at the time and reinstated him. Jesus also asks you, "do you love me more than these?" Look around. What is more important than Jesus? He wants your allegiance to him to be first in your life. Peter was not a perfect man, but God used him in great ways. Peter was the recognized leader of the church movement; he became a fearless messenger of Jesus and the writer of 1 and 2 Peter.

writing tablet, and to everyone's surprise he wrote, "His name is John." [64]Instantly Zechariah could speak again, and he began praising God.

[65]Awe fell upon the whole neighborhood, and the news of what had happened spread throughout the Judean hills. [66]Everyone who heard about it reflected on these

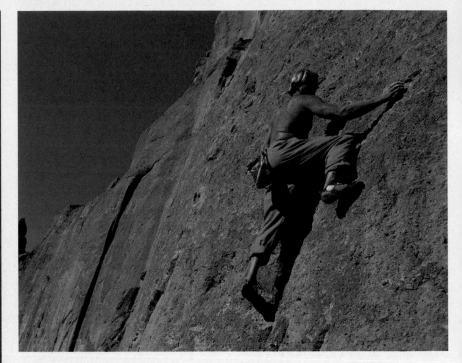

events and asked, "What will this child turn out to be?" For the hand of the Lord was surely upon him in a special way.

Zechariah's Prophecy

[67]Then his father, Zechariah, was filled with the Holy Spirit and gave this prophecy:

[68]"Praise the Lord, the God of Israel,
because he has visited and redeemed his people.
[69]He has sent us a mighty Savior
from the royal line of his servant David,
[70]just as he promised
through his holy prophets long ago.
[71]Now we will be saved from our enemies
and from all who hate us.
[72]He has been merciful to our ancestors
by remembering his sacred covenant—
[73]the covenant he swore with an oath
to our ancestor Abraham.
[74]We have been rescued from our enemies
so we can serve God without fear,
[75]in holiness and righteousness
for as long as we live.

[76]"And you, my little son,
will be called the prophet of the Most High,
because you will prepare the way for the Lord.
[77]You will tell his people how to find salvation
through forgiveness of their sins.
[78]Because of God's tender mercy,
the morning light from heaven is about to break upon us,
[79]to give light to those who sit in darkness and in the shadow of death,
and to guide us to the path of peace."
[80]John grew up and became strong in spirit. And he lived in the wilderness until he began his public ministry to Israel.

The Birth of Jesus

2

At that time the Roman emperor, Augustus, decreed that a census should be taken throughout the Roman Empire. [2](This was the first census taken when Quirinius was governor of Syria.) [3]All returned to their own ancestral towns to register for this census. [4]And because Joseph was a descendant of King David, he had to go to Bethlehem in Judea, David's ancient home. He traveled there from the village of Nazareth in Galilee. [5]He took with him Mary, his fiancée, who was now obviously pregnant.

[6]And while they were there, the time came for her

baby to be born. ⁷She gave birth to her first child, a son. She wrapped him snugly in strips of cloth and laid him in a manger, because there was no lodging available for them.

The Shepherds and Angels

⁸That night there were shepherds staying in the fields nearby, guarding their flocks of sheep. ⁹Suddenly, an angel of the Lord appeared among them, and the radiance of the Lord's glory surrounded them. They were terrified, ¹⁰but the angel reassured them. "Don't be afraid!" he said. "I bring you good news that will bring great joy to all people. ¹¹The Savior—yes, the Messiah, the Lord—has been born today in Bethlehem, the city of David! ¹²And you will recognize him by this sign: You will find a baby wrapped snugly in strips of cloth, lying in a manger."

¹³Suddenly, the angel was joined by a vast host of others—the armies of heaven—praising God and saying,

¹⁴"Glory to God in highest heaven,
and peace on earth to those with whom God is pleased."

¹⁵When the angels had returned to heaven, the shepherds said to each other, "Let's go to Bethlehem! Let's see this thing that has happened, which the Lord has told us about."

¹⁶They hurried to the village and found Mary and Joseph. And there was the baby, lying in the manger. ¹⁷After seeing him, the shepherds told everyone what had happened and what the angel had said to them about this child. ¹⁸All who heard the shepherds' story were astonished, ¹⁹but Mary kept all these things in her heart and thought about them often. ²⁰The shepherds went back to their flocks, glorifying and praising God for all they had heard and seen. It was just as the angel had told them.

For many years the Olympics consisted of only one race, a sprint of 192 meters (210 yards, the length of the stadium) called the stadion.

Always be joyful! This is a tough habit! To have that deep-down-in-your-gut happiness (joy) even when you've blown it or lost a competition . . . how can you do it? By knowing no matter what your circumstances, God totally loves you. "Always be joyful. Never stop praying. Be thankful in all circumstances, for this is God's will for you who belong to Christ Jesus."

(1 Thessalonians 5:16-18)

Jesus Is Presented in the Temple

²¹Eight days later, when the baby was circumcised, he was named Jesus, the name given him by the angel even before he was conceived.

²²Then it was time for their purification offering, as required by the law of Moses after the birth of a child; so his parents took him to Jerusalem to present him to the Lord. ²³The law of the Lord says, "If a woman's first child is a boy, he must be dedicated to the LORD." ²⁴So they offered the sacrifice required in the law of the Lord—"either a pair of turtledoves or two young pigeons."

The Prophecy of Simeon

²⁵At that time there was a man in Jerusalem named Simeon. He was righteous and devout and was eagerly waiting for the Messiah to come and rescue Israel. The Holy Spirit was upon him ²⁶and had revealed to him that he would not die until he had seen the Lord's Messiah. ²⁷That day the Spirit led him to the Temple. So when Mary and Joseph came to present the baby Jesus to the Lord as the law required, ²⁸Simeon was there. He took the child in his arms and praised God, saying,

²⁹"Sovereign Lord, now let your servant die in peace, as you have promised.
³⁰I have seen your salvation,
³¹which you have prepared for all people.
³²He is a light to reveal God to the nations,
and he is the glory of your people Israel!"

³³Jesus' parents were amazed at what was being said about him. ³⁴Then Simeon blessed them, and he said to Mary, the baby's mother, "This child is destined to cause many in Israel to fall, but he will be a joy to many others. He has been sent as a sign from God, but many will oppose him. ³⁵As a result, the deepest thoughts of many hearts will be revealed. And a sword will pierce your very soul."

The Prophecy of Anna

³⁶Anna, a prophet, was also there in the Temple. She was the daughter of Phanuel from the tribe of Asher, and she was very old. Her husband died when they had been married only seven years. ³⁷Then she lived as a widow to the age of eighty-four. She never left the Temple but stayed there day and night, worshiping God with fasting and prayer. ³⁸She came along just as Simeon was talking with Mary and Joseph, and she began praising God. She talked about the child to everyone who had been waiting expectantly for God to rescue Jerusalem.

³⁹When Jesus' parents had fulfilled all the requirements of the law of the Lord, they returned home to Nazareth in Galilee. ⁴⁰There the child grew up healthy and strong. He was filled with wisdom, and God's favor was on him.

Jesus Speaks with the Teachers

⁴¹Every year Jesus' parents went to Jerusalem for the Passover festival. ⁴²When Jesus was twelve years old, they attended the festival as usual. ⁴³After the celebration was over, they started home to Nazareth, but Jesus stayed behind in Jerusalem. His parents didn't miss him at first, ⁴⁴because they assumed he was among the other travelers. But when he didn't show up that evening, they started looking for him among their relatives and friends.

⁴⁵When they couldn't find him, they went back to Jerusalem to search for him there. ⁴⁶Three days later they finally discovered him in the Temple, sitting among the religious teachers, listening to them and asking questions. ⁴⁷All who heard him were amazed at his understanding and his answers.

⁴⁸His parents didn't know what to think. "Son," his mother

said to him, "why have you done this to us? Your father and I have been frantic, searching for you everywhere."

⁴⁹"But why did you need to search?" he asked. "Didn't you know that I must be in my Father's house?" ⁵⁰But they didn't understand what he meant.

⁵¹Then he returned to Nazareth with them and was obedient to them. And his mother stored all these things in her heart. ⁵²Jesus grew in wisdom and in stature and in favor with God and all the people.

John the Baptist Prepares the Way

3

It was now the fifteenth year of the reign of Tiberius, the Roman emperor. Pontius Pilate was governor over Judea; Herod Antipas was ruler over Galilee; his brother Philip was ruler over Iturea and Traconitis; Lysanias was ruler over Abilene. ²Annas and Caiaphas were the high priests. At this time a message from God came to John son of Zechariah, who was living in the wilderness. ³Then John went from place to place on both sides of the Jordan River, preaching that people should be baptized to show that they had turned to God to receive forgiveness for their sins. ⁴Isaiah had spoken of John when he said,

"He is a voice shouting in the wilderness,
'Prepare the way for the LORD's coming!
Clear the road for him!
⁵The valleys will be filled,
and the mountains and hills made level.
The curves will be straightened,
and the rough places made smooth.
⁶And then all people will see
the salvation sent from God.'"

⁷When the crowds came to John for baptism, he said, "You brood of snakes! Who warned you to flee God's coming wrath? ⁸Prove by the way you live that you have repented of your sins and turned to God. Don't just say to each other, 'We're safe, for we are descendants of Abraham.' That means nothing, for I tell you, God can create children of Abraham from these very stones. ⁹Even now the ax of God's judgment is poised, ready to sever the roots of the trees. Yes, every tree that does not produce good fruit will be chopped down and thrown into the fire."

¹⁰The crowds asked, "What should we do?"

¹¹John replied, "If you have two shirts, give one to the poor. If you have food, share it with those who are hungry."

¹²Even corrupt tax collectors came to be baptized and asked, "Teacher, what should we do?"

¹³He replied, "Collect no more taxes than the government requires."

¹⁴"What should we do?" asked some soldiers. John replied, "Don't extort money or make false accusations. And be content with your pay."

¹⁵Everyone was expecting the Messiah to come soon, and they were eager to know whether John might be the Messiah. ¹⁶John answered their questions by saying, "I baptize you with water; but someone is coming soon who is greater than I am—so much greater that I'm not even worthy to be his slave and untie the straps of his sandals. He will baptize you with the Holy Spirit and with fire. ¹⁷He is ready to separate the chaff from the wheat with his winnowing fork. Then he will clean up the threshing area, gathering the wheat into his barn but burning the chaff with never-ending fire." ¹⁸John used many such warnings as he announced the Good News to the people.

¹⁹John also publicly criticized Herod Antipas, the ruler of Galilee, for marrying Herodias, his brother's wife, and for many other wrongs he had done. ²⁰So Herod put John in prison, adding this sin to his many others.

The Baptism of Jesus

²¹One day when the crowds were being baptized, Jesus himself was baptized. As he was praying, the heavens opened, ²²and the Holy Spirit, in bodily form, descended on him like a dove. And a voice from heaven said, "You are my dearly loved Son, and you bring me great joy."

The Ancestors of Jesus

²³Jesus was about thirty years old when he began his public ministry.

Jesus was known as the son of Joseph.
Joseph was the son of Heli.
²⁴Heli was the son of Matthat.
Matthat was the son of Levi.
Levi was the son of Melki.
Melki was the son of Jannai.
Jannai was the son of Joseph.
²⁵Joseph was the son of Mattathias.
Mattathias was the son of Amos.
Amos was the son of Nahum.
Nahum was the son of Esli.
Esli was the son of Naggai.
²⁶Naggai was the son of Maath.
Maath was the son of Mattathias.
Mattathias was the son of Semein.
Semein was the son of Josech.
Josech was the son of Joda.
²⁷Joda was the son of Joanan.
Joanan was the son of Rhesa.
Rhesa was the son of Zerubbabel.
Zerubbabel was the son of Shealtiel.
Shealtiel was the son of Neri.
²⁸Neri was the son of Melki.
Melki was the son of Addi.
Addi was the son of Cosam.
Cosam was the son of Elmadam.
Elmadam was the son of Er.
²⁹Er was the son of Joshua.
Joshua was the son of Eliezer.
Eliezer was the son of Jorim.
Jorim was the son of Matthat.
Matthat was the son of Levi.

Is competition wrong? When you compete at the top level, how do you keep everything in perspective? How do you give it your best shot without treating it like World War Three?

First, in serious competition, we are to give our best and give God the praise for our effort – win, lose or draw. The Christian's purpose is to live out the presence of Christ. For athletes it's in the world of sports – the idea of demonstrating Christ's presence in us and through us in competition to the best of our ability. It is the "What Would Jesus Do?" attitude applied to our sport. It is to love our neighbor (our teammates, our opponents, and even the officials) as ourselves. No one is saying that this is easy. However, it is in the way we conduct ourselves in the heat of the battle that will show the difference Christ makes in our lives.

TIPS

Don't Just Diet:

Hundreds of research studies have shown that a slowdown in metabolism is due to a loss of muscle tissue. And the loss of muscle tissue is directly related to a lack of hard physical activity and healthy nutrition!

[30]Levi was the son of Simeon.
Simeon was the son of Judah.
Judah was the son of Joseph.
Joseph was the son of Jonam.
Jonam was the son of Eliakim.
[31]Eliakim was the son of Melea.
Melea was the son of Menna.
Menna was the son of Mattatha.
Mattatha was the son of Nathan.
Nathan was the son of David.
[32]David was the son of Jesse.
Jesse was the son of Obed.
Obed was the son of Boaz.
Boaz was the son of Salmon.
Salmon was the son of Nahshon.

[33]Nahshon was the son of Amminadab.
Amminadab was the son of Admin.
Admin was the son of Arni.
Arni was the son of Hezron.
Hezron was the son of Perez.
Perez was the son of Judah.
[34]Judah was the son of Jacob.
Jacob was the son of Isaac.
Isaac was the son of Abraham.
Abraham was the son of Terah.
Terah was the son of Nahor.
[35]Nahor was the son of Serug.
Serug was the son of Reu.
Reu was the son of Peleg.
Peleg was the son of Eber.

Eber was the son of Shelah.
[36]Shelah was the son of Cainan.
Cainan was the son of Arphaxad.
Arphaxad was the son of Shem.
Shem was the son of Noah.
Noah was the son of Lamech.
[37]Lamech was the son of Methuselah.
Methuselah was the son of Enoch.
Enoch was the son of Jared.
Jared was the son of Mahalalel.
Mahalalel was the son of Kenan.
[38]Kenan was the son of Enosh.
Enosh was the son of Seth.
Seth was the son of Adam.
Adam was the son of God.

The Temptation of Jesus

4

Then Jesus, full of the Holy Spirit, returned from the Jordan River. He was led by the Spirit in the wilderness, ²where he was tempted by the devil for forty days. Jesus ate nothing all that time and became very hungry.

³Then the devil said to him, "If you are the Son of God, change this stone into a loaf of bread."

⁴But Jesus told him, "No! The Scriptures say, 'People do not live by bread alone.'"

⁵Then the devil took him up and revealed to him all the kingdoms of the world in a moment of time. ⁶"I will give you the glory of these kingdoms and authority over them," the devil said, "because they are mine to give to anyone I please. ⁷I will give it all to you if you will worship me."

⁸Jesus replied, "The Scriptures say,

'You must worship the LORD your God
and serve only him.'"

⁹Then the devil took him to Jerusalem, to the highest point of the Temple, and said, "If you are the Son of God, jump off! ¹⁰For the Scriptures say,

'He will order his angels to protect and guard you.

¹¹And they will hold you up with their hands
so you won't even hurt your foot on a stone.'"

¹²Jesus responded, "The Scriptures also say, 'You must not test the LORD your God.'"

¹³When the devil had finished tempting Jesus, he left him until the next opportunity came.

Jesus Rejected at Nazareth

¹⁴Then Jesus returned to Galilee, filled with the Holy Spirit's power. Reports about him spread quickly through the whole region. ¹⁵He taught regularly in their synagogues and was praised by everyone.

¹⁶When he came to the village of Nazareth, his boyhood home, he went as usual to the synagogue on the Sabbath and stood up to read the Scriptures. ¹⁷The scroll of Isaiah the prophet was handed to him. He unrolled the scroll and found the place where this was written:

¹⁸"The Spirit of the LORD is upon me,

for he has anointed me to bring Good News to the poor.

He has sent me to proclaim that captives will be released,

that the blind will see,

that the oppressed will be set free,

¹⁹and that the time of the LORD's favor has come."

²⁰He rolled up the scroll, handed it back to the attendant, and sat down. All eyes in the synagogue looked at him intently. ²¹Then he began to speak to them. "The Scripture you've just heard has been fulfilled this very day!"

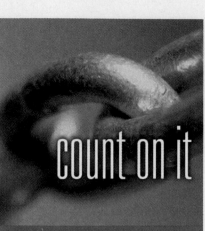

count on it

He will take your troubles!
Have you ever felt so weak that you thought there was no way you could continue? Are there times in your life when you feel so overwhelmed that you are virtually paralyzed? God will give you special strength in those times. Imagine that your life is a walk along the shore with God. If some days there is only one set of footprints in the sand, it's not because God has left you, but because he is carrying you! "My grace is all you need. My power works best in weakness."
(2 Corinthians 12:9)
Count on it!

²²Everyone spoke well of him and was amazed by the gracious words that came from his lips. "How can this be?" they asked. "Isn't this Joseph's son?"

²³Then he said, "You will undoubtedly quote me this proverb: 'Physician, heal yourself'—meaning, 'Do miracles here in your hometown like those you did in Capernaum.' ²⁴But I tell you the truth, no prophet is accepted in his own hometown.

²⁵"Certainly there were many needy widows in Israel in Elijah's time, when the heavens were closed for three and a half years, and a severe famine devastated the land. ²⁶Yet Elijah was not sent to any of them. He was sent instead to a foreigner—a widow of Zarephath in the land of Sidon. ²⁷And there were many lepers in Israel in the time of the prophet Elisha, but the only one healed was Naaman, a Syrian."

²⁸When they heard this, the people in the synagogue were furious. ²⁹Jumping up, they mobbed him and forced him to the edge of the hill on which the town was built. They intended to push him over the cliff, ³⁰but he passed right through the crowd and went on his way.

Jesus Casts Out a Demon

³¹Then Jesus went to Capernaum, a town in Galilee, and taught there in the synagogue every Sabbath day. ³²There, too, the people were amazed at his teaching, for he spoke with authority.

³³Once when he was in the synagogue, a man possessed by a demon—an evil spirit—began shouting at Jesus, ³⁴"Go away! Why are you interfering with us, Jesus of Nazareth? Have you come to destroy us? I know who you are—the Holy One sent from God!"

³⁵Jesus cut him short. "Be quiet! Come out of the man," he ordered. At that, the demon threw the man to the floor as the crowd watched; then it came out of him without hurting him further.

³⁶Amazed, the people exclaimed, "What authority and power this man's words possess! Even evil spirits obey him, and they flee at his command!" ³⁷The news about Jesus spread through every village in the entire region.

Jesus Heals Many People

³⁸After leaving the synagogue that day, Jesus went to Simon's home, where he found Simon's mother-in-law very sick with a high fever. "Please heal her," everyone begged. ³⁹Standing at her bedside, he rebuked the fever, and it left her. And she got up at once and prepared a meal for them.

⁴⁰As the sun went down that evening, people throughout the village brought sick family members to Jesus. No matter what their diseases were, the touch of his hand healed every one. ⁴¹Many were possessed by demons; and the demons came out at his command, shouting, "You are the Son of God!" But because they knew he was the Messiah, he rebuked them and refused to let them speak.

Jesus Continues to Preach

⁴²Early the next morning Jesus went out to an isolated place. The crowds searched everywhere for him, and when they finally found him, they begged him not to leave them. ⁴³But he replied, "I must preach the Good News of the Kingdom of God in other towns, too, because that is why I was sent." ⁴⁴So he continued to travel around, preaching in synagogues throughout Judea.

The First Disciples

5

One day as Jesus was preaching on the shore of the Sea of Galilee, great crowds pressed in on him to listen to the word of God. ²He noticed two empty boats at the water's edge, for the fishermen had left them and were washing their nets. ³Stepping into one of the boats, Jesus asked Simon, its owner, to push it out into the water. So he sat in the boat and taught the crowds from there.

⁴When he had finished speaking, he said to Simon, "Now go out where it is deeper, and let down your nets to catch some fish."

⁵"Master," Simon replied, "we worked hard all last night and didn't catch a thing. But if you say so, I'll let the nets down again." ⁶And this time their nets were so full of fish they began to tear! ⁷A shout for help brought their partners in the other boat, and soon both boats were filled with fish and on the verge of sinking.

⁸When Simon Peter realized what had happened, he fell to his knees before Jesus and said, "Oh, Lord, please leave me—I'm too much of a sinner to be around you." ⁹For he was awestruck by the number of fish they had caught, as were the others with him. ¹⁰His partners, James and John, the sons of Zebedee, were also amazed.

Jesus replied to Simon, "Don't be afraid! From now on you'll be fishing for people!" ¹¹And as soon as they landed, they left everything and followed Jesus.

Jesus Heals a Man with Leprosy

¹²In one of the villages, Jesus met a man with an advanced case of leprosy. When the man saw Jesus, he bowed with his face to the ground, begging to be healed. "Lord," he said, "if you are willing, you can heal me and make me clean."

¹³Jesus reached out and touched him. "I am willing," he said. "Be healed!" And instantly the leprosy disappeared. ¹⁴Then Jesus instructed him not to tell anyone what had happened. He said, "Go to the priest and let him examine you. Take along the offering required in the law of Moses for those who have been healed of leprosy. This will be a public testimony that you have been cleansed."

¹⁵But despite Jesus' instructions, the report of his power spread even faster, and vast crowds came to hear him preach and to be healed of their diseases. ¹⁶But Jesus often withdrew to the wilderness for prayer.

Jesus Heals a Paralyzed Man

¹⁷One day while Jesus was teaching, some Pharisees and teachers of religious law were sitting nearby. (It seemed that these men showed up from every village in all Galilee and Judea, as well as from Jerusalem.) And the Lord's healing power was strongly with Jesus. ¹⁸Some men came carrying a paralyzed man on a sleeping mat. They tried to take him inside to Jesus, ¹⁹but they couldn't reach him because of the crowd. So they went up to the roof and took off some tiles. Then they lowered the sick man on his mat down into the crowd, right in front of Jesus. ²⁰Seeing their faith, Jesus said to the man, "Young man, your sins are forgiven."

²¹But the Pharisees and teachers of religious law said to themselves, "Who does he think he is? That's blasphemy! Only God can forgive sins!"

²²Jesus knew what they were thinking, so he asked them, "Why do you question this in your hearts? ²³Is it easier to say 'Your sins are forgiven,' or 'Stand up and walk'? ²⁴So I will prove to you that the Son of Man has the authority on earth to forgive sins." Then Jesus turned to the paralyzed man and said, "Stand up, pick up your mat, and go home!"

²⁵And immediately, as everyone watched, the man jumped up, picked up his mat, and went home praising God. ²⁶Everyone was gripped with great wonder and awe, and they praised God, exclaiming, "We have seen amazing things today!"

Jesus Calls Levi (Matthew)

²⁷Later, as Jesus left the town, he saw a tax collector named Levi sitting at his tax collector's booth. "Follow me and be my disciple," Jesus said to him. ²⁸So Levi got up, left everything, and followed him.

²⁹Later, Levi held a banquet in his home with Jesus as the guest of honor. Many of Levi's fellow tax collectors and other guests also ate with them. ³⁰But the Pharisees and their teachers of religious law complained bitterly to Jesus' disciples, "Why do you eat and drink with such scum?"

³¹Jesus answered them, "Healthy people don't need a doctor—sick people do. ³²I have come to call not those who think they are righteous, but those who know they are sinners and need to repent."

A Discussion about Fasting

³³One day some people said to Jesus, "John the Baptist's disciples fast and pray regularly, and so do the disciples of the Pharisees. Why are your disciples always eating and drinking?"

³⁴Jesus responded, "Do wedding guests fast while celebrating with the groom? Of course not. ³⁵But someday the groom will be taken away from them, and then they will fast."

³⁶Then Jesus gave them this illustration: "No one tears a piece of cloth from a new garment and uses it to patch an old garment. For then the new garment would be ruined, and the new patch wouldn't even match the old garment. ³⁷And no one puts new wine into old wineskins. For the new wine would burst the wineskins, spilling the wine and ruining the skins. ³⁸New wine must be stored in new wineskins. ³⁹But no one who drinks the old wine seems to want the new wine. 'The old is just fine,' they say."

5:24-26 WHAT'S IT SAYING?

WHAT AM I GOING TO DO ABOUT IT?

A Discussion about the Sabbath

6

One Sabbath day as Jesus was walking through some grainfields, his disciples broke off heads of grain, rubbed off the husks in their hands, and ate the grain. ²But some Pharisees said, "Why are you breaking the law by harvesting grain on the Sabbath?"

³Jesus replied, "Haven't you read in the Scriptures what David did when he and his companions were hungry? ⁴He went into the house of God and broke the law by eating the sacred

loaves of bread that only the priests can eat. He also gave some to his companions." [5]And Jesus added, "The Son of Man is Lord, even over the Sabbath."

Jesus Heals on the Sabbath

[6]On another Sabbath day, a man with a deformed right hand was in the synagogue while Jesus was teaching. [7]The teachers of religious law and the Pharisees watched Jesus closely. If he healed the man's hand, they planned to accuse him of working on the Sabbath.

[8]But Jesus knew their thoughts. He said to the man with the deformed hand, "Come and stand in front of everyone." So the man came forward. [9]Then Jesus said to his critics, "I have a question for you. Does the law permit good deeds on the Sabbath, or is it a day for doing evil? Is this a day to save life or to destroy it?"

[10]He looked around at them one by one and then said to the man, "Hold out your hand." So the man held out his hand, and it was restored! [11]At this, the enemies of Jesus were wild with rage and began to discuss what to do with him.

Jesus Chooses the Twelve Apostles

[12]One day soon afterward Jesus went up on a mountain to pray, and he prayed to God all night. [13]At daybreak he called together all of his disciples and chose twelve of them to be apostles. Here are their names:
[14]Simon (whom he named Peter),
Andrew (Peter's brother),
James,
John,
Philip,
Bartholomew,
[15]Matthew,
Thomas,
James (son of Alphaeus),
Simon (who was called the zealot),
[16]Judas (son of James),
Judas Iscariot (who later betrayed him).

STAND POINT

When you feel like cheating

6:31

Do to others as you would like them to do to you.

Crowds Follow Jesus

[17]When they came down from the mountain, the disciples stood with Jesus on a large, level area, surrounded by many of his followers and by the crowds. There were people from all over Judea and from Jerusalem and from as far north as the seacoasts of Tyre and Sidon. [18]They had come to hear him and to be healed of their diseases; and Jesus also cast out many evil spirits. [19]Everyone tried to touch him, because healing power went out from him, and he healed everyone.

The Beatitudes

[20]Then Jesus turned to his disciples and said,
"God blesses you who are poor,
for the Kingdom of God is yours.
[21]God blesses you who are hungry now,
for you will be satisfied.
God blesses you who weep now,
for in due time you will laugh.
[22]What blessings await you when people hate you and exclude you and mock you and curse you as evil because you follow the Son of Man. [23]When that happens, be happy! Yes, leap for joy! For a great reward awaits you in heaven. And remember, their ancestors treated the ancient prophets that same way.

Sorrows Foretold

[24]"What sorrow awaits you who are rich,
for you have your only happiness now.
[25]What sorrow awaits you who are fat and prosperous now,
for a time of awful hunger awaits you.
What sorrow awaits you who laugh now,
for your laughing will turn to mourning and sorrow.
[26]What sorrow awaits you who are praised by the crowds,
for their ancestors also praised false prophets.

Love for Enemies

[27]"But to you who are willing to listen, I say, love your enemies! Do good to those who hate you. [28]Bless those who curse you. Pray for those who hurt you. [29]If someone slaps you on one cheek, offer the other cheek also. If someone demands your coat, offer your shirt also. [30]Give to anyone who asks; and when things are taken away from you, don't try to get them back. [31]Do to others as you would like them to do to you. [32]"If you love only those who love you, why should you get credit for that? Even sinners love those who love them! [33]And if you do good only to those who do good to you, why should you get credit? Even sinners do that much! [34]And if you lend money only to those who can repay you, why should you get credit? Even sinners will lend to other sinners for a full return. [35]"Love your enemies! Do good to them. Lend to them without expecting to be repaid. Then your reward from heaven will be very great, and you will truly be acting as children of the Most High, for he is kind to those who are unthankful and wicked. [36]You must be compassionate, just as your Father is compassionate.

action

6:32-38 WHAT'S IT SAYING?

WHAT AM I GOING TO DO ABOUT IT?

Do Not Judge Others

[37]"Do not judge others, and you will not be judged. Do not condemn others, or it will all come back against you. Forgive others, and you will be forgiven. [38]Give, and you will receive. Your gift will return to you in full—pressed down, shaken together to make room for more, running over, and poured into your lap. The amount you give will determine the amount you get back."

[39]Then Jesus gave the following illustration: "Can one blind person lead another? Won't they both fall into a ditch? [40]Students are not greater than their teacher. But the student who is fully trained will become like the teacher.

[41]"And why worry about a speck in your friend's eye when you have a log in your own? [42]How can you think of saying, 'Friend, let me help you get rid of that speck in your eye,' when you can't see past the log in your own eye? Hypocrite! First get rid of the log in your own eye; then you will see well enough to deal with the speck in your friend's eye.

The Tree and Its Fruit

[43]"A good tree can't produce bad fruit, and a bad tree can't produce good fruit. [44]A tree is identified by its fruit. Figs never grow on thornbushes, nor grapes on bramble bushes. [45]A good person produces good things from the treasury of a good heart, and an evil person produces evil things from the treasury of an evil heart. What you say flows from what is in your heart.

Building on a Solid Foundation

[46]"So why do you keep calling me 'Lord, Lord!' when you don't do what I say? [47]I will show you what it's like when someone comes to me, listens to my teaching, and then follows it. [48]It is like a person building a house who digs deep and lays the foundation on solid rock. When the floodwaters rise and break against the house, it stands firm because it is well built. [49]But anyone who hears and doesn't obey is like a person who builds a house without a foundation. When the floods sweep down against that house, it will collapse into a heap of ruins."

The Faith of a Roman Officer

7 When Jesus had finished saying all this to the people, he returned to Capernaum. [2]At that time the highly valued slave of a Roman officer was sick and near death. [3]When the officer heard about Jesus, he sent some respected Jewish elders to ask him to come and heal his slave. [4]So they earnestly begged Jesus to help the man. "If anyone deserves your help, he does," they said, [5]"for he loves the Jewish people and even built a synagogue for us."

[6]So Jesus went with them. But just before they arrived at the house, the officer sent some friends to say, "Lord, don't trouble yourself by coming to my home, for I am not worthy of such an honor. [7]I am not even worthy to come and meet you. Just say the word from where you are, and my servant will be healed. [8]I know this because I am under the authority of my superior officers, and I have authority over my soldiers. I only need to say, 'Go,' and they go, or 'Come,' and they come. And if I say to my slaves, 'Do this,' they do it."

[9]When Jesus heard this, he was amazed. Turning to the crowd that was following him, he said, "I tell you, I haven't seen faith like this in all Israel!" [10]And when the officer's friends returned to his house, they found the slave completely healed.

Jesus Raises a Widow's Son

[11]Soon afterward Jesus went with his disciples to the village of Nain, and a large crowd followed him. [12]A funeral procession was coming out as he approached the village gate. The young man who had died was a widow's only son, and a large crowd from the village was with her. [13]When the Lord saw her, his heart overflowed with compassion. "Don't cry!" he said. [14]Then he walked over to the coffin and touched it, and the bearers stopped. "Young man," he said, "I tell you, get up." [15]Then the dead boy sat up and began to talk! And Jesus gave him back to his mother. [16]Great fear swept the crowd, and they praised God, saying, "A mighty prophet has risen among us," and "God has visited his people today." [17]And the news about Jesus spread throughout Judea and the surrounding countryside.

Jesus and John the Baptist

[18]The disciples of John the Baptist told John about everything Jesus was doing. So John called for two of his disciples, [19]and he sent them to the Lord to ask him, "Are you the Messiah we've been expecting, or should we keep looking for someone else?"

[20]John's two disciples found Jesus and said to him, "John the Baptist sent us to ask, 'Are you the Messiah we've been expecting, or should we keep looking for someone else?'"

[21]At that very time, Jesus cured many people of their diseases and illnesses, and he cast out evil spirits and restored sight to many who were blind. [22]Then he told John's disciples, "Go back to John and tell him what you have seen and heard—the blind see, the lame walk, the lepers are cured, the deaf hear, the dead are raised to life, and the Good News is being preached to the poor. [23]And tell him, 'God blesses those who do not turn away because of me.'"

[24]After John's disciples left, Jesus began talking about him to the crowds. "What kind of man did you go into the wilderness to see? Was he a weak reed, swayed by every breath of wind? [25]Or were you expecting to see a man dressed in expensive clothes? No, people who wear beautiful clothes and live in luxury are found in palaces. [26]Were you looking for a prophet? Yes, and he is more than a prophet. [27]John is the man to whom the Scriptures refer when they say,

'Look, I am sending my messenger ahead of you,
and he will prepare your way before you.'

[28]I tell you, of all who have ever lived, none is greater than John. Yet even the least person in the Kingdom of God is greater than he is!"

[29]When they heard this, all the people—even the tax collectors—agreed that God's way was right, for they had been baptized by John. [30]But the Pharisees and experts in religious law rejected God's plan for them, for they had refused John's baptism.

[31]"To what can I compare the people of this generation?" Jesus asked. "How can I describe them? [32]They are like children playing a game in the public square. They complain to their friends,

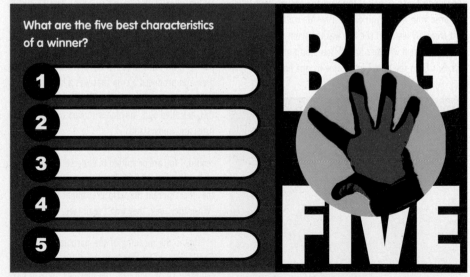

What are the five best characteristics of a winner?

1.
2.
3.
4.
5.

BIG FIVE

'We played wedding songs,
and you didn't dance,
so we played funeral songs,
and you didn't weep.'
[33]For John the Baptist didn't spend his time eating bread or drinking wine, and you say, 'He's possessed by a demon.' [34]The Son of Man, on the other hand, feasts and drinks, and you say, 'He's a glutton and a drunkard, and a friend of tax collectors and other sinners!' [35]But wisdom is shown to be right by the lives of those who follow it."

Jesus Anointed by a Sinful Woman

[36]One of the Pharisees asked Jesus to have dinner with him, so Jesus went to his home and sat down to eat. [37]When a certain immoral woman from that city heard he was eating there, she brought a beautiful alabaster jar filled with expensive perfume. [38]Then she knelt behind him at his feet, weeping. Her tears fell on his feet, and she wiped them off with her hair. Then she kept kissing his feet and putting perfume on them.

[39]When the Pharisee who had invited him saw this, he said to himself, "If this man were a prophet, he would know what kind of woman is touching him. She's a sinner!"

[40]Then Jesus answered his thoughts. "Simon," he said to the Pharisee, "I have something to say to you."

"Go ahead, Teacher," Simon replied.

[41]Then Jesus told him this story: "A man loaned money to two people—500 pieces of silver to one and 50 pieces to the other. [42]But neither of them could repay him, so he kindly forgave them both, canceling their debts. Who do you suppose loved him more after that?"

[43]Simon answered, "I suppose the one for whom he canceled the larger debt."

"That's right," Jesus said. [44]Then he turned to the woman and said to Simon, "Look at this woman kneeling here. When I entered your home, you didn't offer me water to wash the dust from my feet, but she has washed them with her tears and wiped them with her hair. [45]You didn't greet me with a kiss, but from the time I first came in, she has not stopped

kissing my feet. [46]You neglected the courtesy of olive oil to anoint my head, but she has anointed my feet with rare perfume.

[47]"I tell you, her sins—and they are many—have been forgiven, so she has shown me much love. But a person who is forgiven little shows only little love." [48]Then Jesus said to the woman, "Your sins are forgiven."

[49]The men at the table said among themselves, "Who is this man, that he goes around forgiving sins?"

[50]And Jesus said to the woman, "Your faith has saved you; go in peace."

Women Who Followed Jesus

8

Soon afterward Jesus began a tour of the nearby towns and villages, preaching and announcing the Good News about the Kingdom of God. He took his twelve disciples with him, [2]along with some women he had healed and from whom he had cast out evil spirits. Among them were Mary Magdalene, from whom he had cast out seven demons; [3]Joanna, the wife of Chuza, Herod's business manager; Susanna; and many others who were contributing their own resources to support Jesus and his disciples.

Parable of the Farmer Scattering Seed

[4]One day Jesus told a story to a large crowd that had gathered from many towns to hear him: [5]"A farmer went out to plant his seed. As he scattered it across his field, some seed fell on a footpath, where it was stepped on, and the birds ate it. [6]Other seed fell among rocks. It began to grow, but the plant soon wilted and died for lack of moisture. [7]Other seed fell among thorns that grew up with it and choked out the tender plants. [8]Still other seed fell on fertile soil. This seed grew and produced a crop that was a hundred times as much as had been planted!" When he had said this, he called out, "Anyone with ears to hear should listen and understand."

[9]His disciples asked him what this parable meant. [10]He replied, "You are permitted to understand the secrets of the Kingdom of God. But I use parables to teach the others so that the Scriptures might be fulfilled:
'When they look, they won't really see.
When they hear, they won't understand.'
[11]"This is the meaning of the parable: The seed is God's word. [12]The seeds that fell on the footpath represent those who hear the message, only to have

the devil come and take it away from their hearts and prevent them from believing and being saved. [13]The seeds on the rocky soil represent those who hear the message and receive it with joy. But since they don't have deep roots, they believe for a while, then they fall away when they face temptation. [14]The seeds that fell among the thorns represent those who hear the message, but all too quickly the message is crowded out by the cares and riches and pleasures of this life. And so they never grow into maturity. [15]And the seeds that fell on the good soil represent honest, good-hearted people who hear God's word, cling to it, and patiently produce a huge harvest.

action

8:4-15 WHAT'S IT SAYING?

WHAT AM I GOING TO DO ABOUT IT?

Parable of the Lamp

[16]"No one lights a lamp and then covers it with a bowl or hides it under a bed. A lamp is placed on a stand, where its light can be seen by all who enter the house. [17]For all that is secret will eventually be brought into the open, and everything that is concealed will be brought to light and made known to all.

[18]"So pay attention to how you hear. To those who listen to my teaching, more understanding will be given. But for those who are not listening, even what they think they understand will be taken away from them."

In 1970, 127 runners ran the New York Marathon. In 2000, over 32,000 did.

The True Family of Jesus

[19]Then Jesus' mother and brothers came to see him, but they couldn't get to him because of the crowd. [20]Someone told Jesus, "Your mother and your brothers are outside, and they want to see you."

[21]Jesus replied, "My mother and my brothers are all those who hear God's word and obey it."

Jesus Calms the Storm

[22]One day Jesus said to his disciples, "Let's cross to the other side of the lake." So they got into a boat and started out. [23]As they sailed across, Jesus settled down for a nap. But soon a fierce storm came down on the lake. The boat was filling with water, and they were in real danger.

[24]The disciples went and woke him up, shouting, "Master, Master, we're going to drown!"

When Jesus woke up, he rebuked the wind and the raging waves. The storm stopped and all was calm! [25]Then he asked them, "Where is your faith?"

The disciples were terrified and amazed. "Who is this man?" they asked each other. "When he gives a command, even the wind and waves obey him!"

Jesus Heals a Demon-Possessed Man

[26]So they arrived in the region of the Gerasenes, across the lake from Galilee. [27]As Jesus was climbing out of

Bible

The Bible was originally written in three languages – Hebrew, Aramaic, & Greek.

the boat, a man who was possessed by demons came out to meet him. For a long time he had been homeless and naked, living in a cemetery outside the town. [28]As soon as he saw Jesus, he shrieked and fell down in front of him. Then he screamed, "Why are you interfering with me, Jesus, Son of the Most High God? Please, I beg you, don't torture me!" [29]For Jesus had already commanded the evil spirit to come out of him. This spirit had often taken control of the man. Even when he was placed under guard and put in chains and shackles, he simply broke them and rushed out into the wilderness, completely under the demon's power.

[30]Jesus demanded, "What is your name?"

"Legion," he replied, for he was filled with many demons. [31]The demons kept begging Jesus not to send them into the bottomless pit.

[32]There happened to be a large herd of pigs feeding on the hillside nearby, and the demons begged him to let them enter into the pigs.

So Jesus gave them permission. [33]Then the demons came out of the man and entered the pigs, and the entire herd plunged down the steep hillside into the lake and drowned.

[34]When the herdsmen saw it, they fled to the nearby town and the surrounding countryside, spreading the news as they ran. [35]People rushed out to see what had happened. A crowd soon gathered around Jesus, and they saw the man who had been freed from the demons. He was sitting at Jesus' feet, fully clothed and perfectly sane, and they were all afraid. [36]Then those who had seen what happened told the others how the demon-possessed man had been healed. [37]And all the people in the region of the Gerasenes begged Jesus to go away and leave them alone, for a great wave of fear swept over them.

So Jesus returned to the boat and left, crossing back to the other side of the lake. [38]The man who had been freed from the demons begged to go with him. But Jesus sent him home, saying, [39]"No, go back to your family, and tell them everything God has done for you." So he went all through the town proclaiming the great things Jesus had done for him.

Jesus Heals in Response to Faith

[40]On the other side of the lake the crowds welcomed Jesus, because they had been waiting for him. [41]Then a man named Jairus, a leader of the local synagogue, came and fell at Jesus' feet, pleading with him to come home with him. [42]His only daughter, who was twelve years old, was dying.

As Jesus went with him, he was surrounded by the crowds. [43]A woman in the crowd had suffered for twelve years with constant bleeding, and she could find no cure. [44]Coming up behind Jesus, she touched the fringe of his robe. Immediately, the bleeding stopped.

[45]"Who touched me?" Jesus asked.

Everyone denied it, and Peter said, "Master, this whole crowd is pressing up against you."

[46]But Jesus said, "Someone deliberately touched me, for I felt healing power go out from me." [47]When the woman realized that she could not stay hidden, she began to tremble and fell to her knees before him. The whole crowd heard her explain why she had touched him and that she had been immediately healed. [48]"Daughter," he said to her, "your faith has made you well. Go in peace."

[49]While he was still speaking to her, a messenger arrived from the home of Jairus, the leader of the synagogue. He told him, "Your daughter is dead. There's no use troubling the Teacher now."

[50]But when Jesus heard what had happened, he said to Jairus, "Don't be afraid. Just have faith, and she will be healed."

[51]When they arrived at the house, Jesus wouldn't let anyone go in with him except Peter, John, James, and the little girl's father and mother. [52]The house was filled with people weeping and wailing, but he said, "Stop the weeping! She isn't dead; she's only asleep."

[53]But the crowd laughed at him because they all knew she had died. [54]Then Jesus took her by the hand and said in a loud voice, "My child, get up!" [55]And at that moment her life returned, and she immediately stood up! Then Jesus told them to give her something to eat. [56]Her parents were overwhelmed, but Jesus insisted that they not tell anyone what had happened.

Jesus Sends Out the Twelve Disciples

9

One day Jesus called together his twelve disciples and gave them power and authority to cast out demons and to heal all diseases. [2]Then he sent them out to tell everyone about the Kingdom of God and to heal the sick. [3]"Take nothing for your journey," he instructed them. "Don't take a walking stick, a traveler's bag, food, money, or even a change of clothes. [4]Wherever you go, stay in the same house until you leave town. [5]And if a town refuses to welcome you, shake its dust from your feet as you leave to show that you have abandoned those people to their fate."

[6]So they began their circuit of the villages, preaching the Good News and healing the sick.

Herod's Confusion

[7]When Herod Antipas, the ruler of Galilee, heard about everything Jesus was doing, he was puzzled. Some were saying that John the Baptist had been raised from the dead. [8]Others thought Jesus was Elijah or one of the other prophets risen from the dead.

[9]"I beheaded John," Herod said, "so who is this man about whom I hear such stories?" And he kept trying to see him.

Jesus Feeds Five Thousand

[10]When the apostles returned, they told Jesus everything they had done. Then he slipped quietly away with them toward the town of Bethsaida. [11]But the crowds found out where he was going, and they followed him. He welcomed them and taught them about the Kingdom of God, and he healed those who were sick.

[12]Late in the afternoon the twelve disciples came to him and said, "Send the crowds away to the nearby villages and farms, so they can find food and lodging for the night. There is nothing to eat here in this remote place."

[13]But Jesus said, "You feed them."

"But we have only five loaves of bread and two fish," they answered. "Or are you expecting us to go and buy enough food for this whole crowd?" [14]For there were about 5,000 men there.

Jesus replied, "Tell them to sit down in groups of about fifty each." [15]So the people all sat down. [16]Jesus took the five loaves and two fish, looked up toward heaven, and blessed them. Then, breaking the loaves into pieces, he kept giving the bread and fish to the disciples so they could distribute it to the people. [17]They all ate as much as they wanted, and afterward, the disciples picked up twelve baskets of leftovers!

Peter's Declaration about Jesus

[18]One day Jesus left the crowds to pray alone. Only his disciples were with him, and he asked them, "Who do people say I am?"

[19]"Well," they replied, "some say John the Baptist, some say Elijah, and others say you are one of the other ancient prophets risen from the dead."

[20]Then he asked them, "But who do you say I am?" Peter replied, "You are the Messiah sent from God!"

Jesus Predicts His Death

[21]Jesus warned his disciples not to tell anyone who he was. [22]"The Son of Man must suffer many terrible things," he said. "He will be rejected by the elders,

Winners stay in the zone!

Great athletes stay in control; they can keep their cool under pressure. You may remember watching an athlete throw a tantrum, but if you watch closely, you will realize that the majority of professional sports are played with discipline and control. For the best athletes to win, they need to stay focused and master their emotions. God's Spirit will keep you in his zone and under control. Stay in the zone — in the Spirit!

"The Holy Spirit produces this kind of fruit in our lives: love, joy, peace, patience, kindness, goodness, faithfulness, gentleness, and self-control." (Galatians 5:22-23)

Winners stay focused!

the leading priests, and the teachers of religious law. He will be killed, but on the third day he will be raised from the dead."

²³Then he said to the crowd, "If any of you wants to be my follower, you must turn from your selfish ways, take up your cross daily, and follow me. ²⁴If you try to hang on to your life, you will lose it. But if you give up your life for my sake, you will save it. ²⁵And what do you benefit if you gain the whole world but are yourself lost or destroyed? ²⁶If anyone is ashamed of me and my message, the Son of Man will be ashamed of that person when he returns in his glory and in the glory of the Father and the holy angels. ²⁷I tell you the truth, some standing here right now will not die before they see the Kingdom of God."

The Transfiguration

²⁸About eight days later Jesus took Peter, James, and John up on a mountain to pray. ²⁹And as he was praying, the appearance of his face was transformed, and his clothes became dazzling white. ³⁰Then two men, Moses and Elijah, appeared and began talking with Jesus. ³¹They were glorious to see. And they were speaking about his exodus from this world, which was about to be fulfilled in Jerusalem.

³²Peter and the others had fallen asleep. When they woke up, they saw Jesus' glory and the two men

standing with him. ³³As Moses and Elijah were starting to leave, Peter, not even knowing what he was saying, blurted out, "Master, it's wonderful for us to be here! Let's make three shelters as memorials—one for you, one for Moses, and one for Elijah." ³⁴But even as he was saying this, a cloud came over them, and terror gripped them as the cloud covered them.

³⁵Then a voice from the cloud said, "This is my Son, my Chosen One. Listen to him." ³⁶When the voice finished, Jesus was there alone. They didn't tell anyone at that time what they had seen.

Jesus Heals a Demon-Possessed Boy

³⁷The next day, after they had come down the mountain, a large crowd met Jesus. ³⁸A man in the crowd called out to him, "Teacher, I beg you to look at my son, my only child. ³⁹An evil spirit keeps seizing him, making him scream. It throws him into convulsions so that he foams at the mouth. It batters him and hardly ever leaves him alone. ⁴⁰I begged your disciples to cast out the spirit, but they couldn't do it."

⁴¹"You faithless and corrupt people," Jesus said, "how long must I be with you and put up with you?" Then he said to the man, "Bring your son here."

⁴²As the boy came forward, the demon knocked him

to the ground and threw him into a violent convulsion. But Jesus rebuked the evil spirit and healed the boy. Then he gave him back to his father. ⁴³Awe gripped the people as they saw this majestic display of God's power.

Jesus Again Predicts His Death

While everyone was marveling at everything he was doing, Jesus said to his disciples, ⁴⁴"Listen to me and remember what I say. The Son of Man is going to be betrayed into the hands of his enemies." ⁴⁵But they didn't know what he meant. Its significance was hidden from them, so they couldn't understand it, and they were afraid to ask him about it.

The Greatest in the Kingdom

⁴⁶Then his disciples began arguing about which of them was the greatest. ⁴⁷But Jesus knew their thoughts, so he brought a little child to his side. ⁴⁸Then he said to them, "Anyone who welcomes a little child like this on my behalf welcomes me, and anyone who welcomes me also welcomes my Father who sent me. Whoever is the least among you is the greatest."

Using the Name of Jesus

⁴⁹John said to Jesus, "Master, we saw someone using your name to cast out demons, but we told him to stop because he isn't in our group."

⁵⁰But Jesus said, "Don't stop him! Anyone who is not against you is for you."

Did Jesus really rise from the dead?

Nobody could have stolen Jesus' body, as it was guarded by soldiers and a heavy boulder. Once risen, he appeared to many eyewitnesses (1 Corinthians 15:4-8), including 500 at once – they couldn't all have been hallucinating. What is most convincing is that many of these same witnesses were later willing to be tortured and die for their belief that Jesus was resurrected; no one withdrew their faith!

Opposition from Samaritans

[51]As the time drew near for him to ascend to heaven, Jesus resolutely set out for Jerusalem. [52]He sent messengers ahead to a Samaritan village to prepare for his arrival. [53]But the people of the village did not welcome Jesus because he was on his way to Jerusalem. [54]When James and John saw this, they said to Jesus, "Lord, should we call down fire from heaven to burn them up?" [55]But Jesus turned and rebuked them.[*] [56]So they went on to another village.

The Cost of Following Jesus

[57]As they were walking along, someone said to Jesus, "I will follow you wherever you go."

[58]But Jesus replied, "Foxes have dens to live in, and birds have nests, but the Son of Man has no place even to lay his head."

[59]He said to another person, "Come, follow me."

The man agreed, but he said, "Lord, first let me return home and bury my father."

[60]But Jesus told him, "Let the spiritually dead bury their own dead! Your duty is to go and preach about the Kingdom of God."

[61]Another said, "Yes, Lord, I will follow you, but first let me say good-bye to my family."

[62]But Jesus told him, "Anyone who puts a hand to the plow and then looks back is not fit for the Kingdom of God."

Jesus Sends Out His Disciples

10

The Lord now chose seventy-two other disciples and sent them ahead in pairs to all the towns and places he planned to visit. [2]These were his instructions to them: "The harvest is great, but the workers are few. So pray to the Lord who is in charge of the harvest; ask him to send more workers into his fields. [3]Now go, and remember that I am sending you out as lambs among wolves. [4]Don't take any money with you, nor a traveler's bag, nor an extra pair of sandals. And don't stop to greet anyone on the road.

[5]"Whenever you enter someone's home, first say, 'May God's peace be on this house.' [6]If those who live there are peaceful, the blessing will stand; if they are not, the blessing will return to you. [7]Don't move around from home to home. Stay in one place, eating and drinking what they provide. Don't hesitate to accept hospitality, because those who work deserve their pay.

[8]"If you enter a town and it welcomes you, eat whatever is set before you. [9]Heal the sick, and tell them, 'The Kingdom of God is near you now.' [10]But if a town refuses to welcome you, go out into its streets and say, [11]'We wipe even the dust of your town from our feet to show that we have abandoned you to your fate. And know this—the Kingdom of God is near!' [12]I assure you, even wicked Sodom will be better off than such a town on judgment day.

[13]"What sorrow awaits you, Korazin and Bethsaida! For if the miracles I did in you had been done in wicked Tyre and Sidon, their people would have repented of their sins long ago, clothing themselves in burlap and throwing ashes on their heads to show their remorse. [14]Yes, Tyre and Sidon will be better off on judgment day than you. [15]And you people of Capernaum, will you be honored in heaven? No, you will go down to the place of the dead."

[16]Then he said to the disciples, "Anyone who accepts your message is also accepting me. And anyone who rejects you is rejecting me. And anyone who rejects me is rejecting God, who sent me."

[17]When the seventy-two disciples returned, they joyfully reported to him, "Lord, even the demons obey us when we use your name!"

[18]"Yes," he told them, "I saw Satan fall from heaven like lightning! [19]Look, I have given you authority over all the power of the enemy, and you can walk among snakes and scorpions and crush them. Nothing will injure you. [20]But don't rejoice because evil spirits obey you; rejoice because your names are registered in heaven."

Jesus' Prayer of Thanksgiving

[21]At that same time Jesus was filled with the joy of the Holy Spirit, and he said, "O Father, Lord of heaven and earth, thank you for hiding these things from those who think themselves wise and clever, and for revealing them to the childlike. Yes, Father, it pleased you to do it this way.

[22]"My Father has entrusted everything to me. No one truly knows the Son except the Father, and no one truly knows the Father except the Son and those to whom the Son chooses to reveal him."

[23]Then when they were alone, he turned to the disciples and said, "Blessed are the eyes that see what you have seen. [24]I tell you, many prophets and kings longed to see what you see, but they didn't see it. And they longed to hear what you hear, but they didn't hear it."

The Most Important Commandment

[25]One day an expert in religious law stood up to test Jesus by asking him this question: "Teacher, what should I do to inherit eternal life?"

[26]Jesus replied, "What does the law of Moses say? How do you read it?"

[27]The man answered, "'You must love the LORD your God with all your heart, all your soul, all your strength, and all your mind.' And, 'Love your neighbor as yourself.'"

[28]"Right!" Jesus told him. "Do this and you will live!"

[29]The man wanted to justify his actions, so he asked Jesus, "And who is my neighbor?"

Parable of the Good Samaritan

[30]Jesus replied with a story: "A Jewish man was traveling on a trip from Jerusalem to Jericho, and he was attacked by bandits. They stripped him of his clothes, beat him up, and left him half dead beside the road.

[31]"By chance a priest came along. But when he saw the man lying there, he crossed to the other side of the road and passed him by. [32]A Temple assistant walked over and looked at him lying there, but he also passed by on the other side.

[33]"Then a despised Samaritan came along, and when he saw the man, he felt compassion for him. [34]Going over to him, the Samaritan soothed his wounds with olive oil and wine and bandaged them. Then he put the man on his own donkey and took him to an inn,

Put It into Practice (LUKE 11:17–28)
It is time to choose the winning team – and the captain of that team is the Lord Jesus Christ. Always training and never playing makes a sport pretty boring, and the same is true in the Christian faith. You have been training – now is the time to play. USE YOUR WEAPONRY. When it is your turn to bat you don't leave your bat in the dugout! Well don't forget in the spiritual battle, our offensive weapon is the Word of God, the Bible. As we hear and obey the Bible, we experience God's blessing (verse 28). It is not just hearing – it is putting what we hear into action!

9:55 Some manuscripts add *And he said, "You don't realize what your hearts are like.* [56]*For the Son of Man has not come to destroy people's lives, but to save them."*

where he took care of him. ³⁵The next day he handed the innkeeper two silver coins, telling him, 'Take care of this man. If his bill runs higher than this, I'll pay you the next time I'm here.'

³⁶"Now which of these three would you say was a neighbor to the man who was attacked by bandits?" Jesus asked.

³⁷The man replied, "The one who showed him mercy." Then Jesus said, "Yes, now go and do the same."

Jesus Visits Martha and Mary

³⁸As Jesus and the disciples continued on their way to Jerusalem, they came to a certain village where a woman named Martha welcomed them into her home. ³⁹Her sister, Mary, sat at the Lord's feet, listening to what he taught. ⁴⁰But Martha was distracted by the big dinner she was preparing. She came to Jesus and said, "Lord, doesn't it seem unfair to you that my sister just sits here while I do all the work? Tell her to come and help me."

⁴¹But the Lord said to her, "My dear Martha, you are worried and upset over all these details! ⁴²There is only one thing worth being concerned about. Mary has discovered it, and it will not be taken away from her."

11:27-28 WHAT'S IT SAYING?

WHAT AM I GOING TO DO ABOUT IT?

Teaching about Prayer

11

Once Jesus was in a certain place praying. As he finished, one of his disciples came to him and said, "Lord, teach us to pray, just as John taught his disciples."

²Jesus said, "This is how you should pray:
"Father, may your name be kept holy.
May your Kingdom come soon.
³Give us each day the food we need,
⁴and forgive us our sins,
as we forgive those who sin against us.
And don't let us yield to temptation."

⁵Then, teaching them more about prayer, he used this story: "Suppose you went to a friend's house at midnight, wanting to borrow three loaves of bread. You say to him, ⁶'A friend of mine has just arrived for a visit, and I have nothing for him to eat.' ⁷And suppose he calls out from his bedroom, 'Don't bother me. The door is locked for the night, and my family and I are all in bed. I can't help you.' ⁸But I tell you this—though he won't do it for friendship's sake, if you keep knocking long enough, he will get up and give you whatever you need because of your shameless persistence.

⁹"And so I tell you, keep on asking, and you will receive what you ask for. Keep on seeking, and you will find. Keep on knocking, and the door will be opened to you. ¹⁰For everyone who asks, receives. Everyone who seeks, finds. And to everyone who knocks, the door will be opened.

¹¹"You fathers—if your children ask for a fish, do you give them a snake instead? ¹²Or if they ask for an egg, do you give them a scorpion? Of course not! ¹³So if you sinful people know how to give good gifts to your children, how much more will your heavenly Father give the Holy Spirit to those who ask him."

Jesus and the Prince of Demons

¹⁴One day Jesus cast out a demon from a man who couldn't speak, and when the demon was gone, the man began to speak. The crowds were amazed, ¹⁵but some of them said, "No wonder he can cast out demons. He gets his power from Satan, the prince of demons." ¹⁶Others, trying to test Jesus, demanded that he show them a miraculous sign from heaven to prove his authority.

¹⁷He knew their thoughts, so he said, "Any kingdom divided by civil war is doomed. A family splintered by feuding will fall apart. ¹⁸You say I am empowered by Satan. But if Satan is divided and fighting against himself, how can his kingdom survive? ¹⁹And if I am empowered by Satan, what about your own exorcists? They cast out demons, too, so they will condemn you for what you have said. ²⁰But if I am casting out demons by the power of God, then the Kingdom of God has arrived among you. ²¹For when a strong man like Satan is fully armed and guards his palace, his possessions are safe—²²until someone even stronger attacks and overpowers him, strips him of his weapons, and carries off his belongings.

²³"Anyone who isn't with me opposes me, and anyone who isn't working with me is actually working against me.

²⁴"When an evil spirit leaves a person, it goes into the desert, searching for rest. But when it finds none, it says, 'I will return to the person I came from.' ²⁵So it returns and finds that its former home is all swept and in order. ²⁶Then the spirit finds seven other spirits more evil than itself, and they all enter the person and live there. And so that person is worse off than before."

²⁷As he was speaking, a woman in the crowd called out, "God bless your mother—the womb from which you came, and the breasts that nursed you!"

²⁸Jesus replied, "But even more blessed are all who hear the word of God and put it into practice."

The Sign of Jonah

²⁹As the crowd pressed in on Jesus, he said, "This evil generation keeps asking me to show them a miraculous sign. But the only sign I will give them is the sign of Jonah. ³⁰What happened to him was a sign to the people of Nineveh that God had sent him. What happens to the Son of Man will be a sign to these people that he was sent by God.

³¹"The queen of Sheba will stand up against this generation on judgment day and condemn it, for she came from a distant land to hear the wisdom of Solomon. Now someone greater than Solomon is here—but you refuse to listen. ³²The people of Nineveh will also stand up against this generation on judgment day and condemn it, for they repented of their sins at the preaching of Jonah. Now someone greater than Jonah is here—but you refuse to repent.

Receiving the Light

³³"No one lights a lamp and then hides it or puts it under a basket. Instead, a lamp is placed on a stand, where its light can be seen by all who enter the house.

³⁴"Your eye is a lamp that provides light for your body. When your eye is good, your whole body is filled with light. But when it is bad, your body is filled with darkness. ³⁵Make sure that the light you think you have is not actually darkness. ³⁶If you are filled with light, with no dark corners, then your

whole life will be radiant, as though a floodlight were filling you with light."

Jesus Criticizes the Religious Leaders

[37]As Jesus was speaking, one of the Pharisees invited him home for a meal. So he went in and took his place at the table. [38]His host was amazed to see that he sat down to eat without first performing the hand-washing ceremony required by Jewish custom. [39]Then the Lord said to him, "You Pharisees are so careful to clean the outside of the cup and the dish, but inside you are filthy—full of greed and wickedness! [40]Fools! Didn't God make the inside as well as the outside? [41]So clean the inside by giving gifts to the poor, and you will be clean all over.

[42]"What sorrow awaits you Pharisees! For you are careful to tithe even the tiniest income from your herb gardens, but you ignore justice and the love of God. You should tithe, yes, but do not neglect the more important things.

[43]"What sorrow awaits you Pharisees! For you love to sit in the seats of honor in the synagogues and receive respectful greetings as you walk in the marketplaces. [44]Yes, what sorrow awaits you! For you are like hidden graves in a field. People walk over them without knowing the corruption they are stepping on."

[45]"Teacher," said an expert in religious law, "you have insulted us, too, in what you just said."

[46]"Yes," said Jesus, "what sorrow also awaits you experts in religious law! For you crush people with impossible religious demands, and you never lift a finger to ease the burden. [47]What sorrow awaits you! For you build monuments for the prophets your own ancestors killed long ago. [48]But in fact, you stand as witnesses who agree with what your ancestors did. They killed the prophets, and you join in their crime by building the monuments! [49]This is what God in his wisdom said about you: 'I will send prophets and apostles to them, but they will kill some and persecute the others.'

[50]"As a result, this generation will be held responsible for the murder of all God's prophets from the creation of the world—[51]from the murder of Abel to the murder of Zechariah, who was killed between the altar and the sanctuary. Yes, it will certainly be charged against this generation.

[52]"What sorrow awaits you experts in religious law! For you remove the key to knowledge from the people. You don't enter the Kingdom yourselves, and you prevent others from entering."

[53]As Jesus was leaving, the teachers of religious law and the Pharisees became hostile and tried to provoke him with many questions. [54]They wanted to trap him into saying something they could use against him.

A Warning against Hypocrisy

12

Meanwhile, the crowds grew until thousands were milling about and stepping on each other. Jesus turned first to his disciples and warned them, "Beware of the yeast of the Pharisees—their hypocrisy. [2]The time is coming when everything that is covered up will be revealed, and all that is secret will be made known to all. [3]Whatever you have said in the dark will be heard in the light, and what you have whispered behind closed doors will be shouted from the housetops for all to hear!

[4]"Dear friends, don't be afraid of those who want to kill your body; they cannot do any more to you after that. [5]But I'll tell you whom to fear. Fear God, who has the power to kill you and then throw you into hell. Yes, he's the one to fear.

[6]"What is the price of five sparrows—two copper coins? Yet God does not forget a single one of them. [7]And the very hairs on your head are all numbered. So don't be afraid; you are more valuable to God than a whole flock of sparrows.

[8]"I tell you the truth, everyone who acknowledges me publicly here on earth, the Son of Man will also acknowledge in the presence of God's angels. [9]But anyone who denies me here on earth will be denied before God's angels. [10]Anyone who speaks against the Son of Man can be forgiven, but anyone who blasphemes the Holy Spirit will not be forgiven.

[11]"And when you are brought to trial in the synagogues and before rulers and authorities, don't worry about how to defend yourself or what to say, [12]for the Holy Spirit will teach you at that time what needs to be said."

Parable of the Rich Fool

[13]Then someone called from the crowd, "Teacher, please tell my brother to divide our father's estate with me."

[14]Jesus replied, "Friend, who made me a judge over you to decide such things as that?" [15]Then he said, "Beware! Guard against every kind of greed. Life is not measured by how much you own."

[16]Then he told them a story: "A rich man had a fertile farm that produced fine crops. [17]He said to himself, 'What should I do? I don't have room for all my crops.' [18]Then he said, 'I know! I'll tear down my barns and build bigger ones. Then I'll have room enough to store all my wheat and other goods. [19]And I'll sit back and say to myself, "My friend, you have enough stored away for years to come. Now take it easy! Eat, drink, and be merry!"'

[20]"But God said to him, 'You fool! You will die this very night. Then who will get everything you worked for?'

[21]"Yes, a person is a fool to store up earthly wealth but not have a rich relationship with God."

Teaching about Money and Possessions

[22]Then, turning to his disciples, Jesus said, "That is

count on it

You don't have to be good to go to God!
Have you ever felt like you were too messed up to meet with God? Have you ever felt some strange resistance keeping you from praying or reading your Bible? Did you ever feel you had to somehow get your life straight before you could live the Christian life? Don't worry about it! Jesus came to help you in your trouble. He is the great doctor. Go to him with your problems. Not going to him is like waiting until you are cured of a deadly disease before you go to a doctor. Jesus came to help! "Healthy people don't need a doctor – sick people do. I have come to call not those who think they are righteous, but those who know they are sinners." (Mark 2:17)
Count on it!

why I tell you not to worry about everyday life—whether you have enough food to eat or enough clothes to wear. ²³For life is more than food, and your body more than clothing. ²⁴Look at the ravens. They don't plant or harvest or store food in barns, for God feeds them. And you are far more valuable to him than any birds! ²⁵Can all your worries add a single moment to your life? ²⁶And if worry can't accomplish a little thing like that, what's the use of worrying over bigger things?

²⁷"Look at the lilies and how they grow. They don't work or make their clothing, yet Solomon in all his glory was not dressed as beautifully as they are. ²⁸And if God cares so wonderfully for flowers that are here today and thrown into the fire tomorrow, he will certainly care for you. Why do you have so little faith? ²⁹"And don't be concerned about what to eat and what to drink. Don't worry about such things. ³⁰These things dominate the thoughts of unbelievers all over the world, but your Father already knows your needs. ³¹Seek the Kingdom of God above all else, and he will give you everything you need.

³²"So don't be afraid, little flock. For it gives your Father great happiness to give you the Kingdom.

³³"Sell your possessions and give to those in need. This will store up treasure for you in heaven! And the purses of heaven never get old or develop holes. Your treasure will be safe; no thief can steal it and no moth can destroy it. ³⁴Wherever your treasure is, there the desires of your heart will also be.

Be Ready for the Lord's Coming

³⁵"Be dressed for service and keep your lamps burning, ³⁶as though you were waiting for your master to return from the wedding feast. Then you will be ready to open the door and let him in the moment he arrives and knocks. ³⁷The servants who are ready and waiting for his return will be rewarded. I tell you the truth, he himself will seat them, put on an apron, and serve them as they sit and eat! ³⁸He may come in the middle of the night or just before dawn. But whenever he comes, he will reward the servants who are ready.

³⁹"Understand this: If a homeowner knew exactly when a burglar was coming, he would not permit his house to be broken into. ⁴⁰You also must be ready all the time, for the Son of Man will come when least expected."

⁴¹Peter asked, "Lord, is that illustration just for us or for everyone?"

⁴²And the Lord replied, "A faithful, sensible servant is one to whom the master can give the responsibility of managing his other household servants and feeding them. ⁴³If the master returns and finds that the servant has done a good job, there will be a reward. ⁴⁴I tell you the truth, the master will put that servant in charge of all he owns. ⁴⁵But what if the servant thinks, 'My master won't be back for a while,' and he begins beating the other servants, partying, and getting drunk? ⁴⁶The master will return unannounced and unexpected, and he will cut the servant in pieces and banish him with the unfaithful.

⁴⁷"And a servant who knows what the master wants, but isn't prepared and doesn't carry out those instructions, will be severely punished. ⁴⁸But someone who does not know, and then does something wrong, will be punished only lightly. When someone has been given much, much will be required in return; and when someone has been entrusted with much, even more will be required.

Jesus Causes Division

⁴⁹"I have come to set the world on fire, and I wish it were already burning! ⁵⁰I have a terrible baptism of suffering ahead of me, and I am under a heavy burden until it is accomplished. ⁵¹Do you think I have come to bring peace to the earth? No, I have come to divide people against each other! ⁵²From now on families will be split apart, three in favor of me, and two against—or two in favor and three against.

⁵³'Father will be divided against son
and son against father;
mother against daughter
and daughter against mother;
and mother-in-law against daughter-in-law
and daughter-in-law against mother-in-law.'"

⁵⁴Then Jesus turned to the crowd and said, "When you see clouds beginning to form in the west, you say, 'Here comes a shower.' And you are right. ⁵⁵When the south wind blows, you say, 'Today will be a scorcher.' And it is. ⁵⁶You fools! You know how to interpret the weather signs of the earth and sky, but you don't know how to interpret the present times.

⁵⁷"Why can't you decide for yourselves what is right? ⁵⁸When you are on the way to court with your accuser, try to settle the matter before you get there. Otherwise, your accuser may drag you before the judge, who will hand you over to an officer, who will throw you into prison. ⁵⁹And if that happens, you won't be free again until you have paid the very last penny."

A Call to Repentance

13

About this time Jesus was informed that Pilate had murdered some people from Galilee as they were offering sacrifices at the Temple. ²"Do you think those Galileans were worse sinners than all the other people from Galilee?" Jesus asked. "Is that why they suffered? ³Not at all! And you will perish, too, unless you repent of your sins and turn to God. ⁴And what about the eighteen people who died when the tower in Siloam fell on them? Were they the worst sinners in Jerusalem? ⁵No, and I tell you again that unless you repent, you will perish, too."

Parable of the Barren Fig Tree

⁶Then Jesus told this story: "A man planted a fig tree in his garden and came again and again to see if there was any fruit on it, but he was always disappointed. ⁷Finally, he said to his gardener, 'I've waited three years, and there hasn't been a single fig! Cut it down. It's just taking up space in the garden.'

⁸"The gardener answered, 'Sir, give it one more chance. Leave it another year, and I'll give it special attention and plenty of fertilizer. ⁹If we get figs next year, fine. If not, then you can cut it down.'"

Jesus Heals on the Sabbath

¹⁰One Sabbath day as Jesus was teaching in a synagogue, ¹¹he saw a woman who had been crippled by an evil spirit. She had been bent double for eighteen years and was unable to stand up straight. ¹²When Jesus saw her, he called her over and said, "Dear woman, you are healed of your sickness!" ¹³Then he touched her, and instantly she could stand straight. How she praised God!

¹⁴But the leader in charge of the synagogue was indignant that Jesus had healed her on the Sabbath day. "There are six days of the week for working," he said to the crowd. "Come on those days to be healed, not on the Sabbath."

¹⁵But the Lord replied, "You hypocrites! Each of you works on the Sabbath day! Don't you untie your ox or your donkey from its stall on the Sabbath and lead it out for water? ¹⁶This dear woman, a daughter of Abraham, has been held in bondage by Satan for eighteen years. Isn't it right that she be released, even on the Sabbath?"

¹⁷This shamed his enemies, but all the people rejoiced at the wonderful things he did.

Parable of the Mustard Seed

¹⁸Then Jesus said, "What is the Kingdom of God like? How can I illustrate it? ¹⁹It is like a tiny mustard seed that a man planted in a garden; it grows and becomes a tree, and the birds make nests in its branches."

Parable of the Yeast

²⁰He also asked, "What else is the Kingdom of God like? ²¹It is like the yeast a woman used in making bread. Even though she put only a little yeast in three measures of flour, it permeated every part of the dough."

action

13:22-28 WHAT'S IT SAYING?

WHAT AM I GOING TO DO ABOUT IT?

The Narrow Door

²²Jesus went through the towns and villages, teaching as he went, always pressing on toward Jerusalem. ²³Someone asked him, "Lord, will only a few be saved?"

He replied, ²⁴"Work hard to enter the narrow door to God's Kingdom, for many will try to enter but will fail. ²⁵When the master of the house has locked the door, it will be too late. You will stand outside knocking and pleading, 'Lord, open the door for us!' But he will reply, 'I don't know you or where you come from.' ²⁶Then you will say, 'But we ate and drank with you, and you taught in our streets.' ²⁷And he will reply, 'I tell you, I don't know you or where you come from. Get away from me, all you who do evil.'

²⁸"There will be weeping and gnashing of teeth, for you will see Abraham, Isaac, Jacob, and all the prophets in the Kingdom of God, but you will be thrown out. ²⁹And people will come from all over the world—from east and west, north and south—to take their places in the Kingdom of God. ³⁰And note this: Some who seem least important now will be the greatest then, and some who are the greatest now will be least important then."

Jesus Grieves over Jerusalem

³¹At that time some Pharisees said to him, "Get away from here if you want to live! Herod Antipas wants to kill you!"

³²Jesus replied, "Go tell that fox that I will keep on casting out demons and healing people today and tomorrow; and the third day I will accomplish my purpose. ³³Yes, today, tomorrow, and the next day I must proceed on my way. For it wouldn't do for a prophet of God to be killed except in Jerusalem!

³⁴"O Jerusalem, Jerusalem, the city that kills the prophets and stones God's messengers! How often I have wanted to gather your children together as a hen protects her chicks beneath her wings, but you wouldn't let me. ³⁵And now, look, your house is abandoned. And you will never see me again until you say, 'Blessings on the one who comes in the name of the LORD!'"

Jesus Heals on the Sabbath

14

One Sabbath day Jesus went to eat dinner in the home of a leader of the Pharisees, and the people were watching him closely. ²There was a man there whose arms and legs were swollen. ³Jesus asked the Pharisees and experts in religious law, "Is it permitted in the law to heal people on the Sabbath day, or not?" ⁴When they refused to answer, Jesus touched the sick man and healed him and sent him away. ⁵Then he turned to them and said, "Which of you doesn't work on the Sabbath? If your son or your cow falls into a pit, don't you rush to get him out?" ⁶Again they could not answer.

Jesus Teaches about Humility

⁷When Jesus noticed that all who had come to the dinner were trying to sit in the seats of honor near the head of the table, he gave them this advice: ⁸"When you are invited to a wedding feast, don't sit in the seat of honor. What if someone who is more distinguished than you has also been invited? ⁹The host will come and say, 'Give this person your seat.' Then you will be embarrassed, and you will have to take whatever seat is left at the foot of the table!

¹⁰"Instead, take the lowest place at the foot of the table. Then when your host sees you, he will come and say, 'Friend, we have a better place for you!' Then you will be honored in front of all the other guests. ¹¹For those who exalt themselves will be humbled, and those who humble themselves will be exalted."

¹²Then he turned to his host. "When you put on a luncheon or a banquet," he said, "don't invite your friends, brothers, relatives, and rich neighbors. For they will invite you back, and that will be your only reward. ¹³Instead, invite the poor, the crippled, the lame, and the blind. ¹⁴Then at the resurrection of the righteous, God will reward you for inviting those who could not repay you."

Parable of the Great Feast

¹⁵Hearing this, a man sitting at the table with Jesus exclaimed, "What a blessing it will be to attend a banquet in the Kingdom of God!"

¹⁶Jesus replied with this story: "A man prepared a great feast and sent out many invitations. ¹⁷When the banquet was ready, he sent his servant to tell the guests, 'Come, the banquet is ready.' ¹⁸But they all

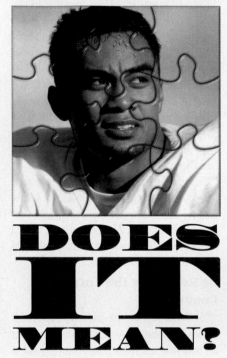

WHAT DOES IT MEAN?

angel

It can mean "messenger," but usually its unique application is to certain heavenly intelligences who God employs to carry out his management of the world. These superior beings are very numerous. As to their nature, they are spirits (Hebrews 1:14), like the soul of man, but they can take a physical form. They are possessed of superhuman intelligence and power (Mark 13:32; 2 Thessalonians 1:7). It is possible you have met an angel without realizing it (Hebrews 13:2), and angels will escort you to paradise (Luke 16:22).

began making excuses. One said, 'I have just bought a field and must inspect it. Please excuse me.' [19]Another said, 'I have just bought five pairs of oxen, and I want to try them out. Please excuse me.' [20]Another said, 'I now have a wife, so I can't come.' [21]"The servant returned and told his master what they had said. His master was furious and said, 'Go quickly into the streets and alleys of the town and invite the poor, the crippled, the blind, and the lame.' [22]After the servant had done this, he reported, 'There is still room for more.' [23]So his master said, 'Go out into the country lanes and behind the hedges and urge anyone you find to come, so that the house will be full. [24]For none of those I first invited will get even the smallest taste of my banquet.'"

14:25-30 WHAT'S IT SAYING?

WHAT AM I GOING TO DO ABOUT IT?

The Cost of Being a Disciple

[25]A large crowd was following Jesus. He turned around and said to them, [26]"If you want to be my disciple, you must hate everyone else by comparison—your father and mother, wife and children, brothers and sisters—yes, even your own life. Otherwise, you cannot be my disciple. [27]And if you do not carry your own cross and follow me, you cannot be my disciple. [28]"But don't begin until you count the cost. For who would begin construction of a building without first calculating the cost to see if there is enough money to finish it? [29]Otherwise, you might complete only the foundation before running out of money, and then everyone would laugh at you. [30]They would say, 'There's the person who started that building and couldn't afford to finish it!' [31]"Or what king would go to war against another king without first sitting down with his counselors to discuss whether his army of 10,000 could defeat the 20,000 soldiers marching against him? [32]And if he can't, he will send a delegation to discuss terms of peace while the enemy is still far away. [33]So you cannot become my disciple without giving up everything you own. [34]"Salt is good for seasoning. But if it loses its flavor, how do you make it salty again? [35]Flavorless salt is good neither for the soil nor for the manure pile. It is thrown away. Anyone with ears to hear should listen and understand!"

Parable of the Lost Sheep

15

Tax collectors and other notorious sinners often came to listen to Jesus teach. [2]This made the Pharisees and teachers of religious law complain that he was associating with such sinful people—even eating with them! [3]So Jesus told them this story: [4]"If a man has a hundred sheep and one of them gets lost, what will he do? Won't he leave the ninety-nine others in the wilderness and go to search for the one that is lost

until he finds it? [5]And when he has found it, he will joyfully carry it home on his shoulders. [6]When he arrives, he will call together his friends and neighbors, saying, 'Rejoice with me because I have found my lost sheep.' [7]In the same way, there is more joy in heaven over one lost sinner who repents and returns to God than over ninety-nine others who are righteous and haven't strayed away!

Parable of the Lost Coin

[8]"Or suppose a woman has ten silver coins and loses one. Won't she light a lamp and sweep the entire house and search carefully until she finds it? [9]And when she finds it, she will call in her friends and neighbors and say, 'Rejoice with me because I have found my lost coin.' [10]In the same way, there is joy in the presence of God's angels when even one sinner repents."

Parable of the Lost Son

[11]To illustrate the point further, Jesus told them this story: "A man had two sons. [12]The younger son told his father, 'I want my share of your estate now before you die.' So his father agreed to divide his wealth between his sons.

[13]"A few days later this younger son packed all his belongings and moved to a distant land, and there he wasted all his money in wild living. [14]About the time his money ran out, a great famine swept over the land, and he began to starve. [15]He persuaded a local farmer to hire him, and the man sent him into his fields to feed the pigs. [16]The young man became so hungry that even the pods he was feeding the pigs looked good to him. But no one gave him anything.

[17]"When he finally came to his senses, he said to himself, 'At home even the hired servants have food enough to spare, and here I am dying of hunger! [18]I will go home to my father and say, "Father, I have sinned against both heaven and you, [19]and I am no longer worthy of being called your son. Please take me on as a hired servant."'

[20]"So he returned home to his father. And while he was still a long way off, his father saw him coming. Filled with love and compassion, he ran to his son, embraced him, and kissed him. [21]His son said to him, 'Father, I have sinned against both heaven and you, and I am no longer worthy of being called your son.'

Brain Power:

The brain is able to learn a new skill, such as walking, talking, or jumping. If we practice walking often enough, then the skill becomes natural and automatic. We no longer have to think how to walk. Walking has become a skill controlled by the subconscious part of our brain. This allows us to look around, talk, and do other things controlled by the conscious part of the brain, all at the same time.

TIPS

We Have a Master (LUKE 17:5)
Jesus reminded the disciples in very graphic language that we are dependent on God. He is the Master and we are servants. The focus of our lives should not be our lack of faith, but God as the object of our faith. The servant coming in from the fields should not have his mind full of his "rights" and his "wants" but of the needs and desires of the Master.

22"But his father said to the servants, 'Quick! Bring the finest robe in the house and put it on him. Get a ring for his finger and sandals for his feet. 23And kill the calf we have been fattening. We must celebrate with a feast, 24for this son of mine was dead and has now returned to life. He was lost, but now he is found.' So the party began.

25"Meanwhile, the older son was in the fields working. When he returned home, he heard music and dancing in the house, 26and he asked one of the servants what was going on. 27'Your brother is back,' he was told, 'and your father has killed the fattened calf. We are celebrating because of his safe return.'

28"The older brother was angry and wouldn't go in. His father came out and begged him, 29but he replied, 'All these years I've slaved for you and never once refused to do a single thing you told me to. And in all that time you never gave me even one young goat for a feast with my friends. 30Yet when this son of yours comes back after squandering your money on prostitutes, you celebrate by killing the fattened calf!'

31"His father said to him, 'Look, dear son, you have always stayed by me, and everything I have is yours. 32We had to celebrate this happy day. For your brother was dead and has come back to life! He was lost, but now he is found!'"

Parable of the Shrewd Manager

16

Jesus told this story to his disciples: "There was a certain rich man who had a manager handling his affairs. One day a report came that the manager was wasting his employer's money. 2So the employer called him in and said, 'What's this I hear about you? Get your report in order, because you are going to be fired.'

3"The manager thought to himself, 'Now what? My boss has fired me. I don't have the strength to dig ditches, and I'm too proud to beg. 4Ah, I know how to ensure that I'll have plenty of friends who will give me a home when I am fired.'

5"So he invited each person who owed money to his employer to come and discuss the situation. He asked the first one, 'How much do you owe him?' 6The man replied, 'I owe him 800 gallons of olive oil.' So the manager told him, 'Take the bill and quickly change it to 400 gallons.'

7"'And how much do you owe my employer?' he asked the next man. 'I owe him 1,000 bushels of wheat,' was the reply.

'Here,' the manager said, 'take the bill and change it to 800 bushels.'

8"The rich man had to admire the dishonest rascal for being so shrewd. And it is true that the children of this world are more shrewd in dealing with the world around them than are the children of the light. 9Here's the lesson: Use your worldly resources to benefit others and make friends. Then, when your earthly possessions are gone, they will welcome you to an eternal home. 10"If you are faithful in little things, you will be faithful in large ones. But if you are dishonest in little things, you won't be honest with greater responsibilities. 11And if you are untrustworthy about worldly wealth, who will trust you with the true riches of heaven? 12And if you are not faithful with other people's things, why should you be trusted with things of your own?

13"No one can serve two masters. For you will hate one and love the other; you will be devoted to one and despise the other. You cannot serve both God and money."

14The Pharisees, who dearly loved their money, heard all this and scoffed at him. 15Then he said to them, "You like to appear righteous in public, but God knows your hearts. What this world honors is detestable in the sight of God.

16"Until John the Baptist, the law of Moses and the messages of the prophets were your guides. But now the Good News of the Kingdom of God is preached, and everyone is eager to get in. 17But that doesn't mean that the law has lost its force. It is easier for heaven and earth to disappear than for the smallest point of God's law to be overturned.

18"For example, a man who divorces his wife and marries someone else commits adultery. And anyone who marries a woman divorced from her husband commits adultery."

Parable of the Rich Man and Lazarus

19Jesus said, "There was a certain rich man who was splendidly clothed in purple and fine linen and who lived each day in luxury. 20At his gate lay a poor man

named Lazarus who was covered with sores. 21As Lazarus lay there longing for scraps from the rich man's table, the dogs would come and lick his open sores.

22"Finally, the poor man died and was carried by the angels to be with Abraham. The rich man also died and was buried, 23and his soul went to the place of the dead. There, in torment, he saw Abraham in the far distance with Lazarus at his side.

24"The rich man shouted, 'Father Abraham, have some pity! Send Lazarus over here to dip the tip of his finger in water and cool my tongue. I am in anguish in these flames.'

25"But Abraham said to him, 'Son, remember that during your lifetime you had everything you wanted, and Lazarus had nothing. So now he is here being comforted, and you are in anguish. 26And besides, there is a great chasm separating us. No one can cross over to you from here, and no one can cross over to us from there.'

27"Then the rich man said, 'Please, Father Abraham, at least send him to my father's home. 28For I have five brothers, and I want him to warn them so they don't end up in this place of torment.'

29"But Abraham said, 'Moses and the prophets have warned them. Your brothers can read what they wrote.'

30"The rich man replied, 'No, Father Abraham! But if someone is sent to them from the dead, then they will repent of their sins and turn to God.'

31"But Abraham said, 'If they won't listen to Moses and the prophets, they won't listen even if someone rises from the dead.'"

Teachings about Forgiveness and Faith

17

One day Jesus said to his disciples, "There will always be temptations to sin, but what sorrow awaits the person who does the tempting! 2It would be better to be thrown into the sea with a millstone hung around your neck than to cause one of these little ones to fall into sin. 3So watch yourselves!

"If another believer sins, rebuke that person; then if there is repentance, forgive. ⁴Even if that person wrongs you seven times a day and each time turns again and asks forgiveness, you must forgive."

⁵The apostles said to the Lord, "Show us how to increase our faith."

⁶The Lord answered, "If you had faith even as small as a mustard seed, you could say to this mulberry tree, 'May you be uprooted and thrown into the sea,' and it would obey you!

⁷"When a servant comes in from plowing or taking care of sheep, does his master say, 'Come in and eat with me'? ⁸No, he says, 'Prepare my meal, put on your apron, and serve me while I eat. Then you can eat later.' ⁹And does the master thank the servant for doing what he was told to do? Of course not. ¹⁰In the same way, when you obey me you should say, 'We are unworthy servants who have simply done our duty.'"

17:1-4 WHAT'S IT SAYING?

WHAT AM I GOING TO DO ABOUT IT?

Ten Healed of Leprosy

¹¹As Jesus continued on toward Jerusalem, he reached the border between Galilee and Samaria. ¹²As he entered a village there, ten lepers stood at a distance, ¹³crying out, "Jesus, Master, have mercy on us!"

¹⁴He looked at them and said, "Go show yourselves to the priests." And as they went, they were cleansed of their leprosy.

¹⁵One of them, when he saw that he was healed, came back to Jesus, shouting, "Praise God!" ¹⁶He fell to the ground at Jesus' feet, thanking him for what he had done. This man was a Samaritan.

¹⁷Jesus asked, "Didn't I heal ten men? Where are the other nine? ¹⁸Has no one returned to give glory to God except this foreigner?" ¹⁹And Jesus said to the man, "Stand up and go. Your faith has healed you."

The Coming of the Kingdom

²⁰One day the Pharisees asked Jesus, "When will the Kingdom of God come?"

Jesus replied, "The Kingdom of God can't be detected by visible signs. ²¹You won't be able to say, 'Here it is!' or 'It's over there!' For the Kingdom of God is already among you."

²²Then he said to his disciples, "The time is coming when you will long to see the day when the Son of Man returns, but you won't see it. ²³People will tell you, 'Look, there is the Son of Man,' or 'Here he is,' but don't go out and follow them. ²⁴For as the lightning flashes and lights up the sky from one end to the other, so it will be on the day when the Son of Man comes. ²⁵But first the Son of Man must suffer terribly and be rejected by this generation.

²⁶"When the Son of Man returns, it will be like it was in Noah's day. ²⁷In those days, the people enjoyed banquets and parties and weddings right up to the time Noah entered his boat and the flood came and destroyed them all.

²⁸"And the world will be as it was in the days of Lot. People went about their daily business—eating and drinking, buying and selling, farming and building— ²⁹until the morning Lot left Sodom. Then fire and burning sulfur rained down from heaven and destroyed them all. ³⁰Yes, it will be 'business as usual' right up to the day when the Son of Man is revealed. ³¹On that day a person out on the deck of a roof must not go down into the house to pack. A person out in the field must not return home. ³²Remember what happened to Lot's wife! ³³If you cling to your life, you will lose it, and if you let your life go, you will save it. ³⁴That night two people will be asleep in one bed; one will be taken, the other left. ³⁵Two women will be grinding flour together at the mill; one will be taken, the other left.*"

³⁷"Where will this happen, Lord?" the disciples asked.

Jesus replied, "Just as the gathering of vultures shows there is a carcass nearby, so these signs indicate that the end is near."

Parable of the Persistent Widow

18

One day Jesus told his disciples a story to show that they should always pray and never give up. ²"There was a judge in a certain city," he said, "who neither feared God nor cared about people. ³A widow of that city came to him repeatedly, saying, 'Give me justice in this dispute with my enemy.' ⁴The judge ignored her for a while, but finally he said to himself, 'I don't fear God or care about people, ⁵but this woman is driving me crazy. I'm going to see that she gets justice, because she is wearing me out with her constant requests!'"

⁶Then the Lord said, "Learn a lesson from this unjust judge. ⁷Even he rendered a just decision in the end. So don't you think God will surely give justice to his chosen people who cry out to him day and night? Will he keep putting them off? ⁸I tell you, he will grant justice to them quickly! But when the Son of Man returns, how many will he find on the earth who have faith?"

Parable of the Pharisee and Tax Collector

⁹Then Jesus told this story to some who had great confidence in their own righteousness and scorned everyone else: ¹⁰"Two men went to the Temple to pray. One was a Pharisee, and the other was a despised tax collector. ¹¹The Pharisee stood by himself and prayed this prayer: 'I thank you, God, that I am not a sinner like everyone else. For I don't cheat, I don't sin, and I don't commit adultery. I'm certainly not like that tax collector! ¹²I fast twice a week, and I give you a tenth of my income.'

STAND POINT

When you need to be pumped up

17:5

The apostles said to the Lord, "Show us how to increase our faith."

17:35 Some manuscripts add verse 36, *Two men will be working in the field; one will be taken, the other left.* Compare Matt 24:40.

APRIL M.A.P.

1
S.D.	P.L.	P.G.	S.G.
P. ☐	F. ☐	F. ☐	T. ☐
F. ☐	W. ☐	W. ☐	P. ☐
B. ☐	P. ☐	C. ☐	C. ☐

2
S.D.	P.L.	P.G.	S.G.
P. ☐	F. ☐	F. ☐	T. ☐
F. ☐	W. ☐	W. ☐	P. ☐
B. ☐	P. ☐	C. ☐	C. ☐

3
S.D.	P.L.	P.G.	S.G.
P. ☐	F. ☐	F. ☐	T. ☐
F. ☐	W. ☐	W. ☐	P. ☐
B. ☐	P. ☐	C. ☐	C. ☐

4
S.D.	P.L.	P.G.	S.G.
P. ☐	F. ☐	F. ☐	T. ☐
F. ☐	W. ☐	W. ☐	P. ☐
B. ☐	P. ☐	C. ☐	C. ☐

9
S.D.	P.L.	P.G.	S.G.
P. ☐	F. ☐	F. ☐	T. ☐
F. ☐	W. ☐	W. ☐	P. ☐
B. ☐	P. ☐	C. ☐	C. ☐

10
S.D.	P.L.	P.G.	S.G.
P. ☐	F. ☐	F. ☐	T. ☐
F. ☐	W. ☐	W. ☐	P. ☐
B. ☐	P. ☐	C. ☐	C. ☐

11
S.D.	P.L.	P.G.	S.G.
P. ☐	F. ☐	F. ☐	T. ☐
F. ☐	W. ☐	W. ☐	P. ☐
B. ☐	P. ☐	C. ☐	C. ☐

12
S.D.	P.L.	P.G.	S.G.
P. ☐	F. ☐	F. ☐	T. ☐
F. ☐	W. ☐	W. ☐	P. ☐
B. ☐	P. ☐	C. ☐	C. ☐

17
S.D.	P.L.	P.G.	S.G.
P. ☐	F. ☐	F. ☐	T. ☐
F. ☐	W. ☐	W. ☐	P. ☐
B. ☐	P. ☐	C. ☐	C. ☐

18
S.D.	P.L.	P.G.	S.G.
P. ☐	F. ☐	F. ☐	T. ☐
F. ☐	W. ☐	W. ☐	P. ☐
B. ☐	P. ☐	C. ☐	C. ☐

19
S.D.	P.L.	P.G.	S.G.
P. ☐	F. ☐	F. ☐	T. ☐
F. ☐	W. ☐	W. ☐	P. ☐
B. ☐	P. ☐	C. ☐	C. ☐

20
S.D.	P.L.	P.G.	S.G.
P. ☐	F. ☐	F. ☐	T. ☐
F. ☐	W. ☐	W. ☐	P. ☐
B. ☐	P. ☐	C. ☐	C. ☐

25
S.D.	P.L.	P.G.	S.G.
P. ☐	F. ☐	F. ☐	T. ☐
F. ☐	W. ☐	W. ☐	P. ☐
B. ☐	P. ☐	C. ☐	C. ☐

26
S.D.	P.L.	P.G.	S.G.
P. ☐	F. ☐	F. ☐	T. ☐
F. ☐	W. ☐	W. ☐	P. ☐
B. ☐	P. ☐	C. ☐	C. ☐

27
S.D.	P.L.	P.G.	S.G.
P. ☐	F. ☐	F. ☐	T. ☐
F. ☐	W. ☐	W. ☐	P. ☐
B. ☐	P. ☐	C. ☐	C. ☐

28
S.D.	P.L.	P.G.	S.G.
P. ☐	F. ☐	F. ☐	T. ☐
F. ☐	W. ☐	W. ☐	P. ☐
B. ☐	P. ☐	C. ☐	C. ☐

Spiritual Disciplines

Prayer

Faith Community

Bible Reading

Prayer List

Friends

World

Personal

(For designing your M.A.P. – Monthly Action Plan – see introduction pages)

Who am I....
Where am I going....
How am I going to get there?

nt:sport

MONTHLY ACTION PLAN

5

S.D.	P.L.	P.G.	S.G.
P. ☐	F. ☐	F. ☐	T. ☐
F. ☐	W. ☐	W. ☐	P. ☐
B. ☐	P. ☐	C. ☐	C. ☐

6

S.D.	P.L.	P.G.	S.G.
P. ☐	F. ☐	F. ☐	T. ☐
F. ☐	W. ☐	W. ☐	P. ☐
B. ☐	P. ☐	C. ☐	C. ☐

7

S.D.	P.L.	P.G.	S.G.
P. ☐	F. ☐	F. ☐	T. ☐
F. ☐	W. ☐	W. ☐	P. ☐
B. ☐	P. ☐	C. ☐	C. ☐

8

S.D.	P.L.	P.G.	S.G.
P. ☐	F. ☐	F. ☐	T. ☐
F. ☐	W. ☐	W. ☐	P. ☐
B. ☐	P. ☐	C. ☐	C. ☐

13

S.D.	P.L.	P.G.	S.G.
P. ☐	F. ☐	F. ☐	T. ☐
F. ☐	W. ☐	W. ☐	P. ☐
B. ☐	P. ☐	C. ☐	C. ☐

14

S.D.	P.L.	P.G.	S.G.
P. ☐	F. ☐	F. ☐	T. ☐
F. ☐	W. ☐	W. ☐	P. ☐
B. ☐	P. ☐	C. ☐	C. ☐

15

S.D.	P.L.	P.G.	S.G.
P. ☐	F. ☐	F. ☐	T. ☐
F. ☐	W. ☐	W. ☐	P. ☐
B. ☐	P. ☐	C. ☐	C. ☐

16

S.D.	P.L.	P.G.	S.G.
P. ☐	F. ☐	F. ☐	T. ☐
F. ☐	W. ☐	W. ☐	P. ☐
B. ☐	P. ☐	C. ☐	C. ☐

21

S.D.	P.L.	P.G.	S.G.
P. ☐	F. ☐	F. ☐	T. ☐
F. ☐	W. ☐	W. ☐	P. ☐
B. ☐	P. ☐	C. ☐	C. ☐

22

S.D.	P.L.	P.G.	S.G.
P. ☐	F. ☐	F. ☐	T. ☐
F. ☐	W. ☐	W. ☐	P. ☐
B. ☐	P. ☐	C. ☐	C. ☐

23

S.D.	P.L.	P.G.	S.G.
P. ☐	F. ☐	F. ☐	T. ☐
F. ☐	W. ☐	W. ☐	P. ☐
B. ☐	P. ☐	C. ☐	C. ☐

24

S.D.	P.L.	P.G.	S.G.
P. ☐	F. ☐	F. ☐	T. ☐
F. ☐	W. ☐	W. ☐	P. ☐
B. ☐	P. ☐	C. ☐	C. ☐

29

S.D.	P.L.	P.G.	S.G.
P. ☐	F. ☐	F. ☐	T. ☐
F. ☐	W. ☐	W. ☐	P. ☐
B. ☐	P. ☐	C. ☐	C. ☐

30

S.D.	P.L.	P.G.	S.G.
P. ☐	F. ☐	F. ☐	T. ☐
F. ☐	W. ☐	W. ☐	P. ☐
B. ☐	P. ☐	C. ☐	C. ☐

Psalm 139:10

Even there your hand will guide me, and your strength will support me.

Personal Goals

Family

Work/School/Social

Challenge

Sport Goals

Training

Performance

Competition Results

[13]"But the tax collector stood at a distance and dared not even lift his eyes to heaven as he prayed. Instead, he beat his chest in sorrow, saying, 'O God, be merciful to me, for I am a sinner.' [14]I tell you, this sinner, not the Pharisee, returned home justified before God. For those who exalt themselves will be humbled, and those who humble themselves will be exalted."

Jesus Blesses the Children

[15]One day some parents brought their little children to Jesus so he could touch and bless them. But when the disciples saw this, they scolded the parents for bothering him. [16]Then Jesus called for the children and said to the disciples, "Let the children come to me. Don't stop them! For the Kingdom of God belongs to those who are like these children. [17]I tell you the truth, anyone who doesn't receive the Kingdom of God like a child will never enter it."

The Rich Man

[18]Once a religious leader asked Jesus this question: "Good Teacher, what should I do to inherit eternal life?" [19]"Why do you call me good?" Jesus asked him. "Only God is truly good. [20]But to answer your question, you know the commandments: 'You must not commit adultery. You must not murder. You must not steal. You must not testify falsely. Honor your father and mother.'"

[21]The man replied, "I've carefully obeyed all these commandments since I was young."

[22]When Jesus heard his answer, he said, "There is still one thing you haven't done. Sell all your possessions and give the money to the poor, and you will have treasure in heaven. Then come, follow me."

[23]But when the man heard this he became sad, for he was very rich.

[24]When Jesus saw this, he said, "How hard it is for the rich to enter the Kingdom of God! [25]In fact, it is easier for a camel to go through the eye of a needle than for a rich person to enter the Kingdom of God!"

STAND POINT

When you are losing

18:27

"What is impossible for people is possible with God."

[26]Those who heard this said, "Then who in the world can be saved?"

[27]He replied, "What is impossible for people is possible with God."

[28]Peter said, "We've left our homes to follow you."

[29]"Yes," Jesus replied, "and I assure you that everyone who has given up house or wife or brothers or parents or children, for the sake of the Kingdom of God, [30]will be repaid many times over in this life, and will have eternal life in the world to come."

Jesus Again Predicts His Death

[31]Taking the twelve disciples aside, Jesus said, "Listen, we're going up to Jerusalem, where all the predictions of the prophets concerning the Son of Man will come true. [32]He will be handed over to the Romans, and he will be mocked, treated shamefully, and spit upon. [33]They will flog him with a whip and kill him, but on the third day he will rise again."

[34]But they didn't understand any of this. The significance of his words was hidden from them, and they failed to grasp what he was talking about.

Jesus Heals a Blind Beggar

[35]As Jesus approached Jericho, a blind beggar was sitting beside the road. [36]When he heard the noise of a crowd going past, he asked what was happening. [37]They told him that Jesus the Nazarene was going by. [38]So he began shouting, "Jesus, Son of David, have mercy on me!"

[39]"Be quiet!" the people in front yelled at him. But he only shouted louder, "Son of David, have mercy on me!"

[40]When Jesus heard him, he stopped and ordered that the man be brought to him. As the man came near, Jesus asked him, [41]"What do you want me to do for you?"

"Lord," he said, "I want to see!"

[42]And Jesus said, "All right, receive your sight! Your faith has healed you." [43]Instantly the man could see, and he followed Jesus, praising God. And all who saw it praised God, too.

Jesus and Zacchaeus

19

Jesus entered Jericho and made his way through the town. [2]There was a man there named Zacchaeus. He was the chief tax collector in the region, and he had become very rich. [3]He tried to get a look at Jesus, but he was too short to see over the crowd. [4]So he ran

count on it

You do not have to be a Bible scholar to understand faith! Jesus loved children and used them often as an example of how to trust. A child who loves a parent puts their entire life in the care of that parent. That is what God wants from you. Like a trusting child, put your whole life (even your sport) in God's hands and allow God to be your Father. He will not let you down! "Let the children come to me. Don't stop them! For the Kingdom of God belongs to those who are like these children." (Mark 10:14) **Count on it!**

ahead and climbed a sycamore-fig tree beside the road, for Jesus was going to pass that way.

[5]When Jesus came by, he looked up at Zacchaeus and called him by name. "Zacchaeus!" he said. "Quick, come down! I must be a guest in your home today."

[6]Zacchaeus quickly climbed down and took Jesus to his house in great excitement and joy. [7]But the people were displeased. "He has gone to be the guest of a notorious sinner," they grumbled.

[8]Meanwhile, Zacchaeus stood before the Lord and said, "I will give half my wealth to the poor, Lord, and if I have cheated people on their taxes, I will give them back four times as much!"

[9]Jesus responded, "Salvation has come to this home today, for this man has shown himself to be a true son of Abraham. [10]For the Son of Man came to seek and save those who are lost."

Parable of the Ten Servants

[11]The crowd was listening to everything Jesus said. And because he was nearing Jerusalem, he told them a story to correct the impression that the Kingdom of

God would begin right away. ¹²He said, "A nobleman was called away to a distant empire to be crowned king and then return. ¹³Before he left, he called together ten of his servants and divided among them ten pounds of silver, saying, 'Invest this for me while I am gone.' ¹⁴But his people hated him and sent a delegation after him to say, 'We do not want him to be our king.'

¹⁵"After he was crowned king, he returned and called in the servants to whom he had given the money. He wanted to find out what their profits were. ¹⁶The first servant reported, 'Master, I invested your money and made ten times the original amount!'

¹⁷"'Well done!' the king exclaimed. 'You are a good servant. You have been faithful with the little I entrusted to you, so you will be governor of ten cities as your reward.'

¹⁸"The next servant reported, 'Master, I invested your money and made five times the original amount.'

¹⁹"'Well done!' the king said. 'You will be governor over five cities.'

²⁰"But the third servant brought back only the original amount of money and said, 'Master, I hid your money and kept it safe. ²¹I was afraid because you are a hard man to deal with, taking what isn't yours and harvesting crops you didn't plant.'

²²"'You wicked servant!' the king roared. 'Your own words condemn you. If you knew that I'm a hard man who takes what isn't mine and harvests crops I didn't plant, ²³why didn't you deposit my money in the bank? At least I could have gotten some interest on it.'

²⁴"Then, turning to the others standing nearby, the king ordered, 'Take the money from this servant, and give it to the one who has ten pounds.'

²⁵"'But, master,' they said, 'he already has ten pounds!'

²⁶"'Yes,' the king replied, 'and to those who use well what they are given, even more will be given. But from those who do nothing, even what little they have will be taken away. ²⁷And as for these enemies of mine who didn't want me to be their king—bring them in and execute them right here in front of me.'"

Jesus' Triumphant Entry

²⁸After telling this story, Jesus went on toward Jerusalem, walking ahead of his disciples. ²⁹As they came to the towns of Bethphage and Bethany on the Mount of Olives, he sent two disciples ahead. ³⁰"Go into that village over there," he told them. "As you enter it, you will see a young donkey tied there that no one has ever ridden. Untie it and bring it here. ³¹If anyone asks, 'Why are you untying that colt?' just say, 'The Lord needs it.'"

³²So they went and found the colt, just as Jesus had said. ³³And sure enough, as they were untying it, the owners asked them, "Why are you untying that colt?" ³⁴And the disciples simply replied, "The Lord needs it." ³⁵So they brought the colt to Jesus and threw their garments over it for him to ride on.

³⁶As he rode along, the crowds spread out their garments on the road ahead of him. ³⁷When they reached the place where the road started down the Mount of Olives, all of his followers began to shout and sing as they walked along, praising God for all the wonderful miracles they had seen.

³⁸"Blessings on the King who comes in the name of the LORD!

Peace in heaven, and glory in highest heaven!"

³⁹But some of the Pharisees among the crowd said, "Teacher, rebuke your followers for saying things like that!"

⁴⁰He replied, "If they kept quiet, the stones along the road would burst into cheers!"

Jesus Weeps over Jerusalem

⁴¹But as they came closer to Jerusalem and Jesus saw the city ahead, he began to weep. ⁴²"How I wish today that you of all people would understand the way to peace. But now it is too late, and peace is hidden from your eyes. ⁴³Before long your enemies will build ramparts against your walls and encircle you and close in on you from every side. ⁴⁴They will crush you into the ground, and your children with you. Your enemies will not leave a single stone in place, because you did not accept your opportunity for salvation."

Jesus Clears the Temple

⁴⁵Then Jesus entered the Temple and began to drive out the people selling animals for sacrifices. ⁴⁶He said to them, "The Scriptures declare, 'My Temple will be a house of prayer,' but you have turned it into a den of thieves."

⁴⁷After that, he taught daily in the Temple, but the leading priests, the teachers of religious law, and the other leaders of the people began planning how to kill him. ⁴⁸But they could think of nothing, because all the people hung on every word he said.

19:45-48 WHAT'S IT SAYING?

WHAT AM I GOING TO DO ABOUT IT?

The Authority of Jesus Challenged

20

One day as Jesus was teaching the people and preaching the Good News in the Temple, the leading priests, the teachers of religious law, and the elders came up to him. ²They demanded, "By what authority are you doing all these things? Who gave you the right?"

³"Let me ask you a question first," he replied. ⁴"Did John's authority to baptize come from heaven, or was it merely human?"

⁵They talked it over among themselves. "If we say it was from heaven, he will ask why we didn't believe John. ⁶But if we say it was merely human, the people will stone us because they are convinced John was a prophet." ⁷So they finally replied that they didn't know.

Olympic badminton rules say that the bird has to have exactly fourteen feathers.

Give to Caesar (LUKE 20:20-26)

Jerusalem had been conquered by Rome, leaving the Jews and their way of life under threat of annihilation. The Pharisees were often walking a tightrope working between the occupying government and the Jews whom they led. Many of the Pharisees had lost sight of their calling and hungered for more power and prestige. Jesus was a threat to their power, and they assumed (along with many of his supporters) that he was trying to take back the power and political structure and make himself, by force or deception, a temporary king. The Pharisees were looking for a way to remove him, so they tried to lay a trap by forcing him to side for or against Roman government. Jesus avoided the trap, and his answer helps Christians understand that they have dual citizenship. They are to be both loyal to their government (unless the civil authority veers from God's direct commandments) and obedient to their supreme authority, God.

BIBLE HIT

[8]And Jesus responded, "Then I won't tell you by what authority I do these things."

Parable of the Evil Farmers

[9]Now Jesus turned to the people again and told them this story: "A man planted a vineyard, leased it to tenant farmers, and moved to another country to live for several years. [10]At the time of the grape harvest, he sent one of his servants to collect his share of the crop. But the farmers attacked the servant, beat him up, and sent him back empty-handed. [11]So the owner sent another servant, but they also insulted him, beat him up, and sent him away empty-handed. [12]A third man was sent, and they wounded him and chased him away.

[13]"'What will I do?' the owner asked himself. 'I know! I'll send my cherished son. Surely they will respect him.'

[14]"But when the tenant farmers saw his son, they said to each other, 'Here comes the heir to this estate. Let's kill him and get the estate for ourselves!' [15]So they dragged him out of the vineyard and murdered him.

"What do you suppose the owner of the vineyard will do to them?" Jesus asked. [16]"I'll tell you—he will come and kill those farmers and lease the vineyard to others."

"How terrible that such a thing should ever happen," his listeners protested.

[17]Jesus looked at them and said, "Then what does this Scripture mean?

'The stone that the builders rejected has now become the cornerstone.'

[18]Everyone who stumbles over that stone will be broken to pieces, and it will crush anyone it falls on." [19]The teachers of religious law and the leading priests wanted to arrest Jesus immediately because they realized he was telling the story against them—they were the wicked farmers. But they were afraid of the people's reaction.

Taxes for Caesar

[20]Watching for their opportunity, the leaders sent spies pretending to be honest men. They tried to get Jesus to say something that could be reported to the Roman governor so he would arrest Jesus. [21]"Teacher," they said, "we know that you speak and teach what is right and are not influenced by what others think. You teach the way of God truthfully. [22]Now tell us—is it right for us to pay taxes to Caesar or not?"

[23]He saw through their trickery and said, [24]"Show me a Roman coin. Whose picture and title are stamped on it?"

"Caesar's," they replied.

[25]"Well then," he said, "give to Caesar what belongs to Caesar, and give to God what belongs to God."

[26]So they failed to trap him by what he said in front of the people. Instead, they were amazed by his answer, and they became silent.

Discussion about Resurrection

[27]Then Jesus was approached by some Sadducees—religious leaders who say there is no resurrection from the dead. [28]They posed this question: "Teacher, Moses gave us a law that if a man dies, leaving a wife but no children, his brother should marry the widow and have a child who will carry on the brother's name. [29]Well, suppose there were seven brothers. The oldest one married and then died without children. [30]So the second brother married the widow, but he also died. [31]Then the third brother married her. This continued with all seven of them, who died without children. [32]Finally, the woman also died. [33]So tell us, whose wife will she be in the resurrection? For all seven were married to her!"

[34]Jesus replied, "Marriage is for people here on earth. [35]But in the age to come, those worthy of being raised from the dead will neither marry nor be given in marriage. [36]And they will never die again. In this respect they will be like angels. They are children of God and children of the resurrection.

[37]"But now, as to whether the dead will be raised—even Moses proved this when he wrote about the burning bush. Long after Abraham, Isaac, and Jacob had died, he referred to the Lord as 'the God of Abraham, the God of Isaac, and the God of Jacob.' [38]So he is the God of the living, not the dead, for they are all alive to him."

Make the Skill Automatic:

The athlete's performance becomes routine as the subconscious part of the brain becomes programmed. This allows the athlete's conscious part of the brain to focus only on the changing variables. Much of sports should be taught to perfection, and with time the skills will become automatic.

TIPS

³⁹"Well said, Teacher!" remarked some of the teachers of religious law who were standing there. ⁴⁰And then no one dared to ask him any more questions.

Whose Son Is the Messiah?

⁴¹Then Jesus presented them with a question. "Why is it," he asked, "that the Messiah is said to be the son of David? ⁴²For David himself wrote in the book of Psalms:

'The LORD said to my Lord,
Sit in the place of honor at my right hand
⁴³until I humble your enemies,
making them a footstool under your feet.'

⁴⁴Since David called the Messiah 'Lord,' how can the Messiah be his son?"

⁴⁵Then, with the crowds listening, he turned to his disciples and said, ⁴⁶"Beware of these teachers of religious law! For they like to parade around in flowing robes and love to receive respectful greetings as they walk in the marketplaces. And how they love the seats of honor in the synagogues and the head table at banquets. ⁴⁷Yet they shamelessly cheat widows out of their property and then pretend to be pious by making long prayers in public. Because of this, they will be severely punished."

The Widow's Offering

21

While Jesus was in the Temple, he watched the rich people dropping their gifts in the collection box. ²Then a poor widow came by and dropped in two small coins.

³"I tell you the truth," Jesus said, "this poor widow has given more than all the rest of them. ⁴For they have given a tiny part of their surplus, but she, poor as she is, has given everything she has."

Jesus Foretells the Future

⁵Some of his disciples began talking about the majestic stonework of the Temple and the memorial decorations on the walls. But Jesus said, ⁶"The time is coming when all these things will be completely demolished. Not one stone will be left on top of another!"

⁷"Teacher," they asked, "when will all this happen? What

sign will show us that these things are about to take place?"

⁸He replied, "Don't let anyone mislead you, for many will come in my name, claiming, 'I am the Messiah,' and saying, 'The time has come!' But don't believe them. ⁹And when you hear of wars and insurrections, don't panic. Yes, these things must take place first, but the end won't follow immediately." ¹⁰Then he added, "Nation will go to war against nation, and kingdom against kingdom. ¹¹There will be great earthquakes, and there will be famines and plagues in many lands, and there will be terrifying things and great miraculous signs from heaven.

¹²"But before all this occurs, there will be a time of great persecution. You will be dragged into synagogues and prisons, and you will stand trial before kings and governors because you are my followers. ¹³But this will be your opportunity to tell them about me. ¹⁴So don't worry in advance about how to answer the charges against you, ¹⁵for I will give you the right words and such wisdom that none of your opponents will be able to reply or refute you! ¹⁶Even those closest to you—your parents, brothers, relatives, and friends—will betray you. They will even kill some of you. ¹⁷And everyone will hate you because you are my followers. ¹⁸But not a hair of your head will perish! ¹⁹By standing firm, you will win your souls.

²⁰"And when you see Jerusalem surrounded by armies, then you will know that the time of its destruction has arrived. ²¹Then those in Judea must flee to the hills. Those in Jerusalem must get out, and those out in the country should not return to the city. ²²For those will be days of God's vengeance, and the prophetic words of the Scriptures will be fulfilled. ²³How terrible it will be for pregnant women and for nursing mothers in those days. For there will be disaster in the land and great anger against this people. ²⁴They will be killed by the sword or sent away as captives to all the nations of the world. And Jerusalem will be trampled down by the Gentiles until the period of the Gentiles comes to an end.

²⁵"And there will be strange signs in the sun, moon, and stars. And here on earth the nations will be in turmoil, perplexed by the roaring seas and strange tides. ²⁶People will be terrified at what they see coming upon the earth, for the powers in the heavens will be shaken. ²⁷Then everyone will see the Son of Man coming on a cloud with power and great glory. ²⁸So when all these things begin to happen, stand and look up, for your salvation is near!"

²⁹Then he gave them this illustration: "Notice the fig tree, or any other tree. ³⁰When the leaves come out,

you know without being told that summer is near. ³¹In the same way, when you see all these things taking place, you can know that the Kingdom of God is near. ³²I tell you the truth, this generation will not pass from the scene until all these things have taken place. ³³Heaven and earth will disappear, but my words will never disappear.

³⁴"Watch out! Don't let your hearts be dulled by carousing and drunkenness, and by the worries of this life. Don't let that day catch you unaware, ³⁵like a trap. For that day will come upon everyone living on the earth. ³⁶Keep alert at all times. And pray that you might be strong enough to escape these coming horrors and stand before the Son of Man."

³⁷Every day Jesus went to the Temple to teach, and each evening he returned to spend the night on the Mount of Olives. ³⁸The crowds gathered at the Temple early each morning to hear him.

21:12-19 WHAT'S IT SAYING?

WHAT AM I GOING TO DO ABOUT IT?

Judas Agrees to Betray Jesus

22

The Festival of Unleavened Bread, which is also called Passover, was approaching. ²The leading priests and teachers of religious law were plotting how to kill

PERSONAL ASSESSMENTS

So where am I at spiritually with the Lord? Am I on God's team?

☐ I am so lost I did not even know there was a game being played.

☐ I know there is a game going on, but I just can't find the stadium.

☐ I found the stadium, but I am on the outside.

☐ I am watching God's team from far away.

☐ I am watching God's team up close.

☐ I want to be on God's team, but I am not sure how to join.

☐ I am on God's team, but I am not making any impact.

☐ I am on God's team and playing as hard as I can!

☐ I am on God's team, but I keep fouling!

Jesus, but they were afraid of the people's reaction. [3]Then Satan entered into Judas Iscariot, who was one of the twelve disciples, [4]and he went to the leading priests and captains of the Temple guard to discuss the best way to betray Jesus to them. [5]They were delighted, and they promised to give him money. [6]So he agreed and began looking for an opportunity to betray Jesus so they could arrest him when the crowds weren't around.

The Last Supper

[7]Now the Festival of Unleavened Bread arrived, when the Passover lamb is sacrificed. [8]Jesus sent Peter and John ahead and said, "Go and prepare the Passover meal, so we can eat it together."

[9]"Where do you want us to prepare it?" they asked him.

[10]He replied, "As soon as you enter Jerusalem, a man carrying a pitcher of water will meet you. Follow him. At the house he enters, [11]say to the owner, 'The Teacher asks: Where is the guest room where I can eat the Passover meal with my disciples?' [12]He will take you upstairs to a large room that is already set up. That is where you should prepare our meal." [13]They went off to the city and found everything just as Jesus had said, and they prepared the Passover meal there.

[14]When the time came, Jesus and the apostles sat down together at the table. [15]Jesus said, "I have been very eager to eat this Passover meal with you before my suffering begins. [16]For I tell you now that I won't eat this meal again until its meaning is fulfilled in the Kingdom of God."

[17]Then he took a cup of wine and gave thanks to God for it. Then he said, "Take this and share it among yourselves. [18]For I will not drink wine again until the Kingdom of God has come."

[19]He took some bread and gave thanks to God for it. Then he broke it in pieces and gave it to the disciples, saying, "This is my body, which is given for you. Do this to remember me."

[20]After supper he took another cup of wine and said, "This cup is the new covenant between God and his people—an agreement confirmed with my blood, which is poured out as a sacrifice for you.

[21]"But here at this table, sitting among us as a friend, is the man who will betray me. [22]For it has been determined that the Son of Man must die. But what sorrow awaits the one who betrays him." [23]The disciples began to ask each other which of them would ever do such a thing.

[24]Then they began to argue among themselves about who would be the greatest among them. [25]Jesus told them, "In this world the kings and great men lord it over their people, yet they are called 'friends of the people.' [26]But among you it will be different. Those who are the greatest among you should take the lowest rank, and the leader should be like a servant. [27]Who is more important, the one who sits at the table or the one who serves? The one who sits at the table, of course. But not here! For I am among you as one who serves.

[28]"You have stayed with me in my time of trial. [29]And just as my Father has granted me a Kingdom, I now grant you the right [30]to eat and drink at my table in my Kingdom. And you will sit on thrones, judging the twelve tribes of Israel.

Jesus Predicts Peter's Denial

[31]"Simon, Simon, Satan has asked to sift each of you like wheat. [32]But I have pleaded in prayer for you, Simon, that your faith should not fail. So when you have repented and turned to me again, strengthen your brothers."

[33]Peter said, "Lord, I am ready to go to prison with you, and even to die with you."

[34]But Jesus said, "Peter, let me tell you something. Before the rooster crows tomorrow morning, you will deny three times that you even know me."

[35]Then Jesus asked them, "When I sent you out to preach the Good News and you did not have money, a traveler's bag, or extra clothing, did you need anything?"

"No," they replied.

[36]"But now," he said, "take your money and a traveler's bag. And if you don't have a sword, sell your cloak and buy one! [37]For the time has come for this prophecy about me to be fulfilled: 'He was counted among the rebels.' Yes, everything written about me by the prophets will come true."

[38]"Look, Lord," they replied, "we have two swords among us."

"That's enough," he said.

Jesus Prays on the Mount of Olives

[39]Then, accompanied by the disciples, Jesus left the upstairs room and went as usual to the Mount of Olives. [40]There he told them, "Pray that you will not give in to temptation."

[41]He walked away, about a stone's throw, and knelt down and prayed, [42]"Father, if you are willing, please take this cup of suffering away from me. Yet I want your will to be done, not mine." [43]Then an angel from heaven appeared and strengthened him. [44]He prayed more fervently, and he was in such agony of spirit that his sweat fell to the ground like great drops of blood.

[45]At last he stood up again and returned to the disciples, only to find them asleep, exhausted from grief. [46]"Why are you sleeping?" he asked them. "Get up and pray, so that you will not give in to temptation."

Jesus Is Betrayed and Arrested

[47]But even as Jesus said this, a crowd approached, led by Judas, one of his twelve disciples. Judas walked over to Jesus to greet him with a kiss. [48]But Jesus said, "Judas, would you betray the Son of Man with a kiss?"

[49]When the other disciples saw what was about to happen, they exclaimed, "Lord, should we fight? We brought the swords!" [50]And one of them struck at the high priest's slave, slashing off his right ear.

[51]But Jesus said, "No more of this." And he touched the man's ear and healed him.

[52]Then Jesus spoke to the leading priests, the captains of the Temple guard, and the elders who had come for him. "Am I some dangerous revolutionary," he asked, "that you come with swords and clubs to arrest me? [53]Why didn't you arrest me in the Temple? I was there

every day. But this is your moment, the time when the power of darkness reigns."

Peter Denies Jesus

[54]So they arrested him and led him to the high priest's home. And Peter followed at a distance. [55]The guards lit a fire in the middle of the courtyard and sat around it, and Peter joined them there. [56]A servant girl noticed him in the firelight and began staring at him. Finally she said, "This man was one of Jesus' followers!"

[57]But Peter denied it. "Woman," he said, "I don't even know him!"

[58]After a while someone else looked at him and said, "You must be one of them!"

"No, man, I'm not!" Peter retorted.

[59]About an hour later someone else insisted, "This must be one of them, because he is a Galilean, too."

[60]But Peter said, "Man, I don't know what you are talking about." And immediately, while he was still speaking, the rooster crowed. [61]At that moment the Lord turned and looked at Peter. Then Peter remembered that the Lord had said, "Before the rooster crows tomorrow morning, you will deny three times that you even know me." [62]And Peter left the courtyard, weeping bitterly.

[63]The guards in charge of Jesus began mocking and beating him. [64]They blindfolded him and said, "Prophesy to us! Who hit you that time?" [65]And they hurled all sorts of terrible insults at him.

Jesus before the Council

[66]At daybreak all the elders of the people assembled, including the leading priests and the teachers of religious law. Jesus was led before this high council, [67]and they said, "Tell us, are you the Messiah?"

But he replied, "If I tell you, you won't believe me. [68]And if I ask you a question, you won't answer. [69]But from now on the Son of Man will be seated in the place of power at God's right hand."

[70]They all shouted, "So, are you claiming to be the Son of God?"

And he replied, "You say that I am."

[71]"Why do we need other witnesses?" they said. "We ourselves heard him say it."

Jesus' Trial before Pilate

23

Then the entire council took Jesus to Pilate, the Roman governor. [2]They began to state their case: "This man has been leading our people astray by telling them not to pay their taxes to the Roman government and

by claiming he is the Messiah, a king."

[3]So Pilate asked him, "Are you the king of the Jews?" Jesus replied, "You have said it."

[4]Pilate turned to the leading priests and to the crowd and said, "I find nothing wrong with this man!"

[5]Then they became insistent. "But he is causing riots by his teaching wherever he goes—all over Judea, from Galilee to Jerusalem!"

[6]"Oh, is he a Galilean?" Pilate asked. [7]When they said that he was, Pilate sent him to Herod Antipas, because Galilee was under Herod's jurisdiction, and Herod happened to be in Jerusalem at the time.

[8]Herod was delighted at the opportunity to see Jesus, because he had heard about him and had been hoping for a long time to see him perform a miracle. [9]He asked Jesus question after question, but Jesus refused to answer. [10]Meanwhile, the leading priests and the teachers of religious law stood there shouting their accusations. [11]Then Herod and his soldiers began mocking and ridiculing Jesus. Finally, they put a royal robe on him and sent him back to Pilate. [12](Herod and Pilate, who had been enemies before, became friends that day.)

[13]Then Pilate called together the leading priests and other religious leaders, along with the people, [14]and he announced his verdict. "You brought this man to me, accusing him of leading a revolt. I have examined him thoroughly on this point in your presence and find him innocent. [15]Herod came to the same conclusion and sent him back to us. Nothing this man has done calls for the death penalty. [16]So I will have him flogged, and then I will release him."*

[18]Then a mighty roar rose from the crowd, and with one voice they shouted, "Kill him, and release Barabbas to us!" [19](Barabbas was in prison for taking part in an insurrection in Jerusalem against the government, and for murder.) [20]Pilate argued with them, because he wanted to release Jesus. [21]But they kept shouting, "Crucify him! Crucify him!"

[22]For the third time he demanded, "Why? What crime has he committed? I have found no reason to sentence him to death. So I will have him flogged, and then I will release him."

[23]But the mob shouted louder and louder, demanding that Jesus be crucified, and their voices prevailed. [24]So Pilate sentenced Jesus to die as they demanded. [25]As

they had requested, he released Barabbas, the man in prison for insurrection and murder. But he turned Jesus over to them to do as they wished.

The Crucifixion

[26]As they led Jesus away, a man named Simon, who was from Cyrene, happened to be coming in from the countryside. The soldiers seized him and put the cross on him and made him carry it behind Jesus. [27]A large crowd trailed behind, including many grief-stricken women. [28]But Jesus turned and said to them, "Daughters of Jerusalem, don't weep for me, but weep for yourselves and for your children. [29]For the days are coming when they will say, 'Fortunate indeed are the women who are childless, the wombs that have not borne a child and the breasts that have never nursed.' [30]People will beg the mountains, 'Fall on us,' and plead with the hills, 'Bury us.' [31]For if these things are done when the tree is green, what will happen when it is dry?"

[32]Two others, both criminals, were led out to be executed with him. [33]When they came to a place called The Skull, they nailed him to the cross. And the criminals were also crucified—one on his right and one on his left.

[34]Jesus said, "Father, forgive them, for they don't know what they are doing." And the soldiers gambled for his clothes by throwing dice.

[35]The crowd watched and the leaders scoffed. "He saved others," they said, "let him save himself if he is really God's Messiah, the Chosen One." [36]The soldiers mocked him, too, by offering him a drink of sour wine. [37]They called out to him, "If you are the King of the Jews, save yourself!" [38]A sign was fastened to the cross above him with these words: "This is the King of the Jews."

[39]One of the criminals hanging beside him scoffed, "So you're the Messiah, are you? Prove it by saving yourself—and us, too, while you're at it!"

[40]But the other criminal protested, "Don't you fear God even when you have been sentenced to die? [41]We deserve to die for our crimes, but this man hasn't done anything wrong." [42]Then he said, "Jesus, remember me when you come into your Kingdom."

[43]And Jesus replied, "I assure you, today you will be with me in paradise."

The Death of Jesus

[44]By this time it was noon, and darkness fell across the whole land until three o'clock. [45]The light from the sun was gone. And suddenly, the curtain in the sanctuary of the Temple was torn down the middle. [46]Then Jesus shouted, "Father, I entrust my spirit into your hands!" And with those words he breathed his last.

[47]When the Roman officer overseeing the execution saw what had happened, he worshiped God and said, "Surely this man

23:16 Some manuscripts add verse 17, *Now it was necessary for him to release one prisoner to them during the Passover celebration.* Compare Matt 27:15; Mark 15:6; John 18:39.

LUKE

was innocent." ⁴⁸And when all the crowd that came to see the crucifixion saw what had happened, they went home in deep sorrow. ⁴⁹But Jesus' friends, including the women who had followed him from Galilee, stood at a distance watching.

The Burial of Jesus

⁵⁰Now there was a good and righteous man named Joseph. He was a member of the Jewish high council, ⁵¹but he had not agreed with the decision and actions of the other religious leaders. He was from the town of Arimathea in Judea, and he was waiting for the Kingdom of God to come. ⁵²He went to Pilate and asked for Jesus' body. ⁵³Then he took the body down from the cross and wrapped it in a long sheet of linen cloth and laid it in a new tomb that had been carved out of rock. ⁵⁴This was done late on Friday afternoon, the day of preparation, as the Sabbath was about to begin.

⁵⁵As his body was taken away, the women from Galilee followed and saw the tomb where his body was placed. ⁵⁶Then they went home and prepared spices and ointments to anoint his body. But by the time they were finished the Sabbath had begun, so they rested as required by the law.

The Resurrection

24

But very early on Sunday morning the women went to the tomb, taking the spices they had prepared. ²They found that the stone had been rolled away from the entrance. ³So they went in, but they didn't find the body of the Lord Jesus. ⁴As they stood there puzzled, two men suddenly appeared to them, clothed in dazzling robes.

⁵The women were terrified and bowed with their faces to the ground. Then the men asked, "Why are you looking among the dead for someone who is alive? ⁶He isn't here! He is risen from the dead! Remember what he told you back in Galilee, ⁷that the Son of Man must be betrayed into the hands of sinful men and be crucified, and that he would rise again on the third day."

⁸Then they remembered that he had said this. ⁹So they rushed back from the tomb to tell his eleven disciples—and everyone else—what had happened. ¹⁰It was Mary Magdalene, Joanna, Mary the mother of James, and several other women who told the apostles what had happened. ¹¹But the story sounded like nonsense to the men, so they didn't believe it. ¹²However, Peter jumped up and ran to the tomb to look. Stooping, he peered in and saw the empty linen wrappings; then he went home again, wondering what had happened.

The Walk to Emmaus

¹³That same day two of Jesus' followers were walking to the village of Emmaus, seven miles from Jerusalem. ¹⁴As they

walked along they were talking about everything that had happened. ¹⁵As they talked and discussed these things, Jesus himself suddenly came and began walking with them. ¹⁶But God kept them from recognizing him.

¹⁷He asked them, "What are you discussing so intently as you walk along?"

They stopped short, sadness written across their faces. ¹⁸Then one of them, Cleopas, replied, "You must be the only person in Jerusalem who hasn't heard about all the things that have happened there the last few days."

¹⁹"What things?" Jesus asked.

"The things that happened to Jesus, the man from Nazareth," they said. "He was a prophet who did powerful miracles, and he was a mighty teacher in the eyes of God and all the people. ²⁰But our leading priests and other religious leaders handed him over to be condemned to death, and they crucified him. ²¹We had hoped he was the Messiah who had come to rescue Israel. This all happened three days ago.

²²"Then some women from our group of his followers were at his tomb early this morning, and they came back with an amazing report. ²³They said his body was missing, and they had seen angels who told them Jesus is alive! ²⁴Some of our men ran out to see, and sure enough, his body was gone, just as the women had said."

²⁵Then Jesus said to them, "You foolish people! You find it so hard to believe all that the prophets wrote in the Scriptures. ²⁶Wasn't it clearly predicted that the Messiah would have to suffer all these things before entering his glory?" ²⁷Then Jesus took them through the writings of Moses and all the prophets, explaining from all the Scriptures the things concerning himself.

²⁸By this time they were nearing Emmaus and the end of their journey. Jesus acted as if he were going on, ²⁹but they begged him, "Stay the night with us, since it is getting late." So he went home with them. ³⁰As they sat down to eat, he took the bread and blessed it. Then he broke it and gave it to them. ³¹Suddenly, their eyes were opened, and they

recognized him. And at that moment he disappeared! ³²They said to each other, "Didn't our hearts burn within us as he talked with us on the road and explained the Scriptures to us?" ³³And within the hour they were on their way back to Jerusalem. There they found the eleven disciples and the others who had gathered with them, ³⁴who said, "The Lord has really risen! He appeared to Peter."

Jesus Appears to the Disciples

³⁵Then the two from Emmaus told their story of how Jesus had appeared to them as they were walking along the road, and how they had recognized him as he was breaking the bread. ³⁶And just as they were telling about it, Jesus himself was suddenly standing there among them. "Peace be with you," he said. ³⁷But the whole group was startled and frightened, thinking they were seeing a ghost!

³⁸"Why are you frightened?" he asked. "Why are your hearts filled with doubt? ³⁹Look at my hands. Look at my feet. You can see that it's really me. Touch me and make sure that I am not a ghost, because ghosts don't have bodies, as you see that I do." ⁴⁰As he spoke, he showed them his hands and his feet.

⁴¹Still they stood there in disbelief, filled with joy and wonder. Then he asked them, "Do you have anything here to eat?" ⁴²They gave him a piece of broiled fish, ⁴³and he ate it as they watched.

⁴⁴Then he said, "When I was with you before, I told you that everything written about me in the law of Moses and the prophets and in the Psalms must be fulfilled." ⁴⁵Then he opened their minds to understand the Scriptures. ⁴⁶And he said, "Yes, it was written long ago that the Messiah would suffer and die and rise from the dead on the third day. ⁴⁷It was also written that this message would be proclaimed in the authority of his name to all the nations, beginning in Jerusalem: 'There is forgiveness of sins for all who repent.' ⁴⁸You are witnesses of all these things.

⁴⁹"And now I will send the Holy Spirit, just as my Father promised. But stay here in the city until the Holy Spirit comes and fills you with power from heaven."

The Ascension

⁵⁰Then Jesus led them to Bethany, and lifting his hands to heaven, he blessed them. ⁵¹While he was blessing them, he left them and was taken up to heaven. ⁵²So they worshiped him and then returned to Jerusalem filled with great joy. ⁵³And they spent all of their time in the Temple, praising God.

Like an old teammate personally recounting past experiences with a famous and historic athlete, John recounts Jesus' life and ministry. John was there and he wants others to know about his hero, Jesus. With a unique flavor and personal touch, the last Gospel was written long after the first three. John, the author and namesake of the book, referred to himself as the "disciple whom Jesus loved," and was nicknamed "Son of Thunder" by Jesus himself. John had seen quite a lot of history. Originally following John the Baptist with his brother James, he had lived closely with and followed Jesus throughout his ministry. The youthful John had a perceptive knack for recognizing and enjoying Jesus. He outlived his friends and fellow disciples, many of whom were executed for their faith. He watched as their precious city of Jerusalem was destroyed by the Romans. John himself had been exiled to the island of Patmos. Finally, advanced in years, it was time for John to write his powerful account of Jesus' life.

Writing both for Jews and Gentiles, John emphasizes how Jesus was God and Savior. One of his key words is *believe*. It is packed with fantastic detail, several other witnesses, and loads of miracles. You are taken into the world of the disciple as he recalls the last days of Jesus' life, crucifixion, and resurrection. Lastly, John gives an intimate account of Jesus' response to Peter, who had denied him earlier. We must act on the same challenge that Peter was given by Jesus: "Follow me!"

John

abundant life
MORE THAN A LIFESTYLE

My purpose is to give them a rich and satisfying life.

JOHN 10:10

JOHN

Prologue: Christ, the Eternal Word

1

¹In the beginning the Word already existed.
The Word was with God,
and the Word was God.
²He existed in the beginning with God.
³God created everything through him,
and nothing was created except through him.
⁴The Word gave life to everything that was created,
and his life brought light to everyone.
⁵The light shines in the darkness,
and the darkness can never extinguish it.

⁶God sent a man, John the Baptist, ⁷to tell about the light so that everyone might believe because of his testimony. ⁸John himself was not the light; he was simply a witness to tell about the light. ⁹The one who is the true light, who gives light to everyone, was coming into the world.

¹⁰He came into the very world he created, but the world didn't recognize him. ¹¹He came to his own people, and even they rejected him. ¹²But to all who believed him and accepted him, he gave the right to become children of God. ¹³They are reborn—not with a physical birth resulting from human passion or plan, but a birth that comes from God.

¹⁴So the Word became human and made his home among us. He was full of unfailing love and faithfulness. And we have seen his glory, the glory of the Father's one and only Son.

¹⁵John testified about him when he shouted to the crowds, "This is the one I was talking about when I said, 'Someone is coming after me who is far greater than I am, for he existed long before me.'"

¹⁶From his abundance we have all received one gracious blessing after another. ¹⁷For the law was given through Moses, but God's unfailing love and faithfulness came through Jesus Christ. ¹⁸No one has ever seen God. But the one and only Son is himself God and is near to the Father's heart. He has revealed God to us.

The Testimony of John the Baptist

¹⁹This was John's testimony when the Jewish leaders sent priests and Temple assistants from Jerusalem to ask John, "Who are you?" ²⁰He came right out and said, "I am not the Messiah."

²¹"Well then, who are you?" they asked. "Are you Elijah?"

"No," he replied.

"Are you the Prophet we are expecting?"

"No."

²²"Then who are you? We need an answer for those who sent us. What do you have to say about yourself?"

²³John replied in the words of the prophet Isaiah:

"I am a voice shouting in the wilderness,
'Clear the way for the LORD's coming!'"

²⁴Then the Pharisees who had been sent ²⁵asked him, "If you aren't the Messiah or Elijah or the Prophet, what right do you have to baptize?"

²⁶John told them, "I baptize with water, but right here in the crowd is someone you do not recognize. ²⁷Though his ministry follows mine, I'm not even worthy to be his slave and untie the straps of his sandal."

²⁸This encounter took place in Bethany, an area east of the Jordan River, where John was baptizing.

On February 6, 1971, the first golf ball was hit on the moon by Alan Shepard.

Jesus, the Lamb of God

²⁹The next day John saw Jesus coming toward him and said, "Look! The Lamb of God who takes away the sin of the world! ³⁰He is the one I was talking about when I said, 'A man is coming after me who is far greater than I am, for he existed long before me.' ³¹I did not recognize him as the Messiah, but I have been baptizing with water so that he might be revealed to Israel."

³²Then John testified, "I saw the Holy Spirit descending like a dove from heaven and resting upon him. ³³I didn't know he was the one, but when God sent me to baptize with water, he told me, 'The one on whom you see the Spirit descend and rest is the one who will baptize with the Holy Spirit.' ³⁴I saw this happen to Jesus, so I testify that he is the Chosen One of God."

The First Disciples

³⁵The following day John was again standing with two of his disciples. ³⁶As Jesus walked by, John looked at him and declared, "Look! There is the Lamb of God!" ³⁷When John's two disciples heard this, they followed Jesus.

³⁸Jesus looked around and saw them following. "What do you want?" he asked them.

They replied, "Rabbi" (which means "Teacher"), "where are you staying?"

³⁹"Come and see," he said. It was about four o'clock in the afternoon when they went with him to the place where he was staying, and they remained with him the rest of the day.

⁴⁰Andrew, Simon Peter's brother, was one of these men who heard what John said and then followed Jesus. ⁴¹Andrew went to find his brother, Simon, and told him, "We have found the Messiah" (which means "Christ").

⁴²Then Andrew brought Simon to meet Jesus. Looking intently at Simon, Jesus said, "Your name is Simon, son of John—but you will be called Cephas" (which means "Peter").

⁴³The next day Jesus decided to go to Galilee. He found Philip and said to him, "Come, follow me." ⁴⁴Philip was from Bethsaida, Andrew and Peter's hometown.

⁴⁵Philip went to look for Nathanael and told him, "We have found the very person Moses and the prophets wrote about! His name is Jesus, the son of Joseph from Nazareth."

⁴⁶"Nazareth!" exclaimed Nathanael. "Can anything good come from Nazareth?"

"Come and see for yourself," Philip replied.

⁴⁷As they approached, Jesus said, "Now here is a genuine son of Israel—a man of complete integrity."

⁴⁸"How do you know about me?" Nathanael asked.

Jesus replied, "I could see you under the fig tree before Philip found you."

⁴⁹Then Nathanael exclaimed, "Rabbi, you are the Son of God—the King of Israel!"

⁵⁰Jesus asked him, "Do you believe this just because I told you I had seen you under the fig tree? You will see greater things than this." ⁵¹Then he said, "I tell you the truth, you will all see heaven open and the angels of God going up and down on the Son of Man, the one who is the stairway between heaven and earth."

The Wedding at Cana

2

The next day there was a wedding celebration in the village of Cana in Galilee. Jesus' mother was there, ²and Jesus and his disciples were also invited to the celebration. ³The wine supply ran out during the festivities, so Jesus' mother told him, "They have no more wine."

⁴"Dear woman, that's not our problem," Jesus replied. "My time has not yet come."

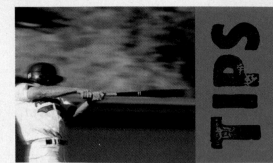

Chewing Gum & Walking:

Have you ever just got it really, really wrong? When both parts of our brain try to control the same skill at the same instant the wires get crossed up and the "program" is corrupted. As it is very difficult to think about two different things at exactly the same instant, the brain will rapidly try to switch between both tasks. That is why practice will help you reduce crossed wires and skills become automatic.

[5]But his mother told the servants, "Do whatever he tells you."

[6]Standing nearby were six stone water jars, used for Jewish ceremonial washing. Each could hold twenty to thirty gallons. [7]Jesus told the servants, "Fill the jars with water." When the jars had been filled, [8]he said, "Now dip some out, and take it to the master of ceremonies." So the servants followed his instructions.

[9]When the master of ceremonies tasted the water that was now wine, not knowing where it had come from (though, of course, the servants knew), he called the bridegroom over. [10]"A host always serves the best wine first," he said. "Then, when everyone has had a lot to drink, he brings out the less expensive wine. But you have kept the best until now!"

[11]This miraculous sign at Cana in Galilee was the first time Jesus revealed his glory. And his disciples believed in him.

[12]After the wedding he went to Capernaum for a few days with his mother, his brothers, and his disciples.

Jesus Clears the Temple

[13]It was nearly time for the Jewish Passover celebration, so Jesus went to Jerusalem. [14]In the Temple area he saw merchants selling cattle, sheep, and doves for sacrifices; he also saw dealers at tables exchanging foreign money. [15]Jesus made a whip from some ropes and chased them all out of the Temple. He drove out the sheep and cattle, scattered the money changers' coins over the floor, and turned over their tables. [16]Then, going over to the people who sold doves, he told them, "Get these things out of here. Stop turning my Father's house into a marketplace!"

[17]Then his disciples remembered this prophecy from the Scriptures: "Passion for God's house will consume me."

[18]But the Jewish leaders demanded, "What are you doing? If God gave you authority to do this, show us a miraculous sign to prove it."

[19]"All right," Jesus replied. "Destroy this temple, and in three days I will raise it up."

[20]"What!" they exclaimed. "It has taken forty-six years to build this Temple, and you can rebuild it in three days?"

[21]But when Jesus said "this temple," he meant his own body. [22]After he was raised from the dead, his disciples remembered he had said this, and they believed both the Scriptures and what Jesus had said.

Jesus and Nicodemus

[23]Because of the miraculous signs Jesus did in Jerusalem at the Passover celebration, many began to trust in him. [24]But Jesus didn't trust them, because he knew human nature. [25]No one needed to tell him what mankind is really like.

3

There was a man named Nicodemus, a Jewish religious leader who was a Pharisee. [2]After dark one evening, he came to speak with Jesus. "Rabbi," he said, "we all know that God has sent you to teach us. Your miraculous signs are evidence that God is with you."

[3]Jesus replied, "I tell you the truth, unless you are born again, you cannot see the Kingdom of God."

[4]"What do you mean?" exclaimed Nicodemus. "How can an old man go back into his mother's womb and be born again?"

[5]Jesus replied, "I assure you, no one can enter the Kingdom of God without being born of water and the Spirit. [6]Humans can reproduce only human life, but the Holy Spirit gives birth to spiritual life. [7]So don't be surprised when I say, 'You must be born again.' [8]The wind blows wherever it wants. Just as you can hear the wind but can't tell where it comes from or where it is going, so you can't explain how people are born of the Spirit."

[9]"How are these things possible?" Nicodemus asked.

[10]Jesus replied, "You are a respected Jewish teacher, and yet you don't understand these things? [11]I assure you, we tell you what we know and have seen, and yet you won't believe our testimony. [12]But if you don't believe me when I tell you about earthly things, how can you possibly believe if I tell you about heavenly things? [13]No one has ever gone to heaven and returned. But the Son of Man has come down from heaven. [14]And as Moses lifted up the bronze snake on a pole in the wilderness, so the Son of Man must be lifted up, [15]so that everyone who believes in him will have eternal life.

[16]"For God loved the world so much that he gave his one and only Son, so that everyone who believes in him will not perish but have eternal life. [17]God sent his Son into the world not to judge the world, but to save the world through him.

[18]"There is no judgment against anyone who believes in him. But anyone who does not believe in him has already been judged for not believing in God's one and only Son. [19]And the judgment is based on this fact: God's light came into the world, but people loved the darkness more than the light, for their actions were evil. [20]All who do evil hate the light and refuse to go near it for fear their sins will be exposed. [21]But those who do what is right come to the light so others can see that they are doing what God wants."

John the Baptist Exalts Jesus

[22]Then Jesus and his disciples left Jerusalem and went into the Judean countryside. Jesus spent some time with them there, baptizing people.

[23]At this time John the Baptist was baptizing at Aenon, near Salim, because there was plenty of water there; and people kept coming to him for baptism. [24](This was before John was thrown into prison.) [25]A debate broke out between John's disciples and a certain Jew over ceremonial cleansing. [26]So John's disciples came to him and said, "Rabbi, the man you met on the other side of the Jordan River, the one you identified as the Messiah, is also baptizing people. And everybody is going to him instead of coming to us."

[27]John replied, "No one can receive anything unless God gives it from heaven. [28]You yourselves know how plainly I told you, 'I am not the Messiah. I am only here to prepare the way for him.' [29]It is the bridegroom who marries the bride, and the best man is simply glad to stand with him and hear his vows. Therefore, I am filled with joy at his success. [30]He must become greater and greater, and I must become less and less.

³¹"He has come from above and is greater than anyone else. We are of the earth, and we speak of earthly things, but he has come from heaven and is greater than anyone else. ³²He testifies about what he has seen and heard, but how few believe what he tells them! ³³Anyone who accepts his testimony can affirm that God is true. ³⁴For he is sent by God. He speaks God's words, for God gives him the Spirit without limit. ³⁵The Father loves his Son and has put everything into his hands. ³⁶And anyone who believes in God's Son has eternal life. Anyone who doesn't obey the Son will never experience eternal life but remains under God's angry judgment."

Look for ways to help: Not doing bad things is not enough! We are responsible to help less fortunate and hurting people. Look for ways to help others today — they are all around you. You will learn the joy of helping others. "So encourage each other and build each other up, just as you are already doing."

1 Thessalonians 5:11

POWER HABITS

action

3:10-21 WHAT'S IT SAYING?

WHAT AM I GOING TO DO ABOUT IT?

Jesus and the Samaritan Woman

4

Jesus knew the Pharisees had heard that he was baptizing and making more disciples than John ²(though Jesus himself didn't baptize them—his disciples did). ³So he left Judea and returned to Galilee. ⁴He had to go through Samaria on the way. ⁵Eventually he came to the Samaritan village of Sychar, near the field that Jacob gave to his son Joseph. ⁶Jacob's well was there; and Jesus, tired from the long walk, sat wearily beside the well about noontime. ⁷Soon a Samaritan woman came to draw water, and Jesus said to her, "Please give me a drink." ⁸He was alone at the time because his disciples had gone into the village to buy some food.

⁹The woman was surprised, for Jews refuse to have anything to do with Samaritans. She said to Jesus, "You are a Jew, and I am a Samaritan woman. Why are you asking me for a drink?"

¹⁰Jesus replied, "If you only knew the gift God has for you and who you are speaking to, you would ask me, and I would give you living water."

¹¹"But sir, you don't have a rope or a bucket," she said, "and this well is very deep. Where would you get this living water? ¹²And besides, do you think you're greater than our ancestor Jacob, who gave us this well? How can you offer better water than he and his sons and his animals enjoyed?"

¹³Jesus replied, "Anyone who drinks this water will soon become thirsty again. ¹⁴But those who drink the water I give will never be thirsty again. It becomes a fresh, bubbling spring within them, giving them eternal life."

¹⁵"Please, sir," the woman said, "give me this water! Then I'll never be thirsty again, and I won't have to come here to get water."

¹⁶"Go and get your husband," Jesus told her.

¹⁷"I don't have a husband," the woman replied.

Jesus said, "You're right! You don't have a husband— ¹⁸for you have had five husbands, and you aren't even married to the man you're living with now. You certainly spoke the truth!"

¹⁹"Sir," the woman said, "you must be a prophet. ²⁰So tell me, why is it that you Jews insist that Jerusalem is the only place of worship, while we Samaritans claim it is here at Mount Gerizim, where our ancestors worshiped?"

²¹Jesus replied, "Believe me, dear woman, the time is coming when it will no longer matter whether you worship the Father on this mountain or in Jerusalem. ²²You Samaritans know very little about the one you worship, while we Jews know all about him, for salvation comes through the Jews. ²³But the time is coming—indeed it's here now—when true worshipers will worship the Father in spirit and in truth. The Father is looking for those who will worship him that way. ²⁴For God is Spirit, so those who worship him must worship in spirit and in truth."

²⁵The woman said, "I know the Messiah is coming—the one who is called Christ. When he comes, he will explain everything to us."

²⁶Then Jesus told her, "I AM the Messiah!"

²⁷Just then his disciples came back. They were shocked to find him talking to a woman, but none of them had the nerve to ask, "What do you want with her?" or "Why are you talking to her?" ²⁸The woman left her water jar beside the well and ran back to the village, telling everyone, ²⁹"Come and see a man who told me everything I ever did! Could he possibly be the Messiah?" ³⁰So the people came streaming from the village to see him.

³¹Meanwhile, the disciples were urging Jesus, "Rabbi, eat something."

³²But Jesus replied, "I have a kind of food you know nothing about."

³³"Did someone bring him food while we were gone?" the disciples asked each other.

³⁴Then Jesus explained: "My nourishment comes from doing the will of God, who sent me, and from finishing his work. ³⁵You know the saying, 'Four months between planting and harvest.' But I say, wake up and look around. The fields are already ripe for harvest. ³⁶The harvesters are paid good

I am the only Christian on the team. I don't really feel like I'm making a difference. Am I?

You are making a massive impact by simply praying for your teammates! Don't be fooled by the idea that you are not being effective. Be super-positive and live out your faith. Both positive and negative attitudes are highly contagious. Negativism can spread through a team like a disease. Carefully guard what you think and say. Start an epidemic of enthusiasm on your team by being optimistic and positive.

Pray, play, and say! Keep asking God for opportunities to reflect and share Jesus.

wages, and the fruit they harvest is people brought to eternal life. What joy awaits both the planter and the harvester alike! ³⁷You know the saying, 'One plants and another harvests.' And it's true. ³⁸I sent you to harvest where you didn't plant; others had already done the work, and now you will get to gather the harvest."

Many Samaritans Believe

³⁹Many Samaritans from the village believed in Jesus because the woman had said, "He told me everything I ever did!" ⁴⁰When they came out to see him, they begged him to stay in their village. So he stayed for two days, ⁴¹long enough for many more to hear his message and believe. ⁴²Then they said to the woman, "Now we believe, not just because of what you told us, but because we have heard him ourselves. Now we know that he is indeed the Savior of the world."

Jesus Heals an Official's Son

⁴³At the end of the two days, Jesus went on to Galilee. ⁴⁴He himself had said that a prophet is not honored in his own hometown. ⁴⁵Yet the Galileans welcomed him, for they had been in Jerusalem at the Passover celebration and had seen everything he did there.

⁴⁶As he traveled through Galilee, he came to Cana, where he had turned the water into wine. There was a government official in nearby Capernaum whose son was very sick. ⁴⁷When he heard that Jesus had come from Judea to Galilee, he went and begged Jesus to come to Capernaum to heal his son, who was about to die.

⁴⁸Jesus asked, "Will you never believe in me unless you see miraculous signs and wonders?"

⁴⁹The official pleaded, "Lord, please come now before my little boy dies."

⁵⁰Then Jesus told him, "Go back home. Your son will live!" And the man believed what Jesus said and started home.

⁵¹While the man was on his way, some of his servants met him with the news that his son was alive and well. ⁵²He asked them when the boy had begun to get better, and they replied, "Yesterday afternoon at one o'clock his fever suddenly disappeared!" ⁵³Then the father realized that that was the very time Jesus had told him, "Your son will live."

And he and his entire household believed in Jesus. ⁵⁴This was the second miraculous sign Jesus did in Galilee after coming from Judea.

action

4:19-24 WHAT'S IT SAYING?

WHAT AM I GOING TO do ABOUT IT?

Jesus Heals a Lame Man

5

Afterward Jesus returned to Jerusalem for one of the Jewish holy days. ²Inside the city, near the Sheep Gate, was the pool of Bethesda, with five covered porches. ³Crowds of sick people—blind, lame, or paralyzed— lay on the porches.[*] ⁵One of the men lying there had been sick for thirty-eight years. ⁶When Jesus saw him

and knew he had been ill for a long time, he asked him, "Would you like to get well?"

⁷"I can't, sir," the sick man said, "for I have no one to put me into the pool when the water bubbles up. Someone else always gets there ahead of me."

⁸Jesus told him, "Stand up, pick up your mat, and walk!"

⁹Instantly, the man was healed! He rolled up his sleeping mat and began walking! But this miracle happened on the Sabbath, ¹⁰so the Jewish leaders objected. They said to the man who was cured, "You can't work on the Sabbath! The law doesn't allow you to carry that sleeping mat!"

¹¹But he replied, "The man who healed me told me, 'Pick up your mat and walk.'"

¹²"Who said such a thing as that?" they demanded.

¹³The man didn't know, for Jesus had disappeared into the crowd. ¹⁴But afterward Jesus found him in the Temple and told him, "Now you are well; so stop sinning, or something even worse may happen to you." ¹⁵Then the man went and told the Jewish leaders that it was Jesus who had healed him.

Jesus Claims to Be the Son of God

¹⁶So the Jewish leaders began harassing Jesus for breaking the Sabbath rules. ¹⁷But Jesus replied, "My Father is always working, and so am I." ¹⁸So the Jewish leaders tried all the harder to find a way to kill him. For he not only broke the Sabbath, he called God his Father, thereby making himself equal with God.

¹⁹So Jesus explained, "I tell you the truth, the Son can do nothing by himself. He does only what he sees the Father doing. Whatever the Father does, the Son also does. ²⁰For the Father loves the Son and shows him everything he is doing. In fact, the Father will show him how to do even greater works than healing this man. Then you will truly be astonished. ²¹For just as the Father gives life to those he raises from the dead, so the Son gives life to anyone he wants. ²²In

5:3 Some manuscripts add *waiting for a certain movement of the water, "for an angel of the Lord came from time to time and stirred up the water. And the first person to step in after the water was stirred was healed of whatever disease he had.*

addition, the Father judges no one. Instead, he has given the Son absolute authority to judge, 23so that everyone will honor the Son, just as they honor the Father. Anyone who does not honor the Son is certainly not honoring the Father who sent him.

24"I tell you the truth, those who listen to my message and believe in God who sent me have eternal life. They will never be condemned for their sins, but they have already passed from death into life.

25"And I assure you that the time is coming, indeed it's here now, when the dead will hear my voice—the voice of the Son of God. And those who listen will live. 26The Father has life in himself, and he has granted that same life-giving power to his Son. 27And he has given him authority to judge everyone because he is the Son of Man. 28Don't be so surprised! Indeed, the time is coming when all the dead in their graves will hear the voice of God's Son, 29and they will rise again. Those who have done good will rise to experience eternal life, and those who have continued in evil will rise to experience judgment. 30I can do nothing on my own. I judge as God tells me. Therefore, my judgment is just, because I carry out the will of the one who sent me, not my own will.

Witnesses to Jesus

31"If I were to testify on my own behalf, my testimony would not be valid. 32But someone else is also testifying about me, and I assure you that everything he says about me is true. 33In fact, you sent investigators to listen to John the Baptist, and his testimony about me was true. 34Of course, I have no need of human witnesses, but I say these things so you might be saved. 35John was like a burning and shining lamp, and you were excited for a while about his message. 36But I have a greater witness than John—my teachings and my miracles. The Father gave me these works to accomplish, and they prove that he sent me. 37And the Father who sent me has testified about me himself. You have never heard his voice or seen him face to face, 38and you do not have his message in your hearts, because you do not believe me—the one he sent to you.

39"You search the Scriptures because you think they give you eternal life. But the Scriptures point to me! 40Yet you refuse to come to me to receive this life.

41"Your approval means nothing to me, 42because I know you don't have God's love within you. 43For I have come to you in my Father's name, and you have rejected me. Yet if others come in their own name, you gladly welcome them. 44No wonder you can't believe! For you gladly honor each other, but you don't care about the honor that comes from the one who alone is God.

45"Yet it isn't I who will accuse you before the Father. Moses will accuse you! Yes, Moses, in whom you put your hopes. 46If you really believed Moses, you would believe me, because he wrote about me. 47But since you don't believe what he wrote, how will you believe what I say?"

Jesus Feeds Five Thousand

6

After this, Jesus crossed over to the far side of the Sea of Galilee, also known as the Sea of Tiberias. 2A huge crowd kept following him wherever he went, because they saw his miraculous signs as he healed the sick. 3Then Jesus climbed a hill and sat down with his disciples around him. 4(It was nearly time for the Jewish Passover celebration.) 5Jesus soon saw a huge crowd of people coming to look for him. Turning to Philip, he asked, "Where can we buy bread to feed all these people?" 6He was testing Philip, for he already knew what he was going to do.

7Philip replied, "Even if we worked for months, we wouldn't have enough money to feed them!"

8Then Andrew, Simon Peter's brother, spoke up. 9"There's a young boy here with five barley loaves and two fish. But what good is that with this huge crowd?"

10"Tell everyone to sit down," Jesus said. So they all sat down on the grassy slopes. (The men alone numbered 5,000.) 11Then Jesus took the loaves, gave thanks to God, and distributed them to the people. Afterward he did the same with the fish. And they all ate as much as they wanted. 12After everyone was full, Jesus told his disciples, "Now gather the leftovers, so that nothing is wasted." 13So they picked up the pieces and filled twelve baskets with scraps left by the people who had eaten from the five barley loaves.

14When the people saw him do this miraculous sign, they exclaimed, "Surely, he is the Prophet we have been expecting!" 15When Jesus saw that they were ready to force him to be their king, he slipped away into the hills by himself.

Jesus Walks on Water

16That evening Jesus' disciples went down to the shore to wait for him. 17But as darkness fell and Jesus still hadn't come back, they got into the boat and headed across the lake toward Capernaum. 18Soon a gale swept down upon them, and the sea grew very rough. 19They had rowed three or four miles when suddenly they saw Jesus walking on the water toward the boat. They were terrified, 20but he called out to them, "Don't be afraid. I am here!" 21Then they were eager to let him in the boat, and immediately they arrived at their destination!

When you feel unfulfilled

6:35

"I am the bread of life. Whoever comes to me will never be hungry again. Whoever believes in me will never be thirsty."

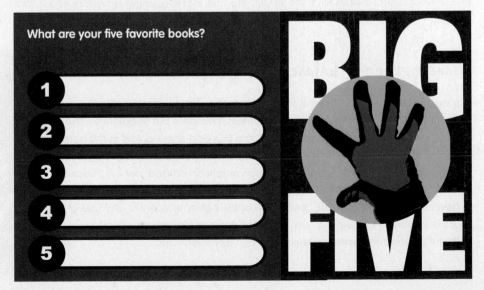

What are your five favorite books?

1
2
3
4
5

BIG FIVE

Jesus, the Bread of Life

22The next day the crowd that had stayed on the far shore saw that the disciples had taken the only boat, and they realized Jesus had not gone with them. 23Several boats from Tiberias landed near the place where the Lord had blessed the bread and the people had eaten. 24So when the crowd saw that neither Jesus nor his disciples were there, they got into the boats and went across to Capernaum to look for him. 25They found him on the other side of the lake and asked, "Rabbi, when did you get here?"

26Jesus replied, "I tell you the truth, you want to be with me because I fed you, not because you understood the miraculous signs. 27But don't be so concerned about perishable things like food. Spend your energy seeking the eternal life that the Son of Man can give you. For God the Father has given me the seal of his approval."

28They replied, "We want to perform God's works, too. What should we do?"

29Jesus told them, "This is the only work God wants from you: Believe in the one he has sent."

30They answered, "Show us a miraculous sign if you want us to believe in you. What can you do? 31After all, our ancestors ate manna while they journeyed through the wilderness! The Scriptures say, 'Moses gave them bread from heaven to eat.'"

32Jesus said, "I tell you the truth, Moses didn't give you bread from heaven. My Father did. And now he offers you the true bread from heaven. 33The true bread of God is the one who comes down from heaven and gives life to the world."

34"Sir," they said, "give us that bread every day."

35Jesus replied, "I am the bread of life. Whoever comes to me will never be hungry again. Whoever believes in me will never be thirsty. 36But you haven't believed in me even though you have seen me. 37However, those the Father has given me will come to me, and I will never reject them. 38For I have come down from heaven to do the will of God who sent me, not to do my own will. 39And this is the will of God, that I should not lose even one of all those he has given me, but that I should raise them up at the last day. 40For it is my Father's will that all who see his Son and believe in him should have eternal life. I will raise them up at the last day."

41Then the people began to murmur in disagreement because he had said, "I am the bread that came down from heaven." 42They said, "Isn't this Jesus, the son of Joseph? We know his father and mother. How can he say, 'I came down from heaven'?"

43But Jesus replied, "Stop complaining about what I said. 44For no one can come to me unless the Father who sent me draws them to me, and at the last day I will raise them up. 45As it is written in the Scriptures, 'They will all be taught by God.' Everyone who listens to the Father and learns from him comes to me. 46(Not that anyone has ever seen the Father; only I, who was sent from God, have seen him.)

47"I tell you the truth, anyone who believes has eternal life. 48Yes, I am the bread of life! 49Your ancestors ate manna in the wilderness, but they all died. 50Anyone who eats the bread from heaven, however, will never die. 51I am the living bread that came down from heaven. Anyone who eats this bread will live forever; and this bread, which I will offer so the world may live, is my flesh."

52Then the people began arguing with each other about what he meant. "How can this man give us his flesh to eat?" they asked.

53So Jesus said again, "I tell you the truth, unless you eat the flesh of the Son of Man and drink his blood, you cannot have eternal life within you. 54But anyone who eats my flesh and drinks my blood has eternal life, and I will raise that person at the last day. 55For my flesh is true food, and my blood is true drink. 56Anyone who eats my flesh and drinks my blood remains in me, and I in him. 57I live because of the living Father who sent me; in the same way, anyone who feeds on me will live because of me. 58I am the true bread that came down from heaven. Anyone who eats this bread will not die as your ancestors did (even though they ate the manna) but will live forever." 59He said these things while he was teaching in the synagogue in Capernaum.

Many Disciples Desert Jesus

60Many of his disciples said, "This is very hard to understand. How can anyone accept it?"

61Jesus was aware that his disciples were complaining, so he said to them, "Does this offend you? 62Then what will you think if you see the Son of Man ascend to heaven again? 63The Spirit alone gives eternal life. Human effort accomplishes nothing. And the very words I have spoken to you are spirit and life. 64But some of you do not believe me." (For Jesus knew from the beginning which ones didn't believe, and he knew who would betray him.) 65Then he said, "That is why I said that people can't come to me unless the Father gives them to me."

66At this point many of his disciples turned away and deserted him. 67Then Jesus turned to the Twelve and asked, "Are you also going to leave?"

68Simon Peter replied, "Lord, to whom would we go? You have the words that give eternal life. 69We believe, and we know you are the Holy One of God."

70Then Jesus said, "I chose the twelve of you, but one is a devil." 71He was speaking of Judas, son of Simon Iscariot, one of the Twelve, who would later betray him.

Winners keep a balanced perspective!

Having God at the center of your life puts everything in perspective. Great athletes don't fall apart when they lose, unless their life is out of balance. The French philosopher Blaise Pascal said, "There is a God-shaped void in the heart of every man." We would certainly never call sport our god, but when we put too much emphasis on anything, or not enough emphasis on God, our lives become lopsided and we create mini-god substitutes. Winning and losing a match can be dangerously overemphasized. Keep God at the center of your life and spend your life in pursuit of pleasing him, and your perspective will be perfect!

"Carefully determine what pleases the Lord." (Ephesians 5:10)

Winners see the big picture!

Jesus and His Brothers

7

After this, Jesus traveled around Galilee. He wanted to stay out of Judea, where the Jewish leaders were plotting his death. ²But soon it was time for the Jewish Festival of Shelters, ³and Jesus' brothers said to him, "Leave here and go to Judea, where your followers can see your miracles! ⁴You can't become famous if you hide like this! If you can do such wonderful things, show yourself to the world!" ⁵For even his brothers didn't believe in him.

⁶Jesus replied, "Now is not the right time for me to go, but you can go anytime. ⁷The world can't hate you, but it does hate me because I accuse it of doing evil. ⁸You go on. I'm not going to this festival, because my time has not yet come." ⁹After saying these things, Jesus remained in Galilee.

Jesus Teaches Openly at the Temple

¹⁰But after his brothers left for the festival, Jesus also went, though secretly, staying out of public view. ¹¹The Jewish leaders tried to find him at the festival and kept asking if anyone had seen him. ¹²There was a lot of grumbling about him among the crowds. Some argued, "He's a good man," but others said, "He's nothing but a fraud who deceives the people." ¹³But no one had the courage to speak favorably about him in public, for they were afraid of getting in trouble with the Jewish leaders.

¹⁴Then, midway through the festival, Jesus went up to the Temple and began to teach. ¹⁵The people were surprised when they heard him. "How does he know so much when he hasn't been trained?" they asked.

¹⁶So Jesus told them, "My message is not my own; it comes from God who sent me. ¹⁷Anyone who wants to do the will of God will know whether my teaching is from God or is merely my own. ¹⁸Those who speak for themselves want glory only for themselves, but a person who seeks to honor the one who sent him speaks truth, not lies. ¹⁹Moses gave you the law, but none of you obeys it! In fact, you are trying to kill me."

²⁰The crowd replied, "You're demon possessed! Who's trying to kill you?"

²¹Jesus replied, "I did one miracle on the Sabbath, and you were amazed. ²²But you work on the Sabbath, too, when you obey Moses' law of circumcision. (Actually, this tradition of circumcision began with the patriarchs, long before the law of Moses.) ²³For if the correct time for circumcising your son falls on the Sabbath, you go ahead and do it so as not to break the law of Moses. So why should you be angry with me for healing a man on the Sabbath? ²⁴Look beneath the surface so you can judge correctly."

Is Jesus the Messiah?

²⁵Some of the people who lived in Jerusalem started to ask each other, "Isn't this the man they are trying to kill? ²⁶But here he is, speaking in public, and they say nothing to him. Could our leaders possibly believe that he is the Messiah? ²⁷But how could he be? For we know where this man comes from. When the Messiah

WHAT DOES IT MEAN?

adultery

An adulterer is a man or woman who has sex with a married or an engaged person. Intercourse between unmarried people is fornication. Adultery and fornication were regarded as great social wrongs in Jesus' time, as well as major sins. It has been inferred from John 8:1-11 that adultery became very common during the age preceding the destruction of Jerusalem.

profiles

John:

At the Last Supper we see a beautiful picture of closeness – a relaxed manner that John had with Jesus. Peter asks John to ask Jesus who is the betrayer. We see John hanging out with Christ in an intimate, easygoing way. John was originally with his (probably older) brother James, a disciple of John the Baptist. It appears that Jesus' mother Mary was John's aunt. We know that Jesus had a special close circle of disciples and an even closer group that accompanied him almost everywhere, which included John. There are insights in John's writings that reveal he knew the master's heart. John had a knack for recognizing Jesus when no one else did (John 21:7), and he was with Jesus at his death. Jesus even charged him to take care of his mother, Mary. Jesus also nicknamed John and his brother "the Sons of Thunder," perhaps after they wanted to blast with lightning a village that spurned Jesus (Luke 9:54). John wrote five books of the New Testament: the Gospel of John, the three letters of John, and Revelation. If Jesus was in the room with you now, could you enjoy the same closeness that John enjoyed or would the relationship be stiff and formal? I hope it would be close, because he is here with you and wants to be close to you.

comes, he will simply appear; no one will know where he comes from."

[28]While Jesus was teaching in the Temple, he called out, "Yes, you know me, and you know where I come from. But I'm not here on my own. The one who sent me is true, and you don't know him. [29]But I know him because I come from him, and he sent me to you." [30]Then the leaders tried to arrest him; but no one laid a hand on him, because his time had not yet come.

[31]Many among the crowds at the Temple believed in him. "After all," they said, "would you expect the Messiah to do more miraculous signs than this man has done?"

[32]When the Pharisees heard that the crowds were whispering such things, they and the leading priests sent Temple guards to arrest Jesus. [33]But Jesus told them, "I will be with you only a little longer. Then I will return to the one who sent me. [34]You will search for me but not find me. And you cannot go where I am going."

[35]The Jewish leaders were puzzled by this statement. "Where is he planning to go?" they asked. "Is he thinking of leaving the country and going to the Jews in other lands? Maybe he will even teach the Greeks! [36]What does he mean when he says, 'You will search for me but not find me,' and 'You cannot go where I am going'?"

Jesus Promises Living Water

[37]On the last day, the climax of the festival, Jesus stood and shouted to the crowds, "Anyone who is thirsty may come to me! [38]Anyone who believes in me may come and drink! For the Scriptures declare, 'Rivers of living water will flow from his heart.'" [39](When he said "living water," he was speaking of the Spirit, who would be given to everyone believing in him. But the Spirit had not yet been given, because Jesus had not yet entered into his glory.)

Division and Unbelief

[40]When the crowds heard him say this, some of them declared, "Surely this man is the Prophet we've been expecting." [41]Others said, "He is the Messiah." Still others said, "But he can't be! Will the Messiah come from Galilee? [42]For the Scriptures clearly state that the Messiah will be born of the royal line of David, in Bethlehem, the village where King David was born." [43]So the crowd was divided about him. [44]Some even wanted him arrested, but no one laid a hand on him. [45]When the Temple guards returned without having arrested Jesus, the leading priests and Pharisees demanded, "Why didn't you bring him in?"

No medals were awarded in the ancient Olympics. A winner received an olive wreath, considered by the Greeks to be a symbol of peace, sustenance, and life, to wear on his head. The apostle Paul mentions this in 1 Corinthians 9:25.

[46]"We have never heard anyone speak like this!" the guards responded.

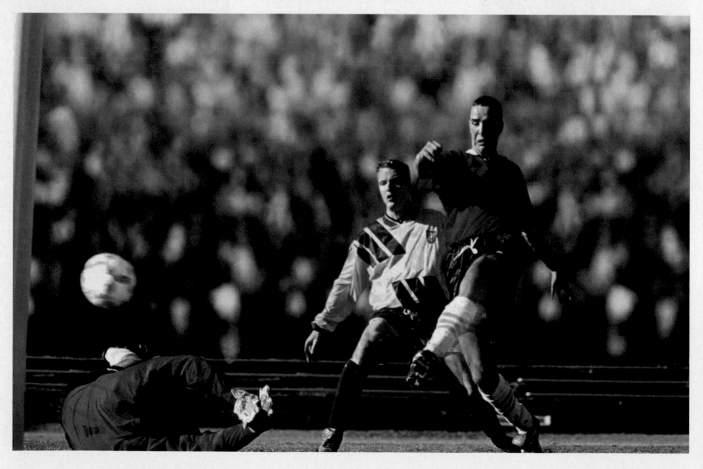

[47]"Have you been led astray, too?" the Pharisees mocked. [48]"Is there a single one of us rulers or Pharisees who believes in him? [49]This foolish crowd follows him, but they are ignorant of the law. God's curse is on them!"

[50]Then Nicodemus, the leader who had met with Jesus earlier, spoke up. [51]"Is it legal to convict a man before he is given a hearing?" he asked.

[52]They replied, "Are you from Galilee, too? Search the Scriptures and see for yourself—no prophet ever comes from Galilee!"

[The most ancient Greek manuscripts do not include John 7:53-8:11.]

[53]Then the meeting broke up, and everybody went home.

8:31-47 WHAT'S IT SAYING?

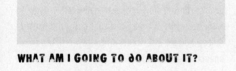

WHAT AM I GOING TO DO ABOUT IT?

A Woman Caught in Adultery

8

Jesus returned to the Mount of Olives, [2]but early the next morning he was back again at the Temple. A crowd soon gathered, and he sat down and taught them. [3]As he was speaking, the teachers of religious law and the Pharisees brought a woman who had been caught in the act of adultery. They put her in front of the crowd.

[4]"Teacher," they said to Jesus, "this woman was caught in the act of adultery. [5]The law of Moses says to stone her. What do you say?"

[6]They were trying to trap him into saying something they could use against him, but Jesus stooped down and wrote in the dust with his finger. [7]They kept demanding an answer, so he stood up again and said, "All right, but let the one who has never sinned throw the first stone!" [8]Then he stooped down again and wrote in the dust.

[9]When the accusers heard this, they slipped away one by one, beginning with the oldest, until only Jesus was left in the middle of the crowd with the woman. [10]Then Jesus stood up again and said to the woman, "Where are your accusers? Didn't even one of them condemn you?"

[11]"No, Lord," she said.

And Jesus said, "Neither do I. Go and sin no more."

Jesus, the Light of the World

[12]Jesus spoke to the people once more and said, "I am the light of the world. If you follow me, you won't have to walk in darkness, because you will have the light that leads to life."

[13]The Pharisees replied, "You are making those claims about yourself! Such testimony is not valid."

[14]Jesus told them, "These claims are valid even though I make them about myself. For I know where I came from and where I am going, but you don't know this about me. [15]You judge me by human standards, but I do not judge anyone. [16]And if I did, my judgment would be correct in every respect because I am not alone. The Father who sent me is with me. [17]Your own law says that if two people agree about something, their witness is accepted as fact. [18]I am one witness, and my Father who sent me is the other."

[19]"Where is your father?" they asked.

Jesus answered, "Since you don't know who I am, you don't know who my Father is. If you knew me, you would also know my Father." [20]Jesus made these statements while he was teaching in the section of the Temple known as the Treasury. But he was not arrested, because his time had not yet come.

The Unbelieving People Warned

[21]Later Jesus said to them again, "I am going away. You will search for me but will die in your sin. You cannot come where I am going."

[22]The people asked, "Is he planning to commit suicide? What does he mean, 'You cannot come where I am going'?"

[23]Jesus continued, "You are from below; I am from above. You belong to this world; I do not. [24]That is why I said that you will die in your sins; for unless you believe that I AM who I claim to be, you will die in your sins."

[25]"Who are you?" they demanded.

Jesus replied, "The one I have always claimed to be. [26]I have much to say about you and much to condemn, but I won't. For I say only what I have heard from the one who sent me, and he is completely truthful." [27]But they still didn't understand that he was talking about his Father.

[28]So Jesus said, "When you have lifted up the Son of Man on the cross, then you will understand that I AM he. I do nothing on my own but say only what the Father taught me. [29]And the one who sent me is with me—he has not deserted me. For I always do what pleases him." [30]Then many who heard him say these things believed in him.

Jesus and Abraham

[31]Jesus said to the people who believed in him, "You are truly my disciples if you remain faithful to my teachings. [32]And you will know the truth, and the truth will set you free."

[33]"But we are descendants of Abraham," they said. "We have never been slaves to anyone. What do you mean, 'You will be set free'?"

[34]Jesus replied, "I tell you the truth, everyone who sins is a slave of sin. [35]A slave is not a permanent member of the family, but a son is part of the family forever. [36]So if the Son sets you free, you are truly free. [37]Yes, I realize that you are descendants of Abraham. And yet some of you are trying to kill me because there's no room in your hearts for my message. [38]I am telling you what I saw when I was with my Father. But you are following the advice of your father."

[39]"Our father is Abraham!" they declared.

"No," Jesus replied, "for if you were really the children of Abraham, you would follow his example. [40]Instead, you are trying to kill me because I told you the truth, which I heard from God. Abraham never did such a thing. [41]No, you are imitating your real father."

They replied, "We aren't illegitimate children! God himself is our true Father."

[42]Jesus told them, "If God were your Father, you would love me, because I have come to you from God. I am not here on my own, but he sent me. [43]Why can't you understand what I am saying? It's because you can't even hear me! [44]For you are the children of your father the devil, and you love to do the evil things he does. He was a murderer from the beginning. He has always hated the truth, because there is no truth in him. When he lies, it is consistent with his character; for he is a liar and the father of lies. [45]So when I tell the truth, you just naturally don't believe me! [46]Which of you can truthfully accuse me of sin? And since I am telling

you the truth, why don't you believe me? [47]Anyone who belongs to God listens gladly to the words of God. But you don't listen because you don't belong to God."

[48]The people retorted, "You Samaritan devil! Didn't we say all along that you were possessed by a demon?"

[49]"No," Jesus said, "I have no demon in me. For I honor my Father—and you dishonor me. [50]And though I have no wish to glorify myself, God is going to glorify me. He is the true judge. [51]I tell you the truth, anyone who obeys my teaching will never die!"

[52]The people said, "Now we know you are possessed by a demon. Even Abraham and the prophets died, but you say, 'Anyone who obeys my teaching will never die!' [53]Are you greater than our father Abraham? He died, and so did the prophets. Who do you think you are?"

[54]Jesus answered, "If I want glory for myself, it doesn't count. But it is my Father who will glorify me. You say, 'He is our God,' [55]but you don't even know him. I know him. If I said otherwise, I would be as great a liar as you! But I do know him and obey him. [56]Your father Abraham rejoiced as he looked forward to my coming. He saw it and was glad."

[57]The people said, "You aren't even fifty years old. How can you say you have seen Abraham?"

[58]Jesus answered, "I tell you the truth, before Abraham was even born, I AM!" [59]At that point they picked up stones to throw at him. But Jesus was hidden from them and left the Temple.

Jesus Heals a Man Born Blind

9

As Jesus was walking along, he saw a man who had been blind from birth. [2]"Rabbi," his disciples asked him, "why was this man born blind? Was it because of his own sins or his parents' sins?"

[3]"It was not because of his sins or his parents' sins," Jesus answered. "This happened so the power of God could be seen in him. [4]We must quickly carry out the tasks assigned us by the one who sent us. The night is coming, and then no one can work. [5]But while I am here in the world, I am the light of the world."

[6]Then he spit on the ground, made mud with the saliva, and spread the mud over the blind man's eyes. [7]He told him, "Go wash yourself in the pool of Siloam" (Siloam means "sent"). So the man went and washed and came back seeing! [8]His neighbors and others who knew him as a blind beggar asked each other, "Isn't this the man who used to sit and beg?" [9]Some said he was, and others said, "No, he just looks like him!"

But the beggar kept saying, "Yes, I am the same one!"

[10]They asked, "Who healed you? What happened?"

[11]He told them, "The man they call Jesus made mud and

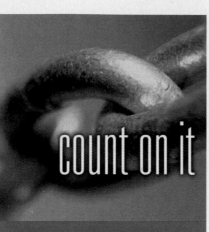

count on it

Try hard!

You do not have to try hard to get God to love you – he loved you so that you would try hard! How much does God love you? Spread out your hands as wide as you can. That much! God sent his son to the cross so that in the bloody sacrifice of Jesus, you would be forgiven! Respond to that love in gratitude. Try hard! "He is so rich in kindness and grace that he purchased our freedom with the blood of his Son and forgave our sins." (Ephesians 1:7)

Count on it!

spread it over my eyes and told me, 'Go to the pool of Siloam and wash yourself.' So I went and washed, and now I can see!"

[12]"Where is he now?" they asked.

"I don't know," he replied.

[13]Then they took the man who had been blind to the Pharisees, [14]because it was on the Sabbath that Jesus had made the mud and healed him. [15]The Pharisees asked the man all about it. So he told them, "He put the mud over my eyes, and when I washed it away, I could see!"

[16]Some of the Pharisees said, "This man Jesus is not from God, for he is working on the Sabbath." Others said, "But how could an ordinary sinner do such miraculous signs?" So there was a deep division of opinion among them.

[17]Then the Pharisees again questioned the man who had been blind and demanded, "What's your opinion about this man who healed you?"

The man replied, "I think he must be a prophet."

[18]The Jewish leaders still refused to believe the man had been blind and could now see, so they called in his parents. [19]They asked them, "Is this your son? Was he born blind? If so, how can he now see?"

[20]His parents replied, "We know this is our son and that he was born blind, [21]but we don't know how he can see or who healed him. Ask him. He is old enough to speak for himself." [22]His parents said this because they were afraid of the Jewish leaders, who had announced that anyone saying Jesus was the Messiah would be expelled from the synagogue. [23]That's why they said, "He is old enough. Ask him."

[24]So for the second time they called in the man who had been blind and told him, "God should get the glory for this, because we know this man Jesus is a sinner."

[25]"I don't know whether he is a sinner," the man replied. "But I know this: I was blind, and now I can see!"

[26]"But what did he do?" they asked. "How did he heal you?"

[27]"Look!" the man exclaimed. "I told you once. Didn't you listen? Why do you want to hear it again? Do you want to become his disciples, too?"

[28]Then they cursed him and said, "You are his disciple, but we are disciples of Moses! [29]We know God spoke to Moses, but we don't even know where this man comes from."

[30]"Why, that's very strange!" the man replied. "He healed my eyes, and yet you don't know where he comes from? [31]We know that God doesn't listen to sinners, but he is ready to hear those who worship him and do his will. [32]Ever since the world began, no one has been able to open the eyes of someone born blind. [33]If this man were not from God, he couldn't have done it."

[34]"You were born a total sinner!" they answered. "Are you trying to teach us?" And they threw him out of the synagogue.

Spiritual Blindness

[35]When Jesus heard what had happened, he found the man and asked, "Do you believe in the Son of Man?"

[36]The man answered, "Who is he, sir? I want to believe in him."

[37]"You have seen him," Jesus said, "and he is speaking to you!"

[38]"Yes, Lord, I believe!" the man said. And he worshiped Jesus.

BIBLE HIT

Life to the Full (JOHN 10:10)

Pro athletes can be the most open to following Christ. They have realized what most athletes dream of: getting to the top. They achieved their dream and climbed the ladder of success. So why are they so open to the gospel? Because the ladder is on the wrong wall! For this reason, they grasp the fact that sporting accomplishments do not make you happy. There is an emptiness in the heart of every person that can only be filled up by God, through Jesus your Lord and Savior. Everyone wants to have life to the max. Having Jesus in your life – life to the full – is the only way to fulfillment.

[39]Then Jesus told him, "I entered this world to render judgment—to give sight to the blind and to show those who think they see that they are blind."

[40]Some Pharisees who were standing nearby heard him and asked, "Are you saying we're blind?"

[41]"If you were blind, you wouldn't be guilty," Jesus replied. "But you remain guilty because you claim you can see.

10:1-10 WHAT'S IT SAYING?

WHAT AM I GOING TO DO ABOUT IT?

The Good Shepherd and His Sheep

10

"I tell you the truth, anyone who sneaks over the wall of a sheepfold, rather than going through the gate, must surely be a thief and a robber! [2]But the one who enters through the gate is the shepherd of the sheep. [3]The gatekeeper opens the gate for him, and the sheep recognize his voice and come to him. He calls his own sheep by name and leads them out. [4]After he has gathered his own flock, he walks ahead of them, and they follow him because they know his voice. [5]They won't follow a stranger; they will run from him because they don't know his voice."

[6]Those who heard Jesus use this illustration didn't understand what he meant, [7]so he explained it to them: "I tell you the truth, I am the gate for the sheep. [8]All who came before me were thieves and robbers. But the true sheep did not listen to them. [9]Yes, I am the gate. Those who come in through me will be saved. They will come and go freely and will find good pastures. [10]The thief's purpose is to steal and kill and destroy. My purpose is to give them a rich and satisfying life.

[11]"I am the good shepherd. The good shepherd sacrifices his life for the sheep. [12]A hired hand will run when he sees a wolf coming. He will abandon the sheep because they don't belong to him and he isn't their shepherd. And so the wolf attacks them and scatters the flock. [13]The hired hand runs away because he's working only for the money and doesn't really care about the sheep.

[14]"I am the good shepherd; I know my own sheep, and they know me, [15]just as my Father knows me and I know the Father. So I sacrifice my life for the sheep. [16]I have other sheep, too, that are not in this sheepfold. I must bring them also. They will listen to my voice, and there will be one flock with one shepherd.

[17]"The Father loves me because I sacrifice my life so I may take it back again. [18]No one can take my life from me. I sacrifice it voluntarily. For I have the authority to lay it down when I want to and also to take it up again. For this is what my Father has commanded."

[19]When he said these things, the people were again divided in their opinions about him. [20]Some said, "He's demon possessed and out of his mind. Why listen to a man like that?" [21]Others said, "This doesn't sound like a man possessed by a demon! Can a demon open the eyes of the blind?"

Jesus Claims to Be the Son of God

[22]It was now winter, and Jesus was in Jerusalem at the time of Hanukkah, the Festival of Dedication. [23]He was in the Temple, walking through the section known as Solomon's Colonnade. [24]The people surrounded him and asked, "How long are you going to keep us in suspense? If you are the Messiah, tell us plainly."

[25]Jesus replied, "I have already told you, and you don't believe me. The proof is the work I do in my Father's name. [26]But you don't believe me because you are not my sheep. [27]My sheep listen to my voice; I know them, and they follow me. [28]I give them eternal life, and they will never perish. No one can snatch them away from me, [29]for my Father has given them to me, and he is more powerful than anyone else. No one can snatch them from the Father's hand. [30]The Father and I are one."

[31]Once again the people picked up stones to kill him. [32]Jesus said, "At my Father's direction I have done many good works. For which one are you going to stone me?"

[33]They replied, "We're stoning you not for any good work, but for blasphemy! You, a mere man, claim to be God."

[34]Jesus replied, "It is written in your own Scriptures that God said to certain leaders of the people, 'I say, you are gods!' [35]And you know that the Scriptures cannot be altered.

STAND POINT

When you want to know God

11:27

"I have always believed you are the Messiah, the Son of God, the one who has come into the world from God."

KNOW it

This Will Not End in Death (JOHN 11)
Jesus had many friends besides his disciples, including the sisters and brother Mary, Martha, and Lazarus, with whom he often stayed. When their brother fell deathly ill, the sisters sent word immediately to Jesus to come and help. Jesus was preaching nearby, across the Jordan River, and could have been with them shortly. But it was not God's timing, and Jesus knew the story was not to end in the death of Lazarus, but to strengthen the faith of many of Jesus' followers. Though Lazarus died and Jesus' delay seemed to be the actions of an insincere, heartless friend, it turned into a marvelous miracle as Jesus raised Lazarus from the dead. God's timing is always perfect. Wait for and trust in that perfect timing.

BIBLE HIT

So if those people who received God's message were called 'gods,' 36why do you call it blasphemy when I say, 'I am the Son of God'? After all, the Father set me apart and sent me into the world. 37Don't believe me unless I carry out my Father's work. 38But if I do his work, believe in the evidence of the miraculous works I have done, even if you don't believe me. Then you will know and understand that the Father is in me, and I am in the Father."

39Once again they tried to arrest him, but he got away and left them. 40He went beyond the Jordan River near the place where John was first baptizing and stayed there awhile. 41And many followed him. "John didn't perform miraculous signs," they remarked to one another, "but everything he said about this man has come true." 42And many who were there believed in Jesus.

The Raising of Lazarus

11

A man named Lazarus was sick. He lived in Bethany with his sisters, Mary and Martha. 2This is the Mary who later poured the expensive perfume on the Lord's feet and wiped them with her hair. Her brother, Lazarus, was sick. 3So the two sisters sent a message to Jesus telling him, "Lord, your dear friend is very sick."

4But when Jesus heard about it he said, "Lazarus's sickness will not end in death. No, it happened for the glory of God so that the Son of God will receive glory from this." 5So although Jesus loved Martha, Mary, and Lazarus, 6he stayed where he was for the next two days. 7Finally, he said to his disciples, "Let's go back to Judea."

8But his disciples objected. "Rabbi," they said, "only a few days ago the people in Judea were trying to stone you. Are you going there again?"

9Jesus replied, "There are twelve hours of daylight every day. During the day people can walk safely. They can see because they have the light of this world. 10But at night there is danger of stumbling because they have no light." 11Then he said, "Our friend Lazarus has fallen asleep, but now I will go and wake him up."

12The disciples said, "Lord, if he is sleeping, he will soon get better!" 13They thought Jesus meant Lazarus was simply sleeping, but Jesus meant Lazarus had died.

14So he told them plainly, "Lazarus is dead. 15And for your sakes, I'm glad I wasn't there, for now you will really believe. Come, let's go see him."

16Thomas, nicknamed the Twin, said to his fellow disciples, "Let's go, too—and die with Jesus."

17When Jesus arrived at Bethany, he was told that Lazarus had already been in his grave for four days. 18Bethany was only a few miles down the road from Jerusalem, 19and many of the people had come to console Martha and Mary in their loss. 20When Martha got word that Jesus was coming, she went to meet him. But Mary stayed in the house. 21Martha said to Jesus, "Lord, if only you had been here, my brother would not have died. 22But even now I know that God will give you whatever you ask."

23Jesus told her, "Your brother will rise again."

24"Yes," Martha said, "he will rise when everyone else rises, at the last day."

25Jesus told her, "I am the resurrection and the life. Anyone who believes in me will live, even after dying. 26Everyone who lives in me and believes in me will never ever die. Do you believe this, Martha?"

27"Yes, Lord," she told him. "I have always believed you are the Messiah, the Son of God, the one who has come into the world from God." 28Then she returned to Mary. She called Mary aside from the mourners and told her, "The Teacher is here and wants to see you." 29So Mary immediately went to him.

30Jesus had stayed outside the village, at the place where Martha met him. 31When the people who were at the house consoling Mary saw her leave so hastily, they assumed she was going to Lazarus's grave to weep. So they followed her there. 32When Mary arrived and saw Jesus, she fell at his feet and said, "Lord, if only you had been here, my brother would not have died."

33When Jesus saw her weeping and saw the other people wailing with her, a deep anger welled up within him, and he was deeply troubled. 34"Where have you put him?" he asked them.

They told him, "Lord, come and see." 35Then Jesus wept. 36The people who were standing nearby said, "See how much he loved him!" 37But some said, "This man healed a blind man. Couldn't he have kept Lazarus from dying?"

38Jesus was still angry as he arrived at the tomb, a cave with

TIPS

Progressively challenge yourself:

Where you have hesitation, lack of control, loss of confidence, or a feeling of tenseness, find a simpler shot, and when you have perfected it move toward a more challenging position, distance, or target. Make small improvements every day!

Access (JOHN 14)

You need to be part of the team if you want to get legitimate access to the field in an important match. You get access to God and a home in heaven through trusting in Jesus. Jesus explains he is the only way to God. With Jesus you have admission – you are on his team and part of his game plan.

BIBLE HIT

a stone rolled across its entrance. ³⁹"Roll the stone aside," Jesus told them.

But Martha, the dead man's sister, protested, "Lord, he has been dead for four days. The smell will be terrible."

⁴⁰Jesus responded, "Didn't I tell you that you would see God's glory if you believe?" ⁴¹So they rolled the stone aside. Then Jesus looked up to heaven and said, "Father, thank you for hearing me. ⁴²You always hear me, but I said it out loud for the sake of all these people standing here, so that they will believe you sent me." ⁴³Then Jesus shouted, "Lazarus, come out!" ⁴⁴And the dead man came out, his hands and feet bound in graveclothes, his face wrapped in a headcloth. Jesus told them, "Unwrap him and let him go!"

The shortest verse is John 11:35: "Then Jesus wept."

The Plot to Kill Jesus

⁴⁵Many of the people who were with Mary believed in Jesus when they saw this happen. ⁴⁶But some went to the Pharisees and told them what Jesus had done. ⁴⁷Then the leading priests and Pharisees called the high council together. "What are we going to do?" they asked each other. "This man certainly performs many miraculous signs. ⁴⁸If we allow him to go on like this, soon everyone will believe in him. Then the Roman army will come and destroy both our Temple and our nation."

⁴⁹Caiaphas, who was high priest at that time, said, "You don't know what you're talking about! ⁵⁰You don't realize that it's better for you that one man should die for the people than for the whole nation to be destroyed."

⁵¹He did not say this on his own; as high priest at that time he was led to prophesy that Jesus would die for the entire nation. ⁵²And not only for that nation, but to bring together and unite all the children of God scattered around the world.

⁵³So from that time on, the Jewish leaders began to plot Jesus' death. ⁵⁴As a result, Jesus stopped his public ministry among the people and left Jerusalem. He went to a place near the wilderness, to the village of Ephraim, and stayed there with his disciples.

⁵⁵It was now almost time for the Jewish Passover celebration, and many people from all over the country arrived in Jerusalem several days early so they could go through the purification ceremony before Passover began. ⁵⁶They kept looking for Jesus, but as they stood around in the Temple, they said to each other, "What do you think? He won't come for Passover, will he?" ⁵⁷Meanwhile, the leading priests and Pharisees had publicly ordered that anyone seeing Jesus must report it immediately so they could arrest him.

Jesus Anointed at Bethany

12

Six days before the Passover celebration began, Jesus arrived in Bethany, the home of Lazarus—the man he had raised from the dead. ²A dinner was prepared in Jesus' honor. Martha served, and Lazarus was among those who ate with him. ³Then Mary took a twelve-ounce jar of expensive perfume made from essence of nard, and she anointed Jesus' feet with it, wiping his feet with her hair. The house was filled with the fragrance.

⁴But Judas Iscariot, the disciple who would soon betray him, said, ⁵"That perfume was worth a year's wages. It should have been sold and the money given to the poor." ⁶Not that he cared for the poor—he was a thief, and since he was in charge of the disciples' money, he often stole some for himself.

⁷Jesus replied, "Leave her alone. She did this in preparation for my burial. ⁸You will always have the poor among you, but you will not always have me."

⁹When all the people heard of Jesus' arrival, they flocked to see him and also to see Lazarus, the man Jesus had raised from the dead. ¹⁰Then the leading priests decided to kill Lazarus, too, ¹¹for it was because of him that many of the people had deserted them and believed in Jesus.

action

12:23-36 WHAT'S IT SAYING?

WHAT AM I GOING TO DO ABOUT IT?

Jesus' Triumphant Entry

¹²The next day, the news that Jesus was on the way to Jerusalem swept through the city. A large crowd of Passover visitors ¹³took palm branches and went down the road to meet him. They shouted,

"Praise God!
Blessings on the one who comes in the name of the LORD!
Hail to the King of Israel!"

¹⁴Jesus found a young donkey and rode on it, fulfilling the prophecy that said:

¹⁵"Don't be afraid, people of Jerusalem.
Look, your King is coming,
riding on a donkey's colt."

¹⁶His disciples didn't understand at the time that this was a fulfillment of prophecy. But after Jesus entered into his glory, they remembered what had happened

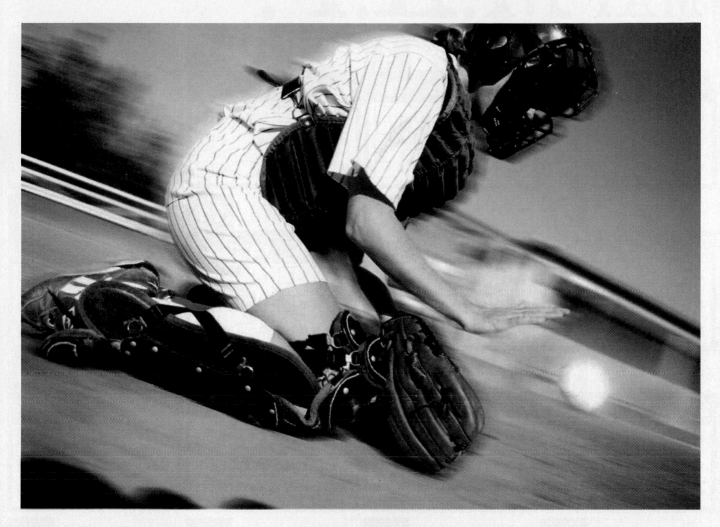

and realized that these things had been written about him.

[17]Many in the crowd had seen Jesus call Lazarus from the tomb, raising him from the dead, and they were telling others about it. [18]That was the reason so many went out to meet him—because they had heard about this miraculous sign. [19]Then the Pharisees said to each other, "There's nothing we can do. Look, everyone has gone after him!"

Jesus Predicts His Death

[20]Some Greeks who had come to Jerusalem for the Passover celebration [21]paid a visit to Philip, who was from Bethsaida in Galilee. They said, "Sir, we want to meet Jesus." [22]Philip told Andrew about it, and they went together to ask Jesus.

[23]Jesus replied, "Now the time has come for the Son of Man to enter into his glory. [24]I tell you the truth, unless a kernel of wheat is planted in the soil and dies, it remains alone. But its death will produce many new kernels—a plentiful harvest of new lives. [25]Those

who love their life in this world will lose it. Those who care nothing for their life in this world will keep it for eternity. [26]Anyone who wants to be my disciple must follow me, because my servants must be where I am. And the Father will honor anyone who serves me. [27]"Now my soul is deeply troubled. Should I pray,

The first ancient Olympic games, held in Olympia, Greece, from 776 BC through AD 393, were part of a religious festival that honored Zeus.

'Father, save me from this hour'? But this is the very reason I came! [28]Father, bring glory to your name."

Then a voice spoke from heaven, saying, "I have already brought glory to my name, and I will do so again." [29]When the crowd heard the voice, some thought it was thunder, while others declared an angel had spoken to him.

[30]Then Jesus told them, "The voice was for your benefit, not mine. [31]The time for judging this world has come, when Satan, the ruler of this world, will be cast out. [32]And when I am lifted up from the earth, I will draw everyone to myself." [33]He said this to indicate how he was going to die.

[34]The crowd responded, "We understood from Scripture that the Messiah would live forever. How can you say the Son of Man will die? Just who is this Son of Man, anyway?"

[35]Jesus replied, "My light will shine for you just a little longer. Walk in the light while you can, so the darkness will not overtake you. Those who walk in the darkness cannot see where they are going. [36]Put your trust in the light while there is still time; then you will become children of the light." After saying these things, Jesus went away and was hidden from them.

MAY M.A.P.

1
S.D.	P.L.	P.G.	S.G.
P. ☐	F. ☐	F. ☐	T. ☐
F. ☐	W. ☐	W. ☐	P. ☐
B. ☐	P. ☐	C. ☐	C. ☐

2
S.D.	P.L.	P.G.	S.G.
P. ☐	F. ☐	F. ☐	T. ☐
F. ☐	W. ☐	W. ☐	P. ☐
B. ☐	P. ☐	C. ☐	C. ☐

3
S.D.	P.L.	P.G.	S.G.
P. ☐	F. ☐	F. ☐	T. ☐
F. ☐	W. ☐	W. ☐	P. ☐
B. ☐	P. ☐	C. ☐	C. ☐

4
S.D.	P.L.	P.G.	S.G.
P. ☐	F. ☐	F. ☐	T. ☐
F. ☐	W. ☐	W. ☐	P. ☐
B. ☐	P. ☐	C. ☐	C. ☐

9
S.D.	P.L.	P.G.	S.G.
P. ☐	F. ☐	F. ☐	T. ☐
F. ☐	W. ☐	W. ☐	P. ☐
B. ☐	P. ☐	C. ☐	C. ☐

10
S.D.	P.L.	P.G.	S.G.
P. ☐	F. ☐	F. ☐	T. ☐
F. ☐	W. ☐	W. ☐	P. ☐
B. ☐	P. ☐	C. ☐	C. ☐

11
S.D.	P.L.	P.G.	S.G.
P. ☐	F. ☐	F. ☐	T. ☐
F. ☐	W. ☐	W. ☐	P. ☐
B. ☐	P. ☐	C. ☐	C. ☐

12
S.D.	P.L.	P.G.	S.G.
P. ☐	F. ☐	F. ☐	T. ☐
F. ☐	W. ☐	W. ☐	P. ☐
B. ☐	P. ☐	C. ☐	C. ☐

17
S.D.	P.L.	P.G.	S.G.
P. ☐	F. ☐	F. ☐	T. ☐
F. ☐	W. ☐	W. ☐	P. ☐
B. ☐	P. ☐	C. ☐	C. ☐

18
S.D.	P.L.	P.G.	S.G.
P. ☐	F. ☐	F. ☐	T. ☐
F. ☐	W. ☐	W. ☐	P. ☐
B. ☐	P. ☐	C. ☐	C. ☐

19
S.D.	P.L.	P.G.	S.G.
P. ☐	F. ☐	F. ☐	T. ☐
F. ☐	W. ☐	W. ☐	P. ☐
B. ☐	P. ☐	C. ☐	C. ☐

20
S.D.	P.L.	P.G.	S.G.
P. ☐	F. ☐	F. ☐	T. ☐
F. ☐	W. ☐	W. ☐	P. ☐
B. ☐	P. ☐	C. ☐	C. ☐

25
S.D.	P.L.	P.G.	S.G.
P. ☐	F. ☐	F. ☐	T. ☐
F. ☐	W. ☐	W. ☐	P. ☐
B. ☐	P. ☐	C. ☐	C. ☐

26
S.D.	P.L.	P.G.	S.G.
P. ☐	F. ☐	F. ☐	T. ☐
F. ☐	W. ☐	W. ☐	P. ☐
B. ☐	P. ☐	C. ☐	C. ☐

27
S.D.	P.L.	P.G.	S.G.
P. ☐	F. ☐	F. ☐	T. ☐
F. ☐	W. ☐	W. ☐	P. ☐
B. ☐	P. ☐	C. ☐	C. ☐

28
S.D.	P.L.	P.G.	S.G.
P. ☐	F. ☐	F. ☐	T. ☐
F. ☐	W. ☐	W. ☐	P. ☐
B. ☐	P. ☐	C. ☐	C. ☐

Spiritual Disciplines

Prayer

Faith Community

Bible Reading

Prayer List

Friends

World

Personal

(For designing your M.A.P. – Monthly Action Plan – see introduction pages)

Who am I....
Where am I going....
How am I going to get there?

nt:sport

MONTHLY ACTION PLAN

5
S.D.	P.L.	P.G.	S.G.
P. ☐	F. ☐	F. ☐	T. ☐
F. ☐	W. ☐	W. ☐	P. ☐
B. ☐	P. ☐	C. ☐	C. ☐

6
S.D.	P.L.	P.G.	S.G.
P. ☐	F. ☐	F. ☐	T. ☐
F. ☐	W. ☐	W. ☐	P. ☐
B. ☐	P. ☐	C. ☐	C. ☐

7
S.D.	P.L.	P.G.	S.G.
P. ☐	F. ☐	F. ☐	T. ☐
F. ☐	W. ☐	W. ☐	P. ☐
B. ☐	P. ☐	C. ☐	C. ☐

8
S.D.	P.L.	P.G.	S.G.
P. ☐	F. ☐	F. ☐	T. ☐
F. ☐	W. ☐	W. ☐	P. ☐
B. ☐	P. ☐	C. ☐	C. ☐

13
S.D.	P.L.	P.G.	S.G.
P. ☐	F. ☐	F. ☐	T. ☐
F. ☐	W. ☐	W. ☐	P. ☐
B. ☐	P. ☐	C. ☐	C. ☐

14
S.D.	P.L.	P.G.	S.G.
P. ☐	F. ☐	F. ☐	T. ☐
F. ☐	W. ☐	W. ☐	P. ☐
B. ☐	P. ☐	C. ☐	C. ☐

15
S.D.	P.L.	P.G.	S.G.
P. ☐	F. ☐	F. ☐	T. ☐
F. ☐	W. ☐	W. ☐	P. ☐
B. ☐	P. ☐	C. ☐	C. ☐

16
S.D.	P.L.	P.G.	S.G.
P. ☐	F. ☐	F. ☐	T. ☐
F. ☐	W. ☐	W. ☐	P. ☐
B. ☐	P. ☐	C. ☐	C. ☐

21
S.D.	P.L.	P.G.	S.G.
P. ☐	F. ☐	F. ☐	T. ☐
F. ☐	W. ☐	W. ☐	P. ☐
B. ☐	P. ☐	C. ☐	C. ☐

22
S.D.	P.L.	P.G.	S.G.
P. ☐	F. ☐	F. ☐	T. ☐
F. ☐	W. ☐	W. ☐	P. ☐
B. ☐	P. ☐	C. ☐	C. ☐

23
S.D.	P.L.	P.G.	S.G.
P. ☐	F. ☐	F. ☐	T. ☐
F. ☐	W. ☐	W. ☐	P. ☐
B. ☐	P. ☐	C. ☐	C. ☐

24
S.D.	P.L.	P.G.	S.G.
P. ☐	F. ☐	F. ☐	T. ☐
F. ☐	W. ☐	W. ☐	P. ☐
B. ☐	P. ☐	C. ☐	C. ☐

29
S.D.	P.L.	P.G.	S.G.
P. ☐	F. ☐	F. ☐	T. ☐
F. ☐	W. ☐	W. ☐	P. ☐
B. ☐	P. ☐	C. ☐	C. ☐

30
S.D.	P.L.	P.G.	S.G.
P. ☐	F. ☐	F. ☐	T. ☐
F. ☐	W. ☐	W. ☐	P. ☐
B. ☐	P. ☐	C. ☐	C. ☐

31
S.D.	P.L.	P.G.	S.G.
P. ☐	F. ☐	F. ☐	T. ☐
F. ☐	W. ☐	W. ☐	P. ☐
B. ☐	P. ☐	C. ☐	C. ☐

Proverbs 1:5

Let the wise listen to these proverbs and become even wiser. Let those with understanding receive guidance.

Personal Goals

Family

Work/School/Social

Challenge

Sport Goals

Training

Performance

Competition Results

The Unbelief of the People

[37]But despite all the miraculous signs Jesus had done, most of the people still did not believe in him. [38]This is exactly what Isaiah the prophet had predicted:

"LORD, who has believed our message?
To whom has the LORD revealed his powerful arm?"

[39]But the people couldn't believe, for as Isaiah also said,

[40]"The Lord has blinded their eyes
and hardened their hearts—
so that their eyes cannot see,
and their hearts cannot understand,
and they cannot turn to me
and have me heal them."

[41]Isaiah was referring to Jesus when he said this, because he saw the future and spoke of the Messiah's glory. [42]Many people did believe in him, however, including some of the Jewish leaders. But they wouldn't admit it for fear that the Pharisees would expel them from the synagogue. [43]For they loved human praise more than the praise of God.

[44]Jesus shouted to the crowds, "If you trust me, you are trusting not only me, but also God who sent me. [45]For when you see me, you are seeing the one who sent me. [46]I have come as a light to shine in this dark world, so that all who put their trust in me will no longer remain in the dark. [47]I will not judge those who hear me but don't obey me, for I have come to save the world and not to judge it. [48]But all who reject me and my message will be judged on the day of judgment by the truth I have spoken. [49]I don't speak on my own authority. The Father who sent me has commanded me what to say and how to say it. [50]And I know his commands lead to eternal life; so I say whatever the Father tells me to say."

Jesus Washes His Disciples' Feet

13

Before the Passover celebration, Jesus knew that his hour had come to leave this world and return to his Father. He had loved his disciples during his ministry on earth, and now he loved them to the very end. [2]It was time for supper, and the devil had already prompted Judas, son of Simon Iscariot, to betray Jesus. [3]Jesus knew that the Father had given him authority over everything and that he had come from God and would return to God. [4]So he got up from the table, took off his robe, wrapped a towel around his waist, [5]and poured water into a basin. Then he began to wash the disciples' feet, drying them with the towel he had around him. [6]When Jesus came to Simon Peter, Peter said to him, "Lord, are you going to wash my feet?"

[7]Jesus replied, "You don't understand now what I am doing, but someday you will."

[8]"No," Peter protested, "you will never ever wash my feet!"

Jesus replied, "Unless I wash you, you won't belong to me."

[9]Simon Peter exclaimed, "Then wash my hands and head as well, Lord, not just my feet!"

[10]Jesus replied, "A person who has bathed all over does not need to wash, except for the feet, to be entirely clean. And you disciples are clean, but not all of you." [11]For Jesus knew who would betray him. That is what he meant when he said, "Not all of you are clean."

[12]After washing their feet, he put on his robe again and sat down and asked, "Do you understand what I was doing? [13]You call me 'Teacher' and 'Lord,' and you are right, because that's what I am. [14]And since

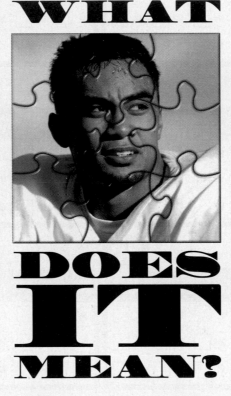

adoption

Adoption is the giving of the family name, place, and privileges of an offspring to someone who is not a descendant by birth. Spiritually, it is an act of God's goodness by which he brings people into his family and allows them to share in all the blessings and inheritance he has provided for them. See 1 Peter 1:14; 2 John 4; Romans 8:15-21.

I, your Lord and Teacher, have washed your feet, you ought to wash each other's feet. [15]I have given you an example to follow. Do as I have done to you. [16]I tell you the truth, slaves are not greater than their master. Nor is the messenger more important than the one who sends the message. [17]Now that you know these things, God will bless you for doing them.

Jesus Predicts His Betrayal

[18]"I am not saying these things to all of you; I know the ones I have chosen. But this fulfills the Scripture that says, 'The one who eats my food has turned against me.' [19]I tell you this beforehand, so that when it happens you will believe that I AM the Messiah. [20]I tell you the truth, anyone who welcomes my messenger is welcoming me, and anyone who welcomes me is welcoming the Father who sent me."

[21]Now Jesus was deeply troubled, and he exclaimed, "I tell you the truth, one of you will betray me!"

[22]The disciples looked at each other, wondering whom he could mean. [23]The disciple Jesus loved was sitting next to Jesus at the table. [24]Simon Peter motioned to him to ask, "Who's he talking about?" [25]So that disciple leaned over to Jesus and asked, "Lord, who is it?"

[26]Jesus responded, "It is the one to whom I give the bread I dip in the bowl." And when he had dipped it, he gave it to Judas, son of Simon Iscariot. [27]When Judas had eaten the bread, Satan entered into him. Then Jesus told him, "Hurry and do what you're going to do." [28]None of the others at the table knew what Jesus meant. [29]Since Judas was their treasurer, some thought Jesus was telling him to go and pay for the food or to give some money to the poor. [30]So Judas left at once, going out into the night.

Jesus Predicts Peter's Denial

[31]As soon as Judas left the room, Jesus said, "The time has come for the Son of Man to enter into his glory, and God will be glorified because of him. [32]And since God receives glory because of the Son, he will soon give glory to the Son. [33]Dear children, I will be with you only a little longer. And as I told the Jewish leaders, you will search for me, but you can't come where I am going. [34]So now I am giving you a new commandment: Love each other. Just as I have loved you, you should love each other. [35]Your love for one another will prove to the world that you are my disciples."

[36]Simon Peter asked, "Lord, where are you going?" And Jesus replied, "You can't go with me now, but you will follow me later."

37"But why can't I come now, Lord?" he asked. "I'm ready to die for you."

38Jesus answered, "Die for me? I tell you the truth, Peter—before the rooster crows tomorrow morning, you will deny three times that you even know me.

Jesus, the Way to the Father

14

"Don't let your hearts be troubled. Trust in God, and trust also in me. 2There is more than enough room in my Father's home. If this were not so, would I have told you that I am going to prepare a place for you? 3When everything is ready, I will come and get you, so that you will always be with me where I am. 4And you know the way to where I am going."

5"No, we don't know, Lord," Thomas said. "We have no idea where you are going, so how can we know the way?"

6Jesus told him, "I am the way, the truth, and the life. No one can come to the Father except through me. 7If you had really known me, you would know who my Father is. From now on, you do know him and have seen him!"

8Philip said, "Lord, show us the Father, and we will be satisfied."

9Jesus replied, "Have I been with you all this time, Philip, and yet you still don't know who I am? Anyone who has seen me has seen the Father! So why are you asking me to show him to you? 10Don't you believe that I am in the Father and the Father is in me? The words I speak are not my own, but my Father who lives in me does his work through me. 11Just believe that I am in the Father and the Father is in me. Or at least believe because of the work you have seen me do.

12"I tell you the truth, anyone who believes in me will do the same works I have done, and even greater works, because I am going to be with the Father. 13You can ask for anything in my name, and I will do it, so that the Son can bring glory to the Father. 14Yes, ask me for anything in my name, and I will do it!

Jesus Promises the Holy Spirit

15"If you love me, obey my commandments. 16And I will ask the Father, and he will give you another Advocate, who will never leave you. 17He is the Holy Spirit, who leads into all truth. The world cannot receive him, because it isn't looking for him and doesn't recognize him. But you know him, because he lives with you now and later will be in you. 18No, I will not abandon you as orphans—I will come to you. 19Soon the world will no longer see me, but you will see me. Since I live, you also will live. 20When I am raised to life again, you will know that I am in my Father, and you are in me, and I am in you. 21Those who accept my commandments and obey them are the ones who love me. And because they love me, my Father will love them. And I will love them and reveal myself to each of them."

22Judas (not Judas Iscariot, but the other disciple with that name) said to him, "Lord, why are you going to reveal yourself only to us and not to the world at large?"

23Jesus replied, "All who love me will do what I say. My Father will love them, and we will come and make our home with each of them. 24Anyone who doesn't love me will not obey me. And remember, my words are not my own. What I am telling you is from the Father who sent me. 25I am telling you these things now while I am still with you. 26But when the Father sends the Advocate as my representative—that is, the Holy Spirit—he will teach you everything and will remind you of everything I have told you.

27"I am leaving you with a gift—peace of mind and heart. And the peace I give is a gift the world cannot give. So don't be troubled or afraid. 28Remember what I told you: I am going away, but I will come back to you again. If you really loved me, you would be happy that I am going to the Father, who is greater than I am. 29I have told you these things before they happen so that when they do happen, you will believe.

30"I don't have much more time to talk to you, because the ruler of this world approaches. He has no power

When people say all religions lead to God

John 14:6

Jesus told him, "I am the way, the truth, and the life. No one can come to the Father except through me."

over me, 31but I will do what the Father requires of me, so that the world will know that I love the Father. Come, let's be going.

Jesus, the True Vine

15

"I am the true grapevine, and my Father is the gardener. 2He cuts off every branch of mine that doesn't produce fruit, and he prunes the branches that do bear fruit so they will produce even more. 3You have already been pruned and purified by the message I have given you. 4Remain in me, and I will remain in you. For a branch cannot produce fruit if it is severed from the vine, and you cannot be fruitful unless you remain in me.

5"Yes, I am the vine; you are the branches. Those who remain in me, and I in them, will produce much fruit. For apart from me you can do nothing. 6Anyone who does not remain in me is thrown away like a useless branch and withers. Such branches are gathered into a pile to be burned. 7But if you remain in me and my words remain in you, you may ask for anything you want, and it will be granted! 8When you produce much fruit, you are my true disciples. This brings great glory to my Father.

9"I have loved you even as the Father has loved me. Remain in my love. 10When you obey my commandments, you remain in my love, just as I obey my Father's commandments and

When you lose your form:

If a skill slump occurs, modify your practice routine to incorporate specific skill training to your troubled area and performance sequence. This suggested solution to the problem may help some athletes, but not all. Some people may require different techniques to solve their particular problem.

remain in his love. [11]I have told you these things so that you will be filled with my joy. Yes, your joy will overflow! [12]This is my commandment: Love each other in the same way I have loved you. [13]There is no greater love than to lay down one's life for one's friends. [14]You are my friends if you do what I command. [15]I no longer call you slaves, because a master doesn't confide in his slaves. Now you are my friends, since I have told you everything the Father told me. [16]You didn't choose me. I chose you. I appointed you to go and produce lasting fruit, so that the Father will give you whatever you ask for, using my name. [17]This is my command: Love each other.

The World's Hatred

[18]"If the world hates you, remember that it hated me first. [19]The world would love you as one of its own if you belonged to it, but you are no longer part of the world. I chose you to come out of the world, so it hates you. [20]Do you remember what I told you? 'A slave is not greater than the master.' Since they persecuted me, naturally they will persecute you. And if they had listened to me, they would listen to you. [21]They will do all this to you because of me, for they have rejected the One who sent me. [22]They would not be guilty if I had not come and spoken to them. But now they have no excuse for their sin. [23]Anyone who hates me also hates my Father. [24]If I hadn't done such miraculous signs among them that no one else could do, they would not be guilty. But as it is, they have seen everything I did, yet they still hate me and my Father. [25]This fulfills what is written in their Scriptures: 'They hated me without cause.'

[26]"But I will send you the Advocate—the Spirit of truth. He will come to you from the Father and will testify all about me. [27]And you must also testify about me because you have been with me from the beginning of my ministry.

16

"I have told you these things so that you won't abandon your faith. [2]For you will be expelled from the synagogues, and the time is coming when those who kill you will think they are doing a holy service for God. [3]This is because they have never known the Father or me. [4]Yes, I'm telling you these things now, so that when they happen, you will remember my warning. I didn't tell you earlier because I was going to be with you for a while longer.

The Work of the Holy Spirit

[5]"But now I am going away to the One who sent me, and not one of you is asking where I am going. [6]Instead, you grieve because of what I've told you. [7]But in fact, it is best for you that I go away, because if I don't, the Advocate won't come. If I do go away, then I will send him to you. [8]And when he comes, he will convict the world of its sin, and of God's righteousness, and of the coming judgment. [9]The world's sin is that it refuses to believe in me. [10]Righteousness is available because I go to the Father, and you will see me no more. [11]Judgment will come because the ruler of this world has already been judged.

[12]"There is so much more I want to tell you, but you can't bear it now. [13]When the Spirit of truth comes, he will guide you into all truth. He will not speak on his own but will tell you what he has heard. He will tell you about the future. [14]He will bring me glory by telling you whatever he receives from me. [15]All that belongs to the Father is mine; this is why I said, 'The Spirit will tell you whatever he receives from me.'

Sadness Will Be Turned to Joy

[16]"In a little while you won't see me anymore. But a little while after that, you will see me again."

[17]Some of the disciples asked each other, "What does he mean when he says, 'In a little while you won't see me, but then you will see me,' and 'I am going to the Father'? [18]And what does he mean by 'a little while'? We don't understand."

[19]Jesus realized they wanted to ask him about it, so he said, "Are you asking yourselves what I meant? I said in a little while you won't see me, but a little while after that you will see me again. [20]I tell you the truth, you will weep and mourn over what is going to happen to me, but the world will rejoice. You will grieve, but your grief will suddenly turn to wonderful joy. [21]It will be like a woman suffering the pains of labor. When her child is born, her anguish gives way to joy because she has brought a new baby into the world. [22]So you have sorrow now, but I will see you again; then you will rejoice, and no one can rob you of that joy. [23]At that time you won't need to ask me for anything. I tell you the truth, you will ask the Father directly, and he will grant your request because you use my name. [24]You haven't done this before. Ask, using my name, and you will receive, and you will have abundant joy.

[25]"I have spoken of these matters in figures of speech, but soon I will stop speaking figuratively and will tell you plainly all about the Father. [26]Then you will ask in my name. I'm not saying I will ask the Father on your behalf, [27]for the Father himself loves you dearly because you love me and believe that I came from God. [28]Yes, I came from the Father into the world, and now I will leave the world and return to the Father."

[29]Then his disciples said, "At last you are speaking plainly and not figuratively. [30]Now we understand that you know everything, and there's no need to question you. From this we believe that you came from God." [31]Jesus asked, "Do you finally believe? [32]But the time is coming—indeed it's here now—when you will be scattered, each one going his own way, leaving me alone. Yet I am not alone because the Father is with me. [33]I have told you all this so that you may have peace in me. Here on earth you will have many trials and sorrows. But take heart, because I have overcome the world."

Is looking at pornography wrong?

Yes, and it's very dangerous. Like trying to drink salt water to quench your thirst, looking at sexually explicit images will not satisfy your sexual desires. Your mind fills with unrealistic and unhealthy images that distort the healthy sexual relationship, which God intended for marriage.

With the Internet, this is a modern land mine. Create ways to block these sites and work hard to control your thoughts. Resist the temptation to look at pornography, and pray for strength.

The Prayer of Jesus

17

After saying all these things, Jesus looked up to heaven and said, "Father, the hour has come. Glorify your Son so he can give glory back to you. ²For you have given him authority over everyone. He gives eternal life to each one you have given him. ³And this is the way to have eternal life—to know you, the only true God, and Jesus Christ, the one you sent to earth. ⁴I brought glory to you here on earth by completing the work you gave me to do. ⁵Now, Father, bring me into the glory we shared before the world began.

⁶"I have revealed you to the ones you gave me from this world. They were always yours. You gave them to me, and they have kept your word. ⁷Now they know that everything I have is a gift from you, ⁸for I have passed on to them the message you gave me. They accepted it and know that I came from you, and they believe you sent me.

⁹"My prayer is not for the world, but for those you have given me, because they belong to you. ¹⁰All who are mine belong to you, and you have given them to me, so they bring me glory. ¹¹Now I am departing from the world; they are staying in this world, but I am coming to you. Holy Father, you have given me your name; now protect them by the power of your name so that they will be united just as we are. ¹²During my time here, I protected them by the power of the name you gave me. I guarded them so that not one was lost, except the one headed for destruction, as the Scriptures foretold.

¹³"Now I am coming to you. I told them many things while I was with them in this world so they would be filled with my joy. ¹⁴I have given them your word. And the world hates them because they do not belong

to the world, just as I do not belong to the world. ¹⁵I'm not asking you to take them out of the world, but to keep them safe from the evil one. ¹⁶They do not belong to this world any more than I do. ¹⁷Make them holy by your truth; teach them your word, which is truth. ¹⁸Just as you sent me into the world, I am sending them into the world. ¹⁹And I give myself as a holy sacrifice for them so they can be made holy by your truth.

²⁰"I am praying not only for these disciples but also for all who will ever believe in me through their message. ²¹I pray that they will all be one, just as you and I are one—as you are in me, Father, and I am in you. And may they be in us so that the world will believe you sent me.

²²"I have given them the glory you gave me, so they may be one as we are one. ²³I am in them and you are in me. May they experience such perfect unity that the world will know that you sent me and that you love them as much as you love me. ²⁴Father, I want these whom you have given me to be with me where I am. Then they can see all the glory you gave me because you loved me even before the world began!

²⁵"O righteous Father, the world doesn't know you, but I do; and these disciples know you sent me. ²⁶I have revealed you to them, and I will continue to do so. Then your love for me will be in them, and I will be in them."

Jesus Is Betrayed and Arrested

18

After saying these things, Jesus crossed the Kidron Valley with his disciples and entered a grove of olive trees. ²Judas, the betrayer, knew this place, because Jesus had often gone there with his disciples. ³The leading priests and Pharisees had given Judas a contingent of Roman soldiers and Temple guards to accompany him. Now with blazing torches, lanterns, and weapons, they arrived at the olive grove.

⁴Jesus fully realized all that was going to happen to him, so he stepped forward to meet them. "Who are you looking for?" he asked.

⁵"Jesus the Nazarene," they replied.

"I AM he," Jesus said. (Judas, who betrayed him, was standing with them.) ⁶As Jesus said "I AM he," they all drew back and fell to the ground! ⁷Once more he asked them, "Who are you looking for?"

And again they replied, "Jesus the Nazarene."

⁸"I told you that I AM he," Jesus said. "And since I am

the one you want, let these others go." ⁹He did this to fulfill his own statement: "I did not lose a single one of those you have given me."

¹⁰Then Simon Peter drew a sword and slashed off the right ear of Malchus, the high priest's slave. ¹¹But Jesus said to Peter, "Put your sword back into its sheath. Shall I not drink from the cup of suffering the Father has given me?"

Jesus at the High Priest's House

¹²So the soldiers, their commanding officer, and the Temple guards arrested Jesus and tied him up. ¹³First they took him to Annas, the father-in-law of Caiaphas, the high priest at that time. ¹⁴Caiaphas was the one who had told the other Jewish leaders, "It's better that one man should die for the people."

Peter's First Denial

¹⁵Simon Peter followed Jesus, as did another of the disciples. That other disciple was acquainted with the high priest, so he was allowed to enter the high priest's courtyard with Jesus. ¹⁶Peter had to stay outside the gate. Then the disciple who knew the high priest spoke to the woman watching at the gate, and she let Peter in. ¹⁷The woman asked Peter, "You're not one of that man's disciples, are you?"

"No," he said, "I am not."

¹⁸Because it was cold, the household servants and the guards had made a charcoal fire. They stood around it, warming themselves, and Peter stood with them, warming himself.

The High Priest Questions Jesus

¹⁹Inside, the high priest began asking Jesus about his followers and what he had been teaching them. ²⁰Jesus replied, "Everyone knows what I teach. I have preached regularly in the synagogues and the Temple, where the people gather. I have not spoken in secret. ²¹Why are you asking me this question? Ask those who heard me. They know what I said."

²²Then one of the Temple guards standing nearby slapped Jesus across the face. "Is that the way to answer the high priest?" he demanded.

²³Jesus replied, "If I said anything wrong, you must prove it. But if I'm speaking the truth, why are you beating me?" ²⁴Then Annas bound Jesus and sent him to Caiaphas, the high priest.

Peter's Second and Third Denials

²⁵Meanwhile, as Simon Peter was standing by the fire, they asked him again, "You're not one of his disciples, are you?" He denied it, saying, "No, I am not."

²⁶But one of the household slaves of the high priest, a relative of the man whose ear Peter had cut off, asked, "Didn't I see you out there in the olive grove with Jesus?" ²⁷Again Peter denied it. And immediately a rooster crowed.

When Jesus was crucified, a sign was posted on the cross. The exact phrase is slightly different in each of the four gospels. "This is Jesus, the King of the Jews." (Matt. 27:37)

Jesus' Trial before Pilate

28Jesus' trial before Caiaphas ended in the early hours of the morning. Then he was taken to the headquarters of the Roman governor. His accusers didn't go inside because it would defile them, and they wouldn't be allowed to celebrate the Passover. 29So Pilate, the governor, went out to them and asked, "What is your charge against this man?"

30"We wouldn't have handed him over to you if he weren't a criminal!" they retorted.

31"Then take him away and judge him by your own law," Pilate told them.

"Only the Romans are permitted to execute someone," the Jewish leaders replied. 32(This fulfilled Jesus' prediction about the way he would die.)

33Then Pilate went back into his headquarters and called for Jesus to be brought to him. "Are you the king of the Jews?" he asked him.

34Jesus replied, "Is this your own question, or did others tell you about me?"

35"Am I a Jew?" Pilate retorted. "Your own people and their leading priests brought you to me for trial. Why? What have you done?"

36Jesus answered, "My Kingdom is not an earthly kingdom. If it were, my followers would fight to keep me from being handed over to the Jewish leaders. But my Kingdom is not of this world."

37Pilate said, "So you are a king?"

Jesus responded, "You say I am a king. Actually, I was born and came into the world to testify to the truth. All who love the truth recognize that what I say is true."

38"What is truth?" Pilate asked. Then he went out again to the people and told them, "He is not guilty of any crime. 39But you have a custom of asking me to release one prisoner each year at Passover. Would you like me to release this 'King of the Jews'?"

40But they shouted back, "No! Not this man. We want Barabbas!" (Barabbas was a revolutionary.)

Jesus Sentenced to Death

19

Then Pilate had Jesus flogged with a lead-tipped whip. 2The soldiers wove a crown of thorns and put it on his head, and they put a purple robe on him. 3"Hail! King of the Jews!" they mocked, as they slapped him across the face.

4Pilate went outside again and said to the people, "I am going to bring him out to you now, but understand clearly that I find him not guilty." 5Then Jesus came out wearing the crown of thorns and the purple robe. And Pilate said, "Look, here is the man!"

6When they saw him, the leading priests and Temple guards began shouting, "Crucify him! Crucify him!"

"Take him yourselves and crucify him," Pilate said. "I find him not guilty."

7The Jewish leaders replied, "By our law he ought to die because he called himself the Son of God."

8When Pilate heard this, he was more frightened than ever. 9He took Jesus back into the headquarters again and asked him, "Where are you from?" But Jesus gave no answer. 10"Why don't you talk to me?" Pilate demanded. "Don't you realize that I have the power to release you or crucify you?"

11Then Jesus said, "You would have no power over me at all unless it were given to you from above. So the one who handed me over to you has the greater sin."

12Then Pilate tried to release him, but the Jewish leaders shouted, "If you release this man, you are no 'friend of Caesar.' Anyone who declares himself a king is a rebel against Caesar."

13When they said this, Pilate brought Jesus out to them again. Then Pilate sat down on the judgment seat on the platform that is called the Stone Pavement (in Hebrew, Gabbatha. 14It was now about noon on the day of preparation for the Passover. And Pilate said to the people, "Look, here is your king!"

15"Away with him," they yelled. "Away with him! Crucify him!"

"What? Crucify your king?" Pilate asked.

"We have no king but Caesar," the leading priests shouted back.

16Then Pilate turned Jesus over to them to be crucified.

The Crucifixion

So they took Jesus away. 17Carrying the cross by himself, he went to the place called Place of the Skull (in Hebrew, Golgotha. 18There they nailed him to the cross. Two others were crucified with him, one on either side, with Jesus between them. 19And Pilate posted a sign over him that read, "Jesus of Nazareth, the King of the Jews." 20The place where Jesus was crucified was near the city, and the sign was written in Hebrew, Latin, and Greek, so that many people could read it. 21Then the leading priests objected and said to Pilate, "Change it from 'The King of the Jews' to 'He said, I am King of the Jews.'"

22Pilate replied, "No, what I have written, I have written."

23When the soldiers had crucified Jesus, they divided his clothes among the four of them. They also took his robe, but it was seamless, woven in one piece from top to bottom. 24So they said, "Rather than tearing it apart, let's throw dice for it. This fulfilled the Scripture that says, "They divided my garments among themselves and threw dice for my clothing." So that is what they did.

25Standing near the cross were Jesus' mother, and his mother's sister, Mary (the wife of Clopas), and Mary Magdalene. 26When Jesus saw his mother standing there beside the disciple he loved, he said to her, "Dear woman, here is your son." 27And he said to this disciple, "Here is your mother." And from then on this disciple took her into his home.

19:28-35 WHAT'S IT SAYING?

WHAT AM I GOING TO DO ABOUT IT?

The Death of Jesus

28Jesus knew that his mission was now finished, and to fulfill Scripture he said, "I am thirsty." 29A jar of sour wine was sitting there, so they soaked a sponge in it, put it on a hyssop branch, and held it up to his lips. 30When Jesus had tasted it, he said, "It is finished!" Then he bowed his head and released his spirit.

31It was the day of preparation, and the Jewish leaders didn't want the bodies hanging there the next day, which was the Sabbath (and a very special Sabbath, because it was the Passover). So they asked Pilate to hasten their deaths by ordering that their legs be broken. Then their bodies could be taken down. 32So the soldiers came and broke the legs of the two men crucified with Jesus. [33]But when they came to Jesus, they saw that he was already dead, so they didn't break his legs. [34]One of the soldiers, however, pierced his side with a spear, and immediately blood and water flowed out. [35](This report is from an eyewitness giving an accurate account. He speaks the truth so that you also can believe.) [36]These things happened in fulfillment of the Scriptures that say, "Not one of his bones will be broken," [37]and "They will look on the one they pierced."

The Burial of Jesus

[38]Afterward Joseph of Arimathea, who had been a secret disciple of Jesus (because he feared the Jewish leaders), asked Pilate for permission to take down Jesus' body. When Pilate gave permission, Joseph came and took the body away. [39]With him came Nicodemus, the man who had come to Jesus at night. He brought seventy-five pounds of perfumed ointment made from myrrh and aloes. [40]Following Jewish burial custom, they wrapped Jesus' body with the spices in long sheets of linen cloth. [41]The place of crucifixion was near a garden, where there was a new tomb, never used before. [42]And so, because it was the day of preparation for the Jewish Passover and since the tomb was close at hand, they laid Jesus there.

The Resurrection

20

Early on Sunday morning, while it was still dark, Mary Magdalene came to the tomb and found that the stone had

PERSONAL ASSESSMENTS

TEAM POSITION (on a scale from 1 to 10, 10 being highest)

Besides playing on the team:

- ☐ I like to "take charge" on a team.

- ☐ I know how to build team spirit even when we are losing.

- ☐ I can help other team members better their skills.

- ☐ I see when a teammate is down and know how to encourage them.

- ☐ I want to encourage others to get involved on my team.

- ☐ I want to help my team succeed.

- ☐ I enjoy planning strategy and plays.

- ☐ I enjoy organizing teams and helping them achieve success.

- ☐ I enjoy teaching techniques and developing the skills of others.

- ☐ I really enjoy hanging around my teammates and having them over to my house.

- ☐ I enjoy initiating and equipping teams.

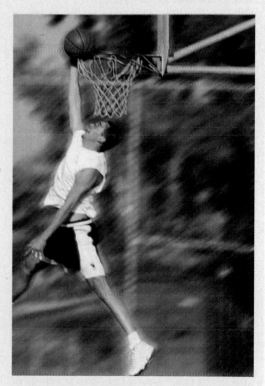

been rolled away from the entrance. ²She ran and found Simon Peter and the other disciple, the one whom Jesus loved. She said, "They have taken the Lord's body out of the tomb, and we don't know where they have put him!"

³Peter and the other disciple started out for the tomb. ⁴They were both running, but the other disciple outran Peter and reached the tomb first. ⁵He stooped and looked in and saw the linen wrappings lying there, but he didn't go in. ⁶Then Simon Peter arrived and went inside. He also noticed the linen wrappings lying there, ⁷while the cloth that had covered Jesus' head was folded up and lying apart from the other wrappings. ⁸Then the disciple who had reached the tomb first also went in, and he saw and believed—⁹for until then they still hadn't understood the Scriptures that said Jesus must rise from the dead. ¹⁰Then they went home.

Jesus Appears to Mary Magdalene

¹¹Mary was standing outside the tomb crying, and as she wept, she stooped and looked in. ¹²She saw two white-robed angels, one sitting at the head and the other at the foot of the place where the body of Jesus had been lying. ¹³"Dear woman, why are you crying?" the angels asked her.

"Because they have taken away my Lord," she replied, "and I don't know where they have put him."

¹⁴She turned to leave and saw someone standing there. It was Jesus, but she didn't recognize him. ¹⁵"Dear woman, why are you crying?" Jesus asked her. "Who are you looking for?"

She thought he was the gardener. "Sir," she said, "if you have taken him away, tell me where you have put him, and I will go and get him."

¹⁶"Mary!" Jesus said.

She turned to him and cried out, "Rabboni!" (which is Hebrew for "Teacher").

¹⁷"Don't cling to me," Jesus said, "for I haven't yet ascended to the Father. But go find my brothers and tell them that I am ascending to my Father and your Father, to my God and your God."

¹⁸Mary Magdalene found the disciples and told them, "I have seen the Lord!" Then she gave them his message.

Jesus Appears to His Disciples

¹⁹That Sunday evening the disciples were meeting behind locked doors because they were afraid of the Jewish leaders. Suddenly, Jesus was standing there among them! "Peace be with you," he said. ²⁰As he spoke, he showed them the wounds in his hands and his side. They were filled with joy when they saw the Lord! ²¹Again he said, "Peace be with you. As the Father has sent me, so I am sending you." ²²Then he breathed on them and said, "Receive the Holy Spirit. ²³If you forgive anyone's sins, they are forgiven. If you do not forgive them, they are not forgiven."

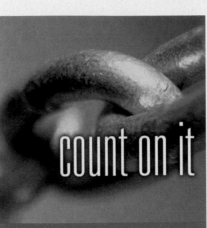

count on it

Open your Eyes!

One of the Holy Spirit's jobs is to illuminate — to open our spiritual eyes. The Spirit's job is to switch on the light and help us see the rich treasures of inheritance we receive. A coach has a similar function. Often training is mundane and repetitious. A good coach has a way of reminding his players what it is all about — the light of a big game at the end of the tunnel. One of the many functions of the Holy Spirit is to remind us that this life is just a mist compared to the greatness of eternal life with our Father. The riches and blessings we enjoy on earth as well as unique blessings to come (our inheritance).

"I pray that your hearts will be flooded with light so that you can understand the confident hope he has given to those he called—his holy people who are his rich and glorious inheritance." (Ephesians 1:18)

Count on it!

Jesus Appears to Thomas

²⁴One of the disciples, Thomas (nicknamed the Twin), was not with the others when Jesus came. ²⁵They told him, "We have seen the Lord!"

But he replied, "I won't believe it unless I see the nail wounds in his hands, put my fingers into them, and place my hand into the wound in his side."

²⁶Eight days later the disciples were together again, and this time Thomas was with them. The doors were locked; but suddenly, as before, Jesus was standing among them. "Peace be with you," he said. ²⁷Then he said to Thomas, "Put your finger here, and look at my hands. Put your hand into the wound in my side. Don't be faithless any longer. Believe!"

²⁸"My Lord and my God!" Thomas exclaimed.

²⁹Then Jesus told him, "You believe because you have seen me. Blessed are those who believe without seeing me."

Purpose of the Book

³⁰The disciples saw Jesus do many other miraculous signs in addition to the ones recorded in this book. ³¹But these are written so that you may continue to believe that Jesus is the Messiah, the Son of God, and that by believing in him you will have life by the power of his name.

Epilogue: Jesus Appears to Seven Disciples

21

Later, Jesus appeared again to the disciples beside the Sea of Galilee. This is how it happened. ²Several of the disciples were there—Simon Peter, Thomas (nicknamed the Twin), Nathanael from Cana in Galilee, the sons of Zebedee, and two other disciples.

³Simon Peter said, "I'm going fishing."

"We'll come, too," they all said. So they went out in the boat, but they caught nothing all night.

⁴At dawn Jesus was standing on the beach, but the disciples couldn't see who he was. ⁵He called out, "Fellows, have you caught any fish?"

"No," they replied.

⁶Then he said, "Throw out your net on the right-hand side of the boat, and you'll get some!" So they did, and they couldn't haul in the net because there were so many fish in it.

⁷Then the disciple Jesus loved said to Peter, "It's the Lord!" When Simon Peter heard that it was the Lord, he put on his tunic (for he had stripped for work), jumped into the water, and headed to shore. ⁸The others stayed with the boat and pulled the loaded net to the shore, for they were only about a hundred yards from shore. ⁹When they got there, they found breakfast waiting for them—fish cooking over a charcoal fire, and some bread.

¹⁰"Bring some of the fish you've just caught," Jesus said. ¹¹So Simon Peter went aboard and dragged the

net to the shore. There were 153 large fish, and yet the net hadn't torn.

¹²"Now come and have some breakfast!" Jesus said. None of the disciples dared to ask him, "Who are you?" They knew it was the Lord. ¹³Then Jesus served them the bread and the fish. ¹⁴This was the third time Jesus had appeared to his disciples since he had been raised from the dead.

¹⁵After breakfast Jesus asked Simon Peter, "Simon son of John, do you love me more than these?"

"Yes, Lord," Peter replied, "you know I love you."

"Then feed my lambs," Jesus told him.

¹⁶Jesus repeated the question: "Simon son of John, do you love me?"

"Yes, Lord," Peter said, "you know I love you."

"Then take care of my sheep," Jesus said.

¹⁷A third time he asked him, "Simon son of John, do you love me?"

Peter was hurt that Jesus asked the question a third time. He said, "Lord, you know everything. You know that I love you."

Jesus said, "Then feed my sheep.

¹⁸I tell you the truth, when you were young, you were able to do as you liked; you dressed yourself and went wherever you wanted to go. But when you are old, you will stretch out your hands, and others will dress you and take you where you don't want to go."

¹⁹Jesus said this to let him know by what kind of death he would glorify God. Then Jesus told him, "Follow me."

²⁰Peter turned around and saw behind them the disciple Jesus loved—the one who had leaned over to Jesus during supper and asked, "Lord, who will betray you?" ²¹Peter asked Jesus, "What about him, Lord?"

²²Jesus replied, "If I want him to remain alive until I return, what is that to you? As for you, follow me."

²³So the rumor spread among the community of believers that this disciple wouldn't die. But that isn't what Jesus said at all. He only said, "If I want him to remain alive until I return, what is that to you?"

²⁴This disciple is the one who testifies to these events and has recorded them here. And we know that his account of these things is accurate.

²⁵Jesus also did many other things. If they were all written down, I suppose the whole world could not contain the books that would be written.

Joining the Team

"I am the way, the truth, and the life. No one can come to the Father except through me."
(John 14:6)

At some point in your life you decided to get involved in sports. Your mother or father may have been sporty; your brothers, sisters, and friends may be sporty; and you may have gone to an athletic school. However, being around sports does not make you an athlete. You may have had athletic attributes — for example, good balance, a keen eye, or an aggressive attitude. But until you join a team, you are not really a sports person; you are more like a fan. At a certain point in your life, you made the transition from fan to participant. You signed up, tried out, and were chosen for some sort of organized sport.

A few legendary sports stars grew up in remote areas of the world. As children they heard vague echoes of the sport and team they would one day compete for in distant lands. But someone noticed them and introduced them to the foreign world and seemingly strange activities they would soon dominate. Other sports stars were almost bred for their sport; they give the impression of coming out of the womb with a racket in their hand. Some great pros are pedigrees from second or third generation sporting heroes. Regardless of where you came from, whether it was a remote African tribe or a famous sporting family, you made up your own mind at some point to join a team. Or you may have been pushed by an overexuberant parent who applied too much pressure. That, too, can be a misery. But I bet if you are reading this, you are probably old enough to make decisions for yourself. You made a conscious effort, at some time, to join a team.

The idea of being picked for a team is not too far off the Christian life. You may have had an overexuberant, religious mom who made you go to Sunday school. You may have had religious family members or friends. Perhaps you went to a religious school or live in a "Christian" country. Or maybe you were raised in an environment (like me) remote from most things Christian. You dreaded thinking about entering that strange religious world and wondered what those people were all about; it may have seemed so foreign, so strange. You may have peeked over the fence into that strange religious world and the changes that may occur in your life. Yet something drew you, or is now drawing you to God. Until you make the decision for yourself (your mom, friend, boyfriend, or girlfriend cannot make that decision), you will merely be a spectator on the sidelines. Until you say, "Yes I want to be on God's team (Team Jesus)," the best you can be is just a religious fan. This book is a challenge to sign up and to compete on Jesus' team . . . to build the inner life and participate with Christ.

Reflection
Where am I in my Christian life? A spectator, an ardent fan, or a participant?

Prayer
Help me, Almighty God, to participate in the spiritual life.

"Come follow me."
Jesus

DEVOTIONAL

Nicked with permission from: A Sporting Guide to Eternity, Steve Connor, Christian Focus Publications - ISBN 1-85792-746-X

Acts

The sequel: *Jesus' Ministry Part II*
So what happened to Jesus' followers after Jesus died and went to heaven? The story isn't over! The Gospel writer Luke (see Luke for more details about the author), with his attention to historical detail, takes up where he left off in the Gospel of Luke. Here we see how Christianity spreads throughout the world by the power of the Holy Spirit. Not only does Luke write about the history of the early church, he lives it, following the apostle Paul in some dangerous and exciting assignments! Read on.

Luke records:
- Jesus' resurrection
- His ascension to heaven
- The obedience of the apostles
- The coming of the Holy Spirit
- The progress of Jesus' followers encouraging the church
- The persecution of Jesus' followers, including Stephen's execution
- The dispersal of Jesus' followers
- The spread of the Good News and the impact it had on new areas
- The dramatic conversion of Paul
- Paul's courage and commitment to spread Christ's message further throughout the world

ACTS

The Promise of the Holy Spirit

1

In my first book I told you, Theophilus, about everything Jesus began to do and teach [2]until the day he was taken up to heaven after giving his chosen apostles further instructions through the Holy Spirit. [3]During the forty days after his crucifixion, he appeared to the apostles from time to time, and he proved to them in many ways that he was actually alive. And he talked to them about the Kingdom of God.

[4]Once when he was eating with them, he commanded them, "Do not leave Jerusalem until the Father sends you the gift he promised, as I told you before. [5]John baptized with water, but in just a few days you will be baptized with the Holy Spirit."

The Ascension of Jesus

[6]So when the apostles were with Jesus, they kept asking him, "Lord, has the time come for you to free Israel and restore our kingdom?"

[7]He replied, "The Father alone has the authority to set those dates and times, and they are not for you to know. [8]But you will receive power when the Holy Spirit comes upon you. And you will be my witnesses, telling people about me everywhere—in Jerusalem, throughout Judea, in Samaria, and to the ends of the earth."

[9]After saying this, he was taken up into a cloud while they were watching, and they could no longer see him. [10]As they strained to see him rising into heaven, two white-robed men suddenly stood among them. [11]"Men of Galilee," they said, "why are you standing here staring into heaven? Jesus has been taken from you into heaven, but someday he will return from heaven in the same way you saw him go!"

Matthias Replaces Judas

[12]Then the apostles returned to Jerusalem from the Mount of Olives, a distance of half a mile. [13]When they arrived, they went to the upstairs room of the house where they were staying.

Here are the names of those who were present: Peter, John, James, Andrew, Philip, Thomas, Bartholomew, Matthew, James (son of Alphaeus), Simon (the Zealot), and Judas (son of James). [14]They all met together and were constantly united in prayer, along with Mary the mother of Jesus, several other women, and the brothers of Jesus.

[15]During this time, when about 120 believers were together in one place, Peter stood up and addressed them. [16]"Brothers," he said, "the Scriptures had to be fulfilled concerning Judas, who guided those who arrested Jesus. This was predicted long ago by the Holy Spirit, speaking through King David. [17]Judas was one of us and shared in the ministry with us."

[18](Judas had bought a field with the money he received

Esther (in the Old Testament) is the only book in the Bible that does not contain the word *God*.

for his treachery. Falling headfirst there, his body split open, spilling out all his intestines. [19]The news of his death spread to all the people of Jerusalem, and they gave the place the Aramaic name *Akeldama*, which means "Field of Blood.")

[20]Peter continued, "This was written in the book of Psalms, where it says, 'Let his home become desolate, with no one living in it.' It also says, 'Let someone else take his position.'

[21]"So now we must choose a replacement for Judas from among the men who were with us the entire time we were traveling with the Lord Jesus—[22]from the time he was baptized by John until the day he was taken from us. Whoever is chosen will join us as a witness of Jesus' resurrection."

[23]So they nominated two men: Joseph called Barsabbas (also known as Justus) and Matthias. [24]Then they all prayed, "O Lord, you know every heart. Show us which of these men you have chosen [25]as an apostle to replace Judas in this ministry, for he has deserted us and gone where he belongs." [26]Then they cast lots, and Matthias was selected to become an apostle with the other eleven.

The Holy Spirit Comes

2

On the day of Pentecost all the believers were meeting together in one place. [2]Suddenly, there was a sound from heaven like the roaring of a mighty windstorm, and it filled the house where they were sitting. [3]Then, what looked like flames or tongues of fire appeared and settled on each of them. [4]And everyone present was filled with the Holy Spirit and began speaking in other languages, as the Holy Spirit gave them this ability.

[5]At that time there were devout Jews from every nation living in Jerusalem. [6]When they heard the loud noise, everyone came running, and they were bewildered to hear their own languages being spoken by the believers.

[7]They were completely amazed. "How can this be?" they exclaimed. "These people are all from Galilee, [8]and yet we hear them speaking in our own native languages! [9]Here we are—Parthians, Medes, Elamites, people from Mesopotamia, Judea, Cappadocia, Pontus, the province of Asia, [10]Phrygia, Pamphylia, Egypt, and the areas of Libya around Cyrene, visitors from Rome (both Jews and converts to Judaism), [11]Cretans, and Arabs. And we all hear these people speaking in our own languages about the wonderful things God has done!" [12]They stood there amazed and perplexed. "What can this mean?" they asked each other.

[13]But others in the crowd ridiculed them, saying, "They're just drunk, that's all!"

Peter Preaches to the Crowd

[14]Then Peter stepped forward with the eleven other apostles and shouted to the crowd, "Listen carefully, all of you, fellow Jews and residents of Jerusalem! Make no mistake about this. [15]These people are not drunk, as some of you are assuming. Nine o'clock in the morning is much too early for that. [16]No, what you see was predicted long ago by the prophet Joel:

[17]'In the last days,' God says,
'I will pour out my Spirit upon all people.
Your sons and daughters will prophesy.

When you need real power

1:8

You will receive power when the Holy Spirit comes upon you. And you will be my witnesses, telling people about me everywhere—in Jerusalem, throughout Judea, in Samaria, and to the ends of the earth.

> You will go the distance: Know that as a Christian you will live forever and your existence will never stop — you have been born into a life that will never die. We may be in the land of the dying, but we are going to the land of the living. "For you have been born again, but not to life that will quickly end. Your new life will last forever because it comes from the eternal, living word of God."
>
> (1 Peter 1:23)

Your young men will see visions,
and your old men will dream dreams.
[18]In those days I will pour out my Spirit
even on my servants—men and women alike—
and they will prophesy.
[19]And I will cause wonders in the heavens above
and signs on the earth below—
blood and fire and clouds of smoke.
[20]The sun will become dark,
and the moon will turn blood red
before that great and glorious day of the LORD arrives.
[21]But everyone who calls on the name of the LORD
will be saved.'
[22]"People of Israel, listen! God publicly endorsed Jesus the Nazarene by doing powerful miracles, wonders, and signs through him, as you well know. [23]But God knew what would happen, and his prearranged plan was carried out when Jesus was betrayed. With the help of lawless Gentiles, you nailed him to a cross and killed him. [24]But God released him from the horrors of death and raised him back to life, for death could not keep him in its grip. [25]King David said this about him:
'I see that the LORD is always with me.
I will not be shaken, for he is right beside me.
[26]No wonder my heart is glad,
and my tongue shouts his praises!
My body rests in hope.
[27]For you will not leave my soul among the dead or allow your Holy One to rot in the grave.
[28]You have shown me the way of life,
and you will fill me with the joy of your presence.'
[29]"Dear brothers, think about this! You can be sure that the patriarch David wasn't referring to himself, for he died and was buried, and his tomb is still here among us. [30]But he was a prophet, and he knew God had promised with an oath that one of David's own descendants would sit on his throne. [31]David was looking into the future and speaking of the Messiah's resurrection. He was saying that God would not leave him among the dead or allow his body to rot in the grave.
[32]"God raised Jesus from the dead, and we are all witnesses of this. [33]Now he is exalted to the place of highest honor in heaven, at God's right hand. And the Father, as he had promised, gave him the Holy Spirit to pour out upon us, just as you see and hear today. [34]For David himself never ascended into heaven, yet he said,
'The LORD said to my Lord,
"Sit in the place of honor at my right hand
[35]until I humble your enemies,
making them a footstool under your feet."'
[36]"So let everyone in Israel know for certain that God has made this Jesus, whom you crucified, to be both Lord and Messiah!"
[37]Peter's words pierced their hearts, and they said to him and to the other apostles, "Brothers, what should we do?"
[38]Peter replied, "Each of you must repent of your sins, turn to God, and be baptized in the name of Jesus Christ to show that you have received forgiveness for your sins. Then you will receive the gift of the Holy Spirit. [39]This promise is to you, and to your children, and even to the Gentiles—all who have been called by the Lord our God." [40]Then Peter continued preaching for a long time, strongly urging all his listeners, "Save yourselves from this crooked generation!"
[41]Those who believed what Peter said were baptized and added to the church that day—about **3,000** in all.

The Believers Form a Community

[42]All the believers devoted themselves to the apostles' teaching, and to fellowship, and to sharing in meals (including the Lord's Supper), and to prayer. [43]A deep sense of awe came over them all, and the apostles performed many miraculous signs and wonders. [44]And all the believers met together in one

place and shared everything they had. ⁴⁵They sold their property and possessions and shared the money with those in need. ⁴⁶They worshiped together at the Temple each day, met in homes for the Lord's Supper, and shared their meals with great joy and generosity—⁴⁷all the while praising God and enjoying the goodwill of all the people. And each day the Lord added to their fellowship those who were being saved.

action

2:37-40 WHAT'S IT SAYING?

WHAT AM I GOING TO DO ABOUT IT?

Peter Heals a Crippled Beggar

3

Peter and John went to the Temple one afternoon to take part in the three o'clock prayer service. ²As they approached the Temple, a man lame from birth was being carried in. Each day he was put beside the Temple gate, the one called the Beautiful Gate, so he could beg from the people going into the Temple. ³When he saw Peter and John about to enter, he asked them for some money.
⁴Peter and John looked at him intently, and Peter said, "Look at us!" ⁵The lame man looked at them eagerly, expecting some money. ⁶But Peter said, "I don't have any silver or gold for you. But I'll give you what I

have. In the name of Jesus Christ the Nazarene, get up and walk!"
⁷Then Peter took the lame man by the right hand and helped him up. And as he did, the man's feet and ankles were instantly healed and strengthened. ⁸He jumped up, stood on his feet, and began to walk! Then, walking, leaping, and praising God, he went into the Temple with them.
⁹All the people saw him walking and heard him praising God. ¹⁰When they realized he was the lame beggar they had seen so often at the Beautiful Gate, they were absolutely astounded! ¹¹They all rushed out in amazement to Solomon's Colonnade, where the man was holding tightly to Peter and John.

Peter Preaches in the Temple

¹²Peter saw his opportunity and addressed the crowd. "People of Israel," he said, "what is so surprising about this? And why stare at us as though we had made this man walk by our own power or godliness? ¹³For it is the God of Abraham, Isaac, and Jacob—the God of all our ancestors—who has brought glory to his servant Jesus by doing this. This is the same Jesus whom you handed over and rejected before Pilate, despite Pilate's decision to release him. ¹⁴You rejected this holy, righteous one and instead demanded the release of a murderer. ¹⁵You killed the author of life, but God raised him from the dead. And we are witnesses of this fact!
¹⁶"Through faith in the name of Jesus, this man was healed—and you know how crippled he was before. Faith in Jesus' name has healed him before your very eyes.

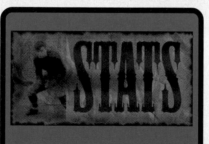

STATS

The huddle was formed due to a deaf football player who used sign language to communicate. His team didn't want the opposition to see the signals he used, so they huddled around him.

¹⁷"Friends, I realize that what you and your leaders did to Jesus was done in ignorance. ¹⁸But God was fulfilling what all the prophets had foretold about the Messiah—that he must suffer these things. ¹⁹Now repent of your sins and turn to God, so that your sins may be wiped away. ²⁰Then times of refreshment will come from the presence of the Lord, and he will again send you Jesus, your appointed Messiah. ²¹For he must remain in heaven until the time for the final restoration of all things, as God promised long ago through his holy prophets. ²²Moses said, 'The LORD your God will raise up for you a Prophet like me from among your own people. Listen carefully to everything he tells you.' ²³Then Moses said, 'Anyone who will not listen to that Prophet will be completely cut off from God's people.'
²⁴"Starting with Samuel, every prophet spoke about what is happening today. ²⁵You are the children of those prophets, and you are included in the covenant God promised to your ancestors. For God said to Abraham, 'Through your descendants all the families on earth will be blessed.' ²⁶When God raised up his servant, Jesus, he sent him first to you people of Israel, to bless you by turning each of you back from your sinful ways."

Peter and John before the Council

4

While Peter and John were speaking to the people, they were confronted by the priests, the captain of the Temple guard, and some of the Sadducees. ²These leaders were very disturbed that Peter and John were teaching the people that through Jesus there is a resurrection of the dead. ³They arrested them and, since it was already evening, put them in jail until morning. ⁴But many of the people who heard their message believed it, so the number of believers now totaled about 5,000 men, not counting women and children.
⁵The next day the council of all the rulers and elders and teachers of religious law met in Jerusalem. ⁶Annas the high priest was there, along with Caiaphas, John, Alexander, and other relatives of the high priest. ⁷They brought in the two disciples and demanded, "By what power, or in whose name, have you done this?"
⁸Then Peter, filled with the Holy Spirit, said to them, "Rulers and elders of our people, ⁹are we being questioned today because we've done a good deed for a crippled man? Do you want to know how he was healed? ¹⁰Let me clearly state to all of you and to all the people of Israel that he was healed by the powerful name of Jesus Christ the Nazarene, the man you crucified but whom God raised from the dead. ¹¹For Jesus is the one referred to in the Scriptures, where it says,
'The stone that you builders rejected
has now become the cornerstone.'
¹²There is salvation in no one else! God has given no other

TIPS

Walk the walk:

Be willing to lead by example. Be an example, and model the desired behavior and performance you want the rest of your team to exhibit. Do not expect your teammates to do something you won't do in front of them.

name under heaven by which we must be saved."

[13]The members of the council were amazed when they saw the boldness of Peter and John, for they could see that they were ordinary men with no special training in the Scriptures. They also recognized them as men who had been with Jesus. [14]But since they could see the man who had been healed standing right there among them, there was nothing the council could say. [15]So they ordered Peter and John out of the council chamber and conferred among themselves.

[16]"What should we do with these men?" they asked each other. "We can't deny that they have performed a miraculous sign, and everybody in Jerusalem knows about it. [17]But to keep them from spreading their propaganda any further, we must warn them not to speak to anyone in Jesus' name again." [18]So they called the apostles back in and commanded them never again to speak or teach in the name of Jesus.

[19]But Peter and John replied, "Do you think God wants us to obey you rather than him? [20]We cannot stop telling about everything we have seen and heard."

[21]The council then threatened them further, but they finally let them go because they didn't know how to punish them without starting a riot. For everyone was praising God [22]for this miraculous sign—the healing of a man who had been lame for more than forty years.

The Believers Pray for Courage

[23]As soon as they were freed, Peter and John returned to the other believers and told them what the leading priests and elders had said. [24]When they heard the report, all the believers lifted their voices together in prayer to God: "O Sovereign Lord, Creator of heaven and earth, the sea, and everything in them—[25]you spoke long ago by the Holy Spirit through our ancestor David, your servant, saying,

'Why were the nations so angry?
Why did they waste their time with futile plans?
[26]The kings of the earth prepared for battle;
the rulers gathered together
against the LORD
and against his Messiah.'

[27]"In fact, this has happened here in this very city! For Herod Antipas, Pontius Pilate the governor, the Gentiles, and the people of Israel were all united against Jesus, your holy servant, whom you anointed. [28]But everything they did was determined beforehand according to your will. [29]And now, O Lord, hear their threats, and give us, your servants, great boldness in preaching your word. [30]Stretch out your hand with healing power; may miraculous signs and wonders be done through the name of your holy servant Jesus."

[31]After this prayer, the meeting place shook, and they were all filled with the Holy Spirit. Then they preached the word of God with boldness.

The Believers Share Their Possessions

[32]All the believers were united in heart and mind. And they felt that what they owned was not their own, so they shared everything they had. [33]The apostles testified powerfully to the resurrection of the Lord Jesus, and God's great blessing was upon them all. [34]There were no needy people among them, because those who owned land or houses would sell them [35]and bring the money to the apostles to give to those in need.

[36]For instance, there was Joseph, the one the apostles nicknamed Barnabas (which means "Son of Encouragement"). He was from the tribe of Levi and came from the island of Cyprus. [37]He sold a field he owned and brought the money to the apostles.

action

4:13-15 WHAT'S IT SAYING?

WHAT AM I GOING TO DO ABOUT IT?

Ananias and Sapphira

5

But there was a certain man named Ananias who, with his wife, Sapphira, sold some property. [2]He brought part of the money to the apostles, claiming it was the full amount. With his wife's consent, he kept the rest. [3]Then Peter said, "Ananias, why have you let Satan fill your heart? You lied to the Holy Spirit, and you kept some of the money for yourself. [4]The property was yours to sell or not sell, as you wished. And after selling it, the money was also yours to give away. How could you do a thing like this? You weren't lying to us but to God!"

[5]As soon as Ananias heard these words, he fell to the floor and died. Everyone who heard about it was

STAND POINT

When you need an example of teamwork

4:32

All the believers were united in heart and mind. And they felt that what they owned was not their own, so they shared everything they had.

WHAT

DOES IT MEAN?

amen

This Hebrew word means firm "rock solid," and hence also "faithful" (Revelation 3:14). It is found singly and sometimes doubly at the end of prayers. In the early churches it was common for the general audience to say "amen" at the close of the prayer (1 Corinthians 14:16). The promises of God are amen rock-solid — they are all true and definite (2 Corinthians 1:20).

terrified. ⁶Then some young men got up, wrapped him in a sheet, and took him out and buried him.
⁷About three hours later his wife came in, not knowing what had happened. ⁸Peter asked her, "Was this the price you and your husband received for your land?" "Yes," she replied, "that was the price."
⁹And Peter said, "How could the two of you even think of conspiring to test the Spirit of the Lord like this? The young men who buried your husband are just outside the door, and they will carry you out, too."
¹⁰Instantly, she fell to the floor and died. When the young men came in and saw that she was dead, they carried her out and buried her beside her husband.
¹¹Great fear gripped the entire church and everyone else who heard what had happened.

The Apostles Heal Many

¹²The apostles were performing many miraculous signs and wonders among the people. And all the believers were meeting regularly at the Temple in the area known as Solomon's Colonnade. ¹³But no one else dared to join them, even though all the people had high regard for them. ¹⁴Yet more and more people believed and were brought to the Lord—crowds of both men and women. ¹⁵As a result of the apostles' work, sick people were brought out into the streets on beds and mats so that Peter's shadow might fall across some of them as he went by. ¹⁶Crowds came from the villages around Jerusalem, bringing their sick and those possessed by evil spirits, and they were all healed.

action

5:1-11 WHAT'S IT SAYING?

WHAT AM I GOING TO DO ABOUT IT?

The Apostles Meet Opposition

¹⁷The high priest and his officials, who were Sadducees, were filled with jealousy. ¹⁸They arrested the apostles and put them in the public jail. ¹⁹But an angel of the Lord came at night, opened the gates of the jail, and brought them out. Then he told them, ²⁰"Go to the Temple and give the people this message of life!"
²¹So at daybreak the apostles entered the Temple, as they were told, and immediately began teaching.

profiles

Paul:

When you open your life to Jesus, you change. Perhaps nobody has ever changed so quickly or dramatically as Paul. Like an athlete, he was single-minded, focused, and intense by nature; in fact in his letters he used sports to illustrate his teaching. Paul, originally named Saul, was a well-trained Jewish Pharisee who saw followers of Jesus as a threat to the Jewish religion. His passion, intensity, and energy were turned toward crushing the Christian movement. He was even part of the stoning of Stephen, a devout follower of Christ. He was heading to the town of Damascus about 160 miles north of the capital, Jerusalem, when Jesus struck him down and he was transformed overnight into a follower of Christ. His zeal for Christ was immediate, and he always carried the knowledge that he at one point had persecuted and killed his Savior's followers. In time he became a zealous, strategic Christian with a passion for telling the Good News of Jesus and encouraging Christian communities to do the same. Besides Christ himself, no one has affected the world more than Paul. What will it be like when we get to heaven and see Stephen and Paul arm in arm praising God?

Can I really control my sex drive?

Yes you can! This may be your longest and toughest challenge. For every encouragement you will have to keep your life pure and follow God's plan for sex, you will have countless negative messages lying to you, telling you just to follow your urges. Remember, Jesus was tempted, and he defeated temptation. Ask God for help! He will give you power and will pick you up if you fall. God has a history of restoring his fallen people to himself. The biggest mistake you can make is when you fail and then withdraw from God. Instead, run to God, apologize, and commit yourself to staying on the right path.

Scripture says next to nothing about masturbation (this may be more of a guy issue), but it is very strong about keeping your thoughts pure and under control. "God's will for you to be holy, so stay away from all sexual sin. Then each of you will control his own body and live in holiness and honor" (1 Thessalonians 4:3-4).

When the high priest and his officials arrived, they convened the high council—the full assembly of the elders of Israel. Then they sent for the apostles to be brought from the jail for trial. [22]But when the Temple guards went to the jail, the men were gone. So they returned to the council and reported, [23]"The jail was securely locked, with the guards standing outside, but when we opened the gates, no one was there!" [24]When the captain of the Temple guard and the leading priests heard this, they were perplexed, wondering where it would all end. [25]Then someone arrived with startling news: "The men you put in jail are standing in the Temple, teaching the people!"

[26]The captain went with his Temple guards and arrested the apostles, but without violence, for they were afraid the people would stone them. [27]Then they brought the apostles before the high council, where the high priest confronted them. [28]"Didn't we tell you never again to teach in this man's name?" he demanded. "Instead, you have filled all Jerusalem with your teaching about him, and you want to make us responsible for his death!"

[29]But Peter and the apostles replied, "We must obey God rather than any human authority. [30]The God of our ancestors raised Jesus from the dead after you killed him by hanging him on a cross. [31]Then God put him in the place of honor at his right hand as Prince and Savior. He did this so the people of Israel would repent of their sins and be forgiven. [32]We are witnesses of these things and so is the Holy Spirit, who is given by God to those who obey him."

[33]When they heard this, the high council was furious and decided to kill them. [34]But one member, a Pharisee named Gamaliel, who was an expert in religious law and respected by all the people, stood up and ordered that the men be sent outside the council chamber for a while. [35]Then he said to his colleagues, "Men of Israel, take care what you are planning to do to these men! [36]Some time ago there was that fellow Theudas, who pretended to be someone great. About 400 others joined him, but he was killed, and all his followers went their various ways. The whole movement came to nothing. [37]After him, at the time of the census, there was Judas of Galilee. He got people to follow him, but he was killed, too, and all his followers were scattered.

[38]"So my advice is, leave these men alone. Let them go. If they are planning and doing these things merely on their own, it will soon be overthrown. [39]But if it is from God, you will not be able to overthrow them. You may even find yourselves fighting against God!"

[40]The others accepted his advice. They called in the apostles and had them flogged. Then they ordered them never again to speak in the name of Jesus, and they let them go.

[41]The apostles left the high council rejoicing that God had counted them worthy to suffer disgrace for the name of Jesus. [42]And every day, in the Temple and from house to house, they continued to teach and preach this message: "Jesus is the Messiah."

Seven Men Chosen to Serve

6

But as the believers rapidly multiplied, there were rumblings of discontent. The Greek-speaking believers complained about the Hebrew-speaking believers, saying that their widows were being discriminated against in the daily distribution of food.

[2]So the Twelve called a meeting of all the believers. They said, "We apostles should spend our time teaching the word of God, not running a food program. [3]And so, brothers, select seven men who are well respected and are full of the Spirit and wisdom. We will give them this responsibility. [4]Then we apostles can spend our time in prayer and teaching the word."

[5]Everyone liked this idea, and they chose the following: Stephen (a man full of faith and the Holy Spirit), Philip, Procorus, Nicanor, Timon, Parmenas, and Nicolas of Antioch (an earlier convert to the Jewish faith). [6]These seven were presented to the apostles, who prayed for them as they laid their hands on them. [7]So God's message continued to spread. The number of believers greatly increased in Jerusalem, and many of the Jewish priests were converted, too.

Stephen Is Arrested

[8]Stephen, a man full of God's grace and power, performed amazing miracles and signs among the people. [9]But one day some men from the Synagogue of Freed Slaves, as it was called, started to debate with him. They were Jews from Cyrene, Alexandria, Cilicia, and the province of Asia. [10]None of them could stand against the wisdom and the Spirit with which Stephen spoke.

[11]So they persuaded some men to lie about Stephen, saying, "We heard him blaspheme Moses, and even God." [12]This roused the people, the elders, and the teachers of religious law. So they arrested Stephen and brought him before the high council.

[13]The lying witnesses said, "This man is always speaking against the holy Temple and against the law of Moses. [14]We have heard him say that this Jesus of Nazareth will destroy the Temple and change the customs Moses handed down to us."

[15]At this point everyone in the high council stared at Stephen, because his face became as bright as an angel's.

Stephen Addresses the Council

7

Then the high priest asked Stephen, "Are these accusations true?"

[2]This was Stephen's reply: "Brothers and fathers, listen to me. Our glorious God appeared to our ancestor Abraham in Mesopotamia before he settled in Haran.

³God told him, 'Leave your native land and your relatives, and come into the land that I will show you.' ⁴So Abraham left the land of the Chaldeans and lived in Haran until his father died. Then God brought him here to the land where you now live.

⁵"But God gave him no inheritance here, not even one square foot of land. God did promise, however, that eventually the whole land would belong to Abraham and his descendants—even though he had no children yet. ⁶God also told him that his descendants would live in a foreign land, where they would be oppressed as slaves for 400 years. ⁷'But I will punish the nation that enslaves them,' God said, 'and in the end they will come out and worship me here in this place.'

⁸"God also gave Abraham the covenant of circumcision at that time. So when Abraham became the father of Isaac, he circumcised him on the eighth day. And the practice was continued when Isaac became the father of Jacob, and when Jacob became the father of the twelve patriarchs of the Israelite nation.

⁹"These patriarchs were jealous of their brother Joseph, and they sold him to be a slave in Egypt. But God was with him ¹⁰and rescued him from all his troubles. And God gave him favor before Pharaoh, king of Egypt. God also gave Joseph unusual wisdom, so that Pharaoh appointed him governor over all of Egypt and put him in charge of the palace.

¹¹"But a famine came upon Egypt and Canaan. There was great misery, and our ancestors ran out of food. ¹²Jacob heard that there was still grain in Egypt, so he sent his sons—our ancestors—to buy some. ¹³The second time they went, Joseph revealed his identity to his brothers, and they were introduced to Pharaoh. ¹⁴Then Joseph sent for his father, Jacob, and all his relatives to come to Egypt, seventy-five persons in all. ¹⁵So Jacob went to Egypt. He died there, as did our ancestors. ¹⁶Their bodies were taken to Shechem and buried in the tomb Abraham had bought for a certain price from Hamor's sons in Shechem.

¹⁷"As the time drew near when God would fulfill his promise to Abraham, the number of our people in Egypt greatly increased. ¹⁸But then a new king came to the throne of Egypt who knew nothing about Joseph. ¹⁹This king exploited our people and oppressed them, forcing parents to abandon their newborn babies so they would die.

²⁰"At that time Moses was born—a beautiful child in God's eyes. His parents cared for him at home for three months. ²¹When they had to abandon him, Pharaoh's daughter adopted him and raised him as her own son. ²²Moses was taught all the wisdom of

the Egyptians, and he was powerful in both speech and action.

²³"One day when Moses was forty years old, he decided to visit his relatives, the people of Israel. ²⁴He saw an Egyptian mistreating an Israelite. So Moses came to the man's defense and avenged him, killing the Egyptian. ²⁵Moses assumed his fellow Israelites would realize that God had sent him to rescue them, but they didn't.

²⁶"The next day he visited them again and saw two men of Israel fighting. He tried to be a peacemaker. 'Men,' he said, 'you are brothers. Why are you fighting each other?'

²⁷"But the man in the wrong pushed Moses aside. 'Who made you a ruler and judge over us?' he asked. ²⁸'Are you going to kill me as you killed that Egyptian yesterday?' ²⁹When Moses heard that, he fled the country and lived as a foreigner in the land of Midian. There his two sons were born.

³⁰"Forty years later, in the desert near Mount Sinai, an angel appeared to Moses in the flame of a burning bush. ³¹When Moses saw it, he was amazed at the sight. As he went to take a closer look, the voice of the LORD called out to him, ³²'I am the God of your ancestors—the God of Abraham, Isaac, and Jacob.' Moses shook with terror and did not dare to look.

³³"Then the LORD said to him, 'Take off your sandals, for you are standing on holy ground. ³⁴I have certainly seen the oppression of my people in Egypt. I have heard their groans and have come down to rescue them. Now go, for I am sending you back to Egypt.'

³⁵"So God sent back the same man his people had previously rejected when they demanded, 'Who made you a ruler and judge over us?' Through the angel who appeared to him in the burning bush, God sent Moses to be their ruler and savior. ³⁶And by means of many wonders and miraculous signs, he led them out of Egypt, through the Red Sea, and through the wilderness for forty years.

³⁷"Moses himself told the people of Israel, 'God will raise up for you a Prophet like me from among your own people.' ³⁸Moses was with our ancestors, the assembly of God's people in the wilderness, when the angel spoke to him at Mount Sinai. And there Moses received life-giving words to pass on to us.

³⁹"But our ancestors refused to listen to Moses. They rejected him and wanted to return to Egypt. ⁴⁰They told Aaron, 'Make us some gods who can lead us, for we don't know what has become of this Moses, who brought us out of Egypt.' ⁴¹So they made an idol shaped like a calf, and they sacrificed to it and celebrated over this thing they had made. ⁴²Then God turned away from them and abandoned them to serve the stars of heaven as their gods! In the book of the prophets it is written,

'Was it to me you were bringing sacrifices and offerings during those forty years in the wilderness, Israel?
⁴³No, you carried your pagan gods—
the shrine of Molech,
the star of your god Rephan,
and the images you made to worship them.
So I will send you into exile
as far away as Babylon.'

⁴⁴"Our ancestors carried the Tabernacle with them through the wilderness. It was constructed according to the plan God had shown to Moses. ⁴⁵Years later, when Joshua led our ancestors in battle against the nations that God drove out of this land, the Tabernacle was taken with them into their new territory. And it stayed there until the time of King David.

STAND POINT

When you need to forgive someone
7:59-60

As they stoned him, Stephen prayed, "Lord Jesus, receive my spirit." He fell to his knees, shouting, "Lord, don't charge them with this sin!" And with that, he died.

⁴⁶"David found favor with God and asked for the privilege of building a permanent Temple for the God of Jacob. ⁴⁷But it was Solomon who actually built it. ⁴⁸However, the Most High doesn't live in temples made by human hands. As the prophet says,

⁴⁹'Heaven is my throne,
and the earth is my footstool.
Could you build me a temple as good as that?'
asks the LORD.
'Could you build me such a resting place?
⁵⁰Didn't my hands make both heaven and earth?'

⁵¹"You stubborn people! You are heathen at heart and deaf to the truth. Must you forever resist the Holy Spirit? That's what your ancestors did, and so do you! ⁵²Name one prophet your ancestors didn't persecute! They even killed the ones who predicted the coming of the Righteous One—the Messiah whom you betrayed and murdered. ⁵³You deliberately disobeyed God's law, even though you received it from the hands of angels."

⁵⁴The Jewish leaders were infuriated by Stephen's accusation, and they shook their fists at him in rage. ⁵⁵But Stephen, full of the Holy Spirit, gazed steadily into heaven and saw the glory of God, and he saw Jesus standing in the place of honor at God's right hand. ⁵⁶And he told them, "Look, I see the heavens opened and the Son of Man standing in the place of honor at God's right hand!"

⁵⁷Then they put their hands over their ears and began shouting. They rushed at him ⁵⁸and dragged him out of the city and began to stone him. His accusers took off their coats and laid them at the feet of a young man named Saul.

⁵⁹As they stoned him, Stephen prayed, "Lord Jesus, receive my spirit." ⁶⁰He fell to his knees, shouting, "Lord, don't charge them with this sin!" And with that, he died.

8

Saul was one of the witnesses, and he agreed completely with the killing of Stephen.

Persecution Scatters the Believers

A great wave of persecution began that day, sweeping over the church in Jerusalem; and all the believers except the apostles were scattered through the regions of Judea and Samaria. ²(Some devout men came and buried Stephen with great mourning.) ³But Saul was going everywhere to destroy the church. He went from house to house, dragging out both men and women to throw them into prison.

Philip Preaches in Samaria

⁴But the believers who were scattered preached the Good News about Jesus wherever they went. ⁵Philip, for example, went to the city of Samaria and told the people there about the Messiah. ⁶Crowds listened intently to Philip because they were eager to hear his message and see the miraculous signs he did. ⁷Many evil spirits were cast out, screaming as they left their victims. And many who had been paralyzed or lame were healed. ⁸So there was great joy in that city.

⁹A man named Simon had been a sorcerer there for many years, amazing the people of Samaria and claiming to be someone great. ¹⁰Everyone, from the least to the greatest, often spoke of him as "the Great One—the Power of God." ¹¹They listened closely to him because for a long time he had astounded them with his magic.

¹²But now the people believed Philip's message of Good News concerning the Kingdom of God and the name of Jesus Christ. As a result, many men and women were baptized. ¹³Then Simon himself believed and was baptized. He began following Philip wherever he went, and he was amazed by the signs and great miracles Philip performed.

¹⁴When the apostles in Jerusalem heard that the people of Samaria had accepted God's message, they sent Peter and John there. ¹⁵As soon as they arrived, they prayed for these new believers to receive the Holy Spirit. ¹⁶The Holy Spirit had not yet come upon any of them, for they had only been baptized in the name of the Lord Jesus. ¹⁷Then Peter and John laid their hands upon these believers, and they received the Holy Spirit. ¹⁸When Simon saw that the Spirit was given when the apostles laid their hands on people, he offered them money to buy this power. ¹⁹"Let me have this power, too," he exclaimed, "so that when I lay my hands on people, they will receive the Holy Spirit!"

²⁰But Peter replied, "May your money be destroyed with you for thinking God's gift can be bought! ²¹You can have no part in this, for your heart is not right with God. ²²Repent of your wickedness and pray to the Lord. Perhaps he will forgive your evil thoughts, ²³for I can see that you are full of bitter jealousy and are held captive by sin."

²⁴"Pray to the Lord for me," Simon exclaimed, "that these terrible things you've said won't happen to me!"

²⁵After testifying and preaching the word of the Lord in Samaria, Peter and John returned to Jerusalem. And they stopped in many Samaritan villages along the way to preach the Good News.

8:18-24 WHAT'S IT SAYING?

WHAT AM I GOING TO DO ABOUT IT?

Philip and the Ethiopian Eunuch

²⁶As for Philip, an angel of the Lord said to him, "Go south down the desert road that runs from Jerusalem to Gaza." ²⁷So he started out, and he met the treasurer of Ethiopia, a eunuch of great authority under the Kandake, the queen of Ethiopia. The eunuch had gone to Jerusalem to worship, ²⁸and he was now returning. Seated in his carriage, he was reading aloud from the book of the prophet Isaiah.

²⁹The Holy Spirit said to Philip, "Go over and walk along beside the carriage."

STATS

The first Wimbledon tennis competition took place in 1877 solely as an amateur competition. Men's singles was the only event that took place. There were 22 competitors, and Spencer Gore won the championship.

³⁰Philip ran over and heard the man reading from the prophet Isaiah. Philip asked, "Do you understand what you are reading?"

³¹The man replied, "How can I, unless someone instructs me?" And he urged Philip to come up into the carriage and sit with him.

³²The passage of Scripture he had been reading was this:

"He was led like a sheep to the slaughter.
And as a lamb is silent before the shearers,
he did not open his mouth.
³³He was humiliated and received no justice.
Who can speak of his descendants?
For his life was taken from the earth."

³⁴The eunuch asked Philip, "Tell me, was the prophet talking about himself or someone else?" ³⁵So beginning with this same Scripture, Philip told him the Good News about Jesus.

³⁶As they rode along, they came to some water, and the eunuch said, "Look! There's some water! Why can't I be baptized?"* ³⁸He ordered the carriage to stop, and they went down into the water, and Philip baptized him.

³⁹When they came up out of the water, the Spirit of the Lord snatched Philip away. The eunuch never saw him again but went on his way rejoicing. ⁴⁰Meanwhile, Philip found himself farther north at the town of Azotus. He preached the Good News there and in every town along the way until he came to Caesarea.

Saul's Conversion

9

Meanwhile, Saul was uttering threats with every breath and was eager to kill the Lord's followers. So he went to the high priest. ²He requested letters addressed to the synagogues in Damascus, asking for their cooperation in the arrest of any followers of the Way he found there. He wanted to bring them—both men and women—back to Jerusalem in chains.

³As he was approaching Damascus on this mission, a light from heaven suddenly shone down around him. ⁴He fell to the ground and heard a voice saying to him, "Saul! Saul! Why are you persecuting me?"

⁵"Who are you, lord?" Saul asked.

And the voice replied, "I am Jesus, the one you are persecuting! ⁶Now get up and go into the city, and you will be told what you must do."

⁷The men with Saul stood speechless, for they heard the sound of someone's voice but saw no one! ⁸Saul picked himself up off the ground, but when he opened his eyes he was blind. So his companions led him by

count on it

You have been adopted!
We in Christ have been adopted onto God's team. We wear his colors, his uniform. We carry all the responsibilities of playing for Christ, for we carry His "seal." When we sin we let down his team. But the Holy Spirit will give us power. He is committed to building us into useful players for the Father. "God decided in advance to adopt us into his own family by bringing us to himself through Jesus Christ." (Ephesians 1:5) **Count on it!**

the hand to Damascus. ⁹He remained there blind for three days and did not eat or drink.

¹⁰Now there was a believer in Damascus named Ananias. The Lord spoke to him in a vision, calling, "Ananias!"

"Yes, Lord!" he replied.

¹¹The Lord said, "Go over to Straight Street, to the house of Judas. When you get there, ask for a man from Tarsus named Saul. He is praying to me right now. ¹²I have shown him a vision of a man named Ananias coming in and laying hands on him so he can see again."

¹³"But Lord," exclaimed Ananias, "I've heard many people talk about the terrible things this man has done to the believers in Jerusalem! ¹⁴And he is authorized by the leading priests to arrest everyone who calls upon your name."

¹⁵But the Lord said, "Go, for Saul is my chosen instrument to take my message to the Gentiles and to kings, as well as to the people of Israel. ¹⁶And I will

show him how much he must suffer for my name's sake."

¹⁷So Ananias went and found Saul. He laid his hands on him and said, "Brother Saul, the Lord Jesus, who appeared to you on the road, has sent me so that you might regain your sight and be filled with the Holy Spirit." ¹⁸Instantly something like scales fell from Saul's eyes, and he regained his sight. Then he got up and was baptized. ¹⁹Afterward he ate some food and regained his strength.

Saul in Damascus and Jerusalem

Saul stayed with the believers in Damascus for a few days. ²⁰And immediately he began preaching about Jesus in the synagogues, saying, "He is indeed the Son of God!"

²¹All who heard him were amazed. "Isn't this the same man who caused such devastation among Jesus' followers in Jerusalem?" they asked. "And didn't he come here to arrest them and take them in chains to the leading priests?"

²²Saul's preaching became more and more powerful, and the Jews in Damascus couldn't refute his proofs that Jesus was indeed the Messiah. ²³After a while some of the Jews plotted together to kill him. ²⁴They were watching for him day and night at the city gate so they could murder him, but Saul was told about their plot. ²⁵So during the night, some of the other believers lowered him in a large basket through an opening in the city wall.

²⁶When Saul arrived in Jerusalem, he tried to meet with the believers, but they were all afraid of him. They did not believe he had truly become a believer! ²⁷Then Barnabas brought him to the apostles and told them how Saul had seen the Lord on the way to Damascus and how the Lord had spoken to Saul. He also told them that Saul had preached boldly in the name of Jesus in Damascus.

²⁸So Saul stayed with the apostles and went all around Jerusalem with them, preaching boldly in the name of the Lord. ²⁹He debated with some Greek-speaking Jews, but they tried to murder him. ³⁰When the believers heard about this, they took him down to Caesarea and sent him away to Tarsus, his hometown.

³¹The church then had peace throughout Judea, Galilee, and Samaria, and it became stronger as the believers lived in the fear of the Lord. And with the encouragement of the Holy Spirit, it also grew in numbers.

Peter Heals Aeneas and Raises Dorcas

³²Meanwhile, Peter traveled from place to place, and he came down to visit the believers in the town of Lydda. ³³There he met a man named Aeneas, who had been paralyzed and bedridden for eight years. ³⁴Peter said to him, "Aeneas, Jesus Christ heals you! Get up, and roll up your sleeping mat!" And he was healed instantly. ³⁵Then the whole population of Lydda and Sharon saw Aeneas walking around, and they turned to the Lord.

8:36 Some manuscripts add verse 37, "You can," Philip answered, "if you believe with all your heart." And the eunuch replied, "I believe that Jesus Christ is the Son of God."

36There was a believer in Joppa named Tabitha (which in Greek is Dorcas). She was always doing kind things for others and helping the poor. 37About this time she became ill and died. Her body was washed for burial and laid in an upstairs room. 38But the believers had heard that Peter was nearby at Lydda, so they sent two men to beg him, "Please come as soon as possible!"

39So Peter returned with them; and as soon as he arrived, they took him to the upstairs room. The room was filled with widows who were weeping and showing him the coats and other clothes Dorcas had made for them. 40But Peter asked them all to leave the room; then he knelt and prayed. Turning to the body he said, "Get up, Tabitha." And she opened her eyes! When she saw Peter, she sat up! 41He gave her his hand and helped her up. Then he called in the widows and all the believers, and he presented her to them alive.

42The news spread through the whole town, and many believed in the Lord. 43And Peter stayed a long time in Joppa, living with Simon, a tanner of hides.

Cornelius Calls for Peter

10

In Caesarea there lived a Roman army officer named Cornelius, who was a captain of the Italian Regiment. 2He was a devout, God-fearing man, as was everyone in his household. He gave generously to the poor and prayed regularly to God. 3One afternoon about three o'clock, he had a vision in which he saw an angel of God coming toward him. "Cornelius!" the angel said.

4Cornelius stared at him in terror. "What is it, sir?" he asked the angel.

And the angel replied, "Your prayers and gifts to the poor have been received by God as an offering! 5Now send some men to Joppa, and summon a man named Simon Peter. 6He is staying with Simon, a tanner who lives near the seashore."

7As soon as the angel was gone, Cornelius called two of his household servants and a devout soldier, one of his personal attendants. 8He told them what had happened and sent them off to Joppa.

Peter Visits Cornelius

9The next day as Cornelius's messengers were nearing the town, Peter went up on the flat roof to pray. It was about noon, 10and he was hungry. But while a meal was being prepared, he fell into a trance. 11He saw the sky open, and something like a large sheet was let down by its four corners. 12In the sheet were all sorts of animals, reptiles, and birds. 13Then a voice said to him, "Get up, Peter; kill and eat them."

14"No, Lord," Peter declared. "I have never eaten anything that our Jewish laws have declared impure and unclean."

15But the voice spoke again: "Do not call something unclean if God has made it clean." 16The same vision was repeated three times. Then the sheet was suddenly pulled up to heaven.

17Peter was very perplexed. What could the vision mean? Just then the men sent by Cornelius found Simon's house. Standing outside the gate, 18they asked if a man named Simon Peter was staying there.

19Meanwhile, as Peter was puzzling over the vision, the Holy Spirit said to him, "Three men have come looking for you. 20Get up, go downstairs, and go with them without hesitation. Don't worry, for I have sent them."

21So Peter went down and said, "I'm the man you are looking for. Why have you come?"

22They said, "We were sent by Cornelius, a Roman officer. He is a devout and God-fearing man, well respected by all the Jews. A holy angel instructed him to summon you to his house so that he can hear your message." 23So Peter invited the men to stay for the night. The next day he went with them, accompanied by some of the brothers from Joppa.

24They arrived in Caesarea the following day. Cornelius was waiting for them and had called together his relatives and close friends. 25As Peter entered his home, Cornelius fell at his feet and worshiped him. 26But Peter pulled him up and said, "Stand up! I'm a human being just like you!" 27So they talked together and went inside, where many others were assembled.

28Peter told them, "You know it is against our laws for a Jewish man to enter a Gentile home like this or to associate with you. But God has shown me that I should no longer think of anyone as impure or unclean. 29So I came without objection as soon as I was sent for. Now tell me why you sent for me."

30Cornelius replied, "Four days ago I was praying in my house about this same time, three o'clock in the afternoon. Suddenly, a man in dazzling clothes was standing in front of me. 31He told me, 'Cornelius, your prayer has been heard, and your gifts to the poor have been noticed by God! 32Now send messengers to Joppa, and summon a man named Simon Peter. He is staying in the home of Simon, a tanner who lives near the seashore.' 33So I sent for you at once, and it was good of you to come. Now we are all here, waiting before God to hear the message the Lord has given you."

The Gentiles Hear the Good News

34Then Peter replied, "I see very clearly that God shows no favoritism. 35In every nation he accepts those who fear him and do what is right. 36This is the message of Good News for the people of Israel—that there is peace with God through Jesus Christ, who is Lord of all. 37You know what happened throughout Judea, beginning in Galilee, after John began preaching his message of baptism. 38And you know that God anointed Jesus of Nazareth with the Holy Spirit and with power. Then Jesus went around doing good and healing all who were oppressed by the devil, for God was with him.

39"And we apostles are witnesses of all he did throughout Judea and in Jerusalem. They put him to death by hanging him on a cross, 40but God raised him to life on the third day. Then God allowed him to appear, 41not to the general public, but to us whom God had chosen in advance to be his witnesses. We were those who ate and drank with him after he rose

Doing Good (ACTS 10:38)
Are you doing good? Jesus always did good. Goodness is the character of God. We can also see glimpses of goodness coming out in people since we are made in God's image. Who are some good role models you can follow and try to be like? What good can you do today?

your best
isn't good
enough

sport

TIPS

When you are being coached, ask yourself:

What's the general skill principle you are focusing on?
What are your objectives?
What are your greatest strengths and weaknesses?

from the dead. [42]And he ordered us to preach everywhere and to testify that Jesus is the one appointed by God to be the judge of all—the living and the dead. [43]He is the one all the prophets testified about, saying that everyone who believes in him will have their sins forgiven through his name."

The Gentiles Receive the Holy Spirit

[44]Even as Peter was saying these things, the Holy Spirit fell upon all who were listening to the message. [45]The Jewish believers who came with Peter were amazed that the gift of the Holy Spirit had been poured out on the Gentiles, too. [46]For they heard them speaking in tongues and praising God.

Then Peter asked, [47]"Can anyone object to their being baptized, now that they have received the Holy Spirit just as we did?" [48]So he gave orders for them to be baptized in the name of Jesus Christ. Afterward Cornelius asked him to stay with them for several days.

Peter Explains His Actions

11

Soon the news reached the apostles and other believers in Judea that the Gentiles had received the word of God. [2]But when Peter arrived back in Jerusalem, the Jewish believers criticized him. [3]"You entered the home of Gentiles and even ate with them!" they said.

[4]Then Peter told them exactly what had happened. [5]"I was in the town of Joppa," he said, "and while I was praying, I went into a trance and saw a vision. Something like a large sheet was let down by its four corners from the sky. And it came right down to me. [6]When I looked inside the sheet, I saw all sorts of small animals, wild animals, reptiles, and birds. [7]And I heard a voice say, 'Get up, Peter; kill and eat them.' [8]"'No, Lord,' I replied. 'I have never eaten anything that our Jewish laws have declared impure or unclean.' [9]"But the voice from heaven spoke again: 'Do not call something unclean if God has made it clean.' [10]This

happened three times before the sheet and all it contained was pulled back up to heaven.

[11]"Just then three men who had been sent from Caesarea arrived at the house where we were staying. [12]The Holy Spirit told me to go with them and not to worry that they were Gentiles. These six brothers here accompanied me, and we soon entered the home of the man who had sent for us. [13]He told us how an angel had appeared to him in his home and had told him, 'Send messengers to Joppa, and summon a man named Simon Peter. [14]He will tell you how you and everyone in your household can be saved!'

[15]"As I began to speak," Peter continued, "the Holy Spirit fell on them, just as he fell on us at the beginning. [16]Then I thought of the Lord's words when he said, 'John baptized with water, but you will be baptized with the Holy Spirit.' [17]And since God gave these Gentiles the same gift he gave us when we believed in the Lord Jesus Christ, who was I to stand in God's way?"

[18]When the others heard this, they stopped objecting and began praising God. They said, "We can see that God has also given the Gentiles the privilege of repenting of their sins and receiving eternal life."

The Church in Antioch of Syria

[19]Meanwhile, the believers who had been scattered during the persecution after Stephen's death traveled as far as Phoenicia, Cyprus, and Antioch of Syria. They preached the word of God, but only to Jews. [20]However, some of the believers who went to Antioch from Cyprus and Cyrene began preaching to the Gentiles about the Lord Jesus. [21]The power of the Lord was with them, and a large number of these Gentiles believed and turned to the Lord.

[22]When the church at Jerusalem heard what had happened, they sent Barnabas to Antioch. [23]When he arrived and saw this evidence of God's blessing, he was filled with joy, and he encouraged the believers to stay true to the Lord. [24]Barnabas was a good man, full of the Holy Spirit and strong in faith. And many

people were brought to the Lord.

[25]Then Barnabas went on to Tarsus to look for Saul. [26]When he found him, he brought him back to Antioch. Both of them stayed there with the church for a full year, teaching large crowds of people. (It was at Antioch that the believers were first called Christians.)

[27]During this time some prophets traveled from Jerusalem to Antioch. [28]One of them named Agabus stood up in one of the meetings and predicted by the Spirit that a great famine was coming upon the entire Roman world. (This was fulfilled during the reign of Claudius.) [29]So the believers in Antioch decided to send relief to the brothers and sisters in Judea, everyone giving as much as they could. [30]This they did, entrusting their gifts to Barnabas and Saul to take to the elders of the church in Jerusalem.

James Is Killed and Peter Is Imprisoned

12

About that time King Herod Agrippa began to persecute some believers in the church. [2]He had the apostle James (John's brother) killed with a sword. [3]When Herod saw how much this pleased the Jewish people, he also arrested Peter. (This took place during the Passover celebration.) [4]Then he imprisoned him, placing him under the guard of four squads of four soldiers each. Herod intended to bring Peter out for public trial after the Passover. [5]But while Peter was in prison, the church prayed very earnestly for him.

Peter's Miraculous Escape from Prison

[6]The night before Peter was to be placed on trial, he was asleep, fastened with two chains between two soldiers. Others stood guard at the prison gate. [7]Suddenly, there was a bright light in the cell, and an angel of the Lord stood before Peter. The angel struck him on the side to awaken him and said, "Quick! Get up!" And the chains fell off his wrists. [8]Then the angel told him, "Get dressed and put on your sandals." And he did. "Now put on your coat and follow me," the angel ordered.

⁹So Peter left the cell, following the angel. But all the time he thought it was a vision. He didn't realize it was actually happening. ¹⁰They passed the first and second guard posts and came to the iron gate leading to the city, and this opened for them all by itself. So they passed through and started walking down the street, and then the angel suddenly left him.

¹¹Peter finally came to his senses. "It's really true!" he said. "The Lord has sent his angel and saved me from Herod and from what the Jewish leaders had planned to do to me!"

¹²When he realized this, he went to the home of Mary, the mother of John Mark, where many were gathered for prayer. ¹³He knocked at the door in the gate, and a servant girl named Rhoda came to open it. ¹⁴When she recognized Peter's voice, she was so overjoyed that, instead of opening the door, she ran back inside and told everyone, "Peter is standing at the door!"

¹⁵"You're out of your mind!" they said. When she insisted, they decided, "It must be his angel."

¹⁶Meanwhile, Peter continued knocking. When they finally opened the door and saw him, they were amazed. ¹⁷He motioned for them to quiet down and told them how the Lord had led him out of prison. "Tell James and the other brothers what happened," he said. And then he went to another place.

¹⁸At dawn there was a great commotion among the soldiers about what had happened to Peter. ¹⁹Herod Agrippa ordered a thorough search for him. When he couldn't be found, Herod interrogated the guards and sentenced them to death. Afterward Herod left Judea to stay in Caesarea for a while.

The Death of Herod Agrippa

²⁰Now Herod was very angry with the people of Tyre and Sidon. So they sent a delegation to make peace with him because their cities were dependent upon Herod's country for food. The delegates won the support of Blastus, Herod's personal assistant, ²¹and an appointment with Herod was granted. When the day arrived, Herod put on his royal robes, sat on his throne, and made a speech to them. ²²The people gave him a great ovation, shouting, "It's the voice of a god, not of a man!"

²³Instantly, an angel of the Lord struck Herod with a sickness, because he accepted the people's worship instead of giving the glory to God. So he was consumed with worms and died. ²⁴Meanwhile, the word of God continued to spread, and there were many new believers.

²⁵When Barnabas and Saul had finished their mission to Jerusalem, they returned, taking John Mark with them.

Barnabas and Saul Are Commissioned

13

Among the prophets and teachers of the church at Antioch of Syria were Barnabas, Simeon (called "the black man"), Lucius (from Cyrene), Manaen (the childhood companion of King Herod Antipas), and Saul. ²One day as these men were worshiping the Lord and fasting, the Holy Spirit said, "Dedicate Barnabas and Saul for the special work to which I have called them." ³So after more fasting and prayer, the men laid their hands on them and sent them on their way.

Paul's First Missionary Journey

⁴So Barnabas and Saul were sent out by the Holy Spirit. They went down to the seaport of Seleucia and then sailed for the island of Cyprus. ⁵There, in the town of Salamis, they went to the Jewish synagogues and preached the word of God. John Mark went with them as their assistant.

⁶Afterward they traveled from town to town across the entire island until finally they reached Paphos, where they met a Jewish sorcerer, a false prophet named Bar-Jesus. ⁷He had attached himself to the governor, Sergius Paulus, who was an intelligent man. The governor invited Barnabas and Saul to visit him, for he wanted to hear the word of God. ⁸But Elymas, the sorcerer (as his name means in Greek), interfered and urged the governor to pay no attention to what Barnabas and Saul said. He was trying to keep the governor from believing.

⁹Saul, also known as Paul, was filled with the Holy Spirit, and he looked the sorcerer in the eye. ¹⁰Then he said, "You son of the devil, full of every sort of deceit and fraud, and enemy of all that is good! Will you never stop perverting the true ways of the Lord? ¹¹Watch now, for the Lord has laid his hand of punishment upon you, and you will be struck blind. You will not see the sunlight for some time." Instantly mist and darkness came over the man's eyes, and he began groping around begging for someone to take his hand and lead him.

¹²When the governor saw what had happened, he became a believer, for he was astonished at the teaching about the Lord.

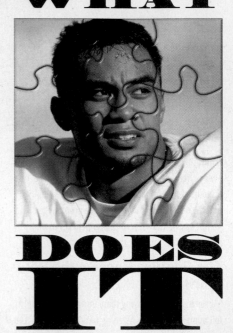

WHAT DOES IT MEAN?

justification

A legal term for God's judicial act, by which he pardons all the sins of those who believe in Christ and accounts for, recognizes, and treats them as righteous in the eyes of the law, i.e., as conformed to all its demands. In addition to the pardon from sin, justification declares that all the claims of the law are satisfied in respect of the justified (Romans 5:1-10). The act of faith that secures our justification secures at the same time our sanctification, so the doctrine of justification by faith does not lead to a license to keep sinning (Romans 6:1-7).

Paul Preaches in Antioch of Pisidia

¹³Paul and his companions then left Paphos by ship for Pamphylia, landing at the port town of Perga. There John Mark left them and returned to Jerusalem. ¹⁴But Paul and Barnabas traveled inland to Antioch of Pisidia.

Individual sports:

Though your sport may mean that you perform on your own, like golf or cycling, it is usually easier and more challenging to train with others.

On the Sabbath they went to the synagogue for the services. [15]After the usual readings from the books of Moses and the prophets, those in charge of the service sent them this message: "Brothers, if you have any word of encouragement for the people, come and give it."

[16]So Paul stood, lifted his hand to quiet them, and started speaking. "Men of Israel," he said, "and you God-fearing Gentiles, listen to me.

[17]"The God of this nation of Israel chose our ancestors and made them multiply and grow strong during their stay in Egypt. Then with a powerful arm he led them out of their slavery. [18]He put up with them through forty years of wandering in the wilderness. [19]Then he destroyed seven nations in Canaan and gave their land to Israel as an inheritance. [20]All this took about 450 years.

"After that, God gave them judges to rule until the time of Samuel the prophet. [21]Then the people begged for a king, and God gave them Saul son of Kish, a man of the tribe of Benjamin, who reigned for forty years. [22]But God removed Saul and replaced him with David, a man about whom God said, 'I have found David son of Jesse, a man after my own heart. He will do everything I want him to do.'

[23]"And it is one of King David's descendants, Jesus, who is God's promised Savior of Israel! [24]Before he came, John the Baptist preached that all the people of Israel needed to repent of their sins and turn to God and be baptized. [25]As John was finishing his ministry he asked, 'Do you think I am the Messiah? No, I am not! But he is coming soon—and I'm not even worthy to be his slave and untie the sandals on his feet.'

[26]"Brothers—you sons of Abraham, and also you God-fearing Gentiles—this message of salvation has been sent to us! [27]The people in Jerusalem and their leaders did not recognize Jesus as the one the prophets had spoken about. Instead, they condemned him, and in doing this they fulfilled the prophets' words that are read every Sabbath. [28]They found no legal reason to execute him, but they asked Pilate to have him killed anyway.

[29]"When they had done all that the prophecies said about him, they took him down from the cross and placed him in a tomb. [30]But God raised him from the dead! [31]And over a period of many days he appeared to those who had gone with him from Galilee to Jerusalem. They are now his witnesses to the people of Israel.

[32]"And now we are here to bring you this Good News. The promise was made to our ancestors, [33]and God has now fulfilled it for us, their descendants, by raising Jesus. This is what the second psalm says about Jesus:

'You are my Son.
Today I have become your Father.'

[34]For God had promised to raise him from the dead, not leaving him to rot in the grave. He said, 'I will give you the sacred blessings I promised to David.' [35]Another psalm explains it more fully: 'You will not allow your Holy One to rot in the grave.' [36]This is not a reference to David, for after David had done the will of God in his own generation, he died and was buried with his ancestors, and his body decayed. [37]No, it was a reference to someone else—someone whom God raised and whose body did not decay.

[38]"Brothers, listen! We are here to proclaim that through this man Jesus there is forgiveness for your sins. [39]Everyone who believes in him is declared right with God—something the law of Moses could never do. [40]Be careful! Don't let the prophets' words apply to you. For they said,

[41]'Look, you mockers,
be amazed and die!
For I am doing something in your own day,
something you wouldn't believe
even if someone told you about it.'"

[42]As Paul and Barnabas left the synagogue that day, the people begged them to speak about these things again the next week. [43]Many Jews and devout converts to Judaism

Winners know they are loved!

You never have to worry about earning God's love by playing well! Fortunately, you do not have to change, grow, or be good to be loved by God! Rather, you are loved by God, so that you will change, grow, and be good. Perhaps you should read the last sentence again! This is quite a hard concept for someone whose whole life has been governed by the teaching that one succeeds by one's own determination! The freedom of knowing you are radically loved by God will give you the security to live life to the full.

"God saved you by his grace when you believed. And you can't take credit for this; it is a gift from God. Salvation is not a reward for the good things we have done, so none of us can boast about it." (Ephesians 2:8-9)

Winners are freed by love!

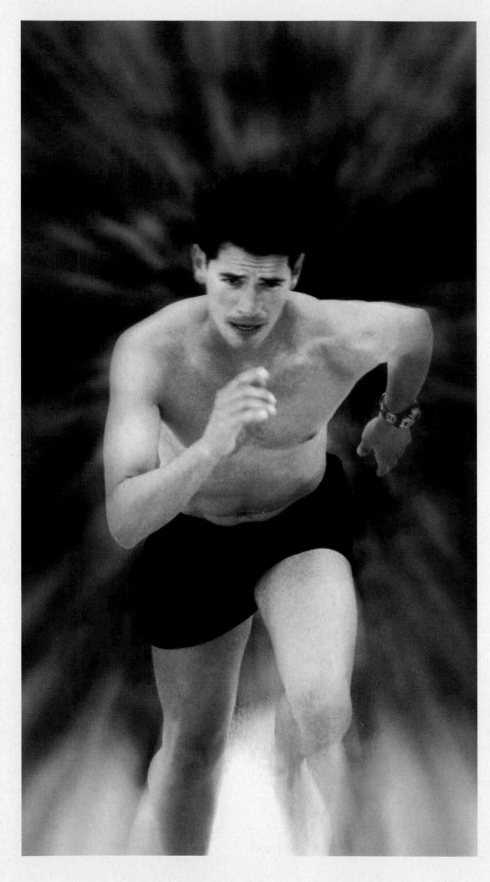

followed Paul and Barnabas, and the two men urged them to continue to rely on the grace of God.

Paul Turns to the Gentiles

⁴⁴The following week almost the entire city turned out to hear them preach the word of the Lord. ⁴⁵But when some of the Jews saw the crowds, they were jealous; so they slandered Paul and argued against whatever he said.

⁴⁶Then Paul and Barnabas spoke out boldly and declared, "It was necessary that we first preach the word of God to you Jews. But since you have rejected it and judged yourselves unworthy of eternal life, we will offer it to the Gentiles. ⁴⁷For the Lord gave us this command when he said,

'I have made you a light to the Gentiles,
to bring salvation to the farthest corners of the earth.'"

⁴⁸When the Gentiles heard this, they were very glad and thanked the Lord for his message; and all who were chosen for eternal life became believers. ⁴⁹So the Lord's message spread throughout that region.

⁵⁰Then the Jews stirred up the influential religious women and the leaders of the city, and they incited a mob against Paul and Barnabas and ran them out of town. ⁵¹So they shook the dust from their feet as a sign of rejection and went to the town of Iconium. ⁵²And the believers were filled with joy and with the Holy Spirit.

Paul and Barnabas in Iconium

14

The same thing happened in Iconium. Paul and Barnabas went to the Jewish synagogue and preached with such power that a great number of both Jews and Greeks became believers. ²Some of the Jews, however, spurned God's message and poisoned the minds of the Gentiles against Paul and Barnabas. ³But the apostles stayed there a long time, preaching boldly about the grace of the Lord. And the Lord proved their message was true by giving them power to do miraculous signs and wonders. ⁴But the people of the town were divided in their opinion about them. Some sided with the Jews, and some with the apostles.

⁵Then a mob of Gentiles and Jews, along with their leaders, decided to attack and stone them. ⁶When the apostles learned of it, they fled to the region of Lycaonia—to the towns of Lystra and Derbe and the surrounding area. ⁷And there they preached the Good News.

Paul and Barnabas in Lystra and Derbe

⁸While they were at Lystra, Paul and Barnabas came upon a man with crippled feet. He had been that way from birth, so he had never walked. He was sitting ⁹and listening as Paul preached. Looking straight at him, Paul realized he had faith to be healed. ¹⁰So Paul called to him in a loud voice, "Stand up!" And the man jumped to his feet and started walking.

¹¹When the crowd saw what Paul had done, they shouted in their local dialect, "These men are gods in human form!" ¹²They decided that Barnabas was the Greek god Zeus and that Paul was Hermes, since he was the chief speaker. ¹³Now the temple of Zeus was located just outside the town. So the priest of the temple and the crowd brought bulls and wreaths of flowers to the town gates, and they prepared to offer sacrifices to the apostles.

¹⁴But when Barnabas and Paul heard what was happening, they tore their clothing in dismay and ran out among the people, shouting, ¹⁵"Friends, why are you doing this? We are merely human beings—just like you! We have come to bring you the Good News that you should turn from these worthless things and turn to the living God, who made heaven and earth, the sea, and everything in them. ¹⁶In the past he permitted all the nations to go their own ways, ¹⁷but he never left them without evidence of himself and his goodness. For instance, he sends you rain and good crops and gives you food and joyful hearts." ¹⁸But even with these words, Paul and Barnabas could scarcely restrain the people from sacrificing to them.

¹⁹Then some Jews arrived from Antioch and Iconium and won the crowds to their side. They stoned Paul and dragged him out of town, thinking he was dead. ²⁰But as the believers gathered around him, he got up and went back into the town. The next day he left with Barnabas for Derbe.

Paul and Barnabas Return to Antioch of Syria

²¹After preaching the Good News in Derbe and making many disciples, Paul and Barnabas returned to Lystra, Iconium, and Antioch of Pisidia, ²²where they strengthened the believers. They encouraged them to continue in the faith, reminding them that we must suffer many hardships to enter the Kingdom of God. ²³Paul and Barnabas also appointed elders in every church. With prayer and fasting, they turned the elders over to the care of the Lord, in whom they had put their trust. ²⁴Then they traveled back through Pisidia

God will speak!

The Christian life is not easy! There will be times when you are laughed at, when you want to lash out against an opponent, and when you are unfairly treated by a coach. But Jesus does promise that when you need to defend yourself and you seek God's power, he will give you the right way to respond. Let God represent you! "Don't worry in advance about what to say. Just say what God tells you at that time, for it is not you who will be speaking, but the Holy Spirit." (Mark 13:11) **Count on it!**

to Pamphylia. ²⁵They preached the word in Perga, then went down to Attalia.

²⁶Finally, they returned by ship to Antioch of Syria, where their journey had begun. The believers there had entrusted them to the grace of God to do the work they had now completed. ²⁷Upon arriving in Antioch, they called the church together and reported everything God had done through them and how he had opened the door of faith to the Gentiles, too. ²⁸And they stayed there with the believers for a long time.

The Council at Jerusalem

15

While Paul and Barnabas were at Antioch of Syria, some men from Judea arrived and began to teach the believers: "Unless you are circumcised as required by the law of Moses, you cannot be saved." ²Paul and Barnabas disagreed with them, arguing vehemently. Finally, the church decided to send Paul and Barnabas to Jerusalem, accompanied by some local believers, to talk to the apostles and elders about this question. ³The church sent the delegates to Jerusalem, and they stopped along the way in Phoenicia and Samaria to visit the believers. They told them—much to everyone's joy—that the Gentiles, too, were being converted.

⁴When they arrived in Jerusalem, Barnabas and Paul were welcomed by the whole church, including the apostles and elders. They reported everything God had done through them. ⁵But then some of the believers who belonged to the sect of the Pharisees stood up and insisted, "The Gentile converts must be circumcised and required to follow the law of Moses."

⁶So the apostles and elders met together to resolve this issue. ⁷At the meeting, after a long discussion, Peter stood and addressed them as follows: "Brothers, you all know that God chose me from among you some time ago to preach to the Gentiles so that they could hear the Good News and believe. ⁸God knows people's hearts, and he confirmed that he accepts Gentiles by giving them the Holy Spirit, just as he did to us. ⁹He made no distinction between us and them, for he cleansed their hearts through faith. ¹⁰So why are you now challenging God by burdening the Gentile believers with a yoke that neither we nor our ancestors were able to bear? ¹¹We believe that we are all saved the same way, by the undeserved grace of the Lord Jesus."

¹²Everyone listened quietly as Barnabas and Paul told about the miraculous signs and wonders God had done through them among the Gentiles.

¹³When they had finished, James stood and said, "Brothers, listen to me. ¹⁴Peter has told you about the time God first visited the Gentiles to take from them a people for himself. ¹⁵And this conversion of Gentiles is exactly what the prophets predicted. As it is written:

¹⁶'Afterward I will return
and restore the fallen house of David.
I will rebuild its ruins
and restore it,
¹⁷so that the rest of humanity might seek the LORD,
including the Gentiles—
all those I have called to be mine.
The LORD has spoken—
¹⁸he who made these things known so long ago.'

¹⁹"And so my judgment is that we should not make it difficult for the Gentiles who are turning to God. ²⁰Instead, we should write and tell them to abstain from eating food offered to idols, from sexual immorality, from eating the meat of strangled animals, and from consuming blood. ²¹For these laws of Moses have been preached in Jewish synagogues in every city on every Sabbath for many generations."

JUNE M.A.P.

1
S.D.	P.L.	P.G.	S.G.
P. ☐	F. ☐	F. ☐	T. ☐
F. ☐	W. ☐	W. ☐	P. ☐
B. ☐	P. ☐	C. ☐	C. ☐

2
S.D.	P.L.	P.G.	S.G.
P. ☐	F. ☐	F. ☐	T. ☐
F. ☐	W. ☐	W. ☐	P. ☐
B. ☐	P. ☐	C. ☐	C. ☐

3
S.D.	P.L.	P.G.	S.G.
P. ☐	F. ☐	F. ☐	T. ☐
F. ☐	W. ☐	W. ☐	P. ☐
B. ☐	P. ☐	C. ☐	C. ☐

4
S.D.	P.L.	P.G.	S.G.
P. ☐	F. ☐	F. ☐	T. ☐
F. ☐	W. ☐	W. ☐	P. ☐
B. ☐	P. ☐	C. ☐	C. ☐

9
S.D.	P.L.	P.G.	S.G.
P. ☐	F. ☐	F. ☐	T. ☐
F. ☐	W. ☐	W. ☐	P. ☐
B. ☐	P. ☐	C. ☐	C. ☐

10
S.D.	P.L.	P.G.	S.G.
P. ☐	F. ☐	F. ☐	T. ☐
F. ☐	W. ☐	W. ☐	P. ☐
B. ☐	P. ☐	C. ☐	C. ☐

11
S.D.	P.L.	P.G.	S.G.
P. ☐	F. ☐	F. ☐	T. ☐
F. ☐	W. ☐	W. ☐	P. ☐
B. ☐	P. ☐	C. ☐	C. ☐

12
S.D.	P.L.	P.G.	S.G.
P. ☐	F. ☐	F. ☐	T. ☐
F. ☐	W. ☐	W. ☐	P. ☐
B. ☐	P. ☐	C. ☐	C. ☐

17
S.D.	P.L.	P.G.	S.G.
P. ☐	F. ☐	F. ☐	T. ☐
F. ☐	W. ☐	W. ☐	P. ☐
B. ☐	P. ☐	C. ☐	C. ☐

18
S.D.	P.L.	P.G.	S.G.
P. ☐	F. ☐	F. ☐	T. ☐
F. ☐	W. ☐	W. ☐	P. ☐
B. ☐	P. ☐	C. ☐	C. ☐

19
S.D.	P.L.	P.G.	S.G.
P. ☐	F. ☐	F. ☐	T. ☐
F. ☐	W. ☐	W. ☐	P. ☐
B. ☐	P. ☐	C. ☐	C. ☐

20
S.D.	P.L.	P.G.	S.G.
P. ☐	F. ☐	F. ☐	T. ☐
F. ☐	W. ☐	W. ☐	P. ☐
B. ☐	P. ☐	C. ☐	C. ☐

25
S.D.	P.L.	P.G.	S.G.
P. ☐	F. ☐	F. ☐	T. ☐
F. ☐	W. ☐	W. ☐	P. ☐
B. ☐	P. ☐	C. ☐	C. ☐

26
S.D.	P.L.	P.G.	S.G.
P. ☐	F. ☐	F. ☐	T. ☐
F. ☐	W. ☐	W. ☐	P. ☐
B. ☐	P. ☐	C. ☐	C. ☐

27
S.D.	P.L.	P.G.	S.G.
P. ☐	F. ☐	F. ☐	T. ☐
F. ☐	W. ☐	W. ☐	P. ☐
B. ☐	P. ☐	C. ☐	C. ☐

28
S.D.	P.L.	P.G.	S.G.
P. ☐	F. ☐	F. ☐	T. ☐
F. ☐	W. ☐	W. ☐	P. ☐
B. ☐	P. ☐	C. ☐	C. ☐

Spiritual Disciplines

Prayer

Faith Community

Bible Reading

Prayer List

Friends

World

Personal

Who am I....
Where am I going....
How am I going to get there?

nt:sport
MONTHLY ACTION PLAN

5
S.D.	P.L.	P.G.	S.G.
P. ☐	F. ☐	F. ☐	T. ☐
F. ☐	W. ☐	W. ☐	P. ☐
B. ☐	P. ☐	C. ☐	C. ☐

6
S.D.	P.L.	P.G.	S.G.
P. ☐	F. ☐	F. ☐	T. ☐
F. ☐	W. ☐	W. ☐	P. ☐
B. ☐	P. ☐	C. ☐	C. ☐

7
S.D.	P.L.	P.G.	S.G.
P. ☐	F. ☐	F. ☐	T. ☐
F. ☐	W. ☐	W. ☐	P. ☐
B. ☐	P. ☐	C. ☐	C. ☐

8
S.D.	P.L.	P.G.	S.G.
P. ☐	F. ☐	F. ☐	T. ☐
F. ☐	W. ☐	W. ☐	P. ☐
B. ☐	P. ☐	C. ☐	C. ☐

13
S.D.	P.L.	P.G.	S.G.
P. ☐	F. ☐	F. ☐	T. ☐
F. ☐	W. ☐	W. ☐	P. ☐
B. ☐	P. ☐	C. ☐	C. ☐

14
S.D.	P.L.	P.G.	S.G.
P. ☐	F. ☐	F. ☐	T. ☐
F. ☐	W. ☐	W. ☐	P. ☐
B. ☐	P. ☐	C. ☐	C. ☐

15
S.D.	P.L.	P.G.	S.G.
P. ☐	F. ☐	F. ☐	T. ☐
F. ☐	W. ☐	W. ☐	P. ☐
B. ☐	P. ☐	C. ☐	C. ☐

16
S.D.	P.L.	P.G.	S.G.
P. ☐	F. ☐	F. ☐	T. ☐
F. ☐	W. ☐	W. ☐	P. ☐
B. ☐	P. ☐	C. ☐	C. ☐

21
S.D.	P.L.	P.G.	S.G.
P. ☐	F. ☐	F. ☐	T. ☐
F. ☐	W. ☐	W. ☐	P. ☐
B. ☐	P. ☐	C. ☐	C. ☐

22
S.D.	P.L.	P.G.	S.G.
P. ☐	F. ☐	F. ☐	T. ☐
F. ☐	W. ☐	W. ☐	P. ☐
B. ☐	P. ☐	C. ☐	C. ☐

23
S.D.	P.L.	P.G.	S.G.
P. ☐	F. ☐	F. ☐	T. ☐
F. ☐	W. ☐	W. ☐	P. ☐
B. ☐	P. ☐	C. ☐	C. ☐

24
S.D.	P.L.	P.G.	S.G.
P. ☐	F. ☐	F. ☐	T. ☐
F. ☐	W. ☐	W. ☐	P. ☐
B. ☐	P. ☐	C. ☐	C. ☐

29
S.D.	P.L.	P.G.	S.G.
P. ☐	F. ☐	F. ☐	T. ☐
F. ☐	W. ☐	W. ☐	P. ☐
B. ☐	P. ☐	C. ☐	C. ☐

30
S.D.	P.L.	P.G.	S.G.
P. ☐	F. ☐	F. ☐	T. ☐
F. ☐	W. ☐	W. ☐	P. ☐
B. ☐	P. ☐	C. ☐	C. ☐

Proverbs 3:6

Seek his will in all you do, and he will show you which path to take.

Personal Goals

Family

Work/School/Social

Challenge

Sport Goals

Training

Performance

Competition Results

(For designing your M.A.P. – Monthly Action Plan – see introduction pages)

FUTURE CHARACTER TRAITS

When I die, if ten different types of people were to say something true and nice at my funeral, I would like them to say I was . . .

- Friend: _____
- Teammate: _____
- Coach: _____
- Minister/Pastor: _____
- Teacher: _____
- Boss: _____
- Work colleague: _____
- Someone who worked for me: _____
- Spouse: _____
- Son: _____
- Daughter: _____
- God: _____

Consider Jesus' words in the Parable of the Three Servants (Matthew 25:14-30)

The Letter for Gentile Believers

22Then the apostles and elders together with the whole church in Jerusalem chose delegates, and they sent them to Antioch of Syria with Paul and Barnabas to report on this decision. The men chosen were two of the church leaders—Judas (also called Barsabbas) and Silas. 23This is the letter they took with them:

"This letter is from the apostles and elders, your brothers in Jerusalem. It is written to the Gentile believers in Antioch, Syria, and Cilicia. Greetings!

24"We understand that some men from here have troubled you and upset you with their teaching, but we did not send them! 25So we decided, having come to complete agreement, to send you official representatives, along with our beloved Barnabas and Paul, 26who have risked their lives for the name of our Lord Jesus Christ. 27We are sending Judas and Silas to confirm what we have decided concerning your question.

28"For it seemed good to the Holy Spirit and to us to lay no greater burden on you than these few requirements: 29You must abstain from eating food offered to idols, from consuming blood or the meat of strangled animals, and from sexual immorality. If you do this, you will do well. Farewell."

30The messengers went at once to Antioch, where they called a general meeting of the believers and delivered the letter. 31And there was great joy throughout the church that day as they read this encouraging message.

32Then Judas and Silas, both being prophets, spoke at length to the believers, encouraging and strengthening their faith. 33They stayed for a while, and then the believers sent them back to the church in Jerusalem with a blessing of peace.* 35Paul and Barnabas stayed in Antioch. They and many others taught and preached the word of the Lord there.

Paul and Barnabas Separate

36After some time Paul said to Barnabas, "Let's go back and visit each city where we previously preached the word of the Lord, to see how the new believers are doing." 37Barnabas agreed and wanted to take along John Mark. 38But Paul disagreed strongly, since John Mark had deserted them in Pamphylia and had not continued with them in their work. 39Their disagreement was so sharp that they separated. Barnabas took John Mark with him and sailed for Cyprus. 40Paul chose Silas, and as he left, the believers

15:33 Some manuscripts add verse 34, *But Silas decided to stay there.*

entrusted him to the Lord's gracious care. ⁴¹Then he traveled throughout Syria and Cilicia, strengthening the churches there.

Paul's Second Missionary Journey

16

Paul went first to Derbe and then to Lystra, where there was a young disciple named Timothy. His mother was a Jewish believer, but his father was a Greek. ²Timothy was well thought of by the believers in Lystra and Iconium, ³so Paul wanted him to join them on their journey. In deference to the Jews of the area, he arranged for Timothy to be circumcised before they left, for everyone knew that his father was a Greek. ⁴Then they went from town to town, instructing the believers to follow the decisions made by the apostles and elders in Jerusalem. ⁵So the churches were strengthened in their faith and grew larger every day.

A Call from Macedonia

⁶Next Paul and Silas traveled through the area of Phrygia and Galatia, because the Holy Spirit had prevented them from preaching the word in the province of Asia at that time. ⁷Then coming to the borders of Mysia, they headed north for the province of Bithynia, but again the Spirit of Jesus did not allow them to go there. ⁸So instead, they went on through Mysia to the seaport of Troas.

⁹That night Paul had a vision: A man from Macedonia in northern Greece was standing there, pleading with him, "Come over to Macedonia and help us!" ¹⁰So we decided to leave for Macedonia at once, having concluded that God was calling us to preach the Good News there.

Lydia of Philippi Believes in Jesus

¹¹We boarded a boat at Troas and sailed straight across to the island of Samothrace, and the next day we landed at Neapolis. ¹²From there we reached Philippi, a major city of that district of Macedonia and a Roman colony. And we stayed there several days. ¹³On the Sabbath we went a little way outside the city to a riverbank, where we thought people would be meeting for prayer, and we sat down to speak with some women who had gathered there. ¹⁴One of them was Lydia from Thyatira, a merchant of expensive purple cloth, who worshiped God. As she listened to us, the Lord opened her heart, and she accepted what Paul was saying. ¹⁵She was baptized along with other

members of her household, and she asked us to be her guests. "If you agree that I am a true believer in the Lord," she said, "come and stay at my home." And she urged us until we agreed.

16:22-40 WHAT'S IT SAYING?

WHAT AM I GOING TO DO ABOUT IT?

Paul and Silas in Prison

¹⁶One day as we were going down to the place of prayer, we met a demon-possessed slave girl. She was a fortune-teller who earned a lot of money for her masters. ¹⁷She followed Paul and the rest of us, shouting, "These men are servants of the Most High God, and they have come to tell you how to be saved." ¹⁸This went on day after day until Paul got so exasperated that he turned and said to the demon within her, "I command you in the name of Jesus Christ to come out of her." And instantly it left her.

¹⁹Her masters' hopes of wealth were now shattered, so they grabbed Paul and Silas and dragged them before the authorities at the marketplace. ²⁰"The whole city is in an uproar because of these Jews!" they shouted to the city officials. ²¹"They are teaching customs that are illegal for us Romans to practice." ²²A mob quickly formed against Paul and Silas, and the city officials ordered them stripped and beaten with wooden rods. ²³They were severely beaten, and then they were thrown into prison. The jailer was ordered to make sure they didn't escape. ²⁴So the jailer

put them into the inner dungeon and clamped their feet in the stocks.

²⁵Around midnight Paul and Silas were praying and singing hymns to God, and the other prisoners were listening. ²⁶Suddenly, there was a massive earthquake, and the prison was shaken to its foundations. All the doors immediately flew open, and the chains of every prisoner fell off! ²⁷The jailer woke up to see the prison doors wide open. He assumed the prisoners had escaped, so he drew his sword to kill himself. ²⁸But Paul shouted to him, "Stop! Don't kill yourself! We are all here!"

²⁹The jailer called for lights and ran to the dungeon and fell down trembling before Paul and Silas. ³⁰Then he brought them out and asked, "Sirs, what must I do to be saved?"

³¹They replied, "Believe in the Lord Jesus and you will be saved, along with everyone in your household." ³²And they shared the word of the Lord with him and with all who lived in his household. ³³Even at that hour of the night, the jailer cared for them and washed their wounds. Then he and everyone in his household were immediately baptized. ³⁴He brought them into his house and set a meal before them, and he and his entire household rejoiced because they all believed in God.

³⁵The next morning the city officials sent the police to tell the jailer, "Let those men go!" ³⁶So the jailer told Paul, "The city officials have said you and Silas are free to leave. Go in peace."

³⁷But Paul replied, "They have publicly beaten us without a trial and put us in prison—and we are Roman citizens. So now they want us to leave secretly? Certainly not! Let them come themselves to release us!"

³⁸When the police reported this, the city officials were alarmed to learn that Paul and Silas were Roman citizens. ³⁹So they came to the jail and apologized to them. Then they brought them out and begged them to leave the city. ⁴⁰When

STAND POINT

When you need an example of boldness

18:9-10

One night the Lord spoke to Paul in a vision and told him, "Don't be afraid! Speak out! Don't be silent! For I am with you, and no one will attack and harm you, for many people in this city belong to me."

Paul and Silas left the prison, they returned to the home of Lydia. There they met with the believers and encouraged them once more. Then they left town.

action

17:10-12 WHAT'S IT SAYING?

WHAT AM I GOING TO DO ABOUT IT?

Paul Preaches in Thessalonica

17

Paul and Silas then traveled through the towns of Amphipolis and Apollonia and came to Thessalonica, where there was a Jewish synagogue. [2]As was Paul's custom, he went to the synagogue service, and for three Sabbaths in a row he used the Scriptures to reason with the people. [3]He explained the prophecies and proved that the Messiah must suffer and rise from the dead. He said, "This Jesus I'm telling you about is the Messiah." [4]Some of the Jews who listened were persuaded and joined Paul and Silas, along with many God-fearing Greek men and quite a few prominent women.

[5]But some of the Jews were jealous, so they gathered some troublemakers from the marketplace to form a mob and start a riot. They attacked the home of Jason, searching for Paul and Silas so they could drag them out to the crowd. [6]Not finding them there, they dragged out Jason and some of the other believers instead and took them before the city council. "Paul and Silas have caused trouble all over the world," they shouted, "and now they are here disturbing our city, too.

[7]And Jason has welcomed them into his home. They are all guilty of treason against Caesar, for they profess allegiance to another king, named Jesus."

[8]The people of the city, as well as the city council, were thrown into turmoil by these reports. [9]So the officials forced Jason and the other believers to post bond, and then they released them.

Paul and Silas in Berea

[10]That very night the believers sent Paul and Silas to Berea. When they arrived there, they went to the Jewish synagogue. [11]And the people of Berea were more open-minded than those in Thessalonica, and they listened eagerly to Paul's message. They searched the Scriptures day after day to see if Paul and Silas were teaching the truth. [12]As a result, many Jews believed, as did many of the prominent Greek women and men.

[13]But when some Jews in Thessalonica learned that

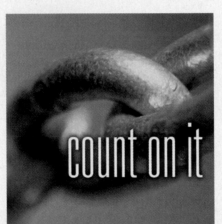

Have you ever felt thirsty?

Wouldn't that suggest you need to get rehydrated? Have you ever felt hungry? Wouldn't that suggest that you need some nutrition? Have you ever felt lonely? Wouldn't that suggest you need companionship? Have you ever felt lonely in a crowd? Wouldn't that suggest that you needed companionship with someone other than another person? God will be there for you! "I will never fail you. I will never abandon you." (Hebrews 13:5)
Count on it!

Paul was preaching the word of God in Berea, they went there and stirred up trouble. [14]The believers acted at once, sending Paul on to the coast, while Silas and Timothy remained behind. [15]Those escorting Paul went with him all the way to Athens; then they returned to Berea with instructions for Silas and Timothy to hurry and join him.

Paul Preaches in Athens

[16]While Paul was waiting for them in Athens, he was deeply troubled by all the idols he saw everywhere in the city. [17]He went to the synagogue to reason with the Jews and the God-fearing Gentiles, and he spoke daily in the public square to all who happened to be there.

[18]He also had a debate with some of the Epicurean and Stoic philosophers. When he told them about Jesus and his resurrection, they said, "What's this babbler trying to say with these strange ideas he's picked up?" Others said, "He seems to be preaching about some foreign gods."

[19]Then they took him to the high council of the city. "Come and tell us about this new teaching," they said. [20]"You are saying some rather strange things, and we want to know what it's all about." [21](It should be explained that all the Athenians as well as the foreigners in Athens seemed to spend all their time discussing the latest ideas.)

[22]So Paul, standing before the council, addressed them as follows: "Men of Athens, I notice that you are very religious in every way, [23]for as I was walking along I saw your many shrines. And one of your altars had this inscription on it: 'To an Unknown God.' This God, whom you worship without knowing, is the one I'm telling you about.

[24]"He is the God who made the world and everything in it. Since he is Lord of heaven and earth, he doesn't live in man-made temples, [25]and human hands can't serve his needs—for he has no needs. He himself gives life and breath to everything, and he satisfies every need. [26]From one man he created all the nations throughout the whole earth. He decided beforehand when they should rise and fall, and he determined their boundaries.

[27]"His purpose was for the nations to seek after God and perhaps feel their way toward him and find him—though he is not far from any one of us. [28]For in him we live and move and exist. As some of your own poets have said, 'We are his offspring.' [29]And since this is true, we shouldn't think of God as an idol designed by craftsmen from gold or silver or stone. [30]"God overlooked people's ignorance about these

things in earlier times, but now he commands everyone everywhere to repent of their sins and turn to him. [31]For he has set a day for judging the world with justice by the man he has appointed, and he proved to everyone who this is by raising him from the dead."

[32]When they heard Paul speak about the resurrection of the dead, some laughed in contempt, but others said, "We want to hear more about this later." [33]That ended Paul's discussion with them, [34]but some joined him and became believers. Among them were Dionysius, a member of the council, a woman named Damaris, and others with them.

Paul Meets Priscilla and Aquila in Corinth

18

Then Paul left Athens and went to Corinth. [2]There he became acquainted with a Jew named Aquila, born in Pontus, who had recently arrived from Italy with his wife, Priscilla. They had left Italy when Claudius Caesar deported all Jews from Rome. [3]Paul lived and worked with them, for they were tentmakers just as he was. [4]Each Sabbath found Paul at the synagogue, trying to convince the Jews and Greeks alike. [5]And after Silas and Timothy came down from Macedonia, Paul spent all his time preaching the word. He testified to the Jews that Jesus was the Messiah. [6]But when they opposed and insulted him, Paul shook the dust from his clothes and said, "Your blood is upon your own heads—I am innocent. From now on I will go preach to the Gentiles."

[7]Then he left and went to the home of Titius Justus, a Gentile who worshiped God and lived next door to the synagogue. [8]Crispus, the leader of the synagogue, and everyone in his household believed in the Lord. Many others in Corinth also heard Paul, became believers, and were baptized.

[9]One night the Lord spoke to Paul in a vision and told him, "Don't be afraid! Speak out! Don't be silent! [10]For

I am with you, and no one will attack and harm you, for many people in this city belong to me." [11]So Paul stayed there for the next year and a half, teaching the word of God.

[12]But when Gallio became governor of Achaia, some Jews rose up together against Paul and brought him before the governor for judgment. [13]They accused Paul of "persuading people to worship God in ways that are contrary to our law."

[14]But just as Paul started to make his defense, Gallio turned to Paul's accusers and said, "Listen, you Jews, if this were a case involving some wrongdoing or a serious crime, I would have a reason to accept your case. [15]But since it is merely a question of words and names and your Jewish law, take care of it yourselves. I refuse to judge such matters." [16]And he threw them out of the courtroom.

[17]The crowd then grabbed Sosthenes, the leader of the synagogue, and beat him right there in the courtroom. But Gallio paid no attention.

Paul Returns to Antioch of Syria

[18]Paul stayed in Corinth for some time after that, then said good-bye to the brothers and sisters and went to nearby Cenchrea. There he shaved his head according to Jewish custom, marking the end of a vow. Then he set sail for Syria, taking Priscilla and Aquila with him. [19]They stopped first at the port of Ephesus, where Paul left the others behind. While he was there, he went to the synagogue to reason with the Jews. [20]They asked him to stay longer, but he declined. [21]As he left, however, he said, "I will come back later, God willing." Then he set sail from Ephesus. [22]The next stop was at the port of Caesarea. From there he went up and visited the church at Jerusalem and then went back to Antioch.

[23]After spending some time in Antioch, Paul went back through Galatia and Phrygia, visiting and strengthening all the believers.

Apollos Instructed at Ephesus

[24]Meanwhile, a Jew named Apollos, an eloquent speaker who knew the Scriptures well, had arrived in Ephesus from Alexandria in Egypt. [25]He had been taught the way of the Lord, and he taught others about Jesus with an enthusiastic spirit and with accuracy. However, he knew only about John's baptism. [26]When Priscilla and Aquila heard him preaching boldly in the synagogue, they took him aside and explained the way of God even more accurately.

[27]Apollos had been thinking about going to Achaia, and the brothers and sisters in Ephesus encouraged him to go. They wrote to the believers in Achaia, asking them to welcome him. When he arrived there, he proved to be of great benefit to those who, by God's grace, had believed. [28]He refuted the Jews with powerful arguments in public debate. Using the Scriptures, he explained to them that Jesus was the Messiah.

Paul's Third Missionary Journey

19

While Apollos was in Corinth, Paul traveled through the interior regions until he reached Ephesus, on the coast, where he found several believers. [2]"Did you receive the Holy Spirit when you believed?" he asked them.

"No," they replied, "we haven't even heard that there is a Holy Spirit."

[3]"Then what baptism did you experience?" he asked.

And they replied, "The baptism of John."

[4]Paul said, "John's baptism called for repentance from sin. But John himself told the people to believe in the one who would come later, meaning Jesus."

[5]As soon as they heard this, they were baptized in the name of the Lord Jesus. [6]Then when Paul laid his hands on them, the Holy Spirit came on them, and they spoke in other tongues and prophesied. [7]There were about twelve men in all.

Paul Ministers in Ephesus

[8]Then Paul went to the synagogue and preached boldly for the next three months, arguing persuasively about the Kingdom of God. [9]But some became stubborn, rejecting his

Will reading my Bible help me in my sport?

Yes, definitely. God's book will help you in every area of your life. God's coaching manual — the Bible — may not help us technically with our game, nor will it give us six principles for effective concentration, but if we live our life by its rules, we will enormously increase our chances of maximizing performance. So playing our sport for Jesus means maintaining a central place in our life for Jesus' book. Serious athletes neglect training at their peril; serious Christians neglect the Bible at their peril.

message and publicly speaking against the Way. So Paul left the synagogue and took the believers with him. Then he held daily discussions at the lecture hall of Tyrannus. [10]This went on for the next two years, so that people throughout the province of Asia—both Jews and Greeks—heard the word of the Lord.

[11]God gave Paul the power to perform unusual miracles. [12]When handkerchiefs or aprons that had merely touched his skin were placed on sick people, they were healed of their diseases, and evil spirits were expelled.

[13]A group of Jews was traveling from town to town casting out evil spirits. They tried to use the name of the Lord Jesus in their incantation, saying, "I command you in the name of Jesus, whom Paul preaches, to come out!" [14]Seven sons of Sceva, a leading priest, were doing this. [15]But one time when they tried it, the evil spirit replied, "I know Jesus, and I know Paul, but who are you?" [16]Then the man with the evil spirit leaped on them, overpowered them, and attacked them with such violence that they fled from the house, naked and battered.

19:19-20 WHAT'S IT SAYING?

WHAT AM I GOING TO DO ABOUT IT?

[17]The story of what happened spread quickly all through Ephesus, to Jews and Greeks alike. A solemn fear descended on the city, and the name of the Lord Jesus was greatly honored. [18]Many who became believers confessed their sinful practices. [19]A number of them who had been practicing sorcery brought their incantation books and burned them at a public bonfire. The value of the books was several million dollars. [20]So the message about the Lord spread widely and had a powerful effect.

[21]Afterward Paul felt compelled by the Spirit to go over to Macedonia and Achaia before going to Jerusalem. "And after that," he said, "I must go on to Rome!" [22]He sent his two assistants, Timothy and Erastus, ahead to Macedonia while he stayed awhile longer in the province of Asia.

The Riot in Ephesus

[23]About that time, serious trouble developed in Ephesus concerning the Way. [24]It began with Demetrius, a silversmith who had a large business manufacturing silver shrines of the Greek goddess Artemis. He kept many craftsmen busy. [25]He called them together, along with others employed in similar trades, and addressed them as follows:

"Gentlemen, you know that our wealth comes from this business. [26]But as you have seen and heard, this man Paul has persuaded many people that handmade gods aren't really gods at all. And he's done this not only here in Ephesus but throughout the entire province! [27]Of course, I'm not just talking about the loss of public respect for our business. I'm also concerned that the temple of the great goddess Artemis will lose its influence and that Artemis—this magnificent goddess worshiped throughout the province of Asia and all around the world—will be robbed of her great prestige!"

[28]At this their anger boiled, and they began shouting, "Great is Artemis of the Ephesians!" [29]Soon the whole city was filled with confusion. Everyone rushed to the amphitheater, dragging along Gaius and Aristarchus, who were Paul's traveling companions from Macedonia. [30]Paul wanted to go in, too, but the believers wouldn't let him. [31]Some of the officials of the province, friends of Paul, also sent a message to him, begging him not to risk his life by entering the amphitheater.

[32]Inside, the people were all shouting, some one thing and some another. Everything was in confusion. In fact, most of them didn't even know why they were there. [33]The Jews in the crowd pushed Alexander forward and told him to explain the situation. He motioned for silence and tried to speak. [34]But when the crowd realized he was a Jew, they started shouting again and kept it up for two hours: "Great is Artemis of the Ephesians! Great is Artemis of the Ephesians!"

[35]At last the mayor was able to quiet them down enough to speak. "Citizens of Ephesus," he said. "Everyone knows that Ephesus is the official guardian of the temple of the great Artemis, whose image fell down to us from heaven. [36]Since this is an undeniable fact, you should stay calm and not do anything rash. [37]You have brought these men here, but they have stolen nothing from the temple and have not spoken against our goddess.

[38]"If Demetrius and the craftsmen have a case against them, the courts are in session and the officials can hear the case at once. Let them make formal charges. [39]And if there are complaints about other matters, they can be settled in a legal assembly. [40]I am afraid we are in danger of being charged with rioting by the Roman government, since there is no cause for all this commotion. And if Rome demands an explanation, we won't know what to say." [41]Then he dismissed them, and they dispersed.

Paul Goes to Macedonia and Greece

20

When the uproar was over, Paul sent for the believers and encouraged them. Then he said good-bye and left for Macedonia. [2]While there, he encouraged the believers in all the towns he passed through. Then he traveled down to Greece, [3]where he stayed for three months. He was preparing to sail back to Syria when he discovered a plot by some Jews against his life, so he decided to return through Macedonia.

[4]Several men were traveling with him. They were Sopater son of Pyrrhus from Berea; Aristarchus and Secundus from Thessalonica; Gaius from Derbe; Timothy; and Tychicus and Trophimus from the province of Asia. [5]They went on ahead and waited for us at Troas. [6]After the Passover ended, we boarded a ship at Philippi in Macedonia and five days later joined them in Troas, where we stayed a week.

Paul's Final Visit to Troas

[7]On the first day of the week, we gathered with the local believers to share in the Lord's Supper. Paul was preaching to them, and since he was leaving the next day, he kept talking until midnight. [8]The upstairs room where we met was lighted with many flickering lamps. [9]As Paul spoke on and on, a young man named Eutychus, sitting on the windowsill, became very drowsy. Finally, he fell sound asleep and dropped three stories to his death below. [10]Paul went down, bent over him, and took him into his arms. "Don't worry,"

he said, "he's alive!" ¹¹Then they all went back upstairs, shared in the Lord's Supper, and ate together. Paul continued talking to them until dawn, and then he left. ¹²Meanwhile, the young man was taken home unhurt, and everyone was greatly relieved.

Paul Meets the Ephesian Elders

¹³Paul went by land to Assos, where he had arranged for us to join him, while we traveled by ship. ¹⁴He joined us there, and we sailed together to Mitylene. ¹⁵The next day we sailed past the island of Kios. The following day we crossed to the island of Samos, and a day later we arrived at Miletus.

¹⁶Paul had decided to sail on past Ephesus, for he didn't want to spend any more time in the province of Asia. He was hurrying to get to Jerusalem, if possible, in time for the Festival of Pentecost. ¹⁷But when we landed at Miletus, he sent a message to the elders of the church at Ephesus, asking them to come and meet him.

¹⁸When they arrived he declared, "You know that from the day I set foot in the province of Asia until now ¹⁹I have done the Lord's work humbly and with many tears. I have endured the trials that came to me from the plots of the Jews. ²⁰I never shrank back from telling you what you needed to hear, either publicly or in your homes. ²¹I have had one message for Jews and Greeks alike—the necessity of repenting from sin and turning to God, and of having faith in our Lord Jesus. ²²"And now I am bound by the Spirit to go to Jerusalem. I don't know what awaits me, ²³except that the Holy Spirit tells me in city after city that jail and suffering lie ahead. ²⁴But my life is worth nothing to me unless I use it for finishing the work assigned me by the Lord Jesus—the work of telling others the Good News about the wonderful grace of God.

The shortest chapter in the Bible is Psalm 117.

²⁵"And now I know that none of you to whom I have preached the Kingdom will ever see me again. ²⁶I declare today that I have been faithful. If anyone suffers eternal death, it's not my fault, ²⁷for I didn't shrink from declaring all that God wants you to know. ²⁸"So guard yourselves and God's people. Feed and shepherd God's flock   his church, purchased with his own blood—over which the Holy Spirit has appointed you as elders. ²⁹I know that false teachers, like vicious wolves, will come in among you after I leave, not sparing the flock. ³⁰Even some men from your own group will rise up and distort the truth in order to draw a following. ³¹Watch out! Remember the three years I was with you—my constant watch and care over you night and day, and my many tears for you.

³²"And now I entrust you to God and the message of his grace that is able to build you up and give you an inheritance with all those he has set apart for himself. ³³"I have never coveted anyone's silver or gold or fine clothes. ³⁴You know that these hands of mine have worked to supply my own needs and even the needs of those who were with me. ³⁵And I have been a constant example of how you can help those in need by working hard. You should remember the words of the Lord Jesus: 'It is more blessed to give than to receive.'"

³⁶When he had finished speaking, he knelt and prayed with them. ³⁷They all cried as they embraced and kissed him good-bye. ³⁸They were sad most of all because he had said that they would never see him again. Then they escorted him down to the ship.

Paul's Journey to Jerusalem

21

After saying farewell to the Ephesian elders, we sailed straight to the island of Cos. The next day we reached Rhodes and then went to Patara. ²There we boarded a ship sailing for Phoenicia. ³We sighted the island of Cyprus, passed it on our left, and landed at the harbor of Tyre, in Syria, where the ship was to unload its cargo.

⁴We went ashore, found the local believers, and stayed with them a week. These believers prophesied through the Holy Spirit that Paul should not go on to Jerusalem. ⁵When we returned to the ship at the end of the week, the entire congregation, including wives and children, left the city and came down to the shore with us. There we knelt, prayed, ⁶and said our farewells. Then we went aboard, and they returned home.

⁷The next stop after leaving Tyre was Ptolemais, where we greeted the brothers and sisters and stayed for one day. ⁸The next day we went on to Caesarea and stayed at the home of Philip the Evangelist, one of the seven men who had been chosen to distribute food. ⁹He had four unmarried daughters who had the gift of prophecy.

¹⁰Several days later a man named Agabus, who also had the gift of prophecy, arrived from Judea. ¹¹He came over, took Paul's belt, and bound his own feet and hands with it. Then he said, "The Holy Spirit declares, 'So shall the owner of this belt be bound by the Jewish leaders in Jerusalem and turned over to the Gentiles.'" ¹²When we heard this, we and the local believers all begged Paul not to go on to Jerusalem. ¹³But he said, "Why all this weeping? You are breaking my

Get good coaching!

The brain is able to learn a new skill, such as walking. If we practice walking often enough, the skill becomes an unconscious reflex. We no longer have to think about how to walk. Walking has become a skill controlled by the subconscious part of our brain. This allows us to look around, talk, and do other things controlled by the conscious part of the brain, all at the same time. Like a computer, the conscious part of the brain learns what is required, writes the program code, and then stores it in the subconscious for instant execution when required. So if you are taught poor technique, it will take more time to root it out and retrain properly.

heart! I am ready not only to be jailed at Jerusalem but even to die for the sake of the Lord Jesus." ¹⁴When it was clear that we couldn't persuade him, we gave up and said, "The Lord's will be done."

Paul Arrives at Jerusalem

¹⁵After this we packed our things and left for Jerusalem. ¹⁶Some believers from Caesarea accompanied us, and they took us to the home of Mnason, a man originally from Cyprus and one of the early believers. ¹⁷When we arrived, the brothers and sisters in Jerusalem welcomed us warmly.

¹⁸The next day Paul went with us to meet with James, and all the elders of the Jerusalem church were present. ¹⁹After greeting them, Paul gave a detailed account of the things God had accomplished among the Gentiles through his ministry.

²⁰After hearing this, they praised God. And then they said, "You know, dear brother, how many thousands of Jews have also believed, and they all follow the law of Moses very seriously. ²¹But the Jewish believers here in Jerusalem have been told that you are teaching all the Jews who live among the Gentiles to turn their backs on the laws of Moses. They've heard that you teach them not to circumcise their children or follow other Jewish customs. ²²What should we do? They will certainly hear that you have come.

²³"Here's what we want you to do. We have four men here who have completed their vow. ²⁴Go with them to the Temple and join them in the purification ceremony, paying for them to have their heads ritually shaved. Then everyone will know that the rumors are all false and that you yourself observe the Jewish laws.

²⁵"As for the Gentile believers, they should do what we already told them in a letter: They should abstain from eating food offered to idols, from consuming blood or the meat of strangled animals, and from sexual immorality."

Paul Is Arrested

²⁶So Paul went to the Temple the next day with the other men. They had already started the purification ritual, so he publicly announced the date when their vows would end and sacrifices would be offered for each of them.

²⁷The seven days were almost ended when some Jews from the province of Asia saw Paul in the Temple and roused a mob against him. They grabbed him, ²⁸yelling, "Men of Israel, help us! This is the man who preaches against our people everywhere and tells everybody to disobey the Jewish laws. He speaks against the Temple—and even defiles this holy place by bringing in Gentiles." ²⁹(For earlier that day they had seen him in the city with Trophimus, a Gentile from Ephesus, and they assumed Paul had taken him into the Temple.)

³⁰The whole city was rocked by these accusations, and a great

riot followed. Paul was grabbed and dragged out of the Temple, and immediately the gates were closed behind him. ³¹As they were trying to kill him, word reached the commander of the Roman regiment that all Jerusalem was in an uproar. ³²He immediately called out his soldiers and officers and ran down among the crowd. When the mob saw the commander and the troops coming, they stopped beating Paul.

³³Then the commander arrested him and ordered him bound with two chains. He asked the crowd who he was and what he had done. ³⁴Some shouted one thing and some another. Since he couldn't find out the truth in all the uproar and confusion, he ordered that Paul be taken to the fortress. ³⁵As Paul reached the stairs, the mob grew so violent the soldiers had to lift him to their shoulders to protect him. ³⁶And the crowd followed behind, shouting, "Kill him, kill him!"

Paul Speaks to the Crowd

³⁷As Paul was about to be taken inside, he said to the commander, "May I have a word with you?"

"Do you know Greek?" the commander asked, surprised. ³⁸"Aren't you the Egyptian who led a rebellion some time ago and took 4,000 members of the Assassins out into the desert?"

³⁹"No," Paul replied, "I am a Jew and a citizen of Tarsus in Cilicia, which is an important city. Please, let me talk to these people." ⁴⁰The commander agreed, so Paul stood on the stairs and motioned to the people to be quiet. Soon a deep silence enveloped the crowd, and he addressed them in their own language, Aramaic.

22

"Brothers and esteemed fathers," Paul said, "listen to me as I offer my defense." ²When they heard him speaking in their own language, the silence was even greater.

The high jump method of jumping headfirst and landing on the back is called the Fosbury Flop.

³Then Paul said, "I am a Jew, born in Tarsus, a city in Cilicia, and I was brought up and educated here in Jerusalem under Gamaliel. As his student, I was carefully trained in our Jewish laws and customs. I became very zealous to honor God in everything I did, just like all of you today. ⁴And I persecuted the followers of the Way, hounding some to death, arresting both men and women and throwing them in prison. ⁵The high priest and the whole council of elders can testify that this is so. For I received letters from them to our Jewish brothers in Damascus, authorizing me to bring the Christians from there to Jerusalem, in chains, to be punished.

⁶"As I was on the road, approaching Damascus about noon, a very bright light from heaven suddenly shone down around me. ⁷I fell to the ground and heard a voice saying to me, 'Saul, Saul, why are you persecuting me?'

⁸"'Who are you, lord?' I asked.

"And the voice replied, 'I am Jesus the Nazarene, the one you are persecuting.' ⁹The people with me saw the light but didn't understand the voice speaking to me.

¹⁰"I asked, 'What should I do, Lord?'

"And the Lord told me, 'Get up and go into Damascus, and there you will be told everything you are to do.' ¹¹I was blinded by the intense light and had to be led by the hand to Damascus by my companions. ¹²A man named Ananias lived there. He was a godly man, deeply devoted to the law, and well regarded by all the Jews of Damascus. ¹³He came and stood beside me and said, 'Brother Saul, regain your sight.' And that very moment I could see him!

¹⁴"Then he told me, 'The God of our ancestors has chosen you to know his will and to see the Righteous One and hear him speak. ¹⁵For you are to be his witness, telling everyone what you have seen and heard. ¹⁶What are you waiting for? Get up and be baptized. Have your sins washed away by calling on the name of the Lord.'

¹⁷"After I returned to Jerusalem, I was praying in the Temple and fell into a trance. ¹⁸I saw a vision of Jesus saying to me, 'Hurry! Leave Jerusalem, for the people here won't accept your testimony about me.'

¹⁹"'But Lord,' I argued, 'they certainly know that in every synagogue I imprisoned and beat those who believed in you. ²⁰And I was in complete agreement when your witness Stephen was killed. I stood by and kept the coats they took off when they stoned him.'

²¹"But the Lord said to me, 'Go, for I will send you far away to the Gentiles!'"

[22] The crowd listened until Paul said that word. Then they all began to shout, "Away with such a fellow! He isn't fit to live!" [23] They yelled, threw off their coats, and tossed handfuls of dust into the air.

Paul Reveals His Roman Citizenship

[24] The commander brought Paul inside and ordered him lashed with whips to make him confess his crime. He wanted to find out why the crowd had become so furious. [25] When they tied Paul down to lash him, Paul said to the officer standing there, "Is it legal for you to whip a Roman citizen who hasn't even been tried?" [26] When the officer heard this, he went to the commander and asked, "What are you doing? This man is a Roman citizen!"

[27] So the commander went over and asked Paul, "Tell me, are you a Roman citizen?"

"Yes, I certainly am," Paul replied.

[28] "I am, too," the commander muttered, "and it cost me plenty!"

Paul answered, "But I am a citizen by birth!"

[29] The soldiers who were about to interrogate Paul quickly withdrew when they heard he was a Roman citizen, and the commander was frightened because he had ordered him bound and whipped.

Paul before the High Council

[30] The next day the commander ordered the leading priests into session with the Jewish high council. He wanted to find out what the trouble was all about, so he released Paul to have him stand before them.

23

Gazing intently at the high council, Paul began: "Brothers, I have always lived before God with a clear conscience!"

[2] Instantly Ananias the high priest commanded those close to Paul to slap him on the mouth. [3] But Paul said to him, "God will slap you, you corrupt hypocrite! What kind of judge are you to break the law yourself by ordering me struck like that?"

[4] Those standing near Paul said to him, "Do you dare to insult God's high priest?"

[5] "I'm sorry, brothers. I didn't realize he was the high priest," Paul replied, "for the Scriptures say, 'You must not speak evil of any of your rulers.'"

[6] Paul realized that some members of the high council were Sadducees and some were Pharisees, so he shouted, "Brothers, I am a Pharisee, as were my ancestors! And I am on trial because my hope is in the resurrection of the dead!" [7] This divided the council—the Pharisees against the Sadducees—[8] for the Sadducees say there is no resurrection or angels or spirits, but the Pharisees believe in all of these. [9] So there was a great uproar. Some of the teachers of religious law who were Pharisees jumped up and began to argue forcefully. "We see nothing wrong with him," they shouted. "Perhaps a spirit or an angel spoke to him." [10] As the conflict grew more violent, the commander was afraid they would tear Paul apart. So he ordered his soldiers to go and rescue him by force and take him back to the fortress.

[11] That night the Lord appeared to Paul and said, "Be encouraged, Paul. Just as you have been a witness to me here in Jerusalem, you must preach the Good News in Rome as well."

The Plan to Kill Paul

¹²The next morning a group of Jews got together and bound themselves with an oath not to eat or drink until they had killed Paul. ¹³There were more than forty of them in the conspiracy. ¹⁴They went to the leading priests and elders and told them, "We have bound ourselves with an oath to eat nothing until we have killed Paul. ¹⁵So you and the high council should ask the commander to bring Paul back to the council again. Pretend you want to examine his case more fully. We will kill him on the way."

¹⁶But Paul's nephew—his sister's son—heard of their plan and went to the fortress and told Paul. ¹⁷Paul called for one of the Roman officers and said, "Take this young man to the commander. He has something important to tell him."

¹⁸So the officer did, explaining, "Paul, the prisoner, called me over and asked me to bring this young man to you because he has something to tell you."

¹⁹The commander took his hand, led him aside, and asked, "What is it you want to tell me?"

²⁰Paul's nephew told him, "Some Jews are going to ask you to bring Paul before the high council tomorrow, pretending they want to get some more information. ²¹But don't do it! There are more than forty men hiding along the way ready to ambush him. They have vowed not to eat or drink anything until they have killed him. They are ready now, just waiting for your consent."

²²"Don't let anyone know you told me this," the commander warned the young man.

Paul Is Sent to Caesarea

²³Then the commander called two of his officers and ordered, "Get 200 soldiers ready to leave for Caesarea at nine o'clock tonight. Also take 200 spearmen and 70 mounted troops. ²⁴Provide horses for Paul to ride, and get him safely to Governor Felix." ²⁵Then he wrote this letter to the governor:

²⁶"From Claudius Lysias, to his Excellency, Governor Felix: Greetings!

²⁷"This man was seized by some Jews, and they were about to kill him when I arrived with the troops. When I learned that he was a Roman citizen, I removed him to safety. ²⁸Then I took him to their high council to try to learn the basis of the accusations against him. ²⁹I soon discovered the charge was something regarding their religious law—certainly nothing worthy of imprisonment or death. ³⁰But when I was informed of a plot to kill him, I immediately sent him on to you. I have told his accusers to bring their charges before you."

³¹So that night, as ordered, the soldiers took Paul as far as Antipatris. ³²They returned to the fortress the next morning, while the mounted troops took him on to Caesarea. ³³When they arrived in Caesarea, they presented Paul and the letter to Governor Felix. ³⁴He read it and then asked Paul what province he was from. "Cilicia," Paul answered.

³⁵"I will hear your case myself when your accusers arrive," the governor told him. Then the governor ordered him kept in the prison at Herod's headquarters.

Paul Appears before Felix

24

Five days later Ananias, the high priest, arrived with some of the Jewish elders and the lawyer Tertullus, to present their case against Paul to the governor. ²When Paul was called in, Tertullus presented the charges against Paul in the following address to the governor: "Your Excellency, you have provided a long period of peace for us Jews and with foresight have enacted reforms for us. ³For all of this we are very grateful to you. ⁴But I don't want to bore you, so please give me your attention for only a moment. ⁵We have found this man to be a troublemaker who is constantly stirring up riots among the Jews all over the world. He is a ringleader of the cult known as the Nazarenes. ⁶Furthermore, he was trying to desecrate the Temple when we arrested him.* ⁸You can find out the truth of our accusations by examining him yourself." ⁹Then the other Jews chimed in, declaring that everything Tertullus said was true.

¹⁰The governor then motioned for Paul to speak. Paul said, "I know, sir, that you have been a judge of Jewish affairs for many years, so I gladly present my defense before you. ¹¹You can quickly discover that I arrived in Jerusalem no more than twelve days ago to worship at the Temple. ¹²My accusers never found me arguing with anyone in the Temple, nor stirring up a riot in any synagogue or on the streets of the city. ¹³These men cannot prove the things they accuse me of doing. ¹⁴But I admit that I follow the Way, which they call a cult. I worship the God of our ancestors, and I firmly believe the Jewish law and everything written in the prophets. ¹⁵I have the same hope in God that these men have, that he will raise both the righteous and the unrighteous. ¹⁶Because of this, I always try to maintain a clear conscience before God and all people.

¹⁷"After several years away, I returned to Jerusalem with money to aid my people and to offer sacrifices to God. ¹⁸My accusers saw me in the Temple as I was completing a purification ceremony. There was no crowd around me and no rioting. ¹⁹But some Jews from the province of Asia were there—and they ought to be here to bring charges if they have anything against me! ²⁰Ask these men here what crime the Jewish high council found me guilty of, ²¹except for the one time I shouted out, 'I am on trial before you today because I believe in the resurrection of the dead!'"

²²At that point Felix, who was quite familiar with the Way, adjourned the hearing and said, "Wait until Lysias, the garrison commander, arrives. Then I will decide the case." ²³He ordered an officer to keep Paul in custody but to give him some freedom and allow his friends to visit him and take care of his needs.

²⁴A few days later Felix came back with his wife, Drusilla, who was Jewish. Sending for Paul, they listened as he told them about faith in Christ Jesus. ²⁵As he reasoned with them about righteousness and self-control and the coming day of judgment, Felix became frightened. "Go away for now," he replied. "When it is more convenient, I'll call for you again." ²⁶He also hoped that Paul would bribe him, so he sent for him quite often and talked with him.

²⁷After two years went by in this way, Felix was succeeded by Porcius Festus. And because Felix wanted to gain favor with the Jewish people, he left Paul in prison.

Cringe Factor (ACTS 24:25)
Felix was curious to find out more about Paul's faith. As Paul spoke about living a righteous life, self-control, and the judgment to come, Felix was terrified. Many will feel awkward and guilty when you speak about the realities of life. Don't be afraid to speak plainly about faith in Christ — a little cringing by your friends now may save them an eternity of cringing later.

BIBLE HIT

24:6 Some manuscripts add We would have judged him by our law, ⁷but Lysias, the commander of the garrison, came and violently took him away from us, ⁸commanding his accusers to come before you.

Paul Appears before Festus

25

Three days after Festus arrived in Caesarea to take over his new responsibilities, he left for Jerusalem, [2]where the leading priests and other Jewish leaders met with him and made their accusations against Paul. [3]They asked Festus as a favor to transfer Paul to Jerusalem (planning to ambush and kill him on the way). [4]But Festus replied that Paul was at Caesarea and he himself would be returning there soon. [5]So he said, "Those of you in authority can return with me. If Paul has done anything wrong, you can make your accusations."

[6]About eight or ten days later Festus returned to Caesarea, and on the following day he took his seat in court and ordered that Paul be brought in. [7]When Paul arrived, the Jewish leaders from Jerusalem gathered around and made many serious accusations they couldn't prove.

[8]Paul denied the charges. "I am not guilty of any crime against the Jewish laws or the Temple or the Roman government," he said.

[9]Then Festus, wanting to please the Jews, asked him, "Are you willing to go to Jerusalem and stand trial before me there?"

[10]But Paul replied, "No! This is the official Roman court, so I ought to be tried right here. You know very well I am not guilty of harming the Jews. [11]If I have done something worthy of death, I don't refuse to die. But if I am innocent, no one has a right to turn me over to these men to kill me. I appeal to Caesar!"

[12]Festus conferred with his advisers and then replied, "Very well! You have appealed to Caesar, and to Caesar you will go!"

[13]A few days later King Agrippa arrived with his sister, Bernice, to pay their respects to Festus. [14]During their stay of several days, Festus discussed Paul's case with the king. "There is a prisoner here," he told him, "whose case was left for me by Felix. [15]When I was in Jerusalem, the leading priests and Jewish elders pressed charges against him and asked me to condemn him. [16]I pointed out to them that Roman law does not convict people without a trial. They must be given an opportunity to confront their accusers and defend themselves.

[17]"When his accusers came here for the trial, I didn't delay. I called the case the very next day and ordered Paul brought in. [18]But the accusations made against him weren't any of the crimes I expected. [19]Instead, it was something about their religion and a dead man named Jesus, who Paul insists is alive. [20]I was at a loss to know how to investigate these things, so I asked him whether he would be willing to stand trial on these charges in Jerusalem. [21]But Paul appealed to have his case decided by the emperor. So I ordered that he be held in custody until I could arrange to send him to Caesar."

[22]"I'd like to hear the man myself," Agrippa said. And Festus replied, "You will—tomorrow!"

Paul Speaks to Agrippa

[23]So the next day Agrippa and Bernice arrived at the auditorium with great pomp, accompanied by military officers and prominent men of the city. Festus ordered that Paul be brought in. [24]Then Festus said, "King Agrippa and all who are here, this is the man whose death is demanded by all the Jews, both here and in Jerusalem. [25]But in my opinion he has done nothing deserving death. However, since he appealed his case to the emperor, I have decided to send him to Rome. [26]But what shall I write the emperor? For there is no clear charge against him. So I have brought him before all of you, and especially you, King Agrippa, so that after we examine him, I might have something to write. [27]For it makes no sense to send a prisoner to the emperor without specifying the charges against him!"

26

Then Agrippa said to Paul, "You may speak in your defense."

So Paul, gesturing with his hand, started his defense: [2]"I am fortunate, King Agrippa, that you are the one hearing my defense today against all these accusations made by the Jewish leaders, [3]for I know you are an expert on all Jewish customs and controversies. Now please listen to me patiently!

[4]"As the Jewish leaders are well aware, I was given a thorough Jewish training from my earliest childhood among my own people and in Jerusalem. [5]If they would admit it, they know that I have been a member of the Pharisees, the strictest sect of our religion. [6]Now I am on trial because of my hope in the fulfillment of God's promise made to our ancestors. [7]In fact, that is why the twelve tribes of Israel zealously worship God night and day, and they share the same hope I have. Yet, Your Majesty, they accuse me for having this hope! [8]Why does it seem incredible to any of you that God can raise the dead?

[9]"I used to believe that I ought to do everything I could to oppose the very name of Jesus the Nazarene. [10]Indeed, I did just that in Jerusalem. Authorized by the leading priests, I caused many believers there to be sent to prison. And I cast my vote against them when they were condemned to death. [11]Many times I had them punished in the synagogues to get them to curse Jesus. I was so violently opposed to them that I even chased them down in foreign cities.

[12]"One day I was on such a mission to Damascus, armed with the authority and commission of the leading priests. [13]About noon, Your Majesty, as I was on the road, a light from heaven brighter than the sun shone down on me and my companions. [14]We all fell down, and I heard a voice saying to me in Aramaic, 'Saul, Saul, why are you persecuting me? It is useless for you to fight against my will.'

[15]"'Who are you, lord?' I asked.

"And the Lord replied, 'I am Jesus, the one you are persecuting. [16]Now get to your feet! For I have appeared to you to appoint you as my servant and witness. You are to tell the world what you have seen and what I will show you in the future. [17]And I will rescue you from both your own people and the Gentiles. Yes, I am sending you to the Gentiles [18]to open their eyes, so they may turn from darkness to light and from the power of Satan to God. Then they will receive forgiveness for their sins and be given a place among God's people, who are set apart by faith in me.'

[19]"And so, King Agrippa, I obeyed that vision from heaven. [20]I preached first to those in Damascus, then in Jerusalem and throughout all Judea, and also to the Gentiles, that all must repent of their sins and turn to God—and prove they have changed by the good things they do. [21]Some Jews arrested me in the Temple for preaching this, and they tried to kill me. [22]But God has protected me right up to this present time so I can testify to everyone, from the least to the greatest. I teach nothing except what the prophets and Moses said would happen—[23]that the Messiah would suffer and be the first to rise from the dead, and in this way announce God's light to Jews and Gentiles alike."

[24]Suddenly, Festus shouted, "Paul, you are insane. Too much study has made you crazy!"

[25]But Paul replied, "I am not insane, Most Excellent Festus. What I am saying is the sober truth. [26]And King Agrippa knows about these things. I speak boldly, for I am sure these events are all familiar to him, for they were not done in a corner! [27]King Agrippa, do you believe the prophets? I know you do—"

[28]Agrippa interrupted him. "Do you think you can persuade me to become a Christian so quickly?"

[29]Paul replied, "Whether quickly or not, I pray to God that both you and everyone here in this audience might become the same as I am, except for these chains."

[30]Then the king, the governor, Bernice, and all the others stood and left. [31]As they went out, they talked it over and agreed, "This man hasn't done anything to deserve death or imprisonment."

³²And Agrippa said to Festus, "He could have been set free if he hadn't appealed to Caesar."

Paul Sails for Rome

27

When the time came, we set sail for Italy. Paul and several other prisoners were placed in the custody of a Roman officer named Julius, a captain of the Imperial Regiment. ²Aristarchus, a Macedonian from Thessalonica, was also with us. We left on a ship whose home port was Adramyttium on the northwest coast of the province of Asia; it was scheduled to make several stops at ports along the coast of the province. ³The next day when we docked at Sidon, Julius was very kind to Paul and let him go ashore to visit with friends so they could provide for his needs. ⁴Putting out to sea from there, we encountered strong headwinds that made it difficult to keep the ship on course, so we sailed north of Cyprus between the island and the mainland. ⁵Keeping to the open sea, we passed along the coast of Cilicia and Pamphylia, landing at Myra, in the province of Lycia. ⁶There the commanding officer found an Egyptian ship from Alexandria that was bound for Italy, and he put us on board.

⁷We had several days of slow sailing, and after great difficulty we finally neared Cnidus. But the wind was against us, so we sailed across to Crete and along the sheltered coast of the island, past the cape of Salmone. ⁸We struggled along the coast with great difficulty and finally arrived at Fair Havens, near the town of Lasea. ⁹We had lost a lot of time. The weather was becoming dangerous for sea travel because it was so late in the fall, and Paul spoke to the ship's officers about it. ¹⁰"Men," he said, "I believe there is trouble ahead if we go on—shipwreck, loss of cargo, and danger to our lives as well." ¹¹But the officer in charge of the prisoners listened more to the ship's captain and the owner than to Paul. ¹²And since Fair Havens was an exposed harbor—a poor place to spend the winter—most of the crew wanted to go on to Phoenix, farther up the coast of Crete, and spend the winter there. Phoenix was a good harbor with only a southwest and northwest exposure.

The Storm at Sea

¹³When a light wind began blowing from the south, the sailors thought they could make it. So they pulled up anchor and sailed close to the shore of Crete. ¹⁴But the weather changed abruptly, and a wind of typhoon strength (called a "northeaster") caught the ship and blew it out to sea. ¹⁵They couldn't turn the ship into the wind, so they gave up and let it run before the gale.

¹⁶We sailed along the sheltered side of a small island named Cauda, where with great difficulty we hoisted aboard the lifeboat being towed behind us. ¹⁷Then the sailors bound ropes around the hull of the ship to strengthen it. They were afraid of being driven across to the sandbars of Syrtis off the African coast, so they lowered the sea anchor to slow the ship and were driven before the wind.

¹⁸The next day, as gale-force winds continued to batter the ship, the crew began throwing the cargo overboard. ¹⁹The following day they even took some of the ship's gear and threw it overboard. ²⁰The terrible storm raged for many days, blotting out the sun and the stars, until at last all hope was gone.

²¹No one had eaten for a long time. Finally, Paul called the crew together and said, "Men, you should have listened to me in the first place and not left Crete. You would have avoided all this damage and loss. ²²But take courage! None of you will lose your lives, even though the ship will go down. ²³For last night an angel of the God to whom I belong and whom I serve stood beside me, ²⁴and he said, 'Don't be afraid, Paul, for you will surely stand trial before Caesar! What's more, God in his goodness has granted safety to everyone sailing with you.' ²⁵So take courage! For I believe God. It will be just as he said. ²⁶But we will be shipwrecked on an island."

The Shipwreck

²⁷About midnight on the fourteenth night of the storm, as we were being driven across the Sea of Adria, the sailors sensed land was near. ²⁸They dropped a weighted line and found that the water was 120 feet deep. But a little later they measured again and found it was only 90 feet deep. ²⁹At this rate they were afraid we would soon be driven against the rocks along the shore, so they threw out four anchors from the back of the ship and prayed for daylight.

³⁰Then the sailors tried to abandon the ship; they lowered the lifeboat as though they were going to put out anchors from the front of the ship. ³¹But Paul said to the commanding officer and the soldiers, "You will all die unless the sailors stay aboard." ³²So the soldiers cut the ropes to the lifeboat and let it drift away.

³³Just as day was dawning, Paul urged everyone to eat. "You have been so worried that you haven't touched food for two weeks," he said. ³⁴"Please eat something now for your own good. For not a hair of your heads will perish." ³⁵Then he took some bread, gave thanks to God before them all, and broke off a piece and ate it. ³⁶Then everyone was encouraged and began to eat—³⁷all 276 of us who were on board. ³⁸After eating, the crew lightened the ship further by throwing the cargo of wheat overboard.

³⁹When morning dawned, they didn't recognize the coastline, but they saw a bay with a beach and wondered if they could get to shore by running the ship aground. ⁴⁰So they cut off the anchors and left them in the sea. Then they lowered the rudders, raised the foresail, and headed toward shore. ⁴¹But they hit a shoal and ran the ship aground too soon. The bow of the ship stuck fast, while the stern was repeatedly smashed by the force of the waves and began to break apart.

⁴²The soldiers wanted to kill the prisoners to make sure they didn't swim ashore and escape. ⁴³But the commanding officer wanted to spare Paul, so he didn't let them carry out their plan. Then he ordered all who could swim to jump overboard first and make for land. ⁴⁴The others held onto planks or debris from the broken ship. So everyone escaped safely to shore.

Paul on the Island of Malta

28

Once we were safe on shore, we learned that we were on the island of Malta. ²The people of the island were very kind to us. It was cold and rainy, so they built a fire on the shore to welcome us.

³As Paul gathered an armful of sticks and was laying them on the fire, a poisonous snake, driven out by the heat, bit him on the hand. ⁴The people of the island saw it hanging from his hand and said to each other, "A murderer, no doubt! Though he escaped the sea, justice will not permit him to live." ⁵But Paul shook off the snake into the fire and was unharmed. ⁶The people waited for him to swell up or suddenly drop dead. But when they had waited a long time and saw that he wasn't harmed, they changed their minds and decided he was a god.

⁷Near the shore where we landed was an estate belonging to Publius, the chief official of the island. He welcomed us and treated us kindly for three days. ⁸As it happened, Publius's father was ill with fever and dysentery. Paul went in and prayed for him, and laying his hands on him, he healed him. ⁹Then all the other sick people on the island came and were healed. ¹⁰As a result we were showered with honors, and when the time came to sail, people supplied us with everything we would need for the trip.

Paul Arrives at Rome

¹¹It was three months after the shipwreck that we set sail on another ship that had wintered at the island— an Alexandrian ship with the twin gods as its

figurehead. ¹²Our first stop was Syracuse, where we stayed three days. ¹³From there we sailed across to Rhegium. A day later a south wind began blowing, so the following day we sailed up the coast to Puteoli. ¹⁴There we found some believers, who invited us to spend a week with them. And so we came to Rome. ¹⁵The brothers and sisters in Rome had heard we were coming, and they came to meet us at the Forum on the Appian Way. Others joined us at The Three Taverns. When Paul saw them, he was encouraged and thanked God.

¹⁶When we arrived in Rome, Paul was permitted to have his own private lodging, though he was guarded by a soldier.

action

28:11-16 WHAT'S IT SAYING?

WHAT AM I GOING TO DO ABOUT IT?

Paul Preaches at Rome under Guard

¹⁷Three days after Paul's arrival, he called together the local Jewish leaders. He said to them, "Brothers, I was arrested in Jerusalem and handed over to the Roman government, even though I had done nothing against our people or the customs of our ancestors. ¹⁸The Romans tried me and wanted to release me, because they found no cause for the death sentence. ¹⁹But when the Jewish leaders protested the decision, I felt it necessary to appeal to Caesar, even though I had no desire to press charges against my own people. ²⁰I asked you to come here today so we could get acquainted and so I could explain to you that I am bound with this chain because I believe that the hope of Israel—the Messiah—has already come."

²¹They replied, "We have had no letters from Judea or reports against you from anyone who has come here. ²²But we want to hear what you believe, for the only thing we know about this movement is that it is denounced everywhere."

²³So a time was set, and on that day a large number of people came to Paul's lodging. He explained and testified about the Kingdom of God and tried to persuade them about Jesus from the Scriptures. Using the law of Moses and the books of the prophets, he spoke to them from morning until evening. ²⁴Some were persuaded by the things he said, but others did not believe. ²⁵And after they had argued back and forth among themselves, they left with this final word from Paul: "The Holy Spirit was right when he said to your ancestors through Isaiah the prophet,

²⁶'Go and say to this people:
When you hear what I say,
you will not understand.
When you see what I do,
you will not comprehend.
²⁷For the hearts of these people are hardened,
and their ears cannot hear,
and they have closed their eyes—
so their eyes cannot see,
and their ears cannot hear,
and their hearts cannot understand,
and they cannot turn to me
and let me heal them.'

²⁸So I want you to know that this salvation from God has also been offered to the Gentiles, and they will accept it."*

³⁰For the next two years, Paul lived in Rome at his own expense. He welcomed all who visited him, ³¹boldly proclaiming the Kingdom of God and teaching about the Lord Jesus Christ. And no one tried to stop him.

28:28 Some manuscripts add verse 29, *And when he had said these words, the Jews departed, greatly disagreeing with each other.*

Commitment

"Again, the Kingdom of Heaven is like a merchant on the lookout for choice pearls. When he discovered a pearl of great value, he sold everything he owned and bought it!" (Matthew 13:45-46)

Jesus keeps trying to explain how his Father lavishes his love on us!

Even though I understand grace, my first impulse is to try to buy my way to heaven. At first glance I treat the parable of the pearl as I was taught to treat life — with a focus on being self-sufficient. In the world of sports we are taught that if we have a dream to play for a certain team or run a certain distance, we should set a goal for ourselves and go for it. Sell out for the dream. When you find that great goal — go for it! So I equate my goal setting with my spiritual life and sell out for God! But if I am brutally honest, I have to admit that I don't have much to sell! I fail too often; I can't really afford the pearl. We will never be able to afford the pearl — we just don't have the cash. Fortunately, God's economy is different than ours.

Why can't you buy this pearl? Because you *are* the pearl! Jesus is talking about you. Do you understand your value in God's eyes? Do you see that you are so

DEVOTIONAL

important to God that he lavished his love on you and sent his Son to die for you? There is no escaping it; you are valued beyond any stretch of your imagination. We can scarcely comprehend that God would sacrifice his Son to purchase (redeem) that which he values so much. Consider that the Creator of the universe would allow his Son to be beaten and cursed by his creation so that you could be redeemed! Look back at the verse and where you see God is like a merchant looking for fine pearls and replace pearls with your name. It becomes clear that you are more precious to God than you can grasp.

Understanding God's commitment to you and the value placed on your life should bring you to your knees in gratitude, ready to give yourself completely to the purchaser.

Reflection
Sell out for the Lord, because he gave his life for you.

Prayer
Lord, I have heard so many times that you died on the cross for me; help me to appreciate its meaning.

"He is so rich in kindness and grace that he purchased our freedom with the blood of his Son and forgave our sins. He has showered his kindness on us, along with all wisdom and understanding."

Ephesians 1:7-8

Nicked with permission from: A Sporting Guide to Eternity, Steve Connor, Christian Focus Publications - ISBN 1-85792-746-X

Romans

Including Romans, the next 13 books of your Bible are written by this passionate follower of Christ: the apostle Paul.

Christianity was spreading around the known world. The spread was systematic, but also because Christians were fleeing from harassment and execution by Jewish leaders in Jerusalem. After Paul's conversion (see Acts 9 for the dramatic account), his single-minded dedication to the elimination of Christianity changed to that of establishing Christianity. Paul became a major advocate for planting faith communities — the church around the known world.

Paul knew that he needed to clearly explain the whys of Christianity. Following Jesus can be hard to explain; many questions need to be answered and made clear. Many people in Paul's time were trying to warp the truth of Jesus and hurt this very important movement of God. In Romans, Paul gave a systematic explanation about man's relationship to God through Jesus to the followers of Christ in Rome. Many famous writings were coming out of the most powerful capital of its time, but nothing changed the world like this letter.

It's a gift
FIND it

For the wages of sin
is death, but the free
gift of God is eternal life
through Christ Jesus our Lord.

ROMANS 6:23

ROMANS

Greetings from Paul

1

This letter is from Paul, a slave of Christ Jesus, chosen by God to be an apostle and sent out to preach his Good News. [2]God promised this Good News long ago through his prophets in the holy Scriptures. [3]The Good News is about his Son, Jesus. In his earthly life he was born into King David's family line, [4]and he was shown to be the Son of God when he was raised from the dead by the power of the Holy Spirit. He is Jesus Christ our Lord. [5]Through Christ, God has given us the privilege and authority as apostles to tell Gentiles everywhere what God has done for them, so that they will believe and obey him, bringing glory to his name. [6]And you are included among those Gentiles who have been called to belong to Jesus Christ. [7]I am writing to all of you in Rome who are loved by God and are called to be his own holy people.

May God our Father and the Lord Jesus Christ give you grace and peace.

God's Good News

[8]Let me say first that I thank my God through Jesus Christ for all of you, because your faith in him is being talked about all over the world. [9]God knows how often I pray for you. Day and night I bring you and your needs in prayer to God, whom I serve with all my heart by spreading the Good News about his Son.

[10]One of the things I always pray for is the opportunity, God willing, to come at last to see you. [11]For I long to visit you so I can bring you some spiritual gift that will help you grow strong in the Lord. [12]When we get together, I want to encourage you in your faith, but I also want to be encouraged by yours.

[13]I want you to know, dear brothers and sisters, that I planned many times to visit you, but I was prevented until now. I want to work among you and see spiritual fruit, just as I have seen among other Gentiles. [14]For I have a great sense of obligation to people in both the civilized world and the rest of the world, to the educated and uneducated alike. [15]So I am eager to come to you in Rome, too, to preach the Good News. [16]For I am not ashamed of this Good News about Christ. It is the power of God at work, saving everyone who believes—the Jew first and also the Gentile. [17]This Good News tells us how God makes us right in his sight. This is accomplished from start to finish by faith. As the Scriptures say, "It is through faith that a righteous person has life."

What are five things you would like to accomplish in your lifetime?

1.
2.
3.
4.
5.

God's Anger at Sin

[18]But God shows his anger from heaven against all sinful, wicked people who suppress the truth by their wickedness. [19]They know the truth about God because he has made it obvious to them. [20]For ever since the world was created, people have seen the earth and sky. Through everything God made, they can clearly see his invisible qualities—his eternal power and divine nature. So they have no excuse for not knowing God.

[21]Yes, they knew God, but they wouldn't worship him as God or even give him thanks. And they began to think up foolish ideas of what God was like. As a result, their minds became dark and confused. [22]Claiming to be wise, they instead became utter fools. [23]And instead of worshiping the glorious, ever-living God, they worshiped idols made to look like mere people and birds and animals and reptiles.

[24]So God abandoned them to do whatever shameful things their hearts desired. As a result, they did vile and degrading things with each other's bodies. [25]They traded the truth about God for a lie. So they worshiped and served the things God created instead of the Creator himself, who is worthy of eternal praise! Amen. [26]That is why God abandoned them to their shameful desires. Even the women turned against the natural way to have sex and instead indulged in sex with each other. [27]And the men, instead of having normal sexual relations with women, burned with lust for each other. Men did shameful things with other men, and as a result of this sin, they suffered within themselves the penalty they deserved.

[28]Since they thought it foolish to acknowledge God, he abandoned them to their foolish thinking and let them do things that should never be done. [29]Their lives became full of every kind of wickedness, sin, greed, hate, envy, murder, quarreling, deception, malicious behavior, and gossip. [30]They

Hang out with encouraging believers. As an athlete you know the value of training with a team. In a group of like-minded athletes competing for the same results, you will be pushed harder and encouraged more than you would be on your own. These same qualities are what God wants for his faith communities (his church). "And let us not neglect our meeting together, as some people do, but encourage one another, especially now that the day of his return is drawing near." (Hebrews 10:25)

are backstabbers, haters of God, insolent, proud, and boastful. They invent new ways of sinning, and they disobey their parents. [31]They refuse to understand, break their promises, are heartless, and have no mercy. [32]They know God's justice requires that those who do these things deserve to die, yet they do them anyway. Worse yet, they encourage others to do them, too.

God's Judgment of Sin

2

You may think you can condemn such people, but you are just as bad, and you have no excuse! When you say they are wicked and should be punished, you are condemning yourself, for you who judge others do these very same things. [2]And we know that God, in his justice, will punish anyone who does such things. [3]Since you judge others for doing these things, why do you think you can avoid God's judgment when you do the same things? [4]Don't you see how wonderfully kind, tolerant, and patient God is with you? Does this mean nothing to you? Can't you see that his kindness is intended to turn you from your sin?

[5]But because you are stubborn and refuse to turn from your sin, you are storing up terrible punishment for yourself. For a day of anger is coming, when God's righteous judgment will be revealed. [6]He will judge everyone according to what they have done. [7]He will give eternal life to those who keep on doing good, seeking after the glory and honor and immortality that God offers. [8]But he will pour out his anger and wrath on those who live for themselves, who refuse to

Soviet gymnast Larissa Latynina holds the record for the most Olympic medals ever won. Competing in three Olympics, between 1956 and 1964, she won 18 medals.

obey the truth and instead live lives of wickedness. [9]There will be trouble and calamity for everyone who keeps on doing what is evil—for the Jew first and also for the Gentile. [10]But there will be glory and honor and peace from God for all who do good—for the Jew first and also for the Gentile. [11]For God does not show favoritism.

[12]When the Gentiles sin, they will be destroyed, even though they never had God's written law. And the Jews, who do have God's law, will be judged by that law when they fail to obey it. [13]For merely listening to the law doesn't make us right with God. It is obeying the

law that makes us right in his sight. [14]Even Gentiles, who do not have God's written law, show that they know his law when they instinctively obey it, even without having heard it. [15]They demonstrate that God's law is written in their hearts, for their own conscience and thoughts either accuse them or tell them they are doing right. [16]And this is the message I proclaim—that the day is coming when God, through Christ Jesus, will judge everyone's secret life.

The Jews and the Law

[17]You who call yourselves Jews are relying on God's law, and you boast about your special relationship with him. [18]You know what he wants; you know what is right because you have been taught his law. [19]You are convinced that you are a guide for the blind and a light for people who are lost in darkness. [20]You think you can instruct the ignorant and teach children the ways of God. For you are certain that God's law gives you complete knowledge and truth.

[21]Well then, if you teach others, why don't you teach yourself? You tell others not to steal, but do you steal? [22]You say it is wrong to commit adultery, but do you commit adultery? You condemn idolatry, but do you use items stolen from pagan temples? [23]You are so proud of knowing the law, but you dishonor God by breaking it. [24]No wonder the Scriptures say, "The Gentiles blaspheme the name of God because of you." [25]The Jewish ceremony of circumcision has value only if you obey God's law. But if you don't obey God's

I have done some pretty bad things. Will God really forgive me?

The Bible is full of God's special people who have messed up and have been restored to God's love. Consider for a moment King David. David had it all: a reputation as a tough warrior, good looks, riches, fame, and God's love and favor. Yet in a heartbeat David messed up. He had an affair with Bathsheba, and she became pregnant. David tried to cover it up, and when that failed, he had Bathsheba's husband, Uriah, killed in battle (2 Samuel 11). No matter what David did, God still loved him greatly. David was confronted with his sin, he paid a deep price for his sin, and he repented of the mistakes he'd made. God said this of David: "I have found David son of Jesse, a man after my own heart" (Acts 13:22).

No matter what we do or how badly we mess up, God still loves us. He tells us "though your sins are like scarlet, I will make them as white as snow. If you will only obey me and let me help you" (Isaiah 1:18-20).

The choice is yours. Today you have the opportunity to turn your life around and have your sins washed away if you follow God. He loves you as much as he loved David. In fact, he sent his Son, Jesus, to the cross to pay the price for your sin. If you take the time to ask for forgiveness, turn away from your sins, and ask God to come into your life, he will wash away those sins forever (see John 3:16). That is a promise you can count on.

TIPS

Cooling down:

Cooling down is defined as performing a group of light exercises immediately after an activity to offer the body a time of transition from exercise to rest. The cool-down period is valuable for athletes who want to maintain or enhance their flexibility. As tissue temperatures rise, stiffness decreases and extensibility increases. Because tissue temperatures will be highest immediately after a workout and during the cool-down phase, stretching is thought to be both safer and more productive at that time.

law, you are no better off than an uncircumcised Gentile. ²⁶And if the Gentiles obey God's law, won't God declare them to be his own people? ²⁷In fact, uncircumcised Gentiles who keep God's law will condemn you Jews who are circumcised and possess God's law but don't obey it.

²⁸For you are not a true Jew just because you were born of Jewish parents or because you have gone through the ceremony of circumcision. ²⁹No, a true Jew is one whose heart is right with God. And true circumcision is not merely obeying the letter of the law; rather, it is a change of heart produced by God's Spirit. And a person with a changed heart seeks praise from God, not from people.

God Remains Faithful

3

Then what's the advantage of being a Jew? Is there any value in the ceremony of circumcision? ²Yes, there are great benefits! First of all, the Jews were entrusted with the whole revelation of God.

³True, some of them were unfaithful; but just because they were unfaithful, does that mean God will be unfaithful? ⁴Of course not! Even if everyone else is a liar, God is true. As the Scriptures say about him,

"You will be proved right in what you say, and you will win your case in court."

⁵"But," some might say, "our sinfulness serves a good purpose, for it helps people see how righteous God is. Isn't it unfair, then, for him to punish us?" (This is merely a human point of view.) ⁶Of course not! If God were not entirely fair, how would he be qualified to judge the world? ⁷"But," someone might still argue, "how can God condemn me as a sinner if my dishonesty highlights his truthfulness and brings him more glory?" ⁸And some people even slander us by claiming that we say, "The more we sin, the better it is!" Those who say such things deserve to be condemned.

All People Are Sinners

⁹Well then, should we conclude that we Jews are better than others? No, not at all, for we have already shown that all people, whether Jews or Gentiles, are under the power of sin. ¹⁰As the Scriptures say,

"No one is righteous—
not even one.
¹¹No one is truly wise;
no one is seeking God.
¹²All have turned away;
all have become useless.
No one does good,
not a single one."
¹³"Their talk is foul, like the stench from an open grave.
Their tongues are filled with lies."
"Snake venom drips from their lips."
¹⁴"Their mouths are full of cursing and bitterness."
¹⁵"They rush to commit murder.
¹⁶Destruction and misery always follow them.
¹⁷They don't know where to find peace."
¹⁸"They have no fear of God at all."

¹⁹Obviously, the law applies to those to whom it was given, for its purpose is to keep people from having excuses, and to show that the entire world is guilty

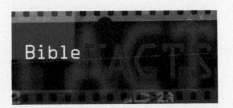

The King James Old Testament consists of 592,439 words and 2,728,100 letters. The New Testament has 181,253 words and 838,380 letters (total 3,566,480 letters).

before God. ²⁰For no one can ever be made right with God by doing what the law commands. The law simply shows us how sinful we are.

action

3:21-31 WHAT'S IT SAYING?

WHAT AM I GOING TO DO ABOUT IT?

Christ Took Our Punishment

²¹But now God has shown us a way to be made right with him without keeping the requirements of the law, as was promised in the writings of Moses and the prophets long ago. ²²We are made right with God by placing our faith in Jesus Christ. And this is true for everyone who believes, no matter who we are.

²³For everyone has sinned; we all fall short of God's glorious

STAND POINT

When you face tough competition

5:3-5

We can rejoice, too, when we run into problems and trials, for we know that they help us develop endurance. And endurance develops strength of character, and character strengthens our confident hope of salvation. And this hope will not lead to disappointment. For we know how dearly God loves us, because he has given us the Holy Spirit to fill our hearts with his love.

standard. [24]Yet God, with undeserved kindness, declares that we are righteous. He did this through Christ Jesus when he freed us from the penalty for our sins. [25]For God presented Jesus as the sacrifice for sin. People are made right with God when they believe that Jesus sacrificed his life, shedding his blood. This sacrifice shows that God was being fair when he held back and did not punish those who sinned in times past, [26]for he was looking ahead and including them in what he would do in this present time. God did this to demonstrate his righteousness, for he himself is fair and just, and he declares sinners to be right in his sight when they believe in Jesus.

[27]Can we boast, then, that we have done anything to be accepted by God? No, because our acquittal is not based on obeying the law. It is based on faith. [28]So we are made right with God through faith and not by obeying the law.

[29]After all, is God the God of the Jews only? Isn't he also the God of the Gentiles? Of course he is. [30]There is only one God, and he makes people right with himself only by faith, whether they are Jews or Gentiles. [31]Well then, if we emphasize faith, does this mean that we can forget about the law? Of course not! In fact, only when we have faith do we truly fulfill the law.

The Faith of Abraham

4

Abraham was, humanly speaking, the founder of our Jewish nation. What did he discover about being made right with God? [2]If his good deeds had made him acceptable to God, he would have had something to boast about. But that was not God's way. [3]For the Scriptures tell us, "Abraham believed God, and God counted him as righteous because of his faith."

[4]When people work, their wages are not a gift, but something they have earned. [5]But people are counted as righteous, not because of their work, but because of their faith in God who forgives sinners. [6]David also spoke of this when he described the happiness of those who are declared righteous without working for it:

[7]"Oh, what joy for those
whose disobedience is forgiven,
whose sins are put out of sight.
[8]Yes, what joy for those
whose record the LORD has cleared of sin."

[9]Now, is this blessing only for the Jews, or is it also for uncircumcised Gentiles? Well, we have been saying that Abraham was counted as righteous by God because of his faith. [10]But how did this happen? Was he counted as righteous only after he was circumcised, or was it before he was circumcised? Clearly, God accepted Abraham before he was circumcised!

[11]Circumcision was a sign that Abraham already had faith and that God had already accepted him and declared him to be righteous—even before he was circumcised. So Abraham is the spiritual father of those who have faith but have not been circumcised. They are counted as righteous because of their faith. [12]And Abraham is also the spiritual father of those who have been circumcised, but only if they have the same kind of faith Abraham had before he was circumcised.

[13]Clearly, God's promise to give the whole earth to Abraham and his descendants was based not on his obedience to God's law, but on a right relationship with God that comes by faith. [14]If God's promise is only for those who obey the law, then faith is not necessary and the promise is pointless. [15]For the law always brings punishment on those who try to obey it. (The only way to avoid breaking the law is to have no law to break!)

[16]So the promise is received by faith. It is given as a free gift. And we are all certain to receive it, whether or not we live according to the law of Moses, if we have faith like Abraham's. For Abraham is the father of all who believe. [17]That is what the Scriptures mean when God told him, "I have made you the father of many nations." This happened because Abraham believed in the God who brings the dead back to life and who creates new things out of nothing.

[18]Even when there was no reason for hope, Abraham kept hoping—believing that he would become the father of many nations. For God had said to him, "That's how many descendants you will have!" [19]And Abraham's faith did not weaken, even though, at about 100 years of age, he figured his body was as good as dead—and so was Sarah's womb.

[20]Abraham never wavered in believing God's promise. In fact, his faith grew stronger, and in this he brought glory to God. [21]He was fully convinced that God is able to do whatever he promises. [22]And because of Abraham's faith, God counted him as righteous. [23]And when God counted him as righteous, it wasn't just for Abraham's benefit. It was recorded [24]for our benefit, too, assuring us that God will also count us as righteous if we believe in him, the one who raised Jesus our Lord from the dead. [25]He was handed over to die because of our sins, and he was raised to life to make us right with God.

Faith Brings Joy

5

Therefore, since we have been made right in God's sight by faith, we have peace with God because of what Jesus Christ our Lord has done for us. [2]Because of our faith, Christ has brought us into this place of undeserved privilege where we now stand, and we confidently and joyfully look forward to sharing God's glory.

[3]We can rejoice, too, when we run into problems and trials, for we know that they help us develop endurance. [4]And endurance develops strength of character, and character strengthens our confident hope of salvation. [5]And this hope will not lead to disappointment. For we know how dearly God loves us, because he has given us the Holy Spirit to fill our hearts with his love.

[6]When we were utterly helpless, Christ came at just the right time and died for us sinners. [7]Now, most people would not be willing to die for an upright person, though someone might perhaps be willing to die for a person who is especially good. [8]But God showed his great love for us by sending Christ to die for us while we were still sinners. [9]And since we have been made right in God's sight by the blood of Christ, he will certainly save us from God's condemnation. [10]For since our friendship with God was restored by the death of his Son while we were still his enemies, we will certainly be saved through the life of his Son. [11]So now we can rejoice in our wonderful new relationship with God because our Lord Jesus Christ has made us friends of God.

Adam and Christ Contrasted

[12]When Adam sinned, sin entered the world. Adam's sin brought death, so death spread to everyone, for everyone sinned. [13]Yes, people sinned even before the law was given. But it was not counted as sin because there was not yet any law to break. [14]Still, everyone died—from the time of Adam to the time of Moses—even those who did not disobey an explicit commandment of God, as Adam did. Now Adam is a symbol, a representation of Christ, who was yet to come. [15]But there is a great difference between Adam's sin and God's gracious gift. For the sin of this one man, Adam, brought death to many. But even greater is God's wonderful grace and his gift of forgiveness to many through this other man, Jesus Christ. [16]And the result of God's gracious gift is very different from the result of that one man's sin. For Adam's sin led to condemnation, but God's free gift leads to our being made right with God, even though we are guilty of many sins. [17]For the sin of this one man, Adam, caused death to rule over many. But even greater is God's wonderful grace and his gift of righteousness, for all who receive it will live in triumph over sin and death through this one man, Jesus Christ.

[18]Yes, Adam's one sin brings condemnation for everyone, but Christ's one act of righteousness brings a right relationship with God and new life for everyone. [19]Because one person disobeyed God, many became sinners. But because one other person obeyed God, many will be made righteous.

[20]God's law was given so that all people could see how sinful they were. But as people sinned more and more, God's wonderful grace became more abundant. [21]So just as sin ruled over all people and brought them to death, now God's wonderful grace rules instead, giving us right standing with God and resulting in eternal life through Jesus Christ our Lord.

Sin's Power Is Broken

6

Well then, should we keep on sinning so that God can show us more and more of his wonderful grace? [2]Of course not! Since we have died to sin, how can we continue to live in it? [3]Or have you forgotten that when we were joined with Christ Jesus in baptism, we joined him in his death? [4]For we died and were buried with Christ by baptism. And just as Christ was raised from the dead by the glorious power of the Father, now we also may live new lives.

[5]Since we have been united with him in his death, we will also be raised to life as he was. [6]We know that our old sinful selves were crucified with Christ so that sin might lose its power in our lives. We are no longer slaves to sin. [7]For when we died with Christ we were set free from the power of sin. [8]And since we died with Christ, we know we will also live with him. [9]We are sure of this because Christ was raised from the dead, and he will never die again. Death no longer has any power over him. [10]When he died, he died once to break the power of sin. But now that he lives, he lives for the glory of God. [11]So you also should consider yourselves to be dead to the power of sin and alive to God through Christ Jesus.

[12]Do not let sin control the way you live; do not give in to sinful desires. [13]Do not let any part of your body become an instrument of evil to serve sin. Instead, give yourselves completely to God, for you were dead, but now you have new life. So use your whole body as an instrument to do what is right for the glory of God. [14]Sin is no longer your master, for you no longer live under the requirements of the law. Instead, you live under the freedom of God's grace.

[15]Well then, since God's grace has set us free from the law, does that mean we can go on sinning? Of course not! [16]Don't you realize that you become the slave of whatever you choose to obey? You can be a slave to sin, which leads to death, or you can choose to obey God, which leads to righteous living. [17]Thank God! Once you were slaves of sin, but now you wholeheartedly obey this teaching we have given you. [18]Now you are free from your slavery to sin, and you have become slaves to righteous living.

[19]Because of the weakness of your human nature, I am using the illustration of slavery to help you understand all this. Previously, you let yourselves be slaves to impurity and

6:15-23 WHAT'S IT SAYING?

WHAT AM I GOING TO DO ABOUT IT?

Miracles (ROMANS 5:8)
The Lord God is the God of miracles. The playbook for life, the Bible, is full of examples. Time and again God has shown his true character by touching a person's life with a miracle. Perhaps the greatest miracle of all is God's love for us. Paul writes, "But God showed his great love for us by sending Christ to die for us while we were still sinners." It is a miracle that God sent his only Son to die on the cross for our sins. It is a miracle that God loves us just the way we are and that we don't have to change before we can receive his love. Eventually everyone Christ healed physically died, but the coolest thing is, those Christ healed spiritually will live forever! Grab on to a miracle. Grab on to Jesus!

BIBLE HIT

lawlessness, which led ever deeper into sin. Now you must give yourselves to be slaves to righteous living so that you will become holy. [20]When you were slaves to sin, you were free from the obligation to do right. [21]And what was the result? You are now ashamed of the things you used to do, things that end in eternal doom. [22]But now you are free from the power of sin and have become slaves of God. Now you do those things that lead to holiness and result in eternal life. [23]For the wages of sin is death, but the free gift of God is eternal life through Christ Jesus our Lord.

No Longer Bound to the Law

7

Now, dear brothers and sisters—you who are familiar with the law—don't you know that the law applies only while a person is living? [2]For example, when a woman marries, the law binds her to her husband as long as he is alive. But if he dies, the laws of marriage no longer apply to her. [3]So while her husband is alive, she would be committing adultery if she married another man. But if her husband dies, she is

Bible FACTS

The Old Testament has 929 chapters; the New Testament 260.

free from that law and does not commit adultery when she remarries.

[4]So, my dear brothers and sisters, this is the point: You died to the power of the law when you died with Christ. And now you are united with the one who was raised from the dead. As a result, we can produce a harvest of good deeds for God. [5]When we were controlled by our old nature, sinful desires were at work within us, and the law aroused these evil desires that produced a harvest of sinful deeds, resulting in death. [6]But now we have been released from the law, for we died to it and are no longer captive to its power.

itself is holy, and its commands are holy and right and good.

[13]But how can that be? Did the law, which is good, cause my death? Of course not! Sin used what was good to bring about my condemnation to death. So we can see how terrible sin really is. It uses God's good commands for its own evil purposes.

Struggling with Sin

[14]So the trouble is not with the law, for it is spiritual and good. The trouble is with me, for I am all too human, a slave to sin. [15]I don't really understand myself, for I want to do what is right, but I don't do it. Instead, I do what I hate. [16]But if I know that what I am doing is wrong, this shows that I agree that the law is good. [17]So I am not the one doing wrong; it is sin living in me that does it.

[18]And I know that nothing good lives in me, that is, in my sinful nature. I want to do what is right, but I can't. [19]I want to do what is good, but I don't. I don't want to do what is wrong, but I do it anyway. [20]But if I do what I don't want to do, I am not really the one doing wrong; it is sin living in me that does it.

Peace (ROMANS 8:6)

Most professional athletes are presumed to live a wild and crazy life. But most pros just want a little peace. Peace is a gift from God and the rightful legacy of all believers. But far too many do not enjoy it. The peace of God flows from a full, unhindered fellowship with God, who is our peace. Allow the Holy Spirit to fill you and keep you in the zone — in peace.

BIBLE HIT

STAND POINT

When you are facing death

8:38

I am convinced that nothing can ever separate us from God's love. Neither death nor life, neither angels nor demons, neither our fears for today nor our worries about tomorrow—not even the powers of hell can separate us from God's love.

Now we can serve God, not in the old way of obeying the letter of the law, but in the new way of living in the Spirit.

God's Law Reveals Our Sin

[7]Well then, am I suggesting that the law of God is sinful? Of course not! In fact, it was the law that showed me my sin. I would never have known that coveting is wrong if the law had not said, "You must not covet." [8]But sin used this command to arouse all kinds of covetous desires within me! If there were no law, sin would not have that power. [9]At one time I lived without understanding the law. But when I learned the command not to covet, for instance, the power of sin came to life, [10]and I died. So I discovered that the law's commands, which were supposed to bring life, brought spiritual death instead. [11]Sin took advantage of those commands and deceived me; it used the commands to kill me. [12]But still, the law

[21]I have discovered this principle of life—that when I want to do what is right, I inevitably do what is wrong. [22]I love God's law with all my heart. [23]But there is another power within me that is at war with my mind. This power makes me a slave to the sin that is still within me. [24]Oh, what a miserable person I am! Who will free me from this life that is dominated by sin and death? [25]Thank God! The answer is in Jesus Christ our Lord. So you see how it is: In my mind I really want to obey God's law, but because of my sinful nature I am a slave to sin.

Life in the Spirit

8

So now there is no condemnation for those who belong to Christ Jesus. [2]And because you belong to him, the power of the life-giving Spirit has freed you from the power of sin that leads to death. ³The law of Moses was unable to save us because of the weakness of our sinful nature. So God did what the law could not do. He sent his own Son in a body like the bodies we sinners have. And in that body God declared an end to sin's control over us by giving his Son as a sacrifice for our sins. ⁴He did this so that the just requirement of the law would be fully satisfied for us, who no longer follow our sinful nature but instead follow the Spirit. ⁵Those who are dominated by the sinful nature think about sinful things, but those who are controlled by the Holy Spirit think about things that please the Spirit. ⁶So letting your sinful nature control your mind leads to death. But letting the Spirit control your mind leads to life and peace. ⁷For the sinful nature is always hostile to God. It never did obey God's laws, and it never will. ⁸That's why those who are still under the control of their sinful nature can never please God.

⁹But you are not controlled by your sinful nature. You are controlled by the Spirit if you have the Spirit of God living in you. (And remember that those who do not have the Spirit of Christ living in them do not belong to him at all.) ¹⁰And Christ lives within you, so even though your body will die because of sin, the Spirit gives you life because you have been made right with God. ¹¹The Spirit of God, who raised Jesus from the dead, lives in you. And just as God raised Christ Jesus from the dead, he will give life to your mortal bodies by this same Spirit living within you.

¹²Therefore, dear brothers and sisters, you have no obligation to do what your sinful nature urges you to do. ¹³For if you live by its dictates, you will die. But if through the power of the Spirit you put to death the deeds of your sinful nature, you will live. ¹⁴For all who are led by the Spirit of God are children of God. ¹⁵So you have not received a spirit that makes you fearful slaves. Instead, you received God's Spirit when he adopted you as his own children. Now we call him, "Abba, Father." ¹⁶For his Spirit joins with our spirit to affirm that we are God's children. ¹⁷And since we are his children, we are his heirs. In fact, together

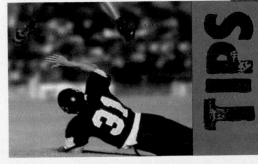

TIPS

Mistakes:

When an athlete makes a mistake that costs the team a game, they feel it more than anyone. The last thing in the world they need is someone yelling at them that they goofed up. They already got that feedback. Even if the mistake is made in a training session, they are probably feeling disappointment. As a player or coach, pick the right time to teach and the right time to encourage.

profiles

Joshua:

Exodus 33:11, "Inside the Tent of Meeting, the LORD would speak to Moses face to face, as a man speaks to his friend. Afterward Moses would return to the camp, but the young man who assisted him, Joshua son of Nun, would remain behind in the Tent of Meeting."

Joshua would later take the baton from the hugest character of the Old Testament and run a faultless race. Moses took the Israelites out of Egypt but was not allowed to enter the Promised Land. But the sign of success is a great successor, and he had that in Joshua. Joshua was trained for greatness, and his commitment to obedience kept him on a successful path. Two of many key ingredients that Joshua had for successful leadership were the desire to stay close to God and the knowledge that no one (not even Moses) was indispensable. We see from Exodus 33 that Joshua stayed in the Tent of Meeting in God's presence. He watched God deal harshly with Moses when he veered from God's rule and consequently was not allowed to cross the Jordan River and enter the land promised to his people. Joshua crossed instead and took on the responsibility of the great leader. In some way you will be called into leadership someday. Don't get arrogant and think the world will not go on without you. Stay close to God and listen to his guidance.

with Christ we are heirs of God's glory. But if we are to share his glory, we must also share his suffering.

The Future Glory

[18]Yet what we suffer now is nothing compared to the glory he will reveal to us later. [19]For all creation is waiting eagerly for that future day when God will reveal who his children really are. [20]Against its will, all creation was subjected to God's curse. But with eager hope, [21]the creation looks forward to the day when it will join God's children in glorious freedom from death and decay. [22]For we know that all creation has been groaning as in the pains of childbirth right up to the present time. [23]And we believers also groan, even though we have the Holy Spirit within us as a foretaste of future glory, for we long for our bodies to be released from sin and suffering. We, too, wait with eager hope for the day when God will give us our full rights as his adopted children, including the new bodies he has promised us. [24]We were given this hope when we were saved. (If we already have something, we don't need to hope for it. [25]But if we look forward to something we don't yet have, we must wait patiently and confidently.)

[26]And the Holy Spirit helps us in our weakness. For example, we don't know what God wants us to pray for. But the Holy Spirit prays for us with groanings that cannot be expressed in words. [27]And the Father who knows all hearts knows what the Spirit is saying, for the Spirit pleads for us believers in harmony with God's own will. [28]And we know that God causes everything to work together for the good of those who love God and are called according to his purpose for them. [29]For God knew his people in advance, and he chose them to become like his Son, so that his Son would be the firstborn among many brothers and sisters. [30]And having chosen them, he called them to come to him. And having called them, he gave them right standing with himself. And having given them right standing, he gave them his glory.

Nothing Can Separate Us from God's Love

[31]What shall we say about such wonderful things as these? If God is for us, who can ever be against us? [32]Since he did not spare even his own Son but gave him up for us all, won't he also give us everything else? [33]Who dares accuse us whom God has chosen for his own? No one—for God himself has given us right standing with himself. [34]Who then will condemn us? No one—for Christ Jesus died for us and was raised to life for us, and he is sitting in the place of

honor at God's right hand, pleading for us.

[35]Can anything ever separate us from Christ's love? Does it mean he no longer loves us if we have trouble or calamity, or are persecuted, or hungry, or destitute, or in danger, or threatened with death? [36](As the Scriptures say, "For your sake we are killed every day; we are being slaughtered like sheep.") [37]No, despite all these things, overwhelming victory is ours through Christ, who loved us.

[38]And I am convinced that nothing can ever separate us from God's love. Neither death nor life, neither angels nor demons, neither our fears for today nor our worries about tomorrow—not even the powers of hell can separate us from God's love. [39]No power in the sky above or in the earth below—indeed, nothing in all creation will ever be able to separate us from the love of God that is revealed in Christ Jesus our Lord.

God's Selection of Israel

9

With Christ as my witness, I speak with utter truthfulness. My conscience and the Holy Spirit confirm it. [2]My heart is filled with bitter sorrow and unending grief [3]for my people, my Jewish brothers and sisters. I would be willing to be forever cursed—cut off from Christ!—if that would save them. [4]They are the people of Israel, chosen to be God's adopted children. God revealed his glory to them. He made covenants with them and gave them his law. He gave them the privilege of worshiping him and receiving his wonderful promises. [5]Abraham, Isaac, and Jacob are their ancestors, and Christ himself was an Israelite as far as his human nature is concerned. And he is God,

WHAT

DOES IT MEAN?

fellowship

We have fellowship with God and other believers. Fellowship with God and one another consists of enjoying God's encouragement, love, joy, interests, sufferings, and spiritual growth (Romans 12:4, 13; Hebrews 13:16). Fellowship among Christians does not mean being in proximity to other Christians, but mutually participating in God's Kingdom.

the one who rules over everything and is worthy of eternal praise! Amen.

⁶Well then, has God failed to fulfill his promise to Israel? No, for not all who are born into the nation of Israel are truly members of God's people! ⁷Being descendants of Abraham doesn't make them truly Abraham's children. For the Scriptures say, "Isaac is the son through whom your descendants will be counted," though Abraham had other children, too. ⁸This means that Abraham's physical descendants are not necessarily children of God. Only the children of the promise are considered to be Abraham's children. ⁹For God had promised, "I will return about this time next year, and Sarah will have a son."

¹⁰This son was our ancestor Isaac. When he married Rebekah, she gave birth to twins. ¹¹But before they were born, before they had done anything good or bad, she received a message from God. (This message shows that God chooses people according to his own purposes; ¹²he calls people, but not according to their good or bad works.) She was told, "Your older son will serve your younger son." ¹³In the words of the Scriptures, "I loved Jacob, but I rejected Esau."

¹⁴Are we saying, then, that God was unfair? Of course not! ¹⁵For God said to Moses,

"I will show mercy to anyone I choose,
and I will show compassion to anyone I choose."

¹⁶So it is God who decides to show mercy. We can neither choose it nor work for it.

¹⁷For the Scriptures say that God told Pharaoh, "I have appointed you for the very purpose of displaying my power in you and to spread my fame throughout the earth." ¹⁸So you see, God chooses to show mercy to some, and he chooses to harden the hearts of others so they refuse to listen.

¹⁹Well then, you might say, "Why does God blame people for not responding? Haven't they simply done what he makes them do?" ²⁰No, don't say that. Who are you, a mere human being, to argue with God? Should the thing that was created say to the one who created it, "Why have you made me like this?" ²¹When a potter makes jars out of clay, doesn't he have a right to use the same lump of clay to make one jar for decoration and another to throw garbage into? ²²In the same way, even though God has the right to show his anger and his power, he is very patient with those on whom his anger falls, who were made for destruction. ²³He does this to make the riches of his glory shine even brighter on those to whom he shows mercy, who were prepared in advance for glory. ²⁴And we are among those whom he selected, both from the Jews and from the Gentiles.

²⁵Concerning the Gentiles, God says in the prophecy of Hosea,

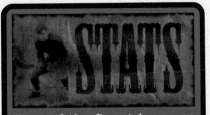

Fans of the Spanish soccer team ONDA are paid to attend games at the local stadium.

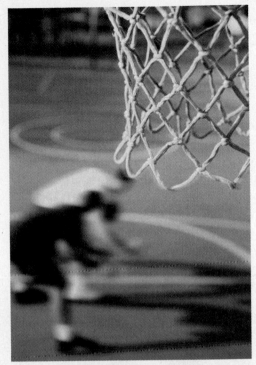

"Those who were not my people,
I will now call my people.
And I will love those
whom I did not love before."

²⁶And,

"Then, at the place where they were told,
'You are not my people,'
there they will be called
'children of the living God.'"

²⁷And concerning Israel, Isaiah the prophet cried out, "Though the people of Israel are as numerous as the sand of the seashore,
only a remnant will be saved.
²⁸For the LORD will carry out his sentence upon the earth quickly and with finality."

²⁹And Isaiah said the same thing in another place:

"If the LORD of Heaven's Armies
had not spared a few of our children,
we would have been wiped out like Sodom,
destroyed like Gomorrah."

Israel's Unbelief

³⁰What does all this mean? Even though the Gentiles were not trying to follow God's standards, they were made right with God. And it was by faith that this took place. ³¹But the people of Israel, who tried so hard to get right with God by keeping the law, never succeeded. ³²Why not? Because they were trying to get right with God by keeping the law instead of by trusting in him. They stumbled over the great rock in

their path. [33]God warned them of this in the Scriptures when he said,

"I am placing a stone in Jerusalem that makes people stumble,
a rock that makes them fall.
But anyone who trusts in him
will never be disgraced."

10

Dear brothers and sisters, the longing of my heart and my prayer to God is for the people of Israel to be saved. [2]I know what enthusiasm they have for God, but it is misdirected zeal. [3]For they don't understand God's way of making people right with himself. Refusing to accept God's way, they cling to their own way of getting right with God by trying to keep the law. [4]For Christ has already accomplished the purpose for which the law was given. As a result, all who believe in him are made right with God.

10:5-15 WHAT'S IT SAYING?

WHAT AM I GOING TO DO ABOUT IT?

Salvation Is for Everyone

[5]For Moses writes that the law's way of making a person right with God requires obedience to all of its commands. [6]But faith's way of getting right with God says, "Don't say in your heart, 'Who will go up to heaven' (to bring Christ down to earth). [7]And don't say, 'Who will go down to the place of the dead' (to bring Christ back to life again)." [8]In fact, it says,

"The message is very close at hand;
it is on your lips and in your heart."

And that message is the very message about faith that we preach: [9]If you confess with your mouth that Jesus is Lord and believe in your heart that God raised him from the dead, you will be saved. [10]For it is by believing in your heart that you are made right with God, and it is by confessing with your mouth that you are saved. [11]As the Scriptures tell us, "Anyone who trusts in him will never be disgraced." [12]Jew and Gentile are the same in this respect. They have the same Lord, who gives generously to all who call on him. [13]For "Everyone who calls on the name of the Lord will be saved."

[14]But how can they call on him to save them unless they believe in him? And how can they believe in him if they have never heard about him? And how can they hear about him unless someone tells them? [15]And how will anyone go and tell them without being sent? That is why the Scriptures say, "How beautiful are the feet of messengers who bring good news!"

[16]But not everyone welcomes the Good News, for Isaiah the prophet said, "Lord, who has believed our message?" [17]So faith comes from hearing, that is, hearing the Good News about Christ. [18]But I ask, have the people of Israel actually heard the message? Yes, they have:

"The message has gone throughout the earth,
and the words to all the world."

[19]But I ask, did the people of Israel really understand? Yes, they did, for even in the time of Moses, God said,
"I will rouse your jealousy through people who are not even a nation.
I will provoke your anger through the foolish Gentiles."

[20]And later Isaiah spoke boldly for God, saying,
"I was found by people who were not looking for me.
I showed myself to those who were not asking for me."

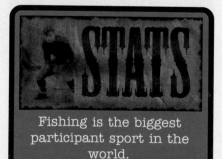

Fishing is the biggest participant sport in the world.

[21]But regarding Israel, God said,
"All day long I opened my arms to them,
but they were disobedient and rebellious."

God's Mercy on Israel

11

I ask, then, has God rejected his own people, the nation of Israel? Of course not! I myself am an Israelite, a descendant of Abraham and a member of the tribe of Benjamin.

[2]No, God has not rejected his own people, whom he chose from the very beginning. Do you realize what the Scriptures say about this? Elijah the prophet complained to God about the people of Israel and said, [3]"Lord, they have killed your prophets and torn down your altars. I am the only one left, and now they are trying to kill me, too."

[4]And do you remember God's reply? He said, "No, I have 7,000 others who have never bowed down to Baal!"

[5]It is the same today, for a few of the people of Israel have remained faithful because of God's grace—his undeserved kindness in choosing them. [6]And since it is through God's kindness, then it is not by their good works. For in that case, God's grace would not be what it really is—free and undeserved.

[7]So this is the situation: Most of the people of Israel have not found the favor of God they are looking for so earnestly. A few have—the ones God has chosen—but the hearts of the rest were hardened. [8]As the Scriptures say,

"God has put them into a deep sleep.
To this day he has shut their eyes so they do not see,
and closed their ears so they do not hear."

[9]Likewise, David said,
"Let their bountiful table become a snare,
a trap that makes them think all is well.
Let their blessings cause them to stumble,
and let them get what they deserve.
[10]Let their eyes go blind so they cannot see,
and let their backs be bent forever."

[11]Did God's people stumble and fall beyond recovery? Of course not! They were disobedient, so God made salvation available to the Gentiles. But he wanted his own people to become jealous and claim it for themselves. [12]Now if the Gentiles were enriched because the people of Israel turned down God's offer of salvation, think how much greater a blessing the world will share when they finally accept it.

[13]I am saying all this especially for you Gentiles. God has appointed me as the apostle to the Gentiles. I

stress this, ¹⁴for I want somehow to make the people of Israel jealous of what you Gentiles have, so I might save some of them. ¹⁵For since their rejection meant that God offered salvation to the rest of the world, their acceptance will be even more wonderful. It will be life for those who were dead! ¹⁶And since Abraham and the other patriarchs were holy, their descendants will also be holy—just as the entire batch of dough is holy because the portion given as an offering is holy. For if the roots of the tree are holy, the branches will be, too.

¹⁷But some of these branches from Abraham's tree—some of the people of Israel—have been broken off. And you Gentiles, who were branches from a wild olive tree, have been grafted in. So now you also receive the blessing God has promised Abraham and his children, sharing in the rich nourishment from the root of God's special olive tree. ¹⁸But you must not brag about being grafted in to replace the branches that were broken off. You are just a branch, not the root.

¹⁹"Well," you may say, "those branches were broken off to make room for me." ²⁰Yes, but remember—those branches were broken off because they didn't believe in Christ, and you are there because you do believe. So don't think highly of yourself, but fear what could happen. ²¹For if God did not spare the original branches, he won't spare you either.

²²Notice how God is both kind and severe. He is severe toward those who disobeyed, but kind to you if you continue to trust in his kindness. But if you stop trusting, you also will be cut off. ²³And if the people of Israel turn from their unbelief, they will be grafted in again, for God has the power to graft them back into the tree. ²⁴You, by nature, were a branch cut from a wild olive tree. So if God was willing to do something contrary to nature by grafting you into his cultivated tree, he will be far more eager to graft the original branches back into the tree where they belong.

Bible Facts

The longest word in the Bible is Maher-shalal-hash-baz. Isaiah 8:1

God's Mercy Is for Everyone

²⁵I want you to understand this mystery, dear brothers and sisters, so that you will not feel proud about yourselves. Some of the people of Israel have hard hearts, but this will last only until the full number of Gentiles comes to Christ. ²⁶And so all Israel will be saved. As the Scriptures say,

"The one who rescues will come from Jerusalem, and he will turn Israel away from ungodliness.
²⁷And this is my covenant with them, that I will take away their sins."

²⁸Many of the people of Israel are now enemies of the Good News, and this benefits you Gentiles. Yet they are still the people he loves because he chose their ancestors Abraham, Isaac, and Jacob. ²⁹For God's gifts and his call can never be withdrawn. ³⁰Once, you Gentiles were rebels against God, but when the people of Israel rebelled against him, God was merciful to you instead. ³¹Now they are the rebels, and God's mercy has come to you so that they, too, will share in God's mercy. ³²For God has imprisoned everyone in disobedience so he could have mercy on everyone.

³³Oh, how great are God's riches and wisdom and knowledge! How impossible it is for us to understand his decisions and his ways!

³⁴For who can know the LORD's thoughts?
Who knows enough to give him advice?
³⁵And who has given him so much
that he needs to pay it back?

³⁶For everything comes from him and exists by his power and is intended for his glory. All glory to him forever! Amen.

action

12:3-11 WHAT'S IT SAYING?

WHAT AM I GOING TO DO ABOUT IT?

A Living Sacrifice to God

12

And so, dear brothers and sisters, I plead with you to give your bodies to God because of all he has done for you. Let them be a living and holy sacrifice—the kind he will find acceptable. This is truly the way to worship him. ²Don't copy the behavior and customs of this world, but let God transform you into a new person by changing the way you think. Then you will learn to know God's will for you, which is good and pleasing and perfect.

³Because of the privilege and authority God has given me, I give each of you this warning: Don't think you are better

Q's AND A's

I feel like the only Christian athlete on the planet. Sometimes I am worn down — what do you suggest?

Be encouraged — you are not the only Christian athlete on the planet, though it may feel like it at times! For this very reason, the Bible encourages Christians to get together and build each other up for encouragement, training, and living. There are several Christian sports Web sites with stories of other athletes who have the same challenges you have. If you are fortunate enough to have a Christian sports camp near you, try to go. Go to the Web site addresses in the resource section of your **nt:sport.** Lastly, encourage others — it is contagious.

JULY M.A.P.

1
S.D.	P.L.	P.G.	S.G.
P. ☐	F. ☐	F. ☐	T. ☐
F. ☐	W. ☐	W. ☐	P. ☐
B. ☐	P. ☐	C. ☐	C. ☐

2
S.D.	P.L.	P.G.	S.G.
P. ☐	F. ☐	F. ☐	T. ☐
F. ☐	W. ☐	W. ☐	P. ☐
B. ☐	P. ☐	C. ☐	C. ☐

3
S.D.	P.L.	P.G.	S.G.
P. ☐	F. ☐	F. ☐	T. ☐
F. ☐	W. ☐	W. ☐	P. ☐
B. ☐	P. ☐	C. ☐	C. ☐

4
S.D.	P.L.	P.G.	S.G.
P. ☐	F. ☐	F. ☐	T. ☐
F. ☐	W. ☐	W. ☐	P. ☐
B. ☐	P. ☐	C. ☐	C. ☐

9
S.D.	P.L.	P.G.	S.G.
P. ☐	F. ☐	F. ☐	T. ☐
F. ☐	W. ☐	W. ☐	P. ☐
B. ☐	P. ☐	C. ☐	C. ☐

10
S.D.	P.L.	P.G.	S.G.
P. ☐	F. ☐	F. ☐	T. ☐
F. ☐	W. ☐	W. ☐	P. ☐
B. ☐	P. ☐	C. ☐	C. ☐

11
S.D.	P.L.	P.G.	S.G.
P. ☐	F. ☐	F. ☐	T. ☐
F. ☐	W. ☐	W. ☐	P. ☐
B. ☐	P. ☐	C. ☐	C. ☐

12
S.D.	P.L.	P.G.	S.G.
P. ☐	F. ☐	F. ☐	T. ☐
F. ☐	W. ☐	W. ☐	P. ☐
B. ☐	P. ☐	C. ☐	C. ☐

17
S.D.	P.L.	P.G.	S.G.
P. ☐	F. ☐	F. ☐	T. ☐
F. ☐	W. ☐	W. ☐	P. ☐
B. ☐	P. ☐	C. ☐	C. ☐

18
S.D.	P.L.	P.G.	S.G.
P. ☐	F. ☐	F. ☐	T. ☐
F. ☐	W. ☐	W. ☐	P. ☐
B. ☐	P. ☐	C. ☐	C. ☐

19
S.D.	P.L.	P.G.	S.G.
P. ☐	F. ☐	F. ☐	T. ☐
F. ☐	W. ☐	W. ☐	P. ☐
B. ☐	P. ☐	C. ☐	C. ☐

20
S.D.	P.L.	P.G.	S.G.
P. ☐	F. ☐	F. ☐	T. ☐
F. ☐	W. ☐	W. ☐	P. ☐
B. ☐	P. ☐	C. ☐	C. ☐

25
S.D.	P.L.	P.G.	S.G.
P. ☐	F. ☐	F. ☐	T. ☐
F. ☐	W. ☐	W. ☐	P. ☐
B. ☐	P. ☐	C. ☐	C. ☐

26
S.D.	P.L.	P.G.	S.G.
P. ☐	F. ☐	F. ☐	T. ☐
F. ☐	W. ☐	W. ☐	P. ☐
B. ☐	P. ☐	C. ☐	C. ☐

27
S.D.	P.L.	P.G.	S.G.
P. ☐	F. ☐	F. ☐	T. ☐
F. ☐	W. ☐	W. ☐	P. ☐
B. ☐	P. ☐	C. ☐	C. ☐

28
S.D.	P.L.	P.G.	S.G.
P. ☐	F. ☐	F. ☐	T. ☐
F. ☐	W. ☐	W. ☐	P. ☐
B. ☐	P. ☐	C. ☐	C. ☐

Spiritual Disciplines

Prayer

Faith Community

Bible Reading

Prayer List

Friends

World

Personal

(For designing your M.A.P. – Monthly Action Plan – see introduction pages)

Who am I....
Where am I going....
How am I going to get there?

nt:sport
MONTHLY ACTION PLAN

5

S.D.	P.L.	P.G.	S.G.
P. ☐	F. ☐	F. ☐	T. ☐
F. ☐	W. ☐	W. ☐	P. ☐
B. ☐	P. ☐	C. ☐	C. ☐

6

S.D.	P.L.	P.G.	S.G.
P. ☐	F. ☐	F. ☐	T. ☐
F. ☐	W. ☐	W. ☐	P. ☐
B. ☐	P. ☐	C. ☐	C. ☐

7

S.D.	P.L.	P.G.	S.G.
P. ☐	F. ☐	F. ☐	T. ☐
F. ☐	W. ☐	W. ☐	P. ☐
B. ☐	P. ☐	C. ☐	C. ☐

8

S.D.	P.L.	P.G.	S.G.
P. ☐	F. ☐	F. ☐	T. ☐
F. ☐	W. ☐	W. ☐	P. ☐
B. ☐	P. ☐	C. ☐	C. ☐

13

S.D.	P.L.	P.G.	S.G.
P. ☐	F. ☐	F. ☐	T. ☐
F. ☐	W. ☐	W. ☐	P. ☐
B. ☐	P. ☐	C. ☐	C. ☐

14

S.D.	P.L.	P.G.	S.G.
P. ☐	F. ☐	F. ☐	T. ☐
F. ☐	W. ☐	W. ☐	P. ☐
B. ☐	P. ☐	C. ☐	C. ☐

15

S.D.	P.L.	P.G.	S.G.
P. ☐	F. ☐	F. ☐	T. ☐
F. ☐	W. ☐	W. ☐	P. ☐
B. ☐	P. ☐	C. ☐	C. ☐

16

S.D.	P.L.	P.G.	S.G.
P. ☐	F. ☐	F. ☐	T. ☐
F. ☐	W. ☐	W. ☐	P. ☐
B. ☐	P. ☐	C. ☐	C. ☐

21

S.D.	P.L.	P.G.	S.G.
P. ☐	F. ☐	F. ☐	T. ☐
F. ☐	W. ☐	W. ☐	P. ☐
B. ☐	P. ☐	C. ☐	C. ☐

22

S.D.	P.L.	P.G.	S.G.
P. ☐	F. ☐	F. ☐	T. ☐
F. ☐	W. ☐	W. ☐	P. ☐
B. ☐	P. ☐	C. ☐	C. ☐

23

S.D.	P.L.	P.G.	S.G.
P. ☐	F. ☐	F. ☐	T. ☐
F. ☐	W. ☐	W. ☐	P. ☐
B. ☐	P. ☐	C. ☐	C. ☐

24

S.D.	P.L.	P.G.	S.G.
P. ☐	F. ☐	F. ☐	T. ☐
F. ☐	W. ☐	W. ☐	P. ☐
B. ☐	P. ☐	C. ☐	C. ☐

29

S.D.	P.L.	P.G.	S.G.
P. ☐	F. ☐	F. ☐	T. ☐
F. ☐	W. ☐	W. ☐	P. ☐
B. ☐	P. ☐	C. ☐	C. ☐

30

S.D.	P.L.	P.G.	S.G.
P. ☐	F. ☐	F. ☐	T. ☐
F. ☐	W. ☐	W. ☐	P. ☐
B. ☐	P. ☐	C. ☐	C. ☐

31

S.D.	P.L.	P.G.	S.G.
P. ☐	F. ☐	F. ☐	T. ☐
F. ☐	W. ☐	W. ☐	P. ☐
B. ☐	P. ☐	C. ☐	C. ☐

Proverbs 8:17

"I love all who love me. Those who search will surely find me."

Personal Goals

Family

Work/School/Social

Challenge

Sport Goals

Training

Performance

Competition Results

STAND POINT

When you need motivation

12:1

And so, dear brothers and sisters, I plead with you to give your bodies to God because of all he has done for you. Let them be a living and holy sacrifice—the kind he will find acceptable. This is truly the way to worship him.

than you really are. Be honest in your evaluation of yourselves, measuring yourselves by the faith God has given us. ⁴Just as our bodies have many parts and each part has a special function, ⁵so it is with Christ's body. We are many parts of one body, and we all belong to each other.

⁶In his grace, God has given us different gifts for doing certain things well. So if God has given you the ability to prophesy, speak out with as much faith as God has given you. ⁷If your gift is serving others, serve them well. If you are a teacher, teach well. ⁸If your gift is to encourage others, be encouraging. If it is giving, give generously. If God has given you leadership ability, take the responsibility seriously. And if you have a gift for showing kindness to others, do it gladly.

⁹Don't just pretend to love others. Really love them. Hate what is wrong. Hold tightly to what is good. ¹⁰Love each other with genuine affection, and take delight in honoring each other. ¹¹Never be lazy, but work hard and serve the Lord enthusiastically. ¹²Rejoice in our confident hope. Be patient in trouble, and keep on praying. ¹³When God's people are in need, be ready to help them. Always be eager to practice hospitality.

¹⁴Bless those who persecute you. Don't curse them; pray that God will bless them. ¹⁵Be happy with those who are happy, and weep with those who weep. ¹⁶Live in harmony with each other. Don't be too proud to enjoy the company of ordinary people. And don't think you know it all!

¹⁷Never pay back evil with more evil. Do things in such a way that everyone can see you are honorable. ¹⁸Do all that you can to live in peace with everyone. ¹⁹Dear friends, never take revenge. Leave that to the righteous anger of God. For the Scriptures say,

"I will take revenge;
I will pay them back,"
says the LORD.

²⁰Instead, "If your enemies are hungry, feed them.
If they are thirsty, give them something to drink.
In doing this, you will heap
burning coals of shame on their heads."

²¹Don't let evil conquer you, but conquer evil by doing good.

Respect for Authority

13

Everyone must submit to governing authorities. For all authority comes from God, and those in positions of authority have been placed there by God. ²So anyone who rebels against authority is rebelling against what God has instituted, and they will be punished. ³For the authorities do not strike fear in people who are doing right, but in those who are doing wrong. Would you like to live without fear of the authorities? Do what is right, and they will honor you. ⁴The authorities are God's servants, sent for your good. But if you are doing wrong, of course you should be afraid, for they have the power to punish you. They are God's servants, sent for the very purpose of punishing those who do what is wrong. ⁵So you must submit to them, not only to avoid punishment, but also to keep a clear conscience.

⁶Pay your taxes, too, for these same reasons. For government workers need to be paid. They are serving God in what they do. ⁷Give to everyone what you owe them: Pay your taxes and government fees to those who collect them, and give respect and honor to those who are in authority.

Winners know humility!

"I don't want my kids to compete because they may get embarrassed." Many leaders and parents want to shelter their kids from humiliation. These attitudes, though generated out of genuine love for kids, can be very unhealthy. We all have to learn to live with embarrassment and humility. Everyone in sport will eventually goof up and be embarrassed and humbled. It is indeed a shame when a youngster (or anyone) is unduly humiliated. Yet humility is also a great virtue. This is nothing to shy away from. Humility comes before honor (Proverbs 15:33). A Dominican monk once wrote, "He who learns to laugh at himself will never cease to be entertained." Many sporting experiences are not glorious, but they do teach us not to take ourselves too seriously! Sport often reveals shortcomings and facing up to these can be a valuable lesson. **"Be honest in your evaluation of yourselves, measuring yourselves by the faith God has given us." (Romans 12:3)**

Winners

Winners can laugh at themselves!

Love Fulfills God's Requirements

⁸Owe nothing to anyone—except for your obligation to love one another. If you love your neighbor, you will fulfill the requirements of God's law. ⁹For the commandments say, "You must not commit adultery. You must not murder. You must not steal. You must not covet." These—and other such commandments—are summed up in this one commandment: "Love your neighbor as yourself." ¹⁰Love does no wrong to others, so love fulfills the requirements of God's law.

¹¹This is all the more urgent, for you know how late it is; time is running out. Wake up, for our salvation is nearer now than when we first believed. ¹²The night is almost gone; the day of salvation will soon be here. So remove your dark deeds like dirty clothes, and put on the shining armor of right living. ¹³Because we belong to the day, we must live decent lives for all to see. Don't participate in the darkness of wild parties and drunkenness, or in sexual promiscuity and immoral living, or in quarreling and jealousy. ¹⁴Instead, clothe yourself with the presence of the Lord Jesus Christ. And don't let yourself think about ways to indulge your evil desires.

14:1-9 WHAT'S IT SAYING?

WHAT AM I GOING TO DO ABOUT IT?

count on it

You are going to live forever!

We all have tough times, but God has given you way more than you can imagine. Remind yourself that in Christ you will live forever in Paradise! This will keep you going! "Anyone with ears to hear must listen to the Spirit and understand what he is saying to the churches. To everyone who is victorious I will give fruit from the tree of life in the paradise of God." (Revelation 2:7)
Count on it!

The Danger of Criticism

14

Accept other believers who are weak in faith, and don't argue with them about what they think is right or wrong. ²For instance, one person believes it's all right to eat anything. But another believer with a sensitive conscience will eat only vegetables. ³Those who feel free to eat anything must not look down on those who don't. And those who don't eat certain foods must not condemn those who do, for God has accepted them. ⁴Who are you to condemn someone else's servants? They are responsible to the Lord, so let him judge whether they are right or wrong. And with the Lord's help, they will do what is right and will receive his approval.

⁵In the same way, some think one day is more holy than another day, while others think every day is alike.

You should each be fully convinced that whichever day you choose is acceptable. ⁶Those who worship the Lord on a special day do it to honor him. Those who eat any kind of food do so to honor the Lord, since they give thanks to God before eating. And those who refuse to eat certain foods also want to please the Lord and give thanks to God. ⁷For we don't live for ourselves or die for ourselves. ⁸If we live, it's to honor the Lord. And if we die, it's to honor the Lord. So whether we live or die, we belong to the Lord. ⁹Christ died and rose again for this very purpose—to be Lord both of the living and of the dead.

¹⁰So why do you condemn another believer? Why do you look down on another believer? Remember, we will all stand before the judgment seat of God. ¹¹For the Scriptures say,

"'As surely as I live,' says the LORD,
'every knee will bend to me,
and every tongue will confess and give praise to God.'"

¹²Yes, each of us will give a personal account to God. ¹³So let's stop condemning each other. Decide instead to live in such a way that you will not cause another believer to stumble and fall.

¹⁴I know and am convinced on the authority of the Lord Jesus that no food, in and of itself, is wrong to eat. But if someone believes it is wrong, then for that person it is wrong. ¹⁵And if another believer is distressed by what you eat, you are not acting in love if you eat it. Don't let your eating ruin someone for whom Christ died. ¹⁶Then you will not be criticized for doing something you believe is good. ¹⁷For the Kingdom of God is not a matter of what we eat or drink, but of living a life of goodness and peace and joy in the Holy Spirit. ¹⁸If you serve Christ with this attitude, you will please God, and others will approve of you, too. ¹⁹So then, let us aim for harmony in the church and try to build each other up.

²⁰Don't tear apart the work of God over what you eat. Remember, all foods are acceptable, but it is wrong to eat something if it makes another person stumble. ²¹It is better not to eat meat or drink wine or do anything else if it might cause another believer to stumble. ²²You may believe there's nothing wrong with what you are doing, but keep it between yourself and God. Blessed are those who don't feel guilty for doing something they have decided is right. ²³But if you have doubts about whether or not you should eat something, you are sinning if you go ahead and do it. For you are not following your convictions. If you do anything you believe is not right, you are sinning.

Living to Please Others

15

We who are strong must be considerate of those who are sensitive about things like this. We must not just please ourselves. ²We should help others do what is right and build them up in the Lord. ³For even Christ didn't live to please himself. As the Scriptures say, "The insults of those who insult you, O God, have fallen on me." ⁴Such things were written in the Scriptures long ago to teach us. And the Scriptures give us hope and encouragement as we wait patiently for God's promises to be fulfilled.

⁵May God, who gives this patience and encouragement, help you live in complete harmony with each other, as is fitting for followers of Christ Jesus. ⁶Then all of you can join together with one voice, giving praise and glory to God, the Father of our Lord Jesus Christ.

⁷Therefore, accept each other just as Christ has accepted you so that God will be given glory. ⁸Remember that Christ came as a servant to the Jews to show that God is true to the promises he made to their ancestors. ⁹He also came so that the Gentiles might give glory to God for his mercies to them. That is what the psalmist meant when he wrote:

"For this, I will praise you among the Gentiles;
I will sing praises to your name."

¹⁰And in another place it is written,

"Rejoice with his people,
you Gentiles."

¹¹And yet again,

"Praise the LORD, all you Gentiles.
Praise him, all you people of the earth."

¹²And in another place Isaiah said,

"The heir to David's throne will come,
and he will rule over the Gentiles.
They will place their hope on him."

¹³I pray that God, the source of hope, will fill you completely with joy and peace because you trust in him. Then you will overflow with confident hope through the power of the Holy Spirit.

Paul's Reason for Writing

¹⁴I am fully convinced, my dear brothers and sisters, that you are full of goodness. You know these things so well you can teach each other all about them. ¹⁵Even so, I have been bold enough to write about some of these points, knowing that all you need is this reminder. For by God's grace, ¹⁶I am a special messenger from Christ Jesus to you Gentiles. I bring you the Good News so that I might present you as an acceptable offering to God, made holy by the Holy Spirit.

¹⁷So I have reason to be enthusiastic about all Christ Jesus has done through me in my service to God. ¹⁸Yet I dare not boast about anything except what Christ has done through me, bringing the Gentiles to God by my message and by the way I worked among them. ¹⁹They were convinced by the power of miraculous signs and wonders and by the power of God's Spirit. In this way, I have fully presented the Good News of Christ from Jerusalem all the way to Illyricum. ²⁰My ambition has always been to preach the Good News

where the name of Christ has never been heard, rather than where a church has already been started by someone else. ²¹I have been following the plan spoken of in the Scriptures, where it says,

"Those who have never been told about him will see,
and those who have never heard of him will understand."

²²In fact, my visit to you has been delayed so long because I have been preaching in these places.

Paul's Travel Plans

²³But now I have finished my work in these regions, and after all these long years of waiting, I am eager to visit you. ²⁴I am planning to go to Spain, and when I do, I will stop off in Rome. And after I have enjoyed

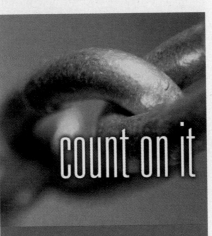

count on it

perfection:
We can never make ourselves completely perfect on our own. But we are made perfect through Jesus Christ. When you have faith in Christ you are complete.
"For by that one offering he forever made perfect those who are being made holy."
(Hebrews 10:14)
Count on it!

your fellowship for a little while, you can provide for my journey.

²⁵But before I come, I must go to Jerusalem to take a gift to the believers there. ²⁶For you see, the believers in Macedonia and Achaia have eagerly taken up an offering for the poor among the believers in Jerusalem. ²⁷They were glad to do this because they feel they owe a real debt to them. Since the Gentiles received the spiritual blessings of the Good News from the believers in Jerusalem, they feel the least they can do in return is to help them financially. ²⁸As soon as I have delivered this money and completed this good deed of theirs, I will come to see you on my way to Spain. ²⁹And I am sure that when I come, Christ will richly bless our time together.

³⁰Dear brothers and sisters, I urge you in the name of our Lord Jesus Christ to join in my struggle by praying to God for me. Do this because of your love for me, given to you by the Holy Spirit. ³¹Pray that I will be rescued from those in Judea who refuse to obey God. Pray also that the believers there will be willing to accept the donation I am taking to Jerusalem. ³²Then, by the will of God, I will be able to come to you with a joyful heart, and we will be an encouragement to each other.

³³And now may God, who gives us his peace, be with you all. Amen.

Paul Greets His Friends

16

I commend to you our sister Phoebe, who is a deacon in the church in Cenchrea. ²Welcome her in the Lord as one who is worthy of honor among God's people. Help her in whatever she needs, for she has been helpful to many, and especially to me.

³Give my greetings to Priscilla and Aquila, my co-workers in the ministry of Christ Jesus. ⁴In fact, they once risked their lives for me. I am thankful to them, and so are all the Gentile churches. ⁵Also give my greetings to the church that meets in their home.

Greet my dear friend Epenetus. He was the first person from the province of Asia to become a follower of Christ. ⁶Give my greetings to Mary, who has worked so hard for your benefit. ⁷Greet Andronicus and Junia, my fellow Jews, who were in prison with me. They are highly respected among the apostles and became followers of Christ before I did. ⁸Greet Ampliatus, my dear friend in the Lord. ⁹Greet Urbanus, our co-worker in Christ, and my dear friend Stachys.

¹⁰Greet Apelles, a good man whom Christ approves. And give my greetings to the believers from the

household of Aristobulus. [11]Greet Herodion, my fellow Jew. Greet the Lord's people from the household of Narcissus. [12]Give my greetings to Tryphena and Tryphosa, the Lord's workers, and to dear Persis, who has worked so hard for the Lord. [13]Greet Rufus, whom the Lord picked out to be his very own; and also his dear mother, who has been a mother to me.

[14]Give my greetings to Asyncritus, Phlegon, Hermes, Patrobas, Hermas, and the brothers and sisters who meet with them. [15]Give my greetings to Philologus, Julia, Nereus and his sister, and to Olympas and all the believers who meet with them. [16]Greet each other in Christian love. All the churches of Christ send you their greetings.

Paul's Final Instructions

[17]And now I make one more appeal, my dear brothers and sisters. Watch out for people who cause divisions and upset people's faith by teaching things contrary to what you have been taught. Stay away from them. [18]Such people are not serving Christ our Lord; they are serving their own personal interests. By smooth talk and glowing words they deceive innocent people. [19]But everyone knows that you are obedient to the Lord. This makes me very happy. I want you to be wise in doing right and to stay innocent of any wrong. [20]The God of peace will soon crush Satan under your feet. May the grace of our Lord Jesus be with you.

[21]Timothy, my fellow worker, sends you his greetings, as do Lucius, Jason, and Sosipater, my fellow Jews. [22]I, Tertius, the one writing this letter for Paul, send my greetings, too, as one of the Lord's followers.

[23]Gaius says hello to you. He is my host and also serves as host to the whole church. Erastus, the city treasurer, sends you his greetings, and so does our brother Quartus.[*]

[25]Now all glory to God, who is able to make you strong, just as my Good News says. This message about Jesus Christ has revealed his plan for you Gentiles, a plan kept secret from the beginning of time. [26]But now as the prophets foretold and as the eternal God has commanded, this message is made known to all Gentiles everywhere, so that they too might believe and obey him. [27]All glory to the only wise God, through Jesus Christ, forever. Amen.

PERSONAL ASSESSMENTS

TRAINING ASSESSMENT:

Pick a sport you want to focus on and see what you need to emphasize:

In my sport power is important:	1 2 3 4 5 6 7 8 9 10
I work hard on developing strength and power:	1 2 3 4 5 6 7 8 9 10
My own strength and power for my age is:	1 2 3 4 5 6 7 8 9 10
In my sport muscular endurance is important:	1 2 3 4 5 6 7 8 9 10
In my sport aerobic fitness is important:	1 2 3 4 5 6 7 8 9 10
In my training I place a lot of emphasis on aerobic fitness:	1 2 3 4 5 6 7 8 9 10
I rate my level of aerobic fitness (for my age):	1 2 3 4 5 6 7 8 9 10
I am maintaining a balanced life style:	1 2 3 4 5 6 7 8 9 10
I have an effective training routine and plan:	1 2 3 4 5 6 7 8 9 10
I understand that if I want to achieve a certain level of skill and performance I will have to work at it:	1 2 3 4 5 6 7 8 9 10

They say that a goal not written down is merely a wish.

Write down five goals you have after completing this assessment:

1 _____

2 _____

3 _____

4 _____

5 _____

16:23 Some manuscripts add verse 24, *May the grace of our Lord Jesus Christ be with you all. Amen.* Still others add this sentence after verse 27.

He's the Boss

"Look! I stand at the door and knock. If you hear my voice and open the door, I will come in, and we will share a meal together as friends." (Revelation 3:20)

Feel your pulse beat and your blood course through you body. Grasp the fact that you not only encompass blood, bone, and tissue. You also house a sophisticated psyche, a complex computer, and a multiplicity of different systems: circulatory, digestive, nervous, respiratory, endocrine, immune, reproductive, lymphatic, and urinary systems. Your body has huge potential.

Another item you contain within your body is a throne. You have the capacity to host the Creator of the universe in the core of your being, the capacity to be in companionship with God almighty.

A rugby player from Keble College in Oxford, England, was the first to show me the famous portrait The Light of the World by William Holman Hunt. It is a beautiful mid-nineteenth century paining of Jesus knocking at a door and carrying a lantern. It was inspired by several Scriptures, including Revelation 3:20. The door symbolizes the entrance to a person's heart or life. The painting took three years to make and when completed was at first misunderstood. The critics laughed at Hunt

and mocked that after three years of detailed work he forgot to paint a handle for the door! A friend, John Ruskin, boldly defended Hunt's symbolic Pre-Raphaelite art in a letter to the London Times. The door handle is on the inside, because Christ will not crash your party or force himself into a place he is not wanted. You have to invite him in.

When Jesus was crucified on the cross, the Temple in Israel had a thick (probably wool) curtain that separated a small exclusive part of the building. It separated the holy area from the Holy of Holies, which hosted the presence of God. At Christ's death the curtain was torn from top to bottom, symbolizing that God would not be contained in a room, but now dwells inside all who ask — inside all who are chosen. But when inviting a king into your life, be careful; he will demand center stage and will want to sit on the throne. Head coaches want what's best for their team, and they call the shots so their team is unified and performs well. God wants to lead you so you will perform the best in life that you can.

Reflection
I want Christ to be my Savior, but do I want him to be my Lord?

Prayer
Father in heaven, give me the courage to answer your Son's calling: "Come follow me."

"All who love me will do what I say. My Father will love them, and we will come and make our home with each of them."
Jesus

Nicked with permission from: A Sporting Guide to Eternity, Steve Connor, Christian Focus Publications - ISBN 1-85792-746-X

Paul's first letter to the Corinthians is an honest, strong, loving, and nurturing response to a church full of problems.

Imagine a great coach sees your potential, recruits you, trains you, and keeps encouraging you long after your sports career is established. The apostle Paul in many ways is like a spiritual coach; in many of his letters he encouraged his "recruits" to follow and be transformed by Christ. God spoke through Paul to instruct believers to live a life worthy of Christ. In this book, Paul was writing to people he knew and loved. He spent a lot of time in Corinth, a very strategic city, and helped establish and care for a young Christian community.

But though the church was started by a great man of God, the movement at Corinth had plenty of problems. We can detect Paul's frustration and shock that the church had turned a blind eye to some clear offenses to God. Corinth was a very immoral community — not unlike the world we live in today. The lessons are as fresh and applicable today as they were in Paul's time.

The book ends with a positive look at the gifts that each believer has and how best to use them to further the cause of Christ. One of the most famous chapters in the Bible is 1 Corinthians 13. Here Paul emphasizes Jesus' teaching about loving and the priority it must have in our lives.

1 Corinthians

Adversity
EXPECT IT

1 CORINTHIANS

Greetings from Paul

1

This letter is from Paul, chosen by the will of God to be an apostle of Christ Jesus, and from our brother Sosthenes.

²I am writing to God's church in Corinth, to you who have been called by God to be his own holy people. He made you holy by means of Christ Jesus, just as he did for all people everywhere who call on the name of our Lord Jesus Christ, their Lord and ours.

³May God our Father and the Lord Jesus Christ give you grace and peace.

Paul Gives Thanks to God

⁴I always thank my God for you and for the gracious gifts he has given you, now that you belong to Christ Jesus. ⁵Through him, God has enriched your church in every way—with all of your eloquent words and all of your knowledge. ⁶This confirms that what I told you about Christ is true. ⁷Now you have every spiritual gift you need as you eagerly wait for the return of our Lord Jesus Christ. ⁸He will keep you strong to the end so that you will be free from all blame on the day when our Lord Jesus Christ returns. ⁹God will do this, for he is faithful to do what he says, and he has invited you into partnership with his Son, Jesus Christ our Lord.

Divisions in the Church

¹⁰I appeal to you, dear brothers and sisters, by the authority of our Lord Jesus Christ, to live in harmony with each other. Let there be no divisions in the church. Rather, be of one mind, united in thought and purpose. ¹¹For some members of Chloe's household have told me about your quarrels, my dear brothers and sisters. ¹²Some of you are saying, "I am a follower of Paul." Others are saying, "I follow Apollos," or "I follow Peter," or "I follow only Christ."

¹³Has Christ been divided into factions? Was I, Paul, crucified for you? Were any of you baptized in the name of Paul? Of course not! ¹⁴I thank God that I did not baptize any of you except Crispus and Gaius, ¹⁵for now no one can say they were baptized in my name. ¹⁶(Oh yes, I also baptized the household of Stephanas, but I don't remember baptizing anyone else.) ¹⁷For Christ didn't send me to baptize, but to preach the Good News—and not with clever speech, for fear that the cross of Christ would lose its power.

The Wisdom of God

¹⁸The message of the cross is foolish to those who are headed for destruction! But we who are being saved know it is the very power of God. ¹⁹As the Scriptures say,

"I will destroy the wisdom of the wise
and discard the intelligence of the intelligent."

²⁰So where does this leave the philosophers, the scholars, and the world's brilliant debaters? God has made the wisdom of this world look foolish. ²¹Since God in his wisdom saw to it that the world would never know him through human wisdom, he has used our foolish preaching to save those who believe. ²²It is foolish to the Jews, who ask for signs from heaven. And it is foolish to the Greeks, who seek human wisdom. ²³So when we preach that Christ was crucified, the Jews are offended and the Gentiles say it's all nonsense.

²⁴But to those called by God to salvation, both Jews and Gentiles, Christ is the power of God and the wisdom of God. ²⁵This foolish plan of God is wiser than the wisest of human plans, and God's weakness is stronger than the greatest of human strength.

²⁶Remember, dear brothers and sisters, that few of you were wise in the world's eyes or powerful or wealthy when God called you. ²⁷Instead, God chose things the world considers foolish in order to shame those who think they are wise. And he chose things that are powerless to shame those who are powerful. ²⁸God chose things despised by the world, things counted as nothing at all, and used them to bring to nothing what the world considers important. ²⁹As a result, no one can ever boast in the presence of God. ³⁰God has united you with Christ Jesus. For our benefit God made him to be wisdom itself. Christ made us right with God; he made us pure and holy, and he freed us from sin. ³¹Therefore, as the Scriptures say, "If you want to boast, boast only about the LORD."

Paul's Message of Wisdom

2

When I first came to you, dear brothers and sisters, I didn't use lofty words and impressive wisdom to tell you God's secret plan. ²For I decided that while I was with you I would forget everything except Jesus Christ, the one who was crucified. ³I came to you in weakness—timid and trembling. ⁴And my message and my preaching were very plain. Rather than using clever and persuasive speeches, I relied only on the power of the Holy Spirit. ⁵I did this so you would trust not in human wisdom but in the power of God.

⁶Yet when I am among mature believers, I do speak with words of wisdom, but not the kind of wisdom that belongs to this world or to the rulers of this world, who are soon forgotten. ⁷No, the wisdom we speak of is the mystery of God—his plan that was previously hidden, even though he made it for our ultimate glory before the world began. ⁸But the rulers of this world have not understood it; if they had, they would not have crucified our glorious Lord. ⁹That is what the Scriptures mean when they say,

"No eye has seen, no ear has heard,
and no mind has imagined
what God has prepared
for those who love him."

¹⁰But it was to us that God revealed these things by his Spirit. For his Spirit searches out everything and shows us God's deep secrets. ¹¹No one can know a person's thoughts except that person's own spirit, and no one can know God's thoughts

Want what God wants! God knows you better than even your mom! He designed you, has a purpose for you, and wants the best for you. Father knows best! "And we are confident that he hears us whenever we ask for anything that pleases him. And since we know he hears us when we make our requests, we also know that he will give us what we ask for."

(1 John 5:14-15)

STAND POINT

When you are jealous

2:9

"No eye has seen, no ear has heard, and no mind has imagined what God has prepared for those who love him."

except God's own Spirit. [12]And we have received God's Spirit (not the world's spirit), so we can know the wonderful things God has freely given us.

[13]When we tell you these things, we do not use words that come from human wisdom. Instead, we speak words given to us by the Spirit, using the Spirit's words to explain spiritual truths. [14]But people who aren't spiritual can't receive these truths from God's Spirit. It all sounds foolish to them and they can't understand it, for only those who are spiritual can understand what the Spirit means. [15]Those who are spiritual can evaluate all things, but they themselves cannot be evaluated by others. [16]For,

"Who can know the LORD's thoughts?
Who knows enough to teach him?"

But we understand these things, for we have the mind of Christ.

Paul and Apollos, Servants of Christ

3

Dear brothers and sisters, when I was with you I couldn't talk to you as I would to spiritual people. I had to talk as

The distance between the pitcher's mound and home plate in baseball is 60 feet 6 inches.

though you belonged to this world or as though you were infants in the Christian life. [2]I had to feed you with milk, not with solid food, because you weren't ready for anything stronger. And you still aren't ready, [3]for you are still controlled by your sinful nature. You are jealous of one another and quarrel with each other. Doesn't that prove you are controlled by your sinful nature? Aren't you living like people of the world? [4]When one of you says, "I am a follower of Paul," and another says, "I follow Apollos," aren't you acting just like people of the world?

[5]After all, who is Apollos? Who is Paul? We are only God's servants through whom you believed the Good News. Each of us did the work the Lord gave us. [6]I planted the seed in your hearts, and Apollos watered it, but it was God who made it grow. [7]It's not important who does the planting, or who does the watering. What's important is that God makes the seed grow. [8]The one who plants and the one who waters work together with the same purpose. And both will be rewarded for their own hard work. [9]For we are both God's workers. And you are God's field. You are God's building.

[10]Because of God's grace to me, I have laid the foundation like an expert builder. Now others are building on it. But whoever is building on this foundation must be very careful. [11]For no one can lay any foundation other than the one we already have—Jesus Christ.

[12]Anyone who builds on that foundation may use a variety of materials—gold, silver, jewels, wood, hay, or straw. [13]But on the judgment day, fire will reveal what kind of work each builder has done. The fire will show if a person's work has any value. [14]If the work survives, that builder will receive a reward. [15]But if the work is burned up, the builder will suffer great loss. The builder will be saved, but like someone barely escaping through a wall of flames.

[16]Don't you realize that all of you together are the temple of God and that the Spirit of God lives in you? [17]God will destroy anyone who destroys this temple. For God's temple is holy, and you are that temple.

[18]Stop deceiving yourselves. If you think you are wise by this world's standards, you need to become a fool to be truly wise. [19]For the wisdom of this world is foolishness to God. As the Scriptures say,

"He traps the wise
in the snare of their own cleverness."

[20]And again,

"The LORD knows the thoughts of the wise;
he knows they are worthless."

[21]So don't boast about following a particular human leader. For everything belongs to you—[22]whether Paul or Apollos or Peter, or the world, or life and death, or the present and the future. Everything belongs to you, [23]and you belong to Christ, and Christ belongs to God.

action

2:14-15 WHAT'S IT SAYING?

WHAT AM I GOING TO DO ABOUT IT?

Paul's Relationship with the Corinthians

4

So look at Apollos and me as mere servants of Christ who have been put in charge of explaining God's mysteries. [2]Now, a person who is put in charge as a manager must be faithful. [3]As for me, it matters very little how I might be evaluated by you or by any human authority. I don't even trust my own judgment on this point. [4]My conscience is clear, but that doesn't prove I'm right. It is the Lord himself who will examine me and decide.

[5]So don't make judgments about anyone ahead of time—before the Lord returns. For he will bring our darkest secrets to light and will reveal our private motives. Then God will give to each one whatever praise is due.

WHAT DOES IT MEAN?

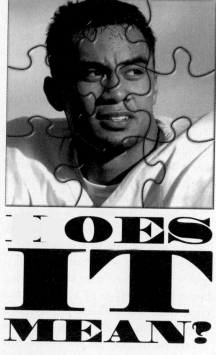

apostle

It is generally agreed to be the body of disciples to whom Jesus entrusted his church and the spreading of his gospel — the Twelve, as they are called (Matthew 10:1-5; Mark 3:14; 6:7; Luke 6:13; 9:1). We have four lists of the apostles, one by each of the synoptic evangelists (Matthew 10:2-4; Mark 3:16-19; Luke 6:14-16) and one in Acts (1:13). Our Lord gave them the keys of the kingdom and by the gift of his Spirit fitted them to be the founders and governors of his church (John 14:16-17, 26; 15:26-27; 16:7-15). Another qualification for apostles was the authority to work miracles (Mark 16:20; Acts 2:43; 1 Corinthians 12:8-11).

[6]Dear brothers and sisters, I have used Apollos and myself to illustrate what I've been saying. If you pay attention to what I have quoted from the Scriptures, you won't be proud of one of your leaders at the expense of another. [7]For what gives you the right to make such a judgment? What do you have that God hasn't given you? And if everything you have is from God, why boast as though it were not a gift?

[8]You think you already have everything you need. You think you are already rich. You have begun to reign in God's kingdom without us! I wish you really were reigning already, for then we would be reigning with you. [9]Instead, I sometimes think God has put us apostles on display, like prisoners of war at the end of a victor's parade, condemned to die. We have become a spectacle to the entire world—to people and angels alike.

[10]Our dedication to Christ makes us look like fools, but you claim to be so wise in Christ! We are weak, but you are so powerful! You are honored, but we are ridiculed. [11]Even now we go hungry and thirsty, and we don't have enough clothes to keep warm. We are often beaten and have no home. [12]We work wearily with our own hands to earn our living. We bless those who curse us. We are patient with those who abuse us. [13]We appeal gently when evil things are said about us. Yet we are treated like the world's garbage, like everybody's trash—right up to the present moment. [14]I am not writing these things to shame you, but to warn you as my beloved children. [15]For even if you had ten thousand others to teach you about Christ, you have only one spiritual father. For I became your father in Christ Jesus when I preached the Good News to you. [16]So I urge you to imitate me.

[17]That's why I have sent Timothy, my beloved and faithful child in the Lord. He will remind you of how I follow Christ Jesus, just as I teach in all the churches wherever I go.

[18]Some of you have become arrogant, thinking I will not visit you again. [19]But I will come—and soon—if the Lord lets me, and then I'll find out whether these arrogant people just give pretentious speeches or whether they really have God's power. [20]For the Kingdom of God is not just a lot of talk; it is living by God's power. [21]Which do you choose? Should I come with a rod to punish you, or should I come with love and a gentle spirit?

Paul Condemns Spiritual Pride

5

I can hardly believe the report about the sexual immorality going on among you—something that even pagans don't do. I am told that a man in your church is living in sin with his stepmother. [2]You are so proud of yourselves, but you should be mourning in sorrow and shame. And you should remove this man from your fellowship.

[3]Even though I am not with you in person, I am with you in the Spirit. And as though I were there, I have already passed judgment on this man [4]in the name of the Lord Jesus. You must call a meeting of the church. I will be present with you in spirit, and so will the power of our Lord Jesus. [5]Then you must throw this man out and hand him over to Satan so that his sinful nature will be destroyed and he himself will be saved on the day the Lord returns.

[6]Your boasting about this is terrible. Don't you realize that this sin is like a little yeast that spreads through the whole batch of dough? [7]Get rid of the old "yeast" by removing this wicked person from among you. Then you will be like a fresh batch of dough made without yeast, which is what you really are. Christ, our Passover Lamb, has been sacrificed for us. [8]So let us celebrate the festival, not with the old bread of wickedness and evil, but with the new bread of sincerity and truth.

[9]When I wrote to you before, I told you not to associate with people who indulge in sexual sin. [10]But I wasn't talking about unbelievers who indulge in sexual sin, or are greedy, or cheat

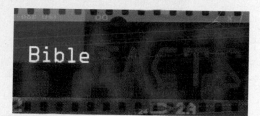

The Bible contains 66 books written by over 40 different authors with one central theme.

people, or worship idols. You would have to leave this world to avoid people like that. [11]I meant that you are not to associate with anyone who claims to be a believer yet indulges in sexual sin, or is greedy, or worships idols, or is abusive, or is a drunkard, or cheats people. Don't even eat with such people.

[12]It isn't my responsibility to judge outsiders, but it certainly is your responsibility to judge those inside the church who are sinning. [13]God will judge those on the outside; but as the Scriptures say, "You must remove the evil person from among you."

Avoiding Lawsuits with Christians

6

When one of you has a dispute with another believer, how dare you file a lawsuit and ask a secular court to decide the matter instead of taking it to other believers! [2]Don't you realize that someday we believers will judge the world? And

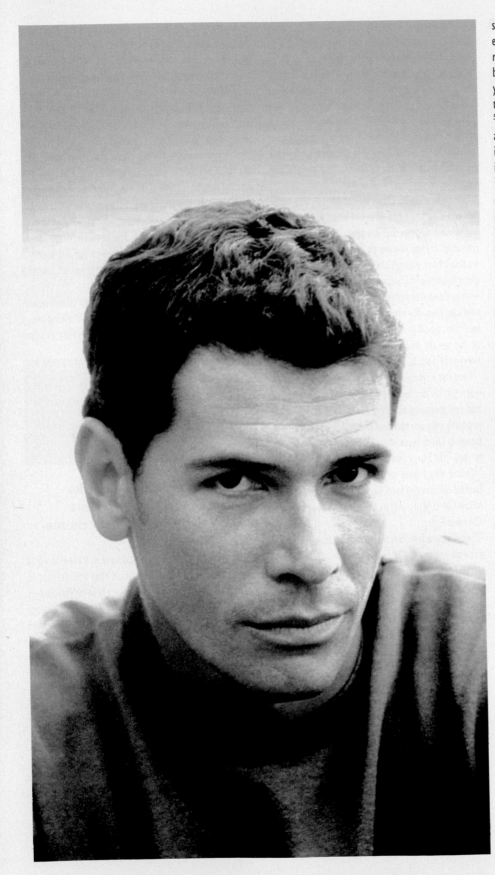

since you are going to judge the world, can't you decide even these little things among yourselves? ³Don't you realize that we will judge angels? So you should surely be able to resolve ordinary disputes in this life. ⁴If you have legal disputes about such matters, why go to outside judges who are not respected by the church? ⁵I am saying this to shame you. Isn't there anyone in all the church who is wise enough to decide these issues? ⁶But instead, one believer sues another—right in front of unbelievers!

⁷Even to have such lawsuits with one another is a defeat for you. Why not just accept the injustice and leave it at that? Why not let yourselves be cheated? ⁸Instead, you yourselves are the ones who do wrong and cheat even your fellow believers.

⁹Don't you realize that those who do wrong will not inherit the Kingdom of God? Don't fool yourselves. Those who indulge in sexual sin, or who worship idols, or commit adultery, or are male prostitutes, or practice homosexuality, ¹⁰or are thieves, or greedy people, or drunkards, or are abusive, or cheat people—none of these will inherit the Kingdom of God. ¹¹Some of you were once like that. But you were cleansed; you were made holy; you were made right with God by calling on the name of the Lord Jesus Christ and by the Spirit of our God.

action

5:9-12 WHAT'S IT SAYING?

WHAT AM I GOING TO DO ABOUT IT?

Avoiding Sexual Sin

[12]You say, "I am allowed to do anything"—but not everything is good for you. And even though "I am allowed to do anything," I must not become a slave to anything. [13]You say, "Food was made for the stomach, and the stomach for food." (This is true, though someday God will do away with both of them.) But you can't say that our bodies were made for sexual immorality. They were made for the Lord, and the Lord cares about our bodies. [14]And God will raise us from the dead by his power, just as he raised our Lord from the dead.

[15]Don't you realize that your bodies are actually parts of Christ? Should a man take his body, which is part of Christ, and join it to a prostitute? Never! [16]And don't you realize that if a man joins himself to a prostitute, he becomes one body with her? For the Scriptures say, "The two are united into one." [17]But the person who is joined to the Lord is one spirit with him.

[18]Run from sexual sin! No other sin so clearly affects the body as this one does. For sexual immorality is a sin against your own body. [19]Don't you realize that your body is the temple of the Holy Spirit, who lives in you and was given to you by God? You do not belong to yourself, [20]for God bought you with a high price. So you must honor God with your body.

Instruction on Marriage

7

Now regarding the questions you asked in your letter. Yes, it is good to live a celibate life. [2]But because there is so much sexual immorality, each man should have his own wife, and each woman should have her own husband.

[3]The husband should fulfill his wife's sexual needs, and the wife should fulfill her husband's needs. [4]The wife gives authority over her body to her husband, and the husband gives authority over his body to his wife.

[5]Do not deprive each other of sexual relations, unless you both agree to refrain from sexual intimacy for a limited time so you can give yourselves more completely to prayer. Afterward, you should come together again so that Satan won't be able to tempt you because of your lack of self-control. [6]I say this as a concession, not as a command. [7]But I wish everyone were single, just as I am. But God gives to some the gift of marriage, and to others the gift of singleness.

[8]So I say to those who aren't married and to widows—it's better to stay unmarried, just as I am. [9]But if they can't control themselves, they should go ahead and marry. It's better to marry than to burn with lust.

6:18-20 WHAT'S IT SAYING?

WHAT AM I GOING TO DO ABOUT IT?

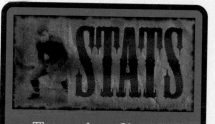

The modern Olympic Games were held for the first time in 1896 in Athens and were followed by the 1900 Paris games. The winter games were added in 1924.

Can sport really be a ministry? Shouldn't I give up my sport and go into missionary work if I am serious about Christ?

Famous English cricket player C. T. Studd said, "Some want to live within the sound of church or chapel bell, I want to run a rescue shop within a yard of hell."

Everything you do should be given up to God. What does it mean to give up everything? Does it, for instance, mean that all of us who love sports should quit playing? It has often been understood in this way, especially if it involves a Sunday sport. Surely what Jesus is getting at is that a real disciple must give Christ full control over his whole life, with everything he is and all that he possesses — including his wealth and his talents. We who are passionate about our sport and our Lord must be prepared to pray, "Lord, I will continue in my sport only if you want me to." There is no point, absolutely no point, in the Christian doing anything that is outside God's will and purpose. Let us get to the place where we put everything into God's hands. He will lead us — some maybe to be missionaries and others to wholehearted discipleship within the culture-shaping arena of sports. Perhaps in a way we are all missionaries. Who best to reach a teammate for Christ than a fellow teammate?

¹⁰But for those who are married, I have a command that comes not from me, but from the Lord. A wife must not leave her husband. ¹¹But if she does leave him, let her remain single or else be reconciled to him. And the husband must not leave his wife.

¹²Now, I will speak to the rest of you, though I do not have a direct command from the Lord. If a Christian man has a wife who is not a believer and she is willing to continue living with him, he must not leave her. ¹³And if a Christian woman has a husband who is not a believer and he is willing to continue living with her, she must not leave him. ¹⁴For the Christian wife brings holiness to her marriage, and the Christian husband brings holiness to his marriage. Otherwise, your children would not be holy, but now they are holy. ¹⁵(But if the husband or wife who isn't a believer insists on leaving, let them go. In such cases the Christian husband or wife is no longer bound to the other, for God has called you to live in peace.) ¹⁶Don't you wives realize that your husbands might be saved because of you? And don't you husbands realize that your wives might be saved because of you?

¹⁷Each of you should continue to live in whatever situation the Lord has placed you, and remain as you were when God first called you. This is my rule for all the churches. ¹⁸For instance, a man who was circumcised before he became a believer should not try to reverse it. And the man who was uncircumcised when he became a believer should not be

that can be trusted, and I will share it with you. ²⁶Because of the present crisis, I think it is best to remain as you are. ²⁷If you have a wife, do not seek to end the marriage. If you do not have a wife, do not seek to get married. ²⁸But if you do get married, it is not a sin. And if a young woman gets married, it is not a sin. However, those who get married at this time will have troubles, and I am trying to spare you those problems.

²⁹But let me say this, dear brothers and sisters: The time that remains is very short. So from now on, those with wives should not focus only on their marriage. ³⁰Those who weep or who rejoice or who buy things should not be absorbed by their weeping or their joy or their possessions. ³¹Those who use the things of the world should not become attached to them. For this world as we know it will soon pass away.

³²I want you to be free from the concerns of this life. An unmarried man can spend his time doing the Lord's work and thinking how to please him. ³³But a married man has to think about his earthly responsibilities and how to please his wife. ³⁴His interests are divided. In the same way, a woman who is no longer married or has never been married can be devoted to the Lord and holy in body and in spirit. But a married woman has to think about her earthly responsibilities and

opinion it would be better for her to stay single, and I think I am giving you counsel from God's Spirit when I say this.

Food Sacrificed to Idols

8

Now regarding your question about food that has been offered to idols. Yes, we know that "we all have knowledge" about this issue. But while knowledge makes us feel important, it is love that strengthens the church. ²Anyone who claims to know all the answers doesn't really know very much. ³But the person who loves God is the one whom God recognizes. ⁴So, what about eating meat that has been offered to idols? Well, we all know that an idol is not really a god and that there is only one God. ⁵There may be so-called gods both in heaven and on earth, and some people actually worship many gods and many lords. ⁶But we know that there is only one God, the Father, who created everything, and we live for him. And there is only one Lord, Jesus Christ, through whom God made everything and through whom we have been given life.

⁷However, not all believers know this. Some are accustomed to thinking of idols as being real, so when

TIPS

I don't get it:

When you do not know the answer to a question, admit it. Asking questions shows you are interested in improving. Don't waste the coach's time or yours by pretending you understand when you don't.

circumcised now. ¹⁹For it makes no difference whether or not a man has been circumcised. The important thing is to keep God's commandments.

²⁰Yes, each of you should remain as you were when God called you. ²¹Are you a slave? Don't let that worry you—but if you get a chance to be free, take it. ²²And remember, if you were a slave when the Lord called you, you are now free in the Lord. And if you were free when the Lord called you, you are now a slave of Christ. ²³God paid a high price for you, so don't be enslaved by the world. ²⁴Each of you, dear brothers and sisters, should remain as you were when God first called you.

²⁵Now regarding your question about the young women who are not yet married. I do not have a command from the Lord for them. But the Lord in his mercy has given me wisdom

how to please her husband. ³⁵I am saying this for your benefit, not to place restrictions on you. I want you to do whatever will help you serve the Lord best, with as few distractions as possible.

³⁶But if a man thinks that he's treating his fiancée improperly and will inevitably give in to his passion, let him marry her as he wishes. It is not a sin. ³⁷But if he has decided firmly not to marry and there is no urgency and he can control his passion, he does well not to marry. ³⁸So the person who marries his fiancée does well, and the person who doesn't marry does even better.

³⁹A wife is bound to her husband as long as he lives. If her husband dies, she is free to marry anyone she wishes, but only if he loves the Lord. ⁴⁰But in my

they eat food that has been offered to idols, they think of it as the worship of real gods, and their weak consciences are violated. ⁸It's true that we can't win God's approval by what we eat. We don't lose anything if we don't eat it, and we don't gain anything if we do.

⁹But you must be careful so that your freedom does not cause others with a weaker conscience to stumble. ¹⁰For if others see you—with your "superior knowledge"—eating in the temple of an idol, won't they be encouraged to violate their conscience by eating food that has been offered to an idol? ¹¹So because of your superior knowledge, a weak believer for whom Christ died will be destroyed. ¹²And when you sin against other believers by encouraging them

to do something they believe is wrong, you are sinning against Christ. [13]So if what I eat causes another believer to sin, I will never eat meat again as long as I live—for I don't want to cause another believer to stumble.

8:7-13 WHAT'S IT SAYING?

WHAT AM I GOING TO DO ABOUT IT?

Paul Gives Up His Rights

9

Am I not as free as anyone else? Am I not an apostle? Haven't I seen Jesus our Lord with my own eyes? Isn't it because of my work that you belong to the Lord?

[2]Even if others think I am not an apostle, I certainly am to you. You yourselves are proof that I am the Lord's apostle.

[3]This is my answer to those who question my authority. [4]Don't we have the right to live in your homes and share your meals? [5]Don't we have the right to bring a Christian wife with us as the other disciples and the Lord's brothers do, and as Peter does? [6]Or is it only Barnabas and I who have to work to support ourselves? [7]What soldier has to pay his own expenses? What farmer plants a vineyard and doesn't have the right to eat some of its fruit? What shepherd cares for a flock of sheep and isn't allowed to drink some of the milk? [8]Am I expressing merely a human opinion, or does the law say the same thing? [9]For the law of Moses says, "You must not muzzle an ox to keep it from eating as it treads out the grain." Was God thinking only about oxen when he said this? [10]Wasn't he actually speaking to us? Yes, it was written for us, so that the one who plows and the one who threshes the grain might both expect a share of the harvest. [11]Since we have planted spiritual seed among you, aren't we entitled to a harvest of physical food and drink? [12]If you support others who preach to you, shouldn't we have an even greater right to be supported? But we have never used this right. We would rather put up with anything than be an obstacle to the Good News about Christ.

[13]Don't you realize that those who work in the temple get their meals from the offerings brought to the temple? And those who serve at the altar get a share of the sacrificial offerings. [14]In the same way, the Lord ordered that those who preach the Good News should be supported by those who benefit from it. [15]Yet I have never used any of these rights. And I am not writing this to suggest that I want to start now. In fact, I would rather die than lose my right to boast about preaching without charge. [16]Yet preaching the Good News is not something I can boast about. I am compelled by God to do it. How terrible for me if I didn't preach the Good News!

[17]If I were doing this on my own initiative, I would deserve payment. But I have no choice, for God has given me this sacred trust. [18]What then is my pay? It is the opportunity to preach the Good News without charging anyone. That's why I never demand my rights when I preach the Good News.

[19]Even though I am a free man with no master, I have become a slave to all people to bring many to Christ. [20]When I was with the Jews, I lived like a Jew to bring the Jews to Christ. When I was with those who follow the Jewish law, I too lived under that law. Even though I am not subject to the law, I did this so I could bring to Christ those who are under the law. [21]When I am with the Gentiles who do not follow the Jewish law, I too live apart from that law so I can bring them to Christ. But I do not ignore the law of God; I obey the law of Christ.

[22]When I am with those who are weak, I share their weakness, for I want to bring the weak to Christ. Yes, I try to find common ground with everyone, doing everything I can to save some. [23]I do everything to spread the Good News and share in its blessings.

[24]Don't you realize that in a race everyone runs, but only one person gets the prize? So run to win! [25]All athletes are disciplined in their training. They do it to win a prize that will fade away, but we do it for an eternal prize. [26]So I run with purpose in every step. I am not just shadowboxing. [27]I discipline my body like an athlete, training it to do what it should. Otherwise, I fear that after preaching to others I myself might be disqualified.

Lessons from Israel's Idolatry

10

I don't want you to forget, dear brothers and sisters, about our ancestors in the wilderness long ago. All of them were guided by a cloud that moved ahead of them, and all of

Winners have fun!

God loves to watch his creation enjoying life! Some people think God's job is finding people who are having a good time and then saying, "Stop doing that!" The truth is our life is the most fun when we stay on God's path. A great pro once said, "I do not want to cheat, because I want to feel good about myself." Trying to keep on God's path is not easy, but it is the best, and wrong turns are no fun at all!

"Whoever abandons the right path will be severely disciplined; whoever hates correction will die." (Proverbs 15:10)

Winners stay on the path!

When you are tempted to cheat

10:13

The temptations in your life are no different from what others experience. And God is faithful. He will not allow the temptation to be more than you can stand. When you are tempted, he will show you a way out so that you can endure.

them walked through the sea on dry ground. [2]In the cloud and in the sea, all of them were baptized as followers of Moses. [3]All of them ate the same spiritual food, [4]and all of them drank the same spiritual water. For they drank from the spiritual rock that traveled with them, and that rock was Christ. [5]Yet God was not pleased with most of them, and their bodies were scattered in the wilderness.

[6]These things happened as a warning to us, so that we would not crave evil things as they did, [7]or worship idols as some of them did. As the Scriptures say, "The people celebrated with feasting and drinking, and they indulged in pagan revelry." [8]And we must not engage in sexual immorality as some of them did, causing 23,000 of them to die in one day. [9]Nor should we put Christ to the test, as some of them did and then died from snakebites. [10]And don't grumble as some of them did, and then were destroyed by the angel of death. [11]These things happened to them as examples for us. They were written down to warn us who live at the end of the age. [12]If you think you are standing strong, be careful not to fall. [13]The temptations in your life are no different from what others experience. And God is faithful. He will not allow the temptation to be more than you can stand. When you are tempted, he will show you a way out so that you can endure. [14]So, my dear friends, flee from the worship of idols. [15]You are reasonable people. Decide for yourselves if what I am saying is true. [16]When we bless the cup at the Lord's Table, aren't we sharing in the blood of Christ? And when we break the bread, aren't we sharing in the body of Christ? [17]And though we are many, we all eat from one loaf of bread, showing that we are one body. [18]Think about the people of Israel. Weren't they united by eating the sacrifices at the altar?

[19]What am I trying to say? Am I saying that food offered to idols has some significance, or that idols are real gods? [20]No, not at all. I am saying that these sacrifices are offered to demons, not to God. And I don't want you to participate with demons. [21]You cannot drink from the cup of the Lord and from the cup of demons, too. You cannot eat at the Lord's Table and at the table of demons, too. [22]What? Do we dare to rouse the Lord's jealousy? Do you think we are stronger than he is?

[23]You say, "I am allowed to do anything"—but not everything is good for you. You say, "I am allowed to do anything"—but not everything is beneficial. [24]Don't be concerned for your own good but for the good of others.

[25]So you may eat any meat that is sold in the marketplace without raising questions of conscience. [26]For "the earth is the LORD's, and everything in it." [27]If someone who isn't a believer asks you home for dinner, accept the invitation if you want to. Eat whatever is offered to you without raising questions of conscience. [28](But suppose someone tells you, "This meat was offered to an idol." Don't eat it, out of consideration for the conscience of the one who told you. [29]It might not be a matter of conscience for you, but it is for the other person.) For why should my freedom be limited by what someone else thinks? [30]If I can thank God for the food and enjoy it, why should I be condemned for eating it?

[31]So whether you eat or drink, or whatever you do, do it all for the glory of God. [32]Don't give offense to Jews or Gentiles or the church of God. [33]I, too, try to please everyone in everything I do. I don't just do what is best for me; I do what is best for others so that many may be saved.

action

10:22-24 WHAT'S IT SAYING?

WHAT AM I GOING TO DO ABOUT IT?

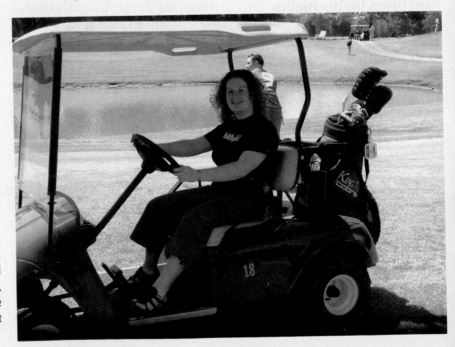

profiles

Deception and Conspiracy, Herod, Pilate and the Jewish Council

Herod Antipas

inherited his power and kingdom along with three other half brothers from his father, Herod the Great. His 1/4 empire was the region of Galilee north of Jerusalem (approximately 40 miles), where Jesus spent his boyhood and early ministry. Herod, who had a partial Jewish upbringing, was shamed by John the Baptist for marrying his brother's wife. Herod, though he liked John, eventually had him beheaded. When Herod heard of Jesus, he immediately thought that it was John coming back to haunt him. Herod, like many others from the outer regions, was in the Holy City to celebrate Passover when he briefly encountered Jesus.

Pilate

was a Roman governor and a corrupt career politician. His rule over Jerusalem, which could be a fragile powder keg of a city, was shaky. He was a weak man who would make judgments not by a code of ethics but by his own selfish interests. Pilate was obviously intimidated by the Jewish council and tried to pacify them and intimidate them at the same time.

Jewish Council

The Jews in Jerusalem were under authority of the occupying power of Rome. The Jewish council had limited power and could not execute anyone without the express authority of Rome. They saw Jesus as a threat to their power and way of life, yet they could not crucify Jesus unless they had it approved by Pilate, who represented Rome. So Jesus went from the Jewish council to Pilate to Herod and back to Pilate. He was never found guilty of anything, but through the pressure put on Pilate he was handed over for execution.

11

¹And you should imitate me, just as I imitate Christ.

Instructions for Public Worship

²I am so glad that you always keep me in your thoughts, and that you are following the teachings I passed on to you. ³But there is one thing I want you to know: The head of every man is Christ, the head of woman is man, and the head of Christ is God. ⁴A man dishonors his head if he covers his head while praying or prophesying. ⁵But a woman dishonors her head if she prays or prophesies without a covering on her head, for this is the same as shaving her head. ⁶Yes, if she refuses to wear a head covering, she should cut off all her hair! But since it is shameful for a woman to have her hair cut or her head shaved, she should wear a covering.

⁷A man should not wear anything on his head when worshiping, for man is made in God's image and reflects God's glory. And woman reflects man's glory. ⁸For the first man didn't come from woman, but the first woman came from man. ⁹And man was not made for woman, but woman was made for man. ¹⁰For this reason, and because the angels are watching, a woman should wear a covering on her head to show she is under authority.

¹¹But among the Lord's people, women are not independent of men, and men are not independent of women. ¹²For although the first woman came from man, every other man was born from a woman, and everything comes from God. ¹³Judge for yourselves. Is it right for a woman to pray to God in public without covering her head? ¹⁴Isn't it obvious that it's disgraceful for a man to have long hair? ¹⁵And isn't long hair a woman's pride and joy? For it has been given to her as a covering. ¹⁶But if anyone wants to argue about this, I simply say that we have no other custom than this, and neither do God's other churches.

Order at the Lord's Supper

¹⁷But in the following instructions, I cannot praise you. For it sounds as if more harm than good is done when you meet together. ¹⁸First, I hear that there are divisions among you when you meet as a church, and to some extent I believe it. ¹⁹But, of course, there must be divisions among you so that you who have God's approval will be recognized! ²⁰When you meet together, you are not really interested in the Lord's Supper. ²¹For some of you hurry to eat your own meal without sharing with others. As a result, some go hungry while others get drunk. ²²What? Don't you have your own homes for eating and drinking? Or do you really want to disgrace God's church and shame the poor? What am I supposed to say? Do you want me to praise you? Well, I certainly will not praise you for this!

²³For I pass on to you what I received from the Lord himself. On the night when he was betrayed, the Lord Jesus took some bread ²⁴and gave thanks to God for it. Then he broke it in pieces and said, "This is my body, which is given for you. Do this to remember me." ²⁵In the same way, he took the cup of wine after supper, saying, "This cup is the new covenant between God and his people—an agreement confirmed with my blood. Do this to remember me as often as you drink it." ²⁶For every time you eat this bread and drink this cup, you are announcing the Lord's death until he comes again.

²⁷So anyone who eats this bread or drinks this cup of the Lord unworthily is guilty of sinning against the body and blood of the Lord. ²⁸That is why you should examine yourself before eating the bread and drinking the cup. ²⁹For if you eat the bread or drink the cup without honoring the body of Christ, you are eating and drinking God's judgment upon yourself. ³⁰That is why many of you are weak and sick and some have even died.

³¹But if we would examine ourselves, we would not be judged by God in this way. ³²Yet when we are judged by the Lord, we are being disciplined so that we will not be condemned along with the world.

³³So, my dear brothers and sisters, when you gather for the Lord's Supper, wait for each other. ³⁴If you are really hungry, eat at home so you won't bring judgment upon yourselves when you meet together. I'll give you instructions about the other matters after I arrive.

Spiritual Gifts

12

Now, dear brothers and sisters, regarding your question about the special abilities the Spirit gives us. I don't want you to misunderstand this. ²You know

Bible

The entire Bible was written over a 1500-year span.

that when you were still pagans, you were led astray and swept along in worshiping speechless idols. ³So I want you to know that no one speaking by the Spirit of God will curse Jesus, and no one can say Jesus is Lord, except by the Holy Spirit.

⁴There are different kinds of spiritual gifts, but the same Spirit is the source of them all. ⁵There are different kinds of service, but we serve the same Lord. ⁶God works in different ways, but it is the same God who does the work in all of us.

⁷A spiritual gift is given to each of us so we can help each other. ⁸To one person the Spirit gives the ability to give wise advice; to another the same Spirit gives a message of special knowledge. ⁹The same Spirit gives great faith to another, and to someone else the one Spirit gives the gift of healing. ¹⁰He gives one person the power to perform miracles, and another the ability to prophesy. He gives someone else the ability to discern whether a message is from the Spirit of God or from another spirit. Still another person is given the ability to speak in unknown languages, while another is given the ability to interpret what is being said. ¹¹It is the one and only Spirit who distributes all these gifts. He alone decides which gift each person should have.

One Body with Many Parts

¹²The human body has many parts, but the many parts make up one whole body. So it is with the body of Christ. ¹³Some of us are Jews, some are Gentiles, some are slaves, and some are free. But we have all been baptized into one body by one Spirit, and we all share the same Spirit.

¹⁴Yes, the body has many different parts, not just one part. ¹⁵If the foot says, "I am not a part of the body because I am not a hand," that does not make it any less a part of the body. ¹⁶And if the ear says, "I am not part of the body because I am not an eye," would that make it any less a part of the body? ¹⁷If the whole body were an eye, how would you hear? Or if your whole body were an ear, how would you smell anything?

¹⁸But our bodies have many parts, and God has put each part just where he wants it. ¹⁹How strange a body would be if it had only one part! ²⁰Yes, there are many parts, but only one body. ²¹The eye can never say to the hand, "I don't need you." The head can't say to the feet, "I don't need you."

²²In fact, some parts of the body that seem weakest and least important are actually the most necessary. ²³And the parts we regard as less honorable are those we clothe with the greatest care. So we carefully

count on it

Do you want to be cool?

Cool under pressure. There are many who just have that touch — a gift that keeps them in the zone and focused. God does not promise that he will give you every physical gift in the world. He doesn't promise that you will get faster or taller — he is not some genie in a bottle. But he does promise peace under pressure. "I am leaving you with a gift — peace of mind and heart. And the peace I give is a gift the world cannot give. So don't be troubled or afraid." (John 14:27)

Count on it!

protect those parts that should not be seen, ²⁴while the more honorable parts do not require this special care. So God has put the body together such that extra honor and care are given to those parts that have less dignity. ²⁵This makes for harmony among the members, so that all the members care for each other. ²⁶If one part suffers, all the parts suffer with it, and if one part is honored, all the parts are glad.

²⁷All of you together are Christ's body, and each of you is a part of it. ²⁸Here are some of the parts God has appointed for the church:

first are apostles,

second are prophets,

third are teachers,

then those who do miracles,

those who have the gift of healing,

those who can help others,

those who have the gift of leadership,

those who speak in unknown languages.

²⁹Are we all apostles? Are we all prophets? Are we all teachers? Do we all have the power to do miracles? ³⁰Do we all have the gift of healing? Do we all have the ability to speak in unknown languages? Do we all have the ability to interpret unknown languages? Of course not! ³¹So you should earnestly desire the most helpful gifts.

But now let me show you a way of life that is best of all.

action

12:12-31 WHAT'S IT SAYING?

WHAT AM I GOING TO DO ABOUT IT?

Love Is the Greatest

13

If I could speak all the languages of earth and of angels, but didn't love others, I would only be a noisy gong or a clanging cymbal. ²If I had the gift of prophecy, and if I understood all of God's secret plans and possessed all knowledge, and if I had such faith that I could move mountains, but didn't love others, I would be nothing. ³If I gave everything I have to the poor and even sacrificed my body, I could boast about it; but if I didn't love others, I would have gained nothing.

⁴Love is patient and kind. Love is not jealous or boastful or proud ⁵or rude. It does not demand its own way. It is not irritable, and it keeps no record of being wronged. ⁶It does not rejoice about injustice but rejoices whenever the truth

wins out. [7]Love never gives up, never loses faith, is always hopeful, and endures through every circumstance.

[8]Prophecy and speaking in unknown languages and special knowledge will become useless. But love will last forever! [9]Now our knowledge is partial and incomplete, and even the gift of prophecy reveals only part of the whole picture! [10]But when full understanding comes, these partial things will become useless.

[11]When I was a child, I spoke and thought and reasoned as a child. But when I grew up, I put away childish things. [12]Now we see things imperfectly as in a cloudy mirror, but then we will see everything with perfect clarity. All that I know now is partial and incomplete, but then I will know everything completely, just as God now knows me completely.

[13]Three things will last forever—faith, hope, and love—and the greatest of these is love.

Tongues and Prophecy

14

Let love be your highest goal! But you should also desire the special abilities the Spirit gives—especially the ability to prophesy. [2]For if you have the ability to speak in tongues, you will be talking only to God, since people won't be able to understand you. You will be speaking by the power of the Spirit, but it will all be mysterious. [3]But one who prophesies strengthens others, encourages them, and comforts them. [4]A person who speaks in tongues is strengthened personally, but one who speaks a word of prophecy strengthens the entire church.

[5]I wish you could all speak in tongues, but even more I wish you could all prophesy. For prophecy is greater than speaking in tongues, unless someone interprets

PERSONAL ASSESSMENTS

WHEN I BLOW IT!

Answer this assessment with T (true) or F (false).

When I blow it (a sin; veering from God's way — not a mistake like a spelling error), I generally:

☐ Ignore it and hope it goes away.

☐ Blame others.

☐ Wallow in self-pity and feel sorry for myself.

☐ Take pride in being a screwup.

☐ Learn from it.

☐ Become overwhelmed by guilt.

☐ Feel bad but in time move on.

☐ Ask forgiveness when it concerns others.

☐ Ask God to forgive me.

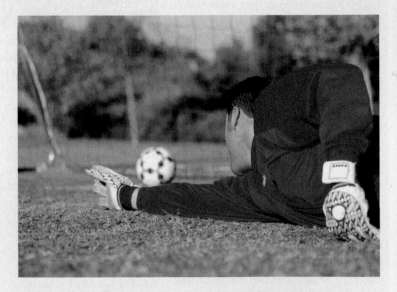

"For the kind of sorrow God wants us to experience leads us away from sin and results in salvation. There's no regret for that kind of sorrow. But worldly sorrow, which lacks repentance, results in spiritual death."
(2 Corinthians 7:10)

what you are saying so that the whole church will be strengthened.

[6]Dear brothers and sisters, if I should come to you speaking in an unknown language, how would that help you? But if I bring you a revelation or some special knowledge or prophecy or teaching, that will be helpful. [7]Even lifeless instruments like the flute or the harp must play the notes clearly, or no one will recognize the melody. [8]And if the bugler doesn't sound a clear call, how will the soldiers know they are being called to battle?

[9]It's the same for you. If you speak to people in words they don't understand, how will they know what you are saying? You might as well be talking into empty space.

[10]There are many different languages in the world, and every language has meaning. [11]But if I don't understand a language, I will be a foreigner to someone who speaks it, and the one who speaks it will be a foreigner to me. [12]And the same is true for you. Since you are so eager to have the special abilities the Spirit gives, seek those that will strengthen the whole church.

[13]So anyone who speaks in tongues should pray also for the ability to interpret what has been said. [14]For if I pray in tongues, my spirit is praying, but I don't understand what I am saying.

[15]Well then, what shall I do? I will pray in the spirit, and I will also pray in words I understand. I will sing in the spirit, and I will also sing in words I understand. [16]For if you praise God only in the spirit, how can those who don't understand you praise God along with you? How can they join you in giving thanks when they don't understand what you are saying? [17]You will be giving thanks very well, but it won't strengthen the people who hear you.

[18]I thank God that I speak in tongues more than any of you. [19]But in a church meeting I would rather speak five understandable words to help others than ten thousand words in an unknown language.

[20]Dear brothers and sisters, don't be childish in your understanding of these things. Be innocent as babies when it comes to evil, but be mature in understanding matters of this kind. [21]It is written in the Scriptures:

"I will speak to my own people
through strange languages
and through the lips of foreigners.
But even then, they will not listen to me,"
says the LORD.

[22]So you see that speaking in tongues is a sign, not for believers, but for unbelievers. Prophecy, however, is for the benefit of believers, not unbelievers. [23]Even so, if unbelievers or people who don't understand these things come into your church meeting and hear everyone speaking in an unknown language, they will

Who have been the five most influential people in your life?

1 _____
2 _____
3 _____
4 _____
5 _____

BIG FIVE

think you are crazy. [24]But if all of you are prophesying, and unbelievers or people who don't understand these things come into your meeting, they will be convicted of sin and judged by what you say. [25]As they listen, their secret thoughts will be exposed, and they will fall to their knees and worship God, declaring, "God is truly here among you."

A Call to Orderly Worship

[26]Well, my brothers and sisters, let's summarize. When you meet together, one will sing, another will teach, another will tell some special revelation God

The Olympic Games were held in St. Louis, Missouri, in 1904, the first time that the games were held in the United States.

has given, one will speak in tongues, and another will interpret what is said. But everything that is done must strengthen all of you.

[27]No more than two or three should speak in tongues. They must speak one at a time, and someone must interpret what they say. [28]But if no one is present who can interpret, they must be silent in your church meeting and speak in tongues to God privately.

[29]Let two or three people prophesy, and let the others evaluate what is said. [30]But if someone is prophesying and another person receives a revelation from the Lord, the one who is speaking must stop. [31]In this way, all who prophesy will have a turn to speak, one after the other, so that everyone will learn and be encouraged. [32]Remember that people who prophesy are in control of their spirit and can take turns. [33]For God is not a God of disorder but of peace, as in all the meetings of God's holy people.

[34]Women should be silent during the church meetings. It is not proper for them to speak. They should be submissive, just as the law says. [35]If they have any questions, they should ask their husbands at home, for it is improper for women to speak in church meetings.

[36]Or do you think God's word originated with you Corinthians? Are you the only ones to whom it was given? [37]If you claim to be a prophet or think you are spiritual, you should recognize that what I am saying is a command from the Lord himself. [38]But if you do not recognize this, you yourself will not be recognized.

[39]So, my dear brothers and sisters, be eager to prophesy, and don't forbid speaking in tongues. [40]But be sure that everything is done properly and in order.

AUGUST M.A.P.

1
S.D.	P.L.	P.G.	S.G.
P. ☐	F. ☐	F. ☐	T. ☐
F. ☐	W. ☐	W. ☐	P. ☐
B. ☐	P. ☐	C. ☐	C. ☐

2
S.D.	P.L.	P.G.	S.G.
P. ☐	F. ☐	F. ☐	T. ☐
F. ☐	W. ☐	W. ☐	P. ☐
B. ☐	P. ☐	C. ☐	C. ☐

3
S.D.	P.L.	P.G.	S.G.
P. ☐	F. ☐	F. ☐	T. ☐
F. ☐	W. ☐	W. ☐	P. ☐
B. ☐	P. ☐	C. ☐	C. ☐

4
S.D.	P.L.	P.G.	S.G.
P. ☐	F. ☐	F. ☐	T. ☐
F. ☐	W. ☐	W. ☐	P. ☐
B. ☐	P. ☐	C. ☐	C. ☐

9
S.D.	P.L.	P.G.	S.G.
P. ☐	F. ☐	F. ☐	T. ☐
F. ☐	W. ☐	W. ☐	P. ☐
B. ☐	P. ☐	C. ☐	C. ☐

10
S.D.	P.L.	P.G.	S.G.
P. ☐	F. ☐	F. ☐	T. ☐
F. ☐	W. ☐	W. ☐	P. ☐
B. ☐	P. ☐	C. ☐	C. ☐

11
S.D.	P.L.	P.G.	S.G.
P. ☐	F. ☐	F. ☐	T. ☐
F. ☐	W. ☐	W. ☐	P. ☐
B. ☐	P. ☐	C. ☐	C. ☐

12
S.D.	P.L.	P.G.	S.G.
P. ☐	F. ☐	F. ☐	T. ☐
F. ☐	W. ☐	W. ☐	P. ☐
B. ☐	P. ☐	C. ☐	C. ☐

17
S.D.	P.L.	P.G.	S.G.
P. ☐	F. ☐	F. ☐	T. ☐
F. ☐	W. ☐	W. ☐	P. ☐
B. ☐	P. ☐	C. ☐	C. ☐

18
S.D.	P.L.	P.G.	S.G.
P. ☐	F. ☐	F. ☐	T. ☐
F. ☐	W. ☐	W. ☐	P. ☐
B. ☐	P. ☐	C. ☐	C. ☐

19
S.D.	P.L.	P.G.	S.G.
P. ☐	F. ☐	F. ☐	T. ☐
F. ☐	W. ☐	W. ☐	P. ☐
B. ☐	P. ☐	C. ☐	C. ☐

20
S.D.	P.L.	P.G.	S.G.
P. ☐	F. ☐	F. ☐	T. ☐
F. ☐	W. ☐	W. ☐	P. ☐
B. ☐	P. ☐	C. ☐	C. ☐

25
S.D.	P.L.	P.G.	S.G.
P. ☐	F. ☐	F. ☐	T. ☐
F. ☐	W. ☐	W. ☐	P. ☐
B. ☐	P. ☐	C. ☐	C. ☐

26
S.D.	P.L.	P.G.	S.G.
P. ☐	F. ☐	F. ☐	T. ☐
F. ☐	W. ☐	W. ☐	P. ☐
B. ☐	P. ☐	C. ☐	C. ☐

27
S.D.	P.L.	P.G.	S.G.
P. ☐	F. ☐	F. ☐	T. ☐
F. ☐	W. ☐	W. ☐	P. ☐
B. ☐	P. ☐	C. ☐	C. ☐

28
S.D.	P.L.	P.G.	S.G.
P. ☐	F. ☐	F. ☐	T. ☐
F. ☐	W. ☐	W. ☐	P. ☐
B. ☐	P. ☐	C. ☐	C. ☐

Spiritual Disciplines

Prayer

Faith Community

Bible Reading

Prayer List

Friends

World

Personal

(For designing your M.A.P. – Monthly Action Plan – see introduction pages)

Who am I....
Where am I going....
How am I going to get there?

MONTHLY ACTION PLAN

5
S.D.	P.L.	P.G.	S.G.
P. ☐	F. ☐	F. ☐	T. ☐
F. ☐	W. ☐	W. ☐	P. ☐
B. ☐	P. ☐	C. ☐	C. ☐

6
S.D.	P.L.	P.G.	S.G.
P. ☐	F. ☐	F. ☐	T. ☐
F. ☐	W. ☐	W. ☐	P. ☐
B. ☐	P. ☐	C. ☐	C. ☐

7
S.D.	P.L.	P.G.	S.G.
P. ☐	F. ☐	F. ☐	T. ☐
F. ☐	W. ☐	W. ☐	P. ☐
B. ☐	P. ☐	C. ☐	C. ☐

8
S.D.	P.L.	P.G.	S.G.
P. ☐	F. ☐	F. ☐	T. ☐
F. ☐	W. ☐	W. ☐	P. ☐
B. ☐	P. ☐	C. ☐	C. ☐

13
S.D.	P.L.	P.G.	S.G.
P. ☐	F. ☐	F. ☐	T. ☐
F. ☐	W. ☐	W. ☐	P. ☐
B. ☐	P. ☐	C. ☐	C. ☐

14
S.D.	P.L.	P.G.	S.G.
P. ☐	F. ☐	F. ☐	T. ☐
F. ☐	W. ☐	W. ☐	P. ☐
B. ☐	P. ☐	C. ☐	C. ☐

15
S.D.	P.L.	P.G.	S.G.
P. ☐	F. ☐	F. ☐	T. ☐
F. ☐	W. ☐	W. ☐	P. ☐
B. ☐	P. ☐	C. ☐	C. ☐

16
S.D.	P.L.	P.G.	S.G.
P. ☐	F. ☐	F. ☐	T. ☐
F. ☐	W. ☐	W. ☐	P. ☐
B. ☐	P. ☐	C. ☐	C. ☐

21
S.D.	P.L.	P.G.	S.G.
P. ☐	F. ☐	F. ☐	T. ☐
F. ☐	W. ☐	W. ☐	P. ☐
B. ☐	P. ☐	C. ☐	C. ☐

22
S.D.	P.L.	P.G.	S.G.
P. ☐	F. ☐	F. ☐	T. ☐
F. ☐	W. ☐	W. ☐	P. ☐
B. ☐	P. ☐	C. ☐	C. ☐

23
S.D.	P.L.	P.G.	S.G.
P. ☐	F. ☐	F. ☐	T. ☐
F. ☐	W. ☐	W. ☐	P. ☐
B. ☐	P. ☐	C. ☐	C. ☐

24
S.D.	P.L.	P.G.	S.G.
P. ☐	F. ☐	F. ☐	T. ☐
F. ☐	W. ☐	W. ☐	P. ☐
B. ☐	P. ☐	C. ☐	C. ☐

29
S.D.	P.L.	P.G.	S.G.
P. ☐	F. ☐	F. ☐	T. ☐
F. ☐	W. ☐	W. ☐	P. ☐
B. ☐	P. ☐	C. ☐	C. ☐

30
S.D.	P.L.	P.G.	S.G.
P. ☐	F. ☐	F. ☐	T. ☐
F. ☐	W. ☐	W. ☐	P. ☐
B. ☐	P. ☐	C. ☐	C. ☐

31
S.D.	P.L.	P.G.	S.G.
P. ☐	F. ☐	F. ☐	T. ☐
F. ☐	W. ☐	W. ☐	P. ☐
B. ☐	P. ☐	C. ☐	C. ☐

Proverbs 11:3

Honesty guides good people; dishonesty destroys treacherous people.

Personal Goals

Family

Work/School/Social

Challenge

Sport Goals

Training

Performance

Competition Results

TIPS

Making adjustments:

A great skill in sports is the ability to adjust to change. Players should be able to apply individual tactics flexibly, adapting their technical and tactical skills to each new situation quickly and correctly. The same tactical flexibility is required for each position and also for the team as a whole.

The Resurrection of Christ

15

Let me now remind you, dear brothers and sisters, of the Good News I preached to you before. You welcomed it then, and you still stand firm in it. [2]It is this Good News that saves you if you continue to believe the message I told you—unless, of course, you believed something that was never true in the first place.

[3]I passed on to you what was most important and what had also been passed on to me. Christ died for our sins, just as the Scriptures said. [4]He was buried, and he was raised from the dead on the third day, just as the Scriptures said. [5]He was seen by Peter and then by the Twelve. [6]After that, he was seen by more than [500] of his followers at one time, most of whom are still alive, though some have died. [7]Then he was seen by James and later by all the apostles. [8]Last of all, as though I had been born at the wrong time, I also saw him. [9]For I am the least of all the apostles. In fact, I'm not even worthy to be called an apostle after the way I persecuted God's church.

[10]But whatever I am now, it is all because God poured out his special favor on me—and not without results. For I have worked harder than any of the other apostles; yet it was not I but God who was working through me by his grace. [11]So it makes no difference whether I preach or they preach, for we all preach the same message you have already believed.

The Resurrection of the Dead

[12]But tell me this—since we preach that Christ rose from the dead, why are some of you saying there will be no resurrection of the dead? [13]For if there is no resurrection of the dead, then Christ has not been raised either. [14]And if Christ has not been raised, then all our preaching is useless, and your faith is useless. [15]And we apostles would all be lying about God—for we have said that God raised Christ from the grave. But that can't be true if there is no resurrection of the dead. [16]And if there is no resurrection of the dead, then Christ has not been raised. [17]And if Christ has not been raised, then your faith is useless and you are still guilty of your sins. [18]In that case, all who have died

believing in Christ are lost! [19]And if our hope in Christ is only for this life, we are more to be pitied than anyone in the world.

[20]But in fact, Christ has been raised from the dead. He is the first of a great harvest of all who have died. [21]So you see, just as death came into the world through a man, now the resurrection from the dead has begun through another man. [22]Just as everyone dies because we all belong to Adam, everyone who belongs to Christ will be given new life. [23]But there is an order to this resurrection: Christ was raised as the first of the harvest; then all who belong to Christ will be raised when he comes back.

[24]After that the end will come, when he will turn the Kingdom over to God the Father, having destroyed every ruler and authority and power. [25]For Christ must reign until he humbles all his enemies beneath his feet. [26]And the last enemy to be destroyed is death. [27]For the Scriptures say, "God has put all things under his authority." (Of course, when it says "all things are under his authority," that does not include God himself, who gave Christ his authority.) [28]Then, when all things are under his authority, the Son will put himself under God's authority, so that God, who gave his Son authority over all things, will be utterly supreme over everything everywhere.

[29]If the dead will not be raised, what point is there in people being baptized for those who are dead? Why do it unless the dead will someday rise again?

[30]And why should we ourselves risk our lives hour by hour? [31]For I swear, dear brothers and sisters, that I face death daily. This is as certain as my pride in what Christ Jesus our Lord has done in you. [32]And what value was there in fighting wild beasts—those people of Ephesus—if there will be no resurrection from the dead? And if there is no resurrection, "Let's feast and drink, for tomorrow we die!" [33]Don't be fooled by those who say such things, for "bad company corrupts good character." [34]Think carefully about what is right, and stop sinning. For to your shame I say that some of you don't know God at all.

The Resurrection Body

[35]But someone may ask, "How will the dead be raised? What kind of bodies will they have?" [36]What a foolish question! When you put a seed into the ground, it doesn't grow into a plant unless it dies first. [37]And what you put in the ground is not the plant that will grow, but only a bare seed of wheat or whatever you are planting. [38]Then God gives it the new body he wants it to have. A different plant grows from each kind of seed. [39]Similarly there are different kinds of flesh—one kind for humans, another for animals, another for birds, and another for fish.

[40]There are also bodies in the heavens and bodies on the earth. The glory of the heavenly bodies is different from the glory of the earthly bodies. [41]The sun has one kind of glory, while the moon and stars each have another kind. And even the stars differ from each other in their glory.

[42]It is the same way with the resurrection of the dead. Our earthly bodies are planted in the ground when we die, but they will be raised to live forever. [43]Our bodies are buried in brokenness, but they will be raised in glory. They are buried in weakness, but they will be raised in strength. [44]They are buried as natural human bodies, but they will be raised as spiritual bodies. For just as there are natural bodies, there are also spiritual bodies.

[45]The Scriptures tell us, "The first man, Adam, became a living person." But the last Adam—that is, Christ—is a life-giving Spirit. [46]What comes first is the natural body, then the spiritual body comes later. [47]Adam, the first man, was made from the dust of the earth, while Christ, the second man, came from heaven. [48]Earthly people are like the earthly man, and heavenly people are like the heavenly man. [49]Just as we are now like the earthly man, we will someday be like the heavenly man.

[50]What I am saying, dear brothers and sisters, is that our physical bodies cannot inherit the Kingdom of God. These dying bodies cannot inherit what will last forever.

⁵¹But let me reveal to you a wonderful secret. We will not all die, but we will all be transformed! ⁵²It will happen in a moment, in the blink of an eye, when the last trumpet is blown. For when the trumpet sounds, those who have died will be raised to live forever. And we who are living will also be transformed. ⁵³For our dying bodies must be transformed into bodies that will never die; our mortal bodies must be transformed into immortal bodies.

⁵⁴Then, when our dying bodies have been transformed into bodies that will never die, this Scripture will be fulfilled:

"Death is swallowed up in victory.
⁵⁵O death, where is your victory?
O death, where is your sting?"

⁵⁶For sin is the sting that results in death, and the law gives sin its power. ⁵⁷But thank God! He gives us victory over sin and death through our Lord Jesus Christ.

⁵⁸So, my dear brothers and sisters, be strong and immovable. Always work enthusiastically for the Lord, for you know that nothing you do for the Lord is ever useless.

The Collection for Jerusalem

16

Now regarding your question about the money being collected for God's people in Jerusalem. You should follow the same procedure I gave to the churches in Galatia. ²On the first day of each week, you should each put aside a portion of the money you have earned. Don't wait until I get there and then try to collect it all at once. ³When I come, I will write letters of recommendation for the messengers you choose to deliver your gift to Jerusalem. ⁴And if it seems appropriate for me to go along, they can travel with me.

Paul's Final Instructions

⁵I am coming to visit you after I have been to Macedonia, for

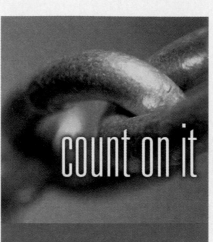

There will be times when you feel all alone.
It might be at school or at work or when you are on the road. It could be when you take that shot in a championship game. But if you love Christ you will never walk alone! "I will never fail you, I will never abandon you." (Hebrews 13:5)
Count on it!

I am planning to travel through Macedonia. ⁶Perhaps I will stay awhile with you, possibly all winter, and then you can send me on my way to my next destination. ⁷This time I don't want to make just a short visit and then go right on. I want to come and stay awhile, if the Lord will let me. ⁸In the meantime, I will be staying here at Ephesus until the Festival of Pentecost. ⁹There is a wide-open door for a great work here, although many oppose me.

¹⁰When Timothy comes, don't intimidate him. He is doing the Lord's work, just as I am. ¹¹Don't let anyone treat him with contempt. Send him on his way with your blessing when he returns to me. I expect him to come with the other believers.

¹²Now about our brother Apollos—I urged him to visit you with the other believers, but he was not willing to go right now. He will see you later when he has the opportunity.

¹³Be on guard. Stand firm in the faith. Be courageous. Be strong. ¹⁴And do everything with love.

¹⁵You know that Stephanas and his household were the first of the harvest of believers in Greece, and they are spending their lives in service to God's people. I urge you, dear brothers and sisters, ¹⁶to submit to them and others like them who serve with such devotion. ¹⁷I am very glad that Stephanas, Fortunatus, and Achaicus have come here. They have been providing the help you weren't here to give me. ¹⁸They have been a wonderful encouragement to me, as they have been to you. You must show your appreciation to all who serve so well.

Paul's Final Greetings

¹⁹The churches here in the province of Asia send greetings in the Lord, as do Aquila and Priscilla and all the others who gather in their home for church meetings. ²⁰All the brothers and sisters here send greetings to you. Greet each other with Christian love. ²¹HERE IS MY GREETING IN MY OWN HANDWRITING—PAUL. ²²If anyone does not love the Lord, that person is cursed. Our Lord, come! ²³May the grace of the Lord Jesus be with you. ²⁴My love to all of you in Christ Jesus.

After his first letter, Paul was curious to know the true response of the people of Corinth and wondered how well it had been received. He sent one of his top workers, Timothy, to find out. Second Corinthians was a response to his scouting. In this letter, through the influence of the Holy Spirit, Paul provided encouragement, guidance and strong leadership.

Paul tirelessly invested a lot of time and energy in the people of Corinth, living there off and on and supporting his ministry, originally by making tents, a major business of the day. The Corinthian church was a lighthouse in a very powerful and wealthy but immoral seaport. Paul established, encouraged, and nurtured the Corinthian faith community for years.

This book expresses his joy that the church was moving forward and his first letter seemed to have been taken in the right attitude and spirit. Paul revealed more of his amazing history and the pain and privileges he had gone through for the cause of Christ. This is another personal and warm letter to a church that needed a lot of leadership, love, and encouragement to progress in the cause of Christ.

2 Corinthians

It's a gift
LIVE it

For the wages
of sin is death,
but the free
gift of God
is eternal life
through
Christ Jesus
our Lord.

ROMANS 6:23

2 CORINTHIANS

Greetings from Paul

1

This letter is from Paul, chosen by the will of God to be an apostle of Christ Jesus, and from our brother Timothy.

I am writing to God's church in Corinth and to all of his holy people throughout Greece.

[2] May God our Father and the Lord Jesus Christ give you grace and peace.

God Offers Comfort to All

[3] All praise to God, the Father of our Lord Jesus Christ. God is our merciful Father and the source of all comfort. [4] He comforts us in all our troubles so that we can comfort others. When they are troubled, we will be able to give them the same comfort God has given us. [5] For the more we suffer for Christ, the more God will shower us with his comfort through Christ. [6] Even when we are weighed down with troubles, it is for your comfort and salvation! For when we ourselves are comforted, we will certainly comfort you. Then you can patiently endure the same things we suffer. [7] We are confident that as you share in our sufferings, you will also share in the comfort God gives us.

[8] We think you ought to know, dear brothers and sisters, about the trouble we went through in the province of Asia. We were crushed and overwhelmed beyond our ability to endure, and we thought we would never live through it. [9] In fact, we expected to die. But as a result, we stopped relying on ourselves and learned to rely only on God, who raises the dead. [10] And he did rescue us from mortal danger, and he will rescue us again. We have placed our confidence in him, and he will continue to rescue us. [11] And you are helping us by praying for us. Then many people will give thanks

There are 43 quintillion (43,252,003,274,489,856,000) different color combinations possible on a Rubik's Cube.

because God has graciously answered so many prayers for our safety.

1:8-11 WHAT'S IT SAYING?

WHAT AM I GOING TO DO ABOUT IT?

Paul's Change of Plans

[12] We can say with confidence and a clear conscience that we have lived with a God-given holiness and sincerity in all our dealings. We have depended on God's grace, not on our own human wisdom. That is how we have conducted ourselves before the world, and especially toward you. [13] Our letters have been straightforward, and there is nothing written between the lines and nothing you can't understand. I hope someday you will fully understand us, [14] even if you don't understand us now. Then on the day when the Lord Jesus returns, you will be proud of us in the same way we are proud of you.

[15] Since I was so sure of your understanding and trust, I wanted to give you a double blessing by visiting you twice—[16] first on my way to Macedonia and again when I returned from Macedonia. Then you could send me on my way to Judea.

[17] You may be asking why I changed my plan. Do you think I make my plans carelessly? Do you think I am like people of the world who say "Yes" when they really mean "No"? [18] As surely as God is faithful, my word to you does not waver between "Yes" and "No." [19] For

Jesus Christ, the Son of God, does not waver between "Yes" and "No." He is the one whom Silas, Timothy, and I preached to you, and as God's ultimate "Yes," he always does what he says. [20] For all of God's promises have been fulfilled in Christ with a resounding "Yes!" And through Christ, our "Amen" (which means "Yes") ascends to God for his glory.

[21] It is God who enables us, along with you, to stand firm for Christ. He has commissioned us, [22] and he has identified us as his own by placing the Holy Spirit in our hearts as the first installment that guarantees everything he has promised us.

[23] Now I call upon God as my witness that I am telling the truth. The reason I didn't return to Corinth was to spare you from a severe rebuke. [24] But that does not mean we want to dominate you by telling you how to put your faith into practice. We want to work together with you so you will be full of joy, for it is by your own faith that you stand firm.

2

So I decided that I would not bring you grief with another painful visit. [2] For if I cause you grief, who will make me glad? Certainly not someone I have grieved. [3] That is why I wrote to you as I did, so that when I do come, I won't be grieved by the very ones who ought to give me the greatest joy. Surely you all know that my joy comes from your being joyful. [4] I wrote that letter in great anguish, with a troubled heart and many tears. I didn't want to grieve you, but I wanted to let you know how much love I have for you.

Forgiveness for the Sinner

[5] I am not overstating it when I say that the man who caused all the trouble hurt all of you more than he hurt me. [6] Most of you opposed him, and that was punishment enough. [7] Now, however, it is time to forgive and comfort him. Otherwise he may be overcome by discouragement. [8] So I urge you now to reaffirm your love for him.

[9] I wrote to you as I did to test you and see if you would fully comply with my instructions. [10] When you forgive this man, I forgive him, too. And when I forgive whatever needs to be forgiven, I do so with Christ's authority for your benefit, [11] so that Satan will not outsmart us. For we are familiar with his evil schemes.

[12] When I came to the city of Troas to preach the Good News of Christ, the Lord opened a door of opportunity for me. [13] But I had no peace of mind because my dear brother Titus hadn't yet arrived with a report from you. So I said good-bye and went on to Macedonia to find him.

Ministers of the New Covenant

[14] But thank God! He has made us his captives and continues to lead us along in Christ's triumphal procession. Now he uses us to spread the knowledge of Christ everywhere, like a

Change! We all have things that need to be put right. You may look at parts of Scripture and think, *No way! I can't do what God wants me to do! I will be a failure!* Don't worry — God knows you can't and does not want you to change alone! He wants to help you change. He will help you if you are courageous enough to let him help you!

"Humanly speaking, it is impossible. But with God everything is possible."

(Matthew 19:26)

sweet perfume. [15]Our lives are a Christ-like fragrance rising up to God. But this fragrance is perceived differently by those who are being saved and by those who are perishing. [16]To those who are perishing, we are a dreadful smell of death and doom. But to those who are being saved, we are a life-giving perfume. And who is adequate for such a task as this? [17]You see, we are not like the many hucksters who preach for personal profit. We preach the word of God with sincerity and with Christ's authority, knowing that God is watching us.

3

Are we beginning to praise ourselves again? Are we like others, who need to bring you letters of recommendation, or who ask you to write such letters on their behalf? Surely not! [2]The only letter of recommendation we need is you yourselves. Your lives are a letter written in our hearts; everyone can read it and recognize our good work among you. [3]Clearly, you are a letter from Christ showing the result of our ministry among you. This "letter" is written not with pen and ink,

When you need an example of boldness

4:9

We are hunted down, but never abandoned by God. We get knocked down, but we are not destroyed.

but with the Spirit of the living God. It is carved not on tablets of stone, but on human hearts.

[4]We are confident of all this because of our great trust in God through Christ. [5]It is not that we think we are qualified to do anything on our own. Our qualification comes from God. [6]He has enabled us to be ministers of his new covenant. This is a covenant not of written laws, but of the Spirit. The old written covenant ends in death; but under the new covenant, the Spirit gives life.

The Glory of the New Covenant

[7]The old way, with laws etched in stone, led to death, though it began with such glory that the people of Israel could not bear to look at Moses' face. For his face shone with the glory of God, even though the brightness was already fading away. [8]Shouldn't we expect far greater glory under the new way, now that the Holy Spirit is giving life? [9]If the old way, which brings condemnation, was glorious, how much more glorious is the new way, which makes us right with God! [10]In fact, that first glory was not glorious at all compared with the overwhelming glory of the new way. [11]So if the old way, which has been replaced, was glorious, how much more glorious is the new, which remains forever!

[12]Since this new way gives us such confidence, we can be very bold. [13]We are not like Moses, who put a veil over his face so the people of Israel would not see the glory, even though it was destined to fade away. [14]But the people's minds were hardened, and to this day whenever the old covenant is being read, the same veil covers their minds so they cannot understand the truth. And this veil can be removed only by believing

in Christ. [15]Yes, even today when they read Moses' writings, their hearts are covered with that veil, and they do not understand.

[16]But whenever someone turns to the Lord, the veil is taken away. [17]For the Lord is the Spirit, and wherever the Spirit of the Lord is, there is freedom. [18]So all of us who have had that veil removed can see and reflect the glory of the Lord. And the Lord—who is the Spirit—makes us more and more like him as we are changed into his glorious image.

Treasure in Fragile Clay Jars

4

Therefore, since God in his mercy has given us this new way, we never give up. [2]We reject all shameful deeds and underhanded methods. We don't try to trick anyone or distort the word of God. We tell the truth before God, and all who are honest know this.

[3]If the Good News we preach is hidden behind a veil, it is hidden only from people who are perishing. [4]Satan, who is the god of this world, has blinded the minds of those who don't believe. They are unable to see the glorious light of the Good News. They don't understand this message about the glory of Christ, who is the exact likeness of God.

[5]You see, we don't go around preaching about ourselves. We preach that Jesus Christ is Lord, and we ourselves are your servants for Jesus' sake. [6]For God, who said, "Let there be light in the darkness," has made this light shine in our hearts so we could know the glory of God that is seen in the face of Jesus Christ. [7]We now have this light shining in our hearts, but we ourselves are like fragile clay jars containing this great treasure. This makes it clear that our great power is from God, not from ourselves.

[8]We are pressed on every side by troubles, but we are not crushed. We are perplexed, but not driven to despair. [9]We are hunted down, but never abandoned by God. We get knocked down, but we are not destroyed. [10]Through suffering, our bodies continue to share in the death of Jesus so that the life of Jesus may also be seen in our bodies.

[11]Yes, we live under constant danger of death because we serve Jesus, so that the life of Jesus will be evident in our dying bodies. [12]So we live in the face of death, but this has resulted in eternal life for you.

[13]But we continue to preach because we have the same kind of faith the psalmist had when he said, "I believed in God, so I spoke." [14]We know that God, who raised the Lord Jesus, will also raise us with Jesus and present

us to himself together with you. [15]All of this is for your benefit. And as God's grace reaches more and more people, there will be great thanksgiving, and God will receive more and more glory.

[16]That is why we never give up. Though our bodies are dying, our spirits are being renewed every day. [17]For our present troubles are small and won't last very long. Yet they produce for us a glory that vastly outweighs them and will last forever! [18]So we don't look at the troubles we can see now; rather, we fix our gaze on things that cannot be seen. For the things we see now will soon be gone, but the things we cannot see will last forever.

New Bodies

5

For we know that when this earthly tent we live in is taken down (that is, when we die and leave this earthly body), we will have a house in heaven, an eternal body made for us by God himself and not by human hands. [2]We grow weary in our present bodies, and we long to put on our heavenly bodies like new clothing. [3]For we will put on heavenly bodies; we will not be spirits without bodies. [4]While we live in these earthly bodies, we groan and sigh, but it's not that we want to die

and get rid of these bodies that clothe us. Rather, we want to put on our new bodies so that these dying bodies will be swallowed up by life. [5]God himself has prepared us for this, and as a guarantee he has given us his Holy Spirit.

[6]So we are always confident, even though we know that as long as we live in these bodies we are not at home with the Lord. [7]For we live by believing and not by seeing. [8]Yes, we are fully confident, and we would rather be away from these earthly bodies, for then we will be at home with the Lord. [9]So whether we are here in this body or away from this body, our goal is to please him. [10]For we must all stand before Christ to be judged. We will each receive whatever we deserve for the good or evil we have done in this earthly body.

Bible FACTS

The Bible contains 1,189 chapters and over 31,000 verses.

We Are God's Ambassadors

[11]Because we understand our fearful responsibility to the Lord, we work hard to persuade others. God knows we are sincere, and I hope you know this, too. [12]Are we commending ourselves to you again? No, we are giving you a reason to be proud of us, so you can answer those who brag about having a spectacular ministry rather than having a sincere heart. [13]If it seems we are crazy, it is to bring glory to God. And if we are in our right minds, it is for your benefit. [14]Either way, Christ's love controls us. Since we believe that Christ died for all, we also believe that we have all died to our old life. [15]He died for everyone so that those who receive his new life will no longer live for themselves. Instead, they will live for Christ, who died and was raised for them.

[16]So we have stopped evaluating others from a human point of view. At one time we thought of Christ merely from a human point of view. How differently we know him now! [17]This means that anyone who belongs to Christ has become a new person. The old life is gone; a new life has begun!

[18]And all of this is a gift from God, who brought us back to himself through Christ. And God has given us this task of reconciling people to him. [19]For God was in Christ, reconciling the world to himself, no longer counting people's sins against them. And he gave us this wonderful message of reconciliation. [20]So we are Christ's ambassadors; God is making his appeal through us. We speak for Christ when we plead, "Come back to God!" [21]For God made Christ, who

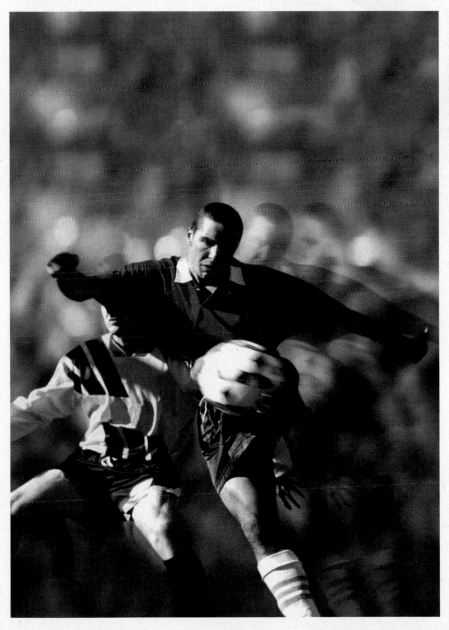

count on it

No fear!

Some people are terrified by the fear of failure. "If I can't win, I will not run!" Others can compete with reckless abandon knowing: "The LORD is my helper, so I will have no fear. What can mere people do to me?" (Hebrews 13:6) **Count on it!**

never sinned, to be the offering for our sin, so that we could be made right with God through Christ.

6

As God's partners, we beg you not to accept this marvelous gift of God's kindness and then ignore it. ²For God says,
"At just the right time, I heard you.
On the day of salvation, I helped you."
Indeed, the "right time" is now. Today is the day of salvation.

Paul's Hardships

³We live in such a way that no one will stumble because of us, and no one will find fault with our ministry. ⁴In everything we do, we show that we are true ministers of God. We patiently endure troubles and hardships and calamities of every kind. ⁵We have been beaten, been put in prison, faced angry mobs, worked to exhaustion, endured sleepless nights, and gone without food. ⁶We prove ourselves by our purity, our understanding, our patience, our kindness, by the Holy Spirit within us, and by our sincere love. ⁷We faithfully preach the truth. God's power is working in us. We use the weapons of righteousness in the right hand for attack and the left hand for defense. ⁸We serve God whether people honor us or despise us, whether they slander us or praise us. We are honest, but they call us impostors. ⁹We are ignored, even though we are well known. We live close to death, but we are

still alive. We have been beaten, but we have not been killed. ¹⁰Our hearts ache, but we always have joy. We are poor, but we give spiritual riches to others. We own nothing, and yet we have everything.

¹¹Oh, dear Corinthian friends! We have spoken honestly with you, and our hearts are open to you. ¹²There is no lack of love on our part, but you have withheld your love from us. ¹³I am asking you to respond as if you were my own children. Open your hearts to us!

action

6:3-13 WHAT'S IT SAYING?

WHAT AM I GOING TO DO ABOUT IT?

The Temple of the Living God

¹⁴Don't team up with those who are unbelievers. How can righteousness be a partner with wickedness? How can light live with darkness? ¹⁵What harmony can there be between Christ and the devil? How can a believer be a partner with an unbeliever? ¹⁶And what union can there be between God's temple and idols? For we are the temple of the living God. As God said:
"I will live in them
and walk among them.
I will be their God,
and they will be my people.
¹⁷Therefore, come out from among unbelievers,
and separate yourselves from them, says the LORD.

Don't touch their filthy things,
and I will welcome you.
¹⁸And I will be your Father,
and you will be my sons and daughters,
says the LORD Almighty."

7

Because we have these promises, dear friends, let us cleanse ourselves from everything that can defile our body or spirit. And let us work toward complete holiness because we fear God.

²Please open your hearts to us. We have not done wrong to anyone, nor led anyone astray, nor taken advantage of anyone. ³I'm not saying this to condemn you. I said before that you are in our hearts, and we live or die together with you. ⁴I have the highest confidence in you, and I take great pride in you. You have greatly encouraged me and made me happy despite all our troubles.

Paul's Joy at the Church's Repentance

⁵When we arrived in Macedonia, there was no rest for us. We faced conflict from every direction, with battles on the outside and fear on the inside. ⁶But God, who encourages those who are discouraged, encouraged us by the arrival of Titus. ⁷His presence was a joy, but so was the news he brought of the encouragement he received from you. When he told us how much you long to see me, and how sorry you are for what happened, and how loyal you are to me, I was filled with joy!

⁸I am not sorry that I sent that severe letter to you, though I was sorry at first, for I know it was painful to you for a little while. ⁹Now I am glad I sent it, not because it hurt you, but because the pain caused you to repent and change your ways. It was the kind of sorrow God wants his people to have, so you were not harmed by us in any way. ¹⁰For the kind of sorrow God wants us to experience leads us away from sin and results in salvation. There's no regret for that kind of sorrow. But worldly sorrow, which lacks repentance, results in spiritual death.

¹¹Just see what this godly sorrow produced in you! Such earnestness, such concern to clear yourselves, such indignation, such alarm, such longing to see me, such zeal, and such a readiness to punish wrong. You showed that you have done everything necessary to make things right. ¹²My purpose, then, was not to write about who did the wrong or who was wronged. I wrote to you so that in the sight of God you could

see for yourselves how loyal you are to us. [13]We have been greatly encouraged by this.

In addition to our own encouragement, we were especially delighted to see how happy Titus was about the way all of you welcomed him and set his mind at ease. [14]I had told him how proud I was of you—and you didn't disappoint me. I have always told you the truth, and now my boasting to Titus has also proved true! [15]Now he cares for you more than ever when he remembers the way all of you obeyed him and welcomed him with such fear and deep respect. [16]I am very happy now because I have complete confidence in you.

A Call to Generous Giving

8

Now I want you to know, dear brothers and sisters, what God in his kindness has done through the churches in Macedonia. [2]They are being tested by many troubles, and they are very poor. But they are also filled with abundant joy, which has overflowed in rich generosity.

[3]For I can testify that they gave not only what they could afford, but far more. And they did it of their own free will. [4]They begged us again and again for the privilege of sharing in the gift for the believers in Jerusalem. [5]They even did more than we had hoped, for their first action was to give themselves to the Lord and to us, just as God wanted them to do.

[6]So we have urged Titus, who encouraged your giving in the first place, to return to you and encourage you to finish this ministry of giving. [7]Since you excel in so many ways—in your faith, your gifted speakers, your knowledge, your enthusiasm, and your love from us—I want you to excel also in this gracious act of giving.

[8]I am not commanding you to do this. But I am testing how genuine your love is by comparing it with the eagerness of the other churches.

[9]You know the generous grace of our Lord Jesus Christ. Though he was rich, yet for your sakes he became poor, so that by his poverty he could make you rich. [10]Here is my advice: It would be good for you to finish what you started a year ago. Last year you were the first who wanted to give, and you were the first to begin doing it. [11]Now you should finish what you started. Let the eagerness you showed in the beginning be matched now by your giving. Give in proportion to what you have. [12]Whatever you give is acceptable if you give it eagerly. And give according to what you have, not what you don't have. [13]Of course, I don't mean your giving should make life easy for others and hard for yourselves. I only mean that there should be some equality. [14]Right now you have plenty and can help those who are in need. Later, they will have plenty and can share with you when you need it. In this way, things will be equal. [15]As the Scriptures say,

"Those who gathered a lot had nothing left over, and those who gathered only a little had enough."

Titus and His Companions

[16]But thank God! He has given Titus the same enthusiasm for you that I have. [17]Titus welcomed our request that he visit you again. In fact, he himself was very eager to go and see you. [18]We are also sending another brother with Titus. All the churches praise him as a preacher of the Good News. [19]He was appointed by the churches to accompany us as we take the offering to Jerusalem—a service that glorifies the Lord and shows our eagerness to help.

[20]We are traveling together to guard against any criticism for the way we are handling this generous gift. [21]We are careful to be honorable before the Lord, but we also want everyone else to see that we are honorable.

[22]We are also sending with them another of our brothers

Who are the top five most influential people in history?

1
2
3
4
5

BIG FIVE

Good Fit (2 CORINTHIANS 6:14)

You would never run a marathon in shoes two sizes too small. Paul is using Jesus' illustration to point out that we should not closely associate with people or organizations that will compromise our friendship with Christ. This is especially relevant to dating and choosing a spouse. Jesus, a master carpenter, used a metaphor that was contemporary to his day (Matthew 11:30). Master carpenters fitted yokes to animals that would plough the farm fields. It was important to get a comfortable fit or a valuable animal could be rendered useless. Many yokes were doubles so there was a team of animals. Jesus said, "My yoke is easy to bear and the burden I give you is light." This does not mean that you should stay away from those who do not follow Jesus; in fact, we are to be an influence on those who do not know him. But all your closest friends — the ones who influence you — should be going in the same direction, a good fit, following Jesus.

BIBLE HIT

who has proven himself many times and has shown on many occasions how eager he is. He is now even more enthusiastic because of his great confidence in you. ²³If anyone asks about Titus, say that he is my partner who works with me to help you. And the brothers with him have been sent by the churches, and they bring honor to Christ. ²⁴So show them your love, and prove to all the churches that our boasting about you is justified.

The Collection for Christians in Jerusalem

9

I really don't need to write to you about this ministry of giving for the believers in Jerusalem. ²For I know how eager you are to help, and I have been boasting to the churches in Macedonia that you in Greece were ready to send an offering a year ago. In fact, it was your enthusiasm that stirred up many of the Macedonian believers to begin giving.

³But I am sending these brothers to be sure you really are ready, as I have been telling them, and that your money is all collected. I don't want to be wrong in my boasting about you. ⁴We would be embarrassed—not to mention your own embarrassment—if some Macedonian believers came with me and found that you weren't ready after all I had told them! ⁵So I thought I should send these brothers ahead of me to make sure the gift you promised is ready. But I want it to be a willing gift, not one given grudgingly.

⁶Remember this—a farmer who plants only a few seeds will get a small crop. But the one who plants generously will get a generous crop. ⁷You must each decide in your heart how much to give. And don't give reluctantly or in response to pressure. "For God loves a person who gives cheerfully." ⁸And God will generously provide all you need. Then you will always have everything you need and plenty left over to share with others. ⁹As the Scriptures say,

"They share freely and give generously to the poor.
Their good deeds will be remembered forever."

¹⁰For God is the one who provides seed for the farmer and then bread to eat. In the same way, he will provide and increase your resources and then produce a great harvest of generosity in you.

The youngest ever Olympian was Greek gymnast Dimitrios Loundras, who competed in the 1896 Athens Olympics. He was 10 years old.

¹¹Yes, you will be enriched in every way so that you can always be generous. And when we take your gifts to those who need them, they will thank God. ¹²So two good things will result from this ministry of giving—the needs of the believers in Jerusalem will be met, and they will joyfully express their thanks to God.

¹³As a result of your ministry, they will give glory to God. For your generosity to them and to all believers will prove that you are obedient to the Good News of Christ. ¹⁴And they will pray for you with deep affection because of the overflowing grace God has given to you. ¹⁵Thank God for this gift too wonderful for words!

Paul Defends His Authority

10

Now I, Paul, appeal to you with the gentleness and kindness of Christ—though I realize you think I am timid in person and bold only when I write from far away. ²Well, I am begging you now so that when I come I won't have to be bold with those who think we act from human motives.

³We are human, but we don't wage war as humans do. ⁴We use God's mighty weapons, not worldly weapons, to knock down the strongholds of human reasoning and to destroy false arguments. ⁵We destroy every proud obstacle that keeps people from knowing God. We capture their rebellious thoughts and teach them to obey Christ. ⁶And after you have become fully obedient, we will punish everyone who remains disobedient.

⁷Look at the obvious facts. Those who say they belong to Christ must recognize that we belong to Christ as much as they do. ⁸I may seem to be boasting too much about the authority given to us by the Lord. But our authority builds you up; it doesn't tear you down. So I will not be ashamed of using my authority.

⁹I'm not trying to frighten you by my letters. ¹⁰For some say, "Paul's letters are demanding and forceful, but in person he is weak, and his speeches are worthless!" ¹¹Those people should realize that our actions when we arrive in person will be as forceful as what we say in our letters from far away.

¹²Oh, don't worry; we wouldn't dare say that we are as wonderful as these other men who tell you how important they are! But they are only comparing themselves with each other, using themselves as the standard of measurement. How ignorant!

¹³We will not boast about things done outside our area of authority. We will boast only about what has happened within the boundaries of the work God has given us, which includes our working with you. ¹⁴We are not reaching beyond these boundaries when we claim authority over you, as if we had never visited you. For we were the first to travel all the way to Corinth with the Good News of Christ.

¹⁵Nor do we boast and claim credit for the work someone else has done. Instead, we hope that your faith will grow so that the boundaries of our work among you will be extended. ¹⁶Then we will be able to go and preach the Good News in other places far beyond you, where no one else is working. Then there will be no question of our boasting about work done in someone else's territory. ¹⁷As the Scriptures say, "If you want to boast, boast only about the LORD." ¹⁸When people commend themselves, it doesn't count for much. The important thing is for the Lord to commend them.

I have real trouble not swearing — I hear it so much on my team.

The language you hear can be a bad influence on you. Asking politely for your teammates to use positive language because you desire to honor God usually creates a stir on the team and will help you to stand up for what you believe. What the Bible repeats over and over is this: If your heart is good, good things will flow out of it! We are commanded to make a difference in this world (to be salt and light), so we cannot shy away from what we are called to influence. But we are to ask for help and strap on God's protection. Go read Ephesians 6.

How to run farther, faster, & smarter:
One of the most important aspects of running is to land more on the whole foot rather than on the heel with the sole of the foot angled upward. This is one of the most frequent errors that leads to injury — and to slower speeds.

Paul and the False Apostles

11

I hope you will put up with a little more of my foolishness. Please bear with me. ²For I am jealous for you with the jealousy of God himself. I promised you as a pure bride to one husband—Christ. ³But I fear that somehow your pure and undivided devotion to Christ will be corrupted, just as Eve was deceived by the cunning ways of the serpent. ⁴You happily put up with whatever anyone tells you, even if they preach a different Jesus than the one we preach, or a different kind of Spirit than the one you received, or a different kind of gospel than the one you believed.

⁵But I don't consider myself inferior in any way to these "super apostles" who teach such things. ⁶I may be unskilled as a speaker, but I'm not lacking in knowledge. We have made this clear to you in every possible way.

⁷Was I wrong when I humbled myself and honored you by preaching God's Good News to you without expecting anything in return? ⁸I "robbed" other churches by accepting their contributions so I could serve you at no cost. ⁹And when I was with you and didn't have enough to live on, I did not become a financial burden to anyone. For the brothers who came from Macedonia brought me all that I needed. I have never been a burden to you, and I never will be. ¹⁰As surely as the truth of Christ is in me, no one in all of Greece will ever stop me from boasting about this. ¹¹Why? Because I don't love you? God knows that I do.

¹²But I will continue doing what I have always done. This will undercut those who are looking for an opportunity to boast that their work is just like ours. ¹³These people are false apostles. They are deceitful workers who disguise themselves as apostles of Christ. ¹⁴But I am not surprised! Even Satan disguises himself as an angel of light. ¹⁵So it is no wonder that his servants also disguise themselves as servants of righteousness. In the end they will get the punishment their wicked deeds deserve.

Paul's Many Trials

¹⁶Again I say, don't think that I am a fool to talk like this. But even if you do, listen to me, as you would to a foolish person, while I also boast a little. ¹⁷Such boasting is not from the Lord, but I am acting like a fool. ¹⁸And since others boast about their human achievements, I will, too. ¹⁹After all, you think you are so wise, but you enjoy putting up with fools! ²⁰You put up with it when someone enslaves you, takes everything you have, takes advantage of you, takes control of everything, and slaps you in the face. ²¹I'm ashamed to say that we've been too "weak" to do that!

But whatever they dare to boast about—I'm talking like a fool again—I dare to boast about it, too. ²²Are they Hebrews? So am I. Are they Israelites? So am I. Are they descendants of Abraham? So am I. ²³Are they servants of Christ? I know I sound like a madman, but I have served him far more! I have worked harder, been put in prison more often, been whipped times without number, and faced death again and again. ²⁴Five different times the Jewish leaders gave me thirty-nine lashes. ²⁵Three times I was beaten with rods. Once I was stoned. Three times I was shipwrecked. Once I spent a whole night and a day adrift at sea. ²⁶I have traveled on many long journeys. I have faced danger from rivers and from robbers. I have faced danger from my own people, the Jews, as well as from the Gentiles. I have faced danger in the cities, in the deserts, and on the seas. And I have faced danger from men who claim to be believers but are not. ²⁷I have worked hard and long, enduring many sleepless nights. I have been hungry and thirsty and have often gone without food. I have shivered in the cold, without enough clothing to keep me warm. ²⁸Then, besides all this, I have the daily burden of my concern for all the churches. ²⁹Who is weak without my feeling that weakness? Who is led astray, and I do not burn with anger?

³⁰If I must boast, I would rather boast about the things that show how weak I am. ³¹God, the Father of our Lord Jesus, who is worthy of eternal praise, knows I am not lying. ³²When I was in Damascus, the governor under King Aretas kept guards at the city gates to catch me. ³³I had to be lowered in a basket through a window in the city wall to escape from him.

When you feel like bragging

11:30

If I must boast, I would rather boast about the things that show how weak I am.

Paul's Vision and His Thorn in the Flesh

12

This boasting will do no good, but I must go on. I will reluctantly tell about visions and revelations from the Lord. ²I was caught up to the third heaven fourteen years ago. Whether I was in my body or out of my body, I don't know—only God knows. ³Yes, only God knows whether I was in my body or outside my body. But I do know ⁴that I was caught up to paradise and heard things so astounding that they cannot be expressed in words, things no human is allowed to tell.

⁵That experience is worth boasting about, but I'm not going to do it. I will boast only about my weaknesses. ⁶If I wanted to boast, I would be no fool in doing so, because I would be telling the truth. But I won't do it, because I don't want anyone to give me credit beyond what they can see in my life or hear in my message, ⁷even though I have received such wonderful revelations from God. So to keep me from becoming proud, I was given a thorn in my flesh, a messenger from Satan to torment me and keep me from becoming proud. ⁸Three different times I begged the Lord to take it away.

WHAT

DOES IT MEAN?

antichrist

Being against Christ or in opposition to Christ, a rival of Christ. The word is used only by the apostle John (1 John 2:18, 22; 4:3; 2 John 1:7), and it has been applied to the beast out of the sea (Revelation 13:1; 17:1-18).

⁹Each time he said, "My grace is all you need. My power works best in weakness." So now I am glad to boast about my weaknesses, so that the power of Christ can work through me. ¹⁰That's why I take pleasure in my weaknesses, and in the insults, hardships, persecutions, and troubles that I suffer for Christ. For when I am weak, then I am strong.

Paul's Concern for the Corinthians

¹¹You have made me act like a fool—boasting like this. You ought to be writing commendations for me, for I am not at all inferior to these "super apostles," even though I am nothing at all. ¹²When I was with you, I certainly gave you proof that I am an apostle. For I patiently did many signs and wonders and miracles among you. ¹³The only thing I failed to do, which I do in the other churches, was to become a financial burden to you. Please forgive me for this wrong!

¹⁴Now I am coming to you for the third time, and I will not be a burden to you. I don't want what you have—I want you. After all, children don't provide for their parents. Rather, parents provide for their children. ¹⁵I will gladly spend myself and all I have for you, even though it seems that the more I love you, the less you love me.

¹⁶Some of you admit I was not a burden to you. But others still think I was sneaky and took advantage of you by trickery. ¹⁷But how? Did any of the men I sent to you take advantage of you? ¹⁸When I urged Titus to visit you and sent our other brother with him, did Titus take advantage of you? No! For we have the same spirit and walk in each other's steps, doing things the same way.

¹⁹Perhaps you think we're saying these things just to defend ourselves. No, we tell you this as Christ's servants, and with God as our witness. Everything we do, dear friends, is to strengthen you. ²⁰For I am afraid that when I come I won't like what I find, and you won't like my response. I am afraid that I will find quarreling, jealousy, anger, selfishness, slander, gossip, arrogance, and disorderly behavior. ²¹Yes, I am afraid that when I come again, God will humble me in your presence. And I will be grieved because many of you have not given up your old sins. You have not repented of your impurity, sexual immorality, and eagerness for lustful pleasure.

Paul's Final Advice

13

This is the third time I am coming to visit you (and as the Scriptures say, "The facts of every case must be established by the testimony of two or three witnesses"). ²I have already warned those who had been sinning when I was there on my second visit. Now I again warn them and all others, just as I did before, that next time I will not spare them.

³I will give you all the proof you want that Christ speaks through me. Christ is not weak when he deals with you; he is powerful among you. ⁴Although he was crucified in weakness, he now lives by the power of God. We, too, are weak, just as Christ was, but when we deal with you we will be alive with him and will have God's power.

The Bible was divided into chapters 800 years ago (by Stephen Langton, not the original writers).

⁵Examine yourselves to see if your faith is genuine. Test yourselves. Surely you know that Jesus Christ is among you; if not, you have failed the test of genuine faith. ⁶As you test yourselves, I hope you will recognize that we have not failed the test of apostolic authority.

⁷We pray to God that you will not do what is wrong by refusing our correction. I hope we won't need to demonstrate our authority when we arrive. Do the right thing before we come—even if that makes it look like we have failed to demonstrate our authority. ⁸For we cannot oppose the truth, but must always stand for the truth. ⁹We are glad to seem weak if it helps show that you are actually strong. We pray that you will become mature.

¹⁰I am writing this to you before I come, hoping that I won't need to deal severely with you when I do come. For I want to use the authority the Lord has given me to strengthen you, not to tear you down.

Paul's Final Greetings

¹¹Dear brothers and sisters, I close my letter with these last words: Be joyful. Grow to maturity. Encourage each other. Live in harmony and peace. Then the God of love and peace will be with you.

¹²Greet each other with Christian love. ¹³All of God's people here send you their greetings.

¹⁴May the grace of the Lord Jesus Christ, the love of God, and the fellowship of the Holy Spirit be with you all.

profiles

Noah:

"So Noah did everything exactly as God had commanded him." (Genesis 6:22)

What a claim to fame! This is what you want the minister to say at your funeral. It is not where you start in your faith that is important but where you finish. God gave Noah a huge challenge: to build a boat in the middle of dry land and fill it full of every type of male and female animal. It must have seemed crazy, but God had a plan and Noah was obedient.

The world was so evil that God had decided to create a flood that would destroy the evil. The perfect world had been quickly destroyed by Adam and Eve's rebellion and disobedience. Noah and his family listened to God and obeyed his commands. Noah's obedience in the face of a seemingly obscure command and a huge task (which took one hundred and twenty years to materialize) is a model of obedience and persistence. Noah was faithful to the vision and, in his enduring obedience, survived the devastating Flood. He and the other survivors went on to repopulate the world.

What task has God given you that seems insurmountable and crazy to the world? Follow Noah's example — be obedient to God and carry out the tasks he sets out for you.

Read more about Noah in the Old Testament in the first book of the Bible, Genesis, starting in Chapter 6.

He's Alive (2 Corinthians 3:3)
Paul's reference to the living God is significant. How much spirit can a dead god have? Is our God alive in your life? Christians should be a living, walking billboard for how awesome the Christian life is. Is God writing a message across your heart?

BIBLE HIT

Can I Impress God?

"For everyone has sinned; we all fall short of God's glorious standard. Yet God, with undeserved kindness, declares that we are righteous. He did this through Christ Jesus when he freed us from the penalty for our sins." (Romans 3:23-24)

An NFL coach once barked at me, "Remember, you're only around here until someone comes along who is a little stronger, faster, or cheaper than you! Then you are gone!"

The sober reality of professional sports is that you have to fight your way up the ranking and you only remain there until someone more talented, cheaper, healthier, or younger than you pushes you out. To compare being picked for God's team as "earning" your salvation or impressing God with your skills as a Christian is poor theology. You cannot climb the ladder to attain anything in God's economy; this idea is not only dangerous, it is also stupid. We do not go up the ranks to meet God; he came down the ranks to meet us. We do not "sign on" to God's team by impressing him with our skill; he offers us a free ticket.

I once heard an amateur golfer desperately trying to impress a certain professional golfer with his play. The amateur was embarrassing himself with his delusional golf skills before a seasoned professional. I believe he thought the pro would not befriend him unless he was a good golfer. The pro was polite but unimpressed with his goodness.

The apostle Paul zealously tried to impress God with his actions before his conversion. He saw Christ's followers as a threat to his cause as a Jewish leader and even helped kill a guy because he followed Jesus. But God was not impressed; he was actually rather unimpressed with Paul. (God does not like it when his people are killed.) Later Paul understood the futility in trying to show off before God. The reformed man was inspired by God to write a part of the Bible to address this very issue of trying to earn or impress your way into heaven. Here are a few small excerpts from one of Paul's many letters in the Bible: "For everyone has sinned; we all fall short of God's glorious standard" (Romans 3:23); "For the wages of sin is death, but the free gift of God is eternal life through Christ Jesus our Lord" (Romans 6:23).

There is nothing we can do to earn our way onto God's team. It is a free gift. Our actions and lifestyle may be impressive in comparison to some. If we compare ourselves to Hitler or the hypocrite who goes to church, we look pretty good. But when we try to make it onto God's team by the standard of a righteous life, we fall short. The good news is it is a free gift. You are chosen for the team because God loves you. He values you. He even likes you and desires you to spend time with him. But you do not make the team because of your skills as a player or as a person.

Reflection
If God loves me just as I am, why do I recoil from his love? Can I relax before God?

Prayer
Lord in heaven, help me to respond to your unconditional love; help me to embrace that love.

"Nothing you can do can make God love you more. Nothing you can do can make God love you less."
Mark Burlingame

Nicked with permission from: A Sporting Guide to Eternity, Steve Connor, Christian Focus Publications - ISBN 1-85792-746-X

Here we find Paul was responding to the lie, "You must follow the law to get to heaven," which was influencing his Galatian church. Don't be like the Galatians to whom Paul said, "Oh foolish Galatians! Who has cast an evil spell on you?" (Galatians 3:1).

Do you belong on God's team? If you do, you got on the team by trusting (having faith) in what Jesus did for you on the cross. You cannot make the team. You cannot earn your way to heaven! The law is the essence of the first five books of the Old Testament. Paul clearly explained the purpose of the law and the futility of trying to earn salvation by obeying the law. Paul was a highly trained Jew; he was very strategic in refuting many problems when Jewish people tried to mix faith in Christ with following Jewish custom. Paul understood the uselessness of trying to earn our way to heaven, and this book clearly points to salvation by faith in Christ alone.

Aren't you glad God gave us a book! Do not be surprised when people try to "add on" to the Christian faith. Fortunately, we have this great Scripture to help us stay in God's boundaries and keep some things out. If you are worried that someone may be trying to add on to your faith, simply see if it is in compliance with his book!

Galatians

In all we do this one's for You

LIVE it

GALATIANS

Greetings from Paul

1

This letter is from Paul, an apostle. I was not appointed by any group of people or any human authority, but by Jesus Christ himself and by God the Father, who raised Jesus from the dead.

[2]All the brothers and sisters here join me in sending this letter to the churches of Galatia.

[3]May God our Father and the Lord Jesus Christ give you grace and peace. [4]Jesus gave his life for our sins, just as God our Father planned, in order to rescue us from this evil world in which we live. [5]All glory to God forever and ever! Amen.

There Is Only One Good News

[6]I am shocked that you are turning away so soon from God, who called you to himself through the loving mercy of Christ. You are following a different way that pretends to be the Good News [7]but is not the Good News at all. You are being fooled by those who deliberately twist the truth concerning Christ.

[8]Let God's curse fall on anyone, including us or even an angel from heaven, who preaches a different kind of Good News than the one we preached to you. [9]I say again what we have said before: If anyone preaches any other Good News than the one you welcomed, let that person be cursed.

[10]Obviously, I'm not trying to win the approval of people, but of God. If pleasing people were my goal, I would not be Christ's servant.

Who are your five favorite sports people of all time?

1
2
3
4
5

Paul's Message Comes from Christ

[11]Dear brothers and sisters, I want you to understand that the gospel message I preach is not based on mere human reasoning. [12]I received my message from no human source, and no one taught me. Instead, I received it by direct revelation from Jesus Christ.

[13]You know what I was like when I followed the Jewish religion—how I violently persecuted God's church. I did my best to destroy it. [14]I was far ahead of my fellow Jews in my zeal for the traditions of my ancestors.

[15]But even before I was born, God chose me and called me by his marvelous grace. Then it pleased him [16]to reveal his Son to me so that I would proclaim the Good News about Jesus to the Gentiles.

When this happened, I did not rush out to consult with any human being. [17]Nor did I go up to Jerusalem to consult with those who were apostles before I was.

Instead, I went away into Arabia, and later I returned to the city of Damascus.

[18]Then three years later I went to Jerusalem to get to know Peter, and I stayed with him for fifteen days. [19]The only other apostle I met at that time was James, the Lord's brother. [20]I declare before God that what I am writing to you is not a lie. [21]After that visit I went north into the provinces of Syria and Cilicia. [22]And still the Christians in the churches in Judea didn't know me personally. [23]All they knew was that people were saying, "The one who used to persecute us is now preaching the very faith he tried to destroy!" [24]And they praised God because of me.

The Apostles Accept Paul

2

Then fourteen years later I went back to Jerusalem again, this time with Barnabas; and Titus came along, too. [2]I went there because God revealed to me that I should go. While I

Winners have hope!

Long before the fish sign, followers of Christ used an anchor as a symbol of their faith in Christ. In the up and down world of sports, what can be more valuable than an anchor? Many athletes live in fear of losing their place on their team or even losing their career. You can see the fear in their face; it says, "What is going to happen to me when my career is over?" Though it can be deeply disappointing when their career comes to an end, many Christian professional athletes know they have an anchor in God that will keep them safe and secure. No matter what level you play at, disappointment is part of sports, but instead of trying to find your happiness in short term success, Christianity offers permanent joy knowing we will spend forever with God!

"This hope is a strong and trustworthy anchor for our souls." (Hebrews 6:19)

Winners hang on to the big picture!

was there I met privately with those considered to be leaders of the church and shared with them the message I had been preaching to the Gentiles. I wanted to make sure that we were in agreement, for fear that all my efforts had been wasted and I was running the race for nothing. ³And they supported me and did not even demand that my companion Titus be circumcised, though he was a Gentile.

⁴Even that question came up only because of some so-called Christians there—false ones, really—who were secretly brought in. They sneaked in to spy on us and take away the freedom we have in Christ Jesus. They wanted to enslave us and force us to follow their Jewish regulations. ⁵But we refused to give in to them for a single moment. We wanted to preserve the truth of the gospel message for you.

⁶And the leaders of the church had nothing to add to what I was preaching. (By the way, their reputation as great leaders made no difference to me, for God has no favorites.) ⁷Instead, they saw that God had given me the responsibility of preaching the gospel to the Gentiles, just as he had given Peter the responsibility of preaching to the Jews. ⁸For the same God who worked through Peter as the apostle to the Jews also worked through me as the apostle to the Gentiles. ⁹In fact, James, Peter, and John, who were known as pillars of the church, recognized the gift God had given me, and they accepted Barnabas and me as their co-workers. They encouraged us to keep preaching to the Gentiles, while they continued their work with the Jews. ¹⁰Their only suggestion was that we keep on helping the poor, which I have always been eager to do.

Paul Confronts Peter

¹¹But when Peter came to Antioch, I had to oppose him to his face, for what he did was very wrong. ¹²When he first arrived, he ate with the Gentile Christians, who were not circumcised. But afterward, when some friends of James came, Peter wouldn't eat with the Gentiles anymore. He was afraid of

The Old Testament was divided into verses in 1448 for ease of use. The New Testament was divided into verses in 1551 for ease of use.

criticism from these people who insisted on the necessity of circumcision. ¹³As a result, other Jewish Christians followed Peter's hypocrisy, and even Barnabas was led astray by their hypocrisy.

¹⁴When I saw that they were not following the truth of the gospel message, I said to Peter in front of all the others, "Since you, a Jew by birth, have discarded the Jewish laws and are living like a Gentile, why are you now trying to make these Gentiles follow the Jewish traditions?

¹⁵"You and I are Jews by birth, not 'sinners' like the Gentiles. ¹⁶Yet we know that a person is made right with God by faith in Jesus Christ, not by obeying the law. And we have believed in Christ Jesus, so that we might be made right with God because of our faith in Christ, not because we have obeyed the law. For no one will ever be made right with God by obeying the law."

¹⁷But suppose we seek to be made right with God through faith in Christ and then we are found guilty because we have abandoned the law. Would that mean Christ has led us into sin? Absolutely not! ¹⁸Rather, I am a sinner if I rebuild the old system of law I already

tore down. ¹⁹For when I tried to keep the law, it condemned me. So I died to the law—I stopped trying to meet all its requirements—so that I might live for God. ²⁰My old self has been crucified with Christ. It is no longer I who live, but Christ lives in me. So I live in this earthly body by trusting in the Son of God, who loved me and gave himself for me. ²¹I do not treat the grace of God as meaningless. For if keeping the law could make us right with God, then there was no need for Christ to die.

action

3:1-5 WHAT'S IT SAYING?

WHAT AM I GOING TO DO ABOUT IT?

Fruit is good for you (GALATIANS 5)

I will endeavor to exhibit Christian behavior in my sport.

LOVE: I will show genuine concern for teammates and ask them how they are doing and mean it.

JOY: I will remind myself that God has given me eternal life.

PEACE: I will prepare harder for competitions and know that I have done all that I could have done to be prepared with the talent God has given me.

PATIENCE: I will remember that teammates may not respond the same way I do.

KINDNESS: I will encourage teammates and competitors.

GOODNESS: I will assert a positive atmosphere in the locker room.

FAITHFULNESS: I will be committed to a training program — spiritual and physical.

GENTLENESS: I will be gracious when I win and lose.

SELF-CONTROL: I will remember that God has given me great power, and I will keep that power within his boundaries.

BIBLE HIT

Warm-up is essential:

A warm-up consisting of exercises performed immediately before an activity to increase circulation and heart rate is an essential part of a good conditioning program.

The Law and Faith in Christ

3

Oh, foolish Galatians! Who has cast an evil spell on you? For the meaning of Jesus Christ's death was made as clear to you as if you had seen a picture of his death on the cross. [2]Let me ask you this one question: Did you receive the Holy Spirit by obeying the law of Moses? Of course not! You received the Spirit because you believed the message you heard about Christ. [3]How foolish can you be? After starting your Christian lives in the Spirit, why are you now trying to become perfect by your own human effort? [4]Have you experienced so much for nothing? Surely it was not in vain, was it? [5]I ask you again, does God give you the Holy Spirit and work miracles among you because you obey the law? Of course not! It is because you believe the message you heard about Christ.

[6]In the same way, "Abraham believed God, and God counted him as righteous because of his faith." [7]The real children of Abraham, then, are those who put their faith in God.

[8]What's more, the Scriptures looked forward to this time when God would declare the Gentiles to be righteous because of their faith. God proclaimed this good news to Abraham long ago when he said, "All nations will be blessed through you." [9]So all who put their faith in Christ share the same blessing Abraham received because of his faith.

[10]But those who depend on the law to make them right with God are under his curse, for the Scriptures say, "Cursed is everyone who does not observe and obey

Until 1967 it wasn't illegal for Olympic athletes to use drugs to enhance their performance during competition.

all the commands that are written in God's Book of the Law." [11]So it is clear that no one can be made right with God by trying to keep the law. For the Scriptures say, "It is through faith that a righteous person has life." [12]This way of faith is very different from the way of law, which says, "It is through obeying the law that a person has life."

[13]But Christ has rescued us from the curse pronounced by the law. When he was hung on the cross, he took upon himself the curse for our wrongdoing. For it is written in the Scriptures, "Cursed is everyone who is hung on a tree." [14]Through Christ Jesus, God has blessed the Gentiles with the same blessing he promised to Abraham, so that we who are believers might receive the promised Holy Spirit through faith.

The Law and God's Promise

[15]Dear brothers and sisters, here's an example from everyday life. Just as no one can set aside or amend an irrevocable agreement, so it is in this case. [16]God gave the promises to Abraham and his child. And notice that the Scripture doesn't say "to his children," as if it meant many descendants. Rather, it says "to his child"—and that, of course, means Christ. [17]This is what I am trying to say: The agreement God

PERSONAL ASSESSMENTS

SPIRITUAL MATURITY

True or False

- I really want to spend time with God.   T/F

- I really want to know more about how to become a stronger Christian.   T/F

- I really believe prayer makes a difference.   T/F

- I really want to encourage others to grow in their faith in Jesus Christ.   T/F

- I really want to go to heaven when I die.   T/F

- I really am grateful for the sacrifices God has made for me by sending his Son to be the sacrifice that takes away my sin and separation from God.   T/F

- Out of gratitude, I really want to obey and serve God.   T/F

---

made with Abraham could not be canceled 430 years later when God gave the law to Moses. God would be breaking his promise. [18]For if the inheritance could be received by keeping the law, then it would not be the result of accepting God's promise. But God graciously gave it to Abraham as a promise. [19]Why, then, was the law given? It was given alongside the promise to show people their sins. But the law was designed to last only until the coming of the child who was promised. God gave his law through angels to Moses, who was the mediator between God and the people. [20]Now a mediator is helpful if more than one party must reach an agreement. But God, who is one, did not use a mediator when he gave his promise to Abraham.

[21]Is there a conflict, then, between God's law and God's promises? Absolutely not! If the law could give us new life, we could be made right with God by obeying it. [22]But the Scriptures declare that we are all prisoners of sin, so we receive God's promise of freedom only by believing in Jesus Christ.

God's Children through Faith

[23]Before the way of faith in Christ was available to us, we were placed under guard by the law. We were kept in protective custody, so to speak, until the way of faith was revealed.

[24]Let me put it another way. The law was our guardian until Christ came; it protected us until we could be made right with God through faith. [25]And now that the way of faith has come, we no longer need the law as our guardian.

[26]For you are all children of God through faith in Christ Jesus. [27]And all who have been united with Christ in baptism have put on the character of Christ, like putting on new clothes. [28]There is no longer Jew or Gentile, slave or free, male and female. For you are all one in Christ Jesus. [29]And now that you belong to Christ, you are the true children of Abraham. You are his heirs, and God's promise to Abraham belongs to you.

4

Think of it this way. If a father dies and leaves an inheritance for his young children, those children are not much better off than slaves until they grow up, even though they actually own everything their father had. [2]They have to obey their guardians until they reach whatever age their father set. [3]And that's the

Until the 1870s, baseball was played without the use of gloves.

way it was with us before Christ came. We were like children; we were slaves to the basic spiritual principles of this world.

[4]But when the right time came, God sent his Son, born of a woman, subject to the law. [5]God sent him to buy freedom for us who were slaves to the law, so that he could adopt us as his very own children. [6]And because we are his children, God has sent the Spirit of his Son into our hearts, prompting us to call out, "Abba, Father." [7]Now you are no longer a slave but God's own child. And since you are his child, God has made you his heir.

Paul's Concern for the Galatians

[8]Before you Gentiles knew God, you were slaves to so-called gods that do not even exist. [9]So now that you know God (or should I say, now that God knows you), why do you want to go back again and become slaves once more to the weak and useless spiritual principles of this world? [10]You are trying to earn favor with God by observing certain days or months or seasons or years. [11]I fear for you. Perhaps all my hard work with you was for nothing. [12]Dear brothers and sisters, I plead with you to live as I do in freedom from these things, for I have become like you Gentiles—free from those laws.

You did not mistreat me when I first preached to you. [13]Surely you remember that I was sick when I first brought you the Good News. [14]But even though my condition tempted you to reject me, you did not despise me or turn me away. No, you took me in and cared for me as though I were an angel from God or even Christ Jesus himself. [15]Where is that joyful and grateful spirit you felt then? I am sure you would have taken out your own eyes and given them to me if it had been possible. [16]Have I now become your enemy because I am telling you the truth?

[17]Those false teachers are so eager to win your favor, but their intentions are not good. They are trying to shut you off from me so that you will pay attention only to them. [18]If someone is eager to do good things for you, that's all right; but let them do it all the time, not just when I'm with you.

[19]Oh, my dear children! I feel as if I'm going through labor pains for you again, and they will continue until Christ is fully developed in your lives. [20]I wish I were with you right now so I could change my tone. But at this distance I don't know how else to help you.

Abraham's Two Children

[21]Tell me, you who want to live under the law, do you know what the law actually says? [22]The Scriptures say

that Abraham had two sons, one from his slave-wife and one from his freeborn wife. [23]The son of the slave-wife was born in a human attempt to bring about the fulfillment of God's promise. But the son of the freeborn wife was born as God's own fulfillment of his promise.

[24]These two women serve as an illustration of God's two covenants. The first woman, Hagar, represents Mount Sinai where people received the law that enslaved them. [25]And now Jerusalem is just like Mount Sinai in Arabia, because she and her children live in slavery to the law. [26]But the other woman, Sarah, represents the heavenly Jerusalem. She is the free woman, and she is our mother. [27]As Isaiah said,

"Rejoice, O childless woman,
you who have never given birth!
Break into a joyful shout,
you who have never been in labor!
For the desolate woman now has more children
than the woman who lives with her husband!"

[28]And you, dear brothers and sisters, are children of the promise, just like Isaac. [29]But you are now being persecuted by those who want you to keep the law, just as Ishmael, the child born by human effort, persecuted Isaac, the child born by the power of the Spirit.

[30]But what do the Scriptures say about that? "Get rid of the slave and her son, for the son of the slave woman will not share the inheritance with the free woman's son." [31]So, dear brothers and sisters, we are not children of the slave woman; we are children of the free woman.

Freedom in Christ

5

So Christ has truly set us free. Now make sure that you stay free, and don't get tied up again in slavery to the law.

[2]Listen! I, Paul, tell you this: If you are counting on circumcision to make you right with God, then Christ will be of no benefit to you. [3]I'll say it again. If you are trying to find favor with God by being circumcised, you must obey every regulation in the whole law of Moses. [4]For if you are trying to make yourselves right with God by keeping the law, you have been cut off from Christ! You have fallen away from God's grace. [5]But we who live by the Spirit eagerly wait to receive by faith the righteousness God has promised to us. [6]For when we place our faith in Christ Jesus, there is no benefit in being circumcised or being uncircumcised. What is important is faith expressing itself in love.

[7]You were running the race so well. Who has held you back from following the truth? [8]It certainly isn't God, for he is the one who called you to freedom. [9]This false teaching is like a little yeast that spreads through the whole batch of dough! [10]I am trusting the Lord to keep you from believing false teachings. God will judge that person, whoever he is, who has been confusing you.

[11]Dear brothers and sisters, if I were still preaching that you must be circumcised—as some say I do—why am I still being persecuted? If I were no longer preaching salvation

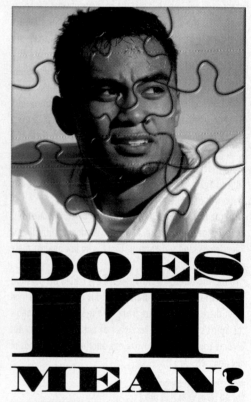

Noah's ark

A building of gopher wood covered with pitch, 300 cubits long, 50 cubits broad, and 30 cubits high (Genesis 6:14-16); an oblong floating house of three stories, with a door in the side and a window in the roof. It took 100 years to build (Genesis 5:32; 7:6). It was intended to preserve certain people and animals from the deluge that God was about to bring over the earth.

through the cross of Christ, no one would be offended. [12]I just wish that those troublemakers who want to mutilate you by circumcision would mutilate themselves.

[13]For you have been called to live in freedom, my brothers and sisters. But don't use your freedom to satisfy your sinful nature. Instead, use your freedom to serve one another in love. [14]For the whole law can be summed up in this one command: "Love your neighbor as yourself." [15]But if you are always biting and devouring one another, watch out! Beware of destroying one another.

Living by the Spirit's Power

[16]So I say, let the Holy Spirit guide your lives. Then you won't be doing what your sinful nature craves. [17]The sinful nature wants to do evil, which is just the opposite of what the Spirit wants. And the Spirit gives us desires that are the opposite of what the sinful nature desires. These two forces are constantly fighting each other, so you are not free to carry out your good intentions. [18]But when you are directed by the Spirit, you are not under obligation to the law of Moses.

[19]When you follow the desires of your sinful nature, the results are very clear: sexual immorality, impurity, lustful pleasures, [20]idolatry, sorcery, hostility, quarreling, jealousy, outbursts of anger, selfish ambition, dissension, division, [21]envy, drunkenness, wild parties, and other sins like these. Let me tell you again, as I have before, that anyone living that sort of life will not inherit the Kingdom of God.

[22]But the Holy Spirit produces this kind of fruit in our lives: love, joy, peace, patience, kindness, goodness, faithfulness, [23]gentleness, and self-control. There is no law against these things!

[24]Those who belong to Christ Jesus have nailed the passions and desires of their sinful nature to his cross and crucified them there. [25]Since we are living by the Spirit, let us follow the Spirit's leading in every part of our lives. [26]Let us not become conceited, or provoke one another, or be jealous of one another.

STAND POINT

When you want to give up

6:9

So let's not get tired of doing what is good. At just the right time we will reap a harvest of blessing if we don't give up.

action

5:16-26 WHAT'S IT SAYING?

WHAT AM I GOING TO DO ABOUT IT?

We Harvest What We Plant

6

Dear brothers and sisters, if another believer is overcome by some sin, you who are godly should gently and humbly help that person back onto the right path. And be careful not to fall into the same temptation yourself. [2]Share each other's burdens, and in this way obey the law of Christ. [3]If you think you are too important to help someone, you are only fooling yourself. You are not that important.

[4]Pay careful attention to your own work, for then you will get the satisfaction of a job well done, and you won't need to compare yourself to anyone else. [5]For we are each responsible for our own conduct. [6]Those who are taught the word of God should provide for their teachers, sharing all good things with them. [7]Don't be misled—you cannot mock the justice of God. You will always harvest what you plant. [8]Those who live only to satisfy their own sinful nature will harvest decay and death from that sinful nature. But those who live to please the Spirit will harvest everlasting life from the Spirit. [9]So let's not get tired

of doing what is good. At just the right time we will reap a harvest of blessing if we don't give up. [10]Therefore, whenever we have the opportunity, we should do good to everyone—especially to those in the family of faith.

Paul's Final Advice

[11]NOTICE WHAT LARGE LETTERS I USE AS I WRITE THESE CLOSING WORDS IN MY OWN HANDWRITING.

[12]Those who are trying to force you to be circumcised want to look good to others. They don't want to be persecuted for teaching that the cross of Christ alone can save. [13]And even those who advocate circumcision don't keep the whole law themselves. They only want you to be circumcised so they can boast about it and claim you as their disciples.

[14]As for me, may I never boast about anything except the cross of our Lord Jesus Christ. Because of that cross, my interest in this world has been crucified, and the world's interest in me has also died. [15]It doesn't matter whether we have been circumcised or not. What counts is whether we have been transformed into a new creation. [16]May God's peace and mercy be upon all who live by this principle; they are the new people of God.

[17]From now on, don't let anyone trouble me with these things. For I bear on my body the scars that show I belong to Jesus.

[18]Dear brothers and sisters, may the grace of our Lord Jesus Christ be with your spirit. Amen.

Bible

What the Bible says about itself: "All Scripture is inspired by God and is useful to teach us what is true and to make us realize what is wrong in our lives. It corrects us when we are wrong and teaches us to do what is right"
(2 Timothy 3:16).

Lock and load! We are a united team, and we have a battle to fight. Paul ends his letter to the Ephesian church (which was located on the beautiful Mediterranean coast of modern-day Turkey) with an order to step it up and get ready for battle — to put on God's full armor! Ephesians was written for the readers to get a glimpse of the majestic works of God and take action in everyday life, with a godly attitude and purpose for living. Paul most likely was writing this book from a Roman prison or when he was under house arrest.

In the first three chapters we see a privileged view of God's grand character and his purpose for our life: "I also pray that you will understand the incredible greatness of God's power for us who believe in him" (Ephesians 1:19). This understanding of God fires us up to live a life worthy of our inheritance in his family. The last three chapters are to be lived out in response to the first three.

As you see the excitement and joy that pours out of Paul, remember that his circumstances do not dictate his attitude; he is suffering and in prison for his faith.

Ephesians

Game Plan

SIN

SIN

ETERNAL LIFE

ETERNAL LIFE

USEFUL INFORMATION

For the wages of sin is death, but the free gift of God is eternal life through Christ Jesus our Lord.
Romans 6:23

sport

EPHESIANS

Greetings from Paul

1

This letter is from Paul, chosen by the will of God to be an apostle of Christ Jesus.

I am writing to God's holy people in Ephesus, who are faithful followers of Christ Jesus.

[2]May God our Father and the Lord Jesus Christ give you grace and peace.

Spiritual Blessings

[3]All praise to God, the Father of our Lord Jesus Christ, who has blessed us with every spiritual blessing in the heavenly realms because we are united with Christ. [4]Even before he made the world, God loved us and chose us in Christ to be holy and without fault in his eyes. [5]God decided in advance to adopt us into his own family by bringing us to himself through Jesus Christ. This is what he wanted to do, and it gave him great pleasure. [6]So we praise God for the glorious grace he has poured out on us who belong to his dear Son. [7]He is so rich in kindness and grace that he purchased our freedom with the blood of his Son and forgave our sins. [8]He has showered his kindness on us, along with all wisdom and understanding.

[9]God has now revealed to us his mysterious plan regarding Christ, a plan to fulfill his own good pleasure. [10]And this is the plan: At the right time he will bring everything together under the authority of Christ—everything in heaven and on earth. [11]Furthermore, because we are united with Christ, we have received an inheritance from God, for he chose us in advance, and he makes everything work out according to his plan.

STATS

Forrest Towns beat a prize cavalry horse, trained as a running jumper, in the 120-yard hurdles. They used only five hurdles to give the horse's longer stride a fair chance.

[12]God's purpose was that we Jews who were the first to trust in Christ would bring praise and glory to God. [13]And now you Gentiles have also heard the truth, the Good News that God saves you. And when you believed in Christ, he identified you as his own by giving you the Holy Spirit, whom he promised long ago. [14]The Spirit is God's guarantee that he will give us the inheritance he promised and that he has purchased us to be his own people. He did this so we would praise and glorify him.

Paul's Prayer for Spiritual Wisdom

[15]Ever since I first heard of your strong faith in the Lord Jesus and your love for God's people everywhere, [16]I have not stopped thanking God for you. I pray for you constantly, [17]asking God, the glorious Father of our Lord Jesus Christ, to give you spiritual wisdom

Eat up! Consider the Word of God as your spiritual food. Would you not eat for a couple days before you ran in a marathon? Would you let a child go without food and stunt their growth? So why starve spiritually? Get in there and eat some more! It's pure power! "You must crave pure spiritual milk so that you will grow into a full experience of salvation. Cry out for this nourishment, now that you have had a taste of the Lord's kindness." (1 Peter 2:2-3)

and insight so that you might grow in your knowledge of God. [18]I pray that your hearts will be flooded with light so that you can understand the confident hope he has given to those he called—his holy people who are his rich and glorious inheritance.

[19]I also pray that you will understand the incredible greatness of God's power for us who believe him. This is the same mighty power [20]that raised Christ from the dead and seated him in the place of honor at God's right hand in the heavenly realms. [21]Now he is far above any ruler or authority or power or leader or anything else—not only in this world but also in the world to come. [22]God has put all things under the authority of Christ and has made him head over all things for the benefit of the church. [23]And the church is his body; it is made full and complete by Christ, who fills all things everywhere with himself.

Made Alive with Christ

2

Once you were dead because of your disobedience and your many sins. [2]You used to live in sin, just like the rest of the world, obeying the devil—the commander of the powers in the unseen world. He is the spirit at work in the hearts of those who refuse to obey God. [3]All of us used to live that way, following the passionate desires and inclinations of our sinful nature. By our very nature we were subject to God's anger, just like everyone else.

[4]But God is so rich in mercy, and he loved us so much, [5]that even though we were dead because of our sins, he gave us life when he raised Christ from the dead. (It is only by God's grace that you have been saved!) [6]For he raised us from the dead along with Christ and seated us with him in the heavenly realms because we are united with Christ Jesus. [7]So God can point to us in all future ages as examples of the incredible wealth of his grace and kindness toward us, as shown in all he has done for us who are united with Christ Jesus.

[8]God saved you by his grace when you believed. And you can't take credit for this; it is a gift from God. [9]Salvation is not a reward for the good things we have done, so none of us can boast about it. [10]For we are God's masterpiece. He has created us anew in Christ Jesus, so we can do the good things he planned for us long ago.

Oneness and Peace in Christ

[11]Don't forget that you Gentiles used to be outsiders. You were called "uncircumcised heathens" by the Jews, who were proud of their circumcision, even though it affected only their bodies and not their hearts. [12]In those days you were living apart from Christ. You were excluded from citizenship among the people of Israel, and you did not know the covenant

promises God had made to them. You lived in this world without God and without hope. [13]But now you have been united with Christ Jesus. Once you were far away from God, but now you have been brought near to him through the blood of Christ.

[14]For Christ himself has brought peace to us. He united Jews and Gentiles into one people when, in his own body on the cross, he broke down the wall of hostility that separated us. [15]He did this by ending the system of law with its commandments and regulations. He made peace between Jews and Gentiles by creating in himself one new people from the two groups. [16]Together as one body, Christ reconciled both groups to God by means of his death on the cross, and our hostility toward each other was put to death.

[17]He brought this Good News of peace to you Gentiles who were far away from him, and peace to the Jews who were near. [18]Now all of us can come to the Father through the same Holy Spirit because of what Christ has done for us.

A Temple for the Lord

[19]So now you Gentiles are no longer strangers and foreigners. You are citizens along with all of God's holy people. You are members of God's family. [20]Together, we are his house, built on the foundation of the apostles and the prophets. And the cornerstone is Christ Jesus himself. [21]We are carefully joined together in him, becoming a holy temple for the Lord. [22]Through him you Gentiles are also being made part of this dwelling where God lives by his Spirit.

God's Mysterious Plan Revealed

3

When I think of all this, I, Paul, a prisoner of Christ Jesus for

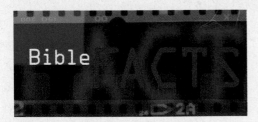

In reading the Bible, it soon becomes apparent that certain numbers occur more frequently than we would expect. FORTY is the number of testing. Jesus was tempted in the wilderness FORTY days and nights. Israel wandered in the wilderness FORTY years. During the flood of Noah, the rain fell FORTY days and nights.

the benefit of you Gentiles . . . [2]assuming, by the way, that you know God gave me the special responsibility of extending his grace to you Gentiles. [3]As I briefly wrote earlier, God himself revealed his mysterious plan to me. [4]As you read what I have written, you will understand my insight into this plan regarding Christ. [5]God did not reveal it to previous generations, but now by his Spirit he has revealed it to his holy apostles and prophets.

[6]And this is God's plan: Both Gentiles and Jews who believe the Good News share equally in the riches inherited by God's children. Both are part of the same body, and both enjoy the promise of blessings because they belong to Christ Jesus. [7]By God's grace and mighty power, I have been given the privilege of serving him by spreading this Good News.

[8]Though I am the least deserving of all God's people, he graciously gave me the privilege of telling the Gentiles about the endless treasures available to them in Christ. [9]I was chosen to explain to everyone this mysterious plan that God, the Creator of all things, had kept secret from the beginning.

[10]God's purpose in all this was to use the church to display his wisdom in its rich variety to all the unseen rulers and authorities in the heavenly places. [11]This was his eternal plan, which he carried out through Christ Jesus our Lord.

[12]Because of Christ and our faith in him, we can now come boldly and confidently into God's presence. [13]So please don't lose heart because of my trials here. I am suffering for you, so you should feel honored.

Paul's Prayer for Spiritual Growth

[14]When I think of all this, I fall to my knees and pray to the Father, [15]the Creator of everything in heaven and on earth. [16]I pray that from his glorious, unlimited resources he will empower you with inner strength through his Spirit. [17]Then Christ will make his home in your hearts as you trust in him. Your roots will grow down into God's love and keep you strong. [18]And may you have the power to understand, as all God's people should, how wide, how long, how high, and how deep his love is. [19]May you experience the love of Christ, though it is too great to understand fully. Then you will be made complete with all the fullness of life and power that comes from God.

[20]Now all glory to God, who is able, through his mighty power at work within us, to accomplish infinitely more than we might ask or think. [21]Glory to him in the church and in Christ Jesus through all generations forever and ever! Amen.

action

2:19-22 WHAT'S IT SAYING?

WHAT AM I GOING TO DO ABOUT IT?

Unity in the Body

4

Therefore I, a prisoner for serving the Lord, beg you to lead a life worthy of your calling, for you have been called by God. [2]Always be humble and gentle. Be patient with each other, making allowance for each other's faults because of your love. [3]Make every effort

STAND POINT

When you are planning your future

3:20

Now all glory to God, who is able, through his mighty power at work within us, to accomplish infinitely more than we might ask or think.

to keep yourselves united in the Spirit, binding yourselves together with peace. ⁴For there is one body and one Spirit, just as you have been called to one glorious hope for the future. ⁵There is one Lord, one

Living as Children of Light

¹⁷With the Lord's authority I say this: Live no longer as the Gentiles do, for they are hopelessly confused. ¹⁸Their minds are full of darkness; they wander far

for we are all parts of the same body. ²⁶And "don't sin by letting anger control you." Don't let the sun go down while you are still angry, ²⁷for anger gives a foothold to the devil. ²⁸If you are a thief, quit stealing. Instead, use your hands for

My sport dominates my life. Should I quit it?

You will fight with idols (things that become more important than God) all your life. Having a sport dominate your life may be the first of many challenges you struggle through. Whenever you have an idol, you have to deal with it severely. Jesus uses hyperbole (overstatement) to demonstrate our immediate need to deal with the problem: "If your eye causes you to sin, gouge it out" (Matthew 18:9). Dealing with an idol in our lives is hard. Sometimes we should stop the activity that becomes an idol, but sometimes we should fight hard to put it in its proper order in our life. Many parents make children more important than God, but they do not quit being a parent. Instead, we need to work out how to make God number one in our heart. Can you do the same with your sport?

faith, one baptism, ⁶and one God and Father, who is over all and in all and living through all.

⁷However, he has given each one of us a special gift through the generosity of Christ. ⁸That is why the Scriptures say,

"When he ascended to the heights,
he led a crowd of captives
and gave gifts to his people."

⁹Notice that it says "he ascended." This clearly means that Christ also descended to our lowly world. ¹⁰And the same one who descended is the one who ascended higher than all the heavens, so that he might fill the entire universe with himself.

¹¹Now these are the gifts Christ gave to the church: the apostles, the prophets, the evangelists, and the pastors and teachers. ¹²Their responsibility is to equip God's people to do his work and build up the church, the body of Christ. ¹³This will continue until we all come to such unity in our faith and knowledge of God's Son that we will be mature in the Lord, measuring up to the full and complete standard of Christ.

¹⁴Then we will no longer be immature like children. We won't be tossed and blown about by every wind of new teaching. We will not be influenced when people try to trick us with lies so clever they sound like the truth. ¹⁵Instead, we will speak the truth in love, growing in every way more and more like Christ, who is the head of his body, the church. ¹⁶He makes the whole body fit together perfectly. As each part does its own special work, it helps the other parts grow, so that the whole body is healthy and growing and full of love.

from the life God gives because they have closed their minds and hardened their hearts against him. ¹⁹They have no sense of shame. They live for lustful pleasure and eagerly practice every kind of impurity.

²⁰But that isn't what you learned about Christ. ²¹Since you have heard about Jesus and have learned the truth that comes from him, ²²throw off your old sinful nature and your former way of life, which is corrupted by lust and deception. ²³Instead, let the Spirit renew your thoughts and attitudes. ²⁴Put on your new nature, created to be like God—truly righteous and holy.

²⁵So stop telling lies. Let us tell our neighbors the truth,

good hard work, and then give generously to others in need. ²⁹Don't use foul or abusive language. Let everything you say be good and helpful, so that your words will be an encouragement to those who hear them.

³⁰And do not bring sorrow to God's Holy Spirit by the way you live. Remember, he has identified you as his own, guaranteeing that you will be saved on the day of redemption.

³¹Get rid of all bitterness, rage, anger, harsh words, and slander, as well as all types of evil behavior. ³²Instead, be kind to each other, tenderhearted, forgiving one another, just as God through Christ has forgiven you.

Who are your five favorite Bible heroes?

1
2
3
4
5

BIG FIVE

SEPTEMBER M.A.P.

1
S.D.	P.L.	P.G.	S.G.
P. ☐	F. ☐	F. ☐	T. ☐
F. ☐	W. ☐	W. ☐	P. ☐
B. ☐	P. ☐	C. ☐	C. ☐

2
S.D.	P.L.	P.G.	S.G.
P. ☐	F. ☐	F. ☐	T. ☐
F. ☐	W. ☐	W. ☐	P. ☐
B. ☐	P. ☐	C. ☐	C. ☐

3
S.D.	P.L.	P.G.	S.G.
P. ☐	F. ☐	F. ☐	T. ☐
F. ☐	W. ☐	W. ☐	P. ☐
B. ☐	P. ☐	C. ☐	C. ☐

4
S.D.	P.L.	P.G.	S.G.
P. ☐	F. ☐	F. ☐	T. ☐
F. ☐	W. ☐	W. ☐	P. ☐
B. ☐	P. ☐	C. ☐	C. ☐

9
S.D.	P.L.	P.G.	S.G.
P. ☐	F. ☐	F. ☐	T. ☐
F. ☐	W. ☐	W. ☐	P. ☐
B. ☐	P. ☐	C. ☐	C. ☐

10
S.D.	P.L.	P.G.	S.G.
P. ☐	F. ☐	F. ☐	T. ☐
F. ☐	W. ☐	W. ☐	P. ☐
B. ☐	P. ☐	C. ☐	C. ☐

11
S.D.	P.L.	P.G.	S.G.
P. ☐	F. ☐	F. ☐	T. ☐
F. ☐	W. ☐	W. ☐	P. ☐
B. ☐	P. ☐	C. ☐	C. ☐

12
S.D.	P.L.	P.G.	S.G.
P. ☐	F. ☐	F. ☐	T. ☐
F. ☐	W. ☐	W. ☐	P. ☐
B. ☐	P. ☐	C. ☐	C. ☐

17
S.D.	P.L.	P.G.	S.G.
P. ☐	F. ☐	F. ☐	T. ☐
F. ☐	W. ☐	W. ☐	P. ☐
B. ☐	P. ☐	C. ☐	C. ☐

18
S.D.	P.L.	P.G.	S.G.
P. ☐	F. ☐	F. ☐	T. ☐
F. ☐	W. ☐	W. ☐	P. ☐
B. ☐	P. ☐	C. ☐	C. ☐

19
S.D.	P.L.	P.G.	S.G.
P. ☐	F. ☐	F. ☐	T. ☐
F. ☐	W. ☐	W. ☐	P. ☐
B. ☐	P. ☐	C. ☐	C. ☐

20
S.D.	P.L.	P.G.	S.G.
P. ☐	F. ☐	F. ☐	T. ☐
F. ☐	W. ☐	W. ☐	P. ☐
B. ☐	P. ☐	C. ☐	C. ☐

25
S.D.	P.L.	P.G.	S.G.
P. ☐	F. ☐	F. ☐	T. ☐
F. ☐	W. ☐	W. ☐	P. ☐
B. ☐	P. ☐	C. ☐	C. ☐

26
S.D.	P.L.	P.G.	S.G.
P. ☐	F. ☐	F. ☐	T. ☐
F. ☐	W. ☐	W. ☐	P. ☐
B. ☐	P. ☐	C. ☐	C. ☐

27
S.D.	P.L.	P.G.	S.G.
P. ☐	F. ☐	F. ☐	T. ☐
F. ☐	W. ☐	W. ☐	P. ☐
B. ☐	P. ☐	C. ☐	C. ☐

28
S.D.	P.L.	P.G.	S.G.
P. ☐	F. ☐	F. ☐	T. ☐
F. ☐	W. ☐	W. ☐	P. ☐
B. ☐	P. ☐	C. ☐	C. ☐

Spiritual Disciplines

Prayer

Faith Community

Bible Reading

Prayer List

Friends

World

Personal

Who am I....
Where am I going....
How am I going to get there?

nt:sport

MONTHLY ACTION PLAN

5

S.D.	P.L.	P.G.	S.G.
P. ☐	F. ☐	F. ☐	T. ☐
F. ☐	W. ☐	W. ☐	P. ☐
B. ☐	P. ☐	C. ☐	C. ☐

6

S.D.	P.L.	P.G.	S.G.
P. ☐	F. ☐	F. ☐	T. ☐
F. ☐	W. ☐	W. ☐	P. ☐
B. ☐	P. ☐	C. ☐	C. ☐

7

S.D.	P.L.	P.G.	S.G.
P. ☐	F. ☐	F. ☐	T. ☐
F. ☐	W. ☐	W. ☐	P. ☐
B. ☐	P. ☐	C. ☐	C. ☐

8

S.D.	P.L.	P.G.	S.G.
P. ☐	F. ☐	F. ☐	T. ☐
F. ☐	W. ☐	W. ☐	P. ☐
B. ☐	P. ☐	C. ☐	C. ☐

13

S.D.	P.L.	P.G.	S.G.
P. ☐	F. ☐	F. ☐	T. ☐
F. ☐	W. ☐	W. ☐	P. ☐
B. ☐	P. ☐	C. ☐	C. ☐

14

S.D.	P.L.	P.G.	S.G.
P. ☐	F. ☐	F. ☐	T. ☐
F. ☐	W. ☐	W. ☐	P. ☐
B. ☐	P. ☐	C. ☐	C. ☐

15

S.D.	P.L.	P.G.	S.G.
P. ☐	F. ☐	F. ☐	T. ☐
F. ☐	W. ☐	W. ☐	P. ☐
B. ☐	P. ☐	C. ☐	C. ☐

16

S.D.	P.L.	P.G.	S.G.
P. ☐	F. ☐	F. ☐	T. ☐
F. ☐	W. ☐	W. ☐	P. ☐
B. ☐	P. ☐	C. ☐	C. ☐

21

S.D.	P.L.	P.G.	S.G.
P. ☐	F. ☐	F. ☐	T. ☐
F. ☐	W. ☐	W. ☐	P. ☐
B. ☐	P. ☐	C. ☐	C. ☐

22

S.D.	P.L.	P.G.	S.G.
P. ☐	F. ☐	F. ☐	T. ☐
F. ☐	W. ☐	W. ☐	P. ☐
B. ☐	P. ☐	C. ☐	C. ☐

23

S.D.	P.L.	P.G.	S.G.
P. ☐	F. ☐	F. ☐	T. ☐
F. ☐	W. ☐	W. ☐	P. ☐
B. ☐	P. ☐	C. ☐	C. ☐

24

S.D.	P.L.	P.G.	S.G.
P. ☐	F. ☐	F. ☐	T. ☐
F. ☐	W. ☐	W. ☐	P. ☐
B. ☐	P. ☐	C. ☐	C. ☐

29

S.D.	P.L.	P.G.	S.G.
P. ☐	F. ☐	F. ☐	T. ☐
F. ☐	W. ☐	W. ☐	P. ☐
B. ☐	P. ☐	C. ☐	C. ☐

30

S.D.	P.L.	P.G.	S.G.
P. ☐	F. ☐	F. ☐	T. ☐
F. ☐	W. ☐	W. ☐	P. ☐
B. ☐	P. ☐	C. ☐	C. ☐

Proverbs 16:9

We can make our plans, but the LORD determines our steps.

Personal Goals

Famlly

Work/School/Social

Challenge

Sport Goals

Training

Performance

Competition Results

(For designing your M.A.P. – Monthly Action Plan – see introduction pages)

Living in the Light

5

Imitate God, therefore, in everything you do, because you are his dear children. [2]Live a life filled with love, following the example of Christ. He loved us and offered himself as a sacrifice for us, a pleasing aroma to God.

[3]Let there be no sexual immorality, impurity, or greed among you. Such sins have no place among God's people. [4]Obscene stories, foolish talk, and coarse jokes—these are not for you. Instead, let there be thankfulness to God. [5]You can be sure that no immoral, impure, or greedy person will inherit the Kingdom of Christ and of God. For a greedy person is an idolater, worshiping the things of this world.

[6]Don't be fooled by those who try to excuse these sins, for the anger of God will fall on all who disobey him. [7]Don't participate in the things these people do. [8]For once you were full of darkness, but now you have light from the Lord. So live as people of light! [9]For this light within you produces only what is good and right and true.

[10]Carefully determine what pleases the Lord. [11]Take no part in the worthless deeds of evil and darkness; instead, expose them. [12]It is shameful even to talk about the things that ungodly people do in secret. [13]But their evil intentions will be exposed when the light shines on them, [14]for the light makes everything visible. This is why it is said,

"Awake, O sleeper,
rise up from the dead,
and Christ will give you light."

Living by the Spirit's Power

[15]So be careful how you live. Don't live like fools, but like those who are wise. [16]Make the most of every opportunity in these evil days. [17]Don't act thoughtlessly, but understand what the Lord wants you to do. [18]Don't be drunk with wine, because that will ruin your life. Instead, be filled with the Holy Spirit, [19]singing psalms and hymns and spiritual songs among yourselves, and making music to the Lord in your hearts. [20]And give thanks for everything to God the Father in the name of our Lord Jesus Christ.

Spirit-Guided Relationships: Wives and Husbands

[21]And further, submit to one another out of reverence for Christ.

[22]For wives, this means submit to your husbands as to the Lord. [23]For a husband is the head of his wife as Christ is the head of the church. He is the Savior of his body, the church. [24]As the church submits to Christ, so you wives should submit to your husbands in everything.

[25]For husbands, this means love your wives, just as Christ

Do you need some guidance?

What team should I play for? What classes should I take? What church should I go to? What job should I take? What person should I marry? Most decisions take time and prayer. If you are living in obedience to God and in fellowship with some wise believers, you are in good shape to allow God to speak to you and give you guidance. Go slow, and as my old coach used to say, "Stay on your knees!" "For that is what God is like. He is our God forever and ever, and he will guide us until we die." (Psalm 48:14)
Count on it!

loved the church. He gave up his life for her [26]to make her holy and clean, washed by the cleansing of God's word. [27]He did this to present her to himself as a glorious church without a spot or wrinkle or any other blemish. Instead, she will be holy and without fault. [28]In the same way, husbands ought to love their wives as they love their own bodies. For a man who loves his wife actually shows love for himself. [29]No one hates his own body but feeds and cares for it, just as Christ cares for the church. [30]And we are members of his body.

[31]As the Scriptures say, "A man leaves his father and mother and is joined to his wife, and the two are united into one." [32]This is a great mystery, but it is an illustration of the way Christ and the church are one. [33]So again I say, each man must love his wife as he loves himself, and the wife must respect her husband.

Children and Parents

6

Children, obey your parents because you belong to the Lord, for this is the right thing to do. [2]"Honor your father and mother." This is the first commandment with a promise: [3]If you honor your father and mother, "things will go well for you, and you will have a long life on the earth."

[4]Fathers, do not provoke your children to anger by the way you treat them. Rather, bring them up with the discipline and instruction that comes from the Lord.

6:10-18 WHAT'S IT SAYING?

WHAT AM I GOING TO DO ABOUT IT?

Slaves and Masters

[5]Slaves, obey your earthly masters with deep respect and fear. Serve them sincerely as you would serve Christ. [6]Try to please them all the time, not just when they are watching you. As slaves of Christ, do the will of God with all your heart. [7]Work with enthusiasm, as though you were working for the Lord rather than for people. [8]Remember that the Lord will reward each one of us for the good we do, whether we are slaves or free.

Athletic star Jesse Owens beat a racehorse over a 100-yard course in 1936.

⁹Masters, treat your slaves in the same way. Don't threaten them; remember, you both have the same Master in heaven, and he has no favorites.

The Whole Armor of God

¹⁰A final word: Be strong in the Lord and in his mighty power. ¹¹Put on all of God's armor so that you will be able to stand firm against all strategies of the devil. ¹²For we are not fighting against flesh-and-blood enemies, but against evil rulers and authorities of the unseen world, against mighty powers in this dark world, and against evil spirits in the heavenly places. ¹³Therefore, put on every piece of God's armor so you will be able to resist the enemy in the time of evil. Then after the battle you will still be standing firm. ¹⁴Stand your ground, putting on the belt of truth and the body armor of God's righteousness. ¹⁵For shoes, put on the peace that comes from the Good News so that you will be fully prepared. ¹⁶In addition to all of these, hold up the shield of faith to stop the fiery arrows of the devil. ¹⁷Put on salvation as your helmet, and take the sword of the Spirit, which is the word of God.

¹⁸Pray in the Spirit at all times and on every occasion. Stay alert and be persistent in your prayers for all believers everywhere.

¹⁹And pray for me, too. Ask God to give me the right words so I can boldly explain God's mysterious plan that the Good News is for Jews and Gentiles alike. ²⁰I am in chains now, still preaching this message as God's ambassador. So pray that I will keep on speaking boldly for him, as I should.

Final Greetings

²¹To bring you up to date, Tychicus will give you a full report about what I am doing and how I am getting along. He is a beloved brother and faithful helper in the Lord's work. ²²I have sent him to you for this very purpose—to let you know how we are doing and to encourage you.

²³Peace be with you, dear brothers and sisters, and may God the Father and the Lord Jesus Christ give you love with faithfulness. ²⁴May God's grace be eternally upon all who love our Lord Jesus Christ.

Bible FACTS

The first Bible translated into English was started by John Wycliffe in 1382 and completed in 1388.

Run for the Prize?

"Don't you realize that in a race everyone runs, but only one person gets the prize? So run to win! All athletes are disciplined in their training. They do it to win a prize that will fade away, but we do it for an eternal prize."
(1 Corinthians 9:24-25)

Here Paul was drawing on his knowledge and understanding of Greek culture in the great city of Corinth. At the time when Paul was writing, the population was estimated to have been about 650,000 people. Over 400,000 were slaves. Competing in the city's games would have been seen as an escape from the oppressive world of slavery. To win a wreath (medal) in the biannual Isthmian Games, the second largest games in Greece, could mean physical emancipation. Performing well in a sport could offer freedom. Paul would have understood the cultural power sports had on the psyche of even the most casual fan in Greece.

The apostle Paul was committed. Paul had a coach's heart: strive, beat your body, look forward, press on — these were all major themes in his letters. It was noted by the historian and Gospel writer Luke that Paul was once nearly beaten to death and driven out of a city. Paul, never to be discouraged, got right back up when

DEVOTIONAL

he had recovered and went back into the city that very night. He was focused and purpose driven. If he were a coach he would expect and get the best from you. He hated a halfhearted, aimless effort.

Paul took everyday illustrations and put them into eternal perspective. Is your goal high enough? Most of us have a yearning for glory — a passion to win. There is an innate longing set in the heart of man to achieve; unfortunately, we often do not aim at eternal achievement, but merely earthly success, which will not satisfy. Paul understood that these noble desires couldn't be satisfied with a wooden wreath or a gold medal. Paul gives us the answer: Run for the eternal prize; live your life with a higher purpose, for a crown that will last forever. The better the athlete you are, the easier it should be to understand that your earthly prizes will not completely satisfy. I know some of you are reading this and saying to yourselves, "Ah Steve, you do not know my goals. If only I could win that prize, play for that team, or break that record — then I would be happy. Then I could sit back and rest on my laurels (trophy)."

I really hope you realize your dream and you make that team or win that prize. Then you will understand that although winning is great, the euphoria does not last. It is easier to explain these concepts to champions than to those who think, "If only." Go for the crown that will last forever.

Reflection
Do I keep chasing after things in life that will not make me happy for long?

Prayer
Lord, there is a yearning in my heart; help me to satisfy it.

"He is no fool who gives what he cannot keep to gain what he could never lose."
Jim Elliot

Nicked with permission from: A Sporting Guide to Eternity, Steve Connor, Christian Focus Publications - ISBN 1-85792-746-X

The theme of *joy* permeates each verse of this book of the Bible. It hardly seems possible that Paul is actually chained to a guard as he writes this letter to the Philippian church, which he founded on his second missionary journey. But when you follow Christ you have a new passport and a new destination. "I press on to reach the end of the race and receive the heavenly prize for which God, through Christ Jesus, is calling us" (Philippians 3:14).

Paul gives us the big picture or, better still, the eternal picture of our life. When you are a citizen of heaven your present difficulties will not get the best of you. Throughout your life, whenever you have troubles (and you will have troubles), no matter whether they are big or small, go to this book. It is a great reminder that in Christ we will live forever and should live in a manner worthy of Christ — that we are teammates and should be in this world in unity and live in joy with the anticipation of going home.

Philippians

it doesn't say it will be easy

sport

LIVE it

PHILIPPIANS

Greetings from Paul

1

This letter is from Paul and Timothy, slaves of Christ Jesus.

I am writing to all of God's holy people in Philippi who belong to Christ Jesus, including the elders and deacons.

²May God our Father and the Lord Jesus Christ give you grace and peace.

Paul's Thanksgiving and Prayer

³Every time I think of you, I give thanks to my God. ⁴Whenever I pray, I make my requests for all of you with joy, ⁵for you have been my partners in spreading the Good News about Christ from the time you first heard it until now. ⁶And I am certain that God, who began the good work within you, will continue his work until it is finally finished on the day when Christ Jesus returns.

⁷So it is right that I should feel as I do about all of you, for you have a special place in my heart. You share with me the special favor of God, both in my imprisonment and in defending and confirming the truth of the Good News. ⁸God knows how much I love you and long for you with the tender compassion of Christ Jesus.

⁹I pray that your love will overflow more and more, and that you will keep on growing in knowledge and understanding. ¹⁰For I want you to understand what really matters, so that you may live pure and blameless lives until the day of Christ's return. ¹¹May you always be filled with the fruit of your salvation—the righteous character produced in your life by Jesus Christ—for this will bring much glory and praise to God.

Paul's Joy That Christ Is Preached

¹²And I want you to know, my dear brothers and sisters, that everything that has happened to me here has helped to spread the Good News. ¹³For everyone here, including the whole palace guard, knows that I am in chains because of Christ. ¹⁴And because of my imprisonment, most of the believers here have gained confidence and boldly speak God's message without fear.

¹⁵It's true that some are preaching out of jealousy and rivalry. But others preach about Christ with pure motives. ¹⁶They preach because they love me, for they know I have been appointed to defend the Good News. ¹⁷Those others do not have pure motives as they preach about Christ. They preach with selfish ambition, not sincerely, intending to make my chains more painful to me. ¹⁸But that doesn't matter. Whether their motives are false or genuine, the message about Christ is being preached either way, so I rejoice. And I will continue to rejoice. ¹⁹For I know that as you pray for me and the Spirit of Jesus Christ helps me, this will lead to my deliverance.

Paul's Life for Christ

²⁰For I fully expect and hope that I will never be ashamed, but that I will continue to be bold for Christ, as I have been in the past. And I trust that my life will bring honor to Christ, whether I live or die. ²¹For to me, living means living for Christ, and dying is even better. ²²But if I live, I can do more fruitful work for Christ. So I really don't know which is better. ²³I'm torn between two desires: I long to go and be with Christ, which would be far better for me. ²⁴But for your sakes, it is better that I continue to live.

²⁵Knowing this, I am convinced that I will remain alive so I can continue to help all of you grow and experience the joy of your faith. ²⁶And when I come to you again, you will have even more reason to take pride in Christ Jesus because of what he is doing through me.

Live as Citizens of Heaven

²⁷Above all, you must live as citizens of heaven, conducting yourselves in a manner worthy of the Good News about Christ. Then, whether I come and see you again or only hear about you, I will know that you are standing side by side, fighting together for the faith, which is the Good News. ²⁸Don't be intimidated in any way by your enemies. This will be a sign to them that they are going to be destroyed, but that you are going to be saved, even by God himself. ²⁹For you have been given not only the privilege of trusting in Christ but also the privilege of suffering for him. ³⁰We are in this struggle together. You have seen my struggle in the past, and you know that I am still in the midst of it.

Have the Attitude of Christ

2

Is there any encouragement from belonging to Christ? Any comfort from his love? Any fellowship together in the Spirit? Are your hearts tender and compassionate?

STAND POINT

When you need the big picture
1:23

I'm torn between two desires: I long to go and be with Christ, which would be far better for me.

WHAT

DOES IT MEAN?

armor

Employed in the Bible to denote military equipment, both offensive and defensive. Reference is made by Paul (Ephesians 6:14-17) that Christians are in battle and need the whole body protected. You would not go into a major competition without the proper equipment; how much more do we have to strap on God's armor for offense and defense. Note, there is no armor for the back, but only for the front. NEVER RETREAT.

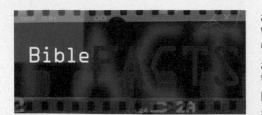

Bible FACTS

About 50 Bibles are sold every minute.

²Then make me truly happy by agreeing wholeheartedly with each other, loving one another, and working together with one mind and purpose.

³Don't be selfish; don't try to impress others. Be humble, thinking of others as better than yourselves. ⁴Don't look out only for your own interests, but take an interest in others, too.

⁵You must have the same attitude that Christ Jesus had.
⁶Though he was God,
he did not think of equality with God
as something to cling to.
⁷Instead, he gave up his divine privileges;
he took the humble position of a slave

action

2:5-11 WHAT'S IT SAYING?

WHAT AM I GOING TO DO ABOUT IT?

and was born as a human being.
When he appeared in human form,
⁸he humbled himself in obedience to God
and died a criminal's death on a cross.
⁹Therefore, God elevated him to the place of highest honor
and gave him the name above all other names,
¹⁰that at the name of Jesus every knee should bow,
in heaven and on earth and under the earth,
¹¹and every tongue confess that Jesus Christ is Lord,
to the glory of God the Father.

Shine Brightly for Christ

¹²Dear friends, you always followed my instructions when I was with you. And now that I am away, it is even more important. Work hard to show the results of your salvation, obeying God with deep reverence and fear. ¹³For God is working in you, giving you the desire and the power to do what pleases him.

¹⁴Do everything without complaining and arguing, ¹⁵so that no one can criticize you. Live clean, innocent lives as children of God, shining like bright lights in a world full of crooked and perverse people. ¹⁶Hold firmly to

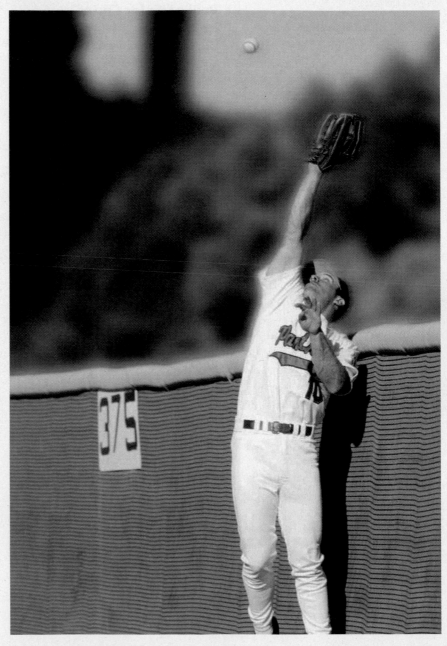

the word of life; then, on the day of Christ's return, I will be proud that I did not run the race in vain and that my work was not useless. [17]But I will rejoice even if I lose my life, pouring it out like a liquid offering to God, just like your faithful service is an offering to God. And I want all of you to share that joy. [18]Yes, you should rejoice, and I will share your joy.

Paul Commends Timothy

[19]If the Lord Jesus is willing, I hope to send Timothy to you soon for a visit. Then he can cheer me up by telling me how you are getting along. [20]I have no one else like Timothy, who genuinely cares about your welfare. [21]All the others care only for themselves and not for what matters to Jesus Christ. [22]But you know how Timothy has proved himself. Like a son with his father, he has served with me in preaching the Good News. [23]I hope to send him to you just as soon as I find out what is going to happen to me here. [24]And I have confidence from the Lord that I myself will come to see you soon.

Paul Commends Epaphroditus

[25]Meanwhile, I thought I should send Epaphroditus back to you. He is a true brother, co-worker, and fellow soldier. And he was your messenger to help me in my need. [26]I am sending him because he has been longing to see you, and he was very distressed that you heard he was ill. [27]And he certainly was ill; in fact, he almost died. But God had mercy on him—and also on me, so that I would not have one sorrow after another. [28]So I am all the more anxious to send him back to you, for I know you will be glad to see him, and then I will not be so worried about you. [29]Welcome him with Christian love and with great joy, and give him the honor that people like him deserve. [30]For he risked his life for the work of Christ, and he was at the point of death while doing for me what you couldn't do from far away.

The Priceless Value of Knowing Christ

3

Whatever happens, my dear brothers and sisters, rejoice in the Lord. I never get tired of telling you these things, and I do it to safeguard your faith. [2]Watch out for those dogs, those people who do evil, those mutilators who say you must be circumcised to be saved. [3]For we who worship by the Spirit of God are the ones who are truly circumcised. We rely on what Christ Jesus has done for us. We put no confidence in human effort, [4]though I could have confidence in my own effort if anyone could. Indeed, if others have reason for confidence in their own efforts, I have even more!

[5]I was circumcised when I was eight days old. I am a pure-blooded citizen of Israel and a member of the tribe of Benjamin—a real Hebrew if there ever was one! I was a member of the Pharisees, who demand the strictest obedience to the Jewish law. [6]I was so zealous that I harshly persecuted the church. And as for righteousness, I obeyed the law without fault.

[7]I once thought these things were valuable, but now I consider them worthless because of what Christ has done. [8]Yes, everything else is worthless when compared with the infinite value of knowing Christ Jesus my Lord. For his sake I have discarded everything else, counting it all as garbage, so that I could gain Christ [9]and become one with him. I no longer count on my own righteousness through obeying the law; rather, I become righteous through faith in Christ. For God's way of making us right with himself depends on faith. [10]I want to know Christ and experience the mighty power that raised him from the dead. I want to suffer with him, sharing in his death, [11]so that one way or another I will experience the resurrection from the dead!

Pressing toward the Goal

[12]I don't mean to say that I have already achieved these things or that I have already reached perfection. But I press on to possess that perfection for which Christ Jesus first possessed me. [13]No, dear brothers and sisters, I have not achieved it, but I focus on this one thing: Forgetting the past and looking forward to what lies ahead, [14]I press on to reach the end of the race and receive the heavenly prize for which God, through Christ Jesus, is calling us.

[15]Let all who are spiritually mature agree on these things. If you disagree on some point, I believe God will make it plain to you. [16]But we must hold on to the progress we have already made.

[17]Dear brothers and sisters, pattern your lives after mine, and learn from those who follow our example. [18]For I have told you often before, and I say it again with tears in my eyes, that there are many whose conduct shows they are really enemies of the cross of Christ. [19]They are headed for destruction. Their god is their appetite, they brag about shameful things, and they think only about this life here on earth. [20]But we are citizens of heaven, where the Lord Jesus Christ lives. And we are eagerly waiting for him to return as our Savior. [21]He will take our weak mortal bodies and change them into glorious bodies like his own, using the same power with which he will bring everything under his control.

4

Therefore, my dear brothers and sisters, stay true to the Lord. I love you and long to see you, dear friends, for you are my joy and the crown I receive for my work.

Words of Encouragement

[2]Now I appeal to Euodia and Syntyche. Please, because you belong to the Lord, settle your disagreement. [3]And I ask you, my true partner, to help these two women, for they worked hard with me in telling others the Good News. They worked along with Clement and the rest of my co-workers, whose names are written in the Book of Life.

The Secret of Living (PHILIPPIANS 4:12-13)

Most superstars realize that all their achievements do not satisfy for long. Are you content only when you are playing well . . . when your team is winning . . . when life is going great? Then the rest of your life will be pretty boring and miserable. The Bible does not promise that your life will be easy or that every time you compete you will win. What the Scripture does say is that you will find fulfillment and satisfaction in Christ and he will give you strength to enjoy life through the good and bad times.

BIBLE HIT

profiles

Abraham:

Imagine walking up a mountain with your precious son, knowing that you are to show obedience to God by sacrificing him. Another model of persistence and obedience, Abraham was promised that, through him, his descendants would create a great nation and all the people on earth would be blessed through him. He was rich and had been given a huge amount of land but could have no offspring. He disobeyed God and had a child with his wife's servant. But God made good on his promise, and when Abraham and his wife were very old they had a true heir: Isaac. But God tested Abraham — and it was a cruel test. He was to show his love for God by sacrificing his son. As Isaac was carrying the wood for the sacrifice up the mountain, he asked, "But where is the lamb for the sacrifice?" Abraham said, "God will provide" (Genesis 22:7-8). Abraham was willing but at the last moment he did not have to sacrifice his son. It was a cruel test — a fact God knew all too well. Fifteen hundred years later God did provide the sacrifice as he sent his own son up the hill carrying a wooden cross. He fulfilled Abraham's promise to Isaac by allowing his own son, a descendant, to die and take away the sin of the world. For more on Abraham, start in chapter 12 of Genesis in the Old Testament.

[4]Always be full of joy in the Lord. I say it again—rejoice! [5]Let everyone see that you are considerate in all you do. Remember, the Lord is coming soon. [6]Don't worry about anything; instead, pray about everything. Tell God what you need, and thank him for all he has done. [7]Then you will experience God's peace, which exceeds anything we can understand. His peace will guard your hearts and minds as you live in Christ Jesus.

[8]And now, dear brothers and sisters, one final thing. Fix your thoughts on what is true, and honorable, and right, and pure, and lovely, and admirable. Think about things that are excellent and worthy of praise. [9]Keep putting into practice all you learned and received from me—everything you heard from me and saw me doing. Then the God of peace will be with you.

action

6:14-18 WHAT'S IT SAYING?

WHAT AM I GOING TO DO ABOUT IT?

Paul's Thanks for Their Gifts

[10]How I praise the Lord that you are concerned about me again. I know you have always been concerned for me, but you didn't have the chance to help me. [11]Not that I was ever in need, for I have learned how to be content with whatever I have. [12]I know how to live on almost nothing or with everything. I have learned the secret of living in every situation, whether it is with a

full stomach or empty, with plenty or little. [13]For I can do everything through Christ, who gives me strength. [14]Even so, you have done well to share with me in my present difficulty.

[15]As you know, you Philippians were the only ones who gave me financial help when I first brought you the Good News and then traveled on from Macedonia. No other church did this. [16]Even when I was in Thessalonica you sent help more than once. [17]I don't say this because I want a gift from you. Rather, I want you to receive a reward for your kindness.

[18]At the moment I have all I need—and more! I am generously supplied with the gifts you sent me with Epaphroditus. They are a sweet-smelling sacrifice that is acceptable and pleasing to God. [19]And this same God who takes care of me will supply all your needs from his glorious riches, which have been given to us in Christ Jesus.

[20]Now all glory to God our Father forever and ever! Amen.

Paul's Final Greetings

[21]Give my greetings to each of God's holy people—all who belong to Christ Jesus. The brothers who are with me send you their greetings. [22]And all the rest of God's people send you greetings, too, especially those in Caesar's household.

[23]May the grace of the Lord Jesus Christ be with your spirit.

STATS

Before they were allowed to compete in the state of Indiana, boxers and pro wrestlers in 1954 had to swear under oath they were not Communists.

Colossians

Have you noticed that Paul used his letters as an opportunity to coach God's faith communities? The overarching theme in this letter is that Christ is supreme. He is the head and center of our faith. No religious activity should take precedence over Christ. We are to keep on the clear path of following Christ. Many religions and cults have come and gone, trying to get people to focus on "good things," like angels, religious ceremonies, or living a certain way. But when "good things" become "god things" (things that become more important than Jesus), then they become bad things.

After Paul addressed the issue of idolatry (putting things ahead of God) and being led astray by empty philosophy, he went back to the theme of growing strong in Christ by getting true spiritual nourishment and living wisely, making the most of every opportunity among those that do not know Jesus. (Colossians 4:5). We maximize our power through feasting on God's Word.

We will only live the Christian life when we focus on the central theme, Jesus. Christ is supreme!

COLOSSIANS

Greetings from Paul

1

This letter is from Paul, chosen by the will of God to be an apostle of Christ Jesus, and from our brother Timothy. [2]We are writing to God's holy people in the city of Colosse, who are faithful brothers and sisters in Christ.
May God our Father give you grace and peace.

Paul's Thanksgiving and Prayer

When you need strength

1:11-12

We also pray that you will be strengthened with all his glorious power so you will have all the endurance and patience you need. May you be filled with joy, always thanking the Father. He has enabled you to share in the inheritance that belongs to his people, who live in the light.

[3]We always pray for you, and we give thanks to God, the Father of our Lord Jesus Christ. [4]For we have heard of your faith in Christ Jesus and your love for all of God's people,

[5]which come from your confident hope of what God has reserved for you in heaven. You have had this expectation ever since you first heard the truth of the Good News.

[6]This same Good News that came to you is going out all over the world. It is bearing fruit everywhere by changing lives, just as it changed your lives from the day you first heard and understood the truth about God's wonderful grace.

[7]You learned about the Good News from Epaphras, our beloved co-worker. He is Christ's faithful servant, and he is helping us on your behalf. [8]He has told us about the love for others that the Holy Spirit has given you.

[9]So we have not stopped praying for you since we first heard about you. We ask God to give you complete knowledge of his will and to give you spiritual wisdom and understanding. [10]Then the way you live will always honor and please the Lord, and your lives will produce every kind of good fruit. All the while, you will grow as you learn to know God better and better.

[11]We also pray that you will be strengthened with all his glorious power so you will have all the endurance and patience you need. May you be filled with joy, [12]always thanking the Father. He has enabled you to share in the inheritance that belongs to his people, who live in the light. [13]For he has rescued us from the kingdom of darkness and transferred us into the Kingdom of his dear Son, [14]who purchased our freedom and forgave our sins.

Christ Is Supreme

[15]Christ is the visible image of the invisible God.
He existed before anything was created and is supreme over all creation,
[16]for through him God created everything
in the heavenly realms and on earth.
He made the things we can see

and the things we can't see—
such as thrones, kingdoms, rulers, and authorities in the unseen world.
Everything was created through him and for him.
[17]He existed before anything else,
and he holds all creation together.
[18]Christ is also the head of the church,
which is his body.
He is the beginning,
supreme over all who rise from the dead.
So he is first in everything.
[19]For God in all his fullness
was pleased to live in Christ,
[20]and through him God reconciled
everything to himself.
He made peace with everything in heaven and on earth
by means of Christ's blood on the cross.
[21]This includes you who were once far away from God. You were his enemies, separated from him by your evil thoughts and actions. [22]Yet now he has reconciled you to himself through the death of Christ in his physical body. As a result, he has brought you into his own presence, and you are holy and blameless as you stand before him without a single fault.
[23]But you must continue to believe this truth and stand firmly in it. Don't drift away from the assurance you received when you heard the Good News. The Good News has been preached all over the world, and I, Paul, have been appointed as God's servant to proclaim it.

Paul's Work for the Church

[24]I am glad when I suffer for you in my body, for I am participating in the sufferings of Christ that continue for his body, the church. [25]God has given me the responsibility of serving his church by proclaiming his entire message to you. [26]This message was kept secret for centuries and generations past, but now it

Winners keep learning!

Competition will push you to be better! Sports have many virtues that can help a person develop in mind, body, and soul. You certainly have to be aware of the pitfalls involved in sports, but enjoy the benefits! Sports create great opportunities to learn and live out God's principles, which develop our Christian character. Winners will never stop learning new skills, life principles, and respectful responses to others.
"Cry out for insight, and ask for understanding. Search for them as you would for silver; seek them like hidden treasures." (Proverbs 2:3-4)

Winners want to know!

Snowboarding made its recent Olympic entrance in the 1998 Winter Games in Nagano, Japan.

has been revealed to God's people. [27]For God wanted them to know that the riches and glory of Christ are for you Gentiles, too. And this is the secret: Christ lives in you. This gives you assurance of sharing his glory.

[28]So we tell others about Christ, warning everyone and teaching everyone with all the wisdom God has given us. We want to present them to God, perfect in their relationship to Christ. [29]That's why I work and struggle so hard, depending on Christ's mighty power that works within me.

2

I want you to know how much I have agonized for you and for the church at Laodicea, and for many other believers who have never met me personally. [2]I want them to be encouraged and knit together by strong ties of love. I want them to have complete confidence that they understand God's mysterious plan, which is Christ himself. [3]In him lie hidden all the treasures of wisdom and knowledge.

[4]I am telling you this so no one will deceive you with well-crafted arguments. [5]For though I am far away from you, my heart is with you. And I rejoice that you are living as you should and that your faith in Christ is strong.

Freedom from Rules and New Life in Christ

[6]And now, just as you accepted Christ Jesus as your Lord, you must continue to follow him. [7]Let your roots grow down into him, and let your lives be built on him. Then your faith will grow strong in the truth you were taught, and you will overflow with thankfulness. [8]Don't let anyone capture you with empty philosophies and high-sounding nonsense that come from human thinking and from the spiritual powers of this world,

rather than from Christ. [9]For in Christ lives all the fullness of God in a human body. [10]So you also are complete through your union with Christ, who is the head over every ruler and authority.

[11]When you came to Christ, you were "circumcised," but not by a physical procedure. Christ performed a spiritual circumcision—the cutting away of your sinful nature. [12]For you were buried with Christ when you were baptized. And with him you were raised to new life because you trusted the mighty power of God, who raised Christ from the dead.

[13]You were dead because of your sins and because your sinful nature was not yet cut away. Then God made you alive with Christ, for he forgave all our sins. [14]He canceled the record of the charges against us and took it away by nailing it to the cross. [15]In this way, he disarmed the spiritual rulers and authorities. He shamed them publicly by his victory over them on the cross.

[16]So don't let anyone condemn you for what you eat or drink, or for not celebrating certain holy days or new moon ceremonies or Sabbaths. [17]For these rules are only shadows of the reality yet to come. And Christ himself is that reality. [18]Don't let anyone condemn you by insisting on pious self-denial or the worship of angels, saying they have had visions about these things. Their sinful minds have made them proud, [19]and they are not connected to Christ, the head of the body. For he holds the whole body together with its joints and ligaments, and it grows as God nourishes it.

[20]You have died with Christ, and he has set you free from the spiritual powers of this world. So why do you keep on following the rules of the world, such as,

[21]"Don't handle! Don't taste! Don't touch!"? [22]Such rules are mere human teachings about things that deteriorate as we use them. [23]These rules may seem wise because they require strong devotion, pious self-denial, and severe bodily discipline. But they provide no help in conquering a person's evil desires.

action

2:13-15 WHAT'S IT SAYING?

WHAT AM I GOING TO DO ABOUT IT?

What would be the five best teams to play for?

1
2
3
4
5

BIG FIVE

Living the New Life

3

Since you have been raised to new life with Christ, set your sights on the realities of heaven, where Christ sits in the place of honor at God's right hand. [2]Think about the things of heaven, not the things of earth. [3]For you died to this life, and your real life is hidden with Christ in God. [4]And when Christ, who is your life, is revealed to the whole world, you will share in all his glory.

[5]So put to death the sinful, earthly things lurking within you. Have nothing to do with sexual immorality, impurity, lust, and evil desires. Don't be greedy, for a greedy person is an idolater, worshiping the things of this world. [6]Because of these sins, the anger of God is coming. [7]You used to do these things when your life was still part of this world. [8]But now is the time to get rid of anger, rage, malicious behavior, slander, and dirty language. [9]Don't lie to each other, for you have stripped off your old sinful nature and all its wicked deeds. [10]Put on your new nature, and be renewed as you learn to know your Creator and become like him. [11]In this new life, it doesn't matter if you are a Jew or a Gentile, circumcised or uncircumcised, barbaric, uncivilized, slave, or free. Christ is all that matters, and he lives in all of us.

[12]Since God chose you to be the holy people he loves, you must clothe yourselves with tenderhearted mercy, kindness, humility, gentleness, and patience. [13]Make allowance for each other's faults, and forgive anyone who offends you. Remember, the Lord forgave you, so you must forgive others. [14]Above all, clothe yourselves with love, which binds us all together in perfect harmony. [15]And let the peace that comes from Christ rule in your hearts. For as members of one body you are called to live in peace. And always be thankful. [16]Let the message about Christ, in all its richness, fill your lives. Teach and counsel each other with all the wisdom he gives. Sing psalms and hymns and spiritual songs to God with thankful hearts. [17]And whatever you do or say, do it as a representative of the Lord Jesus, giving thanks through him to God the Father.

Instructions for Christian Households

[18]Wives, submit to your husbands, as is fitting for those who belong to the Lord.

[19]Husbands, love your wives and never treat them harshly.

[20]Children, always obey your parents, for this pleases the Lord. [21]Fathers, do not aggravate your children, or they will become discouraged.

[22]Slaves, obey your earthly masters in everything you do. Try to please them all the time, not just when they are watching you. Serve them sincerely because of your reverent fear of the Lord. [23]Work willingly at whatever you do, as though you were working for the Lord rather than for people. [24]Remember that the Lord will give you an inheritance as your reward, and that the Master you are serving is Christ. [25]But if you do what is wrong, you will be paid back for the wrong you have done. For God has no favorites.

4

Masters, be just and fair to your slaves. Remember that you also have a Master—in heaven.

An Encouragement for Prayer

[2]Devote yourselves to prayer with an alert mind and a thankful heart. [3]Pray for us, too, that God will give us many opportunities to speak about his mysterious

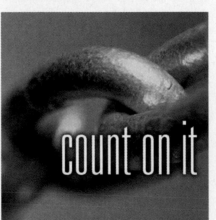

God will supply!

Some days I wish Philippians 4:19 read "my God shall supply all your wants!" But it says "needs." Sometimes what I want is not the thing I most need. Some people will always be richer than you are, some people will always be more skillful than you and some less. But God is rich, it is all his! And out of his wisdom, he will take good care of you. "And this same God who takes care of me will supply all your needs from his glorious riches, which have been given to us in Christ Jesus." (Philippians 4:19)
Count on it!

plan concerning Christ. That is why I am here in chains. [4]Pray that I will proclaim this message as clearly as I should.

[5]Live wisely among those who are not believers, and make the most of every opportunity. [6]Let your conversation be gracious and attractive so that you will have the right response for everyone.

Paul's Final Instructions and Greetings

[7]Tychicus will give you a full report about how I am getting along. He is a beloved brother and faithful helper who serves with me in the Lord's work. [8]I have sent him to you for this very purpose—to let you know how we are doing and to encourage you. [9]I am also sending Onesimus, a faithful and beloved brother, one of your own people. He and Tychicus will tell you everything that's happening here.

[10]Aristarchus, who is in prison with me, sends you his greetings, and so does Mark, Barnabas's cousin. As you were instructed before, make Mark welcome if he comes your way. [11]Jesus (the one we call Justus) also sends his greetings. These are the only Jewish believers among my co-workers; they are working with me here for the Kingdom of God. And what a comfort they have been!

[12]Epaphras, a member of your own fellowship and a servant of Christ Jesus, sends you his greetings. He always prays earnestly for you, asking God to make you strong and perfect, fully confident that you are following the whole will of God. [13]I can assure you that he prays hard for you and also for the believers in Laodicea and Hierapolis.

[14]Luke, the beloved doctor, sends his greetings, and so does Demas. [15]Please give my greetings to our brothers and sisters at Laodicea, and to Nympha and the church that meets in her house.

[16]After you have read this letter, pass it on to the church at Laodicea so they can read it, too. And you should read the letter I wrote to them.

[17]And say to Archippus, "Be sure to carry out the ministry the Lord gave you."

[18]Here is my greeting in my own handwriting—Paul. Remember my chains.

May God's grace be with you.

Work willingly at whatever you do, as though you were working for the Lord rather than for people.

COLOSSIANS 3:23

an audience of ONE

Training

"Those who belong to Christ Jesus have nailed the passions and desires of their sinful nature to his cross and crucified them there. Since we are living by the Spirit, let us follow the Spirit's leading in every part of our lives." (Galatians 5:24-25)

Again we see Paul using a sporting metaphor: keep in step. In athletics (track and field) training, many sprinters and middle distance runners work out together. A common training technique is an Indian line. One runner leads and another half dozen sprinters follow in a straight line, keeping in pace with the leaders. After 300 meters or so the last in the line sprints to the front and sets the new pace. You are caught up in the competition; you do not want to slow down and open up a gap in the line. It is motivating and fun, you dig deep, push further, and challenge each other.

God has you in spiritual training; the Spirit is always pushing you on, challenging you. If you have ever run in a pack you understand the energy of corporate power. Running with others pushes and carries you in a way that you can't get on your own. You are compelled.

The same is true of the life controlled by the Spirit; you feel the pace and the power of God. You are running (spiritually) faster and longer than you have before.

You can almost hear Christ challenging you and advancing your spiritual power, "Come on, live for me." Keeping in step with the Spirit is pure pleasure; you have purpose, direction, and encouragement. You know you're in sync with the Lord, you have kept a short account of sin, and you are seeking to be obedient. Life in sync with the Spirit is never stagnant. You are being stretched; you are aiming for things that you rarely thought of. The presence of God in your life is as necessary as the oxygen in your lungs (if not more so). You now hunger and thirst for righteousness. Keep up the pace — press on!

Reflection
Keep in step and push yourself; you know that God will not run ahead of you and leave you in the dust. Enjoy the progress of the spiritual race.

Prayer
Lord Jesus, thank you that you will help me, guide me, and push me. Thank you that I will never take this trip of life on my own.

"Dance, then, wherever you may be,
I am the Lord of the dance said he,
And I'll lead you all, wherever you may be,
And I'll lead you all in the dance, said he."
Sydney Carter

Nicked with permission from: A Sporting Guide to Eternity, Steve Connor, Christian Focus Publications - ISBN 1-85792-746-X

1 Thessalonians

To better understand the drama and relationship that Paul had with the Thessalonians, read Acts chapter 17. Here again we find Paul going to a strategic city of influence and commerce to start and build up a faith community for the cause of Christ. Thessalonica was a bustling Greek seaport full of international business and a variety of religions. Paul, true to his pattern, based himself at the local synagogue and preached that the fulfillment of the Old Testament was found in Jesus Christ.

We realize from Acts that Paul was only in Thessalonica about three weeks but in that short time established a youthful church. First Thessalonians and second Thessalonians are letters to the church to encourage, shape, and strengthen the truth about the Jesus they were following. Paul stirred up a lot of trouble in his short time there, but the church members blossomed. Paul's mission was to win, build, and mobilize followers of Christ around the world. His message was a joy to many but invoked fury in others. But Paul lived for an audience of one and was motivated to please God, not men. The Thessalonian church had many troubles, but Paul kept them focused and on course, emphasizing the fact that we will be with Christ again. Jesus is coming back!

1 THESSALONIANS

Greetings from Paul

1

This letter is from Paul, Silas, and Timothy.

We are writing to the church in Thessalonica, to you who belong to God the Father and the Lord Jesus Christ.

May God give you grace and peace.

1:2-4 WHAT'S IT SAYING?

WHAT AM I GOING TO DO ABOUT IT?

The Faith of the Thessalonian Believers

[2]We always thank God for all of you and pray for you constantly. [3]As we pray to our God and Father about you, we think of your faithful work, your loving deeds, and the enduring hope you have because of our Lord Jesus Christ.

[4]We know, dear brothers and sisters, that God loves you and has chosen you to be his own people. [5]For when we brought you the Good News, it was not only with words but also with power, for the Holy Spirit gave you full assurance that what we said was true. And you know of our concern for you from the way we lived when we were with you. [6]So you received the message with joy from the Holy Spirit in spite of the severe suffering it brought you. In this way, you imitated both us and the Lord. [7]As a result, you have become an example to all the believers in Greece—throughout both Macedonia and Achaia.

[8]And now the word of the Lord is ringing out from you to people everywhere, even beyond Macedonia and Achaia, for wherever we go we find people telling us about your faith in God. We don't need to tell them about it, [9]for they keep talking about the wonderful welcome you gave us and how you turned away from idols to serve the living and true God. [10]And they speak of how you are looking forward to the coming of God's Son from heaven—Jesus, whom God raised from the dead. He is the one who has rescued us from the terrors of the coming judgment.

Paul Remembers His Visit

2

You yourselves know, dear brothers and sisters, that our visit to you was not a failure. [2]You know how badly we had been treated at Philippi just before we came to you and how much we suffered there. Yet our God gave us the courage to declare his Good News to you boldly, in spite of great opposition. [3]So you can see we were not preaching with any deceit or impure motives or trickery.

[4]For we speak as messengers approved by God to be entrusted with the Good News. Our purpose is to please God, not people. He alone examines the motives of our hearts. [5]Never once did we try to win you with flattery, as you well know. And God is our witness that we were not pretending to be your friends just to get your money! [6]As for human praise, we have never sought it from you or anyone else.

[7]As apostles of Christ we certainly had a right to make some demands of you, but instead we were like children among you. Or we were like a mother feeding and caring for her own children. [8]We loved you so much that we shared with you not only God's Good News but our own lives, too.

[9]Don't you remember, dear brothers and sisters, how hard we worked among you? Night and day we toiled to earn a living so that we would not be a burden to any of you as we preached God's Good News to you. [10]You yourselves are our witnesses—and so is God—that we were devout and honest and faultless toward all of you believers. [11]And you know that we treated each of you as a father treats his own children. [12]We pleaded with you, encouraged you, and urged you to live your lives in a way that God would consider worthy. For he called you to share in his Kingdom and glory.

[13]Therefore, we never stop thanking God that when you received his message from us, you didn't think of our words as mere human ideas. You accepted what we said as the very word of God—which, of course, it is. And this word continues to work in you who believe.

[14]And then, dear brothers and sisters, you suffered persecution from your own countrymen. In this way, you imitated the believers in God's churches in Judea who, because of their belief in Christ Jesus, suffered from their own people, the Jews. [15]For some of the Jews killed the prophets, and some even killed the Lord Jesus. Now they have persecuted us, too. They fail to please God and work against all humanity [16]as they try to keep us from preaching the Good News of salvation to the Gentiles. By doing this, they continue to pile up their sins. But the anger of God has caught up with them at last.

Warm-ups reduce injuries:

Warm-up exercises provide an athlete with time to adjust from rest to exercise. These exercises are designed to improve performance and reduce the chance of injury by preparing the athlete mentally as well as physically for his or her sport. Physiologically, a warm-up elevates body temperature and increases blood flow.

Timothy's Good Report about the Church

[17]Dear brothers and sisters, after we were separated from you for a little while (though our hearts never left you), we tried very hard to come back because of our intense longing to see you again. [18]We wanted very much to come to you, and I, Paul, tried again and again, but Satan prevented us. [19]After all, what gives us hope and joy, and what will be our proud reward and crown as we stand before our Lord Jesus when he returns? It is you! [20]Yes, you are our pride and joy.

3

Finally, when we could stand it no longer, we decided to stay alone in Athens, [2]and we sent Timothy to visit you. He is our brother and God's co-worker in proclaiming the Good News of Christ. We sent him to strengthen you, to encourage you in your faith, [3]and to keep you from being shaken by the troubles you were going through. But you know that we are destined for such troubles. [4]Even while we were with you, we warned you that troubles would soon come—and they did, as you well know. [5]That is why, when I could bear it no longer, I sent Timothy to find out whether your faith was still strong. I was afraid that the tempter had gotten the best of you and that our work had been useless.

[6]But now Timothy has just returned, bringing us good news about your faith and love. He reports that you always remember our visit with joy and that you want to see us as much as we want to see you. [7]So we have been greatly encouraged in the midst of our troubles and suffering, dear brothers and sisters, because you have remained strong in your faith. [8]It gives us new life to know that you are standing firm in the Lord. [9]How we thank God for you! Because of you we have great joy as we enter God's presence. [10]Night and day

we pray earnestly for you, asking God to let us see you again to fill the gaps in your faith.

[11]May God our Father and our Lord Jesus bring us to you very soon. [12]And may the Lord make your love for one another and for all people grow and overflow, just as our love for you overflows. [13]May he, as a result, make your hearts strong, blameless, and holy as you stand before God our Father when our Lord Jesus comes again with all his holy people. Amen.

Live to Please God

4

Finally, dear brothers and sisters, we urge you in the name of the Lord Jesus to live in a way that pleases God, as we have taught you. You live this way already, and we encourage you to do so even more. [2]For you remember what we taught you by the authority of the Lord Jesus.

[3]God's will is for you to be holy, so stay away from all sexual sin. [4]Then each of you will control his own body and live in holiness and honor—[5]not in lustful passion like the pagans who do not know God and his ways. [6]Never harm or cheat a Christian brother in this matter by violating his wife, for the Lord avenges all such sins, as we have solemnly warned you before. [7]God has called us to live holy lives, not impure lives. [8]Therefore, anyone who refuses to live by these rules is not disobeying human teaching but is rejecting God, who gives his Holy Spirit to you.

[9]But we don't need to write to you about the importance of loving each other, for God himself has taught you to love one another. [10]Indeed, you already show your love for all the believers throughout Macedonia. Even so, dear brothers and sisters, we urge you to love them even more.

[11]Make it your goal to live a quiet life, minding your own business and working with your hands, just as we instructed you before. [12]Then people who are not Christians will respect the way you live, and you will not need to depend on others.

The Hope of the Resurrection

[13]And now, dear brothers and sisters, we want you to know what will happen to the believers who have died so you will not grieve like people who have no hope. [14]For since we believe that Jesus died and was raised to life again, we also believe that when Jesus returns, God will bring back with him the believers who have died.

[15]We tell you this directly from the Lord: We who are still living when the Lord returns will not meet him

Dogs are mentioned 14 times in the Bible, and lions 55 times, but domestic cats are not mentioned at all.

profiles

Joseph:

What would you be like if you were spoiled by your father and hated by your brothers, sold into slavery in a strange land, falsely accused of rape, and sent to prison, where you were forgotten by those you'd helped? Would you be bitter toward God or continue to be faithful? Joseph's response transformed his injustices into success. His attitude continued to be faithful to God, and he eventually rose to be the leader of a great and foreign nation: Egypt. He was never bitter and helped to rescue his family from starvation and death.

We all have setbacks and discouragements. We can wallow in self-pity and render ourselves paralyzed in bitterness or we can follow Joseph's example and press on, knowing that God loves us deeply and will use us in those dark times. Joseph gave us a secret to his freedom from bitterness in his two sons Manasseh and Ephraim, whose names translate as "forgiveness" and "fruitfulness." How not to be bitter? Forgive and be fruitful for God. For more information about Joseph, start in the first book of the Old Testament (Genesis) at chapter 37.

ahead of those who have died. [16]For the Lord himself will come down from heaven with a commanding shout, with the voice of the archangel, and with the trumpet call of God.

OCTOBER M.A.P.

1
S.D.	P.L.	P.G.	S.G.
P. ☐	F. ☐	F. ☐	T. ☐
F. ☐	W. ☐	W. ☐	P. ☐
B. ☐	P. ☐	C. ☐	C. ☐

2
S.D.	P.L.	P.G.	S.G.
P. ☐	F. ☐	F. ☐	T. ☐
F. ☐	W. ☐	W. ☐	P. ☐
B. ☐	P. ☐	C. ☐	C. ☐

3
S.D.	P.L.	P.G.	S.G.
P. ☐	F. ☐	F. ☐	T. ☐
F. ☐	W. ☐	W. ☐	P. ☐
B. ☐	P. ☐	C. ☐	C. ☐

4
S.D.	P.L.	P.G.	S.G.
P. ☐	F. ☐	F. ☐	T. ☐
F. ☐	W. ☐	W. ☐	P. ☐
B. ☐	P. ☐	C. ☐	C. ☐

9
S.D.	P.L.	P.G.	S.G.
P. ☐	F. ☐	F. ☐	T. ☐
F. ☐	W. ☐	W. ☐	P. ☐
B. ☐	P. ☐	C. ☐	C. ☐

10
S.D.	P.L.	P.G.	S.G.
P. ☐	F. ☐	F. ☐	T. ☐
F. ☐	W. ☐	W. ☐	P. ☐
B. ☐	P. ☐	C. ☐	C. ☐

11
S.D.	P.L.	P.G.	S.G.
P. ☐	F. ☐	F. ☐	T. ☐
F. ☐	W. ☐	W. ☐	P. ☐
B. ☐	P. ☐	C. ☐	C. ☐

12
S.D.	P.L.	P.G.	S.G.
P. ☐	F. ☐	F. ☐	T. ☐
F. ☐	W. ☐	W. ☐	P. ☐
B. ☐	P. ☐	C. ☐	C. ☐

17
S.D.	P.L.	P.G.	S.G.
P. ☐	F. ☐	F. ☐	T. ☐
F. ☐	W. ☐	W. ☐	P. ☐
B. ☐	P. ☐	C. ☐	C. ☐

18
S.D.	P.L.	P.G.	S.G.
P. ☐	F. ☐	F. ☐	T. ☐
F. ☐	W. ☐	W. ☐	P. ☐
B. ☐	P. ☐	C. ☐	C. ☐

19
S.D.	P.L.	P.G.	S.G.
P. ☐	F. ☐	F. ☐	T. ☐
F. ☐	W. ☐	W. ☐	P. ☐
B. ☐	P. ☐	C. ☐	C. ☐

20
S.D.	P.L.	P.G.	S.G.
P. ☐	F. ☐	F. ☐	T. ☐
F. ☐	W. ☐	W. ☐	P. ☐
B. ☐	P. ☐	C. ☐	C. ☐

25
S.D.	P.L.	P.G.	S.G.
P. ☐	F. ☐	F. ☐	T. ☐
F. ☐	W. ☐	W. ☐	P. ☐
B. ☐	P. ☐	C. ☐	C. ☐

26
S.D.	P.L.	P.G.	S.G.
P. ☐	F. ☐	F. ☐	T. ☐
F. ☐	W. ☐	W. ☐	P. ☐
B. ☐	P. ☐	C. ☐	C. ☐

27
S.D.	P.L.	P.G.	S.G.
P. ☐	F. ☐	F. ☐	T. ☐
F. ☐	W. ☐	W. ☐	P. ☐
B. ☐	P. ☐	C. ☐	C. ☐

28
S.D.	P.L.	P.G.	S.G.
P. ☐	F. ☐	F. ☐	T. ☐
F. ☐	W. ☐	W. ☐	P. ☐
B. ☐	P. ☐	C. ☐	C. ☐

Spiritual Disciplines

Prayer

Faith Community

Bible Reading

Prayer List

Friends

World

Personal

Who am I....
Where am I going....
How am I going to get there?

nt:sport
MONTHLY ACTION PLAN

5
S.D.	P.L.	P.G.	S.G.
P. ☐	F. ☐	F. ☐	T. ☐
F. ☐	W. ☐	W. ☐	P. ☐
B. ☐	P. ☐	C. ☐	C. ☐

6
S.D.	P.L.	P.G.	S.G.
P. ☐	F. ☐	F. ☐	T. ☐
F. ☐	W. ☐	W. ☐	P. ☐
B. ☐	P. ☐	C. ☐	C. ☐

7
S.D.	P.L.	P.G.	S.G.
P. ☐	F. ☐	F. ☐	T. ☐
F. ☐	W. ☐	W. ☐	P. ☐
B. ☐	P. ☐	C. ☐	C. ☐

8
S.D.	P.L.	P.G.	S.G.
P. ☐	F. ☐	F. ☐	T. ☐
F. ☐	W. ☐	W. ☐	P. ☐
B. ☐	P. ☐	C. ☐	C. ☐

13
S.D.	P.L.	P.G.	S.G.
P. ☐	F. ☐	F. ☐	T. ☐
F. ☐	W. ☐	W. ☐	P. ☐
B. ☐	P. ☐	C. ☐	C. ☐

14
S.D.	P.L.	P.G.	S.G.
P. ☐	F. ☐	F. ☐	T. ☐
F. ☐	W. ☐	W. ☐	P. ☐
B. ☐	P. ☐	C. ☐	C. ☐

15
S.D.	P.L.	P.G.	S.G.
P. ☐	F. ☐	F. ☐	T. ☐
F. ☐	W. ☐	W. ☐	P. ☐
B. ☐	P. ☐	C. ☐	C. ☐

16
S.D.	P.L.	P.G.	S.G.
P. ☐	F. ☐	F. ☐	T. ☐
F. ☐	W. ☐	W. ☐	P. ☐
B. ☐	P. ☐	C. ☐	C. ☐

21
S.D.	P.L.	P.G.	S.G.
P. ☐	F. ☐	F. ☐	T. ☐
F. ☐	W. ☐	W. ☐	P. ☐
B. ☐	P. ☐	C. ☐	C. ☐

22
S.D.	P.L.	P.G.	S.G.
P. ☐	F. ☐	F. ☐	T. ☐
F. ☐	W. ☐	W. ☐	P. ☐
B. ☐	P. ☐	C. ☐	C. ☐

23
S.D.	P.L.	P.G.	S.G.
P. ☐	F. ☐	F. ☐	T. ☐
F. ☐	W. ☐	W. ☐	P. ☐
B. ☐	P. ☐	C. ☐	C. ☐

24
S.D.	P.L.	P.G.	S.G.
P. ☐	F. ☐	F. ☐	T. ☐
F. ☐	W. ☐	W. ☐	P. ☐
B. ☐	P. ☐	C. ☐	C. ☐

29
S.D.	P.L.	P.G.	S.G.
P. ☐	F. ☐	F. ☐	T. ☐
F. ☐	W. ☐	W. ☐	P. ☐
B. ☐	P. ☐	C. ☐	C. ☐

30
S.D.	P.L.	P.G.	S.G.
P. ☐	F. ☐	F. ☐	T. ☐
F. ☐	W. ☐	W. ☐	P. ☐
B. ☐	P. ☐	C. ☐	C. ☐

31
S.D.	P.L.	P.G.	S.G.
P. ☐	F. ☐	F. ☐	T. ☐
F. ☐	W. ☐	W. ☐	P. ☐
B. ☐	P. ☐	C. ☐	C. ☐

Proverbs 16:32

Better to be patient than powerful; better to have self-control than to conquer a city.

Personal Goals

Family

Work/School/Social

Challenge

Sport Goals

Training

Performance

Competition Results

(For designing your M.A.P. – Monthly Action Plan – see introduction pages)

Keep alert and under control. Don't disrespect your opponent's ability to whip you! Understand that Satan wants to destroy you! Like a cunning competitor he probably had a reason for playing where he did, so don't blindly ignore moves that appear stupid or attractive. "Stay alert! Watch out for your great enemy, the devil."

(1 Peter 5:8)

Paul's Final Greetings

[23]Now may the God of peace make you holy in every way, and may your whole spirit and soul and body be kept blameless until our Lord Jesus Christ comes again. [24]God will make this happen, for he who calls you is faithful.

[25]Dear brothers and sisters, pray for us.

[26]Greet all the brothers and sisters with Christian love.

[27]I command you in the name of the Lord to read this letter to all the brothers and sisters.

[28]May the grace of our Lord Jesus Christ be with you.

5:16-22 WHAT'S IT SAYING?

WHAT AM I GOING TO DO ABOUT IT?

First, the Christians who have died will rise from their graves. [17]Then, together with them, we who are still alive and remain on the earth will be caught up in the clouds to meet the Lord in the air. Then we will be with the Lord forever. [18]So encourage each other with these words.

5

Now concerning how and when all this will happen, dear brothers and sisters, we don't really need to write you. [2]For you know quite well that the day of the Lord's return will come unexpectedly, like a thief in the night. [3]When people are saying, "Everything is peaceful and secure," then disaster will fall on them as suddenly as a pregnant woman's labor pains begin. And there will be no escape.

[4]But you aren't in the dark about these things, dear brothers and sisters, and you won't be surprised when the day of the Lord comes like a thief. [5]For you are all children of the light and of the day; we don't belong to darkness and night. [6]So be on your guard, not asleep like the others. Stay alert and be clearheaded. [7]Night is the time when people sleep and drinkers get drunk. [8]But let us who live in the light be clearheaded, protected by the armor of faith and love, and

wearing as our helmet the confidence of our salvation. [9]For God chose to save us through our Lord Jesus Christ, not to pour out his anger on us. [10]Christ died for us so that, whether we are dead or alive when he returns, we can live with him forever. [11]So encourage each other and build each other up, just as you are already doing.

Paul's Final Advice

[12]Dear brothers and sisters, honor those who are your leaders in the Lord's work. They work hard among you and give you spiritual guidance. [13]Show them great respect and wholehearted love because of their work. And live peacefully with each other.

[14]Brothers and sisters, we urge you to warn those who are lazy. Encourage those who are timid. Take tender care of those who are weak. Be patient with everyone. [15]See that no one pays back evil for evil, but always try to do good to each other and to all people. [16]Always be joyful. [17]Never stop praying. [18]Be thankful in all circumstances, for this is God's will for you who belong to Christ Jesus.

[19]Do not stifle the Holy Spirit. [20]Do not scoff at prophecies, [21]but test everything that is said. Hold on to what is good. [22]Stay away from every kind of evil.

STAND

Teamwork

5:11

So encourage each other and build each other up, just as you are already doing.

POINT

STATS

Romanian Nadia Comaneci achieved the first ever perfect score of 10 in Olympic gymnastics at the 1976 Montreal Olympics. She won 3 gold medals.

Tough times create a dependence on God. The Thessalonian church began in a whirlwind of tough times. Paul had only been in the great city for three weeks when it was clear he had to move on or what he had established would be destroyed by jealous Greeks who were afraid to embrace the truth of Christ. Though Paul moved on, he was desperate that the church would take root and grow strong. He prayed constantly for the young church and kept reminding them that Christ was going to return. Second Thessalonians was a response to a message he received after sending out his first letter. Here he cleared up some confusion on Jesus' second coming and commended the Thessalonians for their flourishing faith and love for each other.

Though Paul's time in Thessalonica was uncommonly short, it is obvious from this letter that he had developed close and intimate friendships with the church; he never forgot about them. Paul was inspired and delighted that they maintained genuine love and maturity in God in the midst of trying times. Follow Paul's example and keep praying for teammates and friends. Encourage other believers, and when you need encouragement remember that this letter is not just for some ancient Greeks hanging out in the Aegean Sea. Supernaturally, God knew that it would be a letter for you — today. Be encouraged: Jesus is coming back!

2 Thessalonians

2 THESSALONIANS

Greetings from Paul

1

This letter is from Paul, Silas, and Timothy.

We are writing to the church in Thessalonica, to you who belong to God our Father and the Lord Jesus Christ.
[2]May God our Father and the Lord Jesus Christ give you grace and peace.

Encouragement during Persecution

[3]Dear brothers and sisters, we can't help but thank God for you, because your faith is flourishing and your love for one another is growing. [4]We proudly tell God's other churches about your endurance and faithfulness in all the persecutions and hardships you are suffering. [5]And God will use this persecution to show his justice and to make you worthy of his Kingdom, for which you are suffering. [6]In his justice he will pay back those who persecute you.

[7]And God will provide rest for you who are being persecuted and also for us when the Lord Jesus appears from heaven. He will come with his mighty angels, [8]in flaming fire, bringing judgment on those who don't know God and on those who refuse to obey the Good News of our Lord Jesus. [9]They will be punished with eternal destruction, forever separated from the Lord and from his glorious power. [10]When he comes on that day, he will receive glory from his holy people—praise from all who believe. And this includes you, for you believed what we told you about him.

[11]So we keep on praying for you, asking our God to enable you to live a life worthy of his call. May he give you the power to accomplish all the good things your faith prompts you to do. [12]Then the name of our Lord Jesus will be honored because of the way you live, and you will be honored along with him. This is all made possible because of the grace of our God and our Lord Jesus Christ.

[5]Don't you remember that I told you about all this when I was with you? [6]And you know what is holding him back, for he can be revealed only when his time comes. [7]For this lawlessness is already at work secretly, and it will remain secret until the one who is holding it back steps out of the way. [8]Then the man of lawlessness will be revealed, but the Lord Jesus will kill him with the breath of his mouth and destroy him by the splendor of his coming.

[9]This man will come to do the work of Satan with counterfeit power and signs and miracles. [10]He will use every kind of evil deception to fool those on their way to destruction, because they refuse to love and accept the truth that would save them. [11]So God will cause them to be greatly deceived, and they will believe these lies. [12]Then they will be condemned for enjoying evil rather than believing the truth.

Believers Should Stand Firm

[13]As for us, we can't help but thank God for you, dear brothers and sisters loved by the Lord. We are always thankful that God chose you to be among the first to experience salvation—a salvation that came through

Some days I feel close to God and some days far away. What is wrong?
Knowing that God loves you unconditionally whether you feel close to him or not helps your consistency. Pray and read your Bible every day, whether you feel like it or not! Remember that we don't base our faith on how we feel but on the truth of God's Word.

STAND POINT

When you need to encourage your teammates.

2:16-17

May our Lord Jesus Christ himself and God our Father, who loved us and by his grace gave us eternal comfort and wonderful hope, comfort you and strengthen you in every good thing you do and say.

Events prior to the Lord's Second Coming

2

Now, dear brothers and sisters, let us clarify some things about the coming of our Lord Jesus Christ and how we will be gathered to meet him. [2]Don't be so easily shaken or alarmed by those who say that the day of the Lord has already begun. Don't believe them, even if they claim to have had a spiritual vision, a revelation, or a letter supposedly from us. [3]Don't be fooled by what they say. For that day will not come until there is a great rebellion against God and the man of lawlessness is revealed—the one who brings destruction. [4]He will exalt himself and defy everything that people call god and every object of worship. He will even sit in the temple of God, claiming that he himself is God.

the Spirit who makes you holy and through your belief in the truth. [14]He called you to salvation when we told you the Good News; now you can share in the glory of our Lord Jesus Christ.

[15]With all these things in mind, dear brothers and sisters, stand firm and keep a strong grip on the teaching we passed on to you both in person and by letter.

[16]Now may our Lord Jesus Christ himself and God our Father, who loved us and by his grace gave us eternal comfort and a wonderful hope, [17]comfort you and strengthen you in every good thing you do and say.

Paul's Request for Prayer

3

Finally, dear brothers and sisters, we ask you to pray for us. Pray that the Lord's message will spread rapidly and be honored wherever it goes, just as when it came

Prayer and Protection (2 THESSALONIANS 3:1-2)

If God answered every one of your prayers this week, how many new Christians would there be in this world? No, not how many 'old ladies' would get their hips replaced, but how many new converts would be saved from an eternity apart from God? We are to pray that God's message would spread and take hold of the hearts of humanity. We are also charged to pray for protection; there is a very real evil that wants to keep us from our duty to pray and read the Scripture. Pray that you and your friends and loved ones will be strong, and invite God to protect you from evil.

BIBLE HIT

to you. ²Pray, too, that we will be rescued from wicked and evil people, for not everyone is a believer. ³But the Lord is faithful; he will strengthen you and guard you from the evil one. ⁴And we are confident in the Lord that you are doing and will continue to do the things we commanded you. ⁵May the Lord lead your hearts into a full understanding and expression of the love of God and the patient endurance that comes from Christ.

An Exhortation to Proper Living

⁶And now, dear brothers and sisters, we give you this command in the name of our Lord Jesus Christ:

Stay away from all believers who live idle lives and don't follow the tradition they received from us. ⁷For you know that you ought to imitate us. We were not idle when we were with you. ⁸We never accepted food from anyone without paying for it. We worked hard day and night so we would not be a burden to any of you. ⁹We certainly had the right to ask you to feed us, but we wanted to give you an example to follow. ¹⁰Even while we were with you, we gave you this command: "Those unwilling to work will not get to eat."

¹¹Yet we hear that some of you are living idle lives, refusing to work and meddling in other people's business. ¹²We command such people and urge them

in the name of the Lord Jesus Christ to settle down and work to earn their own living. ¹³As for the rest of you, dear brothers and sisters, never get tired of doing good.

¹⁴Take note of those who refuse to obey what we say in this letter. Stay away from them so they will be ashamed. ¹⁵Don't think of them as enemies, but warn them as you would a brother or sister.

Paul's Final Greetings

¹⁶Now may the Lord of peace himself give you his peace at all times and in every situation. The Lord be with you all. ¹⁷HERE IS MY GREETING IN MY OWN HANDWRITING—PAUL. I DO THIS IN ALL MY LETTERS TO PROVE THEY ARE FROM ME. ¹⁸May the grace of our Lord Jesus Christ be with you all.

fight well

Fight well
in the Lord's battles.
Cling to your faith in
Christ, and keep your
conscience clear.

1 TIMOTHY 1:18-19

The Bible is timeless, and the principles that Paul sets forth in the next three books are invaluable to young leaders who want to make an impact for the cause of Christ. Paul is just out of prison and is concerned for the orderly worship and ministry of the churches, particularly the one in Ephesus. Paul encourages Timothy to live in faithfulness and to maintain the truth about Christ in the midst of false teachings. He goes on to give invaluable training on how to maintain and build a faith community.

Coaching the Coaches: 1 Timothy, 2 Timothy, and Titus

A good coach can make your sporting career fantastic, and a bad coach can make it miserable and even put you off sport forever. Paul was aware of that and put a lot of time, prayer, and energy into developing the coaches who would take his teams (faith communities) to the next level. Paul's purpose was to create healthy homegrown churches that could survive and flourish without his being there. He needed leaders who would build on the work that he had started, and he found two such leaders in Timothy and Titus.

Timothy and Titus were both dear to Paul; they had the privilege of living with and learning from the great evangelist and they both experienced many of his adventures and ministries. In the letters to Timothy and Titus, we feel Paul's urgency and responsibility to develop and strengthen these younger future leaders, as well as his instructions on how to organize a community of followers of Jesus Christ.

1 Timothy

1 TIMOTHY

Greetings from Paul

1

This letter is from Paul, an apostle of Christ Jesus, appointed by the command of God our Savior and Christ Jesus, who gives us hope.

[2]I am writing to Timothy, my true son in the faith.

May God the Father and Christ Jesus our Lord give you grace, mercy, and peace.

1:3-7 WHAT'S IT SAYING?

WHAT AM I GOING TO DO ABOUT IT?

Warnings against False Teachings

[3]When I left for Macedonia, I urged you to stay there in Ephesus and stop those whose teaching is contrary to the truth. [4]Don't let them waste their time in endless discussion of myths and spiritual pedigrees. These things only lead to meaningless speculations, which don't help people live a life of faith in God.

[5]The purpose of my instruction is that all believers would be filled with love that comes from a pure heart, a clear conscience, and genuine faith. [6]But some people have missed this whole point. They have turned away from these things and spend their time in meaningless discussions. [7]They want to be known as teachers of the law of Moses, but they don't know what they are talking about, even though they speak so confidently.

[8]We know that the law is good when used correctly. [9]For the law was not intended for people who do what is right. It is for people who are lawless and rebellious, who are ungodly and sinful, who consider nothing sacred and defile what is holy, who kill their father or mother or commit other murders. [10]The law is for people who are sexually immoral, or who practice homosexuality, or are slave traders, liars, promise breakers, or who do anything else that contradicts the wholesome teaching [11]that comes from the glorious Good News entrusted to me by our blessed God.

Paul's Gratitude for God's Mercy

[12]I thank Christ Jesus our Lord, who has given me strength to do his work. He considered me trustworthy and appointed me to serve him, [13]even though I used to blaspheme the name of Christ. In my insolence, I persecuted his people. But God had mercy on me because I did it in ignorance and unbelief. [14]Oh, how generous and gracious our Lord was! He filled me with the faith and love that come from Christ Jesus.

[15]This is a trustworthy saying, and everyone should accept it: "Christ Jesus came into the world to save sinners"—and I am the worst of them all. [16]But God had mercy on me so that Christ Jesus could use me as a prime example of his great patience with even the worst sinners. Then others will realize that they, too, can believe in him and receive eternal life. [17]All honor and glory to God forever and ever! He is the eternal King, the unseen one who never dies; he alone is God. Amen.

Timothy's Responsibility

[18]Timothy, my son, here are my instructions for you, based on the prophetic words spoken about you earlier. May they help you fight well in the Lord's battles. [19]Cling to your faith in Christ, and keep your conscience clear. For some people have deliberately violated their consciences; as a result, their faith has been shipwrecked. [20]Hymenaeus and Alexander are two examples. I threw them out and handed them over to Satan so they might learn not to blaspheme God.

Instructions about Worship

2

I urge you, first of all, to pray for all people. Ask God to help them; intercede on their behalf, and give thanks for them. [2]Pray this way for kings and all who are in authority so that we can live peaceful and quiet lives marked by godliness and dignity. [3]This is good and pleases God our Savior, [4]who wants everyone to be saved and to understand the truth. [5]For there is only one God and one Mediator who can reconcile God and humanity—the man Christ Jesus. [6]He gave his life to purchase freedom for everyone. This is the message God gave to the world at just the right time. [7]And I have been chosen as a preacher and apostle to teach the Gentiles this message about faith and truth. I'm not exaggerating—just telling the truth.

[8]In every place of worship, I want men to pray with holy hands lifted up to God, free from anger and controversy.

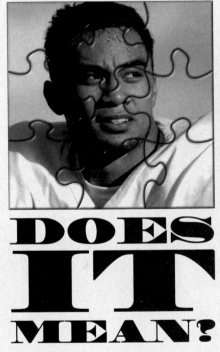

WHAT DOES IT MEAN?

assurance

The resurrection of Jesus (Acts 17:31) is the assurance or promise God has given that his revelation is true and worthy of acceptance. The "complete confidence" in "God's mysterious plan" (Colossians 2:2) is a rock solid assurance of the truth of the declarations of Scripture. This rock-solid conviction of hope is the assurance of a person's salvation through Christ.

⁹And I want women to be modest in their appearance. They should wear decent and appropriate clothing and not draw attention to themselves by the way they fix their hair or by wearing gold or pearls or expensive clothes. ¹⁰For women who claim to be devoted to God should make themselves attractive by the good things they do.

¹¹Women should learn quietly and submissively. ¹²I do not let women teach men or have authority over them. Let them listen quietly. ¹³For God made Adam first, and afterward he made Eve. ¹⁴And it was not Adam who was deceived by Satan. The woman was deceived, and sin was the result. ¹⁵But women will be saved through childbearing, assuming they continue to live in faith, love, holiness, and modesty.

Leaders in the Church

3

This is a trustworthy saying: "If someone aspires to be an elder, he desires an honorable position." ²So an elder must be a man whose life is above reproach. He must be faithful to his wife. He must exercise self-control, live wisely, and have a good reputation. He must enjoy having guests in his home, and he must be able to teach. ³He must not be a heavy drinker or be violent. He must be gentle, not quarrelsome, and not love money. ⁴He must manage his own family well, having children who respect and obey him. ⁵For if a man cannot manage his own household, how can he take care of God's church?

⁶An elder must not be a new believer, because he might become proud, and the devil would cause him to fall. ⁷Also, people outside the church must speak well of him so that he will not be disgraced and fall into the devil's trap.

⁸In the same way, deacons must be well respected and have integrity. They must not be heavy drinkers or dishonest with money. ⁹They must be committed to the mystery of the faith now revealed and must live with a clear conscience. ¹⁰Before they are appointed as deacons, let them be closely examined. If they pass the test, then let them serve as deacons.

What are your five favorite Bible verses?

1
2
3
4
5

BIG FIVE

¹¹In the same way, their wives must be respected and must not slander others. They must exercise self-control and be faithful in everything they do. ¹²A deacon must be faithful to his wife, and he must manage his children and household well. ¹³Those who do well as deacons will be rewarded with respect from others and will have increased confidence in their faith in Christ Jesus.

The Truths of Our Faith

¹⁴I am writing these things to you now, even though I hope to be with you soon, ¹⁵so that if I am delayed, you will know how people must conduct themselves in the household of God. This is the church of the living God, which is the pillar and foundation of the truth. ¹⁶Without question, this is the great mystery of our faith:

Christ was revealed in a human body
and vindicated by the Spirit.
He was seen by angels
and announced to the nations.
He was believed in throughout the world
and taken to heaven in glory.

Warnings against False Teachers

4

Now the Holy Spirit tells us clearly that in the last times some will turn away from the true faith; they will follow deceptive spirits and teachings that come from demons. ²These people are hypocrites and liars, and their consciences are dead.

³They will say it is wrong to be married and wrong to eat certain foods. But God created those foods to be eaten with thanks by faithful people who know the truth. ⁴Since everything God created is good, we should not reject any of it but receive it with thanks. ⁵For we know it is made acceptable by the word of God and prayer.

A Good Servant of Christ Jesus

⁶If you explain these things to the brothers and sisters, Timothy, you will be a worthy servant of Christ Jesus, one who is nourished by the message of faith and the good teaching you have followed. ⁷Do not waste time arguing over godless ideas and old wives' tales. Instead, train yourself to be godly. ⁸"Physical training is good, but training for godliness is much better, promising benefits in this life and

TIPS

Put in extra time:

Don't just rely on your training times. Research suggests that the most significant contributing factor for a dancer, gymnast, or martial artist to improve his or her flexibility is the individual stretches during his or her own time!

Bible Facts

SEVEN is the number of completeness in the old created order. There are seven days of Creation, and in Revelation this number occurs 61 times.

in the life to come." [9]This is a trustworthy saying, and everyone should accept it. [10]This is why we work hard and continue to struggle, for our hope is in the living God, who is the Savior of all people and particularly of all believers. [11]Teach these things and insist that everyone learn them. [12]Don't let anyone think less of you because you are young. Be an example to all believers in what you say, in the way you live, in your love, your faith, and your purity. [13]Until I get there, focus on reading the Scriptures to the church, encouraging the believers, and teaching them. [14]Do not neglect the spiritual gift you received through the prophecy spoken over you when the elders of the church laid their hands on you. [15]Give your complete attention to these matters. Throw yourself into your tasks so that everyone will see your progress. [16]Keep a close watch on how you live and on your teaching. Stay true to what is right for the sake of your own salvation and the salvation of those who hear you.

Advice about Widows, Elders, and Slaves

5

Never speak harshly to an older man, but appeal to him respectfully as you would to your own father. Talk to younger men as you would to your own brothers. [2]Treat older women as you would your mother, and treat younger women with all purity as you would your own sisters.

[3]Take care of any widow who has no one else to care for her. [4]But if she has children or grandchildren, their first responsibility is to show godliness at home and repay their parents by taking care of them. This is something that pleases God.

[5]Now a true widow, a woman who is truly alone in this world, has placed her hope in God. She prays night and day, asking God for his help. [6]But the widow who lives only for pleasure is spiritually dead even while she lives. [7]Give these instructions to the church so that no one will be open to criticism.

[8]But those who won't care for their relatives, especially those in their own household, have denied the true faith. Such people are worse than unbelievers.

[9]A widow who is put on the list for support must be a woman who is at least sixty years old and was faithful to her husband. [10]She must be well respected by everyone because of the good she has done. Has she brought up her children well? Has she been kind to strangers and served other believers humbly? Has she helped those who are in trouble? Has she always been ready to do good?

[11]The younger widows should not be on the list, because their physical desires will overpower their devotion to Christ and they will want to remarry. [12]Then they would be guilty of breaking their previous pledge. [13]And if they are on the list, they will learn to be lazy and will spend their time gossiping from house to house, meddling in other people's business and talking about things they shouldn't. [14]So I advise these younger widows to marry again, have children, and take care of their own homes. Then the enemy will not be able to say anything against them. [15]For I am afraid that some of them have already gone astray and now follow Satan.

[16]If a woman who is a believer has relatives who are widows, she must take care of them and not put the responsibility on the church. Then the church can care for the widows who are truly alone.

[17]Elders who do their work well should be respected and paid well, especially those who work hard at both preaching and teaching. [18]For the Scripture says, "You must not muzzle an ox to keep it from eating as it treads out the grain." And in another place, "Those who work deserve their pay!"

[19]Do not listen to an accusation against an elder unless it is confirmed by two or three witnesses. [20]Those who sin should be reprimanded in front of the whole church; this will serve as a strong warning to others. [21]I solemnly command you in the presence of God and Christ Jesus and the holy angels to obey these instructions without taking sides or showing favoritism to anyone.

[22]Never be in a hurry about appointing a church leader. Do not share in the sins of others. Keep yourself pure. [23]Don't drink only water. You ought to drink a little wine for the sake of your stomach because you are sick so often.

[24]Remember, the sins of some people are obvious, leading them to certain judgment. But there are others whose sins will not be revealed until later. [25]In the same way, the good deeds of some people are obvious. And the good deeds done in secret will someday come to light.

action

5:1-12 WHAT'S IT SAYING?

WHAT AM I GOING TO DO ABOUT IT?

6

All slaves should show full respect for their masters so they will not bring shame on the name of God and his teaching. [2]If the masters are believers, that is no excuse for being disrespectful. Those slaves should work all the harder because their efforts are helping other believers who are well loved.

False Teaching and True Riches

Teach these things, Timothy, and encourage everyone to obey them. [3]Some people may contradict our teaching, but these are the wholesome teachings of the Lord Jesus Christ. These teachings promote a godly life. [4]Anyone who teaches something different is arrogant and lacks understanding. Such a person has an unhealthy desire to quibble over the meaning of words. This stirs up arguments ending in jealousy, division, slander, and evil suspicions. [5]These people always cause trouble. Their minds are corrupt, and they have turned their backs on the truth. To them, a show of godliness is just a way to become wealthy. ⁶Yet true godliness with contentment is itself great wealth. ⁷After all, we brought nothing with us when we came into the world, and we can't take anything with us when we leave it. ⁸So if we have enough food and clothing, let us be content.

⁹But people who long to be rich fall into temptation and are trapped by many foolish and harmful desires that plunge them into ruin and destruction. ¹⁰For the love of money is the root of all kinds of evil. And some people, craving money, have wandered from the true faith and pierced themselves with many sorrows.

Paul's Final Instructions

¹¹But you, Timothy, are a man of God; so run from all these evil things. Pursue righteousness and a godly life, along with faith, love, perseverance, and gentleness. ¹²Fight the good fight for the true faith. Hold tightly to the eternal life to which God has called

you, which you have confessed so well before many witnesses. ¹³And I charge you before God, who gives life to all, and before Christ Jesus, who gave a good testimony before Pontius Pilate, ¹⁴that you obey this command without wavering. Then no one can find fault with you from now until our Lord Jesus Christ comes again. ¹⁵For at just the right time Christ will be revealed from heaven by the blessed and only almighty God, the King of all kings and Lord of all lords. ¹⁶He alone can never die, and he lives in light so brilliant that no human can approach him. No human eye has ever seen him, nor ever will. All honor and power to him forever! Amen.

¹⁷Teach those who are rich in this world not to be proud and not to trust in their money, which is so unreliable. Their trust should be in God, who richly gives us all we need for our enjoyment. ¹⁸Tell them to use their money to do good. They should be rich in good works and generous to those in need, always being ready to share with others. ¹⁹By doing this they will be storing up their treasure as a good foundation for the future

When you are negotiating a contract
6:9

But people who long to be rich fall into temptation and are trapped by many foolish and harmful desires that plunge them into ruin and destruction.

so that they may experience true life.

²⁰Timothy, guard what God has entrusted to you. Avoid godless, foolish discussions with those who oppose you with their so-called knowledge. ²¹Some people have wandered from the faith by following such foolishness.

May God's grace be with you all.

PERSONAL ASSESSMENTS

WHAT DO I REALLY LIKE TO DO?

On a scale from 1 to 10 (1 is never; 10 is always):

- I'd rather watch TV than talk with a friend. [ ]
- I'd rather watch than participate in a sport. [ ]
- I love training and working hard for a goal. [ ]
- I like new adventures more than routine. [ ]
- I do not worry about what others think of me. [ ]
- I prefer team sports over individual sports. [ ]
- I am good at learning new skills and techniques. [ ]
- I listen to my coach. [ ]

Beauty

"Then God looked over all he had made, and he saw that it was very good!" (Genesis 1:31)

Sports can express or reflect certain qualities and virtues that are godly. God gave us an intrinsic desire to appreciate. In sports we have a lot to admire. This may be a faint echo of our Maker: "And [God] saw that it was very good." I believe sport is art. Art can be good and bad — good when we ascribe the qualities properly; bad when we worship the activity rather than the Creator. You need not be a Christian to express these qualities, but a Christian can better understand the origin of these virtues and channel the appreciation accordingly. The sports world is a tool to reach people for Christ, but it is so much more; even the execution and admiration of a sport is a means to glorify the Maker.

On the second day of her gymnastic class, my younger daughter warmed up with cartwheels. She had watched her older sister at home and did her best. The cartwheels were executed poorly in comparison with the more experienced girls, but she was so beautiful in her earnest, heartfelt attempt to complete the work. I knew she was trying, and it was beautiful. If an Olympic gymnast came in, my daughter's skill would pale by comparison, but her beauty would still shine. As I contemplated this, I started to look at the others girls through God's eyes and attempted to see the scene from his vantage point. The beauty was amazing. The laughter became musical, the interaction between girls was merriment, the mistakes were comical, and the skill was profound. I felt as if all my senses were enhanced and I could not wait to share the experience with my wife. The hour and a half flew by, and I wanted to look at everything this way. God gave us so many things to appreciate, enjoy, and attribute to his glory.

Reflection
God is the origin of beauty; find it in your sport.

Prayer
Father, thank you that my canvas to glorify your beauty is in my sport.

"And wherever, in anything God has made, in the glory of it, be it sky or flower or human face, we see the glory of God."
George MacDonald

Nicked with permission from: A Sporting Guide to Eternity, Steve Connor, Christian Focus Publications - ISBN 1-85792-746-X

2 Timothy

This is a passionate letter of encouragement and instruction to someone who is more of an offspring than just a colleague. This letter was probably written about a year or so after the first letter. It was sent from Rome, where Paul was for now in prison, to Timothy by the hands of Tychicus. In it he urges Timothy to come to him before winter and to bring Mark with him! He was predicting that the time of his death was near, and he wanted his "son" Timothy to remain faithful to the things he was taught. In 2 Timothy we get great insights into Paul's missionary method for reaching the world for Christ. "You have heard me teach things that have been confirmed by many reliable witnesses. Now teach these truths to other trustworthy people who will be able to pass them on to others." (2 Timothy 2:2)

2 TIMOTHY

Greetings from Paul

1

This letter is from Paul, chosen by the will of God to be an apostle of Christ Jesus. I have been sent out to tell others about the life he has promised through faith in Christ Jesus. [2]I am writing to Timothy, my dear son.

May God the Father and Christ Jesus our Lord give you grace, mercy, and peace.

Encouragement to Be Faithful

[3]Timothy, I thank God for you—the God I serve with a clear conscience, just as my ancestors did. Night and day I constantly remember you in my prayers. [4]I long to see you again, for I remember your tears as we parted. And I will be filled with joy when we are together again.

[5]I remember your genuine faith, for you share the faith that first filled your grandmother Lois and your mother, Eunice. And I know that same faith continues strong in you. [6]This is why I remind you to fan into flames the spiritual gift God gave you when I laid my hands on you. [7]For God has not given us a spirit of fear and timidity, but of power, love, and self-discipline.

[8]So never be ashamed to tell others about our Lord. And don't be ashamed of me, either, even though I'm in prison for him. With the strength God gives you, be ready to suffer with me for the sake of the Good News. [9]For God saved us and called us to live a holy life. He did this, not because we deserved it, but because that was his plan from before the beginning of time—to show us his grace through Christ Jesus. [10]And now he has made all of this plain to us by the appearing of Christ Jesus, our Savior. He broke the power of death and illuminated the way to life and immortality through the Good News. [11]And God chose me to be a preacher, an apostle, and a teacher of this Good News.

[12]That is why I am suffering here in prison. But I am not ashamed of it, for I know the one in whom I trust, and I am sure that he is able to guard what I have entrusted to him until the day of his return. [13]Hold on to the pattern of wholesome teaching you learned from me—a pattern shaped by the faith and love that you have in Christ Jesus. [14]Through the power of the Holy Spirit who lives within us, carefully guard the precious truth that has been entrusted to you. [15]As you know, everyone from the province of Asia has deserted me—even Phygelus and Hermogenes. [16]May the Lord show special kindness to Onesiphorus and all his family because he often visited and encouraged me. He was never ashamed of me because

Winners work together!

Winners are more interested in the well-being of the team than themselves. One of the most beautiful things to see is a team coordinating their efforts toward a common goal, alternately subordinating and asserting themselves to achieve real harmony in action. Top athletes learn how to work well with others. When you are competing you have a common focus and purpose. The church is also a team (not a building) of fellow believers with a common purpose: to further the cause of Christ.

"Don't be selfish; don't try to impress others. Be humble, thinking of others as better than yourselves. Don't look out only for your own interests, but take an interest in others, too." (Philippians 2:3-4)

Winners create unity!

I was in chains. [17]When he came to Rome, he searched everywhere until he found me. [18]May the Lord show him special kindness on the day of Christ's return. And you know very well how helpful he was in Ephesus.

action

2:14-18 WHAT'S IT SAYING?

WHAT AM I GOING TO DO ABOUT IT?

A Good Soldier of Christ Jesus

2

Timothy, my dear son, be strong through the grace that God gives you in Christ Jesus. [2]You have heard me teach things that have been confirmed by many reliable witnesses. Now teach these truths to other trustworthy people who will be able to pass them on to others.

[3]Endure suffering along with me, as a good soldier of Christ Jesus. [4]Soldiers don't get tied up in the affairs of civilian life, for then they cannot please the officer who enlisted them. [5]And athletes cannot win the prize unless they follow the rules. [6]And hardworking farmers should be the first to enjoy the fruit of their labor. [7]Think about what I am saying. The Lord will help you understand all these things.

[8]Always remember that Jesus Christ, a descendant of King David, was raised from the dead. This is the Good News I preach. [9]And because I preach this Good News, I am suffering and have been chained like a criminal. But the word of God cannot be chained. [10]So I am willing to endure anything if it will bring salvation and eternal glory in Christ Jesus to those God has chosen.

[11]This is a trustworthy saying:
If we die with him,
we will also live with him.
[12]If we endure hardship,
we will reign with him.
If we deny him,
he will deny us.
[13]If we are unfaithful,
he remains faithful,
for he cannot deny who he is.

[14]Remind everyone about these things, and command them in God's presence to stop fighting over words. Such arguments are useless, and they can ruin those who hear them.

An Approved Worker

[15]Work hard so you can present yourself to God and receive his approval. Be a good worker, one who does not need to be ashamed and who correctly explains the word of truth. [16]Avoid worthless, foolish talk that only leads to more godless behavior. [17]This kind of talk spreads like cancer, as in the case of Hymenaeus and Philetus. [18]They have left the path of truth, claiming that the resurrection of the dead has already occurred; in this way, they have turned some people away from the faith.

[19]But God's truth stands firm like a foundation stone with this inscription: "The LORD knows those who are his," and "All who belong to the LORD must turn away from evil."

STAND POINT

When you are frustrated with a teammate.

2:24

A servant of the Lord must not quarrel but must be kind to everyone, be able to teach, and be patient with difficult people.

[20]In a wealthy home some utensils are made of gold and silver, and some are made of wood and clay. The expensive utensils are used for special occasions, and the cheap ones are for everyday use. [21]If you keep yourself pure, you will be a special utensil for honorable use. Your life will be clean, and you will be ready for the Master to use you for every good work.

[22]Run from anything that stimulates youthful lusts. Instead, pursue righteous living, faithfulness, love, and peace. Enjoy the companionship of those who call on the Lord with pure hearts.

[23]Again I say, don't get involved in foolish, ignorant arguments that only start fights. [24]A servant of the Lord must not quarrel but must be kind to everyone, be able to teach, and be patient with difficult people. [25]Gently instruct those who oppose the truth. Perhaps God will change those people's hearts, and they will learn the truth. [26]Then they will come to their senses and escape from the devil's trap. For they have been held captive by him to do whatever he wants.

Let God speak to you. Make a conscious effort to allow the Word of God to occupy your thoughts. Think about it night and day. Speak it to yourself. Ask yourself the meaning of what you read. Ask God to tell you the meaning. Meditating on the Word is like talking to God. It is during these times that the Holy Spirit will drop godly thoughts into your heart. "With all my heart I want your blessings. Be merciful as you promised. I pondered the direction of my life, and I turned to follow your laws."

(Psalm 119:58-59)

POWER HABITS

The Dangers of the Last Days

3

You should know this, Timothy, that in the last days there will be very difficult times. [2]For people will love only themselves and their money. They will be boastful and proud, scoffing at God, disobedient to their parents, and ungrateful. They will consider nothing sacred. [3]They will be unloving and unforgiving; they will slander others and have no self-control. They will be cruel and hate what is good. [4]They will betray their friends, be reckless, be puffed up with pride, and love pleasure rather than God. [5]They will act religious, but they will reject the power that could make them godly. Stay away from people like that!

[6]They are the kind who work their way into people's homes and win the confidence of vulnerable women who are burdened with the guilt of sin and controlled by various desires. [7](Such women are forever following new teachings, but they are never able to understand the truth.) [8]These teachers oppose the truth just as Jannes and Jambres opposed Moses. They have depraved minds and a counterfeit faith. [9]But they won't get away with this for long. Someday everyone will recognize what fools they are, just as with Jannes and Jambres.

Paul's Charge to Timothy

[10]But you, Timothy, certainly know what I teach, and how I live, and what my purpose in life is. You know my faith, my patience, my love, and my endurance. [11]You know how much persecution and suffering I have endured. You know all about how I was persecuted in Antioch, Iconium, and Lystra—but the Lord rescued me from all of it. [12]Yes, and everyone who wants to live a godly life in Christ Jesus will suffer persecution. [13]But evil people and impostors will flourish. They will deceive others and will themselves be deceived.

[14]But you must remain faithful to the things you have been taught. You know they are true, for you know you can trust those who taught you. [15]You have been taught the holy Scriptures from childhood, and they have given you the wisdom to receive the salvation that comes by trusting in Christ Jesus. [16]All Scripture is inspired by God and is useful to teach us what is true and to make us realize what is wrong in our lives. It corrects us when we are wrong and teaches us to do what is right. [17]God uses it to prepare and equip his people to do every good work.

4

I solemnly urge you in the presence of God and Christ Jesus, who will someday judge the living and the dead when he appears to set up his Kingdom: [2]Preach the word of God. Be prepared, whether the time is favorable or not. Patiently

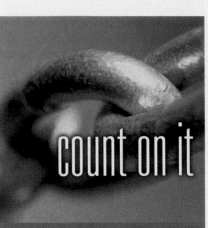

count on it

The Ten Commandments

Then God gave the people all these instructions:

"I am the LORD your God, who rescued you from the land of Egypt, the place of your slavery.

- You must not have any other god but me.
- You must not make for yourself an idol of any kind.
- You must not misuse the name of the LORD your God.
- Remember to observe the Sabbath day by keeping it holy.
- Honor your father and mother. Then you will live a long, full life in the land the LORD your God is giving you.
- You must not murder.
- You must not commit adultery.
- You must not steal.
- You must not testify falsely against your neighbor.
- You must not covet anything that belongs to your neighbor."

(Excerpts from Exodus 20:1-17)

Count on it!

correct, rebuke, and encourage your people with good teaching.

[3]For a time is coming when people will no longer listen to sound and wholesome teaching. They will follow their own desires and will look for teachers who will tell them whatever their itching ears want to hear. [4]They will reject the truth and chase after myths. [5]But you should keep a clear mind in every situation. Don't be afraid of suffering for the Lord. Work at telling others the Good News, and fully carry out the ministry God has given you.

[6]As for me, my life has already been poured out as an offering to God. The time of my death is near. [7]I have fought the good fight, I have finished the race, and I have remained faithful. [8]And now the prize awaits me—the crown of righteousness, which the Lord, the righteous Judge, will give me on the day of his return. And the prize is not just for me but for all who eagerly look forward to his appearing.

Paul's Final Words

[9]Timothy, please come as soon as you can. [10]Demas has deserted me because he loves the things of this life and has gone to Thessalonica. Crescens has gone to Galatia, and Titus has gone to Dalmatia. [11]Only Luke is with me. Bring Mark with you when you come, for he will be helpful to me in my ministry. [12]I sent Tychicus to Ephesus. [13]When you come, be sure to bring the coat I left with Carpus at Troas. Also bring my books, and especially my papers.

[14]Alexander the coppersmith did me much harm, but the Lord will judge him for what he has done. [15]Be careful of him, for he fought against everything we said.

[16]The first time I was brought before the judge, no one came with me. Everyone abandoned me. May it not be counted against them. [17]But the Lord stood with me and gave me strength so that I might preach the Good News in its entirety for all the Gentiles to hear. And he rescued me from certain death. [18]Yes, and the Lord will deliver me from every evil attack and will bring me safely into his heavenly Kingdom. All glory to God forever and ever! Amen.

Paul's Final Greetings

[19]Give my greetings to Priscilla and Aquila and those living in the household of Onesiphorus. [20]Erastus stayed at Corinth, and I left Trophimus sick at Miletus. [21]Do your best to get here before winter. Eubulus sends you greetings, and so do Pudens, Linus, Claudia, and all the brothers and sisters. [22]May the Lord be with your spirit. And may his grace be with all of you.

The letter to Titus was probably written about the same time as 1 Timothy, with which it has many similarities. Both letters are mainly engaged in describing the qualifications required for a church leader. Timothy and Titus were both cautioned against the same widespread false teachings (concerning good works). It is obvious that Paul loved Titus and knew he had been thrown into a particularly hard ministry on the island of Crete. Paul did not just build churches and leave them floundering, but rather we see his long-term concern and personal alliance in maintaining a healthy, active church. Here Paul provides encouragement and leadership to Titus as well as giving the entire church the criteria for leadership and a foundation for the organization of the church.

Titus

TITUS

Greetings from Paul

1

This letter is from Paul, a slave of God and an apostle of Jesus Christ. I have been sent to proclaim faith to those God has chosen and to teach them to know the truth that shows them how to live godly lives. [2]This truth gives them confidence that they have eternal life, which God—who does not lie—promised them before the world began. [3]And now at just the right time he has revealed this message, which we announce to everyone. It is by the command of God our Savior that I have been entrusted with this work for him.

You Are A Messenger (1 THESSALONIANS 2:4)
The time will come when you are asked to stand tall and be a leader at a Bible study, sports camp, or church event. It may simply be a brief opportunity to share your faith with a friend or teammate. Don't be shy. If you are a Christian, God will use you and sanction you as a messenger for his cause. Remember, you are not speaking on your own behalf but as an ambassador for Christ.

When you are tempted to look at pornography

1:15

Everything is pure to those whose hearts are pure. But nothing is pure to those who are corrupt and unbelieving, because their minds and consciences are corrupted.

[4]I am writing to Titus, my true son in the faith that we share.
May God the Father and Christ Jesus our Savior give you grace and peace.

Titus's Work in Crete

[5]I left you on the island of Crete so you could complete our work there and appoint elders in each town as I instructed you. [6]An elder must live a blameless life. He must be faithful to his wife, and his children must be believers who don't have a reputation for being wild or rebellious. [7]For an elder must live a blameless life. He must not be arrogant or quick-tempered; he must not be a heavy drinker, violent, or dishonest with money.

[8]Rather, he must enjoy having guests in his home, and he must love what is good. He must live wisely and be just. He must live a devout and disciplined life. [9]He must have a strong belief in the trustworthy message he was taught; then he will be able to encourage others with wholesome teaching and show those who oppose it where they are wrong.

[10]For there are many rebellious people who engage in useless talk and deceive others. This is especially true of those who insist on circumcision for salvation. [11]They must be silenced, because they are turning whole families away from the truth by their false teaching. And they do it only for money. [12]Even one of their own men, a prophet from Crete, has said about them, "The people of Crete are all liars, cruel animals, and lazy gluttons." [13]This is true. So reprimand them sternly to make them strong in the faith. [14]They must stop listening to Jewish myths and the commands of people who have turned away from the truth.

[15]Everything is pure to those whose hearts are pure. But nothing is pure to those who are corrupt and unbelieving, because their minds and consciences are corrupted. [16]Such people claim they know God, but they deny him by the way they live. They are detestable and disobedient, worthless for doing anything good.

Promote Right Teaching

2

As for you, Titus, promote the kind of living that reflects wholesome teaching. [2]Teach the older men to exercise self-control, to be worthy of respect, and to live wisely. They must have sound faith and be filled with love and patience.

[3]Similarly, teach the older women to live in a way that honors God. They must not slander others or be heavy drinkers. Instead, they should teach others what is good. [4]These older women must train the younger women to love their husbands and their children, [5]to live wisely and be pure, to work in their homes, to do good, and to be submissive to their husbands. Then

What are the five most brutal conditioning workouts?

1.
2.
3.
4.
5.

BIG FIVE

they will not bring shame on the word of God. [6]In the same way, encourage the young men to live wisely. [7]And you yourself must be an example to them by doing good works of every kind. Let everything you do reflect the integrity and seriousness of your teaching. [8]Teach the truth so that your teaching can't be criticized. Then those who oppose us will be ashamed and have nothing bad to say about us.

[9]Slaves must always obey their masters and do their best to please them. They must not talk back [10]or steal, but must show themselves to be entirely trustworthy and good. Then they will make the teaching about God our Savior attractive in every way.

[11]For the grace of God has been revealed, bringing salvation to all people. [12]And we are instructed to turn from godless living and sinful pleasures. We should live in this evil world with wisdom, righteousness, and devotion to God, [13]while we look forward with hope to that wonderful day when the glory of our great God and Savior, Jesus Christ, will be revealed. [14]He gave his life to free us from every kind of sin, to cleanse us, and to make us his very own people, totally committed to doing good deeds.

[15]You must teach these things and encourage the believers to do them. You have the authority to correct them when necessary, so don't let anyone disregard what you say.

Do What Is Good

3

Remind the believers to submit to the government and its officers. They should be obedient, always ready to do what is good. [2]They must not slander anyone and must avoid quarreling. Instead, they should be gentle and show true humility to everyone.

[3]Once we, too, were foolish and disobedient. We were misled and became slaves to many lusts and pleasures. Our lives were full of evil and envy, and we hated each other.

[4]But—"When God our Savior revealed his kindness and love, [5]he saved us, not because of the righteous things we had done, but because of his mercy. He washed away our sins, giving us a new birth and new life through the Holy Spirit. [6]He generously poured out the Spirit upon us through Jesus Christ our Savior. [7]Because of his grace he declared us righteous and gave us confidence that we will inherit eternal life."

[8]This is a trustworthy saying, and I want you to insist on these teachings so that all who trust in God will devote themselves to doing good. These teachings are good and beneficial for everyone.

[9]Do not get involved in foolish discussions about spiritual pedigrees or in quarrels and fights about obedience to Jewish laws. These things are useless and a waste of time. [10]If people are causing divisions among you, give a first and second warning. After that, have nothing more to do with them. [11]For people like that have turned away from the truth, and their own sins condemn them.

action

3:1-2 WHAT'S IT SAYING?

WHAT AM I GOING TO DO ABOUT IT?

Paul's Final Remarks and Greetings

[12]I am planning to send either Artemas or Tychicus to you. As soon as one of them arrives, do your best to meet me at Nicopolis, for I have decided to stay there for the winter. [13]Do everything you can to help Zenas the lawyer and Apollos with their trip. See that they are given everything they need. [14]Our people must learn to do good by meeting the urgent needs of others; then they will not be unproductive.

[15]Everybody here sends greetings. Please give my greetings to the believers—all who love us.

May God's grace be with you all.

WHAT DOES IT MEAN?

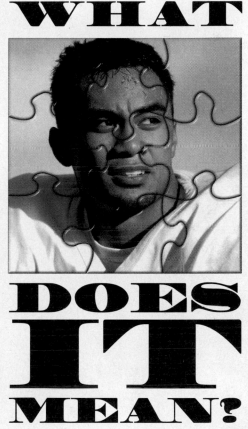

faith

Faith in Jesus Christ is a saving grace, through which we rest on him alone to receive our salvation, as offered to us in the gospel. The object of saving faith is the whole revealed Word of God. Its primary concept is trust. When a thing is true, it is therefore worthy of trust. Faith in Christ is full assurance of truth, in accordance with the evidence on which it rests. Faith is the result of teaching (Romans 10:14-17) and knowledge illuminated by the Holy Spirit. Faith in Christ secures for the believer freedom from condemnation, or justification before God (John 14:19; Romans 6:4-10; Ephesians 1:6-7).

On and off the field

live it

They say sport is the great evener that can break down barriers of race, status, wealth, and privilege. But once you leave the field, many of these barriers rise up again. In this very private letter, Paul explains to the slave owner Philemon, in a most tactful way, that those in Christ are all the same and that there are no walls separating Christians, regardless of social status. This book is also a great lesson on how we should forgive and welcome back those who have hurt us.

Philemon was a faithful man and generous worker for the cause of Christ. He was part of the Colossian church, a convert and dear friend of the apostle Paul. Paul was writing to him pleading that he take back a runaway slave, Onesimus, and not only forgive him but embrace him as a new fellow believer and brother in Christ. Onesimus had fled to Rome, where he met Paul and gave his heart to Christ, but now he willingly returned to Philemon his master. We as Christians also serve a Master. Like Onesimus, our destiny and joy are both found in turning to and serving the Master.

Philemon

PHILEMON

Greetings from Paul

This letter is from Paul, a prisoner for preaching the Good News about Christ Jesus, and from our brother Timothy.

I am writing to Philemon, our beloved co-worker, [2]and to our sister Apphia, and to our fellow soldier Archippus, and to the church that meets in your house.

[3]May God our Father and the Lord Jesus Christ give you grace and peace.

Paul's Thanksgiving and Prayer

[4]I always thank my God when I pray for you, Philemon, [5]because I keep hearing about your faith in the Lord Jesus and your love for all of God's people. [6]And I am praying that you will put into action the generosity that comes from your faith as you understand and experience all the good things we have in Christ. [7]Your love has given me much joy and comfort, my brother, for your kindness has often refreshed the hearts of God's people.

Paul's Appeal for Onesimus

[8]That is why I am boldly asking a favor of you. I could demand it in the name of Christ because it is the right thing for you to do. [9]But because of our love, I prefer simply to ask you. Consider this as a request from me—Paul, an old man and now also a prisoner for the sake of Christ Jesus. [10]I appeal to you to show kindness to my child, Onesimus. I became his father in the faith while here in prison. [11]Onesimus hasn't been of much use to you in the past, but now he is very useful to both of us. [12]I am sending him back to you, and with him comes my own heart.

[13]I wanted to keep him here with me while I am in these chains for preaching the Good News, and he would have helped me on your behalf. [14]But I didn't want to do anything without your consent. I wanted you to help because you were willing, not because you were forced. [15]It seems Onesimus ran away for a little while so that you could have him back forever. [16]He is no longer like a slave to you. He is more than a slave, for he is a beloved brother, especially to me. Now he will mean much more to you, both as a man and as a brother in the Lord.

[17]So if you consider me your partner, welcome him as you would welcome me. [18]If he has wronged you in any way or owes you anything, charge it to me. [19]I, PAUL, WRITE THIS WITH MY OWN HAND: I WILL REPAY IT. AND I WON'T MENTION THAT YOU OWE ME YOUR VERY SOUL! [20]Yes, my brother, please do me this favor for the Lord's sake. Give me this encouragement in Christ.

[21]I am confident as I write this letter that you will do what I ask and even more! [22]One more thing—please prepare a guest room for me, for I am hoping that God will answer your prayers and let me return to you soon.

Paul's Final Greetings

[23]Epaphras, my fellow prisoner in Christ Jesus, sends you his greetings. [24]So do Mark, Aristarchus, Demas, and Luke, my co-workers.

[25]May the grace of the Lord Jesus Christ be with your spirit.

The soccer referee's whistle was introduced in 1878. Prior to this a referee had to rely on waving a handkerchief.

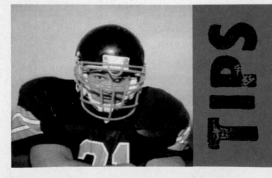

Sports specific training:

Obviously a javelin thrower and a pole-vaulter will need unique and skill-specific training regimens. Ideally, a training program should be individually tailored to meet the needs of each discipline or sport; however, many athletes train in a group or team flexibility program. This team-centered program is great for team building. However, in such cases, it is still essential that each individual athlete be properly instructed to concentrate on specific areas that need additional focus.

Hebrews

In Hebrews we learn how wonderfully God's purpose and plan come together in Jesus. For two thousand years the church has debated the authorship of the book of Hebrews. Now we can answer the big question: God wrote the book! The whole Bible is God's autobiography; he merely used men to pen the manuscript. We really don't know who God used to write this great book. That said, it was God's good pleasure that we should not know the identity of the author, though he certainly writes with apostolic authority. Clearly it was intended for Jewish converts to the faith and probably focused on the converts in Jerusalem. These Christians were being torn by the rich tradition of their old Jewish system and culture and the emergence of Jesus as the fulfillment of the Old Testament.

Its purpose was to show the true meaning of the Mosaic system (the old covenant) and its representative and temporary character. It proves that the Levitical priesthood was a shadow of Christ, and that the Old Testament sacrifices prefigured the great and all-perfect sacrifice: God's Son. In Hebrews we are shown how the Old Testament reveals God and his plan for ultimately redeeming his people — it all points to the Cross.

PROBLEMS

ENDURANCE

STRENGTH

CHARACTER

CONFIDENCE

SALVATION

We can rejoice, too, when we run into `PROBLEMS` and trials, for we know that they help us develop `ENDURANCE`. And endurance develops `STRENGTH` of `CHARACTER,` and character strengthens our `CONFIDENT` hope of `SALVATION.`

`ROMANS 5:3-4`

HEBREWS

Jesus Christ Is God's Son

1

Long ago God spoke many times and in many ways to our ancestors through the prophets. [2]And now in these final days, he has spoken to us through his Son. God promised everything to the Son as an inheritance, and through the Son he created the universe. [3]The Son radiates God's own glory and expresses the very character of God, and he sustains everything by the mighty power of his command. When he had cleansed us from our sins, he sat down in the place of honor at the right hand of the majestic God in heaven. [4]This shows that the Son is far greater than the angels, just as the name God gave him is greater than their names.

The Son Is Greater Than the Angels

[5]For God never said to any angel what he said to Jesus:
"You are my Son.
Today I have become your Father."
God also said,
"I will be his Father,
and he will be my Son."
[6]And when he brought his firstborn Son into the world, God said,
"Let all of God's angels worship him."
[7]Regarding the angels, he says,
"He sends his angels like the winds,
his servants like flames of fire."
[8]But to the Son he says,
"Your throne, O God, endures forever and ever.
You rule with a scepter of justice.
[9]You love justice and hate evil.
Therefore, O God, your God has anointed you,
pouring out the oil of joy on you more than on anyone else."
[10]He also says to the Son,
"In the beginning, Lord, you laid the foundation of the earth
and made the heavens with your hands.
[11]They will perish, but you remain forever.
They will wear out like old clothing.
[12]You will fold them up like a cloak
and discard them like old clothing.
But you are always the same;
you will live forever."
[13]And God never said to any of the angels,

Psalm 118:8 ("It is better to take refuge in the Lᴏʀᴅ than to trust in people") is in the exact middle of the Old and New Testaments.

"Sit in the place of honor at my right hand
until I humble your enemies,
making them a footstool under your feet."
[14]Therefore, angels are only servants—spirits sent to care for people who will inherit salvation.

A Warning against Drifting Away

2

So we must listen very carefully to the truth we have heard, or we may drift away from it. [2]For the message God delivered through angels has always stood firm, and every violation of the law and every act of disobedience was punished. [3]So what makes us think we can escape if we ignore this great salvation that was first announced by the Lord Jesus himself and then delivered to us by those who heard him speak? [4]And God confirmed the message by giving signs and wonders and various miracles and gifts of the Holy Spirit whenever he chose.

Jesus, the Man

[5]And furthermore, it is not angels who will control the future world we are talking about. [6]For in one place the Scriptures say,
"What are people that you should think of them,
or a son of man that you should care for him?
[7]Yet you made them only a little lower than the angels
and crowned them with glory and honor.
[8]You gave them authority over all things."
Now when it says "all things," it means nothing is left out. But we have not yet seen all things put under their authority. [9]What we do see is Jesus, who was given a position "a little lower than the angels"; and because he suffered death for us, he is now "crowned with glory and honor." Yes, by God's grace, Jesus tasted death for everyone. [10]God, for whom and through whom everything was made, chose to bring many children into glory. And it was only right that he should make Jesus, through his suffering, a perfect leader, fit to bring them into their salvation.

[11]So now Jesus and the ones he makes holy have the same Father. That is why Jesus is not ashamed to call them his brothers and sisters. [12]For he said to God,
"I will proclaim your name to my brothers and sisters.
I will praise you among your assembled people."
[13]He also said,
"I will put my trust in him,"
that is, "I and the children God has given me."
[14]Because God's children are human beings—made of flesh and blood—the Son also became flesh and blood. For only as a human being could he die, and only by dying could he break the power of the devil, who had the power of death. [15]Only in this way could he set free all who have lived their lives as slaves to the fear of dying. [16]We also know that the Son did not come to help angels; he came to help the descendants of Abraham. [17]Therefore, it

Be courageous. Courage allows you to be firm when facing danger and temptation. You may feel scared and be tempted to falter; that's a normal part of life. What courage does is allow you to live for God — to speak, react, and perform while under pressure.
"Be on guard. Stand firm in the faith. Be courageous. Be strong."
(1 Corinthians 16:13)

was necessary for him to be made in every respect like us, his brothers and sisters, so that he could be our merciful and faithful High Priest before God. Then he could offer a sacrifice that would take away the sins of the people. [18]Since he himself has gone through suffering and testing, he is able to help us when we are being tested.

Jesus Is Greater Than Moses

3

And so, dear brothers and sisters who belong to God and are partners with those called to heaven, think carefully about this Jesus whom we declare to be God's messenger and High Priest. [2]For he was faithful to God, who appointed him, just as Moses served faithfully when he was entrusted with God's entire house.

[3]But Jesus deserves far more glory than Moses, just as a person who builds a house deserves more praise than the house itself. [4]For every house has a builder, but the one who built everything is God.

[5]Moses was certainly faithful in God's house as a servant.

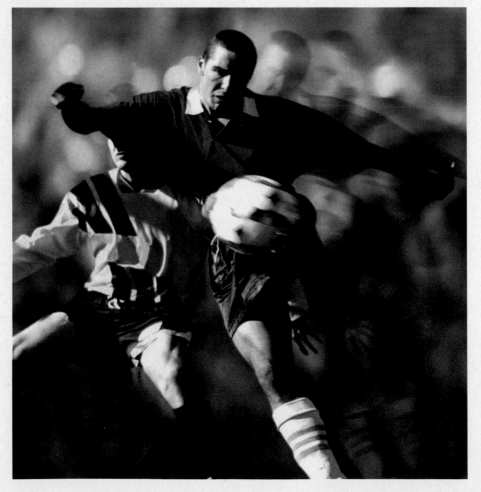

His work was an illustration of the truths God would reveal later. [6]But Christ, as the Son, is in charge of God's entire house. And we are God's house, if we keep our courage and remain confident in our hope in Christ.

[7]That is why the Holy Spirit says,
"Today when you hear his voice,
[8]don't harden your hearts
as Israel did when they rebelled,
when they tested me in the wilderness.
[9]There your ancestors tested and tried my patience,
even though they saw my miracles for forty years.
[10]So I was angry with them, and I said,
'Their hearts always turn away from me.
They refuse to do what I tell them.'
[11]So in my anger I took an oath:
'They will never enter my place of rest.'"
[12]Be careful then, dear brothers and sisters. Make sure that your own hearts are not evil and unbelieving, turning you away from the living God. [13]You must warn each other every day, while it is still "today," so that

none of you will be deceived by sin and hardened against God. [14]For if we are faithful to the end, trusting God just as firmly as when we first believed, we will share in all that belongs to Christ. [15]Remember what it says:

"Today when you hear his voice,
don't harden your hearts
as Israel did when they rebelled."

[16]And who was it who rebelled against God, even though they heard his voice? Wasn't it the people Moses led out of Egypt? [17]And who made God angry for forty years? Wasn't it the people who sinned, whose corpses lay in the wilderness? [18]And to whom was God speaking when he took an oath that they would never enter his rest? Wasn't it the people who disobeyed him? [19]So we see that because of their unbelief they were not able to enter his rest.

Promised Rest for God's People

4

God's promise of entering his rest still stands, so we ought to tremble with fear that some of you might fail to experience it. [2]For this good news—that God has prepared this rest—has been announced to us just as it was to them. But it did them no good because they didn't share the faith of those who listened to God. [3]For only we who believe can enter his rest. As for the others, God said,

"In my anger I took an oath:
'They will never enter my place of rest,'"
even though this rest has been ready since he made the world. [4]We know it is ready because of the place in the Scriptures where it mentions the seventh day:
"On the seventh day God rested from all his work."
[5]But in the other passage God said, "They will never enter my place of rest."

[6]So God's rest is there for people to enter, but those who first heard this good news failed to enter because they disobeyed God. [7]So God set another time for entering his rest, and that time is today. God announced this through David much later in the words already quoted:

"Today when you hear his voice,
don't harden your hearts."

[8]Now if Joshua had succeeded in giving them this rest, God would not have spoken about another day of rest still to come. [9]So there is a special rest still waiting for the people of God. [10]For all who have entered into God's rest have rested from their labors, just as God did after creating the world. [11]So let us do our best to

enter that rest. But if we disobey God, as the people of Israel did, we will fall.

¹²For the word of God is alive and powerful. It is sharper than the sharpest two-edged sword, cutting between soul and spirit, between joint and marrow. It exposes our innermost thoughts and desires. ¹³Nothing in all creation is hidden from God. Everything is naked and exposed before his eyes, and he is the one to whom we are accountable.

4:14-16 WHAT'S IT SAYING?

WHAT AM I GOING TO DO ABOUT IT?

Christ Is Our High Priest

¹⁴So then, since we have a great High Priest who has entered heaven, Jesus the Son of God, let us hold firmly to what we believe. ¹⁵This High Priest of ours understands our weaknesses, for he faced all of the same testings we do, yet he did not sin. ¹⁶So let us

WHAT 5 DOES IT MEAN?

sports in Scripture

Paul frequently drew on sporting analogies to help us better understand the Christian faith (Galatians 2:2; 5:7; Philippians 2:16; 3:14; 1 Timothy 6:12; 2 Timothy 2:5; Hebrews 12:1, 4, 12). Competitions like Grecian gymnastic contests and the numerous Greek Olympic, Pythian, Nemean, and Isthmian Games were of great national importance, and the victors at any of these games were highly respected.

come boldly to the throne of our gracious God. There we will receive his mercy, and we will find grace to help us when we need it most.

5

Every high priest is a man chosen to represent other people in their dealings with God. He presents their gifts to God and offers sacrifices for their sins. ²And he is able to deal gently with ignorant and wayward people because he himself is subject to the same weaknesses. ³That is why he must offer sacrifices for his own sins as well as theirs.

⁴And no one can become a high priest simply because he wants such an honor. He must be called by God for this work, just as Aaron was. ⁵That is why Christ did not honor himself by assuming he could become High Priest. No, he was chosen by God, who said to him,

"You are my Son.
Today I have become your Father."

⁶And in another passage God said to him,

"You are a priest forever in the order of Melchizedek."

⁷While Jesus was here on earth, he offered prayers and pleadings, with a loud cry and tears, to the one who could rescue him from death. And God heard his prayers because of his deep reverence for God. ⁸Even though Jesus was God's Son, he learned obedience from the things he suffered. ⁹In this way, God qualified him as a perfect High Priest, and he became the source of eternal salvation for all those who obey him. ¹⁰And God designated him to be a High Priest in the order of Melchizedek.

A Call to Spiritual Growth

¹¹There is much more we would like to say about this, but it is difficult to explain, especially since you are spiritually dull and don't seem to listen. ¹²You have been believers so long now that you ought to be teaching others. Instead, you need someone to teach you again the basic things about God's word. You are like babies who need milk and cannot eat solid food. ¹³For someone who lives on milk is still an infant and doesn't know how to do what is right. ¹⁴Solid food is for those who are mature, who through training have the skill to recognize the difference between right and wrong.

6

So let us stop going over the basic teachings about Christ again and again. Let us go on instead and become mature in

A Strong and Trustworthy Anchor (HEBREWS 6:16-20)
Early Christians used the sign of an anchor (much like the fish sign) as a symbol for their faith in Christ. Don't flounder through life — hang on to God's assurance of a safe refuge. In the fickle world of sports it is nice to have an anchor — a strong promise from God that those that have faith in Christ are fastened securely to him.

NOVEMBER M.A.P.

1

S.D.	P.L.	P.G.	S.G.
P. ☐	F. ☐	F. ☐	T. ☐
F. ☐	W. ☐	W. ☐	P. ☐
B. ☐	P. ☐	C. ☐	C. ☐

2

S.D.	P.L.	P.G.	S.G.
P. ☐	F. ☐	F. ☐	T. ☐
F. ☐	W. ☐	W. ☐	P. ☐
B. ☐	P. ☐	C. ☐	C. ☐

3

S.D.	P.L.	P.G.	S.G.
P. ☐	F. ☐	F. ☐	T. ☐
F. ☐	W. ☐	W. ☐	P. ☐
B. ☐	P. ☐	C. ☐	C. ☐

4

S.D.	P.L.	P.G.	S.G.
P. ☐	F. ☐	F. ☐	T. ☐
F. ☐	W. ☐	W. ☐	P. ☐
B. ☐	P. ☐	C. ☐	C. ☐

9

S.D.	P.L.	P.G.	S.G.
P. ☐	F. ☐	F. ☐	T. ☐
F. ☐	W. ☐	W. ☐	P. ☐
B. ☐	P. ☐	C. ☐	C. ☐

10

S.D.	P.L.	P.G.	S.G.
P. ☐	F. ☐	F. ☐	T. ☐
F. ☐	W. ☐	W. ☐	P. ☐
B. ☐	P. ☐	C. ☐	C. ☐

11

S.D.	P.L.	P.G.	S.G.
P. ☐	F. ☐	F. ☐	T. ☐
F. ☐	W. ☐	W. ☐	P. ☐
B. ☐	P. ☐	C. ☐	C. ☐

12

S.D.	P.L.	P.G.	S.G.
P. ☐	F. ☐	F. ☐	T. ☐
F. ☐	W. ☐	W. ☐	P. ☐
B. ☐	P. ☐	C. ☐	C. ☐

17

S.D.	P.L.	P.G.	S.G.
P. ☐	F. ☐	F. ☐	T. ☐
F. ☐	W. ☐	W. ☐	P. ☐
B. ☐	P. ☐	C. ☐	C. ☐

18

S.D.	P.L.	P.G.	S.G.
P. ☐	F. ☐	F. ☐	T. ☐
F. ☐	W. ☐	W. ☐	P. ☐
B. ☐	P. ☐	C. ☐	C. ☐

19

S.D.	P.L.	P.G.	S.G.
P. ☐	F. ☐	F. ☐	T. ☐
F. ☐	W. ☐	W. ☐	P. ☐
B. ☐	P. ☐	C. ☐	C. ☐

20

S.D.	P.L.	P.G.	S.G.
P. ☐	F. ☐	F. ☐	T. ☐
F. ☐	W. ☐	W. ☐	P. ☐
B. ☐	P. ☐	C. ☐	C. ☐

25

S.D.	P.L.	P.G.	S.G.
P. ☐	F. ☐	F. ☐	T. ☐
F. ☐	W. ☐	W. ☐	P. ☐
B. ☐	P. ☐	C. ☐	C. ☐

26

S.D.	P.L.	P.G.	S.G.
P. ☐	F. ☐	F. ☐	T. ☐
F. ☐	W. ☐	W. ☐	P. ☐
B. ☐	P. ☐	C. ☐	C. ☐

27

S.D.	P.L.	P.G.	S.G.
P. ☐	F. ☐	F. ☐	T. ☐
F. ☐	W. ☐	W. ☐	P. ☐
B. ☐	P. ☐	C. ☐	C. ☐

28

S.D.	P.L.	P.G.	S.G.
P. ☐	F. ☐	F. ☐	T. ☐
F. ☐	W. ☐	W. ☐	P. ☐
B. ☐	P. ☐	C. ☐	C. ☐

Spiritual Disciplines

Prayer

Faith Community

Bible Reading

Prayer List

Friends

World

Personal

Who am I....
Where am I going....
How am I going to get there?

nt:sport
MONTHLY ACTION PLAN

5

S.D.	P.L.	P.G.	S.G.
P. ☐	F. ☐	F. ☐	T. ☐
F. ☐	W. ☐	W. ☐	P. ☐
B. ☐	P. ☐	C. ☐	C. ☐

6

S.D.	P.L.	P.G.	S.G.
P. ☐	F. ☐	F. ☐	T. ☐
F. ☐	W. ☐	W. ☐	P. ☐
B. ☐	P. ☐	C. ☐	C. ☐

7

S.D.	P.L.	P.G.	S.G.
P. ☐	F. ☐	F. ☐	T. ☐
F. ☐	W. ☐	W. ☐	P. ☐
B. ☐	P. ☐	C. ☐	C. ☐

8

S.D.	P.L.	P.G.	S.G.
P. ☐	F. ☐	F. ☐	T. ☐
F. ☐	W. ☐	W. ☐	P. ☐
B. ☐	P. ☐	C. ☐	C. ☐

13

S.D.	P.L.	P.G.	S.G.
P. ☐	F. ☐	F. ☐	T. ☐
F. ☐	W. ☐	W. ☐	P. ☐
B. ☐	P. ☐	C. ☐	C. ☐

14

S.D.	P.L.	P.G.	S.G.
P. ☐	F. ☐	F. ☐	T. ☐
F. ☐	W. ☐	W. ☐	P. ☐
B. ☐	P. ☐	C. ☐	C. ☐

15

S.D.	P.L.	P.G.	S.G.
P. ☐	F. ☐	F. ☐	T. ☐
F. ☐	W. ☐	W. ☐	P. ☐
B. ☐	P. ☐	C. ☐	C. ☐

16

S.D.	P.L.	P.G.	S.G.
P. ☐	F. ☐	F. ☐	T. ☐
F. ☐	W. ☐	W. ☐	P. ☐
B. ☐	P. ☐	C. ☐	C. ☐

21

S.D.	P.L.	P.G.	S.G.
P. ☐	F. ☐	F. ☐	T. ☐
F. ☐	W. ☐	W. ☐	P. ☐
B. ☐	P. ☐	C. ☐	C. ☐

22

S.D.	P.L.	P.G.	S.G.
P. ☐	F. ☐	F. ☐	T. ☐
F. ☐	W. ☐	W. ☐	P. ☐
B. ☐	P. ☐	C. ☐	C. ☐

23

S.D.	P.L.	P.G.	S.G.
P. ☐	F. ☐	F. ☐	T. ☐
F. ☐	W. ☐	W. ☐	P. ☐
B. ☐	P. ☐	C. ☐	C. ☐

24

S.D.	P.L.	P.G.	S.G.
P. ☐	F. ☐	F. ☐	T. ☐
F. ☐	W. ☐	W. ☐	P. ☐
B. ☐	P. ☐	C. ☐	C. ☐

29

S.D.	P.L.	P.G.	S.G.
P. ☐	F. ☐	F. ☐	T. ☐
F. ☐	W. ☐	W. ☐	P. ☐
B. ☐	P. ☐	C. ☐	C. ☐

30

S.D.	P.L.	P.G.	S.G.
P. ☐	F. ☐	F. ☐	T. ☐
F. ☐	W. ☐	W. ☐	P. ☐
B. ☐	P. ☐	C. ☐	C. ☐

Proverbs 20:24

The LORD directs our steps, so why try to understand everything along the way?

Personal Goals

Family

Work/School/Social

Challenge

Sport Goals

Training

Performance

Competition Results

(For designing your M.A.P. – Monthly Action Plan – see introduction pages)

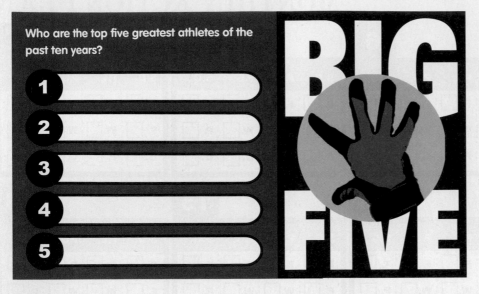

Who are the top five greatest athletes of the past ten years?

1

2

3

4

5

our understanding. Surely we don't need to start again with the fundamental importance of repenting from evil deeds and placing our faith in God. ²You don't need further instruction about baptisms, the laying on of hands, the resurrection of the dead, and eternal judgment. ³And so, God willing, we will move forward to further understanding.

⁴For it is impossible to bring back to repentance those who were once enlightened—those who have experienced the good things of heaven and shared in the Holy Spirit, ⁵who have tasted the goodness of the word of God and the power of the age to come—⁶and who then turn away from God. It is impossible to bring such people back to repentance; by rejecting the Son of God, they themselves are nailing him to the cross once again and holding him up to public shame. ⁷When the ground soaks up the falling rain and bears a good crop for the farmer, it has God's blessing. ⁸But if a field bears

thorns and thistles, it is useless. The farmer will soon condemn that field and burn it.

⁹Dear friends, even though we are talking this way, we really don't believe it applies to you. We are confident that you are meant for better things, things that come with salvation. ¹⁰For God is not unjust. He will not forget how hard you have worked for him and how you have shown your love to him by caring for other believers, as you still do. ¹¹Our great desire is that you will keep on loving others as long as life lasts, in order to make certain that what you hope for will come true. ¹²Then you will not become spiritually dull and indifferent. Instead, you will follow the example of those who are going to inherit God's promises because of their faith and endurance.

God's Promises Bring Hope

¹³For example, there was God's promise to Abraham. Since there was no one greater to swear by, God took an oath in his own name, saying:

¹⁴"I will certainly bless you,

and I will multiply your descendants beyond number."

¹⁵Then Abraham waited patiently, and he received what God had promised.

¹⁶Now when people take an oath, they call on someone greater than themselves to hold them to it. And without any question that oath is binding. ¹⁷God also bound himself with an oath, so that those who received the promise could be perfectly sure that he would never change his mind. ¹⁸So God has given both his promise and his oath. These two things are unchangeable because it is impossible for God to lie. Therefore, we who have fled to him for refuge can have great confidence as we hold to the hope that lies before us.

¹⁹This hope is a strong and trustworthy anchor for our souls. It leads us through the curtain into God's inner sanctuary. ²⁰Jesus has already gone in there for us. He has become our eternal High Priest in the order of Melchizedek.

Melchizedek Is Greater Than Abraham

7

This Melchizedek was king of the city of Salem and also a priest of God Most High. When Abraham was returning home after winning a great battle against the kings, Melchizedek met him and blessed him. ²Then Abraham took a tenth of all he had captured in battle and gave it to Melchizedek. The name Melchizedek means "king of justice," and king of Salem means "king of peace." ³There is no record of his father or mother or any of his ancestors—no beginning or end to his life. He remains a priest forever, resembling the Son of God.

⁴Consider then how great this Melchizedek was. Even Abraham, the great patriarch of Israel, recognized this by giving him a tenth of what he had taken in battle. ⁵Now the law of Moses required that the priests, who are descendants of Levi, must collect a tithe from the rest of the people of Israel, who are also descendants of Abraham. ⁶But Melchizedek, who was not a descendant of Levi, collected a tenth from Abraham. And Melchizedek placed a blessing upon Abraham, the one who had already received the promises of God. ⁷And without question, the person who has the power to give a blessing is greater than the one who is blessed.

⁸The priests who collect tithes are men who die, so Melchizedek is greater than they are, because we are told that he lives on. ⁹In addition, we might even say

STAND POINT

When you are not getting enough playing time

6:10

For God is not unjust. He will not forget how hard you have worked for him and how you have shown your love to him by caring for other believers, as you still do.

Due to World Wars I and II, Summer Olympic Games were not held in 1916, 1940, or 1944.

Winners are patient!

In sports you are constantly waiting and persisting — whether you are waiting for the season to begin, the match to start, a play to develop, an injury to heal, or to be called up for your country. Sport can teach you to persevere and be patient. Knowing God is in control and waiting peacefully is a great way to express faith and worship to God. Patience is a quality for strong people.

"Don't worry about anything; instead, pray about everything. Tell God what you need, and thank him for all he has done." Philippians 4:6

Winners can wait!

that these Levites—the ones who collect the tithe—paid a tithe to Melchizedek when their ancestor Abraham paid a tithe to him. [10]For although Levi wasn't born yet, the seed from which he came was in Abraham's body when Melchizedek collected the tithe from him.

[11]So if the priesthood of Levi, on which the law was based, could have achieved the perfection God intended, why did God need to establish a different priesthood, with a priest in the order of Melchizedek instead of the order of Levi and Aaron? [12]And if the priesthood is changed, the law must also be changed to permit it. [13]For the priest we are talking about belongs to a different tribe, whose members have never served at the altar as priests. [14]What I mean is, our Lord came from the tribe of Judah, and Moses never mentioned priests coming from that tribe.

Jesus Is like Melchizedek

[15]This change has been made very clear since a different priest, who is like Melchizedek, has appeared. [16]Jesus became a priest, not by meeting the physical requirement of belonging to the tribe of Levi, but by the power of a life that cannot be destroyed. [17]And the psalmist pointed this out when he prophesied,

"You are a priest forever in the order of Melchizedek."
[18]Yes, the old requirement about the priesthood was

set aside because it was weak and useless. [19]For the law never made anything perfect. But now we have confidence in a better hope, through which we draw near to God.

[20]This new system was established with a solemn oath. Aaron's descendants became priests without such an oath, [21]but there was an oath regarding Jesus. For God said to him,

"The LORD has taken an oath and will not break his vow:
'You are a priest forever.'"
[22]Because of this oath, Jesus is the one who guarantees this better covenant with God.

[23]There were many priests under the old system, for death prevented them from remaining in office. [24]But because Jesus lives forever, his priesthood lasts forever. [25]Therefore he is able, once and forever, to save those who come to God through him. He lives forever to intercede with God on their behalf.

[26]He is the kind of high priest we need because he is holy and blameless, unstained by sin. He has been set apart from sinners and has been given the highest place of honor in heaven. [27]Unlike those other high priests, he does not need to offer sacrifices every day. They did this for their own sins first and then for the sins of the people. But Jesus did this once for all when he offered himself as the sacrifice for the people's sins.

[28]The law appointed high priests who were limited by human weakness. But after the law was given, God appointed his Son with an oath, and his Son has been made the perfect High Priest forever.

Christ Is Our High Priest

8

Here is the main point: We have a High Priest who sat down in the place of honor beside the throne of the majestic God in heaven. [2]There he ministers in the heavenly Tabernacle, the true place of worship that was built by the Lord and not by human hands.

[3]And since every high priest is required to offer gifts and sacrifices, our High Priest must make an offering, too. [4]If he were here on earth, he would not even be a priest, since there already are priests who offer the gifts required by the law. [5]They serve in a system of worship that is only a copy, a shadow of the real one in heaven. For when Moses was getting ready to build the Tabernacle, God gave him this warning: "Be sure that you make everything according to the pattern I have shown you here on the mountain."

[6]But now Jesus, our High Priest, has been given a ministry that is far superior to the old priesthood, for he is the one who mediates for us a far better covenant with God, based on better promises.

[7]If the first covenant had been faultless, there would have

If you coach, coach positively:

"The things that get rewarded get done." Encourage the athletes that come prepared, ready to learn, and wanting to work, regardless of their skill. Give recognition for effort, not just results. Most improvements come about little by little. Note and reinforce the little victories on the way to the play that wins the championship game.

profiles

Moses:

"Who am I to appear before Pharaoh? Who am I to lead the people of Israel out of Egypt?" (Exodus 3:11). Moses was a giant in history with a privileged upbringing, yet when commanded to free the Israelites and bring them to the Promised Land of their ancestors, he felt inadequate. The sense of unworthiness or weakness is a huge force seen in many successful Bible heroes. We are inadequate, but when that knowledge forces us to beg God for power, then great things can happen. Moses survived the death penalty given by Pharaoh, the ruler of Egypt, who had for years used the people of Joseph (Israelites) to be slaves for Egypt. Moses, after being given a privileged upbringing, eventually fled to the desert. But God had a huge task for Moses in freeing God's special people. Moses conceded and with the help of his brother and God's power led 2 million people out of slavery and into an odyssey that lasted forty years in the wilderness. Moses obeyed God and formed a nation that would influence the world in which we live today.

been no need for a second covenant to replace it. ⁸But when God found fault with the people, he said:
"The day is coming, says the LORD,
when I will make a new covenant
with the people of Israel and Judah.
⁹This covenant will not be like the one

Bible

What the Bible says about itself: "For the word of God is alive and powerful. It is sharper than the sharpest two-edged sword, cutting between soul and spirit, between joint and marrow." (Hebrews 4:12)

I made with their ancestors
when I took them by the hand
and led them out of the land of Egypt.
They did not remain faithful to my covenant,
so I turned my back on them, says the LORD.
¹⁰But this is the new covenant I will make
with the people of Israel on that day, says the LORD:
I will put my laws in their minds,
and I will write them on their hearts.
I will be their God,
and they will be my people.
¹¹And they will not need to teach their neighbors,
nor will they need to teach their relatives,
saying, 'You should know the LORD.'
For everyone, from the least to the greatest,
will know me already.
¹²And I will forgive their wickedness,
and I will never again remember their sins."
¹³When God speaks of a "new" covenant, it means he has made the first one obsolete. It is now out of date and will soon disappear.

Old Rules about Worship

9

That first covenant between God and Israel had regulations for worship and a place of worship here on earth. ²There were two rooms in that Tabernacle. In the first room were a lampstand, a table, and sacred loaves of bread on the table. This room was called the Holy Place. ³Then there was a curtain, and behind the curtain was the second room called the Most Holy Place. ⁴In that room were a gold incense altar and a wooden chest called the Ark of the Covenant, which was covered with gold on all sides. Inside the Ark were a gold jar containing manna, Aaron's staff that

sprouted leaves, and the stone tablets of the covenant. ⁵Above the Ark were the cherubim of divine glory, whose wings stretched out over the Ark's cover, the place of atonement. But we cannot explain these things in detail now.
⁶When these things were all in place, the priests regularly entered the first room as they performed their religious duties. ⁷But only the high priest ever entered the Most Holy Place, and only once a year. And he always offered blood for his own sins and for the sins the people had committed in ignorance. ⁸By these regulations the Holy Spirit revealed that the entrance to the Most Holy Place was not freely open as long as the Tabernacle and the system it represented were still in use.
⁹This is an illustration pointing to the present time. For the gifts and sacrifices that the priests offer are not able to cleanse the consciences of the people who bring them. ¹⁰For that old system deals only with food and drink and various cleansing ceremonies—physical regulations that were in effect only until a better system could be established.

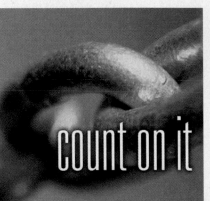

count on it

Brand-new!
When you give yourself to Christ you become brand-new. You get a new set of clothes, a new race to run, and a new finish line to run toward.
"This means that anyone who belongs to Christ has become a new person. The old life is gone; a new life has begun!" (2 Corinthians 5:17)
Count on it!

The first Winter Olympics were in 1924 in Chamonix, France.

Christ Is the Perfect Sacrifice

[11]So Christ has now become the High Priest over all the good things that have come. He has entered that greater, more perfect Tabernacle in heaven, which was not made by human hands and is not part of this created world. [12]With his own blood—not the blood of goats and calves—he entered the Most Holy Place once for all time and secured our redemption forever. [13]Under the old system, the blood of goats and bulls and the ashes of a young cow could cleanse people's bodies from ceremonial impurity. [14]Just think how much more the blood of Christ will purify our consciences from sinful deeds so that we can worship the living God. For by the power of the eternal Spirit, Christ offered himself to God as a perfect sacrifice for our sins. [15]That is why he is the one who mediates a new covenant between God and people, so that all who are called can receive the eternal inheritance God has promised them. For Christ died to set them free from the penalty of the sins they had committed under that first covenant.

[16]Now when someone leaves a will, it is necessary to prove that the person who made it is dead. [17]The will goes into effect only after the person's death. While the person who made it is still alive, the will cannot be put into effect. [18]That is why even the first covenant was put into effect with the blood of an animal. [19]For after Moses had read each of God's commandments to all the people, he took the blood of calves and goats, along with water, and sprinkled both the book of God's law and all the people, using hyssop branches and scarlet wool. [20]Then he said, "This blood confirms the covenant God has made with you." [21]And in the same way, he sprinkled blood on the Tabernacle and on everything used for worship. [22]In fact, according to the law of Moses, nearly everything was purified with blood. For without the shedding of blood, there is no forgiveness.

[23]That is why the Tabernacle and everything in it, which were copies of things in heaven, had to be purified by the blood of animals. But the real things in heaven had to be purified with far better sacrifices than the blood of animals.

[24]For Christ did not enter into a holy place made with human hands, which was only a copy of the true one in heaven. He entered into heaven itself to appear now before God on our behalf. [25]And he did not enter heaven to offer himself again and again, like the high priest here on earth who enters the Most Holy Place year after year with the blood of an animal. [26]If that had been necessary, Christ would have had to die again and again, ever since the world began. But now, once for all time, he has appeared at the end of the age to remove sin by his own death as a sacrifice. [27]And just as each person is destined to die once and after that comes judgment, [28]so also Christ died once for all time as a sacrifice to take away the sins of many people. He will come again, not to deal with our sins, but to bring salvation to all who are eagerly waiting for him.

Christ's Sacrifice Once for All

10

The old system under the law of Moses was only a shadow, a dim preview of the good things to come, not the good things themselves. The sacrifices under that system were repeated again and again, year after year, but they were never able to provide perfect cleansing for those who came to worship. [2]If they could have provided perfect cleansing, the sacrifices would have stopped, for the worshipers would have been purified once for all time, and their feelings of guilt would have disappeared.

[3]But instead, those sacrifices actually reminded them of their sins year after year. [4]For it is not possible for the blood of bulls and goats to take away sins. [5]That is why, when Christ came into the world, he said to God,

"You did not want animal sacrifices or sin offerings.
But you have given me a body to offer.
[6]You were not pleased with burnt offerings
or other offerings for sin.
[7]Then I said, 'Look, I have come to do your will, O God—
as is written about me in the Scriptures.'"

[8]First, Christ said, "You did not want animal sacrifices or sin offerings or burnt offerings or other offerings for sin, nor were you pleased with them" (though they are required by the law of Moses). [9]Then he said, "Look, I have come to do your will." He cancels the first covenant in order to put the second into effect. [10]For God's will was for us to be made holy by the sacrifice of the body of Jesus Christ, once for all time.

When you are losing

10:36

Patient endurance is what you need now, so that you will continue to do God's will. Then you will receive all that he has promised.

Sometimes I feel tempted to do some really bad things. I don't, but I still feel bad. Is there a difference between temptation and sin?

Yes, there is a BIG difference! Remember, Jesus was tempted in the desert by Satan. You will be tempted your whole life. Most of the time temptation will not be blatant and hideous but subtle and seductive. It is your response to temptation that is important. Jesus never gave in to temptation.

Be careful. Are you putting yourself into tempting situations? Be careful what you watch and who you hang around with and what you are putting into your mind.

[11]Under the old covenant, the priest stands and ministers before the altar day after day, offering the same sacrifices again and again, which can never take away sins. [12]But our High Priest offered himself to God as a single sacrifice for sins, good for all time. Then he sat down in the place of honor at God's right hand. [13]There he waits until his enemies are humbled and made a footstool under his feet. [14]For by that one offering he forever made perfect those who are being made holy.

[15]And the Holy Spirit also testifies that this is so. For he says,

[16]"This is the new covenant I will make
with my people on that day, says the LORD:
I will put my laws in their hearts,
and I will write them on their minds."

[17]Then he says,

"I will never again remember
their sins and lawless deeds."

[18]And when sins have been forgiven, there is no need to offer any more sacrifices.

A Call to Persevere

[19]And so, dear brothers and sisters, we can boldly enter heaven's Most Holy Place because of the blood of Jesus. [20]By his death, Jesus opened a new and life-giving way through the curtain into the Most Holy Place. [21]And since we have a great High Priest who rules over God's house, [22]let us go right into the presence of God with sincere hearts fully trusting him. For our guilty consciences have been sprinkled with Christ's blood to make us clean, and our bodies have been washed with pure water.

[23]Let us hold tightly without wavering to the hope we affirm, for God can be trusted to keep his promise. [24]Let us think of ways to motivate one another to acts of love and good works. [25]And let us not neglect our meeting together, as some people do, but encourage one another, especially now that the day of his return is drawing near.

[26]Dear friends, if we deliberately continue sinning after we have received knowledge of the truth, there is no longer any sacrifice that will cover these sins. [27]There is only the terrible expectation of God's judgment and the raging fire that will consume his enemies. [28]For anyone who refused to obey the law of Moses was put to death without mercy on the testimony of two or three witnesses. [29]Just think how much worse the punishment will be for those who have trampled on the Son of God, and have treated the blood of the covenant, which made us holy, as if it were common and unholy, and have insulted and disdained the Holy Spirit who brings God's mercy to us. [30]For we know the one who said,

"I will take revenge.
I will pay them back."

He also said,

"The LORD will judge his own people."

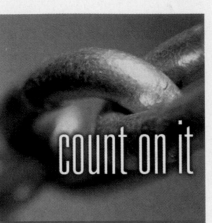

count on it

Forgiveness!

Let's say you ask for forgiveness for doing a bad thing. You ask for forgiveness and it is gone! You still feel bad and you go back to God and ask forgiveness again. God will say, "What bad thing? My Son took it away; now go and live for me! When you are forgiven, you are clean!"

"You know that Jesus came to take away our sins, and there is no sin in him." (1 John 3:5)

Count on it!

[31]It is a terrible thing to fall into the hands of the living God.

[32]Think back on those early days when you first learned about Christ. Remember how you remained faithful even though it meant terrible suffering. [33]Sometimes you were exposed to public ridicule and were beaten, and sometimes you helped others who were suffering the same things. [34]You suffered along with those who were thrown into jail, and when all you owned was taken from you, you accepted it with joy. You knew there were better things waiting for you that will last forever.

[35]So do not throw away this confident trust in the Lord. Remember the great reward it brings you! [36]Patient endurance is what you need now, so that you will continue to do God's will. Then you will receive all that he has promised.

[37]"For in just a little while,
the Coming One will come and not delay.
[38]And my righteous ones will live by faith.
But I will take no pleasure in anyone who turns away."

[39]But we are not like those who turn away from God to their own destruction. We are the faithful ones, whose souls will be saved.

Great Examples of Faith

11

Faith is the confidence that what we hope for will actually happen; it gives us assurance about things we cannot see. [2]Through their faith, the people in days of old earned a good reputation.

[3]By faith we understand that the entire universe was formed at God's command, that what we now see did not come from anything that can be seen.

[4]It was by faith that Abel brought a more acceptable offering to God than Cain did. Abel's offering gave evidence that he was a righteous man, and God showed his approval of his gifts. Although Abel is long dead, he still speaks to us by his example of faith.

[5]It was by faith that Enoch was taken up to heaven

Discipline (HEBREWS 12:6)

If you were a parent would you willfully allow your children to do something that would hurt them? God can never function contrary to his own nature. He will never give you second-best. He can't! His nature will not let him. You are his child, and he wants his children to grow strong and healthy. Never mistake discipline for hatred. He will bring discipline, judgment, and wrath on those who continue in sin and rebellion. His disciplines, however, are always fair and based on love and a desire for his children to have the best.

BIBLE HIT

WHAT

DOES IT MEAN?

fasting

It typically means going without food or drink for a set period of time. Our Lord rebuked the Pharisees for their show and hypocritical pretences in fasting (Matthew 6:16). He himself appointed no mandatory fast, but it is recorded that he did fast. The early Christians observed fasting, especially during times of important decision making (Acts 13:3; 14:23).

without dying—"he disappeared, because God took him." For before he was taken up, he was known as a person who pleased God. [6]And it is impossible to please God without faith. Anyone who wants to come to him must believe that God exists and that he rewards those who sincerely seek him.

[7]It was by faith that Noah built a large boat to save his family from the flood. He obeyed God, who warned him about things that had never happened before. By his faith Noah condemned the rest of the world, and he received the righteousness that comes by faith.

[8]It was by faith that Abraham obeyed when God called him to leave home and go to another land that God would give him as his inheritance. He went without knowing where he was going. [9]And even when he reached the land God promised him, he lived there by faith—for he was like a foreigner, living in tents. And so did Isaac and Jacob, who inherited the same promise. [10]Abraham was confidently looking forward

to a city with eternal foundations, a city designed and built by God.

[11]It was by faith that even Sarah was able to have a child, though she was barren and was too old. She believed that God would keep his promise. [12]And so a whole nation came from this one man who was as good as dead—a nation with so many people that, like the stars in the sky and the sand on the seashore, there is no way to count them.

[13]All these people died still believing what God had promised them. They did not receive what was promised, but they saw it all from a distance and welcomed it. They agreed that they were foreigners and nomads here on earth. [14]Obviously people who say such things are looking forward to a country they can call their own. [15]If they had longed for the country they came from, they could have gone back. [16]But they were looking for a better place, a heavenly homeland. That is why God is not ashamed to be called their God, for he has prepared a city for them.

[17]It was by faith that Abraham offered Isaac as a sacrifice

TIPS

Strength training and flexibility:

Strength training is a vital component for athletes, although misconceptions exist regarding the relationship between strength training and flexibility. Research demonstrates that weight training does not decrease flexibility and in some instances actually improves it. With proper training that is technically correct, an athlete can improve both overall strength and flexibility.

when God was testing him. Abraham, who had received God's promises, was ready to sacrifice his only son, Isaac, [18]even though God had told him, "Isaac is the son through whom your descendants will be counted." [19]Abraham reasoned that if Isaac died, God was able to bring him back to life again. And in a sense, Abraham did receive his son back from the dead.

[20]It was by faith that Isaac promised blessings for the future to his sons, Jacob and Esau.

[21]It was by faith that Jacob, when he was old and dying, blessed each of Joseph's sons and bowed in worship as he leaned on his staff.

[22]It was by faith that Joseph, when he was about to die, said confidently that the people of Israel would leave Egypt. He even commanded them to take his bones with them when they left.

[23]It was by faith that Moses' parents hid him for three months when he was born. They saw that God had given them an unusual child, and they were not afraid to disobey the king's command.

[24]It was by faith that Moses, when he grew up, refused to be called the son of Pharaoh's daughter. [25]He chose to share the oppression of God's people instead of enjoying the fleeting pleasures of sin. [26]He thought it was better to suffer for the sake of Christ than to own the treasures of Egypt, for he was looking ahead to his great reward. [27]It was by faith that Moses left the land of Egypt, not fearing the king's anger. He kept right on going because he kept his eyes on the one who is invisible. [28]It was by faith that Moses commanded the people of Israel to keep the Passover and to sprinkle blood on the doorposts so that the angel of death would not kill their firstborn sons.

[29]It was by faith that the people of Israel went right through the Red Sea as though they were on dry ground. But when the Egyptians tried to follow, they were all drowned.

[30]It was by faith that the people of Israel marched around Jericho for seven days, and the walls came crashing down.

[31]It was by faith that Rahab the prostitute was not destroyed with the people in her city who refused to obey God. For she had given a friendly welcome to the spies.

[32]How much more do I need to say? It would take too long to recount the stories of the faith of Gideon, Barak, Samson, Jephthah, David, Samuel, and all the prophets. [33]By faith these people overthrew kingdoms, ruled with justice, and received what God had promised them. They shut the mouths of lions, [34]quenched the flames of fire, and escaped death by the edge of the sword. Their weakness was turned to strength. They became strong in battle and put whole armies to flight. [35]Women received their loved ones back again from death.

But others were tortured, refusing to turn from God in order to be set free. They placed their hope in a better life after the resurrection. [36]Some were jeered at, and their backs were cut open with whips. Others were chained in prisons. [37]Some died by stoning, some were sawed in half, and others were killed with the sword. Some went about wearing skins of sheep and goats, destitute and oppressed and mistreated. [38]They were too good for this world, wandering over deserts and mountains, hiding in caves and holes in the ground.

[39]All these people earned a good reputation because of their faith, yet none of them received all that God had promised. [40]For God had something better in mind for us, so that they would not reach perfection without us.

God's Discipline Proves His Love

12

Therefore, since we are surrounded by such a huge crowd of witnesses to the life of faith, let us strip off every weight that slows us down, especially the sin that so easily trips us up. And let us run with endurance the race God has set before us. [2]We do this by keeping our eyes on Jesus, the champion who initiates and perfects our faith. Because of the joy awaiting him, he endured the cross, disregarding its shame. Now he is seated in the place of honor beside God's throne. [3]Think of all the hostility he endured from sinful people; then you won't become weary and

A soccer ball is made up of 32 leather panels, held together by 642 stitches.

give up. [4]After all, you have not yet given your lives in your struggle against sin.

[5]And have you forgotten the encouraging words God spoke to you as his children? He said,

"My child, don't make light of the LORD's discipline,
and don't give up when he corrects you.
[6]For the LORD disciplines those he loves,
and he punishes each one he accepts as his child."

[7]As you endure this divine discipline, remember that God is treating you as his own children. Who ever heard of a child who is never disciplined by its father? [8]If God doesn't discipline you as he does all of his children, it means that you are illegitimate and are not really his children at all. [9]Since we respected our earthly fathers who disciplined us, shouldn't we submit even more to the discipline of the Father of our spirits, and live forever?

[10]For our earthly fathers disciplined us for a few years, doing the best they knew how. But God's discipline is always good for us, so that we might share in his holiness. [11]No discipline is enjoyable while it is happening—it's painful! But afterward there will be a peaceful harvest of right living for those who are trained in this way.

[12]So take a new grip with your tired hands and strengthen your weak knees. [13]Mark out a straight path for your feet so that those who are weak and lame will not fall but become strong.

A Call to Listen to God

[14]Work at living in peace with everyone, and work at living a holy life, for those who are not holy will not

Is the Bible trustworthy?

Aren't you glad God gave us this book! Great historians such as Tacitus and Josephus reference the Bible and mention Jesus. Archaeological ruins around Israel verify biblical records. The consistency of the Bible is convincing with some 66 books and 40 different authors spanning 1000 years, all communicating the same general theme. It displays a remarkable unity and claims to be inspired by the Spirit of God. Historians say it is the most authoritative book of its time. If God created us and loves us, wouldn't it make sense that he would want to communicate with us? You can trust it!

see the Lord. [15]Look after each other so that none of you fails to receive the grace of God. Watch out that no poisonous root of bitterness grows up to trouble you, corrupting many. [16]Make sure that no one is immoral or godless like Esau, who traded his birthright as the firstborn son for a single meal. [17]You know that afterward, when he wanted his father's blessing, he was rejected. It was too late for repentance, even though he begged with bitter tears. [18]You have not come to a physical mountain, to a place of flaming fire, darkness, gloom, and whirlwind, as the Israelites did at Mount Sinai. [19]For they heard an awesome trumpet blast and a voice so terrible that they begged God to stop speaking. [20]They staggered back under God's command: "If even an animal touches the mountain, it must be stoned to death." [21]Moses himself was so frightened at the sight that he said, "I am terrified and trembling."

[22]No, you have come to Mount Zion, to the city of the living God, the heavenly Jerusalem, and to countless thousands of angels in a joyful gathering. [23]You have come to the assembly of God's firstborn children, whose names are written in heaven. You have come to God himself, who is the judge over all things. You have come to the spirits of the righteous ones in heaven who have now been made perfect. [24]You have come to Jesus, the one who mediates the new covenant between God and people, and to the sprinkled blood, which speaks of forgiveness instead of crying out for vengeance like the blood of Abel.

[25]Be careful that you do not refuse to listen to the One who is speaking. For if the people of Israel did not escape when they refused to listen to Moses, the earthly messenger, we will certainly not escape if we reject the One who speaks to us from heaven! [26]When God spoke from Mount Sinai his voice shook the earth, but now he makes another promise: "Once again I will shake not only the earth but the heavens also." [27]This means that all of creation will be shaken and removed, so that only unshakable things will remain. [28]Since we are receiving a Kingdom that is unshakable, let us be thankful and please God by worshiping him with holy fear and awe. [29]For our God is a devouring fire.

Concluding Words

13

Keep on loving each other as brothers and sisters. [2]Don't forget to show hospitality to strangers, for some who have done this have entertained angels without realizing it! [3]Remember those in prison, as if you were there yourself. Remember also those being mistreated, as if you felt their pain in your own bodies.

[4]Give honor to marriage, and remain faithful to one another in marriage. God will surely judge people who are immoral and those who commit adultery.

[5]Don't love money; be satisfied with what you have. For God has said,

"I will never fail you.
I will never abandon you."

[6]So we can say with confidence,
"The LORD is my helper,
so I will have no fear.
What can mere people do to me?"

[7]Remember your leaders who taught you the word of God. Think of all the good that has come from their lives, and follow the example of their faith.

[8]Jesus Christ is the same yesterday, today, and forever. [9]So do not be attracted by strange, new ideas. Your strength comes from God's grace, not from rules about food, which don't help those who follow them.

[10]We have an altar from which the priests in the Tabernacle have no right to eat. [11]Under the old system,

STAND POINT

When you need confidence

13:6

So we can say with confidence, "The LORD is my helper, so I will have no fear. What can mere people do to me?"

the high priest brought the blood of animals into the Holy Place as a sacrifice for sin, and the bodies of the animals were burned outside the camp. [12]So also Jesus suffered and died outside the city gates to make his people holy by means of his own blood. [13]So let us go out to him, outside the camp, and bear the disgrace he bore. [14]For this world is not our permanent home; we are looking forward to a home yet to come.

[15]Therefore, let us offer through Jesus a continual sacrifice of praise to God, proclaiming our allegiance to his name. [16]And don't forget to do good and to share with those in need. These are the sacrifices that please God.

[17]Obey your spiritual leaders, and do what they say. Their work is to watch over your souls, and they are accountable to God. Give them reason to do this with joy and not with sorrow. That would certainly not be for your benefit.

[18]Pray for us, for our conscience is clear and we want to live honorably in everything we do. [19]And especially pray that I will be able to come back to you soon.

[20]Now may the God of peace—
who brought up from the dead our Lord Jesus,
the great Shepherd of the sheep,
and ratified an eternal covenant with his blood—
[21]may he equip you with all you need
for doing his will.
May he produce in you,
through the power of Jesus Christ,
every good thing that is pleasing to him.
All glory to him forever and ever! Amen.

[22]I urge you, dear brothers and sisters, to pay attention to what I have written in this brief exhortation.

[23]I want you to know that our brother Timothy has been released from jail. If he comes here soon, I will bring him with me to see you.

[24]Greet all your leaders and all the believers there. The believers from Italy send you their greetings.

[25]May God's grace be with you all.

Standing firm

"With all these things in mind, dear brothers and sisters, stand firm and keep a strong grip on the teaching we passed on to you both in person and by letter."

(2 Thessalonians 2:15)

How encouraging it is to find someone standing firm in his or her faith in the world of sports. It is obvious that people are drifting spiritually. Many athletes are looking for a new gimmick to improve their performance, so they try Jesus the same way they might try a lucky charm or a new color of running shoes. Often a superstitious faith is a brand of religion that comes with feigned or halfhearted devotion to God. They do not want to obey their Creator; they prefer to have a "genie in a bottle" that will obey them. When it is convenient, they may go to church or read their Bible, but they are often merely drifting with the current. Sometimes the drifters get anchored to God, and sometimes they flounder and fade away.

An eccentric friend who annoyingly talks in Christian jargon asked a colleague of mine, "When did you wake up?" The colleague was baffled and said, "6:00 a.m."

My friend was a bit frustrated that he did not catch his line of inquiry and again repeated the question with more emphasis, "No man, when did you WAKE UP, WAKE UP SPIRITUALLY! When did you become a Christian?" My colleague was quick and fired back, "Ah, I woke up in '76 but did not get out of bed until '80!" There are plenty of Christian weaklings getting pushed around by every new fad or temptation. We need some spiritual tough guys who will not get pushed around and who will hang on to their faith in times of adversity. So get out of bed! Stand firm in your faith, hang on tight to the Word of God, and be a blessing to someone else — someone who has just woken up!

"This hope is a strong and trustworthy anchor for our souls." (Hebrews 6:19)

Reflection
I can stand firm because my feet are on a secure foundation.

Prayer
Father, you are the rock on which I stand.

"The difference between a successful person and others is not a lack of strength . . . but rather a lack of will."
Vince Lombardi

Nicked with permission from: A Sporting Guide to Eternity, Steve Connor, Christian Focus Publications - ISBN 1-85792-746-X

Imagine growing up with Jesus! He was not an only child — he had a big family, and James was his half brother. When the time came for Jesus to start his formal ministry, James was not ready to follow his older brother. But after Jesus' resurrection we find James so changed that he ended up leading the strategic church in Jerusalem (see Acts 15) and later, as recorded by the great historian Josephus, died a painful death for his faith in Jesus — his brother, Lord, and Savior.

Faith works! Unlike the person who learns all about fishing but never goes fishing, you can't just read about it. James wrote his relatively small book to encourage believers to live it. No more lip service — if you do not live out your faith, do you really have a faith? James shows us how to live our lives and how our actions (good deeds) reflect our faith. Throughout this book we hear echoes of Jesus' life and teachings: "I tell you the truth, when you refused to help the least of these my brothers and sisters, you were refusing to help me." (Matthew 25:45)

James

JAMES

Greetings from James

1

This letter is from James, a slave of God and of the Lord Jesus Christ.

I am writing to the "twelve tribes"—Jewish believers scattered abroad. Greetings!

Let it Go! If you live on planet earth you will be hurt by others; but holding a grudge or deep bitterness will only rot your guts. You do not gain anything but misery and frustration. Allow God's love into your heart and ask for power to wash away the bad feelings. This is not an option, this is imperative for you to enjoy the forgiveness God gives you. "And forgive us our sins, as we have forgiven those who sin against us."

(Matthew 6:12)

Faith and Endurance

²Dear brothers and sisters, when troubles come your way, consider it an opportunity for great joy. ³For you know that when your faith is tested, your endurance has a chance to grow. ⁴So let it grow, for when your endurance is fully developed, you will be perfect and complete, needing nothing.

⁵If you need wisdom, ask our generous God, and he will give it to you. He will not rebuke you for asking. ⁶But when you ask him, be sure that your faith is in God alone. Do not waver, for a person with divided

When you need direction

1:5-8

If you need wisdom, ask our generous God, and he will give it to you. He will not rebuke you for asking. But when you ask him, be sure that your faith is in God alone. Do not waver, for a person with divided loyalty is as unsettled as a wave of the sea that is blown and tossed by the wind. Such people should not expect to receive anything from the Lord. Their loyalty is divided between God and the world, and they are unstable in everything they do.

loyalty is as unsettled as a wave of the sea that is blown and tossed by the wind. ⁷Such people should not expect to receive anything from the Lord. ⁸Their loyalty is divided between God and the world, and they are unstable in everything they do.

⁹Believers who are poor have something to boast about, for God has honored them. ¹⁰And those who are rich should boast that God has humbled them. They will fade away like a little flower in the field. ¹¹The hot sun rises and the grass withers; the little flower droops and falls, and its beauty fades away. In the same way, the rich will fade away with all of their achievements.

¹²God blesses those who patiently endure testing and temptation. Afterward they will receive the crown of life that God has promised to those who love him. ¹³And remember, when you are being tempted, do not say, "God is tempting me." God is never tempted to do wrong, and he never tempts anyone else. ¹⁴Temptation comes from our own desires, which entice us and drag us away. ¹⁵These desires give birth to sinful actions. And when sin is allowed to grow, it gives birth to death.

¹⁶So don't be misled, my dear brothers and sisters. ¹⁷Whatever is good and perfect comes down to us from God our Father, who created all the lights in the heavens. He never changes or casts a shifting shadow. ¹⁸He chose to give birth to us by giving us his true word. And we, out of all creation, became his prized possession.

Listening and Doing

¹⁹Understand this, my dear brothers and sisters: You must all be quick to listen, slow to speak, and slow to get angry. ²⁰Human anger does not produce the righteousness God desires. ²¹So get rid of all the filth and evil in your lives, and humbly accept the word God has planted in your hearts, for it has the power to save your souls.

²²But don't just listen to God's word. You must do what it says. Otherwise, you are only fooling yourselves. ²³For if you listen to the word and don't obey, it is like glancing at your face in a mirror. ²⁴You see yourself, walk away, and forget what you look like. ²⁵But if you look carefully into the perfect law that sets you free, and if you do what it says and don't forget what you heard, then God will bless you for doing it.

²⁶If you claim to be religious but don't control your tongue, you are fooling yourself, and your religion is worthless. ²⁷Pure and genuine religion in the sight of God the Father means caring for orphans and widows in their distress and refusing to let the world corrupt you.

A Warning against Prejudice

2

My dear brothers and sisters, how can you claim to have faith in our glorious Lord Jesus Christ if you favor some people over others?

²For example, suppose someone comes into your meeting dressed in fancy clothes and expensive jewelry, and another comes in who is poor and dressed in dirty clothes. ³If you give special attention and a good seat to the rich person, but you say to the poor one, "You can stand over there, or else sit on the floor"—well, ⁴doesn't this discrimination show that your judgments are guided by evil motives?

⁵Listen to me, dear brothers and sisters. Hasn't God chosen the poor in this world to be rich in faith? Aren't they the ones who will inherit the Kingdom he promised to those who love him? ⁶But you dishonor the poor! Isn't it the rich who oppress you and drag

you into court? ⁷Aren't they the ones who slander Jesus Christ, whose noble name you bear?

⁸Yes indeed, it is good when you obey the royal law as found in the Scriptures: "Love your neighbor as yourself." ⁹But if you favor some people over others, you are committing a sin. You are guilty of breaking the law.

¹⁰For the person who keeps all of the laws except one is as guilty as a person who has broken all of God's laws. ¹¹For the same God who said, "You must not commit adultery," also said, "You must not murder." So if you murder someone but do not commit adultery, you have still broken the law.

¹²So whatever you say or whatever you do, remember that you will be judged by the law that sets you free. ¹³There will be no mercy for those who have not shown mercy to others. But if you have been merciful, God will be merciful when he judges you.

2:14-26 WHAT'S IT SAYING?

WHAT AM I GOING TO DO ABOUT IT?

Faith without Good Deeds Is Dead

¹⁴What good is it, dear brothers and sisters, if you say you have faith but don't show it by your actions? Can that kind of faith save anyone? ¹⁵Suppose you see a brother or sister who has no food or clothing, ¹⁶and you say, "Good-bye and have a good day; stay warm and eat well"—but then you don't give that person any food or clothing. What good does that do?

¹⁷So you see, faith by itself isn't enough. Unless it produces good deeds, it is dead and useless.

¹⁸Now someone may argue, "Some people have faith; others have good deeds." But I say, "How can you show me your faith if you don't have good deeds? I will show you my faith by my good deeds."

¹⁹You say you have faith, for you believe that there is one God. Good for you! Even the demons believe this, and they tremble in terror. ²⁰How foolish! Can't you see that faith without good deeds is useless?

²¹Don't you remember that our ancestor Abraham was shown to be right with God by his actions when he offered his son Isaac on the altar? ²²You see, his faith and his actions worked together. His actions made his faith complete. ²³And so it happened just as the Scriptures say: "Abraham believed God, and God counted him as righteous because of his faith." He was even called the friend of God. ²⁴So you see, we are shown to be right with God by what we do, not by faith alone.

²⁵Rahab the prostitute is another example. She was shown to be right with God by her actions when she hid those messengers and sent them safely away by a different road. ²⁶Just as the body is dead without breath, so also faith is dead without good works.

Controlling the Tongue

3

Dear brothers and sisters, not many of you should become teachers in the church, for we who teach will be judged more strictly. ²Indeed, we all make many mistakes. For if we could control our tongues, we would be perfect and could also control ourselves in every other way.

³We can make a large horse go wherever we want by means of a small bit in its mouth. ⁴And a small rudder makes a huge ship turn wherever the pilot chooses to go, even though the winds are strong. ⁵In the same way, the tongue is a small thing that makes grand speeches.

But a tiny spark can set a great forest on fire. ⁶And the tongue is a flame of fire. It is a whole world of wickedness, corrupting your entire body. It can set your whole life on fire, for it is set on fire by hell itself.

⁷People can tame all kinds of animals, birds, reptiles, and fish, ⁸but no one can tame the tongue. It is restless and evil, full of deadly poison. ⁹Sometimes it praises our Lord and Father, and sometimes it curses those

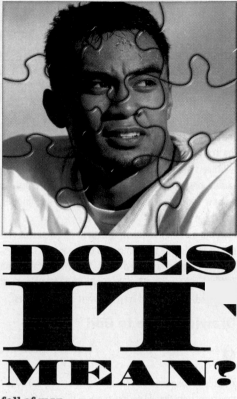

WHAT DOES IT MEAN?

fall of man

This is an expression arguably gleaned from the Apocryphal Book of Wisdom to express the rebellion of Adam and Eve against God, and the consequent sin and misery that they and all their offspring inherited. The history of the Fall is recorded in Genesis 2 and 3. The effects of this first sin on our first parents themselves were shame, humiliation, and contamination. We inherited the disease of sin and are by our very nature spiritually dead. We must be restored to life through faith in Christ.

who have been made in the image of God. ¹⁰And so blessing and cursing come pouring out of the same mouth. Surely, my brothers and sisters, this is not right! ¹¹Does a spring of water bubble out with both fresh water and bitter water? ¹²Does a fig tree produce olives, or a grapevine produce figs? No, and you can't draw fresh water from a salty spring.

True Wisdom Comes from God

¹³If you are wise and understand God's ways, prove it by living an honorable life, doing good works with the humility

BIBLE HIT

Spiritual Fitness Test (JAMES 1:2-4)
Have you ever taken a fitness test? They can be pretty tough and revealing. James reminds us that our faith will be tested too. A test will reveal shortcomings and strengths and can create endurance. Troubles will come your way — that's a promise! Troubles will either pulverize or polish you. With God's strength, take on life's challenges with joy, knowing they will transform you into a person who is ready for anything!

that comes from wisdom. [14]But if you are bitterly jealous and there is selfish ambition in your heart, don't cover up the truth with boasting and lying. [15]For jealousy and selfishness are not God's kind of wisdom. Such things are earthly, unspiritual, and demonic. [16]For wherever there is jealousy and selfish ambition, there you will find disorder and evil of every kind.

[17]But the wisdom from above is first of all pure. It is also peace loving, gentle at all times, and willing to yield to others. It is full of mercy and good deeds. It shows no favoritism and is always sincere. [18]And those who are peacemakers will plant seeds of peace and reap a harvest of righteousness.

Drawing Close to God

4

What is causing the quarrels and fights among you? Don't they come from the evil desires at war within you? [2]You want what you don't have, so you scheme and kill to get it. You are jealous of what others have, but you can't get it, so you fight and wage war to take it away from them. Yet you don't have what you want because you don't ask God for it. [3]And even when you ask, you don't get it because your motives are all wrong—you want only what will give you pleasure.

[4]You adulterers! Don't you realize that friendship with the world makes you an enemy of God? I say it again: If you want to be a friend of the world, you make yourself an enemy of God. [5]What do you think the Scriptures mean when they say that the spirit God has placed within us is filled with envy? [6]But he gives us even more grace to stand against such evil desires. As the Scriptures say,

"God opposes the proud
but favors the humble."

[7]So humble yourselves before God. Resist the devil, and he will flee from you. [8]Come close to God, and God will come close to you. Wash your hands, you sinners; purify your hearts, for your loyalty is divided between God and the world. [9]Let there be tears for what you have done. Let there be sorrow and deep grief. Let there be sadness instead of laughter, and gloom instead of joy. [10]Humble yourselves before the Lord, and he will lift you up in honor.

Warning against Judging Others
[11]Don't speak evil against each other, dear brothers and sisters. If you criticize and judge each other, then you are criticizing and judging God's law. But your job is to obey the law, not to judge whether it applies to you. [12]God alone, who gave the law, is the Judge. He alone has the power to save or to destroy. So what right do you have to judge your neighbor?

Warning about Self-Confidence

[13]Look here, you who say, "Today or tomorrow we are going to a certain town and will stay there a year. We will do business there and make a profit." [14]How do you know what your life will be like tomorrow? Your life is like the morning fog—it's here a little while, then it's gone. [15]What you ought to say is, "If the Lord wants us to, we will live and do this or that." [16]Otherwise you are boasting about your own plans, and all such boasting is evil.

[17]Remember, it is sin to know what you ought to do and then not do it.

action

5:7-20 WHAT'S IT SAYING?

WHAT AM I GOING TO dO ABOUT IT?

What are the five most important skills for your sport?

1.
2.
3.
4.
5.

BIG FIVE

Warning to the Rich

5

Look here, you rich people: Weep and groan with anguish because of all the terrible troubles ahead of you. [2]Your wealth is rotting away, and your fine clothes are moth-eaten rags. [3]Your gold and silver have become worthless. The very wealth you were counting on will eat away your flesh like fire. This treasure you have accumulated will stand as evidence against you on the day of judgment. [4]For listen! Hear the cries of the field workers whom you have cheated of their pay. The wages you held back cry out against you. The cries of those who harvest your fields have reached the ears of the Lord of Heaven's Armies.

[5]You have spent your years on earth in luxury, satisfying your every desire. You have fattened yourselves for the day of slaughter. [6]You have condemned and killed innocent people, who do not resist you.

Patience and Endurance

[7]Dear brothers and sisters, be patient as you wait for the Lord's return. Consider the farmers who patiently wait for the rains in the fall and in the spring. They eagerly look for the valuable harvest to ripen. [8]You, too, must be patient. Take courage, for the coming of the Lord is near.

[9]Don't grumble about each other, brothers and sisters, or you will be judged. For look—the Judge is standing at the door!

[10]For examples of patience in suffering, dear brothers and sisters, look at the prophets who spoke in the name of the Lord. [11]We give great honor to those who endure under suffering. For instance, you know about Job, a man of great endurance. You can see how the Lord was kind to him at the end, for the Lord is full of tenderness and mercy.

[12]But most of all, my brothers and sisters, never take

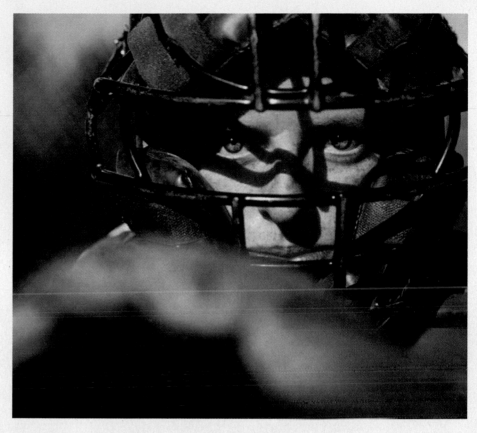

an oath, by heaven or earth or anything else. Just say a simple yes or no, so that you will not sin and be condemned.

The Power of Prayer

[13]Are any of you suffering hardships? You should pray. Are any of you happy? You should sing praises. [14]Are any of you sick? You should call for the elders of the church to come and pray over you, anointing you with oil in the name of the Lord. [15]Such a prayer offered in faith will heal the sick, and the Lord will make you well. And if you have committed any sins, you will be forgiven.

[16]Confess your sins to each other and pray for each other so that you may be healed. The earnest prayer of a righteous person has great power and produces wonderful results. [17]Elijah was as human as we are, and yet when he prayed earnestly that no rain would fall, none fell for three and a half years! [18]Then, when he prayed again, the sky sent down rain and the earth began to yield its crops.

Restore Wandering Believers

[19]My dear brothers and sisters, if someone among you wanders away from the truth and is brought back, [20]you can be sure that whoever brings the sinner back will save that person from death and bring about the forgiveness of many sins.

I think about sex all the time. Am I messed up?

This is totally normal (although arguably more of a guy issue).

They say the average male adolescent thinks about sex one out of every seven seconds. It is hard to figure out what they think about in the other six seconds! Probably sports and food! How you control and direct your thoughts is what counts. Hang in there and ask God to help you with this issue (you may have to ask for help one out of every seven seconds!).

It's a long road
LIVE it

A sportswriter reflecting on his long friendship with a particular boxer once wrote: "He started out mean, inarticulate, narcissistic, and shallow. But after his conversion to Christianity he miraculously became generous, articulate, and selfless, and he cared deeply for others." Be careful — when you hang around Jesus, you change! Similarly, Peter the fisherman — boastful, hasty, strong-tempered, inarticulate, and at times cowardly — hung around Jesus and changed! Peter, now filled with the Holy Spirit (read Acts 1–3) became articulate, lion-hearted, thoughtful and a missionary and spokesman for the Christian church. In 1 Peter he was strengthening the persecuted believers in their faith and reminding all of us that our worth, our significance, and our security are found only in God who, out of love, has given us salvation through his Son, Jesus.

1 Peter

1 PETER

Greetings from Peter

1

This letter is from Peter, an apostle of Jesus Christ.

I am writing to God's chosen people who are living as foreigners in the provinces of Pontus, Galatia, Cappadocia, Asia, and Bithynia. ²God the Father knew you and chose you long ago, and his Spirit has made you holy. As a result, you have obeyed him and have been cleansed by the blood of Jesus Christ.

May God give you more and more grace and peace.

The Hope of Eternal Life

³All praise to God, the Father of our Lord Jesus Christ. It is by his great mercy that we have been born again, because God raised Jesus Christ from the dead. Now we live with great expectation, ⁴and we have a priceless inheritance—an inheritance that is kept in heaven for you, pure and undefiled, beyond the reach of change and decay. ⁵And through your faith, God is protecting you by his power until you receive this salvation, which is ready to be revealed on the last day for all to see.

⁶So be truly glad. There is wonderful joy ahead, even though you have to endure many trials for a little while. ⁷These trials will show that your faith is genuine. It is being tested as fire tests and purifies gold—though your faith is far more precious than mere gold. So when your faith remains strong through many trials, it will bring you much praise and glory and honor on the day when Jesus Christ is revealed to the whole world.

⁸You love him even though you have never seen him. Though

Jeanne Genevieve Garnerin was the first female parachutist. She jumped from a hot-air balloon in 1799.

salvation prepared for you. ¹¹They wondered what time or situation the Spirit of Christ within them was talking about when he told them in advance about Christ's suffering and his great glory afterward.

¹²They were told that their messages were not for themselves, but for you. And now this Good News has been announced to you by those who preached in the power of the Holy Spirit sent from heaven. It is all so wonderful that even the angels are eagerly watching these things happen.

A Call to Holy Living

¹³So think clearly and exercise self-control. Look forward to the gracious salvation that will come to you when Jesus Christ is revealed to the world. ¹⁴So you must live as God's obedient children. Don't slip back into your old ways of living to satisfy your own desires. You didn't know any better then. ¹⁵But now you must be holy in everything you do, just as God who chose you is holy. ¹⁶For the Scriptures say, "You

in the land." ¹⁸For you know that God paid a ransom to save you from the empty life you inherited from your ancestors. And the ransom he paid was not mere gold or silver. ¹⁹It was the precious blood of Christ, the sinless, spotless Lamb of God. ²⁰God chose him as your ransom long before the world began, but he has now revealed him to you in these last days.

²¹Through Christ you have come to trust in God. And you have placed your faith and hope in God because he raised Christ from the dead and gave him great glory.

²²You were cleansed from your sins when you obeyed the truth, so now you must show sincere love to each other as brothers and sisters. Love each other deeply with all your heart.

²³For you have been born again, but not to a life that will quickly end. Your new life will last forever because it comes from the eternal, living word of God. ²⁴As the Scriptures say,

"People are like grass;
their beauty is like a flower in the field.
The grass withers and the flower fades.
²⁵But the word of the Lord remains forever."

And that word is the Good News that was preached to you.

2

So get rid of all evil behavior. Be done with all deceit, hypocrisy, jealousy, and all unkind speech. ²Like newborn babies, you must crave pure spiritual milk so that you will grow into a full experience of salvation. Cry out for this nourishment, ³now that you have had a taste of the Lord's kindness.

Overcome your fear of failure:

Many athletes do not fulfill their potential due to their inability to overcome their fear of failure. In order to succeed, an athlete must accept that if they want to learn and improve they must encounter failure. The process of learning how to handle their disappointment and how the lessons learned can improve them will develop a healthy drive. In other words, they do not like failure, but at the same time they do not fear it.

you do not see him now, you trust him; and you rejoice with a glorious, inexpressible joy. ⁹The reward for trusting him will be the salvation of your souls.

¹⁰This salvation was something even the prophets wanted to know more about when they prophesied about this gracious

must be holy because I am holy."

¹⁷And remember that the heavenly Father to whom you pray has no favorites. He will judge or reward you according to what you do. So you must live in reverent fear of him during your time as "foreigners

Living Stones for God's House

⁴You are coming to Christ, who is the living cornerstone of God's temple. He was rejected by people, but he was chosen by God for great honor.

⁵And you are living stones that God is building into

Winners are fair!

When someone is cheating against us, fair play is important! But the quality of fairness comes in the measure that we are fair to others. Being truthful, keeping our promises, being empathetic, reporting cheats, and playing by the rules are marks of a winner. Competing as hard as you can is totally fair, as long as you play within the confines of the rules. You may win or lose by one hundred points, but don't scream "It's not fair!" if both teams agreed to play under the same rules. What is unfair is when you try to win or lose outside of the rules. You may choose to keep the score under control — that may be wise. When you commit a foul, you must be honest. In the long run it will pay off. **"The Lord detests the use of dishonest scales, but he delights in accurate weights."** (Proverbs 11:1)

Winners live by the rules!

his spiritual temple. What's more, you are his holy priests. Through the mediation of Jesus Christ, you offer spiritual sacrifices that please God. [6]As the Scriptures say,

"I am placing a cornerstone in Jerusalem,
chosen for great honor,
and anyone who trusts in him
will never be disgraced."

[7]Yes, you who trust him recognize the honor God has given him. But for those who reject him,

"The stone that the builders rejected
has now become the cornerstone."

[8]And,

"He is the stone that makes people stumble,
the rock that makes them fall."

They stumble because they do not obey God's word, and so they meet the fate that was planned for them. [9]But you are not like that, for you are a chosen people. You are royal priests, a holy nation, God's very own possession. As a result, you can show others the goodness of God, for he called you out of the darkness into his wonderful light.

[10]"Once you had no identity as a people;
now you are God's people.
Once you received no mercy;
now you have received God's mercy."

[11]Dear friends, I warn you as "temporary residents and foreigners" to keep away from worldly desires that wage war against your very souls. [12]Be careful to live properly among your unbelieving neighbors. Then even if they accuse you of doing wrong, they will see your honorable behavior, and they will give honor to God when he judges the world.

Respecting People in Authority

[13]For the Lord's sake, respect all human authority— whether the king as head of state, [14]or the officials he has appointed. For the king has sent them to punish those who do wrong and to honor those who do right. [15]It is God's will that your honorable lives should silence those ignorant people who make foolish accusations against you. [16]For you are free, yet you are God's slaves, so don't use your freedom as an excuse to do evil. [17]Respect everyone, and love your Christian brothers and sisters. Fear God, and respect the king.

Slaves

[18]You who are slaves must accept the authority of your masters with all respect. Do what they tell you—not only if they are kind and reasonable, but even if they are cruel. [19]For God is pleased with you when you do what you know is right and patiently endure unfair treatment. [20]Of course, you get no credit for being patient if you are beaten for doing wrong. But if you suffer for doing good and endure it patiently, God is pleased with you.

[21]For God called you to do good, even if it means suffering, just as Christ suffered for you. He is your example, and you must follow in his steps.

[22]He never sinned,
nor ever deceived anyone.

[23]He did not retaliate when he was insulted,
nor threaten revenge when he suffered.
He left his case in the hands of God,
who always judges fairly.

[24]He personally carried our sins
in his body on the cross
so that we can be dead to sin
and live for what is right.
By his wounds
you are healed.

[25]Once you were like sheep
who wandered away.
But now you have turned to your Shepherd,
the Guardian of your souls.

Stay right with God. Forgiveness is a benefit that we should love to receive. Satan will try to tell you that you are not worthy to go to God for forgiveness. He is half right — we are not worthy, and we never will be worthy. But we must turn back to God when we sin and he will gladly and faithfully forgive us. Once forgiven, we have a freedom that comes from purity. **"But if we confess our sins to him, he is faithful and just to forgive us our sins and to cleanse us from all wickedness."** (1 John 1:9)

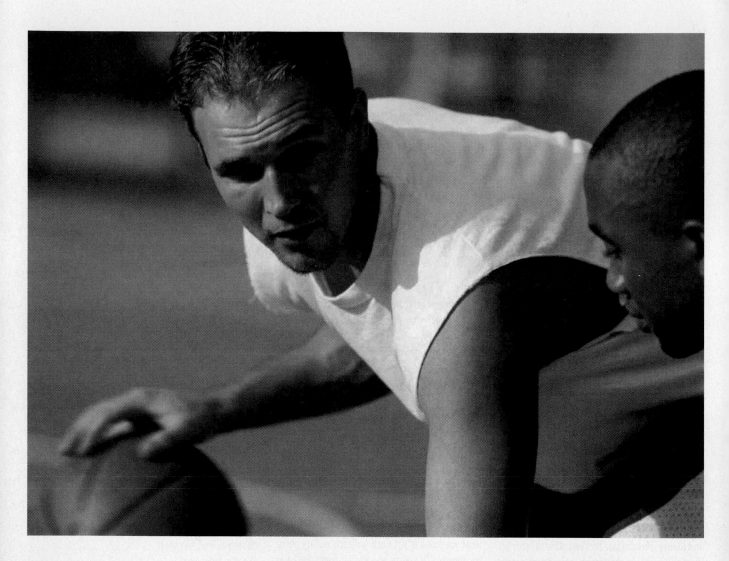

Wives

3

In the same way, you wives must accept the authority of your husbands. Then, even if some refuse to obey the Good News, your godly lives will speak to them without any words. They will be won over ²by observing your pure and reverent lives.

³Don't be concerned about the outward beauty of fancy hairstyles, expensive jewelry, or beautiful clothes. ⁴You should clothe yourselves instead with the beauty that comes from within, the unfading beauty of a gentle and quiet spirit, which is so precious to God. ⁵This is how the holy women of old made themselves beautiful. They trusted God and accepted the authority of their husbands. ⁶For instance, Sarah obeyed her husband, Abraham, and called him her master. You are her daughters when you do what is right without fear of what your husbands might do.

Husbands

⁷In the same way, you husbands must give honor to your wives. Treat your wife with understanding as you live together. She may be weaker than you are, but she is your equal partner in God's gift of new life. Treat her as you should so your prayers will not be hindered.

All Christians

⁸Finally, all of you should be of one mind. Sympathize with each other. Love each other as brothers and sisters. Be tenderhearted, and keep a humble attitude. ⁹Don't repay evil for evil. Don't retaliate with insults when people insult you. Instead, pay them back with a blessing. That is what God has called you to do, and he will bless you for it. ¹⁰For the Scriptures say,
"If you want to enjoy life
and see many happy days,
keep your tongue from speaking evil

and your lips from telling lies.
¹¹Turn away from evil and do good.
Search for peace, and work to maintain it.
¹²The eyes of the Lord watch over those who do right,
and his ears are open to their prayers.
But the Lord turns his face
against those who do evil."

In 1975 Junko Tabei from Japan became the first woman to reach the top of Mount Everest.

Suffering for Doing Good

[13]Now, who will want to harm you if you are eager to do good? [14]But even if you suffer for doing what is right, God will reward you for it. So don't worry or be afraid of their threats. [15]Instead, you must worship Christ as Lord of your life. And if someone asks about your Christian hope, always be ready to explain it. [16]But do this in a gentle and respectful way. Keep your conscience clear. Then if people speak against you, they will be ashamed when they see what a good life you live because you belong to Christ. [17]Remember, it is better to suffer for doing good, if that is what God wants, than to suffer for doing wrong!

[18]Christ suffered for our sins once for all time. He never sinned, but he died for sinners to bring you safely home to God. He suffered physical death, but he was raised to life in the Spirit.

[19]So he went and preached to the spirits in prison— [20]those who disobeyed God long ago when God waited patiently while Noah was building his boat. Only eight people were saved from drowning in that terrible flood. [21]And that water is a picture of baptism, which now saves you, not by removing dirt from your body, but as a response to God from a clean conscience. It is effective because of the resurrection of Jesus Christ. [22]Now Christ has gone to heaven. He is seated in the place of honor next to God, and all the angels and authorities and powers accept his authority.

Living for God

4

So then, since Christ suffered physical pain, you must arm yourselves with the same attitude he had, and be ready to suffer, too. For if you have suffered physically for Christ, you have finished with sin. [2]You won't spend the rest of your lives chasing your own desires, but you will be anxious to do the will of God. [3]You have had enough in the past of the evil things that godless people enjoy—their immorality and lust, their

Today, the complete Bible is available in 400 of the 6,500 languages spoken in the world.

feasting and drunkenness and wild parties, and their terrible worship of idols. [4]Of course, your former friends are surprised when you no longer plunge into the flood of wild and destructive things they do. So they slander you. [5]But remember that they will have to face God, who will judge everyone, both the living and the dead. [6]That is why the Good News was preached to those who are now dead—so although they were destined to die like all people, they now live forever with God in the Spirit.

[7]The end of the world is coming soon. Therefore, be earnest and disciplined in your prayers. [8]Most important of all, continue to show deep love for each other, for love covers a multitude of sins. [9]Cheerfully share your home with those who need a meal or a place to stay.

[10]God has given each of you a gift from his great variety of spiritual gifts. Use them well to serve one another. [11]Do you have the gift of speaking? Then speak as though God himself were speaking through you. Do you have the gift of helping others? Do it with all the strength and energy that God supplies. Then everything you do will bring glory to God through Jesus Christ. All glory and power to him forever and ever! Amen.

4:7-11 WHAT'S IT SAYING?

WHAT AM I GOING TO DO ABOUT IT?

STAND POINT

When you need to listen to your coach

5:5

You younger men must accept the authority of the elders. And all of you, serve each other in humility, for "God opposes the proud but favors the humble."

Suffering for Being a Christian

[12]Dear friends, don't be surprised at the fiery trials you are going through, as if something strange were happening to you. [13]Instead, be very glad—for these trials make you partners with Christ in his suffering, so that you will have the wonderful joy of seeing his glory when it is revealed to all the world.

[14]So be happy when you are insulted for being a Christian, for then the glorious Spirit of God rests upon you. [15]If you suffer, however, it must not be for murder, stealing, making trouble, or prying into other people's affairs. [16]But it is no shame to suffer for being a Christian. Praise God for the privilege of being called by his name! [17]For the time has come for judgment, and it must begin with God's household. And if judgment begins with us, what terrible fate awaits those who have never obeyed God's Good News? [18]And also,

"If the righteous are barely saved,
what will happen to godless sinners?"

[19]So if you are suffering in a manner that pleases God, keep on doing what is right, and trust your lives to the God who created you, for he will never fail you.

Advice for Elders and Young Men

5

And now, a word to you who are elders in the churches. I, too, am an elder and a witness to the sufferings of Christ. And I, too, will share in his glory when he is revealed to the whole world. As a fellow elder, I appeal to you: [2]Care for the flock that God has entrusted to you. Watch over it willingly, not grudgingly—not for what you will get out of it, but because you are eager to serve God. [3]Don't lord it over the people assigned to your care, but lead them by your own good example. [4]And when the Great Shepherd appears, you will receive a crown of never-ending glory and honor.

[5]In the same way, you younger men must accept the authority of the elders. And all of you, serve each other in humility, for "God opposes the proud
but favors the humble."

[6]So humble yourselves under the mighty power of God, and at the right time he will lift you up in honor. [7]Give all your worries and cares to God, for he cares about you.

[8]Stay alert! Watch out for your great enemy, the devil. He prowls around like a roaring lion, looking for someone to devour. [9]Stand firm against him, and be strong in your faith. Remember that your Christian brothers and sisters all over the world are going through the same kind of suffering you are.

[10]In his kindness God called you to share in his eternal glory by means of Christ Jesus. So after you have suffered a little while, he will restore, support, and strengthen you, and he will place you on a firm foundation. [11]All power to him forever! Amen.

Peter's Final Greetings

[12]I have written and sent this short letter to you with the help of Silas, whom I commend to you as a faithful brother. My purpose in writing is to encourage you and assure you that what you are experiencing is truly part of God's grace for you. Stand firm in this grace. [13]Your sister church here in Babylon sends you greetings, and so does my son Mark. [14]Greet each other with Christian love.

Peace be with all of you who are in Christ.

PERSONAL ASSESSMENTS

SPIRITUAL GIFTS SURVEY:

God has given us all unique ways to build his Kingdom. Pick out five from this list that you feel you have or may have a special talent for.

Ask God to help you develop these or other talents for his Kingdom.

Missionary: the use of other spiritual gifts to minister in other unique cultures. (See 1 Corinthians 9:19-23.)

Healing: gift whereby the Spirit works through Christians to restore health to the sick. (See James 5:13-16; Luke 9:1-2.)

Intercession: gift that enables Christians to pray with great and unique positive effect for the building of the Kingdom. (See 1 Thessalonians 3:10-13; 1 Timothy 2:1-2.)

Craftsmanship: the ability to use hands and minds to build up the Kingdom through artistic, creative means. (See Exodus 28:3-4.)

Hospitality: the ability to cheerfully and willingly open one's home and offer lodging, food, and comfort to other people. (See Genesis 18:1-15.)

Faith: extraordinary confidence in God's promises, power, and presence. (See Hebrews 11.)

Discernment: knowledge with assurance whether some behavior is of God or of Satan. (See Acts 5:3-6; 16:16-18.)

Mercy: empathy and compassion for those who are suffering. (See Luke 10:30-37.)

Giving: the cheerful and liberal offering of material blessings for the work of the church. (See 2 Corinthians 8:1-5.)

Administration: the ability to understand and effectively direct the goals and big picture of a given faith community. (See Acts 15:12-21.)

Leadership: the gift of motivating, directing and inspiring God's people in such a way that they harmoniously work together to do the church's work effectively. (See Hebrews 13:7; Judges 3:10; Exodus 18:13-16.)

Helps: assistance in bearing the burdens of other Christians and helping them in such a way that they can do their tasks more effectively. (See Acts 6:2-4; Galatians 6:1-2.)

Knowledge: understanding in an exceptional way the great truths of God's Word and making them real to others. (See Ephesians 3:14-19.)

Wisdom: an understanding of God's will and work as it relates to the life of the individual and faith community. (See James 3:13-17.)

Exhortation: the ability to bring comfort, counsel, and encouragement. (See Acts 11:23-24; 14:21-22.)

Teacher: the gift of communicating the truths of God's Word so that others can learn and apply it to their lives. (See Hebrews 5:12-14.)

Pastor: taking responsibility for the spiritual welfare of a group of believers. (See 1 Peter 5:1-11.)

Evangelist: expressing faith in Christ to unbelievers in a spiritually effective manner. (See Acts 8:26-40.)

Prophet: interpreting and applying God's revelation in a given situation. (See 1 Corinthians 14:1-5; 14:30-33; 14:37-40.)

2 Peter

What is the biggest problem for a coach whose team is winning? It is keeping his players from becoming complacent and cocky. In his final words, Peter reminds Christians at large not to become complacent. "So I will work hard to make sure you always remember these things" (2 Peter 1:5); "I will always remind you about these things" (2 Peter 1:12).

Our job as Christians is to keep God number one! Peter, like a good coach, encourages us to push on and have victory in Jesus. Allow God to take command in your life every day. Read the Scriptures for encouragement, training, and transformation. Allow Peter to "always remind you."

2 PETER

Greetings from Peter

1

This letter is from Simon Peter, a slave and apostle of Jesus Christ.

I am writing to you who share the same precious faith we have. This faith was given to you because of the justice and fairness of Jesus Christ, our God and Savior.

[2]May God give you more and more grace and peace as you grow in your knowledge of God and Jesus our Lord.

When you need discipline

1:6

. . . knowledge with self-control, and self-control with patient endurance, and patient endurance with godliness . . .

Growing in Faith

[3]By his divine power, God has given us everything we need for living a godly life. We have received all of this by coming to know him, the one who called us to himself by means of his marvelous glory and excellence. [4]And because of his glory and excellence, he has given us great and precious promises. These are the promises that enable you to share his divine nature and escape the world's corruption caused by human desires.

[5]In view of all this, make every effort to respond to God's promises. Supplement your faith with a generous provision of moral excellence, and moral excellence with knowledge, [6]and knowledge with self-control, and self-control with patient endurance, and patient endurance with godliness, [7]and godliness with brotherly affection, and brotherly affection with love for everyone.

[8]The more you grow like this, the more productive and useful you will be in your knowledge of our Lord Jesus Christ. [9]But those who fail to develop in this way are shortsighted or blind, forgetting that they have been cleansed from their old sins.

[10]So, dear brothers and sisters, work hard to prove that you really are among those God has called and chosen. Do these

Soccer is the most attended and watched sport in the world.

things, and you will never fall away. [11]Then God will give you a grand entrance into the eternal Kingdom of our Lord and Savior Jesus Christ.

Paying Attention to Scripture

[12]Therefore, I will always remind you about these things—even though you already know them and are standing firm in the truth you have been taught. [13]And it is only right that I should keep on reminding you as long as I live. [14]For our Lord Jesus Christ has shown me that I must soon leave this earthly life, [15]so I will work hard to make sure you always remember these things after I am gone.

[16]For we were not making up clever stories when we told you about the powerful coming of our Lord Jesus Christ. We saw his majestic splendor with our own eyes [17]when he received honor and glory from God the Father. The voice from the majestic glory of God said to him, "This is my dearly loved Son, who brings me great joy." [18]We ourselves heard that voice from heaven when we were with him on the holy mountain. [19]Because of that experience, we have even greater confidence in the message proclaimed by the prophets. You must pay close attention to what they wrote, for their words are like a lamp shining in a dark place—until the Day dawns, and Christ the Morning Star shines in your hearts. [20]Above all, you must realize that no prophecy in Scripture ever came from the prophet's own understanding, [21]or from human initiative. No, those prophets were moved by the Holy Spirit, and they spoke from God.

The Danger of False Teachers

2

But there were also false prophets in Israel, just as there will be false teachers among you. They will cleverly teach destructive heresies and even deny the Master who bought them. In this way, they will bring sudden destruction on themselves. [2]Many will follow

their evil teaching and shameful immorality. And because of these teachers, the way of truth will be slandered. [3]In their greed they will make up clever lies to get hold of your money. But God condemned them long ago, and their destruction will not be delayed.

[4]For God did not spare even the angels who sinned. He threw them into hell, in gloomy pits of darkness, where they are being held until the day of judgment. [5]And God did not spare the ancient world—except for Noah and the seven others in his family. Noah warned the world of God's righteous judgment. So God protected Noah when he destroyed the world of ungodly people with a vast flood. [6]Later, God condemned the cities of Sodom and Gomorrah and turned them into heaps of ashes. He made them an example of what will happen to ungodly people. [7]But God also rescued Lot out of Sodom because he was a righteous man who was sick of the shameful immorality of the wicked people around him. [8]Yes, Lot was a righteous man who was tormented in his soul by the wickedness he saw and heard day after day. [9]So you see, the Lord knows how to rescue godly people from their trials, even while keeping the wicked under punishment until the day of final judgment. [10]He is especially hard on those who follow their own twisted sexual desire, and who despise authority.

These people are proud and arrogant, daring even to scoff at supernatural beings without so much as trembling. [11]But the angels, who are far greater in power and strength, do not dare to bring from the Lord a charge of blasphemy against those supernatural beings.

[12]These false teachers are like unthinking animals, creatures of instinct, born to be caught and destroyed. They scoff at things they do not understand, and like animals, they will be destroyed. [13]Their destruction is their reward for the harm they have done. They love to indulge in evil pleasures in broad daylight. They are a disgrace and a stain among you. They delight in deception even as they eat with you in your fellowship meals. [14]They commit adultery with their eyes, and their desire for sin is never satisfied. They lure unstable people into sin, and they are well trained in greed. They live under God's curse. [15]They have wandered off the right road and followed the footsteps of Balaam son of Beor, who loved to earn money by doing wrong. [16]But Balaam was stopped from his mad course when his donkey rebuked him with a human voice.

[17]These people are as useless as dried-up springs or as mist blown away by the wind. They are doomed to blackest darkness. [18]They brag about themselves with

empty, foolish boasting. With an appeal to twisted sexual desires, they lure back into sin those who have barely escaped from a lifestyle of deception. [19]They promise freedom, but they themselves are slaves of sin and corruption. For you are a slave to whatever controls you. [20]And when people escape from the wickedness of the world by knowing our Lord and Savior Jesus Christ and then get tangled up and enslaved by sin again, they are worse off than before. [21]It would be better if they had never known the way to righteousness than to know it and then reject the command they were given to live a holy life. [22]They prove the truth of this proverb: "A dog returns to its vomit." And another says, "A washed pig returns to the mud."

The Day of the Lord Is Coming

3

This is my second letter to you, dear friends, and in both of them I have tried to stimulate your wholesome thinking and refresh your memory. [2]I want you to remember what the holy prophets said long ago and what our Lord and Savior commanded through your apostles.

[3]Most importantly, I want to remind you that in the last days scoffers will come, mocking the truth and following their own desires. [4]They will say, "What happened to the promise that Jesus is coming again? From before the times of our ancestors, everything has remained the same since the world was first created."

[5]They deliberately forget that God made the heavens by the word of his command, and he brought the earth out from the water and surrounded it with water. [6]Then he used the water to destroy the ancient world with a mighty flood. [7]And by the same word, the present heavens and earth have been stored up for fire. They are being kept for the day of judgment, when ungodly people will be destroyed.

[8]But you must not forget this one thing, dear friends: A day is like a thousand years to the Lord, and a thousand years is like a day. [9]The Lord isn't really being slow about his promise, as some people think. No, he is being patient for your sake. He does not want anyone to be destroyed, but wants everyone to repent. [10]But the day of the Lord will come as unexpectedly as a thief. Then the heavens will pass away with a terrible noise, and the very elements themselves will disappear in fire, and the earth and everything on it will be found to deserve judgment.

[11]Since everything around us is going to be destroyed like this, what holy and godly lives you should live, [12]looking forward to the day of God and hurrying it along. On that day, he will set the heavens on fire, and the elements will melt away in the flames. [13]But we are looking forward to the new heavens and new earth he has promised, a world filled with God's righteousness.

[14]And so, dear friends, while you are waiting for these things to happen, make every effort to be found living peaceful lives that are pure and blameless in his sight. [15]And remember, the Lord's patience gives people time to be saved. This is what our beloved brother Paul also wrote to you with the wisdom God gave him— [16]speaking of these things in all of his letters. Some of his comments are hard to understand, and those who are ignorant and unstable have twisted his letters to mean something quite different, just as they do with other parts of Scripture. And this will result in their destruction.

3:1-16 WHAT'S IT SAYING?

WHAT AM I GOING TO dO ABOUT IT?

Peter's Final Words

[17]I am warning you ahead of time, dear friends. Be on guard so that you will not be carried away by the errors of these wicked people and lose your own secure footing. [18]Rather, you must grow in the grace and knowledge of our Lord and Savior Jesus Christ. All glory to him, both now and forever! Amen.

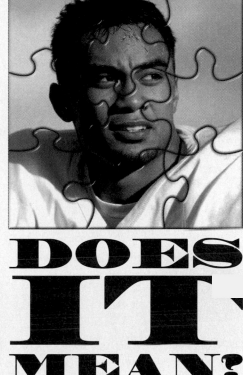

WHAT DOES IT MEAN?

inspiration of Scripture

Inspiration is the extraordinary or supernatural, divine influence of those who wrote the Holy Scriptures, making their writings without error (2 Timothy 3:16). The writers were supernaturally guided and prompted to express exactly what God intended them to communicate as a revelation of his mind and will.

Bible

The concept of HELL occurs 23 times in the New Testament.

Wearing the Uniform

"Quick! Bring the finest robe in the house and put it on him. Get a ring for his finger and sandals for his feet. And kill the calf we have been fattening. We must celebrate with a feast, for this son of mine was dead and has now returned to life." (Luke 15:22-24)

Do you remember receiving your first sports uniform? I didn't want to take mine off and probably wore it to bed! There is something about us humans that loves definition and validation. One of the great things about sports is that it sets margins. You're either part of the team or you're not. You win or lose. You have a low handicap or a high one. We enjoy being part of a group. The more others want to be part of a group the more esteemed the group is. Even anti-group types form their own countercultures and wear antisocial clothing (which is just another uniform), jewelry, haircuts, etc. Ironically, the antiestablishment uniform usually becomes the next generation's establishment kit. At one time not wearing a tie to watch a sporting event was considered socially outrageous!

DEVOTIONAL

Being adopted into God's family gives you certain rights, privileges, and responsibilities. You wear a new uniform. If you are a Christian you have been adopted into God's family. You are now a princess or a prince. You belong to God and you have a new allegiance, a new title, and a new citizenship. And, like enjoying being part of a team, you also have new duties and responsibilities that come with the uniform.

"Now you are no longer a slave but God's own child. And since you are his child, God has made you his heir." (Galatians 4:7)

Nicked with permission from: A Sporting Guide to Eternity, Steve Connor, Christian Focus Publications - ISBN 1-85792-746-X

1,2,3 John

John had seen it all: he had witnessed Jesus' crucifixion, he'd been banished to the island of Patmos, his brother and many of his closest friends had been martyred, and legend has it that he was boiled in oil. Yet at around one hundred years of age he was still going strong, and his central theme was: love God and love others as dear children of God. These three small letters are powerfully condensed; John does not waste a word.

Perhaps **1 John** is a supplement to his wonderful Gospel (see introduction to the Gospel of John). The letter gives us an intimate understanding of the privilege that those who follow Christ have: "See how very much our Father loves us, for he calls us his children" (3:1). But it also contains strict warnings: "Dear children, keep away from anything that might take God's place in your hearts" (5:21). As always, the early church leaders were dogged by problems with bogus teachers trying to corrupt Christians and entire churches. And again we find John addressing the issue and correcting his "dear children." But this is no bad thing. If John, Paul, and Peter did not have to deal with these idiots, we would not have the rich, strong instruction in the Scriptures that we apply to our lives today.

Second John and 3 John are very intimate and concise letters, perhaps originally written on one sheet of papyrus each. Though they are short, meditate on them, allow God's power to transform your being, and apply them to your life.

1 JOHN

Introduction

1

We proclaim to you the one who existed from the beginning, whom we have heard and seen. We saw him with our own eyes and touched him with our own hands. He is the Word of life. [2]This one who is life itself was revealed to us, and we have seen him. And now we testify and proclaim to you that he is the one who is eternal life. He was with the Father, and then he was revealed to us. [3]We proclaim to you what we ourselves have actually seen and heard so that you may have fellowship with us. And our fellowship is with the Father and with his Son, Jesus Christ. [4]We are writing these things so that you may fully share our joy.

1:5-10 WHAT'S IT SAYING?

WHAT AM I GOING TO DO ABOUT IT?

Living in the Light

[5]This is the message we heard from Jesus and now declare to you: God is light, and there is no darkness in him at all. [6]So we are lying if we say we have fellowship with God but go on living in spiritual darkness; we are not practicing the truth. [7]But if we are living in the light, as God is in the light, then we have fellowship with each other, and the blood of Jesus,

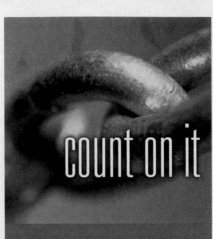

The big win!

Championships come and go but the disarming of sin on the Cross is the mother of all victories. So what can you do about that great win, how should you respond, and does Christ's victory have anything to do with you?

It can — by nailing your sins to the Cross. Christ has victory over sin which has eternal consequences (big win), and you enter into that victory by nailing your sins to the Cross. It happens to be the answer to the universe, the key to life, the only victory that will last. Enter in with a few nails.

"He canceled the record of the charges against us and took it away by nailing it to the cross." (Colossians 2:14)

Count on it!

his Son, cleanses us from all sin.

[8]If we claim we have no sin, we are only fooling ourselves and not living in the truth. [9]But if we confess our sins to him, he is faithful and just to forgive us our sins and to cleanse us from all wickedness. [10]If we claim we have not sinned, we are calling God a liar and showing that his word has no place in our hearts.

2

My dear children, I am writing this to you so that you will not sin. But if anyone does sin, we have an advocate who pleads our case before the Father. He is Jesus Christ, the one who is truly righteous. [2]He himself is the sacrifice that atones for our sins—and not only our sins but the sins of all the world.

[3]And we can be sure that we know him if we obey his commandments. [4]If someone claims, "I know God," but doesn't obey God's commandments, that person is a liar and is not living in the truth. [5]But those who obey God's word truly show how completely they love him. That is how we know we are living in him. [6]Those who say they live in God should live their lives as Jesus did.

A New Commandment

[7]Dear friends, I am not writing a new commandment for you; rather it is an old one you have had from the very beginning. This old commandment—to love one another—is the same message you heard before. [8]Yet it is also new. Jesus lived the truth of this commandment, and you also are living it. For the darkness is disappearing, and the true light is already shining.

[9]If anyone claims, "I am living in the light," but hates a Christian brother or sister, that person is still living in darkness. [10]Anyone who loves another brother or sister is living in the light and does not cause others to stumble. [11]But anyone who hates another brother or sister is still living and walking in darkness. Such a person does not know the way to go, having been blinded by the darkness.

[12]I am writing to you who are God's children because your sins have been forgiven through Jesus. [13]I am writing to you who are mature in the faith because you know Christ, who existed from the beginning.

I am writing to you who are young in the faith because you have won your battle with the evil one. [14]I have written to you who are God's children because you know the Father.

I have written to you who are mature in the faith because you know Christ, who existed from the beginning.

I have written to you who are young in the faith because you are strong.

God's word lives in your hearts, and you have won your battle with the evil one.

Do Not Love This World

[15]Do not love this world nor the things it offers you, for when you love the world, you do not have the love of the Father in you. [16]For the world offers only a craving for physical pleasure, a craving for everything we see, and pride in our achievements and possessions.

These are not from the Father, but are from this world. [17]And this world is fading away, along with everything that people crave. But anyone who does what pleases God will live forever.

Warning about Antichrists

[18]Dear children, the last hour is here. You have heard that the Antichrist is coming, and already many such antichrists have appeared. From this we know that the last hour has come. [19]These people left our churches, but they never really belonged with us; otherwise they would have stayed with us. When they left, it proved that they did not belong with us.

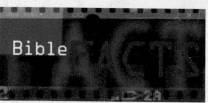

The word *gospel* means "good news."

[20]But you are not like that, for the Holy One has given you his Spirit, and all of you know the truth. [21]So I am writing to you not because you don't know the truth but because you know the difference between truth and lies. [22]And who is a liar? Anyone who says that Jesus is not the Christ. Anyone who denies the Father and the Son is an antichrist. [23]Anyone who denies the Son doesn't have the Father, either. But anyone who acknowledges the Son has the Father also.

[24]So you must remain faithful to what you have been taught from the beginning. If you do, you will remain in fellowship with the Son and with the Father. [25]And in this fellowship we enjoy the eternal life he promised us.

[26]I am writing these things to warn you about those who want to lead you astray. [27]But you have received the Holy Spirit, and he lives within you, so you don't need anyone to teach you what is true. For the Spirit teaches you everything

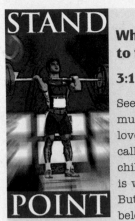

STAND POINT

When you need to feel loved

3:1

See how very much our Father loves us, for he calls us his children, and that is what we are! But the people who belong to this world don't recognize that we are God's children because they don't know him.

---

you need to know, and what he teaches is true—it is not a lie. So just as he has taught you, remain in fellowship with Christ.

Living as Children of God

²⁸And now, dear children, remain in fellowship with Christ so that when he returns, you will be full of courage and not shrink back from him in shame.

²⁹Since we know that Christ is righteous, we also know that all who do what is right are God's children.

3

See how very much our Father loves us, for he calls us his children, and that is what we are! But the people who belong to this world don't recognize that we are God's children because they don't know him. ²Dear friends, we are already

God's children, but he has not yet shown us what we will be like when Christ appears. But we do know that we will be like him, for we will see him as he really is. ³And all who have this eager expectation will keep themselves pure, just as he is pure.

⁴Everyone who sins is breaking God's law, for all sin is contrary to the law of God. ⁵And you know that Jesus came to take away our sins, and there is no sin in him. ⁶Anyone who continues to live in him will not sin. But anyone who keeps on sinning does not know him or understand who he is.

⁷Dear children, don't let anyone deceive you about this: When people do what is right, it shows that they are righteous, even as Christ is righteous. ⁸But when people keep on sinning, it shows that they belong to the devil, who has been sinning since the beginning. But the Son of God came to destroy the works of the devil. ⁹Those who have been born into God's family do not make a practice of sinning, because God's life is in them. So they can't keep on sinning, because they are children of God. ¹⁰So now we can tell who are children of God and who are children of the devil. Anyone who does not live righteously and does not love other believers does not belong to God.

Love One Another

¹¹This is the message you have heard from the beginning: We should love one another. ¹²We must not be like Cain, who belonged to the evil one and killed his brother. And why did he kill him? Because Cain had been doing what was evil, and his brother had been doing what was righteous. ¹³So don't be surprised, dear brothers and sisters, if the world hates you. ¹⁴If we love our Christian brothers and sisters, it proves that we have passed from death to life. But a person

who has no love is still dead. ¹⁵Anyone who hates another brother or sister is really a murderer at heart. And you know that murderers don't have eternal life within them.

¹⁶We know what real love is because Jesus gave up his life for us. So we also ought to give up our lives for our brothers and sisters. ¹⁷If someone has enough money to live well and sees a brother or sister in need but shows no compassion—how can God's love be in that person?

¹⁸Dear children, let's not merely say that we love each other; let us show the truth by our actions. ¹⁹Our actions will show that we belong to the truth, so we will be confident when we stand before God. ²⁰Even if we feel guilty, God is greater than our feelings, and he knows everything.

²¹Dear friends, if we don't feel guilty, we can come to God with bold confidence. ²²And we will receive from him whatever we ask because we obey him and do the things that please him.

²³And this is his commandment: We must believe in the name of his Son, Jesus Christ, and love one another,

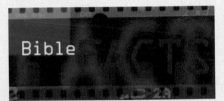

In ancient times, a chariot imported from Egypt cost around 600 shekels of silver (that would be about the same as the cost of a luxury car today).

just as he commanded us. ²⁴Those who obey God's commandments remain in fellowship with him, and he with them. And we know he lives in us because the Spirit he gave us lives in us.

Discerning False Prophets

4

Dear friends, do not believe everyone who claims to speak by the Spirit. You must test them to see if the spirit they have comes from God. For there are many false prophets in the world. ²This is how we know if they have the Spirit of God: If a person claiming to be a prophet acknowledges that Jesus Christ came in a real body, that person has the Spirit of God. ³But if someone claims to be a prophet and does not

---

Who are five people you want to encourage this year?

1. _____
2. _____
3. _____
4. _____
5. _____

BIG FIVE

TIPS

Fundamentals are key:

The mental aspect of the game will, and does, affect your performance. For example, for various reasons, when golfers put a driver in their hands they tend to tense up. Before you begin to count on your driver to help you lower your score, you need to develop a comfort level with it. The same is true in all sports; work hard on fundamentals and slowly pull out the big plays (or clubs) as your confidence and skills develop.

acknowledge the truth about Jesus, that person is not from God. Such a person has the spirit of the Antichrist, which you heard is coming into the world and indeed is already here.

⁴But you belong to God, my dear children. You have already won a victory over those people, because the

Roger Bannister broke the 4-minute mile barrier in 1954.

Spirit who lives in you is greater than the spirit who lives in the world. ⁵Those people belong to this world, so they speak from the world's viewpoint, and the world listens to them. ⁶But we belong to God, and those who know God listen to us. If they do not belong to God, they do not listen to us. That is how we know if someone has the Spirit of truth or the spirit of deception.

Loving One Another

⁷Dear friends, let us continue to love one another, for love comes from God. Anyone who loves is a child of God and knows God. ⁸But anyone who does not love does not know God, for God is love.

⁹God showed how much he loved us by sending his one and only Son into the world so that we might

have eternal life through him. ¹⁰This is real love—not that we loved God, but that he loved us and sent his Son as a sacrifice to take away our sins.

¹¹Dear friends, since God loved us that much, we surely ought to love each other. ¹²No one has ever seen God. But if we love each other, God lives in us, and his love is brought to full expression in us.

¹³And God has given us his Spirit as proof that we live in him and he in us. ¹⁴Furthermore, we have seen with our own eyes and now testify that the Father sent his Son to be the Savior of the world. ¹⁵All who confess that Jesus is the Son of God have God living in them, and they live in God. ¹⁶We know how much God loves us, and we have put our trust in his love.

God is love, and all who live in love live in God, and God lives in them. ¹⁷And as we live in God, our love grows more

DECEMBER M.A.P.

1
S.D.		P.L.		P.G.		S.G.	
P.	☐	F.	☐	F.	☐	T.	☐
F.	☐	W.	☐	W.	☐	P.	☐
B.	☐	P.	☐	C.	☐	C.	☐

2
S.D.		P.L.		P.G.		S.G.	
P.	☐	F.	☐	F.	☐	T.	☐
F.	☐	W.	☐	W.	☐	P.	☐
B.	☐	P.	☐	C.	☐	C.	☐

3
S.D.		P.L.		P.G.		S.G.	
P.	☐	F.	☐	F.	☐	T.	☐
F.	☐	W.	☐	W.	☐	P.	☐
B.	☐	P.	☐	C.	☐	C.	☐

4
S.D.		P.L.		P.G.		S.G.	
P.	☐	F.	☐	F.	☐	T.	☐
F.	☐	W.	☐	W.	☐	P.	☐
B.	☐	P.	☐	C.	☐	C.	☐

9
S.D.		P.L.		P.G.		S.G.	
P.	☐	F.	☐	F.	☐	T.	☐
F.	☐	W.	☐	W.	☐	P.	☐
B.	☐	P.	☐	C.	☐	C.	☐

10
S.D.		P.L.		P.G.		S.G.	
P.	☐	F.	☐	F.	☐	T.	☐
F.	☐	W.	☐	W.	☐	P.	☐
B.	☐	P.	☐	C.	☐	C.	☐

11
S.D.		P.L.		P.G.		S.G.	
P.	☐	F.	☐	F.	☐	T.	☐
F.	☐	W.	☐	W.	☐	P.	☐
B.	☐	P.	☐	C.	☐	C.	☐

12
S.D.		P.L.		P.G.		S.G.	
P.	☐	F.	☐	F.	☐	T.	☐
F.	☐	W.	☐	W.	☐	P.	☐
B.	☐	P.	☐	C.	☐	C.	☐

17
S.D.		P.L.		P.G.		S.G.	
P.	☐	F.	☐	F.	☐	T.	☐
F.	☐	W.	☐	W.	☐	P.	☐
B.	☐	P.	☐	C.	☐	C.	☐

18
S.D.		P.L.		P.G.		S.G.	
P.	☐	F.	☐	F.	☐	T.	☐
F.	☐	W.	☐	W.	☐	P.	☐
B.	☐	P.	☐	C.	☐	C.	☐

19
S.D.		P.L.		P.G.		S.G.	
P.	☐	F.	☐	F.	☐	T.	☐
F.	☐	W.	☐	W.	☐	P.	☐
B.	☐	P.	☐	C.	☐	C.	☐

20
S.D.		P.L.		P.G.		S.G.	
P.	☐	F.	☐	F.	☐	T.	☐
F.	☐	W.	☐	W.	☐	P.	☐
B.	☐	P.	☐	C.	☐	C.	☐

25
S.D.		P.L.		P.G.		S.G.	
P.	☐	F.	☐	F.	☐	T.	☐
F.	☐	W.	☐	W.	☐	P.	☐
B.	☐	P.	☐	C.	☐	C.	☐

26
S.D.		P.L.		P.G.		S.G.	
P.	☐	F.	☐	F.	☐	T.	☐
F.	☐	W.	☐	W.	☐	P.	☐
B.	☐	P.	☐	C.	☐	C.	☐

27
S.D.		P.L.		P.G.		S.G.	
P.	☐	F.	☐	F.	☐	T.	☐
F.	☐	W.	☐	W.	☐	P.	☐
B.	☐	P.	☐	C.	☐	C.	☐

28
S.D.		P.L.		P.G.		S.G.	
P.	☐	F.	☐	F.	☐	T.	☐
F.	☐	W.	☐	W.	☐	P.	☐
B.	☐	P.	☐	C.	☐	C.	☐

Spiritual Disciplines

Prayer

Faith Community

Bible Reading

Prayer List

Friends

World

Personal

(For designing your M.A.P. – Monthly Action Plan – see introduction pages

Who am I....
Where am I going....
How am I going to get there?

nt:sport
MONTHLY ACTION PLAN

5

S.D.	P.L.	P.G.	S.G.
P. ☐	F. ☐	F. ☐	T. ☐
F. ☐	W. ☐	W. ☐	P. ☐
B. ☐	P. ☐	C. ☐	C. ☐

6

S.D.	P.L.	P.G.	S.G.
P. ☐	F. ☐	F. ☐	T. ☐
F. ☐	W. ☐	W. ☐	P. ☐
B. ☐	P. ☐	C. ☐	C. ☐

7

S.D.	P.L.	P.G.	S.G.
P. ☐	F. ☐	F. ☐	T. ☐
F. ☐	W. ☐	W. ☐	P. ☐
B. ☐	P. ☐	C. ☐	C. ☐

8

S.D.	P.L.	P.G.	S.G.
P. ☐	F. ☐	F. ☐	T. ☐
F. ☐	W. ☐	W. ☐	P. ☐
B. ☐	P. ☐	C. ☐	C. ☐

13

S.D.	P.L.	P.G.	S.G.
P. ☐	F. ☐	F. ☐	T. ☐
F. ☐	W. ☐	W. ☐	P. ☐
B. ☐	P. ☐	C. ☐	C. ☐

14

S.D.	P.L.	P.G.	S.G.
P. ☐	F. ☐	F. ☐	T. ☐
F. ☐	W. ☐	W. ☐	P. ☐
B. ☐	P. ☐	C. ☐	C. ☐

15

S.D.	P.L.	P.G.	S.G.
P. ☐	F. ☐	F. ☐	T. ☐
F. ☐	W. ☐	W. ☐	P. ☐
B. ☐	P. ☐	C. ☐	C. ☐

16

S.D.	P.L.	P.G.	S.G.
P. ☐	F. ☐	F. ☐	T. ☐
F. ☐	W. ☐	W. ☐	P. ☐
B. ☐	P. ☐	C. ☐	C. ☐

21

S.D.	P.L.	P.G.	S.G.
P. ☐	F. ☐	F. ☐	T. ☐
F. ☐	W. ☐	W. ☐	P. ☐
B. ☐	P. ☐	C. ☐	C. ☐

22

S.D.	P.L.	P.G.	S.G.
P. ☐	F. ☐	F. ☐	T. ☐
F. ☐	W. ☐	W. ☐	P. ☐
B. ☐	P. ☐	C. ☐	C. ☐

23

S.D.	P.L.	P.G.	S.G.
P. ☐	F. ☐	F. ☐	T. ☐
F. ☐	W. ☐	W. ☐	P. ☐
B. ☐	P. ☐	C. ☐	C. ☐

24

S.D.	P.L.	P.G.	S.G.
P. ☐	F. ☐	F. ☐	T. ☐
F. ☐	W. ☐	W. ☐	P. ☐
B. ☐	P. ☐	C. ☐	C. ☐

29

S.D.	P.L.	P.G.	S.G.
P. ☐	F. ☐	F. ☐	T. ☐
F. ☐	W. ☐	W. ☐	P. ☐
B. ☐	P. ☐	C. ☐	C. ☐

30

S.D.	P.L.	P.G.	S.G.
P. ☐	F. ☐	F. ☐	T. ☐
F. ☐	W. ☐	W. ☐	P. ☐
B. ☐	P. ☐	C. ☐	C. ☐

31

S.D.	P.L.	P.G.	S.G.
P. ☐	F. ☐	F. ☐	T. ☐
F. ☐	W. ☐	W. ☐	P. ☐
B. ☐	P. ☐	C. ☐	C. ☐

Proverbs 21:30

No human wisdom or understanding or plan can stand against the LORD.

Personal Goals

Family

Work/School/Social

Challenge

Sport Goals

Training

Performance

Competition Results

WHAT

DOES IT MEAN?

Jerusalem

Jerusalem is a city of contrasts, called at times the "city of God" and the "holy city." It is one of the most famous cities in the world and considered sacred by Jews, Christians, and Muslims. It embodies a powerful mixture of East and West at the same time. The great city has been under siege for over four thousand years. It became King David's capital, and after his death, his son Solomon built the Temple, a house for God. Jerusalem has been rebuilt over and over on the immense beds of rubbish resulting from blockades, destruction, and wars. In Jesus' time, Jerusalem was the Jewish cultural center and capital and a powder keg of tension because of Roman occupation and domination. Jesus visited as a boy, taught in the Temple, celebrated festivals, was crucified, and showed himself after his resurrection in the holy city.

perfect. So we will not be afraid on the day of judgment, but we can face him with confidence because we live like Jesus here in this world.

[18]Such love has no fear, because perfect love expels all fear. If we are afraid, it is for fear of punishment, and this shows that we have not fully experienced his perfect love. [19]We love each other because he loved us first.

[20]If someone says, "I love God," but hates a Christian brother or sister, that person is a liar; for if we don't love people we can see, how can we love God, whom we cannot see? [21]And he has given us this command: Those who love God must also love their Christian brothers and sisters.

4:1-21 WHAT'S IT SAYING?

WHAT AM I GOING TO DO ABOUT IT?

Faith in the Son of God

5

Everyone who believes that Jesus is the Christ has become a child of God. And everyone who loves the Father loves his children, too. [2]We know we love God's children if we love God and obey his commandments. [3]Loving God means keeping his commandments, and his commandments are not burdensome. [4]For every child of God defeats this evil world, and we achieve this victory through our faith. [5]And who can win this

battle against the world? Only those who believe that Jesus is the Son of God.

[6]And Jesus Christ was revealed as God's Son by his baptism in water and by shedding his blood on the cross—not by water only, but by water and blood. And the Spirit, who is truth, confirms it with his testimony. [7]So we have these three witnesses—[8]the Spirit, the water, and the blood—and all three agree. [9]Since we believe human testimony, surely we can believe the greater testimony that comes from God. And God has testified about his Son. [10]All who believe in the Son of God know in their hearts that this testimony is true. Those who don't believe this are actually calling God a liar because they don't believe what God has testified about his Son.

[11]And this is what God has testified: He has given us eternal life, and this life is in his Son. [12]Whoever has the Son has life; whoever does not have God's Son does not have life.

Conclusion

[13]I have written this to you who believe in the name of the Son of God, so that you may know you have eternal life. [14]And we are confident that he hears us whenever we ask for anything that pleases him. [15]And since we know he hears us when we make our requests, we also know that he will give us what we ask for.

[16]If you see a Christian brother or sister sinning in a way that does not lead to death, you should pray, and God will give that person life. But there is a sin that leads to death, and I am not saying you should pray for those who commit it. [17]All wicked actions are sin, but not every sin leads to death.

[18]We know that God's children do not make a practice of sinning, for God's Son holds them securely, and the evil one cannot touch them. [19]We know that we are children of God and that the world around us is under the control of the evil one.

[20]And we know that the Son of God has come, and he has given us understanding so that we can know the true God. And now we live in fellowship with the true God because we live in fellowship with his Son, Jesus Christ. He is the only true God, and he is eternal life. [21]Dear children, keep away from anything that might take God's place in your hearts.

2 JOHN

Greetings

This letter is from John, the elder.

I am writing to the chosen lady and to her children, whom I love in the truth—as does everyone else who knows the truth—²because the truth lives in us and will be with us forever.

³Grace, mercy, and peace, which come from God the Father and from Jesus Christ—the Son of the Father—will continue to be with us who live in truth and love.

Live in the Truth

⁴How happy I was to meet some of your children and find them living according to the truth, just as the Father commanded.

⁵I am writing to remind you, dear friends, that we should love one another. This is not a new commandment, but one we have had from the beginning. ⁶Love means doing what God has commanded us, and he has commanded us to love one another, just as you heard from the beginning.

⁷I say this because many deceivers have gone out into the world. They deny that Jesus Christ came in a real body. Such a person is a deceiver and an antichrist. ⁸Watch out that you do not lose what we have worked so hard to achieve. Be diligent so that you receive your full reward. ⁹Anyone who wanders away from this teaching has no relationship with God. But anyone who remains in the teaching of Christ has a relationship with both the Father and the Son.

¹⁰If anyone comes to your meeting and does not teach the truth about Christ, don't invite that person into your home or give any kind of encouragement. ¹¹Anyone who encourages such people becomes a partner in their evil work.

Conclusion

¹²I have much more to say to you, but I don't want to do it with paper and ink. For I hope to visit you soon and talk with you face to face. Then our joy will be complete.

¹³Greetings from the children of your sister, chosen by God.

3 JOHN

Greetings

This letter is from John, the elder.

I am writing to Gaius, my dear friend, whom I love in the truth.

²Dear friend, I hope all is well with you and that you are as healthy in body as you are strong in spirit. ³Some of the traveling teachers recently returned and made me very happy by telling me about your faithfulness and that you are living according to the truth. ⁴I could have no greater joy than to hear that my children are following the truth.

Caring for the Lord's Workers

⁵Dear friend, you are being faithful to God when you care for the traveling teachers who pass through, even though they are strangers to you. ⁶They have told the church here of your loving friendship. Please continue providing for such teachers in a manner that pleases God. ⁷For they are traveling for the Lord, and they accept nothing from people who are not believers. ⁸So we ourselves should support them so that we can be their partners as they teach the truth.

⁹I wrote to the church about this, but Diotrephes, who loves to be the leader, refuses to have anything to do with us. ¹⁰When I come, I will report some of the things he is doing and the evil accusations he is making against us. Not only does he refuse to welcome the traveling teachers, he also tells others not to help them. And when they do help, he puts them out of the church.

¹¹Dear friend, don't let this bad example influence you. Follow only what is good. Remember that those who do good prove that they are God's children, and those who do evil prove that they do not know God. ¹²Everyone speaks highly of Demetrius, as does the truth itself. We ourselves can say the same for him, and you know we speak the truth.

1:11-12 WHAT'S IT SAYING?

WHAT AM I GOING TO DO ABOUT IT?

Conclusion

¹³I have much more to say to you, but I don't want to write it with pen and ink. ¹⁴For I hope to see you soon, and then we will talk face to face. ¹⁵Peace be with you.

Your friends here send you their greetings. Please give my personal greetings to each of our friends there.

My friends say that Christians are too uptight about watching movies and listening to music.

Our intake affects our output. The goal of sports nutrition is to "eat to compete" — to fuel the body for maximum performance. What we feed our minds is just as important as what we feed our bodies. The kind of books we read, the people we hang out with, the music we listen to, and the films and television shows we watch are all part of our mental diet. You are what you eat.

"A wise person is hungry for knowledge, while the fool feeds on trash." (Proverbs 15:14)

find the power
LIVE it

Jude

Jude was the brother of James and half brother of Jesus (see Mark 6:3). Plainly his target audience was the Christian movement that was spreading around the world. Like other Bible writers, Jude had to stop the spread of false teaching that can spread like a cancer. We can feel his concern and sense of urgency to stop the raging disease of lies. But in this struggle for the hearts of people, adversity creates strength and endurance.

You do not become a champion by listening to and following liars. You cannot be successful and lazy. The same is true in your walk with God — the Bible never says it will be easy, and there is a spiritual evil that is going to wage war against you . . . "dangerous reefs that can shipwreck you." (Jude 1:12) But we are not to be scared because we have a God who will "keep us from stumbling" and bring us into his presence.

JUDE

Greetings from Jude

This letter is from Jude, a slave of Jesus Christ and a brother of James.

I am writing to all who have been called by God the Father, who loves you and keeps you safe in the care of Jesus Christ. [2]May God give you more and more mercy, peace, and love.

STAND

When a friend is weak

1:22

You must show mercy to those whose faith is wavering.

POINT

The Danger of False Teachers

[3]Dear friends, I had been eagerly planning to write to you about the salvation we all share. But now I find that I must write about something else, urging you to defend the faith that God has entrusted once for all time to his holy people. [4]I say this because some ungodly people have wormed their way into your churches, saying that God's marvelous grace allows us to live immoral lives. The condemnation of such people was recorded long ago, for they have denied our only Master and Lord, Jesus Christ.

[5]So I want to remind you, though you already know these things, that Jesus first rescued the nation of Israel from Egypt, but later he destroyed those who did not remain faithful. [6]And I remind you of the angels who did not stay within the limits of authority God gave them but left the place where they belonged. God has kept them securely chained in prisons of darkness, waiting for the great day of judgment. [7]And don't forget Sodom and Gomorrah and their neighboring towns, which were filled with immorality and every kind of sexual perversion. Those cities were destroyed by fire and serve as a warning of the eternal fire of God's judgment.

[8]In the same way, these people—who claim authority from their dreams—live immoral lives, defy authority, and scoff at supernatural beings. [9]But even Michael, one of the mightiest of the angels, did not dare accuse the devil of blasphemy, but simply said, "The Lord rebuke you!" (This took place when Michael was arguing with the devil about Moses' body.) [10]But these people scoff at things they do not understand. Like unthinking animals, they do whatever their instincts tell them, and so they bring about their own destruction. [11]What sorrow awaits them! For they follow in the footsteps of Cain, who killed his brother. Like Balaam, they deceive people for money. And like Korah, they perish in their rebellion.

[12]When these people eat with you in your fellowship meals commemorating the Lord's love, they are like dangerous reefs that can shipwreck you. They are like shameless shepherds who care only for themselves. They are like clouds blowing over the land without giving any rain. They are like trees in autumn that are doubly dead, for they bear no fruit and have been pulled up by the roots. [13]They are like wild waves of the sea, churning up the foam of their shameful deeds. They are like wandering stars, doomed forever to blackest darkness.

[14]Enoch, who lived in the seventh generation after Adam, prophesied about these people. He said, "Listen! The Lord is coming with countless thousands of his holy ones [15]to execute judgment on the people of the world. He will convict every person of all the ungodly things they have done and for all the insults that ungodly sinners have spoken against him."

[16]These people are grumblers and complainers, living only to satisfy their desires. They brag loudly about themselves, and they flatter others to get what they want.

action

1:12-16 WHAT'S IT SAYING?

WHAT AM I GOING TO DO ABOUT IT?

Bible FACTS

The 10 Plagues of Egypt:

1. **Water turns to blood**
2. **Frogs**
3. **Gnats**
4. **Flies**
5. **Livestock die of diseases**
6. **Boils and sores**
7. **Hail**
8. **Locusts**
9. **Darkness**
10. **Death of firstborn**

A Call to Remain Faithful

[17]But you, my dear friends, must remember what the apostles of our Lord Jesus Christ said. [18]They told you that in the last times there would be scoffers whose purpose in life is to satisfy their ungodly desires. [19]These people are the ones who are creating divisions among you. They follow their natural instincts because they do not have God's Spirit in them.

[20]But you, dear friends, must build each other up in your most holy faith, pray in the power of the Holy Spirit, [21]and await the mercy of our Lord Jesus Christ, who will bring you eternal life. In this way, you will keep yourselves safe in God's love.

[22]And you must show mercy to those whose faith is wavering. [23]Rescue others by snatching them from the flames of judgment. Show mercy to still others, but do so with great caution, hating the sins that contaminate their lives.

A Prayer of Praise

[24]Now all glory to God, who is able to keep you from falling away and will bring you with great joy into his glorious presence without a single fault. [25]All glory to him who alone is God, our Savior through Jesus Christ our Lord. All glory, majesty, power, and authority are his before all time, and in the present, and beyond all time! Amen.

Revelation

Read this book if you want to be blessed! It expressly promises that all who read and all who listen and obey the message of this book will be given blessing (Rev. 1:3). It also promises that anybody who adds to or removes anything from this book will be cursed (Rev. 22:18)! The word *revelation* means "unveiling" or "revealing" (*apocalypse* is the Greek name). This book is a disclosure of truth that Jesus Christ possesses and is giving to us, his church. The central theme is Jesus Christ's reign and his complete and eternal victory over Satan. God gives us a glimpse at the end of the match, and the scoreboard reads: God wins!

The author of this book was undoubtedly John the apostle. As to the relation between this book and the Gospel of John, it has been well observed that the leading ideas of both are the same: the ultimate clash between good and evil and God's solution. The Gospel gives us a magnificent historical drama, and Revelation gives us the amazing vision and foretelling. In both, Jesus Christ is the key figure, whose victory through the Cross is central!

OUTLINE:

- 1   Jesus revealed in glory
- 2–3   Scope of church history
- 4–5   Christ and his church
- 6–17   Christ and the world
- 18–22   Christ's return

REVELATION

Prologue

1

This is a revelation from Jesus Christ, which God gave him to show his servants the events that must soon take place. He sent an angel to present this revelation to his servant John, [2]who faithfully reported everything he saw. This is his report of the word of God and the testimony of Jesus Christ.

[3]God blesses the one who reads the words of this prophecy to the church, and he blesses all who listen to its message and obey what it says, for the time is near.

John's Greeting to the Seven Churches

[4]This letter is from John to the seven churches in the province of Asia.

Grace and peace to you from the one who is, who always was, and who is still to come; from the sevenfold Spirit before his throne; [5]and from Jesus Christ. He is the faithful witness to these things, the first to rise from the dead, and the ruler of all the kings of the world.

All glory to him who loves us and has freed us from our sins by shedding his blood for us. [6]He has made us a Kingdom of priests for God his Father. All glory and power to him forever and ever! Amen.

[7]Look! He comes with the clouds of heaven.
And everyone will see him—
even those who pierced him.
And all the nations of the world
will mourn for him.
Yes! Amen!

[8]"I am the Alpha and the Omega—the beginning and the end," says the Lord God. "I am the one who is, who always was, and who is still to come—the Almighty One."

Vision of the Son of Man

[9]I, John, am your brother and your partner in suffering and in God's Kingdom and in the patient endurance to which Jesus calls us. I was exiled to the island of Patmos for preaching the word of God and for my testimony about Jesus. [10]It was the Lord's Day, and I was worshiping in the Spirit. Suddenly, I heard behind me a loud voice like a trumpet blast. [11]It said, "Write in a book everything you see, and send it to the seven churches in the cities of Ephesus, Smyrna, Pergamum, Thyatira, Sardis, Philadelphia, and Laodicea."

[12]When I turned to see who was speaking to me, I saw seven gold lampstands. [13]And standing in the middle of the lampstands was someone like the Son of Man. He was wearing a long robe with a gold sash across his chest. [14]His head and

count on it

Christ came for you!
Jesus Christ had a purpose, a focus, and a finish line. He completed his race, and the end result was that those who receive his love and forgiveness, in faith, will have eternal life. You are a sinner, but . . .
"This is a trustworthy saying, and everyone should accept it: 'Christ Jesus came into the world to save sinners.'" (1 Timothy 1:15)
Count on it!

his hair were white like wool, as white as snow. And his eyes were like flames of fire. [15]His feet were like polished bronze refined in a furnace, and his voice thundered like mighty ocean waves. [16]He held seven stars in his right hand, and a sharp two-edged sword came from his mouth. And his face was like the sun in all its brilliance.

[17]When I saw him, I fell at his feet as if I were dead.

STAND POINT

When you face death
1:18
I am the living one. I died, but look—I am alive forever and ever! And I hold the keys of death and the grave.

But he laid his right hand on me and said, "Don't be afraid! I am the First and the Last. [18]I am the living one. I died, but look—I am alive forever and ever! And I hold the keys of death and the grave.

[19]"Write down what you have seen—both the things that are now happening and the things that will happen. [20]This is the meaning of the mystery of the seven stars you saw in my right hand and the seven gold lampstands: The seven stars are the angels of the seven churches, and the seven lampstands are the seven churches.

action

2:2-7 WHAT'S IT SAYING?

WHAT AM I GOING TO DO ABOUT IT?

The Message to the Church in Ephesus

2

"Write this letter to the angel of the church in Ephesus. This is the message from the one who holds the seven stars in his right hand, the one who walks among the seven gold lampstands:

[2]"I know all the things you do. I have seen your hard work and your patient endurance. I know you don't tolerate evil people. You have examined the claims of those who say they are apostles but are not. You have discovered they are liars. [3]You have patiently suffered for me without quitting.

4"But I have this complaint against you. You don't love me or each other as you did at first! 5Look how far you have fallen! Turn back to me and do the works you did at first. If you don't repent, I will come and remove your lampstand from its place among the churches. 6But this is in your favor: You hate the evil deeds of the Nicolaitans, just as I do.

7"Anyone with ears to hear must listen to the Spirit and understand what he is saying to the churches. To everyone who is victorious I will give fruit from the tree of life in the paradise of God.

The Message to the Church in Smyrna

8"Write this letter to the angel of the church in Smyrna. This is the message from the one who is the First and the Last, who was dead but is now alive:

9"I know about your suffering and your poverty— but you are rich! I know the blasphemy of those opposing you. They say they are Jews, but they are not, because their synagogue belongs to Satan. 10Don't be afraid of what you are about to suffer. The devil will throw some of you into prison to test you. You will suffer for ten days. But if you remain faithful even when facing death, I will give you the crown of life.

11"Anyone with ears to hear must listen to the Spirit and understand what he is saying to the churches. Whoever is victorious will not be harmed by the second death.

The Message to the Church in Pergamum

12"Write this letter to the angel of the church in Pergamum. This is the message from the one with the sharp two-edged sword:

13"I know that you live in the city where Satan has his throne, yet you have remained loyal to me. You refused to deny me even when Antipas, my faithful witness, was martyred among you there in Satan's city.

14"But I have a few complaints against you. You tolerate some among you whose teaching is like that of Balaam, who showed Balak how to trip up the people of Israel. He taught them to sin by eating food offered to idols and by committing sexual sin. 15In a similar way, you have some Nicolaitans among you who follow the same teaching. 16Repent of your sin, or I will come to you suddenly and fight against them with the sword of my mouth.

17"Anyone with ears to hear must listen to the Spirit and understand what he is saying to the churches. To everyone who is victorious I will give some of the manna that has been hidden away in heaven. And I

Give it to God: When anything starts to bug you — anything — ask God for help. There is nothing too big or small for him to help you with. Worry should be an alarm ringing in your head to remind you to pray. "Don't worry about anything; instead, pray about everything. Tell God what you need, and thank him for all he has done. Then you will experience God's peace, which exceeds anything we can understand. His peace will guard your hearts and minds as you live in Christ Jesus." (Philippians 4:6-7)

Who are the five coolest athletes under pressure?

1
2
3
4
5

BIG FIVE

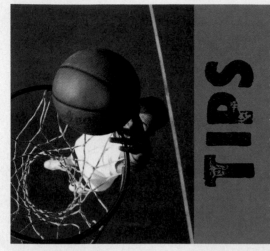

How to improve your anticipation:

Good anticipation is a primary reason why great players make their game look so easy. They always seem to be moving in the right direction toward their opponents' shots and rarely seem surprised by what is happening in competition. Many players think of anticipation as knowing exactly what type of delivery will come at them. Anticipation is not so much knowing the exact shot your opponent is about to throw you, but reducing the possibilities to a few of the likeliest ones. This comes with time and experience. Watch professionals, your opponents, and teammates compete. Don't just watch the game — put yourself in their shoes; feel their footwork and their responses. You will soon learn that there are only a few realistic options that will come at you.

will give to each one a white stone, and on the stone will be engraved a new name that no one understands except the one who receives it.

The Message to the Church in Thyatira

[18]"Write this letter to the angel of the church in Thyatira. This is the message from the Son of God, whose eyes are like flames of fire, whose feet are like polished bronze:
[19]"I know all the things you do. I have seen your love, your faith, your service, and your patient endurance. And I can see your constant improvement in all these things.
[20]"But I have this complaint against you. You are permitting that woman—that Jezebel who calls herself a prophet—to lead my servants astray. She teaches them to commit sexual sin and to eat food offered to idols. [21]I gave her time to repent, but she does not want to turn away from her immorality.
[22]"Therefore, I will throw her on a bed of suffering, and those who commit adultery with her will suffer greatly unless they repent and turn away from her evil deeds. [23]I will strike her children dead. Then all the churches will know that I am the one who searches out the thoughts and intentions of every person. And I will give to each of you whatever you deserve.
[24]"But I also have a message for the rest of you in Thyatira who have not followed this false teaching ('deeper truths,' as they call them—depths of Satan, actually). I will ask nothing more of you [25]except that you hold tightly to what you have until I come. [26]To all who are victorious, who obey me to the very end,
To them I will give authority over all the nations.
[27]They will rule the nations with an iron rod
and smash them like clay pots.
[28]They will have the same authority I received from my Father, and I will also give them the morning star!
[29]"Anyone with ears to hear must listen to the Spirit and understand what he is saying to the churches.

The Message to the Church in Sardis

3

"Write this letter to the angel of the church in Sardis. This is the message from the one who has the sevenfold Spirit of God and the seven stars:
"I know all the things you do, and that you have a reputation for being alive—but you are dead. [2]Wake up! Strengthen what little remains, for even what is left is almost dead. I find that your actions do not meet the requirements of my God. [3]Go back to what you heard and believed at first; hold to it firmly. Repent and turn to me again. If you don't wake up, I will come to you suddenly, as unexpected as a thief.
[4]"Yet there are some in the church in Sardis who have not soiled their clothes with evil. They will walk with me in white, for they are worthy. [5]All who are victorious will be clothed in white. I will never erase their names from the Book of Life, but I will announce before my Father and his angels that they are mine.

Volleyball was invented by William George Morgan of Holyoke, Massachusetts, in 1895, for the Young Men's Christian Association.

[6]"Anyone with ears to hear must listen to the Spirit and understand what he is saying to the churches.

The Message to the Church in Philadelphia

[7]"Write this letter to the angel of the church in Philadelphia.
This is the message from the one who is holy and true, the one who has the key of David.
What he opens, no one can close;
and what he closes, no one can open.
[8]"I know all the things you do, and I have opened a door for you that no one can close. You have little strength, yet you obeyed my word and did not deny me. [9]Look, I will force those who belong to Satan's synagogue—those liars who say they are Jews but are not—to come and bow down at your feet. They will acknowledge that you are the ones I love.
[10]"Because you have obeyed my command to persevere, I will protect you from the great time of testing that will come upon the whole world to test those who belong to this world. [11]I am coming soon. Hold on to what you have, so that no one will take away your crown. [12]All who are victorious will become pillars in the Temple of my God, and they will never have to leave it. And I will write on them the name of my God, and they will be citizens in the city of my God—the new Jerusalem that comes down from heaven from my God. And I will also write on them my new name.
[13]"Anyone with ears to hear must listen to the Spirit and understand what he is saying to the churches.

The Message to the Church in Laodicea

[14]"Write this letter to the angel of the church in

Laodicea. This is the message from the one who is the Amen—the faithful and true witness, the beginning of God's new creation:

[15]"I know all the things you do, that you are neither hot nor cold. I wish that you were one or the other! [16]But since you are like lukewarm water, neither hot nor cold, I will spit you out of my mouth! [17]You say, 'I am rich. I have everything I want. I don't need a thing!' And you don't realize that you are wretched and miserable and poor and blind and naked. [18]So I advise you to buy gold from me—gold that has been purified by fire. Then you will be rich. Also buy white garments from me so you will not be shamed by your nakedness, and ointment for your eyes so you will be able to see. [19]I correct and discipline everyone I love. So be diligent and turn from your indifference.

[20]"Look! I stand at the door and knock. If you hear my voice and open the door, I will come in, and we will share a meal together as friends. [21]Those who are victorious will sit with me on my throne, just as I was victorious and sat with my Father on his throne.

[22]"Anyone with ears to hear must listen to the Spirit and understand what he is saying to the churches."

Worship in Heaven

4

Then as I looked, I saw a door standing open in heaven, and the same voice I had heard before spoke to me like a trumpet blast. The voice said, "Come up here, and I will show you what must happen after this." [2]And instantly I was in the Spirit, and I saw a throne in heaven and someone sitting on it. [3]The one sitting on the throne was as brilliant as gemstones—like jasper and carnelian. And the glow of an emerald circled his throne like a rainbow. [4]Twenty-four thrones surrounded him, and twenty-four elders sat on them. They were all clothed in white and had gold crowns on their heads. [5]From the throne came flashes of lightning and the rumble of thunder. And in front of the throne were seven torches with burning flames. This is the sevenfold Spirit of God. [6]In front of the throne was a shiny sea of glass, sparkling like crystal. In the center and around the throne were four living beings, each covered with eyes, front and back. [7]The first of these living beings was like a lion; the second was like an ox; the third had a human face; and the fourth was like an eagle in flight. [8]Each of these living beings had six wings, and their wings were covered all over with eyes, inside and out. Day after day and night after night they keep on saying,

"Holy, holy, holy is the Lord God, the Almighty—
the one who always was, who is, and who is still to come."

[9]Whenever the living beings give glory and honor and thanks to the one sitting on the throne (the one who lives forever and ever), [10]the twenty-four elders fall down and worship the one sitting on the throne (the one who lives forever and ever). And they lay their crowns before the throne and say,

[11]"You are worthy, O Lord our God,
to receive glory and honor and power.
For you created all things,
and they exist because you created what you pleased."

5:1-14 WHAT'S IT SAYING?

WHAT AM I GOING TO DO ABOUT IT?

The Lamb Opens the Scroll

5

Then I saw a scroll in the right hand of the one who was sitting on the throne. There was writing on the inside and the outside of the scroll, and it was sealed with seven seals. [2]And I saw a strong angel, who shouted with a loud voice: "Who is worthy to break the seals on this scroll and open it?" [3]But no one in heaven or on earth or under the earth was able to open the scroll and read it.

profiles

David:

1 Samuel 17:45: "David replied to the Philistine, 'You come to me with sword, spear, and javelin, but I come to you in the name of the LORD of Heaven's Armies.'" If you were to write a story for your own religion you would not show yourself and your colleagues constantly failing. But the Bible was written by God, not men, and God allows us to see that he will use flawed but faithful people for great things. David was fearless in the face of seemingly great odds. Have you ever faced a struggle that was apparently impossible to overcome? David faced these struggles over and over, but instead of relying on his own strength he relied on God. Samuel, a high priest and a prophet, was commissioned by God to find a good king to lead the Israelites. 1 Samuel 16:7: "But the Lord said to Samuel, 'Don't judge by his appearance or height, for I have rejected him. The Lord doesn't see things the way you see them. People judge by outward appearance, but the Lord looks at the heart.'" David was a shepherd, a poet, a giant-killer, a king, and a commander. But his failures include liar, adulterer, and murderer. He learned from his mistakes. The consequences of his sin were painful, but the joy of his life was glorious.

Should Christians consider themselves better or superior to those who aren't?
Of course not. We should consider ourselves as beggars who have found a lasting source of food. Christians should be aware of their shortcomings. The classic answer to "I don't want to go to church — it is full of hypocrites" should be, "No it's not — there is always room for one more!" How do we know it is full of hypocrites? Because we are flawed people, falling down in our faith every day. Fortunately, we have a perfect Redeemer.

⁴Then I began to weep bitterly because no one was found worthy to open the scroll and read it. ⁵But one of the twenty-four elders said to me, "Stop weeping! Look, the Lion of the tribe of Judah, the heir to David's throne, has won the victory. He is worthy to open the scroll and its seven seals."

⁶Then I saw a Lamb that looked as if it had been slaughtered, but it was now standing between the throne and the four living beings and among the twenty-four elders. He had seven horns and seven eyes, which represent the sevenfold Spirit of God that is sent out into every part of the earth. ⁷He stepped forward and took the scroll from the right hand of the one sitting on the throne. ⁸And when he took the scroll, the four living beings and the twenty-four elders fell down before the Lamb. Each one had a harp, and they held gold bowls filled with incense, which are the prayers of God's people. ⁹And they sang a new song with these words:

"You are worthy to take the scroll
and break its seals and open it.
For you were slaughtered, and your blood has ransomed people for God
from every tribe and language and people and nation.
¹⁰And you have caused them to become
a Kingdom of priests for our God.
And they will reign on the earth."

¹¹Then I looked again, and I heard the voices of thousands and millions of angels around the throne and of the living beings and the elders. ¹²And they sang in a mighty chorus:

"Worthy is the Lamb who was slaughtered—
to receive power and riches

Revelation, written about AD 95, is the youngest book in the New Testament.

and wisdom and strength
and honor and glory and blessing."

¹³And then I heard every creature in heaven and on earth and under the earth and in the sea. They sang:

"Blessing and honor and glory and power
belong to the one sitting on the throne
and to the Lamb forever and ever."

¹⁴And the four living beings said, "Amen!" And the twenty-four elders fell down and worshiped the Lamb.

The Lamb Breaks the First Six Seals

6

As I watched, the Lamb broke the first of the seven seals on the scroll. Then I heard one of the four living beings say with a voice like thunder, "Come!" ²I looked up and saw a white horse standing there. Its rider carried a bow, and a crown was placed on his head. He rode out to win many battles and gain the victory. ³When the Lamb broke the second seal, I heard the second living being say, "Come!" ⁴Then another horse appeared, a red one. Its rider was given a mighty sword and the authority to take peace from the earth. And there was war and slaughter everywhere.

⁵When the Lamb broke the third seal, I heard the third living being say, "Come!" I looked up and saw a black horse, and its rider was holding a pair of scales in his hand. ⁶And I heard a voice from among the four living beings say, "A loaf of wheat bread or three loaves of barley will cost a day's pay. And don't waste the olive oil and wine."

⁷When the Lamb broke the fourth seal, I heard the fourth living being say, "Come!" ⁸I looked up and saw a horse whose color was pale green. Its rider was named Death, and his companion was the Grave. These two were given authority over one-fourth of the earth, to kill with the sword and famine and disease and wild animals.

⁹When the Lamb broke the fifth seal, I saw under the altar the souls of all who had been martyred for the word of God and for being faithful in their testimony. ¹⁰They shouted to the Lord and said, "O Sovereign Lord, holy and true, how long before you judge the people who belong to this world and avenge our blood for what they have done to us?" ¹¹Then a white robe was given to each of them. And they were told to rest a little longer until the full number of their brothers and sisters—their fellow servants of Jesus who were to be martyred—had joined them.

¹²I watched as the Lamb broke the sixth seal, and there was a great earthquake. The sun became as dark as black cloth, and the moon became as red as blood. ¹³Then the stars of the sky fell to the earth like green figs falling from a tree shaken by a strong wind. ¹⁴The sky was rolled up like a scroll, and all of the mountains and islands were moved from their places.

¹⁵Then everyone—the kings of the earth, the rulers, the generals, the wealthy, the powerful, and every slave and free person—all hid themselves in the caves and among the rocks of the mountains. ¹⁶And they cried to the mountains and the rocks, "Fall on us and hide us from the face of the one who sits on the throne and from the wrath of the Lamb. ¹⁷For the great day of their wrath has come, and who is able to survive?"

God's People Will Be Preserved

7

Then I saw four angels standing at the four corners of the earth, holding back the four winds so they did not

WHAT

DOES IT MEAN?

judgment

Judgment is the sentence that will be passed on our actions at the last day (Matthew 25; Romans 14:10-11; 2 Corinthians 5:10; 2 Thessalonians 1:7-10). The judge is Jesus Christ. All judgment is committed to him (Acts 17:31; John 5:22, 27; Revelation 1:7). The people to be judged are the whole race of Adam, without a single exception (Matthew 25:31 46; 1 Corinthians 15:51-52; Revelation 20:11-15) and the fallen angels (2 Peter 2:4; Jude 1:6). The rule of judgment is the standard of God's law as revealed to humans and written on their hearts (Luke 12:47-48; Romans 2:12-16). Since the Scriptures represent the final judgment as certain, universal, decisive, and having eternal consequences (Hebrews 6:2), let us be concerned for the welfare of our immortal interests and the interests of our friends. Let's run to Jesus' mercy, make the most of our time on earth, rely on Jesus' faithfulness to change us, and stick close to his commands.

blow on the earth or the sea, or even on any tree. [2]And I saw another angel coming up from the east, carrying the seal of the living God. And he shouted to those four angels, who had been given power to harm land and sea, [3]"Wait! Don't harm the land or the sea or the trees until we have placed the seal of God on the foreheads of his servants."

[4]And I heard how many were marked with the seal of God—144,000 were sealed from all the tribes of Israel:

[5]	from Judah	12,000
	from Reuben	12,000
	from Gad	12,000
[6]	from Asher	12,000
	from Naphtali	12,000
	from Manasseh	12,000
[7]	from Simeon	12,000
	from Levi	12,000
	from Issachar	12,000
[8]	from Zebulun	12,000
	from Joseph	12,000
	from Benjamin	12,000

Praise from the Great Crowd

[9]After this I saw a vast crowd, too great to count, from every nation and tribe and people and language, standing in front of the throne and before the Lamb. They were clothed in white robes and held palm branches in their hands. [10]And they were shouting with a mighty shout,

"Salvation comes from our God who sits on the throne and from the Lamb!"

[11]And all the angels were standing around the throne and around the elders and the four living beings. And they fell before the throne with their faces to the ground and worshiped God. [12]They sang,

"Amen! Blessing and glory and wisdom
and thanksgiving and honor
and power and strength belong to our God
forever and ever! Amen."

[13]Then one of the twenty-four elders asked me, "Who are these who are clothed in white? Where did they come from?"

[14]And I said to him, "Sir, you are the one who knows." Then he said to me, "These are the ones who died in the great tribulation. They have washed their robes in the blood of the Lamb and made them white. [15]"That is why they stand in front of God's throne and serve him day and night in his Temple. And he who sits on the throne will give them shelter. [16]They will never again be hungry or thirsty;

they will never be scorched by the heat of the sun. [17]For the Lamb on the throne
will be their Shepherd.
He will lead them to springs of life-giving water.
And God will wipe every tear from their eyes."

The Lamb Breaks the Seventh Seal

8

When the Lamb broke the seventh seal on the scroll, there was silence throughout heaven for about half an hour. [2]I saw the seven angels who stand before God, and they were given seven trumpets.

[3]Then another angel with a gold incense burner came and stood at the altar. And a great amount of incense was given to him to mix with the prayers of God's people as an offering on the gold altar before the throne. [4]The smoke of the incense, mixed with the prayers of God's holy people, ascended up to God from the altar where the angel had poured them out. [5]Then the angel filled the incense burner with fire from the altar and threw it down upon the earth; and thunder crashed, lightning flashed, and there was a terrible earthquake.

The First Four Trumpets

[6]Then the seven angels with the seven trumpets prepared to blow their mighty blasts.

[7]The first angel blew his trumpet, and hail and fire mixed with blood were thrown down on the earth. One-third of the earth was set on fire, one-third of the trees were burned, and all the green grass was burned.

[8]Then the second angel blew his trumpet, and a great mountain of fire was thrown into the sea. One-third of the water in the sea became blood, [9]one-third of all things living in the sea died, and one-third of all the ships on the sea were destroyed.

When you need guidance

7:17

For the Lamb on the throne will be their Shepherd. He will lead them to springs of life-giving water. And God will wipe every tear from their eyes.

[10]Then the third angel blew his trumpet, and a great star fell from the sky, burning like a torch. It fell on one-third of the rivers and on the springs of water. [11]The name of the star was Bitterness. It made one-third of the water bitter, and many people died from drinking the bitter water.

[12]Then the fourth angel blew his trumpet, and one-third of the sun was struck, and one-third of the moon, and one-third of the stars, and they became dark. And one-third of the day was dark, and also one-third of the night.

[13]Then I looked, and I heard a single eagle crying loudly as it flew through the air, "Terror, terror, terror to all who belong to this world because of what will happen when the last three angels blow their trumpets."

The Fifth Trumpet Brings the First Terror

9

Then the fifth angel blew his trumpet, and I saw a star that had fallen to earth from the sky, and he was given the key to the shaft of the bottomless pit. [2]When he opened it, smoke poured out as though from a huge furnace, and the sunlight and air turned dark from the smoke.

[3]Then locusts came from the smoke and descended on the earth, and they were given power to sting like scorpions. [4]They were told not to harm the grass or plants or trees, but only the people who did not have the seal of God on their foreheads. [5]They were told not to kill them but to torture them for five months with pain like the pain of a scorpion sting. [6]In those days people will seek death but will not find it. They will long to die, but death will flee from them!

[7]The locusts looked like horses prepared for battle. They had what looked like gold crowns on their heads, and their faces

STAND POINT

When you feel like procrastinating

10:6

He swore an oath in the name of the one who lives forever and ever, who created the heavens and everything in them, the earth and everything in it, and the sea and everything in it. He said, "There will be no more delay."

count on it

Hang on to the power!

In the Christian life, like water-skiing, you have to hang onto the rope — the power. It is not your power that will make you fly, it is God's! God's power is what will give you life. You will be pulled out of polluted water and your skill will improve, but Christ is the only source of power that pulls you out of your sin and evil. "Let us hold tightly without wavering to the hope we affirm, for God can be trusted to keep his promise." (Hebrews 10:23)
Count on it!

looked like human faces. [8]They had hair like women's hair and teeth like the teeth of a lion. [9]They wore armor made of iron, and their wings roared like an army of chariots rushing into battle. [10]They had tails that stung like scorpions, and for five months they had the power to torment people. [11]Their king is the angel from the bottomless pit; his name in Hebrew is *Abaddon*, and in Greek, *Apollyon*—the Destroyer.

[12]The first terror is past, but look, two more terrors are coming!

The Sixth Trumpet Brings the Second Terror

[13]Then the sixth angel blew his trumpet, and I heard a voice speaking from the four horns of the gold altar that stands in the presence of God. [14]And the voice said to the sixth angel who held the trumpet, "Release

the four angels who are bound at the great Euphrates River." [15]Then the four angels who had been prepared for this hour and day and month and year were turned loose to kill one-third of all the people on earth. [16]I heard the size of their army, which was 200 million mounted troops.

[17]And in my vision, I saw the horses and the riders sitting on them. The riders wore armor that was fiery red and dark blue and yellow. The horses had heads like lions, and fire and smoke and burning sulfur billowed from their mouths. [18]One-third of all the people on earth were killed by these three plagues—by the fire and smoke and burning sulfur that came from the mouths of the horses. [19]Their power was in their mouths and in their tails. For their tails had heads like snakes, with the power to injure people. [20]But the people who did not die in these plagues still refused to repent of their evil deeds and turn to God. They continued to worship demons and idols made of gold, silver, bronze, stone, and wood—idols that can neither see nor hear nor walk! [21]And they did not repent of their murders or their witchcraft or their sexual immorality or their thefts.

The Angel and the Small Scroll

10

Then I saw another mighty angel coming down from heaven, surrounded by a cloud, with a rainbow over his head. His face shone like the sun, and his feet were like pillars of fire. [2]And in his hand was a small scroll that had been opened. He stood with his right foot on the sea and his left foot on the land. [3]And he gave a great shout like the roar of a lion. And when he shouted, the seven thunders answered.

[4]When the seven thunders spoke, I was about to write. But I heard a voice from heaven saying, "Keep secret what the seven thunders said, and do not write it down."

[5]Then the angel I saw standing on the sea and on the land raised his right hand toward heaven. [6]He swore an oath in the name of the one who lives forever and ever, who created the heavens and everything in them, the earth and everything in it, and the sea and everything in it. He said, "There will be no more delay.
[7]When the seventh angel blows his trumpet, God's mysterious plan will be fulfilled. It will happen just as he announced it to his servants the prophets."

[8]Then the voice from heaven spoke to me again: "Go and take the open scroll from the hand of the angel

Winners have that touch!

Self-control: temperance; the skill of taking things only as far as is appropriate. Imagine: Tiger Woods drops the ball six feet from the ninth hole at St. Andrews golf course. He walks up to the green, pulls out a wood, and blasts the ball into the North Sea! That is intemperance! God gave us good things to enjoy, not to abuse. We can be intemperate about so many things: sports, clothes, work, sex. Yes, there are certain things that are prohibited and things that are to be done only within God's plan. There are certain things that are better to stay away from because they will influence or discourage others. Self-control is the attitude of keeping yourself together: to stay on God's path and enjoy the journey he has for you. **"Take hold of my instructions; don't let them go. Guard them, for they are the key to life."** (Proverbs 4:13)

Winners have self-control!

who is standing on the sea and on the land."
⁹So I went to the angel and told him to give me the small scroll. "Yes, take it and eat it," he said. "It will be sweet as honey in your mouth, but it will turn sour in your stomach!" ¹⁰So I took the small scroll from the hand of the angel, and I ate it! It was sweet in my mouth, but when I swallowed it, it turned sour in my stomach.
¹¹Then I was told, "You must prophesy again about many peoples, nations, languages, and kings."

The Two Witnesses

11

Then I was given a measuring stick, and I was told, "Go and measure the Temple of God and the altar, and count the number of worshipers. ²But do not measure the outer courtyard, for it has been turned over to the nations. They will trample the holy city for 42 months. ³And I will give power to my two witnesses, and they will be clothed in burlap and will prophesy during those 1,260 days."
⁴These two prophets are the two olive trees and the two lampstands that stand before the Lord of all the earth. ⁵If anyone tries to harm them, fire flashes from their mouths and consumes their enemies. This is how anyone who tries to harm them must die. ⁶They have power to shut the sky so that no rain will fall for as long as they prophesy. And they have the power to turn the rivers and oceans into blood, and to strike the earth with every kind of plague as often as they wish.
⁷When they complete their testimony, the beast that

comes up out of the bottomless pit will declare war against them, and he will conquer them and kill them. ⁸And their bodies will lie in the main street of Jerusalem, the city that is figuratively called "Sodom" and "Egypt," the city where their Lord was crucified. ⁹And for three and a half days, all peoples, tribes, languages, and nations will stare at their bodies. No one will be allowed to bury them. ¹⁰All the people who belong to this world will gloat over them and give presents to each other to celebrate the death of the two prophets who had tormented them.
¹¹But after three and a half days, God breathed life into them, and they stood up! Terror struck all who were staring at them. ¹²Then a loud voice from heaven called to the two prophets, "Come up here!" And they

The very first Olympic race, held in 776 BC, was won by Corubus, a chef.
•
About 42,000 tennis balls are used in the 650 or so matches in the Wimbledon Championship.

rose to heaven in a cloud as their enemies watched.
¹³At the same time there was a terrible earthquake that destroyed a tenth of the city. Seven thousand people died in that earthquake, and everyone else was terrified and gave glory to the God of heaven.
¹⁴The second terror is past, but look, the third terror is coming quickly.

The Seventh Trumpet Brings the Third Terror

¹⁵Then the seventh angel blew his trumpet, and there were loud voices shouting in heaven:
"The world has now become the Kingdom of our Lord and of his Christ,
and he will reign forever and ever."
¹⁶The twenty-four elders sitting on their thrones before God fell with their faces to the ground and worshiped him. ¹⁷And they said,
"We give thanks to you, Lord God, the Almighty,
the one who is and who always was,
for now you have assumed your great power
and have begun to reign.
¹⁸The nations were filled with wrath,
but now the time of your wrath has come.
It is time to judge the dead
and reward your servants the prophets,
as well as your holy people,
and all who fear your name,
from the least to the greatest.
It is time to destroy
all who have caused destruction on the earth."
¹⁹Then, in heaven, the Temple of God was opened and the Ark

of his covenant could be seen inside the Temple. Lightning flashed, thunder crashed and roared, and there was an earthquake and a terrible hailstorm.

The Woman and the Dragon

12

Then I witnessed in heaven an event of great significance. I saw a woman clothed with the sun, with the moon beneath her feet, and a crown of twelve stars on her head. [2]She was pregnant, and she cried out because of her labor pains and the agony of giving birth.

[3]Then I witnessed in heaven another significant event. I saw a large red dragon with seven heads and ten horns, with seven crowns on his heads. [4]His tail swept away one-third of the stars in the sky, and he threw them to the earth. He stood in front of the woman as she was about to give birth, ready to devour her baby as soon as it was born.

[5]She gave birth to a son who was to rule all nations with an iron rod. And her child was snatched away from the dragon and was caught up to God and to his throne. [6]And the woman fled into the wilderness, where God had prepared a place to care for her for 1,260 days.

[7]Then there was war in heaven. Michael and his angels fought against the dragon and his angels. [8]And the dragon lost the battle, and he and his angels were forced out of heaven. [9]This great dragon—the ancient serpent called the devil, or Satan, the one deceiving the whole world—was thrown down to the earth with all his angels.

[10]Then I heard a loud voice shouting across the heavens,

"It has come at last—
salvation and power
and the Kingdom of our God,
and the authority of his Christ.
For the accuser of our brothers and sisters
has been thrown down to earth—
the one who accuses them
before our God day and night.
[11]And they have defeated him by the blood of the Lamb
and by their testimony.
And they did not love their lives so much
that they were afraid to die.
[12]Therefore, rejoice, O heavens!
And you who live in the heavens, rejoice!
But terror will come on the earth and the sea,
for the devil has come down to you in great anger,
knowing that he has little time."

[13]When the dragon realized that he had been thrown down to the earth, he pursued the woman who had given birth to the male child. [14]But she was given two wings like those of a great eagle so she could fly to the place prepared for her in the wilderness. There she would be cared for and protected

from the dragon for a time, times, and half a time. [15]Then the dragon tried to drown the woman with a flood of water that flowed from his mouth. [16]But the earth helped her by opening its mouth and swallowing the river that gushed out from the mouth of the dragon. [17]And the dragon was angry at the woman and declared war against the rest of her children—all who keep God's commandments and maintain their testimony for Jesus.

[18]Then the dragon took his stand on the shore beside the sea.

13:3-10 WHAT'S IT SAYING?

WHAT AM I GOING TO DO ABOUT IT?

The Beast out of the Sea

13

Then I saw a beast rising up out of the sea. It had seven heads and ten horns, with ten crowns on its horns. And written on each head were names that blasphemed God. [2]This beast looked like a leopard, but it had the feet of a bear and the mouth of a lion! And the dragon gave the beast his own power and throne and great authority.

[3]I saw that one of the heads of the beast seemed wounded beyond recovery—but the fatal wound was healed! The whole world marveled at this miracle and

gave allegiance to the beast. [4]They worshiped the dragon for giving the beast such power, and they also worshiped the beast. "Who is as great as the beast?" they exclaimed. "Who is able to fight against him?" [5]Then the beast was allowed to speak great blasphemies against God. And he was given authority to do whatever he wanted for forty-two months. [6]And he spoke terrible words of blasphemy against God, slandering his name and his temple—that is, those who live in heaven. [7]And the beast was allowed to wage war against God's holy people and to conquer them. And he was given authority to rule over every tribe and people and language and nation. [8]And all the people who belong to this world worshiped the beast. They are the ones whose names were not written in the Book of Life before the world was made—the Book that belongs to the Lamb who was slaughtered.

[9]Anyone with ears to hear
should listen and understand.
[10]Anyone who is destined for prison
will be taken to prison.
Anyone destined to die by the sword
will die by the sword.

This means that God's holy people must endure persecution patiently and remain faithful.

The Beast out of the Earth

[11]Then I saw another beast come up out of the earth. He had two horns like those of a lamb, but he spoke with the voice of a dragon. [12]He exercised all the authority of the first beast. And he required all the earth and its people to worship the first beast, whose fatal wound had been healed. [13]He did astounding miracles, even making fire flash down to earth from the sky while everyone was watching. [14]And with all the miracles he was allowed to perform on behalf of the first beast, he deceived all the people who belong to this world. He ordered the people to make a great statue of the first beast, who was fatally wounded and then came back to life. [15]He was then permitted to give life to this statue so that it could speak. Then

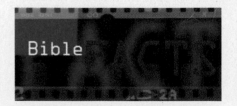

In Old Testament times the Mediterranean Sea was called the Great Sea.

14:12

STAND POINT

When you need endurance

14:12

This means that God's holy people must endure persecution patiently, obeying his commands and maintaining their faith in Jesus.

name of the beast or the number representing his name. [18]Wisdom is needed here. Let the one with understanding solve the meaning of the number of the beast, for it is the number of a man. His number is 666.

The Lamb and the 144,000

14

Then I saw the Lamb standing on Mount Zion, and with him were 144,000 who had his name and his Father's name written on their foreheads. [2]And I heard a sound from heaven like the roar of mighty ocean waves or the rolling of loud thunder. It was like the sound of many harpists playing together.

[3]This great choir sang a wonderful new song in front of the throne of God and before the four living beings and the twenty-four elders. No one could learn this song except the 144,000 who had been redeemed from the earth. [4]They have kept themselves as pure as virgins, following the Lamb wherever he goes. They have been purchased from among the people on the earth as a special offering to God and to the Lamb. [5]They have told no lies; they are without blame.

The Three Angels

[6]And I saw another angel flying through the sky, carrying the eternal Good News to proclaim to the people who belong to this world—to every nation, tribe, language, and people.

the statue of the beast commanded that anyone refusing to worship it must die.

[16]He required everyone—small and great, rich and poor, free and slave—to be given a mark on the right hand or on the forehead. [17]And no one could buy or sell anything without that mark, which was either the

Tactical knowledge:

TIPS

Players should develop a broad tactical understanding of the game to quickly assess situations on the field and make the correct choices for their team. Rigid team roles and positions will not succeed in the future; therefore, players will be required to be flexible in where and how they play.

⁷"Fear God," he shouted. "Give glory to him. For the time has come when he will sit as judge. Worship him who made the heavens, the earth, the sea, and all the springs of water."

⁸Then another angel followed him through the sky, shouting, "Babylon is fallen—that great city is fallen—because she made all the nations of the world drink the wine of her passionate immorality."

⁹Then a third angel followed them, shouting, "Anyone who worships the beast and his statue or who accepts his mark on the forehead or on the hand ¹⁰must drink the wine of God's anger. It has been poured full strength into God's cup of wrath. And they will be tormented with fire and burning sulfur in the presence of the holy angels and the Lamb. ¹¹The smoke of their torment will rise forever and ever, and they will have no relief day or night, for they have worshiped the beast and his statue and have accepted the mark of his name."

¹²This means that God's holy people must endure persecution patiently, obeying his commands and maintaining their faith in Jesus.

¹³And I heard a voice from heaven saying, "Write this down: Blessed are those who die in the Lord from now on. Yes, says the Spirit, they are blessed indeed, for they will rest from their hard work; for their good deeds follow them!"

The Harvest of the Earth

¹⁴Then I saw a white cloud, and seated on the cloud was someone like the Son of Man. He had a gold crown on his head and a sharp sickle in his hand.

¹⁵Then another angel came from the Temple and shouted to the one sitting on the cloud, "Swing the sickle, for the time of harvest has come; the crop on earth is ripe." ¹⁶So the one sitting on the cloud swung his sickle over the earth, and the whole earth was harvested.

¹⁷After that, another angel came from the Temple in heaven, and he also had a sharp sickle. ¹⁸Then another angel, who had power to destroy with fire, came from the altar. He shouted to the angel with the sharp sickle, "Swing your sickle now to gather the clusters of grapes from the vines of the earth, for they are ripe for judgment." ¹⁹So the angel swung his sickle over the earth and loaded the grapes into the great winepress of God's wrath. ²⁰The grapes were trampled in the winepress outside the city, and blood flowed from the winepress in a stream about 180 miles long and as high as a horse's bridle.

The Song of Moses and of the Lamb

15

Then I saw in heaven another marvelous event of great significance. Seven angels were holding the seven last plagues, which would bring God's wrath to completion. ²I saw before

WHAT

DOES IT MEAN?

Bethlehem and Nazareth

Jesus' birthplace and hometown. The birth of our Lord took place at the time and town predicted by the Old Testament prophets. Joseph and Mary were providentially led to go up to Bethlehem because Joseph was a descendant of King David and had to register for an official census in Bethlehem. He traveled with his fiancée, Mary, who was heavily pregnant, and there the baby Jesus was born. (For more on Jesus' birth, read Matthew 2 and Luke 2.)

Though Jesus was destined to be born in Bethlehem, he was raised approximately 60 miles to the north in the town of Nazareth, in the region of Galilee. This was the home of Joseph and Mary (Luke 2:39), and here the angel announced to the virgin the birth of the Christ (Luke 1:26-28). Jesus grew up from his infancy to manhood (Luke 4:16) and here he began his public ministry in the synagogue (Matthew 13:54).

me what seemed to be a glass sea mixed with fire. And on it stood all the people who had been victorious over the beast and his statue and the number representing his name. They were all holding harps that God had given them. ³And they were singing the song of Moses, the servant of God, and the song of the Lamb:

"Great and marvelous are your works,
O Lord God, the Almighty.
Just and true are your ways,
O King of the nations.
⁴Who will not fear you, Lord,
and glorify your name?
For you alone are holy.
All nations will come and worship before you,
for your righteous deeds have been revealed."

The Seven Bowls of the Seven Plagues

⁵Then I looked and saw that the Temple in heaven, God's Tabernacle, was thrown wide open. ⁶The seven angels who were holding the seven plagues came out of the Temple. They were clothed in spotless white linen with gold sashes across their chests. ⁷Then one of the four living beings handed each of the seven angels a gold bowl filled with the wrath of God, who lives forever and ever. ⁸The Temple was filled with smoke from God's glory and power. No one could enter the Temple until the seven angels had completed pouring out the seven plagues.

16

Then I heard a mighty voice from the Temple say to the seven angels, "Go your ways and pour out on the earth the seven bowls containing God's wrath."

²So the first angel left the Temple and poured out his bowl on the earth, and horrible, malignant sores broke out on everyone who had the mark of the beast and who worshiped his statue.

³Then the second angel poured out his bowl on the sea, and it became like the blood of a corpse. And everything in the sea died.

⁴Then the third angel poured out his bowl on the rivers and springs, and they became blood. ⁵And I heard the angel who had authority over all water saying,

"You are just, O Holy One, who is and who always was, because you have sent these judgments.
⁶Since they shed the blood
of your holy people and your prophets,
you have given them blood to drink.
It is their just reward."

⁷And I heard a voice from the altar, saying,

"Yes, O Lord God, the Almighty,
your judgments are true and just."

[8]Then the fourth angel poured out his bowl on the sun, causing it to scorch everyone with its fire. [9]Everyone was burned by this blast of heat, and they cursed the name of God, who had control over all these plagues. They did not repent of their sins and turn to God and give him glory.

[10]Then the fifth angel poured out his bowl on the throne of the beast, and his kingdom was plunged into darkness. His subjects ground their teeth in anguish, [11]and they cursed the God of heaven for their pains and sores. But they did not repent of their evil deeds and turn to God.

[12]Then the sixth angel poured out his bowl on the great Euphrates River, and it dried up so that the kings from the east could march their armies toward the west without hindrance. [13]And I saw three evil spirits that looked like frogs leap from the mouths of the dragon, the beast, and the false prophet. [14]They are demonic spirits who work miracles and go out to all the rulers of the world to gather them for battle against the Lord on that great judgment day of God the Almighty. [15]"Look, I will come as unexpectedly as a thief! Blessed are all who are watching for me, who keep their clothing ready so they will not have to walk around naked and ashamed."

[16]And the demonic spirits gathered all the rulers and their armies to a place with the Hebrew name *Armageddon*.

[17]Then the seventh angel poured out his bowl into the air. And a mighty shout came from the throne in the Temple, saying, "It is finished!" [18]Then the thunder

An ice skater revolving at 270 revolutions per minute will need 5 full turns a second!

crashed and rolled, and lightning flashed. And a great earthquake struck—the worst since people were placed on the earth. [19]The great city of Babylon split into three sections, and the cities of many nations fell into heaps of rubble. So God remembered all of Babylon's sins, and he made her drink the cup that was filled with the wine of his fierce wrath. [20]And every island disappeared, and all the mountains were leveled. [21]There was a terrible hailstorm, and hailstones weighing seventy-five pounds fell from the sky onto the people below. They cursed God because of the terrible plague of the hailstorm.

The Great Prostitute

17

One of the seven angels who had poured out the seven bowls came over and spoke to me. "Come with me," he said, "and I will show you the judgment that is going to come on the great prostitute, who rules over many waters. [2]The kings of the world have committed adultery with her, and the people who belong to this world have been made drunk by the wine of her immorality."

[3]So the angel took me in the Spirit into the wilderness. There I saw a woman sitting on a scarlet beast that had seven heads and ten horns, and blasphemies against God were written all over it. [4]The woman wore purple and scarlet clothing and beautiful jewelry made of gold and precious gems and pearls. In her hand she held a gold goblet full of obscenities and the impurities of her immorality. [5]A mysterious name was written on her forehead: "Babylon the Great, Mother of All Prostitutes and Obscenities in the World." [6]I could see that she was drunk—drunk with the blood of God's holy people who were witnesses for Jesus. I stared at her in complete amazement.

[7]"Why are you so amazed?" the angel asked. "I will tell you the mystery of this woman and of the beast with seven heads and ten horns on which she sits. [8]The beast you saw was once alive but isn't now. And yet he will soon come up out of the bottomless pit and go to eternal destruction. And the people who belong to this world, whose names were not written in the Book of Life before the world was made, will be amazed at the reappearance of this beast who had died. [9]This calls for a mind with understanding: The seven heads of the beast represent the seven hills where the woman rules. They also represent seven kings. [10]Five kings have already fallen, the sixth now reigns, and the seventh is yet to come, but his reign will be brief.

[11]"The scarlet beast that was, but is no longer, is the eighth king. He is like the other seven, and he, too, is headed for destruction. [12]The ten horns of the beast are ten kings who have not yet risen to power. They will be appointed to their kingdoms for one brief moment to reign with the beast. [13]They

I have faith in Jesus, but how do I answer my friends when they say all religions lead to the same thing?

We are commanded to love everyone, but we are not commanded to believe everyone. Look up John 14:6: "Jesus told him, 'I am the way, the truth, and the life. No one can come to the Father except through me.'" Jesus said he was mutually exclusive (the only way to God): that makes him a liar, a lunatic, or the real deal — the Lord. Many world religions:

- agree that God made the earth and the rules
- agree that mankind broke the rules and the consequence is separation from God
- depart from Christianity at the step needed to get back to God
- say, "Do this, this, and this, and you will attain a higher place in heaven."

Christianity tells us the truth. We will never attain a restored relationship with God from anything we do. **"For everyone has sinned; we all fall short of God's glorious standard" (Romans 3:23).** Yet now God in his gracious kindness declares us not guilty. He has done this through Christ Jesus, who has freed us by taking away our sins. **"For God presented Jesus as the sacrifice for sin" (Romans 3:23-25).**

will all agree to give him their power and authority. [14]Together they will go to war against the Lamb, but the Lamb will defeat them because he is Lord of all lords and King of all kings. And his called and chosen and faithful ones will be with him."

[15]Then the angel said to me, "The waters where the prostitute is ruling represent masses of people of every nation and language. [16]The scarlet beast and his ten horns all hate the prostitute. They will strip her naked, eat her flesh, and burn her remains with fire. [17]For God has put a plan into their minds, a plan that will carry out his purposes. They will agree to give their authority to the scarlet beast, and so the words of God will be fulfilled. [18]And this woman you saw in your vision represents the great city that rules over the kings of the world."

18:1-24 WHAT'S IT SAYING?

WHAT AM I GOING TO DO ABOUT IT?

The Fall of Babylon

18

After all this I saw another angel come down from heaven with great authority, and the earth grew bright with his splendor. [2]He gave a mighty shout:

"Babylon is fallen—that great city is fallen!
She has become a home for demons.
She is a hideout for every foul spirit,
a hideout for every foul vulture
and every foul and dreadful animal.
[3]For all the nations have fallen
because of the wine of her passionate immorality.
The kings of the world
have committed adultery with her.
Because of her desires for extravagant luxury,
the merchants of the world have grown rich."

[4]Then I heard another voice calling from heaven,
"Come away from her, my people.
Do not take part in her sins,
or you will be punished with her.
[5]For her sins are piled as high as heaven,
and God remembers her evil deeds.
[6]Do to her as she has done to others.
Double her penalty for all her evil deeds.
She brewed a cup of terror for others,
so brew twice as much for her.
[7]She glorified herself and lived in luxury,
so match it now with torment and sorrow.
She boasted in her heart,
'I am queen on my throne.
I am no helpless widow,
and I have no reason to mourn.'
[8]Therefore, these plagues will overtake her in a single day—
death and mourning and famine.
She will be completely consumed by fire,
for the Lord God who judges her is mighty."

[9]And the kings of the world who committed adultery with her and enjoyed her great luxury will mourn for her as they see the smoke rising from her charred remains. [10]They will stand at a distance, terrified by her great torment. They will cry out,

"How terrible, how terrible for you,
O Babylon, you great city!
In a single moment
God's judgment came on you."

[11]The merchants of the world will weep and mourn for her, for there is no one left to buy their goods. [12]She bought great quantities of gold, silver, jewels, and pearls; fine linen, purple, silk, and scarlet cloth; things made of fragrant thyine wood, ivory goods, and objects made of expensive wood; and bronze, iron, and marble. [13]She also bought cinnamon, spice, incense, myrrh, frankincense, wine, olive oil, fine flour, wheat, cattle, sheep, horses, chariots, and bodies—that is, human slaves.

[14]"The fancy things you loved so much
are gone," they cry.
"All your luxuries and splendor
are gone forever,
never to be yours again."

[15]The merchants who became wealthy by selling her these things will stand at a distance, terrified by her great torment. They will weep and cry out,

[16]"How terrible, how terrible for that great city!
She was clothed in finest purple and scarlet linens,
decked out with gold and precious stones and pearls!
[17]In a single moment
all the wealth of the city is gone!"

And all the captains of the merchant ships and their passengers and sailors and crews will stand at a distance. [18]They will cry out as they watch the smoke ascend, and they will say, "Where is there another city as great as this?" [19]And they will weep and throw dust on their heads to show their grief. And they will cry out,

"How terrible, how terrible for that great city!
The shipowners became wealthy
by transporting her great wealth on the seas.
In a single moment it is all gone."

[20]Rejoice over her fate, O heaven
and people of God and apostles and prophets!
For at last God has judged her
for your sakes.

[21]Then a mighty angel picked up a boulder the size of a huge millstone. He threw it into the ocean and shouted,

"Just like this, the great city Babylon
will be thrown down with violence
and will never be found again.
[22]The sound of harps, singers, flutes, and trumpets
will never be heard in you again.
No craftsmen and no trades
will ever be found in you again.
The sound of the mill
will never be heard in you again.
[23]The light of a lamp
will never shine in you again.
The happy voices of brides and grooms
will never be heard in you again.
For your merchants were the greatest in the world,
and you deceived the nations with your sorceries.
[24]In your streets flowed the blood of the prophets and of God's holy people
and the blood of people slaughtered all over the world."

Songs of Victory in Heaven

19

After this, I heard what sounded like a vast crowd in

heaven shouting,
"Praise the LORD!
Salvation and glory and power belong to our God.
[2]His judgments are true and just.
He has punished the great prostitute
who corrupted the earth with her immorality.
He has avenged the murder of his servants."
[3]And again their voices rang out:
"Praise the LORD!
The smoke from that city ascends forever and ever!"
[4]Then the twenty-four elders and the four living beings fell down and worshiped God, who was sitting on the throne. They cried out, "Amen! Praise the LORD!"
[5]And from the throne came a voice that said,
"Praise our God,
all his servants,
all who fear him,
from the least to the greatest."
[6]Then I heard again what sounded like the shout of a vast crowd or the roar of mighty ocean waves or the crash of loud thunder:
"Praise the LORD!
For the Lord our God, the Almighty, reigns.
[7]Let us be glad and rejoice,
and let us give honor to him.
For the time has come for the wedding feast of the Lamb,
and his bride has prepared herself.
[8]She has been given the finest of pure white linen to wear."
For the fine linen represents the good deeds of God's holy people.
[9]And the angel said to me, "Write this: Blessed are those who are invited to the wedding feast of the Lamb." And he added, "These are true words that come from God."
[10]Then I fell down at his feet to worship him, but he said, "No, don't worship me. I am a servant of God, just like you and your brothers and sisters who testify about their faith in Jesus. Worship only God. For the essence of prophecy is to give a clear witness for Jesus."

The Rider on the White Horse

[11]Then I saw heaven opened, and a white horse was standing there. Its rider was named Faithful and True, for he judges fairly and wages a righteous war. [12]His eyes were like flames of fire, and on his head were many crowns. A name was written on him that no one understood except himself. [13]He wore a robe dipped in blood, and his title was the Word of God. [14]The armies of heaven, dressed in the finest of pure white linen, followed him on white horses. [15]From his mouth

The Bible, the world's best-selling book, is also the world's most shoplifted book.

came a sharp sword to strike down the nations. He will rule them with an iron rod. He will release the fierce wrath of God, the Almighty, like juice flowing from a winepress. [16]On his robe at his thigh was written this title: King of all kings and Lord of all lords.
[17]Then I saw an angel standing in the sun, shouting to the vultures flying high in the sky: "Come! Gather together for the great banquet God has prepared. [18]Come and eat the flesh of kings, generals, and strong warriors; of horses and their riders; and of all humanity, both free and slave, small and great."
[19]Then I saw the beast and the kings of the world and their armies gathered together to fight against the one sitting on the horse and his army. [20]And the beast was captured, and with him the false prophet who did mighty miracles on behalf of the beast—miracles that deceived all who had accepted the mark of the beast and who worshiped his statue. Both the beast and his false prophet were thrown alive into the fiery lake of burning sulfur. [21]Their entire army was killed by the sharp sword that came from the mouth of the one riding the white horse. And the vultures all gorged themselves on the dead bodies.

The Thousand Years

20

Then I saw an angel coming down from heaven with the key to the bottomless pit and a heavy chain in his hand. [2]He seized the dragon—that old serpent, who is the devil, Satan—and bound him in chains for a thousand years. [3]The angel threw him into the bottomless pit, which he then shut and locked so Satan could not deceive the nations anymore until the thousand years were finished. Afterward he must be released for a little while.
[4]Then I saw thrones, and the people sitting on them had been given the authority to judge. And I saw the souls of those who had been beheaded for their testimony about Jesus and for proclaiming the word of God. They had not worshiped the beast or his statue,

nor accepted his mark on their forehead or their hands. They all came to life again, and they reigned with Christ for a thousand years.
[5]This is the first resurrection. (The rest of the dead did not come back to life until the thousand years had ended.) [6]Blessed and holy are those who share in the first resurrection. For them the second death holds no power, but they will be priests of God and of Christ and will reign with him a thousand years.

The Defeat of Satan

[7]When the thousand years come to an end, Satan will be let out of his prison. [8]He will go out to deceive the nations—called Gog and Magog—in every corner of the earth. He will gather them together for battle—a mighty army, as numberless as sand along the seashore. [9]And I saw them as they went up on the broad plain of the earth and surrounded God's people and the beloved city. But fire from heaven came down on the attacking armies and consumed them.
[10]Then the devil, who had deceived them, was thrown into the fiery lake of burning sulfur, joining the beast and the false prophet. There they will be tormented day and night forever and ever.

The Final Judgment

[11]And I saw a great white throne and the one sitting on it. The earth and sky fled from his presence, but they found no place to hide. [12]I saw the dead, both great and small, standing before God's throne. And the books were opened, including the Book of Life. And the dead were judged according to what they had done, as recorded in the books. [13]The sea gave up its dead, and death and the grave gave up their dead. And all were judged according to their deeds. [14]Then death and the grave were thrown into the lake of fire. This lake of fire is the second death. [15]And anyone whose name was not found recorded in the Book of Life was thrown into the lake of fire.

The New Jerusalem

21

Then I saw a new heaven and a new earth, for the old heaven and the old earth had disappeared. And the sea was also gone. [2]And I saw the holy city, the new Jerusalem, coming down from God out of heaven like a bride beautifully dressed for her husband.
[3]I heard a loud shout from the throne, saying, "Look, God's home is now among his people! He will live with them, and they will be his people. God himself will be with them. [4]He will wipe every tear from their eyes, and there will be no more death or sorrow or crying or pain. All these things are gone forever."

And the one sitting on the throne said, "Look, I am making everything new!" And then he said to me, "Write this down, for what I tell you is trustworthy and true." ⁶And he also said, "It is finished! I am the Alpha and the Omega—the Beginning and the End. To all who are thirsty I will give freely from the springs of the water of life. ⁷All who are victorious will inherit all these blessings, and I will be their God, and they will be my children.

⁸"But cowards, unbelievers, the corrupt, murderers, the immoral, those who practice witchcraft, idol worshipers, and all liars—their fate is in the fiery lake of burning sulfur. This is the second death."

⁹Then one of the seven angels who held the seven bowls containing the seven last plagues came and said to me, "Come with me! I will show you the bride, the wife of the Lamb."

¹⁰So he took me in the Spirit to a great, high mountain, and he showed me the holy city, Jerusalem, descending out of heaven from God. ¹¹It shone with the glory of God and sparkled like a precious stone—like jasper as clear as crystal. ¹²The city wall was broad and high, with twelve gates guarded by twelve angels. And the names of the twelve tribes of Israel were written on the gates. ¹³There were three gates on each side—east, north, south, and west. ¹⁴The wall of the city had twelve foundation stones, and on them were written the names of the twelve apostles of the Lamb.

¹⁵The angel who talked to me held in his hand a gold measuring stick to measure the city, its gates, and its wall. ¹⁶When he measured it, he found it was a square, as wide as it was long. In fact, its length and width and height were each 1,400 miles. ¹⁷Then he measured the walls and found them to be 216 feet thick (according to the human standard used by the angel).

¹⁸The wall was made of jasper, and the city was pure gold, as clear as glass. ¹⁹The wall of the city was built on foundation stones inlaid with twelve precious stones: the first was jasper, the second sapphire, the third agate, the fourth emerald, ²⁰the fifth onyx, the sixth carnelian, the seventh chrysolite, the eighth beryl, the ninth topaz, the tenth chrysoprase, the eleventh jacinth, the twelfth amethyst.

²¹The twelve gates were made of pearls—each gate from a single pearl! And the main street was pure gold, as clear as glass.

²²I saw no temple in the city, for the Lord God Almighty and the Lamb are its temple. ²³And the city has no need of sun or moon, for the glory of God illuminates the city, and the Lamb is its light. ²⁴The nations will walk in its light, and the kings of the world will enter the city in all their glory. ²⁵Its gates will never be closed at the end of day because there is no night there. ²⁶And all the nations will bring their glory and honor into the city. ²⁷Nothing evil will be allowed to enter, nor anyone who practices shameful idolatry and dishonesty—but only those whose names are written in the Lamb's Book of Life.

22

Then the angel showed me a river with the water of life, clear as crystal, flowing from the throne of God and of the Lamb. ²It flowed down the center of the main street. On each side of the river grew a tree of life, bearing twelve crops of fruit, with a fresh crop each month. The leaves were used for medicine to heal the nations.

³No longer will there be a curse upon anything. For the throne of God and of the Lamb will be there, and his servants will worship him. ⁴And they will see his face, and his name will be written on their foreheads. ⁵And there will be no night there—no need for lamps or sun—for the Lord God will shine on them. And they will reign forever and ever.

⁶Then the angel said to me, "Everything you have heard and seen is trustworthy and true. The Lord God, who inspires his prophets, has sent his angel to tell his servants what will happen soon."

Jesus Is Coming

⁷"Look, I am coming soon! Blessed are those who obey the words of prophecy written in this book."

⁸I, John, am the one who heard and saw all these things. And when I heard and saw them, I fell down to worship at the feet of the angel who showed them to me. ⁹But he said, "No, don't worship me. I am a servant of God, just like you and your brothers the prophets, as well as all who obey what is written in this book. Worship only God!"

¹⁰Then he instructed me, "Do not seal up the prophetic words in this book, for the time is near. ¹¹Let the one who is doing harm continue to do harm; let the one who is vile continue to be vile; let the one who is righteous continue to live righteously; let the one who is holy continue to be holy."

¹²"Look, I am coming soon, bringing my reward with me to repay all people according to their deeds. ¹³I am the Alpha and the Omega, the First and the Last, the Beginning and the End."

¹⁴Blessed are those who wash their robes. They will be permitted to enter through the gates of the city and eat the fruit from the tree of life. ¹⁵Outside the city are the dogs—the sorcerers, the sexually immoral, the murderers, the idol worshipers, and all who love to live a lie.

¹⁶"I, Jesus, have sent my angel to give you this message for the churches. I am both the source of David and the heir to his throne. I am the bright morning star."

¹⁷The Spirit and the bride say, "Come." Let anyone who hears this say, "Come." Let anyone who is thirsty come. Let anyone who desires drink freely from the water of life. ¹⁸And I solemnly declare to everyone who hears the words of prophecy written in this book: If anyone adds anything to what is written here, God will add to that person the plagues described in this book. ¹⁹And if anyone removes any of the words from this book of prophecy, God will remove that person's share in the tree of life and in the holy city that are described in this book.

²⁰He who is the faithful witness to all these things says, "Yes, I am coming soon!"

Amen! Come, Lord Jesus!

²¹May the grace of the Lord Jesus be with God's holy people.

STAND POINT

When you need something to look forward to

21:4

He will wipe every tear from their eyes, and there will be no more death or sorrow or crying or pain. All these things are gone forever.

notes

resource

To The Next Level

To The Next Level is a ministry dedicated to educate, inspire and motivate athletes and coaches, and all whom they influence to achieve their full human, spiritual, and athletic potential in reaching to the next level through a life changing relationship with Jesus Christ.

Performance Principles *WWW.TOTHENEXTLEVEL.ORG*

What does it take to be a champion? Countless athletes take to the pitch, court, rink, pool, and mat each year — all hoping to be crowned a champion. But few actually achieve their goals. Athletic Performance Principles for Life are the keys to being a champion — not only in athletics, but in life as well. Study these areas and plug this wisdom into your own life — you'll be glad you did!

www.tothenextlevel.org

Monthly Action Plan: Goals List M.A.P.

SPIRITUAL DISCIPLINES:

_____

Prayer:

_____

Faith Community:

_____

Bible Reading:

_____

PRAYER LIST

_____

Friends:

_____

World:

_____

Personal:

_____

Monthly Action Plan: Goals List

M.A.P.

PERSONAL GOALS

Family:

Work/School/Social:

Challenge:

SPORT GOALS:

Training:

Performance:

Competition Results:

notes